BIOGRAPHY OF A BATTALION

THE LIFE AND TIMES OF AN
INFANTRY BATTALION IN EUROPE
IN WORLD WAR II

BIOGRAPHY OF A BATTALION

THE LIFE AND TIMES OF AN
INFANTRY BATTALION IN EUROPE
IN WORLD WAR II

BY

JAMES A. HUSTON

Assistant Professor of History, Purdue University

STACKPOLE
BOOKS

Published by
STACKPOLE BOOKS
5067 Ritter Road
Mechanicsburg, PA 17055
www.stackpolebooks.com

Jacket design by Wendy A. Reynolds

Printed in the United States of America

10 9 8 7 6 5 4 3 2 1

FIRST EDITION

Library of Congress Cataloging-in-Publication Data

Huston, James A. (James Alvin), 1918–
      Biography of a battalion : the life and times of an infantry battalion in Europe in
   World War II / by James A. Huston ; with a new foreword by James W. Huston—
   1 st ed.
         p.   cm.
      Originally published: Gering, Nebr. : Courier Press, 1950.
      Includes bibliographical references.
      ISBN 0-8117-2694-0
      1. United States. Army. Infantry, 134th. 2. World War, 1939–1945—Regimental
   histories—United States. 3. World War, 1939–1945—Campaigns—Western Front.
   I. Title.

D769.31 134th .H87 2003
940.54'1273—dc21   2002030247

BIOGRAPHY OF A BATTALION

To the Memory of

ALFRED THOMSEN,

Lieutenant Colonel, Infantry

CONTENTS

CHAPTER   PAGE

Preface xxi

PROLOGUE

INTO THE MAELSTROM...................................... 1

A summary of the organization and training of the battalion and its movement overseas.

Part One

NORMANDY

I   Hedgerows and Sunken Roads............................ 14

The Battalion moves up to relieve elements of the 29th Division before St. Lo.

II   "Assemble at Emelie"..................................... 22

The Battalion is ordered to assemble and prepare to exploit the success of
the First Battalion, and runs into trouble—almost ambushed.

III On to St. Lo... 30

The final attack in the capture of St. Lo, key to the Normandy defenses.

IV   "Bloody Sunday" 47

The Battalion suffers 120 casualties—command group hit: battalion commander mortally wounded.

V   "Pinched out" across the Vire River....................... 56

Crossing of the Vire River—Company I runs into trouble at Pont Bellenger—
pinched out by British and 2nd Armored Division—assemble to join Third
Army.

VI   Detour to Mortain...................................... 63

Motor column turned back to help stop the Nazi counteroffensive toward
Avranches and the sea.

CONTENTS

Part Two

RACE ACROSS FRANCE

CHAPTER   PAGE

VII   Into a New War.. 75

Staff changed—the FBI—on the right flank of the Third Army—prisoners by
the thousand around St. Florentine and Joigny—out of gasoline.

VIII   The Bridge at Flavigny................................. 84

Attack again—bridge blown out behind most of the 2nd Battalion at the
Moselle River.

IX   Liberation of Nancy..................................... 90

Formation of task force with regiment from 80th Division—the underground
inside Nancy—move through the forest—the wild, happy crowds in Nancy
welcoming their liberators.

X   Pain de Sucre ("Sugar Loaf" Hill)...................... 96

Crossing the Meurthe River: Company L in Malzeville: attack on the Plateau
de Malzeville; the "perfect attack" of infantry and tanks to recapture the
Sugar Loaf after 1st Battalion was driven off.

XI   Defensive in the Foret de Gremecey...................... 106

Stretched lines along edge of forest—repeated counterattacks.

Part Three

LORRAINE TO THE SAARLAND

XII   "Blue Monday" on Red Hill.............................. 124

First attack over snow—battle against the weather.

XIII   Capture of Morhange.................................... 131

In friendly artillery fire—machine-gunned by tanks of 4th Armored Division
—first shelter since the jump-off.

XIV   "Task Force Lagrew".................................... 136

Attached to 6th Armored Division—tank-infantry attack on Puttelange.

XV   Crossing the Saar River.................................. 144

A night crossing over a fallen railway bridge.

XVI   Habkirchen 153

Attempt to cross the Blies River in two-man rubber boats—house to house
fighting in Habkirchen: first entry into Germany: German artillery.

Part Four

THE ARDENNES BULGE

XVII   Toward Bastogne 164

Christmas in Metz—with the 4th Armored Division south of Bastogne.

XVIII Counterattacks at Lutrebois.............................. 173

Threat to the Arlon-Bastogne Highway: Company L—heroic stand of machine
gun platoon—the pocket broken . . . "Battle of the C.P."

XIX   Steel on Ice... 192

Attached to 6th Armored Division again—the skyline drive—scouts in snow-
suits—attack on Kilborn.

Part Five

ROER TO THE RHINE

XX   With the Ninth Army..................................... 201

Relief of British unit—the Roer River line; preparations for attack.

XXI   Across the Roer at Hilfarth.............................. 210

Crossing the Roer River to turn the enemy's flank.

XXII The Wesel Pocket....................................... 216

The final push to the Rhine.

Part Six

THE FIFTH STAR: EAST OF THE RHINE

CHAPTER   PAGE

XXIII   Urban Offensive 224

Rest period; combat through built-up areas: Gladbeck—Buer—Reckling-hausen.

XXIV   The Ruhr Pocket.. 241

Eliminating an encircled army; to the banks of the Ruhr.

XXV   The Dash to the Elbe.................................... 251

Long-distance motor move—tactical move to the banks of the Elbe—counter-attacks—waiting for the Russians.

XXVI   War's End 266

Back to Hannover for occupation duty.

EPILOGUE

Occupation in the Coblenz area; Redeployment: return to the United States 270

Reflections—attitudes of returning infantrymen............... 275

"The Queen of Battles"—pride of the infantry................. 281

Appreciation 287

Some Comparisons with combat in World War I.............. 288

Some thoughts on Universal Military Training................ 293

New Organization: eyes on the future...................... 296

Summary 300

APPENDIX

Table of Organization, Infantry Battalion.................... 302

BIBLIOGRAPHY 303

MAPS

PAGE

Moving into position; Objective: St. Lo............................. 26

Opening phase of attack for St. Lo................................. 26

On July 16 the Third Battalion made the main effort.................. 40

On the 18th they swept into St. Lo................................. 40

Nancy and Pain de Sucre... 98

Defense in Foret de Gremecey.................................116-117

South of Bastogne...170-171

The Ruhr Pocket—Recklinghausen..............................238-239

The Dash to the Elbe.. 252

On the Elbe... 257

Photos by U. S. Army Signal Corps

FOREWORD

Perhaps it was the Nazi flag that never let me forget World War II, the flag that stayed folded up in the corner of our musty basement, my father's office, where he sat surrounded by his thousands of books that I got paid to dust every now and then. Growing up in Indiana I remember always knowing that my father had fought as an infantry officer in Europe in the war. Our family vacations were often to Army bases where my father would do his two-week active duty as a Reserve Army Officer.

When I was a boy I would ask my father where he got the Nazi flag. He would always say it was from the war. I would ask how he got it in the war, and he would say they "gave it to him" in a German town. For reasons which now escape me, I was satisfied with that answer.

As I grew older, my curiosity about that answer—and whatever else I didn't know about his role in the war—increased. I remember asking him what *he* had done. He told me he had written most of it down, and I should read it. He gave me a manuscript entitled *Biography of a Battalion*. I kept it on my lone bookcase in my room, and later in my life on whatever bookcase I had wherever I lived. I never did read that manuscript. At least not back then.

He wasn't much of a talker or storyteller. He was mostly quiet. But he did try to convey to me some of his experiences. When I was ten, and then twelve, my family traveled to Europe, and he showed me the hedgerows of Normandy where he fought and the cities he liberated, and Bastogne, Belgium, where he fought in the Battle of the Bulge. Those memories are still vivid from my youth. As I would stand over those battlefields and think of him being involved in a massive, mechanical, destructive battle, it would jar me. It just went against everything he was. Although he is a large man—six feet four inches tall—he is the most gentle, humble, unpretentious human being I have ever met. It is very difficult to envision such a person planning a night attack on a Nazi position.

As I grew older my military interests tended toward the nautical. Rather than playing with toy soldiers, I would build models of battleships, aircraft carriers, and airplanes. I wanted to fly in the Navy, and ultimately did. My fascination with World War II was more with the Pacific Theater.

In looking back now though, that feels like an excuse for never having read my father's manuscript about the war. He published many books on World War II and is a well regarded military and diplomatic historian. But I still never read his personal story. At some point it became embarrassing. I couldn't very well tell my father that I was so interested in what he did in the war that I had never even found the time to read what he had written and given to me as a child. It almost made it impossible to talk about the war at all, because he would reasonably assume I already knew most of it from reading his manuscript.

So we would discuss the war in general: military tactics, why Hitler foolishly invaded Russia thereby ensuring a two front war, the kinds of discussions you might hear in a course on military history. But we wouldn't talk about what *he*, as an individual experienced.

Now that I have five children of my own—ages eleven through nineteen—I had begun to wonder if they had any appreciation for World War II at all, and in particular what their grandfather had gone through. He was the only officer in his battalion that landed at Normandy and fought all the way to the Elbe river—fifty miles from Berlin—that wasn't killed, wounded, or sent home. How do you convey that to children? It was time.

Last year I called my father and asked him to return to Europe with me and my family. It was time for them to hear his story. But even as I was asking, haunting me still was the fact that even then, at forty-seven years of age, I hadn't read his manuscript. Our family was going to the British Isles first for vacation, and we would rendezvous with my father in Paris two weeks later.

I tossed the manuscript in my suitcase vowing to read every word or die in the process. When we sat down on our nonstop British Air flight out of San Diego I pulled it out and started reading. I couldn't stop. I was riveted. Here was something different. I have continued to read all kinds of military history books over the years. I read Ambrose who writes in an anecdotal, storytelling way, or John Keegan, the British military historian who has written some splendid works, or Richard Frank who wrote *Guadalcanal*, my favorite book dealing with an island campaign in the Pacific, or even individual accounts of soldiers or marines such as *With the Old Breed*, by E. B. Sledge, perhaps the best of the genre, that gives you the gory gritty day to day slaughter of the marines fighting on the islands. All different styles. All fine and useful.

Biography of a Battalion was different. But how? What distinguished it? Then it hit me. My father grew up and was educated in the depression. He attended Indiana University and received his BA in History and completed Army ROTC. He receive a reserve commission as a second lieutenant in the Army long before the United States became involved in the war. In fact he went on to graduate school at IU and received his MA in history, then applied for a Penfield Fellowship to study for his Ph.D. at New York University and was accepted. This young man from tiny Fairmount, Indiana, was going to Manhattan to study history at one of the premier universities in the country. He was hard at work on his doctorate in history at NYU when the war started. In fact he was walking out of the subway stop at Times Square on December 7, 1941, and learned of the attack on Pearl Harbor on the lighted ticker at Times Square. He knew his summons would come, and he was right. His reserve commission was activated and he headed to Fort Benning two months later.

How many Ph.D. history candidates fought as infantry officers in World War II? And how many of them went on to get their final degrees, and become military historians and write about the war? The historians we generally read didn't fight in the war, not Ambrose, not Keegan, not Frank. Many people who did fight in the war and wrote about it weren't trained as historians. Eisenhower's book is fine, as are many others. But they are usually written as memoirs to explain their thought processes in large questions of strategy, not to let us see how the Army worked at the soldier level, how they kept their feet warm in flooded or frozen foxholes. If fact most of them were never in a foxhole in the war.

What makes my father's book different is that he writes with the eye of a trained historian and the experience of a foot soldier.

During our travels from London to the mandatory journey to one's town of origin—Houston, Scotland in Renfrewshire—I read *Biography of a Battalion* every night. I read about my father's division, the 35th Division, a division that fought across the entire face of France. Perhaps less well known than some other divisions, they had nominally fifteen thousand men, and over the course of just fourteen months of fighting gave out fifteen thousand purple hearts. They fought in the hardest and bloodiest battles of the war, and took twenty five percent casualties on several days.

When my family rendezvoused with my father in Paris and prepared for our train ride to Caen, I was finished with the manuscript and in awe of the man who was my father. Brokaw calls them the greatest generation. Here is another story that confirms that in spades.

I wanted my children to have the same appreciation I did. They would listen, but they didn't really get it yet. Sitting in the courtyard in our Paris hotel, or eating dinner at the sidewalk cafes while we talked about the American soldiers fighting on D-Day, or the much higher casualties suffered during the rest of the Battle of Normandy campaign at places such as St. Lô where my father's division fought, were too abstract. Then we headed for Normandy.

Traveling with a large family is always a challenge, not the least of which is not forcing people to do what they don't want to do. My father thought our first morning should be spent on the beaches. Omaha. Utah. D-Day landing sites. And since we were there in June, he thought we should be there when the landing occurred—6:30 in the morning. Needless to say, the children were unenthusiastic about getting up in time to be on the beach that early. My father thought that perhaps since Americans had ridden around in ships and landing craft all night to prepare for the landing, most seasick, all to get dumped out on the beach and shot at or killed back in 1944, perhaps we could honor that effort by getting ourselves out of bed in time to *look* at the beach at 6:30. The family relented and we spent the next morning staring out into the hazy June morning listening to my father explain the landing and how landing in one spot on the beach ensured almost certain destruction, while five hundred yards away men walked ashore untouched. We walked in the wide sands and examined remaining gun emplacements and bunkers, built only to kill those who would come to liberate France and the continent from the Nazi death grip.

We went on from the beaches to the hedgerows. We drove to the very spot where my father's battalion was trucked for their drive to St. Lô, a city that was being attacked by the U.S. 29th Division against the heavily defended German positions. The battle had reached a stalemate and casualties were climbing. The 35th Division was to join the assault on St. Lô. As they got out of the trucks, my father was sent forward to see if the intelligence reports were true, that there weren't any Germans in the area. He walked down across two or three fields and peered over a massive hedgerow. The entire area was crawling with Germans.

He backed away silently and reported to the battalion commander who immediately began calling for reinforcements. One battalion wasn't enough against the enemy in front of them. Just then a German tank came rumbling down the road. The battalion commander wasn't going to have that. He ran into the field and drew his sidearm, a .45 caliber automatic pistol. He ran at the tank and, with his men yelling "Colonel! No!" began firing. His bullets plinked harmlessly off the side of the tank, but it was enough to confuse the tank—the Germans didn't know there was any opposition nearby either, and weren't about to charge into whatever it was without seeing it. The tank backed away and returned to its line.

The colonel replaced his sidearm and was very pleased with himself. He was killed a few weeks later, the first of three commanders of the 3rd Battalion, 134th Infantry killed or wounded before the end of the war.

We went on, and found the field I had come to learn from his book was referred to as Bloody Sunday. His battalion (about three hundred fifty strong at the time) lost twenty-five percent of the battalion on that day in a four-hour period. We looked for the specific field, and a farm called La Buste, that sat on the corner of the picturesque French country road. We couldn't find it so we stopped at another farm to ask directions. The man who came to the door not only knew where the field was, he had *been there* in 1944 and had watched the entire battle as a seventeen-year-old Frenchman. He and my father discussed the German machine gun positions and the ferocity of the battle. I knew most of that from the manuscript. But then I learned two things that weren't in the book.

The farm was still there. Same house. My father told us on the evening of that battle, the Germans had taken over the farmhouse and had ordered the woman of the house to kill her chickens and fix them a chicken dinner. She had reluctantly complied, but when the Germans heard my father's battalion approaching, they quickly abandoned their position in the farmhouse. When the battalion checked at the farmhouse to learn where the Germans had gone, they were happily offered the chicken dinner that had been fixed for the Germans. They gladly accepted, sat and ate the chicken dinner, then turned their attention on the German army.

I and the French farmer also learned that a few hours later, during that battle, my father was in a foxhole with two other soldiers under a withering artillery barrage when his battalion commanding officer told him to go back to HQ to get reinforcements. He jumped in a jeep and headed off. He returned a few minutes later and dashed through the continuing artillery fire to the safety of the foxhole he had recently abandoned. The two men he had left were dead.

On we went through the fields and up to St. Lô, with me driving one of our Peugeots and my father navigating. "Turn here!" "Left here! Right! Up into that cemetery!" The cemetery? Okay, Dad. We pulled up deep into the cemetery and my father was out of the car before we had stopped. He hurried toward the top of small rise, to a mausoleum. It was made of stone and was fifteen feet high with pillars and an ominous door. He disappeared inside. We hurried in behind him, and couldn't find him. Then we saw a narrow staircase, not wide enough for one man's shoulders, descending underneath the mausoleum. We went down after him, and found him standing in a tiny room, containing the sarcophagus of a Frenchman, a stone bathtub like structure with a lid and some sculptured likeness of the man on top. His legs and arms were broken off. My father was staring around the room. He put his hands on his hips and stared. He spoke quietly. "This was our battalion headquarters for the attack on St. Lô. We got shelled all night. It was the only safe place. We used this guy's sarcophagus here as our map table. The battalion staff slept here—my sleeping bag was right *there*." Although he had been back to this cemetery a few times since the war, this room had never been open before. It was the first time he had been there since 1944.

There was something almost spiritual about the experience. To look at the place where the battalion staff lay on the floor underneath the German artillery making their plans to liberate this French city, and to see the thriving city now, almost without signs of the carnage of the forties is a testament to so many people and such dedication to a clear mission.

On we went to the museum in St. Lô dedicated to the 29th and 35th Divisions. When the curator of the museum heard my father was in town, he called the president of the 35th Division society in St. Lô and notified him. They immediately planned a massive dinner for the members of their society and our entire group.

That night at the quickly organized dinner they showered my father with praise and gratefulness, and repeatedly told him how they wouldn't be there today if it weren't for him and people like him. They told him it is the Americans to whom they owe their freedom, and how they will never forget him or us. They gave him a sealed bottle of sand from Normandy, and toasted his bravery, friendship, and character. It was one of the most moving things I have ever seen. I have never been more proud.

The French have the reputation in the United States, I think it is fair to say, of being ingrates, of not appreciating what the United States has done for them. Perhaps certain French deserve that reputation, I don't know. But it must be said that there is a deep, lingering, heartfelt gratitude verging on hero worship in many French people for what the Americans did for them in World War II. These are not just people who were of the generation who fought in the war. Many of them were either not born, or were small children during the war, yet they know more about my father's division than any in America do, except perhaps military historians.

The journey was a wonderful one. My children got to see where their grandfather fought, where his headquarters were from cemeteries to stately mansions now weathered and beaten. They saw how even though things are far away from home, they can be pivotal in how your life and your family has developed.

After exploring Normandy, we rode the train back to Paris. As the clean French train raced through the lush countryside I sat across the table from my father. I asked him about the manuscript. I asked him if he had ever tried to get it published. He said he had had a few run off for some members of the 35th Division who wanted to read it. I asked him if he had ever tried to write it in the first person instead of the third person. He told me he wrote the first draft in a tower at the student union at Indiana University after returning from the war. The first draft was in first person. He said he would send me a copy of it.

When we got back to the States he sent me that first draft. I opened it, and nearly had a stroke. There in the front of the manuscript, bound in with the rest of it, was a letter on White House stationary. It was handwritten from Harry Truman as the sitting president of the United States. My father had sent him a copy of the manuscript, and Truman had read it and wrote his note. He remarked how it was better than Eichelberger's work (Commanding General of the Australia America corps under MacArthur, the Eighth Army that took back the Philippines and occupied Japan), and several others. Perhaps he was biased—Truman was in the 35th Division in World War I— but still, how many sitting presidents would read such a work and send their regards in a handwritten note on White House stationary?

It was then I knew others needed to read my father's work. As I have said, it is not the usual war memoir, nor is it the book of an after-the-fact historian. Those are fine as well. But this one is different. It is written by an historian trained in his craft before being sent off to the biggest war in history and finished after he completed his Ph.D. in history at NYU. It carries the authenticity of someone who saw and experienced things first hand, yet it is carefully understated and objective. I can think of no other book about World War II that contains both.

But back to the man. The greatest generation. I've thought that for a long time, and not just because of World War II. I've thought that because he is a man of character and honesty, integrity and humor. He went on to become a professor of history at Purdue for a number of years, and received an award as the best teacher in the university while I was in high school. He left there to become Dean of Lynchburg College in Lynchburg, Virginia, where he finished out his academic career. He continues to write both military history books and fiction. His most recent history book is called *A Historian's Handbook,* and his most recent work of fiction (written with Anne Marshall Huston) is called *Violet Storm,* an epic about South Carolina during reconstruction.

For how many of us will it be said by others that the longer they knew us the deeper their admiration grows for us? That is true of almost everyone who encounters my father. How much of that is because of what he went through in World War II? Is that generation great today because of what they went through? Did they see the worst humanity could do and took it upon themselves to make the world a better place simply through the force of their character?

We can only hope to carry on that legacy. It is for that reason that we need to honor them, to listen to them, to read their books, and most importantly, reflect their character in who we are, from one generation to another. If there is any greatness there, we must do what we can to pass it on to make sure the generations that come after us are able to summon up such character, such dedication and yes, heroism, when called upon to do so.

I for one am grateful to have seen such character close up for my entire life. And I am grateful to be able to pass a small part of it on to the public in the form of this book. I have finally read it, and encourage you to do so much faster than I did.

As Andre Malraux said of Joan of Arc, "The monuments for heroes are in the hearts of the living." I am hopeful that this book allows us to keep the heroism of the men my father fought with in World War II in our hearts a little more than we otherwise might. If those monuments are tended, they may inspire in us the same sort of character the next time it is called for in the defense of freedom.

James W. Huston

PREFACE

Early in World War II steps were taken to insure an adequate historical coverage for the events and implications of this great conflict.

At a meeting in August, 1943, the committee [on Records of War Administration] considered the broader aspects of the history of World War II and agreed upon six over-all objectives. The committee took no responsibility for the wide coverage indicated by the following objectives, but did call attention to certain principles:

1. All of the major Federal Agencies should gather data relating to their development and their most significant activities during the war period in order to create a central historical file.

2. There should be several non-official and popular accounts of World War II written from different standpoints, showing the military operations of the war, the civilian administration of the war, and the diplomatic phases of the war.

3. There should be a series of scholarly monographs analyzing the effect of the war on important phases of our social and economic life.

4. Studies should be made on a selected list of topics that are the concern of no one government or private organization.

5. State historical groups should prepare accounts of state activities in World War I.

6. Leading American industrial firms should have histories written recounting their war work.

The objectives outlined above conform closely to those approved in the business meeting of the American Historical Association on December 30, 1942.[1]

The War Department's *American Forces in Action* series provides some excellent studies of action in specific operations, and its projected 99 volume history promises results in quality to equal its magnitude in quantity. Nevertheless, an adequate treatment should include accounts of infantry units carried throughout the war. A large number of infantry divisions already have published histories, and these do have a definite value to anyone seeking an understanding of the military phase of the war; however, these accounts frequently display a temptation to dwell too much on self-glorification at the expense of more complete accuracy and perspective.

But the story of the "typical" infantry battalion is one which deserves to be told. "Battalion," because the battalion is the largest unit whose commander habitually follows the troops on the ground. It is the smallest unit whose commander has a staff to assist him in his duties—a fact which lends a measure of continuity to the battalion in spite of the rapid turnover of its personnel. It is the level where the interplay of strategy and large unit tactics with the tactics of the small unit can be seen most clearly.

If any infantry battalion can be called "typical," perhaps the 3rd Battalion, 134th Infantry (35th Division) has as good a claim to that description as any. The story of this battalion includes participation in the Normandy campaign and the capture of St. Lo under General Omar Bradley's First Army; the dash across France, the advance through Lorraine, and then the

1. **The American Historical Review**, LLIX (January 1944), 249-51. See also William C. Dinkley, "Two World Wars and Historical Scholarship," The Mississippi Valley Historical Review, XXXIII (June 1946), 3-26.

relief of Bastogne in the Ardennes "Bulge" under General George S. Patton Jr.'s Third Army; the drive from the Roer to the Rhine, the fighting in the Ruhr valley, and the race to the Elbe, little more than fifty miles from Berlin, under Lieutenant General William H. Simpson's Ninth Army. The story of the "typical" battalion must include each of the major compaigns, for in some ways they were so diffeernt as to seem almost different wars.

Infantry units seemed to have a great deal in common—in battle experiences as well as in the common background of training. Each seemed to have its "St. Lo," its "Bloody Sunday," its "Blue Monday."

My own position to relate this story is, perhaps, unique. Aside from the motor officer and the supply officer, I was the only officer in the Battalion to survive its whole period of combat. After completing the Basic course, as a reserve officer, at the Infantry School, Fort Benning, I joined the regiment in California as a rifle platoon leader in May, 1942. After subsequent assignments as battalion antitank platoon leader, rifle company executive officer, and rifle company commander, I joined the Third Battalion as temporary S-3 (operations officer) at the termination of maneuvers in Tennessee in January, 1944. On the return of the regular operations officer (Captain Merle R. Carroll) from another course at Fort Benning, I remained as Battalion intelligence officer (S-2).

It was in this position that I entered combat with the Battalion in Normandy in July, 1944. As S-2 I was concerned primarily with information of the enemy—reconnaissance, prisoners, map distribution. Then early in September the Battalion operations officer was wounded and I succeeded to that assignment. Now it was my duty to accompany the Battalion commander wherever he went—to regimental meetings to make notes on the regimental orders, to conferences with other commanders, to the companies on visits or inspections, to the observation posts, behind the advancing companies during attacks. The day's work included preparation of field orders, transmission of orders and directions to the company commanders, coordination with supporting units and friendly units on the flanks, preparation of training schedules and supervision of training.

In the preparation of this history every effort has been made to corroborate my statements by reference to reliable documents or the observations of others. However, statements which rest on no other authority depend upon my personal observation. My own experience, then, has served in a positive way to supplement other information, and in a negative way to afford a critical evaluation of the available documents.

The main source for the activities of the Battalion in combat is the Battalion Journal. The completeness of this journal grew out of the insistence on the part of Lt. Col. Alfred Thomsen, the commanding officer, on the keeping of a detailed "log" in his headquarters whether in garrison or on maneuvers or in operations. It was through this instrument that the commander and members of the staff were able to keep themselves informed and to make available information to the others by making a notation in the "log." This procedure was found to be so valuable during combat—the commander or staff officer, after a few hours' sleep, could bring himself completely up to date on the situation merely by reading the entries in the journal—that succeeding commanders likewise insisted upon its maintenance. The result was a detailed record of a kind likely to be found in very few infantry battalions. It was standard staff procedure to keep a unit journal, but a journal was not required by regulations in units smaller than a regiment (or independent battalion), and it is not likely that very many journals, complete in detail, were kept in infantry battalions. Even in the Third Battalion, unfortunately, there is a gap in the journal for the period of the Normandy campaign. During those first days of combat the sergeant-major kept a brief journal merely on loose sheets of paper, and when he was killed, his records were lost. It was not until September, then, that a complete journal was begun in permanent form, i.e., in bound books.

But complete as it seems to be, even the Battalion Journal which has been preserved is not without its shortcomings. One will find that for quiet periods, entries in the journal are quite complete, but during important battle actions frequently the number of entries will be disappointing, for during the intense action there is little time for attention to the journal in a battalion headquarters. In regimental and division headquarters, on the other hand, this situation is not so likely, for there it is possible often to make the keeping of the journals full-time jobs for persons in the headquarters organization.

Therefore, even for the combat action, it is necessary to supplement the Battalion Journal with other sources. Fortunately, the Regimental S-3 Journal gives a rather complete record of the Normandy campaign with frequent references to the Third Battalion. Kept for the information of the regimental operations officer, this journal may be accepted with the same authenticity as that granted the Battalion Journal.

Another unofficial record which gives a wealth of information concerning all kinds of activities of the regiment—training, combat, recreation, speeches, traditions, humorous incidents—is the 134th Infantry *Daily Log and Diary*. Anxious to keep members of the regiment informed of regimental activities, and at the same time to keep a valuable historical record, Colonel B. B. Miltonberger, the regimental commander, demanded the preparation of this "Daily Log." It was a typewritten summary prepared each day by the assistant adjutant (S-1) of the regiment. Distributed to the units, it served to disseminate news of the regiment. The original copies, then, were bound, together with copies of operation reports, newspaper clippings, and some official correspondence, into six volumes.

Perhaps of less value as historical sources than those records mentioned above, because of the very fact that they were "official," and so prepared for higher headquarters and the permanent record, were the official documents which are preserved in The Adjutant General's Office in the Pentagon, Washington, D. C. These include the regimental After Action Reports, Unit Journal, S-2 Periodic Reports, and S-3 Situation Reports.

Of these, probably the Unit Journal is most valuable, for it is in manuscript form—that is entries of events were made at the time of their occurrence. The After Action Reports were prepared each month for submission to higher headquarters to cover the action of the preceding month. The S-3 situation reports were concise daily summaries of the friendly situation, and ordinarily were accompanied by situation maps (or overlays) which are of considerable historical importance. The S-2 periodic reports were similar daily summaries of enemy activity, of estimates of the enemy situation and capabilities, the handling of prisoners and captured equipment, and again were accompanied by overlays showing enemy dispositions.

In a treatment of this kind—seeking to present the total picture of the infantry battalion, I have felt it desirable to include a number of minor personal incidents. Aside from personal observation and conversation, it is necessary to depend almost wholly on General Orders—i.e., citations for awards—for that kind of information. I have attempted to include only those incidents of which I had personal knowledge, or reason to believe their authenticity. General Orders, in most cases, will serve as a valuable guide for those individual exploits. It must be recognized, however, that those citations were written from recommendations whose sole purpose was the winning of an award for the individual concerned, and no doubt there sometimes was a tendency to add color to the facts. In the Third Battalion, the company commanders wrote the recommendations for awards, and then these were re-written in the formal language of citations by an officer at regimental headquarters. On the other hand, it should be noted that probably more individual acts of heroism went without recognition than otherwise. It was necessary to wait for a relatively quiet day before the commanders could find any time to give their attention to writing recommendations, and even then, under the pressure of other duties, it was easy to procrastinate. Moreover it was not infrequent that there would be a change in commanders in the midst of an action, or witnesses would become casualties before they had an opportunity to make a report, or action could continue so long without a break that some such details would be forgotten.

My source for casualty figures was the Regimental Battle Casualty Report, a running account, on a bookkeeping basis, of the strength of all companies of the regiment. I was able to make notes from that record before the de-activation of the unit.

Earlier I alluded to the difficulty of recording events in the midst of battle. In order to supplement those important battle details the Army organized an Information and Historical Service which sent out teams to gather that information by means of combat interviews. Captain Jacob L. Goldman paid several visits to the Third Battalion to get the stories of the unit's action from the commander or staff officers. With a complete set of maps to refresh his memory, then, the officer concerned would dictate his story to a stenographer. But a word of caution is necessary regarding the use of this material (now filed in the Historical Records Section, War Department Records Branch, The Adjutant General's Office). These interviews necessarily had to take place some time after the action described—sometimes there was a lapse of several months—so that there may have been minor errors resulting from faulty recollection. Again, some officers may have been tempted to color the story slightly in favor of their own units, or to make second judgments and assign motives or considerations which actually did not operate to influence the decisions. But for the most part, the combat interviews may be regarded as a valuable supplementary source.

For additional material—particularly treating phases not adequately covered in journals or combat interviews, I have resorted to correspondence with men who held key positions in the Battalion—Battalion commander, staff officers, company commanders, platoon leader (see Acknowledgements). I accept the observations of these officers as completely reliable, with the reservation that they were depending upon their memories as much as two years after the events. Some were able to refer to their maps and notebooks for their information, and the other information corroborates my own observations or personal knowledge.

I have used freely my own notebooks which I kept at various times as rifle company officer, antitank officer and operations officer during training in the United States and as intelligence officer and operations officer overseas. Again I have found my own private correspondence with friends and relatives in the United States a rather useful source.

Particular mention ought also to be made of the use of field manuals, tables of organization, and other War Department publications. As far as weapons are concerned, they give an accurate description of the various weapons which the Third Battalion—or any rifle battalion—carried. But reference to manuals and tables on points of organization or tactics or equipment of the Battalion as a whole is not made for the purpose of supporting statements concerning the Third Battalion as such, but rather to indicate the "normal" or authorized strength or equipment and to suggest how the Third Battalion conformed, or failed to conform, to the standard in that particular case. In a number of instances, more recent field manuals have been published than those to which I have referred; I have used the older editions because the newer ones retain a classification of "Restricted" which makes them unavailable to the general public.

In this connection I should mention that the historical records on file in The Adjutant General's Office all were classified originally as "secret," but this classification is being removed as rapidly as those responsible can work through the mass of documents deposited there. It was my good fortune to find that all documents pertinent to the history of the Third Battalion had been declassified—or were declassified while I was there. Therefore the historical records are as open as they ever will be, and one of the obstacles to writing contemporary history is removed.

Perhaps I could describe my attempt as one in which I essay to combine the method of Thucydides—the father of accurate military history, who described events in which he participated and depended for his information upon his own observations or conversations and reports of other trustworthy witnesses—with the methods of modern research which puts its faith in the written document. Thus one approach is available to correct or confirm or evaluate the conclusions of the other.

The object here, then, is to present an accurate picture of an infantry battalion in combat, and to attempt to provide some understanding of the infantry soldier—of how he lived, how he fought, how he died; what he wore, what arms and equipment he carried, what he ate, and some idea as to what he felt and thought. In following the movements of a battalion, we shall seek to escape the impersonality of corps and armies; here we find the meaning of symbols on maps and decisions of higher headquarters as they affect the men on the ground.

The basic battle units of infantry are battalions. They are the tactical units of the regiment, the yardstick of a division commander, and the barometer of divisional combat-power to a corps commander. In the number, condition, and disposition of infantry battalions, hostile and friendly, rests a basis of estimate, decision, plan, order, and execution. In and around the infantry battalion are found the means, organic and supporting, for the application of the speculative idea (the scheme of maneuver) to the terrain.[2]

No matter what size the unit, infantry operations of all types depend upon battalion efficiency and culminate in the solutions of battalion problems.[3]

The combined result of the actions of infantry battalions went far toward determining the nature of the war in Europe. The outcome of these efforts in bringing the war to a successful military conclusion, and the combined results of the attitudes and impressions and lessons which the participants brought home may go far in determining the nature of the policies of the country which they represented.

James A. Huston

2. Lt. Col. H. E. Dager, "Modern Infantry," The Command and General Staff School Military Review 11 (March 1940), 5.
3. Ibid., p. 11.

ACKNOWLEDGEMENTS

A debt of gratitude must be expressed to all those persons whose interest and cooperation has made such a project possible, and its execution enjoyable.

No praise could be too high for the courtesy and helpfulness which prevailed uniformly throughout the sections of the War Department in making material accessible. Specific thanks must be expressed to Major General Butler B. Miltonberger, Chief of the National Guard Bureau, War Department Special Staff, who commanded the 134th Infantry Regiment during most of its training and combat, for access to his papers relating to the regiment's activities. Likewise must be mentioned the helpfulness of Lieutenant Colonel Dan E. Craig, executive of the National Guard Bureau, and of Major Lysle I. Abbott of the personnel section, National Guard Bureau.

Similar cooperation was to be found among the other persons concerned in the War Department. These would include, among others, Lieutenant Colonel John Kemper, Chief of planning branch, Major James M. Whitmire, executive, and Mr. Israel Wise, of the Historical Division, War Department Special Staff; Mr. R. L. Thompson of the Historical Records Sections, War Department Records Branch, The Adjutant General's Office; Mrs. Rogers of the Army Pictorial Service, Still Picture Branch, and E. J. Seymour, acting chief, Army Map Service.

Among those who cooperated in the way of making available certain information through correspondence were Lieutenant Colonel Charles A. Brown, executive, Office of Public Relations, Director of Information, Army Air Forces; D. B. Grant, Assistant vice president, Beech-Nut Packing Company, Canajoharie, New York, and Leona A. Wehrheim, administrative assistant, information section, Quartermaster Food and Container Institute for the Armed Forces, Chicago.

In addition there were a number who had served with the Battalion in key positions who undertook personal correspondence to relate personal recollections and make suggestions. One taking a most active interest and of greatest assistance in these suggestions and details was Brigadier General Warren C. Wood, Gering, Nebraska, who commanded the Battalion during most of its combat and who is now assistant division commander, 34th Division. Others on this list will include:

Major John C. Campbell, Chicago, Illinois. (Platoon leader with Company L, and company commander, Company K).

Major Merle Ray Carroll, Decatur, Illinois. (Battalion operations officer until September 1944, and then regimental operations officer).

Capt. Michael Hanna, Masontown, Pennsylvania. (Battalion intelligence officer, and later, adjutant).

Capt. Warren B. Hodges, Honor Guard, GHQ, FEC, Tokyo. (Platoon leader and company commander, Company I).

Lt. Lawrence P. Langdon, Omaha, Nebraska. (Platoon sergeant and platoon leader, Company K).

Lt. Eldephonse C. Reischel, Glidden, Wisconsin. (Battalion motor officer).

Chaplain (Capt.) Alexander C. Walker, 10th Infantry, Camp Campbell, Kentucky. (Chaplain with the Third Battalion).

Technical Sergeant Ralph Van Landingham, Mission, Kansas. (Platoon sergeant, Company L).

Finally, thanks are due Florence Webb Huston for assistance in preparing material for publication.

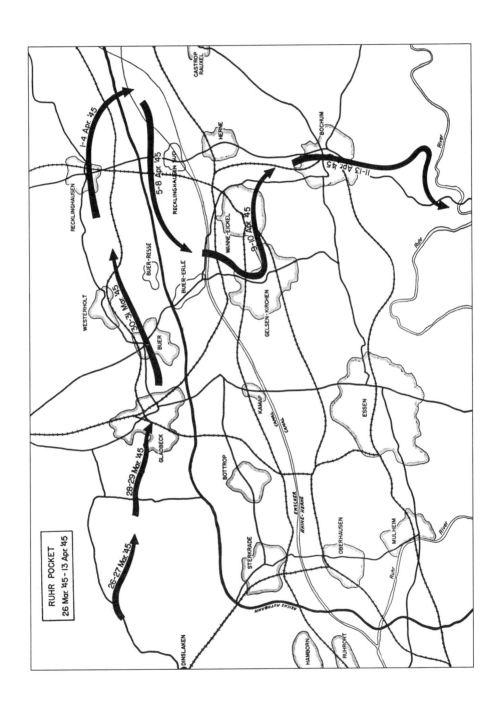

RUHR POCKET
26 Mar. '45 - 13 Apr. '45

26-27 Mar. '45
28-29 Mar. '45
30-31 Mar. '45
1-4 Apr. '45
5-8 Apr. '45
9-10 Apr. '45
11-13 Apr. '45

DINSLAKEN
HAMBORN
RUHRORT
STERKRADE
OBERHAUSEN
MULHEIM
BOTTROP
KAMAP
ESSEN
GLADBECK
BUER
WESTERHOLT
BUER-RESSE
BUER-ERLE
GELSEN-KIRCHEN
WANNE-EICKEL
RECKLINGHAUSEN
RECKLINGHAUSEN SUD
HERNE
CASTROP RAUXEL
BOCHUM

REICHS AUTOBAHN
RHINE-HERNE CANAL
EMSCHER
CANAL
Ruhr River
River
Ruhr

July 7, 1951

Dear Mr. Huston:

About a month ago, on June 6 you sent me your book, "Biography of a Battalion." I have been reading it, and I like it. It is a great contribution to the history of World War II.

General Bradley sent me his book, so did General Eichelberger. Both are excellent historical accounts from the viewpoints of a four star and a three star general.

But your "Battalion Biography" gives an account that makes the higher command possible and gives the reason for the success of these very great generals.

I believe I can understand your account better because I was one third of a Battalion of Field Artillery in World War I in the same Division as the 134th in World War II.

After our return and discharge from the Army in 1919, Jay M. Lee a 1st Lieutenant of Field Artillery wrote a history of the 129th Field Artillery in World War I.

Lt. Lee didn't get his money back for his effort and the publication costs — but his book is now selling for fifty dollars a copy! A certain Battery Commander is the cause.

I hope that you will use your experience and talents for further publications.

Sincerely,

Harry Truman

PROLOGUE

★ ★ ★

INTO THE MAELSTROM

★ ★ ★

Leading elements of the Third Battalion were moving out in a thin column of files on each side of a narrow, muddy road in Normandy. Members of the command group—the 12 to 15 officers and men of the Battalion Staff who ordinarily accompanied the battalion commander—adjusted their equipment and fell into their places in the column.

"Thank God for Tennessee; thank God for Tennessee." Lieutenant Colonel Alfred Thomsen of Omaha, Nebraska entered the road from the meadow gate and moved off with his battalion.

The battalion commander was alluding to the similarity which he sensed between the situation in which he now found himself and the marches which he had led through the mud of Tennessee during maneuvers. He was thankful that his battalion had had the experience of long and rigorous training.

That training had begun at Camp Joseph T. Robinson in Arkansas when the 35th Infantry Division first had been called into Federal service. Nebraska's National Guard regiment—the 134th Infantry—had entered upon active service in the Army of the United States two days before Christmas in 1940. Those first days the companies had gathered at local armories for organization, inoculations, lectures on the Articles of War, preparation for movement.[1]

Of the five companies of the Third Battalion which had assembled that day, two were from Omaha—Company K, and Company L. Headquarters and Company I came from Lincoln, and Company M, the heavy weapons company, came from Seward.[2]

Arriving at Camp Robinson on January 6, 1941, members of the Third Battalion had entered at once upon their long training program. On July 26th they had participated in the first division review before the division commander, Major General R. E. Truman (cousin to Harry S. Truman, the future President). Then the large-scale Louisiana maneuvers had come in August. On completion of those exercises the division had returned to Camp Robinson and the men had found themselves greeted with open arms in welcomes and parties by the chamber of commerce and the citizens of Little Rock. The governor had even gone so far as to proclaim them adopted sons of Arkansas.[3]

It had been like leaving home a second time when, seven days after the Japanese attack on Pearl Harbor, orders had come to move to the west coast—to Fort Ord, California. At first it had appeared that the division was going to move straightway to the Pacific Ocean area. However, shipping difficulties ruled this out, and the threat to the California coast made it desirable to deploy troops there. After short stays at San Francisco, Camp San Luis Obispo and Bakersfield, the division had taken over the Southern California Sector of the Western Defense Command.[4]

1. Dan E. Rowley and Robert H. Price, "The Cornhuskers". (A narrative in typescript of a company of the 134th Infantry, appended to 134th Infantry, **Daily Log and Dairy,** III, 114-122.)
2. Lt. Col. Dan E. Craig, executive, National Guard Bureau, to the author, July 10, 1946.
3. Rowley and Rice, **loc. cit.**
4. **ibid.**; History of the 134th Infantry Regiment (prep. by Information and Education Section, 134th Inf.; mimeographed) in The Information Section, (Analysis Branch) Headquarters Army Ground Forces.

Inducted as a "square" division (i.e., of two brigades, each composed of two infantry regiments, or a total of four regiments), the 35th had been reorganized March 1, 1942 as a "triangular" division with three infantry regiments and no brigade organization.[5]

There had been "stand-to's," alerts, patrols. The Third Battalion had taken up duties of patrolling the beaches north and south from Ventura—Elwood Oil Fields . . . Santa Barbara . . . Gaviota . . . Surf . . . Oxnard . . . Point Magu . . . Malibu. Those had been the days of bulky S-2 (intelligence) journals filled with notations of alleged submarines (which frequently turned out to be sea lions—though the shelling near Santa Barbara had shown that there was some danger) and of mysterious lights reported along the blacked-out coast.[6] Those had been days of growth under the command of Lt. Col. William G. Utterback.

Then an exchange in assignments with another battalion had taken the Third to the Los Angeles area where it had been on security duty at Mines Field and the North American Aircraft plant and at the Northrop plant at Hawthorne.[7]

And of course there had been training periods back at the Ojai Country Club. Here there had been squad problems and rifle and machine gun field firing; there had been firing with 60 mm and 81 mm mortars (which frequently seemed to amount to a few minutes of firing the weapon and then spending the remainder of the day in fighting brush and grass fires).[8]

And Ojai had been the scene of the inevitable formal guard mounts and battalion and regimental retreat parades. Hundreds of friends would gather on Sunday afternoons—on January 10th they numbered a thousand—for the ceremonial parades.[9]

And then had come rumors that the unit was to move, and there had been divergent speculation as to the destination. On January 20th the Third Battalion had arrived at Camp San Luis Obispo again. The 35th Division —less the 140th Infantry—had left the Southern California Sector and had assembled for a new period of training. Major General Maxwell Murray, former division commander, had remained in command of the Sector, and Brig. Gen. Paul W. Baade assumed command of the division. At San Luis there had been reviews of basic training, and small unit training, and a week of firing of weapons on the ranges—during which the breakfast hour had been moved from 6:50 to 5:30 A.M. There had been the California winter rains, and then a return of fine weather. And throughout the period Colonel Butler B. Miltonberger, the regimental commander, had continued his emphasis on discipline. Concluding one of his talks to the officers of the regiment he had remarked: "Any member of this unit found dead in battle will be found properly dressed."[10]

Now the self-styled "Hollywood Commandos"[11] had left Hollywood and California far behind, when, late in March, a trans-continental rail movement had taken them to Camp Rucker, Alabama.[12] Soon after arrival there, Colonel Miltonberger had assembled the officers to explain the new training program.

5. "35th Division" (typescript memorandum) in The Information Section—Analysis Branch—Headquarters Army Ground Forces.
6. Rowley and Rice, *loc. cit.*; 134th Inf., **Daily Log and Diary**, III, May-July 1942.
7. *ibid.*, July-November, 1942.
8. *ibid.*, December, 1942.
9. e.g., 134th Inf., **Daily Log and Diary**, IV, Jan. 3, 1943, Jan. 10, 1943.
10. *ibid.*, Jan. 13-Feb. 1; Feb. 4; March 1-6, 1943.
11. Rowley and Rice, *loc. cit.*
12. 134th Inf., **Daily Log and Diary**, IV, 20.

Noting that this was the third time that the regiment had undertaken a program of basic training, he had said: "I can tell you frankly that I think this is the last time we will train a regiment before going overseas."[13]

Camp Rucker had meant excessive heat and rigorous physical tests; from April to November the training had been intensive. More basic training at first—scouting and patrolling, first aid, military courtesy and discipline, Saturday morning inspections . . . and reviews of weapons training. An observer passing Company I one morning might have heard a lieutenant or a sergeant instructing groups gathered around BAR's:

"This weapon is called the Browning Automatic Rifle, caliber .30, model 1918A2, it is a gas-operated, air-cooled, magazine-fed, shoulder weapon of the automatic type," he would know all of this by heart after his numerous repetitions, "it has a normal cyclic rate of fire of 550 rounds per minute, and a slow cyclic rate of 350 rounds per minute. Total weight, with bipod: 21 pounds; overall length, 47 inches. . ."[14]

Or at Company M one might have heard about another weapon:

"We call this the Browning or Heavy Machine Gun, caliber .30, model 1917. It is a recoil-operated, belt-fed, water-cooled weapon fired from a tripod mount. Its fire is automatic; that is, it fires continuously as long as the trigger is held back. Its water jacket holds seven pints of water. Weight of gun and pintle, with water: 40.75 pounds; weight of tripod: 51 pounds; weight of loaded belt and chest: 20.5 pounds; length of barrel: 24 inches; muzzle velocity: approximately 2,700 feet per second."[15]

But Camp Rucker had meant more than a review of weapons training; ranger training and realistic combat training were in the vogue, and that had meant many weary miles over dusty roads in the summer heat of the Alabama sun. There had been obstacle courses . . . platoon proficiency tests . . . battalion proficiency tests (in which the Third had gained a high position in the division) . . . regimental combat team problems . . . the infiltration course (crawling under machine gun fire) . . . the combat reaction course (individual soldier would run along trail through the woods and engage surprise dummy targets with bayonet or grenade or rifle, and would surmount physical obstacles, such as crossing a stream by a tricky rope bridge while charges of dynamite exploded about him) . . . the attack of a Nazi village . . . the attack of a fortified position, where assault platoons would attack mock pill boxes with bazookas (rocket launchers) satchel charges, pole charges, flame throwers, grenades . . . the severe test of marching 25 miles in 8 hours carrying full field packs on the night of 7-8 August. . .the exacting regimental combat team exercises in the Conecuh National Forest—on the Florida-Alabama boundary, near Andalusia—late in August. And there had been more weapons firing, and inspections and drives for national service life insurance and for war bond purchases and allotments.[16]

In an address to the assembled regiment in the Camp Rucker Bowl, Colonel Miltonberger had adapted the remark of General Hale during the Philippine Insurrection—"There goes the First Nebraska, and all hell can't stop them!"—to be the regimental battle cry. Within a month the legend "All Hell Can't

13. *Ibid.*, March 30, 1943.
14. War Department, Basic Field Manual 23-35, **Browning Automatic Rifle, Caliber** 30, **M1918A2, with Bipod** (Washington: U. S. Govt. Printing office, 1940) pp. 1ff.
15. Basic Field Manual 23-35 (1940) pp. 1ff.
16. 134th Inf., **Daily Log and Diary**, IV, May 3, 22, April 1, 24, June 1, 9, July 1, 27, 29, August 7, 22, Sept. 16, 28, 1943; J. Huston to F. E. Webb, Oct. 4, Oct. 31, Nov. 9, Nov. 13, 1943.

Stop Us"—white on blue—had been placed over the door of every orderly room in the regimental area.[17]

It had been during this period that the Battalion had developed into a well-knit team. The MTP series (Mobilization Training Program) had been an integrated training program which had begun with individual training, and then had progressed through the various command units from squad to regiment and division. The "final examination" had been in the Tennessee Maneuvers—a phase whose successful completion was required of all units before movement overseas.[18]

Those maneuvers had been in the discomfort of rain and mud and cold and snow—November, December, January. There, near the scenes of celebrated engagements of the Civil War, troops of a new age had participated in war games as nearly like the real thing as could be devised. Foxholes and shelter tents had afforded little comfort in that cold and wet winter . . . but at the termination of a problem, fires (only "small fires, not more than six inches high" had been authorized during tactical conditions) would grow to great size, and some men would get passes to Nashville, and others would be taken to some school or other facility for showers (and some would combine in groups to hunt rabbits, and on finding one would send a cry through the woods: "Get that rabbit!") There had been river crossings and withdrawals and attacks and defenses.[19]

It had been a happy day for men of the Third Battalion when they, with the rest of the regiment and division, had set off for the long, cold, motor movement to Camp Butner, North Carolina. Through clear weather the motor column had begun moving at 6:00 A. M. on January 19th. They had camped near Knoxville the first night, and then had continued through attractive towns, scenic farm homes, and arresting mountain scenery; at the schools along the way children would gather to wave and shout greetings as though an army of liberators were entering. Another bivouac east of Asheville, North Carolina; another near Lexington, and at last through Chapel Hill and Durham to Camp Butner. Reconditioning of weapons and equipment had been the first order of business at the new station.[20] Once again the training schedule had taken on the aspects of basic training as review of elementary subjects was emphasized. Training in antitank mines, marksmanship and physical conditioning predominated, for example, in the Battalion schedule for the week ending February 19th:

BATTALION COMPOSITE SCHEDULE			WEEK ENDING: 19 February 1944		
(Date)	(Unit)	(Subject)	(Reference)	(Instructor)	(Area)
Mon. 14 Feb 44					
0800	All	See 60th Eng Schedule	[Instruction on antitank mine fields]		
Tues. 15 Feb 44					
0800	All	See 60th Eng Schedule			
Wedn. 16 Feb 44					
0800	All	Calisthenics	FM21-20 par 72-81	Plat Ldrs	Co Trng Areas
0815	All	Close order drill	FM22-5 par 114-158	" "	Areas
0900	All	15 Mile March	FM21-100 par 195-199	Regtl Control	

---

17. 134th Inf., **Daily Log and Diary**, IV, May 22, June 23, 1943.
18. Ray Carroll to the author, July 15, 1946.
19. 134th Inf., **Daily Log and Diary**, IV, V, Nov. 15, 1943-Jan. 18, 1944.
20. J. A. Huston to F. E. Webb, Jan. 22, 1944.

Thurs. 17 Feb 44

Time	Co	Activity	Reference	Instructor	Location
0800	All	Calisthenics	FM21-20 par 72-81	Plt Ldrs	Co Trng Areas
0815	All	Close order drill	FM22-5 par 114-158	" "	"
0900	Hq Co	Physical Training	FM21-20 par 72-81	Sgt Mumm	"
0900	I Co	Rifle Marksmanship	FM23-5 par 63-67	Plt Ldrs	"
0900	K Co	Rifle Marksmanship	FM23-5 par 63-67	Lt MacIvor	"
0900	L Co	Air Grd-Iden Trng	FM30-30, AG-12	Lt McCollister	"
0900	M Co	Rifle & Crew Svd marksmanship	FM23-5 par 63-67 FM23-55 par 99-100, FM23-90 par 83-104	Plt Ldrs	Co Trng Areas
1000	L Co	Rifle Marksmanship Trigger squeeze, positions	FM23-5 par 63-67	Lt Detterman	Areas
1000	M Co	Physical Training	FM21-20 par 72-81	Plat Ldrs	"
1100	M Co	Rifle & crew svd Marksmanship	FM23-5 par 63-67 FM23-55 par 99-110, FM23-90 par 83-104	" "	"
1100	Hq Co	Rifle Marksmanship	FM23-5 par 63-67	Cpl Mandis	"
1300	I Co	Air-Grd Iden Trng	FM30-30, AG-12	Lt Guice	"
1300	K Co	Air-Grd Iden Trng	FM30-30, AG-12	Capt Melcher	"
1300	L Co	Rifle Marksmanship Trigger squeeze, position	FM23-5 par 63-67	Plat Sgts	"
1400	I Co	Rifle Marksmanship	FM23-5 par 63-67	Plat Ldrs	"
1400	K Co	Rifle Marksmanship	FM23-5 par 63-67	" "	"
1500	I Co	Physical Training	FM21-20 par 72-81 TC #87 - '42	" "	"
1530	L Co	Physical Training	TC #87 - '42	" "	"
1600	Hq Co	Air-Grd Iden Trng	FM30-30, AG-12	Lt Juroe	"
1600	M Co	Air-Grd Iden Trng	FM30-30, AG-12	Lt Hyde	"

Fri. 18 Feb. 44

Time	Co	Activity	Reference	Instructor	Location
0800	All	Calisthenics	FM21-20 par 72-81	Plt Ldrs	Co Trng Areas
0815	All	Close order drill	FM22-5 par 114-158	" "	"
0900	Hq Co	Rifle Marksmanship	FM23-5 par 63-67	Sgt Stephan	"
0900	I Co	Rifle Marksmanship	FM23-5 par 63-67	Plat Ldrs	"
0900	K Co	Rifle Marksmanship	FM23-5 par 63-67	" "	"
0900	L Co	Rifle Marksmanship	FM23-5 par 63-67	Lt Detterman	"
0900	M Co	Rifle & crew served marksmanship	FM23-5 par 63-67 FM23-55 par 99-110 FM23-90 par 83-104	Plat Ldrs	"
1000	M Co	Physical Trng	FM21-20 par 72-81	Plat Ldrs	Co Trng Areas
1100	M Co	Rifle and crew served marksmanship	FM23-5 par 63-67 FM23-5 par 63-67 FM23-55 par 99-110,	" "	"
1300	I Co	Rifle Marksmanship	FM23-5 par 63-67	Plat Ldrs	"
1300	K Co	Rifle Marksmanship	FM23-5 par 63-67	" "	"
1300	L Co	Rifle Marksmanship	FM23-5 par 63-67	" "	Stadium
1400	I Co	Obstacle Course		" "	2d Bn Area
1425	K Co	Obstacle Course		" "	2d Bn Area
1425	I Co	Physical Trng	FM21-20 par 72-87	" "	Co Trng Areas
1400	Hq Co	Physical Trng	TC #87 - '42	Cpl Mandis	"
1525	Hq Co) & (M Co)	Obstacle Course	TC #87 - '42	Plat Ldrs	2d Bn Area
1500	I Co	Rifle Marksmanship	FM23-5 par 63-67	" "	Co Trng Area
1500	L Co	Obstacle Course		" "	2d Bn Area
1500	K Co	Rifle Marksmanship	FM23-5 par 63-67	" "	Co Trng Area
1525	L Co	Physical Training	FM21-20 par 72-81	" "	"
1600	Hq Co &) K Co & (M Co)	Physical Training	TC #87 - '42		

Sat. 19 Feb. 44

0800	All	Calisthenics	FM21-20 par 72-81	
0815	All	Close order drill	FM22-5 par 114-158	
0900	All	Ordnance inspection	Bn Control, Regtl	Regtl Control Theatre #6
NOTES:			Spot Check	
0800		Motor Call		T. O. Motor Pool
1630		Motor Call		" " "

Anti Tank Platoon under Anti Tank Company Control.[20a]

Very soon there had been another interlude in garrison life: mountain maneuvers in West Virginia. There, carrying rucksacks with a load of 60 to 70 pounds which included sleeping bags, rubberized mountain tents, aluminum tent pins, gasoline cooking stoves, and provisions, the trainees had marched over the rough terrain, climbed cliffs—with the aid of nylon ropes and hammers and pitons—and engaged in tactical exercises: defense of hill positions, attacks through the snow, crossing treacherous mountain rivers; these had given experience under trying conditions of maintaining communications, living on combat and emergency rations—C, K, and D—evacuating wounded (mostly simulated). Dressed in mountain jackets, trousers, and caps of herringbone twill, and heavy ski socks and shoepacs (rubber feet and leather uppers) with felt inner soles, they had been able to endure sudden blizzards and deep snows without suffering from frostbite or exposure.[21]

Back in Camp Butner again, the emphasis had been upon "POM" (Preparation for Overseas Movement), and another full program of range firing for all weapons soon was underway. All companies had been issued charts and each individual given a POM card to insure that he had completed all requirements specified for a soldier before overseas movement. These check cards had listed 25 items (each to be initialed by an appropriate authority):

Identification Tags O.K.
Identification Card O.K. (officers)
Immunization Register complete
Has extra glasses (if applicable)
Teeth O.K.
Infiltration Course
Fired own weapon for record
Familiarization firing
Has proper clothing and equipment
Pay Data Card on record O.K.
Emergency Addressee Card O.K.
Will, power of attorney
Medical officer's certificate
Insignia removed
Clothing and equipment marked
Baggage marked
Section VIII AR 380-5 [on safeguarding military information]
Article of War 28 [on soldier shirking hazardous duty guilty of desertion]
Allotments, insurance
Malaria control
Furloughs and leaves
Dependents allowance
Military censorship

20a. Copy, Battalion Training Schedule, 19 Feb., 1944.
21. **The Santa Fe Express,** April 1, 1944, p. 1; J. A. Huston, to F. E. Webb, March 11, 1944, March 13, 1944.

On the outside of the folded card were the words—

THIS CERTIFIES THAT
I AM POM QUALIFIED
FIT TO FIGHT
AND READY TO GO
ALL HELL
CAN'T STOP US[22]

And this had brought the inevitable "showdown" inspections for checking the completeness and serviceability of clothing and equipment. During those numerous inspections company officers would go through the barracks with check sheets for each man and then there would be "spot checks" by members of the Battalion, regimental, and division staffs and representatives from the Inspector-General's Department.[23] They would look at the displays and run down their check sheets—

	PER EM
Belt, waist, web	1
CAP, garrison, wool	1
*CAP, HBT (or Hat) [Herringbone Twill]	1
CAP, wool, knit	1
COAT, wool, serge, O.D.	1
DRAWERS, cotton, short	3
DRAWERS, wool	2
GLOVES, wool, O.D.	1
INSIGNIA, collar, branch	1
INSIGNIA, collar, U.S.	1
*JACKETS, herringbone twill	2
JACKETS, field, O.D.	1
LEGGINGS, canvas, dismounted	2
NECKTIE, cotton, mohair	2
*OVERCOATS, wool, O.D.	1
RAINCOATS, dismounted	1
SHIRTS, flannel, O.D.	2
SHOES, service, type 2 or 3	2
SOCKS, cotton, tan	3
SOCKS, wool, light or heavy	3
*TROUSERS, HBT	2
TROUSERS, wool, serge, O.D.	2
UNDERSHIRTS, cotton, summer	3
UNDERSHIRTS, wool	2
OVERSHOES, Arctic	1

CLOTHING PROTECTIVE

COVERS, (CELLOPHANE TYPE)	2
DRAWERS, wool, Prot.	1
GLOVES, cotton, Prot.	1
HOOD, wool, Prot.	1
*JACKET, HBT, Prot.	1
LEGGINGS, dismounted, cvs. Prot.	1
SOCKS, wool, light, Prot.	1
*TROUSERS, HBT, Prot.	1
UNDERSHIRT, wool, Prot.	1

EQUIPMENT

BAG, barrack	1
BAG, duffel	1
*BAG, field, canvas	1

22. 134th Inf., POM Qualification Card. (1944)
23. 134th Inf., **Daily Log and Diary,** IV, April-May, 1944.

```
BANDS, head  .......................................... 1
BANDS, neck  .......................................... 1
BELT, cartridge, 30rd................................. 1
BELT, pistol  ......................................... 1
BLANKETS, wool, O.D.................................. 2
CAN, meat  ........................................... 1
CANTEEN, almn, S/S or plastic........................ 1
*CARRIER, pack  ...................................... 1
COVER, canteen  ...................................... 1
CUP, canteen, almn or S/S............................ 1
FORK, M-26  .......................................... 1
*HAVERSACK  .......................................... 1
HELMET, steel, M-1................................... 1
KNIFE, M-26  ......................................... 1
LINER, helmet, M-1................................... 1
LINES, guy tent S/H (shelterhalf) .................... 1
NECKLACE, identification tag.......................... 1
PINS, tent, S/H....................................... 5
POLES, tent, S/H...................................... 1
POUCH, meat can....................................... 1
POUCH, first aid, packet M-42......................... 1
ROLL, bed, waterproof................................. 1
SPOON, M-26  ......................................... 1
STRAP, bag, field..................................... 1
*SUSPENDER belt  ..................................... 1
TENT, S/H  ........................................... 1
TOWELS, bath, O.D..................................... 2
```

EQUIPMENT WHEN AUTHORIZED

```
BAG, carrying ammunition.............................. 1
BELT. B.A.R.  ........................................ 3
POCKET, Mag. for carbine
POCKET, Mag. double web
```

*NOTES: *As authorized in T/E 21.[24]

As the troops prepared to leave Camp Butner, there had been another division review on the parade grounds. It was there that the division commander, Major General Paul W. Baade, had said in his address, "You have a record through training and maneuvers of which to be proud . . . this is a good division . . . in the days to come I shall at times probably call upon you to do what seems humanly impossible."[25]

From this point developments had been rapid, and on May 2nd a train carrying members of the Third Battalion had arrived in Camp Kilmer, New Jersey—at the New York Port of Embarkation. Here processing had included checking and correcting all unit records, further inspections of clothing and equipment and the drawing of new items to fill shortages, additional medical examinations and inoculations, lectures on censorship and security, abandon ship drills, issue of new type gas masks, final replacements to bring all units up to authorized strength.[26]

The Third Battalion, with the regiment, had sailed May 12th aboard the U. S. S. *General A. E. Anderson,* a naval transport of 26,000 tons. After a quiet voyage, in convoy, the vessel had docked at Avonmouth (the Port of Bristol) on May 26th where an Army Transportation Corps officer had boarded

24. 134th Inf., Individual Clothing and Equipment Check Sheet—Table of Equipment 21, 15 Dec. 1943.
25. 35th Div., **Attack!** (Orientation Section, Information and Education Division, European Theater of Operations, United States Army, 1945) p. i.
26. Carroll, loc. cit.; Staging Area Requirements (reproduced by S-3 Section, 134th Infantry, April 26, 1944); Army Service Forces, New York Port of Embarkation, **Instruction Bulletin** (1 Nov. 1943).

the vessel with complete instructions for deployment, movement, and billeting of the Battalion in Cornwall. Battalion Headquarters Company and Company M (-) had gone to Prah Sands; Company K and one platoon of M to Marazion; Company L to Porthleven; Company I to Lizard Point—all along the southern coast with billets in hotels, private homes, estates.[27]

Such dispersion of troops had made control and training difficult, but every opportunity for furthering preparation for the tasks which lay ahead had been exploited. Training had consisted mainly of marches, athletics, small unit problems.[28] An inspection of training had been the occasion for a visit to the Battalion of General Dwight D. Eisenhower, the supreme commander, and Lieutenant General George S. Patton, Jr., commander of the Third United States Army to which the 35th Division had been assigned upon its arrival in England. One of the points of interest for the generals had been a platoon of Company L which was running squad problems. The visitors reached the scene just as an "enemy" machine gun opened fire, at which an attacking squad was to take actions to reduce it. One Private Liffrieg fell to the ground as the machine gun fired, but he became confused and started crawling in the wrong direction. Immediately noticing the action, Patton shouted, "Where in the hell do you think you're going? The U. S. gives you a brand new uniform and you crawl all over the damned ground with it. Where in hell did you ever learn that?"

"In the States, sir," the soldier answered back without hesitating.

"That's just where the hell you ought to be now."

"I wish to hell I was, sir!"

Any further exchange was interrupted when Eisenhower spoke a few words to the Third Army commander.[29]

Back in training it always had seemed that movements of the regiment to new stations had been calculated to come on Sunday—so that there would be no loss in training time, but only of a day of rest. The regimental motto, "Lah We Lah His," officially translated as Pawnee Indian for "The Strong, the Brave" then had been given a new "translation"—"Lah We Lah His: We move on Sunday!" There had been no question as to meaning, then, when Colonel Miltonberger telephoned Lt. Col. Thomsen one Saturday night and said, "Lah We Lah His, 6:00 A.M.; meeting at Regimental C P in two hours. Understand, Tommy?"[30]

The 35th Division had not participated in the "D" Day assault landings on June 6th, but after that, orders had been expected momentarily for shipment across the English Channel for a role in the build-up of the Normandy beachhead. However, the "Lah We Lah His" message had been the result of a change in schedule which had moved up the departure date for the division by several days. After that midnight meeting at the regimental command post there had been much to do in little time to get the Battalion to the port. The short notice,—about five hours—the wide dispersion of the troops, separate movements of organic vehicles by highway, and foot troops by rail, all combined to make this the most difficult administrative move in the Battalion's career. But with one exception the operation had been conducted smoothly; in one of the few instances in which the Transportation Corps per-

27. Carroll, **loc. cit. For an Account of U.S.S. General A. E. Anderson,** see Arthur Gordon, "Troopships Are Never Dull," **Infantry Journal,** Aug. 1949, pp. 9-12.
28. Carroll, **loc. cit.**
29. Capt. John Campbell to the author, July 15, 1946.
30. Carroll, **loc. cit.**

sonnel erred in their contacts with the Third Battalion, Company M had turned up at Plymouth instead of Falmouth where it was assigned to go.[31]

Wearing oily, smelly, protective clothing (herringbone twill treated to protect against mustard gas) over their regular woolen uniforms to insure warmth on the channel crossing and to protect the woolens from dirt and salt water, men of the Third Battalion had boarded ships on July 3rd. Distant bombing reflections in the sky that night had seemed a fitting display as a prelude to Independence Day.

Battalion Headquarters and Headquarters Company had filed onto a Liberty Ship which carried the Battalion's motor vehicles and, as well, a part of the regimental trains. The ship had sailed on the 4th of July, and the cross-channel voyage was completed safely, though rather vigorously. As the vessel had approached the crowded beach, it had begun swerving through the maze of shipping, while the captain of the ship mounted the bridge to shout profanatory epithets at the other vessels anchored or plying near his course. Still proceeding forward in good speed, then, he had cried out, "Drop the damn anchor!—there, by God, that does it."[32]

Omaha beach had stood as testimony of the superiority of the Allied Air Forces as hundreds of ships and small craft of every kind plyed back and forth and discharged cargo; transport planes took off from a landing strip every few minutes; and the whole beach, marked by a canopy of barrage balloons, seethed with activity, practically immune to hostile air attacks. Men and equipment had gone ashore by lighters and rafts—the last group had "hitch-hiked" part of the way on a Coast Guard cutter and then had transferred to a DUKW or "Duck" (2½-ton amphibious truck) to land with their feet dry—and as they had marched up the first hill, men of the Third Battalion had sensed the debt which they owed to their predecessors (116th Infantry, 29th Division)— on the forward slope there remained a knocked-out German pill box with its gun covering the beach.[33]

Now, July 9th, the "Santa Fe" Division was being committed. But the regiment—the 134th Infantry—was being held out for the time being as corps reserve for Major General Charles N. Corlett's XIX Corps; it was marching up to an assembly area near Ste. Marguerite - d'Elle where it would be available for action on short notice. The two sister regiments—137th under Colonel Grant Layng, and the 320th, under Colonel Bernard A. Byrne, were to make an attack in a zone to the left (east) of the Vire River between LaMeauffe and La Nicollerie. The division was going into action between the 30th ("Old Hickory") Division on the right, and the 29th ("Blue and Grey") Division on the left.[34]

Here, marching through the rain that Sunday (!) afternoon in Normandy was an infantry battalion practically at full strength. This strength was authorized to be 825 enlisted men and 35 officers.[35] Its three rifle companies— I, K, L—[36] led off in order. Each of these companies included three rifle platoons—each with three 12-man squads armed with 11 M-1 (Garand) rifles

31. ibid.
32. ibid.
33. J. Huston to F. E. Webb, July 8, 1944.
34. 35th Div., Attack! p. 5; 134th Inf., **Daily Log and Diary**, V, 9 July 1944; Carroll, **loc. cit.**
35. War Department, Table of Organization and Equipment 7-15, 26 Feb. 1944, with changes 30 June 1944. See appendix.
36. In the rifle regiment, the company designations went successively, (omitting J) from A to M: A, B, C, and D comprised the 1st battalion; E, F, G, and H, the 2nd, and I, K, L, and M, the 3rd.

and one Browning Automatic Rifle—and one weapons platoon with a machine gun section of two light machine guns and a mortar section of three 60 mm mortars—plus headquarters personnel. Of the total strength of six officers and 187 men authorized each rifle company, 15 to 20 normally performed their duties in the rear areas; this included the mess sergeant and cooks, the supply sergeant and artificer, and often a few physically unfit for front-line duty. This group ordinarily was with the regimental train bivouac where, under most conditions, all the kitchens of the regiment were set up under the regimental S-4 (supply officer). The company clerk remained with the personnel section— with the company records—at division rear echelon headquarters.[37]

Then came the heavy weapons company—Company M. The greater number of its eight officers and 152 men were riding with the weapons on the company's transportation—19 jeeps,[38] and 14 ¼-ton trailers, and one ¾-ton maintenance truck. Those trailers carried the eight heavy machine guns for the two machine gun platoons (each platoon included two sections each of two squads), and the six 81 mm mortars for the mortar platoon.[39]

The fifth company was Battalion Headquarters Company. In addition to its company headquarters it had a battalion headquarters section whose members assisted the officers of the battalion staff, a communications platoon, an ammunition and pioneer platoon, and an antitank platoon. The antitank platoon had three 57 mm guns (designed after the British six-pounder). For prime movers to tow the guns and carry the crews, the platoon had three 1½-ton trucks, 6 x 6 (six-wheeled, six-wheel drive).[40]

Lieutenant Eldephonse Reischel, battalion motor officer, was bringing up the battalion's organic transportation at the rear of the column. In addition to the heavy weapons company and antitank platoon vehicles, there were two jeeps and trailers from each rifle company, nine jeeps from Battalion Headquarters and Headquarters Company,—five for the communications platoon, one carrying the antitank platoon leader, one for the S-1 (adjutant and headquarters company commander), one for the S-2 (intelligence officer), and one for the battalion commander—two jeeps from the battalion section of the regimental medical detachment, the 1½-ton A & P (Ammunition and Pioneer) truck carrying engineer tools and equipment, two 2½-ton ammunition trucks from the regimental train, and the chaplain's jeep.[41]

The triangular organization (largely borrowed from the Germans) could be seen all the way up from small to large units: three basic elements and added special troops at each level. Thus we have seen that a rifle platoon included three rifle squads, that the rifle company included three rifle platoons plus special troops—the weapons platoon, and that the battalion included three rifle companies plus special troops—the heavy weapons company and the headquarters company. Similarly the regiment consisted of three battalions and additional special troops—a headquarters company, a service company, a cannon company (105 mm howitzers), an antitank company (57 mm guns), and a

37. See Table of Organization and Equipment 7-17 (26 Feb. 1944) War Department, Infantry Field Manual 7-10; Rifle Company, Rifle Regiment, 1942) pp. 1-5; 186-188.
38. The small, powerful ¼-ton truck. Different units used different terms to name this sturdy all-purpose vehicle, and individuals usually persisted in calling it by the name they first learned. Thus some called it the "beep", and still others, the "peep". The more generally accepted term (e.g. in General Marshall's Report, p. 98) is said to have been derived from the letter-markings, "G.P." for "government property."
39. Table of Organization and Equipment 7-1S, 26 Feb. 1 1944, Change 1, 30 June 1944.
40. Table of Organization and Equipment 7-16, 26 Feb. 1944, Change 1, 30 June 1944; War Department, Infantry Field Manual 7-20: Rifle Battalion (1942) pp. 24-32.
41. See Table of Organization and Equipment 7-15; The Infantry School, Fort Benning, Georgia, Reference Data, (1942) pp. 39-43.

medical detachment and chaplains (formed into battalion sections, the medical personnel actually operated with the battalion; likewise the three chaplains each accompanied one battalion). The division—the largest unit formed under a permanent table of organization, and the smallest to include the several arms and services as organic parts—was composed of three infantry regiments plus the division artillery,[42] an engineer battalion, a medical battalion, a mechanized cavalry reconnaissance troop, an ordnance company, a quartermaster company, a signal company, a military police platoon, and a headquarters company.[43]

At the culmination of long travel and long periods of training, men were marching up soon to become engaged in new battles in the tradition of the 134th Infantry. The regiment traced its history back to 1854, and its crest depicted service (in the earlier years as the First Nebraska Volunteer or the Nebraska Infantry Regiment) in the Indian Wars, the Spanish-American War, the Philippine Insurrection, on the Mexican Border in 1916-17, in World War I as a part of the 34th Division (but did not participate in combat action as a unit).[44] On their shoulders, men of the Battalion wore the insignia of the 35th Division—a white "Santa Fe cross" upon a wagon wheel with four quadrant projections on a blue field. The cross was supposed to be taken from the white crosses which had been used to mark the Santa Fe Trail; and the insignia to symbolize the courage, hardiness, and pioneer spirit of the people whose descendants—from Kansas, Nebraska, and Missouri—formed the nucleus of the division.[45]

If any battalion could claim, on the basis of its composition, to represent a "typical" American infantry battalion, then no doubt the Third Battalion, 134th Infantry, could qualify to that description as well as any. Its antecedants lay in the Middle West—the "common denominator of America"; its original membership had come from Omaha, Lincoln, and Seward, Nebraska; but before it sailed from New York its ranks included men from every section —and most states—of the nation.[46] Its officers—all of whom shared the common experience of a course at The Infantry School, Fort Benning, Georgia— included National Guard Officers, reserve officers who had been commissioned upon graduation from Reserve Officers Training Corps courses, and those who held temporary commissions in the Army of the United States by virtue of having risen from the ranks to win an appointment to Officer Candidate School (at the Infantry School) and having completed the rigorous three-month's course of instruction.

Men of the Third Battalion were aware that they were approaching nearer and nearer. They had been aware of it since the departure from California, but then it had seemed so far away. Vaguely they had known that they were coming closer to the center of conflict as they passed the training tests at Camp Rucker and the rugged maneuvers of Tennessee and West Virginia. Inexorably they were being drawn toward that conflict by a tremendous force over which they had no control. They were but ships floating on the outer edges of a gigantic whirlpool. They were being drawn—slowly at first, then more and more rapidly—ever nearer its center. There could be no turning back, no

42. "Divarty" included three battalions (each of three four-gun batteries) of light artillery— 105 mm howitzers,—and one battalion of medium artillery—155 mm howitzers.
43. War Department, Infantry Field Manual 7-20: **Rifle Regiment** (1942) pp.1ff.; Table of Organization and Equipment 7, 26 Feb. 1944.
44. History of the 134th Infantry Regiment (mimeo.)
45. **ibid.**; 35th Div., **Attack!**, p. 2.
46. 134th Infantry Roster.

struggling against the current, no changing its course. Faster and faster they whirled toward that foreboding center. Camp Kilmer . . . inspections . . . new equipment . . . the convoy . . . Cornwall . . . the channel . . . Now they knew that the death and misery which they had been dreading were close at hand; soon they would begin "a descent into the maelstrom"—a descent to the very gates of Hades.

PART ONE—NORMANDY
★ ★ ★
CHAPTER I
★ ★ ★
HEDGEROWS AND SUNKEN ROADS
★ ★ ★

During the days of grace while the Battalion was in assembly areas prior to its commitment into active combat, the companies continued to advance their preparation for the problems ahead. The leaders had an opportunity to observe and get information from the initial attacks of the two sister regiments, and to appraise themselves from the reports of divisions already in combat. Although the Cornish countryside had been broken up into small fields by systems of hedgerows, and it was known that the terrain of Normandy would present similar obstacles, thinking had progressed little beyond the stage of speculation. Now the problem was real. It soon became obvious that certain added advantages would accrue to the defender.

This was an area whose characteristic feature was the hedgerows. Those usually consisted of banks of dirt, sometimes with stones in them, three to five feet thick, and four to six feet high. The embankments were surmounted with shrubs or trees—frequently full-grown trees—and the sides as well were covered with grass or shrubs. These earth and plant fences enclosed fields—usually meadows or orchards—of irregular shapes and sizes which seemed to average toward a quadrilateral about 100 yards long and 50 yards wide.[1]

By digging a deep foxhole—a covered one—behind and in these hedgerows, the defender could make himself almost immune from all kinds of small arms or shell fire. But that was not his only, nor his greatest advantage. There was the observation which he denied his attackers but enjoyed himself. He could have his guns zeroed in, put an observer up in a tree and wait. The attacker, on the other hand, usually could not see more than one hedgerow ahead, and could almost never see any enemy activity; and then when he did discover the enemy's presence by suddenly finding himself pinned down by enemy fire, he was too close to employ his own artillery. At the same time, the enemy found that these hedgerows provided him with covered routes for supply and evacuation and withdrawal. There were numerous roads and lanes—always running between hedgerows—leading in all directions. Frequently these would be considerably below the level of the adjacent fields—forming "sunken roads"—while the walls formed by the hedgerows would be relatively that much higher. Often the rows of trees would bend toward each other overhead and thus conceal the route from aerial observation. In a hedgerow system of defense the first dike usually was held by only a few men as an outpost line—frequently armed with machine pistols. The second row was likely to be defended more fully; it would have riflemen and machine guns well dug-in, with firing slits through the hedgerows. The third, also held with machine guns and rifles, was more thoroughly prepared with extensive tun-

---

1. 2nd Lt. David Garth, **St. Lo** (mimeographed copy of MS. scheduled for publication in 1947 by Historical Division, War Department Special Staff.)—Appendix, "Hedgerow Terrain" (prep. by 12 Army Group) p. ii; 35th Inf. Div. **Santa Fe** (Typescript. The History of the 35th Division, scheduled for publication in 1946) pp. 16-17; Ernie Pyle, **Brave Men** (New York, 1944) pp. 302ff.; Harold Denny in The New York Times, July 23, 1944, p. E5.

neling and digging. The entire position was covered by well-coordinated artillery and mortar fire. Snipers, mines, booby traps, filled in the defensive pattern. In a heavy attack, men from the first hedgerow tended to withdraw to the second or third and continue the defense. Key positions were those at the corners—near junctions of hedgerows—whence machine guns could cover the entire field in an exchange of fire with a machine gun at the next corner. Above, denying advance to the attacking troops, these automatic weapons would pin them down—fix them on a target where they would become easy prey to the bursting shells of high-angle mortar fire.[2]

Manning these defenses would be German battalions which, though they would vary in details from time to time, generally followed an organization very similar to that of the Third Battalion, 134th Infantry. Thus a full-strength infantry battalion contained 850 officers and men organized into a headquarters group and communications platoon, three rifle companies (each of three rifle platoons and special weapons) whose armament included 12 light machine guns (one for each rifle squad and platoon headquarters) three 60 mm mortars, three antitank rifles (cf. with the American rifle company's 15 Browning automatic rifles, three 60 mm mortars, and two light machine guns), and a machine gun company armed with 12 heavy machine guns (heavy machine guns were the same as light except they were mounted on heavy tripods) and six 80 mm mortars (cf. with American heavy weapons company's eight heavy machine guns and six 81 mm mortars). Most striking difference was in transportation. As against the American battalion's 40 motor vehicles (plus other attached trucks) the German battalion had 11 motor vehicles and 45 horse-drawn vehicles—and 120 horses—plus 39 motorcycles.[3]

Though the organization of the rifle squads and platoons was similar, there was a difference in emphasis between the American and German units. In the American unit the automatic weapon was a base of fire; its function was to secure the advance of the riflemen so that they could close with the enemy for a decision. In the German unit, on the other hand, it was the role of the riflemen to secure the advance of the machine gun in order to facilitate maintenance of complete fire superiority.

This difference in emphasis, together with certain other factors, was reflected in the difference in production of weapons. The American Army, with several hundred thousand Browning automatic rifles in war reserve, decided to retain this weapon of World War I as the base of fire for its rifle squad and to concentrate manufacturing efforts on the production of a new semi-automatic rifle—the M-1, or Garand. The Germans, on the other hand, retained their World War I bolt-operated rifle, but turned out quantities of a superior light machine gun, and a machine pistol. However, the American infantry fire power was able to maintain its superiority through the semi-automatic rifle.[4] The German answer was the development of a light, (air-cooled) machine gun second to none. This became the most important single weapon of the Nazi infantryman. The older model—the MG 34—weighed only 26.5

2. Garth, St. Lo; p. ii; "German Defensive Positions," (In zone of the 35th Division south of La Meauffe) The Infantry Journal, LVI, (March 1945) pp. 33-35; David Anderson, (an account of the 137th Infantry's battle for La Meauffe) in The New York Times, July 13, 1944, p. 2. An aerial photograph appended to the After Action Report, VIII Corps, July 1944, showed more than 3,900 hedged enclosures in less than eight square miles—Garth, op. cit., p. 6.
3. Lt. Col. C. R. Warndof, "German and Japanese Infantry Divisions," The Infantry Journal, LIV (April 1944) p. 34; et. al.
4. General George C. Marshall, The Winning of the War in Europe and the Pacific: Biennial Report of the Chief of Staff of the United States Army, 1943 to 1945, to the Secretary of War. (New York: Simon and Schuster, 1945) p. 98.

pounds with its bipod mount, or only five and one half pounds more than the American Browning Automatic rifle; but it could spit out bullets—loaded in non-disintegrating link belts—at a rate of 900 rounds per minute. (The American light machine gun—the Browning air-cooled found in the rifle company weapons platoons—weighed 42.25 pounds with its tripod mount, and its cyclic rate was 400 to 500 rounds per minute.—Basic Field Manual 23 - 45 (1942) pp. 1ff). With its heavy tripod mount for use as a heavy machine gun in the machine gun company, the M G 34 weighed 68.5 pounds. (cf. with the American heavy—the water-cooled Browning found in the heavy weapons company, which weighed, with its tripod, 91.75 pounds.) A newer model, the M G 42, was similar, but was of simpler construction, and was capable of firing at the very high rate of 1,200 to 1,500 rounds per minute.[5]

The German battalion, like the American, carried two types of mortars. The smaller, the one found in rifle companies, was a 50 mm piece weighing 31 pounds with a range of 55 to 550 yards (cf. with U. S. 60 mm mortar which weighed 42 pounds and had a range of 100 to 1,935 yards.—Basic Field Manual 23 - 83 (1942) pp. 1ff.). The 80 mm mortar, carried in the machine gun company, was very similar to the American 81 mm mortar found in the heavy weapons company, but it did not have the varieties of ammunition, nor the range of the American weapon. Its total weight was 125 pounds, and its range was 425 to 1,300 yards.[6] (The U. S. 81 mm mortar had a total weight of 136 pounds, and was provided with a heavy shell and a white phosphorous shell in addition to the regular HE light; with the light ammunition its range was 100 to 3,290 yards.—Basic Field Manual 23 - 90, pp. 1ff.).

Though the Germans did develop a semi-automatic rifle, it never reached the battlefield in any quantity.[7] The standard rifle continued to be the Mauser Karbiner 98. It was very similar to the American Springfield (model 1903) which, after all, was patterned after the German rifle: 23.4-inch barrel, nine-pound weight, muzzle velocity of 2,800 feet per second, bolt-operated, ammunition loaded in five-round clips, leaf sight. Its bore was of 7.92 mm (caliber .312).[8]

In their development of automatic weapons the Germans also beat the Americans to mass production of the machine pistol.[9] There were two German models: The Schmeisser MP 38 and MP 40. They carried 32-round clips, and fired 9 mm parabellum cartridges; their grips and handguards were of plastic. (Just recently the American Battalion had receievd 20—six for each rifle company and two for headquarters company—new caliber .45 submachine guns, M 3.—Table of Organization and Equipment 7 - 15, Change 1, 30 June 1944.) In addition the Germans had two 9 mm pistols (favorite items among souvenir collectors)—the Luger, 1908, and the Walther P 38.[10]

The Third Battalion practiced during those days at attacking over the hedgerows with rifle squads, the use of supporting weapons, methods of breaking through the embankments—with charges of TNT—to assist the advance of tanks. Other final preparations included the disposal of excess baggage. All clothing and equipment which was not going to be needed in combat was put

5. Lt. John Scofield, "German Infantry Weapons," **The Infantry Journal**, LIV, (Jan. 1944) pp. 37-40, et. al.
6. **Ibid.** p. 40.
7. General Marshall's Report, p. 98.
8. Scofield, **loc. cit.**, pp. 35-36.
9. Marshall, **op. cit.**
10. Scofield, **loc. cit.**, pp. 36-37.

into duffle bags and stored in the custody of a regimental Service Company officer.[11]

Some of the officers, feeling that the carbine with which they were armed would not provide them with sufficient fire power, began looking around for other weapons. Some traded for a Garand; others found Thompson submachine guns. Actually the carbine was not such an unsatisfactory weapon for an officer. It was easy to handle—only 35½ inches long, and weighed only 5½ pounds—but had the necessary volume of fire (carried a magazine of 15 rounds) and was a semi-automatic (self-feeding) weapon; with an effective range of 300 yards and a maximum range of 2,200 yards, and with a muzzle velocity of 2000 feet per second for its .30-caliber bullet, it had the power requisite for its purpose.[12] It was not intended that an officer should engage habitually in a fire fight; his weapon was for his personal protection or other emergencies. If he were out firing at the enemy it usually would mean that his men were being neglected; his job was to run a platoon and direct the fire of several weapons. (Later, many officers carried only pistols.)

The heavier (9½ pounds) and longer (43.6 inches) M-1 or Garand rifle was harder to handle. Its presence would make it more difficult for the officer to refer to his map, to use his compass and field glasses, to make notes, to move about quickly. But in the hands of the rifleman it was unexcelled. It too was a semi-automatic weapon, carrying eight-round clips. Firing the ordinary M-2 ball ammunition (caliber .30) it had a muzzle velocity of about 2,800 feet per second, and a maximum range of approximately 3,500 yards.[13]

After four days in the assembly area, there still was no word as to when the Third Battalion might be expected to move. Colonel Miltonberger paid a visit to division headquarters on the night of July 12th, but called back to his command post to say that there was no change in the situation. There was no change until the following night when Colonel Thomsen and Captain Carroll (S-3) were called to a meeting at the regimental command post at 10:30. One battalion—the Third—was to relieve elements of the 29th Division that same night; the other two battalions were to prepare to attack on the 15th.[14]

On the return of the battalion commander, the company commanders and members of the battalion staff gathered in the command post tent to hear his instructions. Here were the leaders of the Third Battalion on whose shoulders rested the responsibility for 800 men in battle and for the accomplishment of the assigned missions. Focal point for troop responsibility was in the company commander. A myriad of details demanded his personal attention; he had no staff, but he had an executive officer to assist him, and he could call upon his platoon leaders, and the enlisted men of his headquarters. He had to be a small-unit tactician, a combat leader, an administrator. His general duties were extensive:

> The commander is responsible for the discipline, administration, supply, training, tactical employment, and control of his company. He is responsible that his company is trained to accomplish its combat tasks decisively; to function as an effective unit in the military team. He must anticipate and plan in order to prepare his company for prospective missions; his supervision must be continuous to insure that all subordinates properly execute their part in the company task. Decision as to a specific course of

11. M. R. Carroll to the Author, July 15, 1946; 134th Infantry, S-3 Journal, 9 July 1944.
12. War Department, Basic Field Manual 23-7, pp. 1ff.
13. War Department, Basic Field Manual 23-5 (1940) pp. 1ff.
14. 134th Inf., S-3 Journal, 12 July 1944; 134th Inf., Unit Journal, 13 July 1944; Carroll, loc. cit.

action is his responsibility in conformity with orders from higher headquarters. While he may accept advice and suggestions from any of his subordinates, he alone is responsible for what his unit does or fails to do.[15]

The Third Battalion's three rifle company commanders were Captain Joseph P. Hartung, Company I; Captain Richard D. Melcher of Omaha, Nebraska, Company K; and Captain James Lassiter of Massachusetts, Company L. Commander of Company M, the heavy weapons company, was First Lieutenant Earl J. Ruby of Grand Island, Nebraska.

To Captain O. H. Bruce of Maryland, adjutant and S-1 fell the dual functions of chief administrative officer of the battalion staff and commander of the battalion headquarters company. He was concerned primarily with personnel reports—strength and casualties, replacements, morale, making reconnaissance for movement of the battalion command post and supervising its set-up and security, arranging for quartering parties, allotting space to the companies in bivouac and assembly area.[16] As commander of the headquarters company he was responsible for its administration, discipline, and training, but not for its tactical employment.[17] (The antitank, communications, and ammunition and pioneer platoon leaders operated directly under the battalion commander, coordinating through S-3.)

As operations officer (S-3), Captain Ray Carroll of Illinois was the battalion commander's principal assistant in matters pertaining to training and tactical operations. He had to keep himself informed of the situation and be prepared to give the commander information of friendly troops in the area, to make detailed plans based on the battalion commander's decision, and to recommend possible lines of action. He would have to prepare operation maps and overlays and supervise communications; he would prepare field orders and transmit orders and instructions for the battalion commander to the company commanders and coordinate their execution. And his function of planning and supervising all training assured him of duties during periods when the Battalion was not engaged in combat.[18]

The Battalion's supply officer was First Lieutenant G. I. Stoneburner of Virginia. Technically assigned to Service Company, he served two masters: the regimental S-4, who commanded the regimental supply section, and the battalion commander whose demands he was trying to satisfy. Then there was the intelligence officer (S-2) whose principal duties were concerned with information of the enemy.[19]

Chief of this Battalion Staff was Major Foster H. Weyand of Nebraska, executive officer. A veteran of World War I and of the 2nd Battalion's expedition to the Aleutians in 1942, he was the second-in-command. He usually would remain at the command post to coordinate activities of the staff while the battalion commander went forward.[20]

In addition to the regular battalion staff, there was the "special staff" which included officers commanding certain special units: motor transport officer (Lt. Eldephonse Reischel of Wisconsin), antitank officer (Lt. Clyde Payne of Nebraska), communications officer (Lt. Floyd Garner of Arizona), ammunition and pioneer officer (Lt. Charles D. Hall of South Carolina), the battalion surgeon (Capt. John Matthew of Indiana), the heavy weapons com-

15. War Department, Infantry Field Manual, 7-10: **Rifle Company, Rifle Regiment**, pp. 7-8.
16. War Department, Infantry Field Manual, 7-20: **Rifle Battalion** (1942) p. 6.
17. **ibid.** pp. 24-25.
18. **ibid.**, p. 7.
19. **ibid.**, pp. 6-8.
20. **ibid.**, pp. 5-6.

pany commander, and the artillery liaison officer.[21] And of course there was the chaplain: Alexander C. Walker, a Southern Baptist from Virginia.

But the responsibility for the Battalion centered in its commander, Lt. Col. Alfred Thomsen of Omaha; functions of command could not be delegated. Colonel Thomsen appeared to be big enough to handle the responsibilities. His height was over six feet two inches, and his big frame carried more than 225 pounds. He had been a railroad blacksmith in the Union Pacific shops; but his physique was that of the traditional village blacksmith. He was proud of his enormous strength and agility. This he used to demonstrate back at Camp Butner by walking over to his office doorway and kicking the top of it. He delighted in enticing young lieutenants half his age into trying to imitate this feat. Invariably they would fail, and frequently would fall flat on their backs in the attempt. His short hair left an island of baldness in the center which he blamed onto the old-type steel helmet which he had worn in training during the First World War and the early part of this.

The colonel always was fixing up some kind of device for added comfort or convenience. Back in California he had invented an instrument for passing up written messages from a jeep to the cab of a big truck in a moving convoy: it was a clothes pin on a stick. One member of the group was wearing a wrist watch whose strap was secured not by sewing, but by an application of Colonel Thomsen's glue—and it worked. He used his favorite glue for everything—on metal, paper, cloth, wood, or leather; the substance did not matter. This was his panacea for all mending. When a member of the Battalion found himself confronted with a broken part of a weapon or a damaged vehicle, he was likely to call out for some of "Colonel Thomsen's glue." In order that he could have shelter in which to sit up during maneuvers, he had had an additional strip of canvas sewed to his pup tent. Disgusted with the perpetual shortness of raincoats, he obtained two of the waterproof garments and had the lower half of the second sewed onto the bottom of the first. It fell all the way to the heels of his shoes; when he wore it he looked as though he were peering out of the top of a pyramidal tent. The men would refer to things of the Colonel's in making comparisons in the superlative: an especially large tent or balloon was "as big as Colonel Thomsen's raincoat"; a massive pack or bulky load was "as heavy as Colonel Thomsen's bed roll"; a big collection of papers was "as thick as Colonel Thomsen's notebook"; all the men had known exactly the type of lifejacket they were to be issued on the transport ship when Major Weyand told them, "They look just like Colonel Thomsen's field jacket."

When he wished, the Colonel could command all of polish ever required of a lieutenant colonel of the United States Army at the most correct social function. But in the field he preferred to let his boisterous, swashbuckling nature dominate. At the same time Alfred Thomsen was as strong in his principles as he was boisterous in his talk. He was a "rugged individual" and he would stand firmly against all odds for what he believed to be right. When the chaplain held church services in the battalion, he and the major always would go and sit on the front row. He urged his officers to do the same thing. Once in England a few days before the Battalion's departure, Headquarters and "M" Company officers were sitting at the dinner table when he paused in the conversation and then said, "We all have our fun with Chappie, but you know

21. *Ibid.*, pp. 4-5.

it wouldn't hurt any of us to go down to his services and help him out; it is not going to be very long now until we are going to be needing help from Somebody up there who is a lot bigger than any of us; then we've got to have something to believe in to give us hope."

That the Third Battalion now was about to enter the line in Normandy rather than in some other section of western France was the result of long study on the part of the high-level planners. A basic consideration had been the need for port facilities to maintain a force of some 26 to 30 divisions and to enable augmentation by three to five divisions a month. Other factors included the type of beaches, the location with respect to an offensive against Germany, and the extent of the enemy defenses. The Pas-de-Calais region presented the advantages of proximity to England, favorable beaches, and the most direct route to Germany. But, on the other hand, that area was the most formidably defended on the whole French coast. Normandy, then, represented something of a compromise. Its military geography was not as favorable, but neither were the defenses so strong. From here it had been considered that necessary port facilities could be obtained by the seizure of Cherbourg and then of the Brittany ports; but in the meantime supplies were being brought into the beach areas through two artificial harbors—Mulberry A and B.[22]

After initial successes, the attacks in Normandy were falling behind schedule. Allied planners had hoped for the fall of Cherbourg by D-plus-8; it had not come until D-plus-21 (June 27th). The V Corps was to have taken St. Lo by D-plus-9, but now, on D-plus-37 the German II Parachute Corps had rallied to prevent any breakthrough to St. Lo as the First Army continued its drive; indeed Panzer Lehr, the pride of German armored divisions, had just been committed to launch a counterattack on July 11th, but the 9th and 30th Divisions had been able to repel it.[23] Actually, gains had been slow and costly in all sectors since the capture of Cherbourg. The VIII Corps had been able to take La-Haye-du-Puit only after a week's heavy fighting; the VII Corps had made slight gains along the Carentan-Periers highway; XIX Corps—for which the 134th Infantry and the Third Battalion had been serving as reserve— had established a bridgehead across the Vire River at St.-Jean-de-Daye and now was attacking astride the river southward toward St. Lo. Meanwhile in the sector farther east, the British Second Army was making little progress in the Caen area.[24]

Soon after receiving the orders, the Third Battalion was ready to move. While the troops marched through the darkness toward the front, Colonel Thomsen and members of his staff went forward by jeep to coordinate the relief with the commander and staff of the 115th Infantry (29th Division) and the two front-line battalions in positions east of a village called Villiers-Fossard (a little over three miles northeast of St. Lo) which would be concerned. Captain Carroll, the S-3, then went down to coordinate with the left battalion, while the battalion commander supervised the details on the right (with the 115th Infantry's 2nd Battalion). This meant a total frontage of about 2,000 yards for the Battalion, and to cover it, Colonel Thomsen disposed all three companies on the line: Company L on the right, Company I in the center, and Company K on the left. Officers and men alike of the battalions being relieved bore the

22. Brig. Gen. Paul W. Thompson, "Why Normandy," **The Infantry Journal**, LVIII (Feb. 1946) p. 10; General Eisenhower's Report, pp. 1-2, 12.
23. ibid., pp. 7, 33.
24. ibid., p. 33.

mark of weariness from weeks of continuous battle in the hedgerows; news that they were to be relieved was about the only kind which could have evoked any expression in their countenances. Relief was not completed until about 10:30 the next morning (July 14th), but it was accomplished without incident and without confusion. The Battalion command post moved into the place vacated by the 2nd Battalion, 115th Infantry—a well-constructed dugout, lighted from automobile batteries, beside a hedgerow—and took over the existing communications systems.[25]

During the day, leaders of the 1st and 2nd Battalions made reconnaissance —insofar as the hedgerows and enemy would permit—and completed preparations for their attack toward the regimental objective: St. Lo.

25. Carroll, loc. cit.; 134th Inf., Unit Journal, 14 July 1944.

CHAPTER II

★ ★ ★

"ASSEMBLE AT EMELIE"

★ ★ ★

Saint Lo was the key to the Normandy defenses. The town was not a very large one (peace time population: about 12,000[1]) but it was the most important road center in the area. It was the anchor of the German defenses in Normandy. Not only did the main defense line of the Cotentin Peninsula—along the St. Lo-Periers-Lessay highway—hinge there, but so did the secondary line—along the St. Lo-Coutances highway—as well.[2] About 47 miles southeast of Cherbourg, St. Lo lay to the west of a horseshoe bend in the Vire River at the base of the Cotentin Peninsula. It was the capital of the French department of Manche.[3] Moreover, it was from St. Lo that it seemed most likely that the Germans would launch a counterattack against the Americans. It was known that headquarters for the German LXXXIV Corps were located there, and it appeared to be the command center for Military Administrative Area A. The Air Forces therefore had been instructed to prevent movement through the city. In consequence of this action, 60 per cent of the buildings of St. Lo already had been destroyed by the beginning of July.[4]

Its beachhead established and the port of Cherbourg captured, the First Army's problem in July was to extend its area—by continued attacks to the south—in order to gain the terrain required for maneuver, build-up, and traffic. Earlier plans—late in June—had contemplated capture of the St. Lo-Marigny-Coutances line; however, early in July this objective was modified to the St. Lo-Periers-Lessay line—now the American commanders considered that the terrain along the St. Lo-Periers road was satisfactory for mounting operation COBRA—the blow designed to produce a breakout.[5] But St. Lo had to be taken in any case. It figured as prominently in the American offensive plans as it did in German defensive strategy.

The 30th Division inaugurated the XIX Corps' battle for St. Lo with an attack on July 7th against a German salient which pointed toward the corps right (west) flank. In addition to the desirability of reducing the German salient, the necessity of gaining time to permit the arrival of the 35th Division into the line and for coordination with the 2nd and 29th Divisions had recommended this preliminary attack.[6]

The 29th had had difficulty in launching any attack at all. Itself the victim of a night attack by German paratroopers, the 29th Division had been combatting the main enemy defenses. The 116th Infantry had been able to advance satisfactorily in the left of that division's zone on July 11th, but the 115th, on the right, had been unable to achieve such progress. The next day (July 12th) had been no better.

---

1. Encyclopedia Britannica World Atlas (Chicago, 1942) p. 104.
2. Drew Middleton in **The New York Times**, July 16, 1944, p. 1, and July 18, 1944, p. 1.
3. Lippincott's Gazetteer, p. 1611.
4. **St. Lo** (MS), p. 3.
5. **ibid.**, p. 4.
6. **ibid.**, pp. 16-17. An unfortunate incident in this attack occurred on July 9th when tanks of the 3rd Armored Division made the wrong turn at the Pont Hebert road and drove back toward St. Jean de Daye and the oncoming infantry of the 30th Division who were thrown into confusion when hit by this surprise armored "counterattack."—p. 17.

The 2nd Battalion, 115th Infantry, fighting on the west of the St. Lo-Isigny road ended the day without advance. Twice it attacked across a stream at Bourg d'Énfer and each time artillery, mortar, and small arms drove it back. An enemy counterattack caused a platoon on the left to break, a rumor of withdrawal spread, and other platoons pulled out. The retreat finally was stopped on the line of departure, where Colonel Ordway ordered the Battalion C. O. to reorganize and prepare to resume the attack, but the battalion could not get going.[7]

It was in these circumstances, then, that the Third Battalion effected its relief.

By July 11th the enemy units in front of the elements of the 35th Division who were attacking on the right of the 29th appeared to be the 897th, 898th, and 899th Infantry, comprising Kampgruppe Kenthner, and the Panzer Lehr Division.[8]

American pushes toward St. Lo from both north and east had come practically to a standstill at distances of from two to three miles from the city. The British had been meeting the same kind of resistance in the Caen area— the Nazis were holding all along the front. A Vichy radio broadcast on the 12th announced that Von Kluge, German commander in Normandy, was expecting "an all-out American drive for St. Lo." Another German source added that a new German panzer division had been thrown into the battle in the St. Lo area.[9] Indeed the Germans had reason for concern.

A powerful and coordinated corps attack, the "Sunday Punch," had been ordered for July 15th. And in the 35th Division's attack, the 134th Infantry was to make the main effort toward St. Lo itself—with the immediate objective of taking the high ground: Hill 122, before the city—while the 137th made a feint on the right.[10]

Colonel Miltonberger received the division attack order at 4:30 P.M. on the 14th, and he issued his order to the battalion commanders two hours later. The attack south for St. Lo would jump off at 5:15 with the 1st Battalion on the right and the 2nd Battalion on the left. The Third Battalion was to remain in position prepared to assist, and would assemble on order to continue the attack. Additional battalions of artillery were to join the Division Artillery in laying down a virtual rolling barrage in front of the infantry. Each battalion was to have a company of tanks[11] attached, and there was to be a company of TD's (tank destroyers) and Company A of the 60th Engineer Battalion.[12]

The noisy armor moved up to forward assembly positions during the night, but drew only slight artillery fire. The 1st and 2nd Battalions prepared to go.

7. Ibid., pp. 86, 116.
8. 35th Division, After Action Report, 5 Aug. 1944. Panzer Lehr had been activated in France early in 1944 with completely new equipment. Assigned the unique mission of driving the Allied invaders back into the sea, it had received completely new equipmnet—and it was 100 per cent armored (including its infantry). Its commander described it as the best equipped panzer division that Germany ever had. And its personnel had been teachers and demonstrators of armored tactics. However, this crack division had suffered some misfortunes since the invasion. It had suffered heavy losses in the Caen sector, and then had been hit by air attack while shifting to the St. Lo sector. Nevertheless it had launched a counterattack on July 11th which had been quite effective initially—it had accidentally attacked through a gap between the 29th and 30th Divisions (as its commander sought to strike at the 29th Division which he considered to be less effective at this time) and so was in a position to move against the flanks. Finally, however, those American divisions had been able to strike back with such vigour as to eliminate it practically as a serious threat in the St. Lo area—it was estimated that the German elite unit suffered losses of 50 per cent during one day's action.—St. Lo, MS. p. 63.
9. The Stars and Stripes (ETO ed.), July 13, 1944, p. 1.
10. St. Lo, (MS) pp. 123, 128.
11. It was normal now for each infantry division to have a battalion of tanks (a tank strength equal to one-third that of an armored division) and a battalion of tank destroyers.—General Eisenhower's Report, p. 122. Units working with the 35th Division were the 737th Tank Battalion and the 654th Tank Destroyer Battalion—Santa Fe, p. 207.
12. 3rd Bn. Notebook, I; M. R. Carroll to the author, July 15, 1946.

At 5:15 the artillery opened fire and the troops started to move; the 115th Infantry, on the left, jumped off at the same time to renew its assault from the east.[13] Von Kluge's "all-out American drive for St. Lo" was on.

But the German artillery had opened up as soon as the American; the chatter of small-arms fire followed. It appeared that the enemy was launching an attack of his own! Already men of the Third Battalion, even as they lay in their foxholes, were getting it. Men of Company I could see Germans starting to move, but the threat to the position actually was not permitted to become serious. However, the German shelling claimed its toll. First casualty was Captain Joseph Hartung, commander of Company I. An "old Army man," Hartung had been preparing for this day during all the years of his training; and now, minutes after the first combat operation had begun, he lay helpless. Ordinarily when the company commander was hit, the executive officer would take command. However, within a few minutes after Hartung had been hit, a high explosive shell fell almost in the midst of the area—a few foxholes along a hedgerow—being used for a company command post, First Lieutenant Billy Guice of Louisiana, executive officer, was wounded; First Sergeant Connors—a veteran of World War I—was wounded so severely that he was at first reported dead.[14] This was the first in a series of events which was to make Company I the ill-fated company of the Battalion for its company commanders.

When this news reached Colonel Thomsen he called Captain Philip Bauer. Assigned to the Battalion back at Camp Butner, Bauer had been designated "on paper" as commander of Company M. Actually he had been retained at Battalion headquarters where he had proved his capabilities in staff work. Now the colonel handed him one of the most difficult assignments in combat:

"Go up and take command of Company I, and get it reorganized."

"Yes, sir."

Bauer did not know a noncommissioned officer up there; the company was in confusion after losing its commander, its executive officer, its first sergeant; as a matter of fact that shell practically had eliminated all of the company headquarters personnel. But the company's new commander—the third within an hour—went forward immediately and got the position reorganized.[15]

Meanwhile the attacking battalions had become engaged in some terrific fire fights. The 1st Battalion had been able to make considerable initial progress behind the heavy rolling barrage, but the 2nd was having difficulty even getting beyond the Third Battalion's lines. Both sides were laying down intense artillery, mortar, and small arms fire.[16]

Communications were difficult because shell fire kept breaking the telephone lines. And so much credence had been given to stories about how radios drew artillery fire that those instruments had been ordered kept silent. This order was modified somewhat when a message came at 6:35 authorizing radios to be used to transmit position locations (in code, of course) and flash warnings.[17]

Shortly before 8 o'clock a message reached the Battalion command post which directed First Lieutenant William Brodbeck, executive officer of Company L—schooled under Captain James Lassiter—to report to the 2nd Battalion

13. 134th Inf., S-3 Journal, July 15, 1944.
14. Carroll, loc. cit.
15. Carroll, loc. cit.
16. Ibid.
17. 134th Inf., S-3 Journal.

to take command of Company G whose C.O. had just been wounded. (Later it was learned that the original commander was killed by a second shell as he was being carried away on a litter.) By noon Brodbeck himself was back at the aid station with a wounded leg.[18]

The 1st Battalion was having a difficult time of it. It was reported that "C" Company had suffered more than 65 casualties during the first three hours, and the other companies had been hit hardly less severely. Nevertheless they continued to make progress. At 12:50 Colonel Boatsman reported that his 1st Battalion had advanced some 2200 yards and was now only 600 yards from the top of strongly-defended Hill 122—key terain feature before St. Lo, and immediate regimental objective. Colonel Miltonberger decided to assemble the Third Battalion to exploit the success of the 1st. It began to look as though this might be a long-awaited break.[19]

The Battalion Commander sent Captain Carroll, S-3; Captain Bruce, S-1; Captain Ruby, heavy weapons company commander, together with some enlisted men of battalion headquarters, forward to reconnoiter for an assembly area for the Battalion. They moved off toward Emelie while the companies prepared to assemble for the march up to the new position. Actually it was nearly 5 P.M. before the companies began to move, and, concerned lest there might be some delay in finding the party which had gone forward, Colonel Thomsen sent Lt. Reischel (motor officer) and Lt. Payne (antitank officer) to locate the first group and to select a site for the battalion motor park somewhere south of Villiers-Fossard.

These preparatory measures taken, Colonel Thomsen moved up to the head of the column which Headquarters Company was forming, and, accompanied by the remaining members of his staff, began to lead the troops over to the Villiers-Fossard road. Remembering his training habits, the Colonel sent out a "point"—a patrol of three or four men—as a security measure. The leading scout turned out to be Sgt. Donald Buckley—the Headquarters Company supply sergeant![20]

The column was moving parallel to the front—moving over to the right to find the road. The men passed some soldiers who said that they were from Company A. The only answer to an inquiry by one of the officers as to how the 1st Battalion troops were doing was, "Oh, they're all shot to hell, sir."

A few minutes later there was some rapid cracking noises over the heads of the men of the Third Battalion,—followed a second later by a similar succession in a lower key. It was one of the hated German machine pistols or "burp guns." It sounded like the noise of a flicker working at top speed on a telephone pole while a second answered on the trunk of a hollow tree. The first burst of noise was the sound of the bullets cracking overhead; the "echo" —moments later—was the report of the gun itself. That made it difficult— especially for the uninitiated—to guess from what direction the fire was coming.

---

18. **Ibid.**
19. **Ibid.**, Some of the afternoon's entries in the Regimental S-3 Journal were:
"1320—Gen. Baade (division commander) comes to CP of 134th to study plans and coordinate the exploitation of the 1st Bn. advance.
1325—Talked with artillery executive officer—authorized one arty. Bn. to 2nd Bn. until follow-up on right starts.
1345—Gen. Corlett (corps commander)—Just talked to 115th Inf. and they have not advanced materially. He believes we have something here. Supplement this thing to the fullest. To break this defense would save lots of casualties in units on right and left.
1440—516659 (map cordinates) Counter-attack forming.
1630—F Company held off the counter-attack, NCO, Company F report Capt. Scully the bravest sunofabitch they ever saw. 2nd Bn. going ahead."
20. A supply sergeant's duties ordinarily kept him at the regimental train bivouac during combat.

"Nothing but a sniper or two," Colonel Thomsen said, "let's go."

Soon the leading men dropped down to a road. To be sure it ran in the direction of St. Lo, but the Colonel was not sure that this was the road which he had pointed out on the map. Now Colonel Thomsen took great pride in

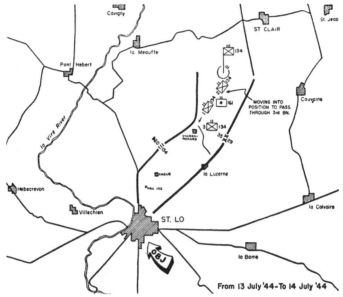

Moving into position. Objective: St. Lo.

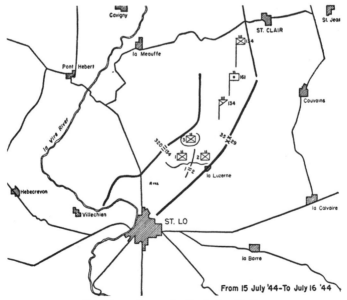

Opening phase of attack for St. Lo.

his map and aerial photograph reading—he probably knew no peer in the regiment; but this gravel road was so apparently unused that he was not sure that it was the one for which he was looking—there was no way of knowing how many roads and lanes there might be on the ground which did not appear on the map. The commander then led his column on across the road. Either he should find a more promising road, or should find the unit on the right—the 320th Infantry.

Actually, on crossing another series of hedged meadows he did contact troops of the sister regiment, and so was assured that that road was the one being sought. But as the column turned about to recross a field, the close crackling of a Nazi machine gun sent everyone down in the tall grass. Some of the men crawled a short way, hesitated, got up, hit the ground again in response to another burst. Finally they made it over the next hedgerow and down to the road by advancing in short rushes: four or five men at a time would get up and run at full speed until behind new cover. This presented too poor a target to draw any more fire.

Now Reischel hurried up to tell the battalion commander that he had run into German soldiers in the area where he had hoped to locate the motor park. The colonel's reaction was that the motor officer had gone to the wrong place. Reischel then set out to find that machine gun; again he found German soldiers moving about—he fired a few times, but the only result was another burst of machine gun fire over the Battalion Staff.[21] It did not improve the situation any when Carroll, Bruce, and Ruby returned to say that they had begun to allocate company areas in a new forward assembly position when they too noticed numerous enemy soldiers in the vicinity—"and their actions were definitely not friendly."[22]

The proposed assembly area was behind the zone of advance of the 1st Battalion, and supposedly had been cleared out during the day's attack. Confident that the enemy troops which had been seen were only a few which the other battalion had by-passed, the colonel determined to advance to the new area. He sent the S-2 and a couple of his intelligence scouts forward to see if they could locate and neutralize the machine gun which had been making the trouble. Impatient after a few minute's wait, he called for a platoon from Company L to go up to help out the intelligence section on the right of the road, and then formed the remainder of the Battalion—less Company I who apparently had become involved in a fight alongside the 1st Battalion up to the front—into a route column along the road. Company K furnished the advance guard, and Colonel Thomsen took his staff up to accompany the point.[23]

Meanwhile Reischel led a squad from Company L up to the place where earlier he had seen two enemy soldiers along a hedgerow in some bushes. These had departed, but now the motor officer directed the fire of the squad to assist Lt. Lou Dailey's platoon which had gone forward. Suddenly a burp gun opened fire from the same side of the hedgerow; Reischel quickly returned the fire, but missed, and his antagonist scampered over the hedge and then threw a "potato masher" grenade. Fortunately for the Third Battalion's motor officer, the grenade hit the hedgerow and bounced back before it exploded. Reischel's reply was a grenade of his own.[24]

21. Reischel, loc. cit.
22. Carroll, loc. cit.
23. Ibid.
24. Reischel, loc. cit.

By now the battalion column was approaching. As the point reached the vicinity where the reconnaissance party had observed the enemy soldiers, it came under intense cross fire from well-located machine guns. The Battalion Staff, as well as the leading elements of Company K, were pinned to the ground. Already the platoon of "L" Company—in an orchard on the right above the sunken road—were in a vigorous fire fight. The head of the Battalion (the troops were in a column of twos—one on each side of the road) was at a slight bend in the road, and now machine guns, commanding the road from a large brick house some 150 yards beyond, began spraying the road; "burp guns" rattled to the left and rear; shell fire began to drop along the road to add to the confusion. Small mortar shells were bursting along the adjacent fields, on the tops of the hedgerows, and then down the road. Larger caliber mortar and light artillery shells began to burst all around—they seemed to have a way of hitting the tops of hedgerows, and, bursting in red flames and black smoke, would send fragments and dirt on the men who were seeking cover in the shallow side-ditches below. Wounded men—those who could—began making their way to the rear.

Two men, assigned the mission of working up to the brick house to destroy the machine guns, scrambled up the bank and over the hedgerow on the left. But just as their heads disappeared on the other side, a large-caliber shell burst at precisely the same spot.

Now a new threat appeared. A quick-firing, direct-fire gun was searching down the shoulder of the road where the men lay seeking cover against the bank. Captain Ray Carroll drew his .45-caliber pistol. What was it? A tank! Colonel Thomsen had disappeared from the sight of his staff. He had found an opening in the hedgerow and made his way forward along the edge of the meadow. There he saw the approaching armored vehicle; but there was a group of four or five soldiers accompanying it on foot. Traditionally the best pistol marksman in the Batallion, he drew his Colt .45 and took aim; he fired—and missed. Six more rounds he fired, and missed every time.

The men were hearing of this tank, and began drawing back. Obviously this was no place for a rifle battalion. Down in this narrow cut, strung out in a column where it could not fight back, with a tank approaching which was capable of laying down a devastating enfilade fire, and automatic weapons and mortars playing on every side, the Battalion was in a good position to be completely cut up—to be annihilated without having even been committed to action! It was imperative that the Battalion be withdrawn in time to permit reorganization in a formation in which it could fight. The column turned back toward Villiers-Fossard and the companies moved off the road to take up defensive positions north of the creek which ran across the zone about 400 yards to the front (south) of the village. A command post was established along a hedgerow in a field immediately south of Villiers-Fossard. Inasmuch as the whereabouts of Colonel Thomsen were, at this point, unknown, the reorganization was undertaken under the supervision of the executive officer, Major Weyand.

However, the reorganization was a difficult enough task itself now. Word came that Company I was up on the flank of the 1st Battalion which still was attacking for Hill 122. Captain Melcher of "K" Company tapped in his company telephone on the regimental wire to try to find out where the Third Battalion now was located. And amidst all of this, regimental and division staff officers were discussing sending the Third Battalion into an immediate attack for Hill 122![25]

It was dusk by the time Captain Carroll got to the C.P. after coordinating the defenses of the companies, and after a vain effort to find Colonel Thomsen. At 8:25 the field telephone rang. It was Brigadier General Edmund B. Sebree, assistant division commander. Carroll, out of breath, and still not fully oriented on the new position of the Battalion, took the call, and tried to explain the situation. The general was not interested in alleged obstacles, but was blunt and to the point. "Be in Emelie by 2200 (10 P.M.) tonight," he said.[26]

Shortly after, Colonel Thomsen appeared. Cut off for a time behind German lines, the C. O. had made his way back by creeping and crawling through mortar and machine gun fire to safety. Now, after learning what he could of the situation in a few minutes, he called regimental headquarters to give a vigorous explanation of what had happened. Nevertheless he thought that the Battalion would be able to give some assistance when the 1st Battalion renewed its assault at 8:45.[27]

At 10:30 Colonel Boatsman reported that Companies A and B had reached Hill 122 only to be driven back 200 yards.[28]

There were efforts at infiltration and sporadic firing going on during most of the night.[29]

The Third Battalion was reorganizing. There had been 57 casualties during the day[30]—and that without even being committed to action! It prepared to renew its advance toward Emelie—a small village about one and a half miles down the road toward St. Lo—on the morrow; but this time it would not be a march in route column for a covered assembly area—it would be an attack!

25. 134th Inf. S-3 Journal.
26. Carroll, loc. cit.
27. 134th Inf., S-3 Journal.
28. ibid.
29. ibid.
30. 134th Inf., Battle Casualty Report.

CHAPTER III

★ ★ ★

ON TO SAINT LO

★ ★ ★

The Third Battalion's mission for the next day (July 16th) was to "clear the rear areas in the right zone" (the area through which the 1st Battalion supposedly had gone) and assemble in an orchard northwest of Emelie. A platoon of tank destroyers was to be attached. Colonel Thomsen tried to emphasize that this was not going to be a question of cleaning out a few snipers and moving up to an assembly area. He had found that out the previous day when the Battalion had been stopped by about a dozen machine guns, he pointed out, and he was expecting a great deal of opposition in this attempt.[1] And Colonel Thomsen was one who leaned over backwards to avoid any accusation of exaggerating his enemy opposition to higher headquarters.

The time for moving out was set for 7:30 A. M.[2]

The battalion commander had been hoping to make use of some of the tanks which had been working with the 1st Battalion. But shortly after 7 o'clock their commander indicated that they were going to withdraw, and efforts to hold them were to no avail, because they were acting on division orders. At 7:15 Lieutenant Davoe, liaison officer from the supporting field artillery battalion, the 161st, called in to request artillery to support the attack. This was refused because the location of the 1st Battalion was not known definitely enough. The company commanders were at the C. P. awaiting the final word. It was 7:20, and the attached TD platoon had not appeared. Colonel Thomsen called regimental headquarters: he was called upon to make an attack, yet he had no tanks, tank destroyers had not arrived, and he could not even have artillery support.[3]

It was after 10 o'clock by the time the TD's arrived and the Battalion moved off. Companies K and L were in the assault—K on the right—and Company I in reserve. They met immediate and intense opposition, but began to work small groups slowly forward. They were working forward in groups, or sometimes even singly. Pfc Darwin Mohorich found himself and all the other members of his "K" Company platoon pinned down by one of those rapid-firing machine guns. Not content to lie there and take that, Mohorich crept along the edge of the field until he was opposite the right flank of that enemy position. Two hand grenades put an end to that particular trouble spot.[4] Gradually the men were learning their way in that unfamiliar hedgerow country where each little patch was "a separate battlefield to be laboriously conquered and mopped up before passing on to the next."[5] Around 2 o'clock the TD's were getting up there and firing their powerful 3-inch guns into the defended hedgerows with telling effect—ten prisoners came out.[6]

These looked like beaten creatures. They were bareheaded or wore soft caps,[7] their green-gray uniforms were dirty and wrinkled, but they nearly always

1. 134th Inf., S-3 Journal, 16 July 1944.
2. **ibid.**
3. **ibid.**
4. 35th Div., General Orders No. 31, 12 Sept. 1944.
5. Harold Denny in **The New York Times**, July 23, 1944, p. E 5.
6. 134th Inf., S-3 Journal.
7. Prisoners of war were entitled to retain their steel helmets until they were back out of artillery range; however, a German coming in to surrender almost never wore a helmet; in fact he was usually recognized as wishing to surrender by his lack of a helmet.

wore good boots. Most of them carried the cylindrical gas mask container, but it likely contained some foul cheese and stale bread. Many of them came saying, "me Ruski" or "me Polski." Members of the Battalion were aware of the formation of the "East Battalion" in the German army. These units were about two-thirds or more, Russian or Polish, but of course their leaders were German.

Whatever pressure had been brought to bear on them, it was difficult for men of the Third Battalion to overlook the fact that they had been shooting Americans. And they could hardly conceive that Russian armies were encountering any groups of Americans fighting against them on the Eastern front.

Hostile artillery fire was coming in and the companies were practically at a standstill. Shortly before 3 o'clock the battalion commander decided to commit the reserve—Company I—in an effort to break through. They were to go in on the left, but intense fire on that flank prevented any maneuver. By 4:30 regimental and division commanders recognized that this was going to take a major attack. Word came to consolidate and hold the gains made thus far.[8]

That evening members of the Battalion learned that they were to renew the attack at 4:30 A.M. with a company of tanks, a platoon of TD's, and a 4.2-inch chemical mortar company attached. The Third Battalion was to make the main effort.[9]

Fog delayed the coming of dawn, but the battalion commander was determined to attack on time. At 4:15 the men were finishing their breakfast unit of "K" ration and were beginning to form up preparatory to the jump-off. It was not necessary to begin to stir very much before zero. Sleeping in a foxhole (or slit trench) fully clothed—the helmet for a pillow and the rifle for a bedfellow—and with hair clipped short, there was little else to making one's toilet than simply getting up. Men were traveling light now. Most of the packs had been sent to the rear. Usually a soldier would wear a fieldjacket during the cool nights but it would come off during the warm day and be draped around the cartridge belt. The wool O. D. uniform seldom was too warm. Two or three boxes of "K" ration went into the back of the shirt—at the small of the back. The bosom and sides probably would be bulging with hand grenades, and riflemen would be carrying two bandoliers of ammunition which, slung over opposite shoulders, would cross over the chest. The web cartridge belt was a general catch-all. In addition to its eight pockets containing clips of ammunition, most of its eyes were carrying hooks for other suspended equipment—most important of these was the canteen of water on the right hip. At the right side was a bayonet or trench knife. Seldom fixed on the rifles, the bayonet was more frequently used as a machete or a can opener than as a combat weapon. On the left side there usually would be an entrenching tool—a short handled shovel or pick-mattock. On the left hip (later changed to front) was the first aid packet containing a packet of sulfa "wound pills" and the sterile compress and bandage and sulfa "wound powder." There probably would be a raincoat hanging over the back of the belt. Certain leaders or designated men would carry other special equipment like a compass or wire cutters. This belt had to be kept tight in order to hold the field jacket securely; otherwise K rations and hand grenades would be dropped all over the field. Officers carried a compass and field glasses (which they liked to conceal when in view of the

8. 134th Inf., S-3 Journal.
9. Ibid.

enemy). A net with a few weeds or leaves eliminated the shine and broke the regular outline of the steel helmet.[10]

Colonel Thomsen called for his command group—those headquarters personnel who accompany the battalion commander. There was the S-3, the artillery liaison section (officer and radio crew), two intelligence scouts, in addition to the intelligence officer; a radio man, carrying the SCR300; a wire crew to follow along stringing wire so that the commander could have telephone communication with the CP and with regiment; four company runners. He called for a message center man to look after the runners, Sgt. Drew (the Sergeant Major) and then Leemhuis, his orderly.

The command group was growing to a size too large for a party whose primary job was not actual fighting, but who, nevertheless, would be exposed to movement under enemy fire.

But it was 4:30 and the companies were moving on. Almost immediately they were pinned down by hostile fire. They did not even get away from the line of departure—the creek—before they drew withering fire from those machine guns. The fog was still on and it was impossible to use the tanks with any effect without observation. This fog likewise made it impossible for the artillery liaison planes— the little L-4 "Piper Cubs"—to get into the air. There was no question but that those observation planes were highly effective in directing fires:[11] But the infantryman came to attach an almost phenomenal importance to them. He wanted one of those Grasshoppers up there all the time— he felt sure that the enemy's artillery would be less intense if those aerial spotters were watching for gun flashes.

"L" Company had been able to advance a short distance, but was hit hard by a counterattack on the left. Colonel Thomsen called into regiment to see if this was a "hold at all costs affair." Company L's men were falling back.[12] Fire became intense all over the area. Men sought what protection they could from previously dug holes—when there were any—along the hedgerows. The Colonel was trying to move Company I up into an effective position but its platoons became separated as they moved through the hollow—an area thick with trees and bushes down along the creek. Burp guns seemed to be everywhere. Many soldiers declared that enemy snipers transmitted signals by systems of regular long and short bursts of those machine pistols. However that might have been, the Nazis were demonstrating a clever coordination between automatic weapons and mortars. The machine guns and pistols would open up, pinning the troops to the ground, and then the mortars would traverse and search over the whole area to exact casualties among the soldiers who were held on the target by the streams of bullets cracking over their heads.[13] Men

10. c.f. Ralph Ingersoll, **The Battle is the Pay-Off** (New York: Harcourt, Brace and Company, 1943 pp. 99-104.
11. Later a letter was found in which a German soldier had described his reactions: "The artillery observers destroy our positions. Here our artillery is shooting a little more, but the answer always comes and in much greater quantities. We would all be very happy to see a few of our fighter planes which would bring an end to the "stueren" which we call the artillery observers. Without any interference these dogs fly around all day in our sky. Against that one can only hide like a little mouse and do the rest at night.—161st Field Artillery Battalion, 35th Division, **Lessons Learned,** pp. 11-12.
12. At 8:35 the keeper of the regimental S-3 Journal made these notations: "Having difficulty with TD but are moving now.
Co. L men coming back.
Lay mortars—lay on draw just in case.
Shall we move switchboard back w/o (without) breaking comc (communication).
A temporary lull at this time.
Col. states he must reorganize and try something else. He has a plan that may work. He sure needs (one.)"
13. cf.—"They put their MG's so as to hold us up at a certain hedgerow and as soon as we'd stop, down it came. That's how we got our heaviest casualties."—"It's a Tough Racket," **The Infantry Journal,** LVI (March 1945) pp. 27-28.

had to fight down fear within them under those circumstances.

Some had been afraid long before they ever had been under fire; fear mounted in others as they approached the danger zone. Some had conditioned themselves strongly not to be affected by the death and pain which they knew they would see about them; and then suddenly, perhaps after several hours or days of such conditioned nonchalance, the terrifying fact would seize upon them—the next one might be me! Some were horrified at the thought of being mangled as they had seen their comrades mangled. To others it was not so much death itself that they feared, but it was the thought of the effect on loved ones at home. They wanted so much to live; there were so many things they wanted to do, if only they could be at home again!

Prior to entering into combat, the greatest dread of some had been of fear itself, and as they approached the battlefields an agony would seize them that they might be overcome by fear and thus appear ridiculous in the eyes of their comrades. They would seek solace in attempting to discover signs of fear in others.[13a]

As the fears of combat took different forms, so fear found its expression in different reactions. Some could steel themselves to show little or no signs of fear at all. Others froze and quivered. Many felt an almost over-powering desire to get back—back away from those bursting shells and cracking bullets; a few yielded, and became stragglers. Some became angered at their plight and wanted to fight hard—to do everything they could to get the ordeal over the right way; those heart-breaking thoughts did not have time to linger in a mind in the thick of active fight. Many were simply well-disciplined, conscientious soldiers intent on doing their best. Some soldiers hoped for a wound —a light one. If a wounded soldier were not doomed to death or to be permanently and seriously maimed, he found little sympathy from his comrades; indeed, he considered himself a lucky fellow; some wanted to lift an arm or a foot out of a foxhole in the hopes of getting it hit. Those wounds in the foot or hand which had broken bones requiring a long enough period to mend to warrant return to a hospital in the United States were known as "million dollar wounds." There were a few who resorted to the unsoldierly expedient of inflicting a wound upon themselves in order to find an escape.

Some of the men lay under that fire shaking with fear, unable to move. They lay and let those thoughts race through their heads, and that only added to their misery. Others knew they must keep moving to avoid destruction, and they intended to do something about it. Some took what comfort they could from a fatalistic view. A great many—perhaps all, in one way or another,— prayed. Aware that they were involved in something bigger than any man, they felt that they must turn to some Greater Power if they were to find any

13a. The Army, in its training program, made a great effort—particularly through the medium of training film—to show that fear was a very general feeling, and that no soldier should suffer misgivings over thoughts that such fears were unique to himself.

It should be observed, however, that such an approach—the attempt to persuade soldiers of the universality of their feelings of fear—might be carried too far. When a frightened soldier's eyes searched the countenance of his captain, it was not an attempt to find consolation through perceiving signs of a similar fear; it was a quest for reassurance from signs of confidence in that leader. Fear nourished on further fear easily can give way to panic.

Perhaps resulting mainly from fear is also the inertia of men in combat—a small minority really does the fighting. S. L. A. Marshall, after conducting scores of post-battle mass interviews found: "In an average experienced infantry company in an average stern day's action, the number engaging with any and all weapons was approximately 15 percent of total strength. In the most aggressive infantry companies under the most intense local pressure, the number rarely rose above 25 per cent of total strength from the opening to the close of the action."—**Men Against Fire** (New York, 1947) p. 56. (Another reason some men did not fire probably was that they did not want to clean their rifles!)

relief or any escape from certain destruction.[14]

It was nearly 9 o'clock before the tanks started rolling up. By then visibility had cleared. Of the company's 17 tanks, 15 were in action and ready to go.[15] Demolition crews from the A & P platoon— the men who knew how to blast a hole through the hedgerows—boarded the leading tanks and they rumbled on down the road across the little bridge spanning the creek and started up the opposite slope.

A leading tank halted in a flash of flame and smoke. It had hit a mine. The tank was burning.

But others were able to make it into the fields. And the TD's got into firing position. A tank tried to blast its way through a hedgerow with its 75 mm gun, but it was to no avail. A well-placed charge of TNT was effective, and the tank roared through to begin covering the opposite hedgerow with machine gun and high explosive fire.[16] Company L was approaching that same large house where the battalion column had been held up two days before. Captain Lassiter called for the 4.2-inch chemical mortars to put some white phosphorus shells onto the place. Minutes later the mortar officer called "on the way!" and huge billows of thick white smoke began to rise over the target.[17]

A few prisoners came in around noon. They were concerned mostly in being assured that they were not going to be killed. They wanted to get back someday to see their wives and families. They illustrated their devotion to their families by displaying dozens of photographs. One little German who appeared to be about 40 years old said that he used to live in Chicago—out by the stockyards—but that he had returned to Germany in 1933.[18]

"L" Company was starting to move again. Leading the attack was 2nd Lt. Louis Dailey and his platoon. Dailey was of small stature and—as a second lieutenant traditionally is depicted—young. He was another who had served as an enlisted man on the old 2nd Battalion's expedition to the Aleutians. He was up at the head of his platoon now leading his men up against those next hedgerows. They were drawing fire, but the platoon kept on moving until it had driven a wedge into the enemy's position. This brought down intense mortar fire. And Lou Dailey, leading his platoon, died in that mortar barrage.[19] Now the whole company was stopped under intense mortar, artillery and machine gun fire. There was one particularly troublesome machine gun to the front, and Private Buster E. Brown, who already had distinguished himself by silencing a machine gun single-handedly the previous day, now advanced alone to make another try with his automatic rifle. Yet 150 yards from the enemy position, he was struck by a bullet, but he opened fire and continued moving

14. c.f. Edwin G. Boring, ed., **Psychology for the Armed Forces** (Prepared under supervision of National Research Council, Washington: **The Infantry Journal**, 1945) pp. 383-393; Norman C. Meier, Military Psychology (New York: Harper and Brothers, 1943) pp. 253-283; John Dollard, **Fear in Battle** (New Haven: Institute of Human Relations, Yale University, 1943); Emilio Mira, **Psychiatry in War** (New York: W. W. Norton and Company, 1943); "The Mind in Combat", **The Infantry Journal**, LII (Feb. 1944) p. 52.

15. 134th Inf., S-3 Journal.

16. c.f. Francis Trevelyn Miller, **History of World War II** (Philadelphia, 1945) p. 750.

"In the campaign leading to the capture of St. Lo our forces worked out a new tank technique that greatly speeded up the conquest of these little fields and cut our losses in taking them.

"In present-day tank tactics, infantry and tanks support each other. Machine guns are deadly to infantry but ineffective against tanks, so tanks spray the hedges to knock out the machine guns and suppress the enemy infantry. Antitank guns will kill a tank but infantry can slip up and destroy them. Now the engineers have been added to the infantry-tank team. They go in with both and blow holes in the hedgerow with demolition charges, enabling the tanks to break through."—Harold Denny in **The New York Times**, July 23, 1944, p. 5E.

17. This particular mortar unit—Company C, 92nd Chemical Battalion—accounted for four machine guns with 26 rounds of ammunition; the elapsed time from "target sighted" to "mission accomplished" was 11 minutes.—Twelfth Army Group, **"Battle Experiences**, No. 40, Sept. 8, 1944.

18. 3rd Bn., S-2 Notebook.

19. 35th Div., General Orders, No. 36, Sept. 24, 1944.

forward until a second wound forced him out of action. Nevertheless he already had succeeded in neutralizing this obstacle to his platoon's advance. As a result, to Buster Brown of the Third Battalion's Company L went the division's first Distinguished Service Cross.[20]

The Third Battalion was in the midst of one of the most difficult battles which it, or any battalion, had faced thus far in France: "The July battling all along the front involved some of the fiercest and most sanguinary fighting of the war."[20a] Correspondents wrote:

> The battle for St. Lo is proving the hardest since our men once established themselves on D-Day—much harder than at Cherbourg or La Haye du Puits.[21]
>
> St. Lo was under its sixth successive day of siege yesterday. The fighting was as hard in its way as the first landings on the toughest beaches on D-Day, one field dispatch said. The dispatch added that the whole story of the bloody battle could be summed up in one report which reached a command post outside St. Lo: "Advanced three hedgerows"—a sizeable, bitterly contested advance in this kind of fighting.[22]

Now over on the right, Company K was moving. Melcher had moved his company wide to the right, so that Colonel Thomsen called for Company I to move up on his left and Company L reverted to reserve. By early afternoon they had advanced 500 to 800 yards beyond the creek where they had seen so much trouble earlier in the day.

During these attacks, Company M's machine gun platoons had been attached to the assault companies. The heavy machine guns were being mounted on light machine gun tripods or on improvised bipods, or with no mounts at all, were fired by laying them on the tops of the hedgerows. By this time, however, the heavy weapons company had become practically a "light" automatic weapons company. Through battle-field recovery, salvage, repairing, and shrewd trading in the rear areas (of enemy pistols or machine guns for U. S. automatic rifles), executive officer Virgil Hyde had been able to replace most of the heavies with light machine guns or with BAR's—a popular favorite in the hedgerows; and he had added a few Thompson submachine guns for good measure.

Supporting this advance on the left was Second Lieutenant Halley Dickey's First Machine Gun platoon. Dickey had been wounded during this action but he refused evacuation so that he could get his platoon organized. Then noticing a wounded soldier lying out in the open, exposed to enemy fire, Dickey crawled over to him and dragged him to cover. But now he found himself in the midst of a field of "S" mines—those deadly"Bouncing Betties!" Fine trip-wires were running all along the ground. Dickey lay quiet.[23]

Major Weyand, growing impatient back at the CP had walked up forward to see the reserve company.[24] He heard about Dickey's plight and immediately got some medical men with a litter and went over to where Dickey lay. A team had evacuated the man whom Dickey had dragged back. Now they put him on a litter and Major Weyand walked alongside. Then that tremendous blast of a mine beside them. Only the major was able to walk away, but fragments had torn painful wounds into his arm—now he added a Purple Heart from this war to the wound stripes he already wore. His only concern was for the men still in that mine field. Other medics, and some pioneers, went back to get them

20. Third U. S. Army, General Orders, No. 59, 13 Sept. 1944.
20a. Dwight D. Eisenhower, **Crusade in Europe** (New York, 1948) pp. 271-272.
21. Harold Denny in **The New York Times**, July 18, 1944, p. 3.
22. **The Stars and Stripes** (London ed.) July 17, 1944, p. 2.
23. 35th Div., General Orders, No. 18, 12 Aug. 1944.
24. 134th Inf., S-3 Journal.

out. While they were dressing his wounds at the aid station, the major kept asking, "How is Dickey, and how are those two medics?"

Dickey and one of the medics were dead.

As the afternoon wore on there seemed to be no diminishing of the enemy resistance. There would be lulls, to be sure, and sometimes there would be minutes of silence so complete as to be almost as frightening as the loudest noises. But each time that the companies would begin a new movement, they would find themselves "stirring up a hornets' nest."

Company I, coming up on the left, had lost contact with Company K. Lieutenant Norman Wardwell made his way over to the right to make contact and establish the relative positions of the two companies. On his return he found that Captain Bauer had been hit. With enemy fire still falling in the area, he knew that they must move forward to get out of it. Quickly organizing the men in the vicinity, he led them forward. They moved forward steadily, over one hedgerow, then over another. Wardwell moved on out in front. A small cluster of farm buildings looming ahead appeared to him a likely site for an enemy strong point. He crouched behind hedgerows and worked his way forward. He saw no sign of life; he ran quickly over to the barn—then edging his way around to the opposite side he came upon a German 81 mm mortar. It looked as though the crew was preparing to make a hasty departure. Reaching in his shirt, he brought out a hand grenade and pulled the pin. Other men were coming nearer now and the Germans started to leave. But Wardwell's grenade stopped most of them—they would not be back to fight another day.[25]

Meanwhile Company K was making good progress on the right. It made good progress as far as a road which ran across its front between LeMesnl-Rouxelin, a village on the right, and Emelie, on the left. Then it was another of those wicked machine guns. Firing from the right flank, the German 42 had the whole company pinned down. Captain Richard D. Melcher moved up to determine the trouble. He saw that the machine gun fire was coming from the edge of the village (LeMesnl). His whole company frozen in place, the Captain started after the machine gun himself. He found himself going through a real "infiltration course"—more trying than those of Camp Rucker and Camp Butner combined—for when he saw that the fire was coming from a church, he had to creep and crawl through an open field—under the machine gun's stream of bullets—in order to get to it. He got out three hand grenades. Dragging oneself across a field like a reptile was exhausting enough in itself—not to mention the nervous strain of stalking a deadly machine gun! Melcher raised himself and in rapid succession hurled the three grenades through a church window. Result: complete destruction of the enemy.[26]

It was growing dusk, but the companies moved on another two hedgerows before consolidating their positions for the night. They were on a part of Hill 122. Colonel Thomsen moved up with the command group to a sunken trail near the farm buildings which Company K had overrun. One of the buildings was on fire. Almost immediately an enemy direct-fire gun—a dreaded "88" began firing. Its shells, bursting every few feet on the ground, and sometimes overlapping, pock-marked the whole field. Most of the men could recognize the "88" (88 mm gun—tank gun, antitank gun, or dual purpose antitank, anti-

25. 35th Div., General Orders, No. 34, 22 May, 1945.
26. 35th Div., General Orders, No. 25, 25 Aug. 1944.

aircraft gun) now for its loud "zip-bang." There was no long whistle of the shell; in fact the shell arrived first, and then would come the sound of the gun. At first every enemy bursting shell—mortar, howitzer, gun—was attributed to the "88". But the real effectiveness of the gun was second only to the stories about it.[27]

In two days the Third Battalion had gone a mile and a half to Emelie— two days after the general had made his demand.

The hard fighting was finished for that day, but that did not mean that the work was finished. There were supplies—ammunition and rations—to be brought up. Preparations had to be made for attack on the morrow. No, no orders had been received, but there was no question about it: it would be attack, attack until St. Lo had fallen.

Twilight was adding its shadows of gloom to the already grotesque pattern of shelled and torn Villiers-Fossard when someone came up the road near the Battalion CP to say that there were some wounded men in a knocked-out tank about a thousand yards to the front. The tank still was exposed to enemy fire. Immediately Edward Thill, a technician in the medical detachment, volunteered to go get them. Without allowing time for any refusal he jumped into his jeep and "took off". Once a Milwaukee taxicab driver, "Mouse" Thill now drove his jeep with as much disregard to mines and enemy fire as he would have given to yellow traffic lights. Two considerations demanded speed: to get the wounded men back to the aid station as quickly as possible, and to limit 'the time of exposure to enemy fire. Thill felt no reluctance to apply speed. Flying a red cross over the hood, the jeep sped down the road until it neared the tank. Then, disregarding the enemy fire, Thill raced to the tank, and was able to extract two wounded men. He got them into the jeep, and half-standing, half-sitting on the back of the seat, he came roaring back with his precious cargo. This feat won a silver star medal for Thill.[28] His work was typical of the "medics". All of them had won a high regard for themselves in the hearts of the doughboys. This regard was especially keen for the company aid men—one for each rifle platoon when they were fortunate enough to be at full strength—who, unarmed, went along with the rifle platoons and crawled from one wounded man to another to administer first aid: and for the litter teams who came up to carry the wounded to safety.

As night fell the periphery of the glowing light from the burning house up near Emelie extended farther and farther outward. The flames became a reference point which could be seen for miles in the clear night. Then ammunition in the house began to explode. This fireworks display continued sporadically almost all night.

Engineers were working on the road to remove mines from the vicinity of the American tank which had hit one. Third Battalion's supply train—a jeep and trailer for each company—started up from the motor park. Leading the column, Company I's truck started to drive around the tank. A quaking ex-

27. The improved, dual-purpose 88 mm flak 41 fired a 22.5-pound-projectile at a muzzle velocity of 3,400 feet per second; against tanks, it could penetrate 7 inches of armor at 1,000 yards; it was effective against aircraft flying at 36,000 feet. "What the world had not seen in Spain, or rather had not understood, was a 'new' and apparently orthodox antiaircraft gun which had been secretly designed a decade before Hitler came to power. This 88 mm gun—the Flak 36— later to become the big stick of German artillery power—was still unappreciated at the end of the Spanish War . . . Certainly no piece of equipment can be given as much credit for Allied defeats as those erstwhile Nazi antiaircraft guns."—Lt. John Scofield, "German Infantry Weapons," **The Infantry Journal**, LIV. (Jan. 1944), 41.
28. Robert Cromie, Chicago Tribune Press Service, Dec. 13, 1944, reprinted in **The Santa Fe Express**, May 1945, p. 2.

plosion rent the air: another mine had claimed its toll.[29]

Men from the Regimental Antitank Company's Mine Platoon and engineers tried to find another route, but met with no success. Engineers went to work on the main route again. But at 6 A.M. Colonel Thomsen had to call regimental headquarters to say that he had been unable to get his supplies up yet. Finally Motor Officer Reischel was able to get over a detour route which the First Battalion had used.[30]

The attack on the 18th was to be a continuation of the previous day's, but the delay in getting up supplies had caused some delay in launching the new assault. Some changes in position caused other delay. The 2nd Battalion of the 320th had been attached to the 134th for the renewal of the operation against Hill 122.[31] Now, as the Third Battalion awaited for the attack, the men crouching behind the hedgerows, a battalion of the 320th appeared in the zone —men from the sister regiment, apparently confused in direction, were marching across the front of the Third Battalion! The error discovered, the visitors counter-marched to retrace their steps, again across the front. Miraculously, this whole maneuver was completed without bringing down a barrage of enemy fire. Minutes later, the Third Battalion attacked, and not 300 yards beyond, ran into a tremendous volume of mortar and machine gun fire.[32] The companies were able to advance only a hedgerow or two and then it was the old story of confronting those well dug-in, coordinated positions.

The doughboys had been apprehensive about the presence of tanks in the attack at first. In fact it had seemed initially that men of the First Battalion did not want to attack without tanks, while men of the Third Battalion did not want to attack with them. Actually the Third Battalion soldier wanted the tanks near, but not in his own particular sector. He was afraid of the way they would draw enemy fire. This fear was deepened this afternoon when men of Company I found themselves under the machine gun fire of friendly tanks. If there were anything worse than stalking a firing German machine gun, it would be approaching an American machine gun. There was the same danger, but the danger could not be eliminated with a hand grenade. Technical Sergeant Milton Bates, recognizing the slower-firing weapons as American, braved the bullets to go back to the tanks and have them call off their fire.[33]

Company L moved up to the assault position in place of Company I, on "K" Company's left. Both companies pressed forward. It was hard going. There were probably no men who were unafraid;—unless it was Colonel Thomsen—there were strong men who had the courage to go on in spite of fear, and there were some weaker men who could not go on. It took discipline of the highest order to keep going in the face of that machine gun and artillery fire. It was a question of which side could give the most and take the most. Company L's light machine guns were sputtering out their support for the advance. Always they became priority targets for enemy artillery fire. When one salvo came in, one of the company's machine guns stopped firing. Private Thomas Hudson had been hit in the shoulder. He looked up and found all the other members of his squad wounded. But those enemy riflemen had to be kept pinned down in their holes if "L" Company's men were to keep going. Hudson

29. 134th Inf., S-3 Journal, 18 July 1944.
30. Ibid.
31. Santa Fe, p. 31; hills usually were called by the number appearing on the map which indicated their height in meters.
32. Carroll, loc. cit.
33. 30th Div., General Orders, No. 18, 12 Aug. 1944.

moved the gun to an alternate position and opened fire. He had to handle the ammunition, and keep the gun firing all alone. He kept spraying the hedge-rows, supporting the attack, until he collapsed from loss of blood.[34]

By 6 P. M. the attack had carried well down the forward (southern) slope of Hill 122. The principal defense before St. Lo had been taken. This was not a tall, forebidding hill, but it did command the northern approaches to St. Lo, and the well-organized Nazi defenses made it forbidding enough. It was re-garded as the key to the situation.[35] Now the way was open to St. Lo. But here the enemy had shown "a lively anxiety to hold this important road junction, the capture of which was essential to the success of the plan for a break-through."[36]

The German's ability to maintain a static defense position across the base of the Cherbourg Peninsula depends on their retention of St. Lo, hinge for their present line through Periers to Lessay....

There is a great test of strength going on between the Americans and German armies at St. Lo.... Here the Germans have thrown in artillery, tanks, and infantry without stint. Here American doughboys are proving themselves superior to the finest German troops.[37]

Now the capture of Hill 122, together with the enveloping movement of the 2nd Battalion, 115th Infantry and 116th Infantry (29th Division) to the left (east) put the German 3rd Paratroop Division in a precarious position—a position in which a cutting off of communications while these vigorous at-tacks continued from the north loomed as a distinct possibility.[38]

This advance left the Third Battalion hardly a thousand yards north of the edge of St. Lo. Colonel Thomsen was as anxious as higher headquarters to push on and complete this big initial assignment; he could look down and see shattered roof-tops and spires beckoning to him. He notified the companies to reorganize and then go for St. Lo at 7:30.[39] However, they were cautioned to go only to the edge of town and not on down to the principal parts—the 29th Division was attacking from the east and it was to have the honor of entering the town which had been marked as its objective originally. More than that, there would be danger of mingling troops and getting into each other's fire if both divisions had troops going into the town.[40]

Pairs of Thunderbolts had gone in earlier to drop their pairs of bombs on the already much cratered town. The time was growing near for the re-newal of the attack. Tired soldiers were called upon for another big effort.

The men of Company K, after some hesitation, were jolted into action: over the hedgerow they went and started moving for the opposite one. Melcher looked to his left. He could not see Company L moving. "Lassiter, let's go!"

"L" Company was having the same trouble. Days of fighting were be-ginning to tell. Weariness had taken the edge off the discipline of the men which forced them to go forward without regard for themselves. Yet, it was just as that 29th Division intelligence officer had said—"They freeze in their foxholes and you can't do anything with them."

But now one of "L" Company's platoons was leading out. First Lieutenant Francis Greenlief had his platoon on the way. They went over the hedgerow and started across the next field. When a man hesitated Greenlief called out

34. 35th Div., General Orders, No. 20, 15 Aug. 1944.
35. Santa Fe., pp. 31 ff.
36. General Eisenhower's Report, p. 34.
37. Drew Middleton in The New York Times, July 18, 1944, p. 1.
38. St. Lo (MS) p. 117.
39. 134th Inf., Unit Journal, 18 July 1944.
40. Carroll, loc. cit.

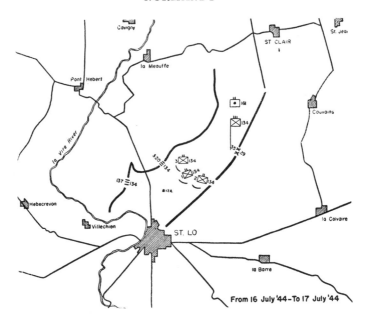

On 16 July the Third Battalion made the main effort.

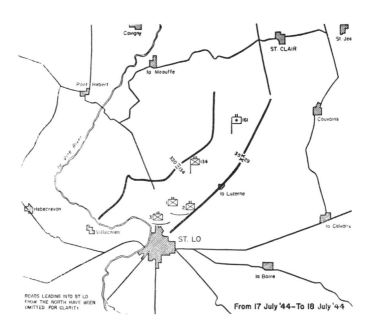

On the 18th they swept into St. Lo.

to him. His voice could be heard above everything else in the area. As "L" Company's First Platoon advanced across the field a German machine gun 42 suddenly opened up with a long burst from an opposite corner. It caught most of a squad. Four of them fell dead. The remainder of the platoon hit the ground and froze. Greenlief shouted to urge them on, but they could not face that machine gun. He crawled to a wounded soldier and picked up his Browning Automatic Rifle—always a favorite weapon. The big platoon leader, still shouting to his men, jumped up and opened fire—firing from the hip. He stood up and sprayed the whole hedgerow ahead of him, and then, still firing in order to keep the Germans' heads down—he knew they would "freeze" as much as his own men—he rushed to the corner where the machine gun had been firing. He went in fast and destroyed the entire enemy crew.[41] With the immediate danger removed, and such an example of heroism as this, the men no longer could remain down.

They began moving all along the line. Each took confidence as he saw his comrades moving with him. Now they were moving in short rushes, from cover to cover. No longer was it a pair of scouts or half a squad working forward along the hedgerow—it was fire and movement all along the battalion front. Tired men forgot their fatigue. Scared men forgot their fear. All of them brave men now kept shooting and going forward.[42]

An "L" Company man leaped over the next hedgerow, but he dropped his rifle on the wrong side. When he looked up he saw three Nazi soldiers standing beside him. They were as surprised as he; but they had one important advantage—they were armed. Acting quickly—almost by reflex action—he grabbed a burp gun from the hands of his nearest adversary and with a single burst shot all three of them.

Dolan Boggs' usual place was with the CP or command group of Company L, for he was the communication sergeant. But he wanted to help to get the company moving on this drive. He volunteered to man a BAR. Soon after he had moved up behind a hedgerow and opened fire, an enemy machine gun burst hit him; but he kept on firing—kept on until his wounds forced him out of action.[43]

A frightened German jumped up in front of Company K and fled over a hedge. "Get that rabbit! Get that rabbit!" Two or three riflemen paused for a shot; he fell violently.

The call carried on down to Company L; then someone started yelling the old war cry, "All hell can't stop us!" . . . "Lah We Lah His!" The Kraut was on the run, and when he was on the run he could not very well shoot back.

Company commanders cautioned their men to halt at the edge of the town; but the assault now was out of their hands. It swept into the outskirts of St. Lo and scouts probed through the acres of rubble. After some effort, the company commanders were able to recall their men back up to the edge of town and organize a defensive position.[44]

During the night the keeper of the Regimental S-3 Journal made these entries:

41. 35th Div., General Orders, No. 28, 2 Sept. 1944.
42. Carroll, loc. cit.
43. 35th Div., General Orders, No. 21, 19 Aug. 1944.
44. Carroll, loc. cit.

2400—Blue 3[45] wants to be sure liaison planes will be in the air at day-break

0115—Capt. Heffelfinger [First Battalion S-3] reports Strader [C.O., Co. A] tied in on to Lassiter in St. Lo—cemetery on outskirts—out of our boundary. Strader is requesting AT guns to be there by daylight.

0130—Called Blue 6—Lassiter is tied on a church about 1000 ft due N of St. Lo—K is on his right. Strader and Davis on the left.

FO #7

XIX Corps defends along line Vire R.—St. Lo—35th on right, 29th on left.

134th w/Co A, 60 Engr. complete occupation of St. Lo in zone; organize to defend line of Vire R.—St. Lo in zone. Establish limiting point on MLR,[Main Line of Resistance]. RRL [Regimental Reserve Line]. Tie in w/29th Div.[46]

This was among the toughest battles in the history of American armies. For almost a week the Americans had laid siege to St. Lo....

The final entry into the city came from the north, as the Germans on heights were pouring shells into the town and its approaches.[47]

Those three weeks of painful slugging to get St. Lo.... proved that our earlier swift cutting of the Cherbourg Peninsula was no prelude to an easy victory. Instead it was the beginning of about as hard fighting as American troops have ever had to face. Perhaps our men in the Solomons had a harder time. I don't know. I have never been there. But certainly the last few days have been harder than almost anything we endured in World War I.[48]

For its success in carrying Hill 122 and forcing entry in to St. Lo, the regiment was awarded the French Croix de Guerre with Palm.[49] The War Department announced later that "two former National Guard regiments, the 134th and the 115th Infantry, had distinguished themselves in the capture of St. Lo."[50] The day after the fall of the city, the division received a commendation from Maj. Gen. Charles H. Corlett, commander of the XIX Corps.[51]

The success of the 134th Infantry in the Battle for St. Lo might question the value of so-called "veteran" units. Here green troops had won their objective where elements of the "veteran" 29th Division had failed to gain in three successive attempts. Some would say that the Third Battalion never at any time—unless it was during the latter phases of the war—was as effective an organization as it was in its first battle. No, its members were not battle-experienced, but all had had at least a year's training, and some as much as four years' and more. After that battle the casualties had been such that its ranks were filled mostly not with "battle-wise veterans," but with replacements.

This being the case, a valid question would be, was that much training necessary? Was it not a waste to undertake that much training only to have

45. "Blue 3" was a reference to S-3, Third Battalion. Telephone code names were assigned to all units, and these names came to be used widely in referring to the unit, by number, to individuals. Thus the code name for the 35th Division was "Justice"; all its subordinate units had names also beginning with "J"; 320 Infantry was "Juniper", 137th Infantry, "Jury", and 134th, "Joplin". The three battalions of a regiment were referred to respectively as "Red," "White", and "Blue". In the battalion, "Blue 1", "Blue 2", "Blue 3", "Blue 4" referred to S-1, S-2, S-3, S-4. "Blue 5" referred to the executive, and "Blue 6" to the commander. Similarly, "Joplin 6" referred to the regimental commander.

46. 134th Inf., S-3 Journal, 19 July 1944.

47. Miller, **History of World War II**, pp. 751-752.

48. Harold Denny in **The New York Times**, July 23, 1944, p. 5E. See also Denny, "Normandy; Grim School of Battle", **The New York Times Magazine**, XXV, (July 23, 1944), 4-5; "Hedgerow Fighting," **The Infantry Journal**, LV (Oct. 1944), 9-18; "Battle of the Hedgerows," **Life** XVII (Aug. 7, 1944), 17-23; First U. S. Army, Report of Operations, 20 Oct. 43—1 Aug. 44, p. 90.

49. Col. A. J. P. Le Bel (Acting French Military Attache in Washington) to Maj. Gen. Butler B. Miltonberger, 22 Aug. 1946 (photostat).

50. **The Stars and Stripes** (ETO edition), Aug. 9, 1944, p. 4.

51. The text of the letter of commendations:
"1. The capture of St. Lo climaxes an operation of major importance to the American cause, and brings to a successful conclusion the initial combat action of the 35th Infantry Division.
"2. It was marked by repeated instances of personal and group heroism of the highest order and has earned for your division a place among the great organizations of American military history.
"3. Please convey to the veteran officers and men of your division my pride in their achievements, and my sincere congratulations on a job well done."
Senator Harry S. Truman obtained permission to have this commendation inserted in the **Congressional Record.—Santa Fe**, p. 37.

its value lost in the first battle? Answers would be valid only in terms of the combat to come—when men with 13-weeks of training would predominate. But even then, conditions would vary so much, and so many factors would be involved, that it would defy accurate correlation.

On the other hand, there always were survivors to any engagement, and though in a few week's time casualties might approach a figure equal to 100 per cent, that would not mean that all of the original men were involved— turnover would be high among the replacements too. It was this minority of survivors, then, that made a unit "veteran." In the enlisted ranks, survivors became noncommissioned officers almost by default—and even then there were not always enough to fill the vacancies satisfactorily. Surviving lieutenants became company commanders, and so the company had the guidance of a battle-experienced leader.

The battalion staff, in a position to escape with a greater proportion of survivors, soon did become a "battle wise" group which permitted the battalion a measure of continuity in spite of rapid turnover. The staff soon developed procedures and methods found to be most efficient and became an important influence in battalion operations. Battle-wise soldiers learned to tell friendly fire from enemy, and what to do under fire.

There was loss and gain, then, to be had in battle experience. Perhaps the results would indicate a greater importance in developing leadership and staff procedures in pre-battle training than in the individual training of infantry soldiers. Given expert commanders and staffs, in other words, it is to be doubted whether the unit would have been any less efficient in battle if its individual soldiers had had no more than 13 weeks of training than it would if those soldiers had been trained a whole year as members of *various other units.*

Being on the regimental right, the Third Battalion was assigned the mission of maintaining contact with the 137th Infantry on the right, and of operating foot patrols along the horseshoe bend of the Vire River from a point south of St. Georges-Montcocq to the right flank of the 1st Battalion in St. Lo.[52] While a patrol was working its way over to establish that contact, a Nazi airplane paid a visit to the regimental area. A colorful display of red and green tracer bullets raced across the darkening sky as the lone airman came in to strafe the hedgerows. Two men of the Battalion were hit; but he had greater success in the Service Company area—the regimental kitchen and supply train. There bombs and machine gun bullets killed one man and wounded eight others; the 2nd Battalion had nine casualties as well, but none was serious.[53]

The next day was the first since coming up to the front that there had been any relaxation possible. To be sure the patrols had to keep going, the enemy remained on the opposite side of the river, and artillery shells came in— usually in the early morning or evening, but now for the first time everyone had a chance to shave—in the cool water of Normandy wells—and Lt. Stone-burner could bring up hot chow.

Colonel Thomsen even directed that the Battalion CP move into a large house standing in a lot adjacent to the orchard where the Pioneers had dug out a shelter for the CP. This was the first time that any part of the Battalion had occupied a building. Fear of booby-traps and fear that they would be

52. 134th Inf., S-3 Journal, 20 July 1944.
53. 134th Inf., S-3 Journal, 20 July 1944.

artillery targets had put a taboo on all buildings. There were signs of anti-personnel mines in this yard, but none was discovered in the house. This made much easier the installation' and operations of telephones and radios[54] and working with maps and notes.

Occupying this position on the high ground at the edge of the town, the Third Battalion had reverted to a reserve position, with the First and Second Battalions occupying the main parts of the city. After three days in this position the Third Battalion received orders to relieve the First. The companies moved down to occupy basements and occasional lower rooms in the shattered houses and buildings—an undamaged building was not to be found.[55]

The Battalion CP took over from the 1st Battalion in a small tomb or mausoleum in the cemetery near the northeast edge of the town. Telephone lines ran down the marble steps to the crypt where officers and assistants crowded over maps in the light of a gasoline lantern. The vault left little room for movement about the sides, but in spite of its stone-carved figures, it served as desk for maps and papers and as table for "K" rations. The air was heavy. Colonel Thomsen had his bedroll brought up and this, put down at the foot of the vault, served as a mattress for staff members who took turns at catching a nap when the situation permitted.[56]

Some of the men slept in the small upper room. Others prefered to dig foxholes outside—some were digging their own graves.

Even the dead could have no rest. Ghoulish German artillery was more furious than ever. "The gravestones and religious emblems had gone through a furious pounding."[57] Usually it seemed that the German tried to send in the artillery during early morning and evening when he thought chow was coming up; but it was coming at all hours now. Going between companies, or between the Battalion CP and the companies, was a precarious undertaking; everyone dreaded "running the gauntlet" down the street past "88 corner". Bursting shells crumbled tombstones and dug craters among the graves. The mausoleum itself proved its worth by sustaining a number of direct hits.

St. Lo itself was almost in complete ruins.[58] The Germans already had evacuated all civilians from St. Lo and vicinity. They were making use of the destruction of the towns which accompanied their expulsion from Normandy for propaganda purposes. They were taking photographs of ruins and were circulating them through occupied France under such captions as "This Is Liberation."[59]

Each night supply parties would have to carry rations, water, ammunition, radio batteries, from a quary about a mile outside of town.

The Colonel decided to move the CP back about 300 yards to get out of the cemetery and back behind the hill. Once more the Pioneers and all hands dug in.[60]

54. In addition to the SCR 300, the 32-pound set for communication with the companies, the battalion had a larger SCR 284 for the regimental net. The 284 was primarily a vehicular set—normally it was mounted in a jeep—but it was equipped with a hand generator and receiver dry battery for ground use. As a portable set it weighed approximately 130 pounds, and could be broken down into two or three-man loads for carrying. Capable of use either with voice or key, this radio's range was listed as being about 15 miles for the former and 30 miles for the latter. —The Infantry School, Fort Benning, Ga., **Reference Data**, Table 21.
55. 134th Inf., S-3 Journal, 22-23 July 1944.
56. Carroll, **loc. cit.**
57. Sgt. Saul Levitt, "St. Lo was No Cinch," **Yank** (Brit. Ed.), III (Aug. 13, 1944), 2.
58. Drew Middleton in **The New York Times**, July 19, 1944, p. 3; Battle of France—Ruins of St. Lo," **Life**, XVII (Aug. 21, 1944), 36-37.
59. Harold Denny in **The New York Times**, July 18, 1944, p. 3.
60. Carroll, **loc. cit.**

War had left its mark along this highway which ran out of St. Lo to the northeast. The body of an old woman in black dress and bonnet lay along a shoulder of the road; a little farther up was another knocked-out jeep of the 29th Division. A damaged winery stood down by a small creek 300 yards to the rear of the CP site; on its walls, scrawled in big letters, was the motto of the predecessors in this sector: "Let's Go 29th!"[61]

The Germans had fought tenaciously to hold St. Lo, and now, if they could not hold it themselves they were determined to deny it to the Americans to the greatest possible extent. They continued to pound the town from a ridge slightly over two miles to the southeast. "The position in St. Lo was described as 'hell' by troops at the front."[62]

But the German defenders had not been strong enough to withstand the terrible attacks to which they had been subjugated. The German side of the fall of St. Lo is revealed in a captured report from the 3rd Parachute Division:

On the 17th the Americans renewed their attacks. After several attacks against the 2 Co. of the 5 Para Regt, the 1 Co of the 8 Para Regt and the 3 Para Engr Bn, they succeeded in breaking through on the front of the 2 Co of the 8 Para Regt. This time the Americans gained ground all through Martinville and south to the village of la Madeleine.[63] The available reserves were too weak to beat back the advancing troops. All our counterattacks during the day were unsuccessful.

With great difficulty we succeeded in occupying the MLR by noon and held off all attacks. We also accomplished contact with the units on our left. The continuous, agile, harassing fire by the Americans aggravated our already tired troops.... At the same time the foe succeeded in advancing on our left to St. Lo.[64] After having lost contact on the left flank, owing to this penetration and the danger of being fired on from the rear, the MLR had to be pulled back beyond the road to St. Lo-Bayeux. After building up a weak flank support we succeeded in holding off the coming decisive breakthrough to the south of St. Lo and to form [sic] a new MLR with the troops to the left. Only the 3 Para Engr Bn in an advance position blocked all traffic east and west on the main road.[65]

The temporary pause in St. Lo found Lt. E. R. Reischel and his party of men hard at work to clear the battlefields over which the Battalion had been fighting. They were working eight to ten hours a day just removing the dead and picking up equipment. Some of the men could work through the stench only by wearing gas masks. About five loads—¼-ton trailers with discarded rifles being used for staves—of bodies (usually about five German to one American) were being removed each day, and then there would be as many loads of American equipment to salvage.[66]

Men of the Third Battalion knew that this defensive situation could not last much longer. They heard that "something big" was up. General Bradley was going to try for a break-through—as soon as he had a good flying day. Infantry and armored divisions—the first prominent mention of armored *divisions*—were "stacked up" behind St. Lo: the armor would go through and carry on. The capture of St. Lo had made this operation—referred to as "Operation Cobra"—feasible. Now that the anchor of the German defenses had

61. "There was a fantastically twisted body on the other side of the road—sex, nationality, and color indeterminate—the product of a direct shell hit. During the first hours after St. Lo fell, that body became a road marker, and now when somebody wants to indicate how far into town he was able to get under German shellfire, he refers to 'that body on the side of the road.' "—Levitt, "St. Lo Was No Cinch," **Yank,** Aug. 13, 1944.
62. Drew Middleton in **The New York Times,** July 20, 1944, p. 1.
63. This refers to the advances of the 29th Division from the east.
64. The American editor comments that this apparently refers to the threat of the 30th Division's push toward the Vire. It would seem as likely that this would refer to the attack of the 35th Division from the north—which would be the left as the defender faced the 29th's attacks from the east. It was the 35th that was attacking directly toward the city; the 30th was on the "wrong," i.e., the west, side of the Vire River to make an attack directly to St. Lo.
65. From XIX Corps Historical File, reproduced in St. Lo (MS), p. 183.
66. E. C. Reischel to the author, July 14, 1946.

fallen, American infantry, armor, and air forces were to combine for the big break-through. In addition to 15 American infantry divisions, there were three armored divisions now coiled for the strike.[67]

Each day artillery fire was claiming its toll in casualties. On Tuesday morning, July 24th, four men of the Third Battalion were killed and five were wounded in heavy shelling between 5:30 and 6:00 o'clock.[68] That evening Lieutenant Edgar Keltner, regimental assistant S-3 called:

"The snake is going to begin to uncoil soon."

67. General Eisenhower's Report, p. 34; Ingersoll, **Top Secret**, p. 178.
68. 134th Inf., S-3 Journal, 24 July 1944.

CHAPTER IV

★ ★ ★

"BLOODY SUNDAY"

★ ★ ★

The 2,000 planes—fighters to Flying Fortresses—were in the air. Their bombs began to fall. One could feel them almost more than hear them. They kept coming in a seemingly endless stream. It appeared that some of them were falling very close to friendly troops—in the area of the 30th Division to the right. For 75 minutes the great air assault continued to loose nearly 5,000 tons of bombs on an area five miles long and one mile wide.[1]

The plan of attack was that, following a heavy air bombardment of the enemy positions, the First Army was to advance on a three-divisional front west of St. Lo, with the general line Marigny-St. Gilles as the primary objective. Three more divisions were then to pass through the first wave, turn westward, and strike for Coutances and Granville, thus cutting off the enemy in the Area Periers-Lessay. These first two waves were to be launched by VII Corps, with VIII Corps subsequently taking up the battle in the Lessay sector and advancing along the coast on the right.

. . . .

At the same time our VIII, XIX, and V Corps maintained their pressure along the remainder of the army front.[2]

Reports came in during the afternoon and next morning that the attack was going well, and that the armor was on its way. Obviously it would be necessary to maintain pressure to the immediate front in order not to permit the transfer of any troops to the area of the main break-through.

On Thursday morning, the 27th, men of the Third Battalion were surprised to see officers from the 28th ("Keystone"—Pennsylvania) Division coming up to the Battalion CP. They had orders to relieve the Battalion. This doubtless seemed a little strange; but perhaps the Battalion was going to follow-up the break-through while this newer unit would take over the defensive mission. Hardly had these reconniassance parties left until a call came from regimental headquarters.[3]

"Previous instructions on relief cancelled; we attack at 1500."

The 134th Infantry was to make the main effort in taking the high ground to the south of St. Lo. Nineteen battalions of artillery were available to support the attack.[4]

Colonel Thomsen took his command group and moved down through the rubble to Company I's CP.[5] Passing the old, once beautiful Church of Notre Dame, men paused to point out to those who followed an inspiring curiosity of the ruins: stone dust had clouded what was left of the beautiful blue and white and gold of the interior; most of the roof was demolished; the walls were crumbling; but amidst this destruction, rose the great crucifix, unbroken.[6]

In a thin single-file, the battalion column moved over the deep rubble which filled the streets, wound down narrow steps to get down to the river

1. Sgt. Bill Davidson, "Barrage by Bombers", **Yank** (British ed.) III (Aug. 13, 1944), 5; E. C. Daniel in **The New York Times,** July 26, 1944, p. 1; Frederick Graham in **The New York Times,** p. 4; Ralph Ingersoll, **Top Secret,** pp. 178ff; General Eisenhower's Report, p. 36.
2. General Eisenhower's Report, pp. 36, 38.
3. 134th Inf., S-3 Journal, 27 July 1944.
4. ibid.
5. ibid.
6. see **Time** XLVIII (Nov. 4, 1944) p. 63; see **Lost Treasures of Europe** (New York: Pantheon, 1946) pp. 227, 228. Formerly a cathedral, the church dated from the 14th Century, and had been restored in the 17th Century.—Lippincott's Gazetteer, p. 1611.

level, and then moved down along the highway to the southwest. A small field of teller anti-tank mines laid on the road surface near the edge of town suggested that the German withdrawal had been a hasty one.

A TD platoon had been attached to the Third Battalion, but it was unable to move through the rubble of St. Lo. A tank reconaissance officer went down to look over the conditions and estimated that it would take two days to get any armor through St. Lo. Division engineers went to work with bulldozers and shovels and trucks—and mine detectors. Though the principal route had been heavily mined, the debris had covered the mines so completely that they could not be detonated. The engineers worked through the night to clear a vehicular route in good time—though it required eight hours' work even to clear a path for jeeps.[7]

Company L deployed on the left of Company I and the Battalion moved warily ahead more than a thousand yards before running into any trouble. Here after a brisk fire fight, Company I knocked out a machine gun and took some prisoners.[8] But another machine gun was holding up Company L. Lieutenant Jack Campbell, platoon leader, sent one of his squads to the left flank of the enemy position in an effort to destroy it. However, the squad was unable to advance far enough to bring any effective fire to bear on its antagonist. Thereupon Campbell determined to make an attack against the right flank—a personal attack. Armed only with hand grenades, the lieutenant crawled toward his objective until he was in a position to hurl two of the deadly missiles against the foe. The result was a continuation of its advance on the part of Company L.[9] Now leaving the highway upon which it had been guiding, the Battalion moved southeast through orchards and hedgerows. Here and there the Battalion would run into a pocket of resistance and then move on. Prisoners in groups of four or five to 20 were taken, and of course, more men were getting hurt.

It was such a pocket of resistance that the Battalion found as it crossed another of those sunken roads. During this series of fire fights through the hedgerow terrain, it was difficult to maintain contact. Colonel Thomsen had gone forward to contact Company L, and members of the command group, left to wait in the sunken road, were not sure of his whereabouts. A burst of small arms fire cracked overhead and cut through the tree leaves. Radiomen and telephone men lifted their rifles or carbines. They started to move around a slight curve in the sunken road; there was another burst of fire from the other direction. Now the volume of fire became intense. Men had to fight off panic as a sickening feeling of being caught in a trap sought to possess them. Then they recognized the familiarity of the sounds of the weapons. They all were American!

A platoon of "K" and a platoon of "L" were shooting at each other! The command group was in the sunken road between the two platoons. Leaders hurried to the radio to get word to the two companies to cease firing. In due course this was successful before there had been actual casualties on either side.

Division orders came directing that the attack be continued until 10:30 o'clock. At that hour the Third Battalion was in another brisk fire fight, and darkness had applied its own envelopment before quiet returned.[10] Then, with

7. M. R. Carroll to the Author, July 15, 1946; 134th Inf., S-3 Journal.
8. ibid.
9. 35th Div., General Orders, No. 38, 29 Sept. 1944.
10. 134th Inf., S-3 Journal.

the companies' assigned hedgerows surrounding two fields, and the Battalion CP along the middle hedgerow, the Battalion formed a "wagon-wheel," all-around, defense—for the night.

Hardly had the men dug their foxholes before that bothersome German airplane was circling overhead. Again came those brilliant yellow, everlasting flares, and then the bombs, and then the machine gun bullets. It was awe-inspiring to watch as long as he kept at a safe distance, but when he came over the Battalion's orchard it was more comforting to hide the head ostrich-like in the foxhole and shut out that disrobing light. This night he seemed to be interested particularly in the supporting 161st Field Artillery Battalion. One bomb tore a huge crater in the very center of a field which scattered mud all over trucks and guns around the edges. So regular had these visits become— 11 o'clock each evening—that everyone referred to the hostile airman as "Bed-check Charlie." And men were asking where was the famed "Black Widow" night-fighter?

A regrouping of troops during the night (27-28 July) brought the 29th Division out of the line and shifted it—by motor—to a sector on the right.[11] This move was to carry that division down through the Brittany Peninsula. The 35th now was in Major General Leonard T. Gerow's V Corps; withdrawal of the 29th left the 2nd Division on the left.[12]

Moving off at 10 A.M., the Third Battalion deployed on either side of the road leading to Ste. Suzanne sur Vire and Conde Sur Vire and met only scattered, slight opposition. Colonel Thomsen was moving behind the assault companies with the same energy as always. Sometimes he would give his command group—and especially the wire crew—a difficult time as they tried to keep up. Often it took something akin to mind-reading to know when to follow and when to wait for him. The wiremen and messengers of course, could carry only a limited amount of wire—even with the light wire it could be no more than three or four miles, and the wiremen had a difficult time of it in trying to follow the Colonel as he would siz-zag from one company's zone to the other. Sometimes he would say "Wait here, I'll be right back," but he would just keep going. It came to be a game to try to cut across his turns in order to save wire and keep up with him—and he always insisted on having that telephone wirehead with him.

Approaching the village of Ste. Suzanne, the Colonel decided that he was nearing the day's objective—the high ground between Ste. Suzanne and Conde sur Vire—and by radio he called the company commanders to meet him on the road.

The command group continued down the road. Sending his S-2 back to see if he could find "K" Company, the Colonel sat down on the shoulder of the road.

The intelligence officer contacted Captain Melcher of Company K 200 yards to the rear of Ste. Suzanne. The Colonel was acting as the point. He was sitting up there along the road about four hundred yards in front of everybody.

Just before sunset the Battalion moved up on the high ground and reported "On objective." The Americans were north of Conde sur Vire.[13] Taking over some abandoned German foxholes (theirs were always better,

11. ibid.
12. ibid.
13. ibid.; E. C. Daniel in **The New York Times**, July 30, 1944, p. 3.

deeper, and with thick coverings) and digging some new ones, the men prepared for the night.

During the afternoon the 1st Battalion had been held up, and this had left a big gap—both in width and in depth—between the two battalions. Accordingly the Second Battalion, in reserve, had been ordered to move up on the left of the Third and take over the objective originally assigned to the 1st Battalion.[14]

The Battalion was getting organized on its position when there was a close, nerve-racking burst from a burp gun. Always it was difficult to distinguish between the sound of the bullets and the sound of the weapon, and the use of smokeless powder made a German weapon a hard thing to locate. Men started looking for a sniper. There was nothing hated worse than a sniper—a "lost soldier" who would hide himself in a tree or in a house or in a chimney to shoot down Americans until his ammunition was exhausted when he would come down with his hands up to beg mercy. Some Americans began firing in the area. Colonel Thomsen ordered all firing ceased so that he could hear this sniper.

A man thought that he had located the enemy in a tree. He pointed, and other men along the hedgerow lifted their rifles toward the tree. Just then a man jumped out of the tree and looked around at all those rifles trained on him—it was Johnson, one of the intelligence scouts.

By this fear of snipers in trees, men of the Third Battalion denied themselves the use of trees for observation—one of the few means at hand for taking a look over the hedgerows.

An increase in the tempo of the firing to the left rear told them that there was something more than a sniper or two there. The 2nd Battalion, coming up, was encountering real trouble in an area immediately to the left of the route over which the Third had come. The firing was intense on both sides.[15]

Not till the next morning were the three battalions able to make contact with each other. By that time the Germans, now following a regular pattern, had withdrawn. But there was no intention of permitting the enemy any respite.

An "L" Company patrol reported at 6:50 A.M. that an enemy tank had moved in alongside the church in Conde sur Vire. The attack moved off without any opposition two hours later. Another patrol at 10:20 was able to describe the steel monster as a self-propelled "88". Company K was moving in at the same time, and now the Battalion Antitank Platoon was looking for a place to get in a shot with a 57 mm gun. The result was a couple of antitank rockets (from "bazookas") from one group, some antitank grenades from another and some 57 mm slugs from the third. No one was quite sure who delivered the knock-out blow, but the Battalion had "bagged" its first tank. Company L found the tank crew in the church and routed them out.[16]

At 4 o'clock, orders came to continue the attack—the regiment was to keep going until it had taken the town of Torigni-sur-Vire. Lieutenant Campbell of "L" Company took a patrol on through Conde sur Vire to reconnoiter the ground beyond. He found no enemy on the high ground to the south; the 35th Cavalry Reconnaissance Troop was working down the highway to his right.[17]

By 7 o'clock the companies were through Conde. But once again darkness

14. Carroll, *loc. cit.*; 134th Inf., S-3 Journal.
15. 134th Inf., S-3 Journal.
16. 134th Inf., S-3 Journal, 29 July 1944; 134th Inf., Unit Journal, 29 July 1944
17. 134th Inf., S-3 Journal.

was overtaking an attack. The companies moved forward about a thousand yards during each of the next two hours. At 9:30 they passed through a small cluster of farm dwellings and barns noted as "le Bust" on the map.[18] French people—men, women and children—came out to greet them. Here, for the first time, French families were found occupying their homes. Villiers-Fossard had been almost completely abandoned; St. Lo a ghost town;[1] Ste Suzanne and Conde sur Vire practically lifeless. But not this little farm hamlet—its people were out to greet the Yanks.

Fifteen minutes later there was machine gun fire ahead, but it was of short duration. The battalion commander directed the companies to "tie-in" and await orders. He walked over to the wirehead and picked up the field telephone to call regimental headquarters. He felt sure that trouble lay ahead, and he was opposed to continuing an attack at night over strange ground without benefit of any reconnaissance.[19]

The regimental commander was wholly in sympathy with the objection to a night attack without any prior reconnaissance,[20] and after another telephone conference with the Division Chief of Staff, he was able to have continuation of the attack postponed until 9 o'clock the next morning.[21]

The halt came none too soon, for a hostile airplane was approaching. Men were scattering among the buildings and hedgerows; the 2nd Battalion was moving along the road beyond a railroad underpass when a string of flares cast its bright yellow light over the landscape. There was a burst of machine gun fire from near the railway. The airplane answered by swooping down low with its machine guns strafing over the 2nd Battalion; a bomb sent tremors through the earth. The bomb, rather than hitting the nearby house, had made a direct hit in the very center of the bridge; crumbled stone from the demolished span lay amongst the twisted rails below. Now it was necessary for headquarters men coming to the rear to climb down into the deep cut and out again over the rubble on the other side.[22] It appeared that the Third Battalion had suffered a few casualties during the raid, but parts of the Second had been hit hard.[23]

Guards posted, the men snuggled down in their slit trenches to claim a few short hours of nature's escape from warfare. But the drone of another airplane interrupted their sleep. To the front they could see a green flare; soon a similar flare burst to the right side—then to the left—finally to the rear.[24] Then came the bright yellow flares from the plane as he searched for prey; fortunately there was no firing on the area. The Battalion, evidently, was well-concealed.

Having finished eating their "K" ration breakfast, the men were putting on their equipment preparatory to moving off with a 9 o'clock Sunday-morning attack. Colonel Thomsen walked up to the corner of the field, plastic map case in one hand, long field coat slung over the back of his belt, paused momentarily to collect his command group, and moved up a hedgerow to a sunken road where he stopped to direct the attack.

18. **ibid.**
19. Carroll, **loc. cit.**
20. "A battalion should have a minimum of 3 hours for daylight preparation . . . . Night attacks are seldom justified without ample time for daylight preparation—Infantry Field Manual 7-20: **Rifle Battalion,** p. 112.
21. 134th Inf., S-3 Journal.
22. Carroll, **loc. cit.**
23. 134th Inf., S-3 Journal.
24. **ibid.**

The companies jumped off at 9 o'clock, but the German withdrawal pattern had been altered: there were immediate bursts of hostile fire all along the line. The enemy added artillery to his small arms fire. What made the situation immediately worse was the relative compactness of the Battalion's formation. It had not even had an opportunity to deploy fully from its compact wagon-wheel formation which it had taken up for night security. This meant that the Battalion CP was only about one hedgerow in rear of the front line, and the aid station and other headquarters personnel were only the distance of a small orchard to the left rear—across the road. Nearly the whole Battalion, therefore, was under fire when any great volume was directed at any part of it.[25]

An hour and a half later the situation had not improved. "K" and "L" Companies unable to advance, Colonel Thomsen sent Company "I" around to attack on the left of "L"; but there was no flank and "I" was under fire before it even came abreast.[26] All companies were suffering casualties, and were gaining nothing. Artillery fire had cut telephone lines, and communications between Battalion and regiment broke.

At the Battalion CP the medics were busy. A litter team was lifting the battalion clerk from his foxhole onto their litter; he had painful wounds in his arm and thigh. Someone lit a cigarette for him, and he thanked them cheerfully as he was carried away. Lieutenant Garner was hit—wounded seriously. A company runner, eyes closed, sat stiffly in a fox hole where a shell had killed him. The tank officer who had come up to cordinate was in a hole nearby, and he got hit; Captain Carroll had gone up to see Colonel Thomsen, and the S-2 had gone back to regimental headquarters; Pfc. Johnson was the only one there who did not get hit.

Meanwhile the companies were trying hard to advance. Company K was still on the right, and trying to make the next hedgerow. Technical Sergeant Paul Forney of Nebraska, platoon sergeant, had found himself in command of his platoon when the lieutenant had been hit. He led the platoon out across the orchard toward the next hedgerow. Moving through enemy fire, Forney was wounded; but he kept right on going to throw his hand grenades over the next hedgerow. He rallied his men to continue the assault, but the next burst of fire killed him.[27] Pfc. Edward Abraham of Ohio was a little more fortunate. When his platoon was pinned down by an enemy machine gun, he leaped over the hedgerow, and although wounded, crawled down near the German gun and destroyed the crew with a hand grenade.[28]

Four automatic riflemen were wounded in quick succession at a vital position protecting the left flank of Company L's 2nd Platoon. Immediately Pfc. Luverne Strand of Minnesota, and Robert Hanlon of Washington, D. C., ran up to take over the BAR. They opened fire, and kept the weapon going until a direct hit from an enemy mortar killed both of them.[29]

Over in Company I one platoon had been able to drive a short gain, but heavy fire from front and flank forced it to give this up. Technical Sergeant Leonard Oseik of Ohio, the platoon sergeant, grabbed a light machine gun to cover the withdrawal of his platoon. He remained in position until all the other members of his platoon had taken cover behind the hedgerow to the rear.

25. Carroll, loc. cit.
26. ibid.
27. 35th Div., General Orders, No. 25, 25 Aug. 1944.
28. 35th Div., General Orders, No. 22, 20 Aug. 1944.
29. 35th Div., General Orders, No. 25, 25 Aug. 1944.

Then, firing the machine gun from his hip, he walked backwards until he reached the hedgerow. But as he started to climb over, enemy fire killed him.[30]

Colonel Thomsen was becoming worried over the Battalion's situation. Tanks were coming up; they were able to cross the railroad over a grade crossing about a half mile to the west of the knocked-out overpass, but the sunken road which ran parallel to the railroad was too narow for them in some places, and there it was necessary for pioneer demolition crews to blast openings in the hedgerow. All of this was taking time, and in the meantime the accurate enemy fire was sapping the Battalion's strength. The battalion commander was hoping that Colonel Miltonberger would commit the Second Battalion which was being held in regimental reserve.[31] To this Colonel Miltonberger readily agreed when he saw the gravity of the situation. However, the commander of the 2nd Battalion had been wounded in the previous night's bombing attack, and now the executive officer was near nervous exhaustion; it was not until Captain Carroll, after repeated trips, got hold of the S-3, Captain Frederick Roecker, a young West Pointer from Washington that he was able to get any action.[32]

A long whistle announced the approach of another shell. It burst on a barn. Splinters of wood, timber fragments, smoke and dust rose high into the air. Members of the Pioneer Platoon came running out of the old building; several were injured—Lieutenant Hall had a gash in his hand. Already motor personnel, Pioneers, and others, had been pressed into service to deliver supplies of ammunition to the companies.[33]

The battalion medical section was having its busiest day at the aid station which was in a small building about a hundred yards off the road to the immediate left. Now a barrage hit the aid station. One man was holding out his hand having a finger bandaged; a big shell fragment took off the hand. Wounded men lying helplessly on the floor were wounded a second and a third time; medics were wounded so that they could not care for them. Captain Matthew decided he must move the aid station back. The assistant surgeon gathered up the party and started down the road while Matthew jumped in his jeep and went on down to find another site. A pathetic group it was that emerged from the damaged building and filed out to the road. Bloody bandages fluttering from arms or heads or shoulders . . . wounded medics carrying men on litters . . . everyone in a hurry, but no one could run . . . out to the road to join a stream of God-forsaken human beings . . . The walking wounded from the Pioneer platoon, and additional ones coming from the companies, added their number to the battered column . . . French civilians from the little hamlet—the ones who had been so gay the night before—now added to the general confusion by coming out onto the road pulling carts stacked high with bedclothes, utensils, what foodstuffs they might have. They all trudged down the dusty road in the hot sun toward the railroad. Matthew set up his aid station in an orchard along the tracks.

It took some time to get any part of the 2nd Battalion started up, but presently Captain McDannel approached the area of the battalion CP with Company E. But another barrage was on the way. Tree bursts sent leaves and boughs fluttering to the ground, and sent steel fragments about the men below.

30. **ibid.**
31. 134th Inf., S-3 Journal; Carroll, **loc. cit.**
32. **ibid.**
33. E. C. Reischel to the Author, July 14, 1946.

Torn bodies writhed upon the ground. A man cried out in a loud voice, "Oh, Jesus, someone help me!" And then he died. An "M" company mortar crew was knocked out on the other side of the hedgerow to the right. Other shells hit on top of the hedgerow and on the ground beside it—they cut down that column of men.

It was nearing 5 o'clock now, and Colonel Thomsen was worried about the situation. He chafed at being unable to advance; he was impatient that neither the tanks nor the 2nd Battalion had been able to give any assistance, and he was concerned about the loss of men. There had been nearly a hundred casualties so far during the day. Captain Lassiter of Company L had been seriously wounded, and so had First Sergeant Benjamin Miller. Colonel Thomsen was standing behind a tree in the sunken trail. A barrage burst among the trees to scatter its lethal fragments on the sunken trail. Nearly everyone in the command group had been hit. Colonel Thomsen was wounded, Lt. Davis, "K" Company executive, was hit. Captain Bruce, the adjutant, had been knocked out by a shell farther to the rear.

Captain Carroll went up to take over. Medics were at work quickly, but they had a big job on their hands. Colonel Thomsen was unconscious from a wound in his head; the artillery liaison radio had been destroyed, and all the members of the liaison group wounded. Drew, the Battalion Sergeant Major, had been killed. The intelligence sergeant was wounded; but when the medics came for him he refused to be evacuated until all the other wounded men had been cared for. Then, while he was being carried to safety some minutes later, another shell came in to end his life and those of the men carrying him.

With the approach of dusk, the regimental commander ordered the 2nd Battalion to relieve the Third to give the latter an opportunity for reorganization.[34]

Throughout the day the Battalion had been receiving shell fire from time to time from the rear. The men could hear the report of the gun distinctly, and the shells would come ripping through with deadly effect. Immediately they had accused friendly artillery, but later investigation showed this not to be the case. They concluded that there was an enemy mobile gun somewhere in the rear area.[35]

It was dark before the relieving companies started up, and it was a slow process. Elements of the Third Battalion's companies had become intermingled during the heavy fighting, and it was a task to get the platoons reorganized so that they could move out in an orderly fashion. And any intimation to the enemy that a relief of battalions was going on would have invited disaster. Lt. Ruby had taken the available members of Company M as well as much of Headquarters Company to act as guides. At last members of Company I came back to the vicinity of the farm houses, formed a column, and set off down the muddy sunken trail and turned into the dry gravel road. The night was calm and clear—with a partial moon, and it was cool as always. Carrol and the S-2 waited another hour—"sweating out" "Bed-check Charlie"; fortunately, they received word that there would be friendly night-fighters up,[36] and "Charlie" missed a call. Presently the sticking, slippery sound of feet upon mud told them that Company L was coming out. It was well after 5 A.M. before all the Battalion was back in the assembly area. Lieutenant Colonel Sheppard, regi-

34. Carroll, *loc. cit.*
35. *ibid.*; 134th Inf., S-3 Journal.
36. *ibid.*

mental executive officer, was sitting by a lamp in a dugout; he was to remain with the battalion until its new commander arrived.[37] Members of the earlier companies already were asleep when the later ones started digging their foxholes. Some men had to be sent up to outpost the gap between the First and Second Battalions. Everyone was physically and mentally exhausted. Men had seen about 115 casualties leave the Battalion during the day;[38] they were wondering when their turn would be—percentages looked well enough when the figures were dealing with the whole Army,[39] for most of the Army does not fight, but in the fighting elements of an infantry battalion they began to see that they had no odds in their favor. It was becoming a question not *if* they were going to get hit, but *when,* and *how badly.* Would he be one of the lucky ones, or would he be killed or permanently maimed? During these two weeks of combat the Battalion had suffered 574 casualties—86 were wounded fatally.[40]

37. Carroll, loc cit.; Reischel, loc. cit.; 134th Inf., S-3 Journal.
38. 134th Inf., Battle Casualty Report.
39. "It is reassuring to know that of all men in an army comparatively few are killed. The chances that any one man will be among those mortally wounded in any one battle are relatively small."—"Psychology for the Fighting Man," **The Infantry Journal,** LII (Jan. 1943), 60.
40. 134th Inf., Battle Casualty Report.

CHAPTER V

★ ★ ★
"PINCHED OUT" ACROSS THE VIRE RIVER
★ ★ ★

There scarcely could have been any greater stimuli to a soldier's morale than hot food and mail. Both items came up for the Battalion on that Monday morning following "Bloody Sunday."

Yet, in spite of its desirability, mail could have the effect of magnifying one's sense of frustration. Now when one had a few minutes to reflect on the happenings of the preceding day, he became keenly aware of the odds against him. Letters from loved ones reminded him that all this would affect more than merely himself; he wanted so much to be back with them again, but they seemed so very, very far away; he wondered if he even dared hope. Some men received packages of candy or cakes in the mail; and they hastened to eat them quickly, for tomorrow might be too late to enjoy them.

A group of replacements had come up to replenish partially the weakened companies. These newly-arrived soldiers were joining the Battalion now as the result of the functioning of the army's replacement system. This system represented something of a departure from practice in earlier wars, and of most armies in this.

> In past wars it had been the accepted practice to organize as many divisions as manpower resources would permit, fight those divisions until casualties had reduced them to bare skeletons, then withdraw them from the line and rebuild them in a rear area. In 1918 the AEF was forced to reduce the strength of divisions and finally to disband newly arrived divisions in France in order to maintain the already limited strength of those engaged in battle. The system we adopted for this war involved a flow of individual replacements from training centers to the divisions so they would be constantly at full strength.[1]

Among those replacements was blonde, medium-sized Elton H. Ridge, a school teacher from Denver, Missouri.[2] The process which now brought Ridge to the Third Battalion already had begun to function while the Battalion still was in training at Camp Rucker. He had been inducted on September 24, 1943, and had entered into active service three weeks later at Fort Leavenworth, Kansas.[3] On October 28th, he had left Reception Center 1773 to go to the Infantry Replacement Training Center at Camp Wolters, Texas,[4] where he would receive his basic infantry training program. After about four months of this training, he had been assigned to the 69th Division at Camp Shelby, Mississippi[5] where he had joined the 272nd Infantry Regiment.[6] Six weeks later he had found himself shifted into the stream whose ultimate destination would be Europe—he had been sent to Army Ground Forces Personnel Replacement Depot No. 1 at Fort George G. Meade, Maryland.[7] Early in May, then he had gone to the Hampton Roads Port of Embarkation, Camp Patrick Henry, Virginia where he had become a member of a group designated merely as GI-040(a)-A.[8] For the overseas voyage he had been transferred to a "packet"—

1. General Marshall's Report, p. 103.
2. Enlisted Record and Report of Separation, 396-38 (War Department, Adjutant General's Office Form 53-55, 1 November 1944 (Photostat).
3. ibid.
4. Service Record, 1st Indorsement, 28 Oct., 1943 (Photostat).
5. ibid., 2nd Ind., 6 March 1944.
6. ibid., 3rd Ind., Apr. 24, 1944.
7. ibid.
8. ibid., 4th Ind., 2 May 1944.

GS-150(a).[9] Actually, Ridge had sailed from the Hampton Roads on May 21st—only nine days after the Third Battalion had departed from New York, and had arrived in England, June 2nd.[10] From here he had joined the 11th Replacement Depot, and on June 15th had been assigned to Replacement Detachment X-24-B[11] for the cross-channel voyage to France. Then through the 12th Replacement Depot and the 89th Replacement Battalion and through the 86th Replacement[12] Battalion to the 35th Division[13] where he only had arrived on July 30th— just in time to be available to join the group of replacements so badly needed by the Third Battalion on this Monday morning. In the Battalion, he was retained in Battalion Headquarters in the S-2 section—i.e., as an intelligence scout.

This replacement system proved its worth in some respects, but there were certain disadvantages within it. Principal ones were the difficult questions of anticipating requirements accurately, and delay in arrival of new men.[14] Consequently the division came to be fought "until casualties had reduced them to bare skeletons" in spite of the new system. Another had to do with the maintenance of *esprit de corps* in the face of very rapid turnovers. Some officers recommended that replacements should be organized and sent into combat as battalions or companies—possibly having already been assigned to some regiment as a replacement battalion while in training. Some saw an advantage to maintaining a continuity, of spreading out replacements among men who already had seen some combat—but others would point out that sometimes the so-called "veterans" were not a desirable influence. On the other hand, there is no question but that the effect of divisions continuing to fight day after day in spite of heavy casualties was a serious threat to German morale.

At 8:00 Lieutenant Colonel Robert E. Moore of Missouri arrived in the area to take command of the Battalion.[15] He had been assigned to the sister 137th Infantry back in the States, but then had gone to an assignment with higher headquarters. A veteran of World War I, he had been clamoring for action—he wanted to command an infantry battalion. Now he was going to have it. Colonel Moore was of less than average stature, but well-built and his hair and mustache were gray. He did not propose to introduce any radical changes into the way the Battalion operated.

Two hours later young, stocky, Captain Harlan B. Heffelfinger of Beatrice, Nebraska came to join the Battalion.[16] He was leaving his place as 1st Battalion S-3 to be Third Battalion executive officer.

Lieutenant Frank Snyder of New York, who had been 1st Battalion communications officer was with Captain Heffelfinger—Snyder was to take over the same job in the Third.

The injury of Captain Bruce had left another vacancy in Battalion headquarters: S-1 (adjutant). The S-2 was to assume these duties for the time being. He called Sergeant Buckley up from the supply section to take over his old place as Sergeant Major, and sent a message back to Division headquarters, rear echelon, to have a young clerk there named Bartash return to the Company as Battalion clerk.

9. Ibid., 5th Ind., 9 May 1944.
10. Enlisted Record and Report of Separation.
11. Service Record, 6th Ind., 15 June 1944.
12. Ibid., 7th Ind.
13. Ibid., 8th Ind., 30 July 1944.
14. At one time in August, the total replacement pool of riflemen in France was down to one man. Fortunately a ship load arrived the next morning.—Randolph Leigh, 48 Million Tons to Eisenhower (Washington: The Infantry Journal, 1945) p. 112.
15. 134th Inf., S-3 Journal, 31 July 1944.
16. Ibid.

During the morning the men took advantage of this opportunity to shave and wash. Unfortunately the luxury of relaxation never could last very long. A telephone call came from regimental headquarters. The Battalion would be moving again shortly after noon.[17] The watchword was "push, push." The enemy must be allowed no respite.

Apparently the German had been hurt as much as the Third Battalion during the previous day's fighting, for when the 1st and 2nd Battalions attacked at 12 o'clock, the opposition had withdrawn from the front.

A change in boundaries gave the city of Torigni-sur-Vire to the 320th Infantry,[18] and by evening it was cleared out.[19]

The advance continued the next day without any real opposition. Down the sunken trails, over unused highways, across hedgerows, through meadows and orchards, the columns moved through the Bocage country.[20] During one temporary halt an artillery liaison plane fluttering earthward like a stricken sparrow—the pilot was trying to land with the greatest possible speed—gave notice that enemy aircraft were approaching. Seconds later two Messerschmitt 109's streaked across the sky. And then two Thunderbolts—P-47's—recognizable only through field glasses—appeared and shot down one of the intruders; the other turned about and sped in the opposite direction.

Opposition on the ground did not develop until evening when the 1st Battalion ran into some small arms fire.[21] The Third was able to go up on the left of the 1st to dig in for the night, but at twilight there were heavy barrages of artillery and mortar fire. This was somewhat disconcerting for a column of replacements coming up, and other shells fell into the motor park—this knocked out a jeep, and hit an ammunition trailer which only quick work by the A & P men saved—and forced the aid station to move to the rear. This would mean more work for the Battalion's motor maintenance men, and those motor vehicles were essential to the Battalion's efficiency. Usually it would take two to three weeks to get a replacement when a truck was so badly damaged as to be beyond immediate repair. And even then, the mechanics[22] frequently would be able to make the replacement vehicle satisfactory for combat use only after a great deal of effort. Sometimes it was difficult to get needed parts; there would be delays and difficulties, but by improvization and experiment, most of the motors were kept functioning most of the time, and in emergencies it frequently was possible to get replacements and make repairs in a remarkably short time.[23]

Colonel Moore said that he was through with having his CP in a hole behind a hedgerow, and he directed battalion headquarters to move into a small farm house and its out buildings—they soon discovered that a house was better protection against artillery than was a foxhole. Quilts and comforters over the windows provided the necessary blackout, and the farmer's kerosene lamps (sometimes they burned gasoline in them) gave the necessary light. An old dining table, covered with a blanket (they were careful to protect it from scratches and spots although a few shells might have reduced it to splinters at

17. Ibid.
18. Ibid.
19. E. C. Daniel in The New York Times, Aug. 1, 1944, p. 1.
20. "La Bocage", a name referring to the brush and thickets of the country, was a term applied to the whole area centering about Vire.
21. 134th Inf., S-3 Journal, 1 Aug. 1944.
22. Motor personnel under the supervision of the motor officer included a motor transport sergeant and a mechanic (technician, grade 4) in battalion headquarters, and a mechanic in the heavy weapons company, plus all the drivers of the Battalion.—T. O. And E. 7-16 and 7-16, 26 Feb. 1944.
23. E. C. Reischel to the Author, July 14, 1946.

any moment) afforded a place to install telephones and work over maps and notes.

Hardly had the command post been set up when the regimental S-3 came down to visit the battalion commander—the regiment had orders to continue the attack during the night to seize the Vire River line.[24] Third Battalion officers were apprehensive about undertaking any night attack without prior reconnaissance.

Jeeps and trailers came up with hot chow—hot meals whenever at all possible was another "must" of the new battalion commander—and then the companies were told to be alert and prepared to move at 2 A.M., the time given for the night attack.

At 2 o'clock Colonel Moore reported to regiment that he was ready to go, but was waiting on the 1st Battalion.[25] He had one of the companies send out a patrol, and kept in close radio and physical contact with Red battalion.[26] The 1st Battalion reported that it was unable to advance on account of heavy mortar and machine gun fire.[27]

Actually the main body of troops moved out sometime after 7 o'clock.[28] They encountered French people returning to their homes, and interpreted this as a good sign. The Pioneers had to clear a big tree which had been felled across the road before the vehicles could come up, but no other obstacles barred the way, and by noon the Battalion had reached high Hill 201 overlooking the Vire River Valley. A main highway leading to Villedieu-les-Poels and Avranches ran across the front.

Leaders at higher headquarters were getting excited about crossing the Vire River: The V Corps Chief of staff was at the regimental CP, the Division G-3 was making calls to regiment, and soon General Baade, the Division commander, came down to visit the battalions. "There's nothing out there," he said, "and we must cross that river this afternoon; stop for nothing; the enemy is withdrawing." The objective was the city of Vire, some 10 or 12 miles away.[29] That always was the depressing thing about capturing an objective—there always was another, bigger and farther away than ever.

It was true that there had been no opposition to the advance during the morning, and there was no shell fire of any kind now; but the battalion commanders had little enthusiasm for going down into that deep valley to face those commanding hills (the river itself was reported to be narrow and shallow here —no obstacle to foot troops) without any preparation or reconnaissance. They determined to take enough time to make a short preliminary reconnaissance.

Colonel Moore came back and called for an officer and three men from Company I—he was going to lead a patrol himself to check on a route down to the river. Having lost one battalion commander already, his staff did not look upon this project with much favor, but the Colonel was determined to go. Lieutenant Wardwell reported with his men within a few minutes, and the patrol was ready. They carried a 536[30] hand radio, and were able to relay

24. 134th Inf., S-3 Journal.
25. Ibid., 2 Aug. 1944.
26. Ibid.
27. Ibid.
28. Ibid.
29. Ibid.
30. Each company had six of these small five-pound hand radios. The whole set was held to the side of the head where the telephone-like mouthpiece and receiver would come to a convenient position. Depression of a large button switched the set from receiving to sending. (It operated on a single pre-set frequency.) The SCR 536 had a range of about one mile.—T.O. and E. 7-17, 26 Feb. 1944, p. 10; The Infantry School, **Reference Data** (1942) p. 33.

messages back through Company I; however, they were soon out of range when
they started down the hill.

After they had been gone long enough to arouse considerable anxiety the
battalion commander and his party finally returned. The Colonel was carrying a burp gun slung over his shoulder—as the patrol had been moving along
down near the river, the alert Wardwell suddenly had lifted his rifle to fire into
a bush and felled a would-be assassin whose machine pistol had been pointed
directly at Colonel Moore; three or four associates had fled. But now the
Colonel was able to report it "all clear" to the river.

The battalion column—I, K, L—in single file, wound down into the valley
like a huge serpent. Communications men had to carry the 284 radio by hand.
Machine guns and ammunition became greater loads as their bearers filed down
the slopes.

Here, for the first time, it was possible to find an observation post from
which one could watch the Battalion's advance. Captain Heffelfinger and Lieutenant Blackburn of Company M remained here to observe. Should the Battalion run into trouble, Blackburn could open fire immediately with his 81
mm mortars and the executive officer could call for artillery or other assistance.
It was another bright day and observation was good. Men followed the path—
if there was no path originally, there was one by the time these companies had
passed in single file—down through shoulder-high grass and bushes to the
water's edge . The stream was only a narrow creek here, ("Is this the Vire?" a
soldier said. "Hell, I can spit across this.") but there was a feeling of dread
throughout the Battalion. All regarded the high, commanding hills on either
side as they started down the side of the valley. It was difficult to imagine why
the enemy should not defend these heights.

Still without any kind of enemy opposition, the column followed along
the side of the valley toward Pont Bellenger 1500 yards to the south.[31] As "I"
and "K" companies uncovered from behind the nose of the hill and began to
approach the town, the enemy opened fire. Machine guns and rifles sent bullets
crackling through the valley and shell fire was quick to follow. Mortars searched
the column all the way back to the stream. Fortunately the enemy had failed
to set the trap at his disposal, and there was no direct fire from the tops of the
riverside hills. However, that coming from the vicinity of Pont Bellenger was
sufficient to be costly. Company I, in the lead, had 25 casualties within a few
minutes.[32] Nearly the whole Battalion was pinned down.

Blackburn, observing from the high ground on the other side of the river,
had his mortars open fire on the town with white phosphorus and high explosive.

Captain Melcher of Company K crawled up to his 300 radio operator, but
as he reached for the handset, a shell fragment tore away the mouthpiece and
killed the radio operator.

Colonel Moore and most of his command group were pinned down in a
little shed. Just outside in the meadow lay Elton Ridge, the new intelligence
man, and now he was getting his initiation. Company I men were coming back,
and Ridge was crawling toward the relative safety of the little shed, where he

31. The Vire River flowed generally west in this area, and turned north at Ponfaroy—thus
previously it had been generally parallel to the direction of advance, but now that change in direction caused it to run generally perpendicular to the direction of advance. But though its general
direction in this area was west, it followed a very crooked course, and at this particular point its
direction was south-north for some thousand yards.—Map: France, 1:50,000, Torigni-sur-Vire,
Sheet 6 F/4.

32. 134th Inf., Battle Casualty Report.

would join the other members of the command group when an "I" company
sergeant came upon him.

Naturally all the new men in the companies had not had a chance as yet
to become acquainted with each other and the sergeant apparently thought
Ridge one of his own replacements. At any rate the new intelligence scout
found himself on the "I" Company firing line shooting away. Men still were
falling about him . . . rapid bursts of machine gun fire barely grazing over his
back . . . a shell hit within ten feet and set his ears to ringing. He glanced up
and saw a wounded man lying a few yards ahead of him out in the meadow.
In spite of all the natural fear which was crushing down upon him, Ridge
crawled out under that machine gun fire and amidst the shell fire, to drag the
stricken man back to safety. The wounded comrade looked up and said, "What's
your name, soldier?—that was a great thing you did."

The companies withdrew back around the nose of the hill to reorganize.[33]
Captain Craig, who had been commanding Company I, had been killed; Lieutenant Bickford, who had taken over command, had been wounded—a machine
gun burst had broken his leg; a second lieutenant who had come up only the
night before had been killed. Only Lieutenant Wardwell was left, but he was
badly shaken up, and felt that he could not assume the command. That left
Company I without a commander, and the Colonel was determined to renew
the attack. Captain Carroll, Battalion S-3, volunteered to undertake the difficult assignment of taking over a strange, disorganized company, and lead it into
an attack.[34]

Colonel Moore shifted Company L up to the left of K in assault, and left
I in reserve for the new attack at 8:30. By this time the 2nd Battalion had
come up on the high ground to the right, and the opposition subsided. The
assault companies reached the edge of Pont Bellenger within an hour and the
battalion dug in to wait for renewal of the advance at 8 o'clock the next morning.[35]

Bridging difficulties made it necessary for carrying parties to take up
ammunition, water, and rations during the night. There were no bridges or
roads or even trails available for vehicles. Engineers did build a bridge of
planks and timbers, but it could not be used until the following day. Men
from the kitchens and motor park, then, had to carry the supplies more than
a mile through tall grass and weeds, and finally up the hill which had been the
companies' objective—a hill so steep that it required two men to carry a five-
gallon can of water to the top. The task of carrying up supplies and evacuating wounded and dead was not completed before 8:30 o'clock the next morning.[36] "Bed-check Charlie" made his usual visit, but inflicted no local damage. The sister regiments continued to advance; the 320th came up on the
high ground to the left and before 7 o'clock the next morning the 320th reported that it had men on high, commanding, Hill 203, to the southeast of
Pont Bellenger, and the 137th had elements on Hill 193 to the southwest of
Pont Bellenger.[37] Now it did begin to look as though enemy opposition was
broken.

The Battalion moved out the next day following the road through Pont
Bellenger—the Pioneers had to make a route around a mine field there where

33. 134th Inf., S-3 Journal.
34. 35th Div., General Orders.
35. 134th Inf., S-3 Journal.
36. Reischel, loc. cit.
37. 134th Inf., S-3 Journal.

one man already had been killed—and continued southward over the nose of Hill 203.[38] There the odor of broken tree limbs, torn green leaves, and burnt gun powder—an aroma which now had become so closely associated with death—was heavy in the air where terrific artillery barrages had pounded this key terrain feature all during the night. Careful of mines which might lay concealed beneath the fallen leaves and branches, the column moved on.

There was some resistance down near the town of Annebecq—the town received a heavy German shelling while the Battalion remained safely to the left (east) of it—in the evening, but the advance moved on at 6:30 (August 4) the next morning without difficulty.[39]

Rumors had been spreading that Vire no longer was to be a division objective—that the British and the 2nd Division were to take it. The 134th had heard so many rumors in the course of this campaign about being "pinched out"—that is to have other friendly units maneuver across the front and thus cut off contact with the enemy—that the term had become a by-word. Now, however, as the Battalion advanced, queer-looking British vehicles began to appear along the roads to the left. Before noon orders came down to hold up —elements of the Second Armored ("Hell on Wheels") Division were approaching from the right; they were heading for Vire down the Tessy-Vire highway.[40] The Battalion went into a defensive position in some orchards and meadows; the command post set up in a farm house which had escaped the destruction of war.

It was as though a tremendous weight had been lifted from the shoulders. Men washed and shaved, and built small fires, and got fresh water (always putting in the purifying halazone tablets, of course), and basked in the warm afternoon sun. For the first time there was something besides enemy out in front. For the first time in nine days it looked as though there would be no order coming down calling for a resumption of the attack. Men of the Third Battalion knew that the Third Army was racing across the Brest Peninsula;[41] the situation now called for a change in sector for the 35th Division and they speculated on the possibility of mounting trucks and returning to the Third Army to follow General Patton's armor.

The pause gave the companies a chance to look about with a view to adding some fowl or game to the menu for supper. Hon, a "K" Company messenger of Chinese extraction was drafted to prepare a fowl for Battalion Headquarters. Hon had received wide radio and newspaper publicity back in his native Chicago, when he had been a holder of the first number drawn in the 1940 draft lottery. After he had served his bird his assignment became permanent—he was to become a Third Battalion Headquarters fixture.

Looking out through the clear night, members of the Third Battalion could see Vire burning, and the flashes of artillery barrages, but the sounds were scarcely audible. They munched on chicken and rabbit and contemplated on the end of the Normandy campaign.

38. Ibid.
39. Ibid.
40. Ibid., 4 Aug. 1944.
41. The Stars and Stripes (ETO Ed.), Aug. 3, 1944, p. 1. The Third Army, under General Patton, had become operational at noon on Aug. 1st.—Third U. S. Army, After Action Report, I, 16. (Delivery of Stars and Stripes to the troops—copies usually went up with the rations—was one of the Army's steps in a very conscientious effort to keep its soldiery informed. Other projects included a widespread "orientation" program under the supervision of specially-trained officers, radio newscasters, Yank magazine.) See General Marshal's Report, pp. 111-113.

CHAPTER VI
★ ★ ★
DETOUR TO MORTAIN
★ ★ ★

The Battalion moved into its assigned assembly area along the hedgerows northeast of Annebecq after a rapid, warm, afternoon march from its latest defensive position on August 5th. Indications were that the 35th Division would be moving by motor late the next day to join in the spectacular drive of the Third Army.[1]

So far removed from the scenes of combat that the roar of cannon now were reduced to peals as of distant thunder, the feeling of safety added to the brilliance of the sunshine on that bright Sunday morning. Everyone seemed to be intensely conscious that he was alive.

This was the chaplain's first opportunity to hold any kind of a church service since the Battalion had entered combat. The Catholic Chaplain, Father Hayes, who was accompanying the 2nd Battalion, came over to the Battalion area to hold a service at 9 o'clock, and then Chaplain Walker prepared for his Protestant service at 10 o'clock.

As the hour approached, men began to gather at the designated spot in an open meadow. This was near the center of the battalion area, and streams of men came from all directions. Trained never to be without their protection, the men were wearing their steel helmets, and carrying their rifles— it reminded one of the stories of the Pilgrims going to church back in Plymouth Colony.

It appeared that every man in the Battalion was attending church. The chaplain almost was overcome as he stood up to face his greatest military congregation. Actually it was too large a group to have together this close to the front, but no one was afraid. Several hundred male voices joined in singing some old hymns, and then the solo voice of Corporal Cross, battalion medical technician, carried clearly across the countryside in a special number.

The men sat in that sun-bathed meadow looking at the hills in the distance. A pair of airplanes flew over the hills and flashed their sides in the sun as they circled back—they were friendly. Here was the beauty of quiet such as had not been experienced in three weeks—in three weeks which seemed longer than months. The monotony of continuous violence of attack, the sameness of fear and pain, had been exchanged for the serenity of quiet worship.

"We are all very much aware of how fortunate we are to be able to come together for worship on this beautiful morning," the chaplain said, "and we remember in our hearts and in our prayers our comrades who are not here today. We turn to the only source we know to find a strength to see us through the trials in the days to come." The period closed with a communion service; later, three men were baptized.[2]

Considerations which usually would dictate a night move actually called for a daylight move under the circumstances then prevailing in Normandy. The Germans always had made their withdrawals and troop movements at

1. 134th Inf., S-3 Journal, 5 Aug. 1946.
2. Chaplain Alexander C. Walker to the Author, July 15, 1946.

night in order to escape Allied air forces. No one ever explained why it was that American aircraft could not operate with flares at night just as effectively as a few scattered Germans could, but the fact was that in that sector the air at night usually was left for the enemy—not only did American aircraft refrain from carrying out any offensive operations at night to the front, but they even refrained from sending up any defense a great deal of the time. Regular as he was, "Bed-check Charlie" never seemed to run into any night-fighters. The Germans then found that most of the time they could fill the roads with troops and wagons at night in perfect immunity. The Third Battalion, on the other hand, never had any trouble from German air attacks during the daytime.

Whatever the reason might have been, men of the Third Battalion played ball and rested during that Sunday until evening. Then they boarded trucks. The destination was in the vicinity of Louvigne—Lieutenant Hall had gone ahead with a quartering party to select an assembly area and then guide the Battalion.[3]

No one was surprised when the familiar slow drone of an enemy airplane came over the motor column at about 11 o'clock. Fortunately, the Third Battalion's trucks were able to find some concealment in the shadows of high hedgerows and bushes along the narrow road. The plane's particular target was a bridge which they had crossed about a mile and a half to the rear, but he missed that; however, he was able to inflict some costly casualties on some of the division special troops in the vicinity.

By August 7th it was reported that six American spearheads were driving eastward on a 53-mile front less than 135 miles from Paris. But on this same day it also was reported that four German armored divisions had opened a "large-scale counter-offensive" toward Avranches and the sea. Aimed at seizing that key point at the juncture of the Cotentin and Croton Peninsulas, the Nazis already had re-captured Mortain and penetrated three miles toward the sea.[4]

Avranches was the focal and critical communications point between the supply bases at the beaches and at Cherbourg, on the one hand, and the fast-moving columns of the Third Army which were racing across Brittany and turning toward Paris. Hitler was making a desperate gamble. If successful, it would cut off the Third Army from its supplies. Lieutenant General Omar N. Bradley, commander of the American Army Group, decided to match Hitler's gamble with one of his own: The Third Army's columns would race on; he would divert other troops to meet the counter-offensive—an Army and a campaign were at stake.[5]

Now the 35th Division, in assembly areas near Louvigne, awaited word to continue its move to join the Third Army. But the big gamble required that it be diverted first to the Mortain sector to help stop that dangerous German drive. Actually the division had been stopped, together with General Jacques Leclerc's 2nd French Armored Division, as parts of the newly-formed XX Corps, by Lt. Gen. George S. Patton, Jr., as a precautionary measure, but now was returning to the First Army for a few days. It was 3:20 P.M. on that same August 7th when the Battalion's motor column began to move back north.

3. 134th Inf., S-3 Journal.
4. The Stars and Stripes, Aug. 8, 1944, p. 1.
5. Lawrence Youngman in the Omaha World-Herald, reprinted in Santa Fe Express, May, 1945, p. 1; General Eisenhower's Report, p. 42.

Within 30 minutes after its receipt of orders, the Division had formed into its three regimental combat teams.[6]

Smaller units—doubtless because of lack of time—had not been very well oriented nor given very clear orders. As they rolled through St. Hilaire and headed east and southeast toward the area marked on the map as their "goose-egg," they were not sure whether they were moving up to an assembly position preparatory to attack, or into a defensive position, or to await further orders. They only knew vaguely that there was some kind of German counter-offensive on: they were told that there was a "pocket of resistance" in the Mortain area.

They began to notice civilians in greater and greater numbers trudging along the roads pushing carts or pulling small wagons stacked high with their effects. Were these people returning to their liberated homes, or were they fleeing the German offensive? One inquiry was sufficient to clear up this question. They would point to the direction whence they came (i.e., the direction in which the column was going) and cry "Boche!" One civilian report had no less than 80,000 Germans in the Foret de Mortain.[7]

The Battalion went into a defensive position on some high hills above a small creek. The attached 2½-ton trucks were to be retained, and they assembled in the protection of the valley. However, it was not the American policy to meet a counterattack with defense—but with attack. At 8:20 o'clock that same evening, the Battalion received orders to move.[8] Hardly more than an hour later, the Battalion, mounted in the trucks, was back on the road. It was to move tactically by motor as far as practical, and then dismount and continue on foot to an area just west of Notre Dame de Touchet. Lieutenant Kennedy of Company K was out in front with the point.

In the vicinity of Villechien—where the 35th Reconnaissance Troop had reported enemy less than half an hour before—the Battalion now came upon scores of armored vehicles—some turning around, others starting and stopping in a roar and a cloud of dust, others setting quietly—of the 2nd French Armored Division. It was necessary to infiltrate through that armored column to get to the Notre Dame road.[9] As the motor column turned to the east—toward Notre Dame—machine gun bursts could be heard, and tracers could be seen streaking across the road to the north. A cavalry[10] unit was involved in a brush farther up the road.

Trucks were released a mile or two short of the objective, and then the companies moved up to the edge of Notre Dame without any difficulty.

6. First U. S. Army, Report of operations, 1 Aug. 44—22 Feb. 45, pp. 6-7; 134th Inf., Unit Journal, 6 Aug. 1944: 134th Inf., After Action Report, 1 Sept. 1944; 35th Div., **Attack!** p. 11; George S. Patton, Jr., **War As I Knew It** (Boston, 1947), p. 102; Robert S. Allen, **Lucky Forward** (New York, 1947) p. 99.

The regimental combat team included the Artillery battalion (the 161st), a platoon of engineers, a medical collecting company, and a signal team, all attached to the regiment under the command of the infantry regimental commander.

7. 134th Inf., S-3 Journal.
8. **ibid.**
9. **ibid.**

General Leclerc's newly-arrived 2nd French Armored Division was receiving an enthusiastic welcome as it passed through a small town that afternoon (August 7th).

"As each tank rolled by, crowds lining the sidewalks would read aloud the name stenciled on the front and shout it to those in the rear."

" 'Vive Bordeaux!' they shouted, and a cheer went up. 'Vive Lorraine!' Another cheer."

"Somewhere along the route a G.I. supply truck had slipped into the convoy. Stenciled on the radiator was the familiar sign, 'Prestone 1943,' indicating that Prestone had been put into the cooling system.

" 'Vive La Prestone!' shouted the crowd wildly."

—Tom Hoge in **The Stars and Stripes,** Aug. 15, 1944, p. 1.

10. All "cavalry" was mechanized with six-wheeled armored cars (M-8's) or light tanks, or other vehicles.

It was a little surprising when the Battalion resumed its advance at 6 o'clock the next morning, went through Notre Dame, and on down the warm, dusty road toward its objective beyond the Barenton-St. Jean du Cordl highway without meeting any opposition. Object for the greatest resentment of the marching infantrymen was a platoon of tanks which moved through the column churning up choking dust over the "dog-faces." Tanks were regarded as another of those things which "you can't get along with, and can't get along without."

During a temporary halt after about three hours of marching, a formation of high-flying B-17's—Flying Fortresses—appeared overhead. The regular pattern of faint silver crosses presented a striking beauty against the bright blueness of the sky. But the picture of innocent beauty was marred presently by a series of dark blotches. Antiaircraft shells were bursting beneath the big bombers; soon it became intense—puffs of smoke appeared all through the formation. But not a plane wavered from its course; straight through the flak they flew. Then one was crippled; it lost its speed, seemed to pause for a moment there in the air, and then its nose turned down and it plunged earthward—there was no spinning, no turning, no pauses; in ever increasing speed it fell straight down until it disappeared behind trees on the horizon. Seconds later there was the noise of a tremendous explosion and a pall of smoke rose above the trees. "How well put," someone remarked, " 'Queens Die Proudly' ".

As the Battalion neared the highway other planes appeared. This time they were fighter-bombers—three pairs circled over a high, wooded hill southeast of Mortain. First the P-51's (Mustangs), guided by smoke shells, went in to dive toward the positions and drop their bombs, and then zoom upward. The German hardly had time to shake his head after that before the P-47 Thunderbolts came in to "lay their eggs." And that was not all yet: most beautiful of all (thought members of the Third Battalion who had made their acquaintance in California) were the P-38's (the twin tail-boomed Lightnings) diving down, then streaking up again as an earth-shaking roar came across the valley and clouds of dust and smoke billowed into the air.[11]

The Third Battalion went into position on its objective before noon and sat down to await developments.[12] The only trouble there during the day was in the afternoon when parts of the Battalion were moving farther forward to better positions and drew some shelling. Tree bursts caught parts of Company L coming down a sunken road and killed one man and wounded some others.

The other battalions had not fared so well during the day. They had run into strong opposition and had made little progress in their attack toward St. Jean du Cordl. Young Captain Frederick Roecker, who had succeeded to the command of the 2nd Battalion, had been wounded during the morning.[13] Now the Third Battalion, alone on the objective, was sticking out like the proverbial sore thumb. Anxious to take advantage of this favorable, if precarious, position, the regimental commander made a plan to have the Third Battalion form a task force to take up a position to the southeast of St. Jean where it could cut off any enemy withdrawal and annihilate him as the 1st and 2nd Battalions attacked from the west.[14] A part of Company I, with some "M" Company

11. J. Huston, to F. E. Webb, Aug. 11, 1944.
12. 134th Inf., S-3 Journal.
13. ibid.
14. ibid.

machine guns and a platoon of tank destroyers, moved up the highway and deployed to the southwest of St. Jean. The Battalion CP was set up in a small, fragile shed. Other headquarters men moved into a nearby barn.

During the afternoon and evening of August 8th the enemy showed no signs of letting up. Groups of enemy infiltrated into the rear of the 1st and 2nd Battalions. They captured the 2nd Battalion's aid station, chaplain, and some motor personnel. At 8 o'clock tanks were reported in the 1st Battalion's motor park.[15] Another enemy group approached the Third Battalion's task force, fired a few rounds and withdrew.[16] All this was enough to keep most men on the alert during the hours of darkness.

The division order which came down the next morning was the kind which one learned to expect in those situations where attack was meeting attack. (The division had been assigned to the VII Corps the previous day.)[17] The 320 Infantry was to go in on the north of the 134th; the 3rd Battalion, 137th Infantry, was attached to the 134th Infantry, and took over the 1st Battalion's mission while the latter reverted to reserve and was to follow closely behind the 2nd Battalion. The Third Battalion, alone on its objective, was attached to the 137th Infantry which was operating northwest from Barenton. The Third Battalion, however, was to remain in position for the time being while the rest of the Division launched a new attack at 9 A.M.[18]

The task force did become active enough to draw fire, though it had to be careful not to move into the zone of one of the battalions coming from the other direction. Colonel Moore went up to direct the fight, and had a narrow escape from machine gun bullets. The artillery liaison officer, Lieutenant Vernon Freitas of California went up to see if he could assist the effort.[19] Freitas advanced alone 300 yards, climbed up on a house top, and there found that he could see St. Jean—the focal point toward which all these attacks were directed. He set to work to bring some observed fire down on the town. However, his own position became perilous when enemy shells began to fall in the area and then the machine gun fire started up again below. Some of the men pulled back from the vicinity of the house to seek better cover. But Freitas, out in front of his own infantry, remained there to bring in the artillery on the enemy. This proved to be effective and he was able to get back to the CP without injury.[20]

Meanwhile the 1st and 2nd Battalions were in trouble again. It was another counterattack.[21] The regimental commander sent Captain O'Keefe, regimental assistant operations officer, up to find out the situation and report back. O'Keefe arrived as tanks seemed to start closing in from all directions. Colonel Boatsman, 1st Battalion commander, reported the number to be anything between "15 and 50".[22] The 2nd Battalion was pinned down on a sunken road to the front[23] and now the enemy tanks, attacking the rear of the 1st, had both

15. ibid.
16. ibid.; Youngman, loc. cit.
17. 35th Div., **Attack!**, p. 11.
18. 134th Inf., S-3 Journal, 9 Aug. 1944.
19. Ordinarily there were one or two artillery forward observers to go with the leading companies. These worked with the company commanders under the supervision of the liaison officer, who normally remained near the battalion commander. The FO (forward observer) had radio communication (and could get wire when the situation warranted) by which he could call directly to the artillery fire control center; however, the liaison officer frequently fired missions himself when he was not assisting the FO's; the liaison officer's job was to get the needed artillery for the infantry battalion commander.—Infantry Field Manual 7-20, **Rifle Battalion**, pp. 11-12.
20. 35th Div., General Orders, No. 28, 2 Sept. 1944.
21. 134th Inf., S-3 Journal.
22. ibid.
23. ibid.

battalions cut off. Already men had heard that there was a "lost battalion" of the 30th Division surrounded in or near Mortain. Now it looked as though there was to be a pair of lost battalions here. Radio communications were good, but it was not wise to give too much of a bad situation over the air. Colonel Miltonberger was getting impatient. He went to his regimental radio and contacted Captain O'Keefe at the 1st Battalion.

"O'Keefe, you get back here right away," he said.

"Yes, sir, I sure would like to, but I am afraid it would take an armored division to accomplish that right now."

A German tank came up to the 1st Battalion's motor park and, pointing its long gun over the hedgerow, fired right down the line of jeeps in the other field. First Battalion lost four attached tanks and three tank destroyers, five jeeps, and five other vehicles.[24]

Heavy artillery fire and vigorous fighting back forced an enemy withdrawal during the night.[25]

All of this was happening to the west of the Third Battalion. To the east were some units of the 2nd Armored Division, and they too were receiving an attack by the next morning, but here the situation was a little different. The tank men heard the enemy preparing for an attack, and set themselves for it. Light and medium tanks were deployed all along the forward slope of the hill, but concealed behind hedgerows and shrubbery, they were not visible to the enemy in the dim light of pre-dawn. The enemy came rushing across the field in an old infantry charge. The tankmen held their fire until the shouting Nazis were within 200 yards, and then 30 caliber machine guns, 50 caliber machine guns, 37 mm guns, and 75 mm guns opened fire all down the line. This quickly broke the charge and was said to have left about 200 dead Germans on the field.

How the Third Battalion escaped all these attacks remained a mystery. The Battalion was having casualties every day, to be sure, but it had been able to march right up on its objective and remain there free of strong counterattacks while the other units were having a most difficult time making any progress at all. It had taken several prisoners—they were from the vaunted S.S. "Das Reich" and "Deutschland" divisions.[26] From the observation post, Battalion observers could look across the valley to a high enemy occupied hill and plainly see enemy activity. It was most trying to watch German vehicles going up the road or troops on bicycles[27] pedaling around the curve and then to be unable to get artillery on them. Other sectors had the priority for artillery just then. One afternoon, however, the commander of the division's medium artillery battalion (155 mm howitzers)—the 127th F.A.Bn., came up to visit the OP. As a matter of fact, the observation post was so well-situated that it attracted all kinds of visitors; when an OP has too many visitors they are likely to draw fire, and then it becomes useless—the men nicknamed this one "Yankee Stadium" and declared that it was a sell-out every day. At any rate, the artillery commander was in good spirits this day, and he wanted to shoot.

He saw the activity out across the valley and fired several volleys. Then

24. **ibid.**
25. **ibid.**, 11 Aug. 1944.
26. 3rd Bn. S-2 Notebook; J. Huston to F. E. Webb, Aug. 11, 1944.
27. The bicycle was another common item of German equipment. The Battalion Medical Detachment had collected some 30 of them and this had made the whole detachment mobile; when the Battalion was moving south from St. Lo, the medical men would mount their bicycles and follow down the road by bounds; much to their disappointment, they had had to abandon them at the crossing of the Vire River.

he sent one last message down for another—"Make that TOT," he said. Later the infantrymen learned that TOT meant "time on target"—all the guns of a battalion, or a dozen battalions, were fired at such a time that all shells would hit the target at the same moment. Thus the whole target was covered in an instant, and there was no chance for victims to run for cover.[28]

Attached to the 137th Infantry, the Third Battalion moved late in the afternoon of the 11th to join in attack with that regiment. The Battalion assembled back along the St. Jean-Barenton highway and marched to the southwest through Barenton, then followed the main Barenton-Mortain highway back northwest. A turn off the highway to the left would take it to the west and it would be heading for that hill on which the Colonel had been firing artillery from the opposite direction.

Vehicles of the 2nd Armored Division were all through Barenton and strung out along the highway which the Battalion followed out. An ammunition truck had been hit at a particularly dangerous corner ahead, and this delayed the march for a few minutes. Shortly after, the Battalion left the road, and with Companies K and I abreast advanced in the direction of the hill objective. By this time dusk was closing down.

The companies moved out across the meadows and tied in for the night in the edge of a woods. The Battalion CP was established in a pile of rails— the center rails were pulled out, and raincoats spread over to insure blackout.

As members of the staff were walking down a small lane toward the CP they heard a strange, weird sound in the west. It sounded like some gigantic spring cog winding up. A loud, awe-inspiring scream, and then a huge flash of light, as sheet lightning, came up behind a hill to precede a rapid series of thunderous explosions. It was the "screaming meemie" or rockets. Immediately there was an answer. From the rear came the hollow-sounding reports of a rapid-firing gun—it was a sound which had become familiar in nightly harassing and interdiction fire back at St. Lo; none of the Battalion had been able to see the weapon, but men heard that it was a recently developed 4.5 inch gun—and the bursts of its shells sounded to be at the precise spot whence the sounds of the "winding up" had come. They heard nothing more from the "screaming meemie" that night.

The attack was scheduled to be resumed at 7 o'clock the next morning,[29] but Colonel Moore felt that a little night activity might make the task easier. He determined to send a combat patrol—a full rifle platoon—to the hill which was the objective. If they ran into opposition they were to return to the area, but if they could sneak up the hill without hitting anyone, they were to set up an all-around defense to hold it and radio word back to the Battalion. The Battalion then would move up the next morning quickly. A few hours after the patrol's departure the reassuring word came over the 300 radio: it had reached the hill without opposition.

Only a few Nazis were to be found in the path of the Battalion the next day as it moved up to occupy its objective. The command post moved into a small, but neatly-built farm house. Its sole occupant—at least on this day—was a tiny, white-haired old woman. She was happy to see the Americans come. She led some of the men up to a loft in the little barn where they found some discarded German uniforms and equipment. The old woman could not under-

28. For a description of these artillery "serenades" at Mortain, see Ralph Ingersoll, **Top Secret.** p. 181.
29. 134th Inf., S-3 Journal, 12 Aug. 1944.

stand any English, but she was keenly interested in the friendly soldiers. When they broke out their "K" rations at noon, she insisted on clearing off part of her long board table for them to set their cardboard boxes and tins on. Then she set to building a fire in her fireplace so that they could heat their food— until they made her understand that smoke from the chimney might bring in shells from the Boche.

As a matter of fact it was not long until shells started to come; and they were shells of large caliber. One of the men brought in a fragment so that members of the staff could see how large they were; this warm, jagged piece of metal was longer than a man's fore-arm and three or four inches wide. The old lady looked on with interest, and then suddenly her face lit up and she hurried outdoors. No one noticed her until she returned a few minutes later struggling with something heavy. It was a dud! She sensed that something was wrong when everyone scattered from the unexploded shell. She set it down on the concrete floor. Finally ammunition expert Lieutenant Hall picked up the dangerous missile and carried it to a safe spot.

Shells started coming in again and the frightened old French woman knelt beside her fireplace to pray most of the afternoon. From time to time she would look up and her eyes would search the men's faces for some sign of reassurance.

Captain Heffelfinger decided that the shelling had subsided enough to permit him to make a visit up to the positions of the forward companies. He took a messenger and an intelligence man and started up the hill. They were nearing the top when the whistle of a low shell came in fast upon them. It was coming right for them. The messenger winced and fell to the ground; the shell bounced crazily on down the hill. Unable to get up, the man found that he had a broken leg. The shell had hit his leg! But its angle had been just the precise one which left the leg reparable and yet prevented the shell from exploding; had the round hit the ground it is probable that all three would have been killed.

Later in the afternoon, Lieutenant Clyde Payne came into the CP with a bundle of papers. He had found a stack of Nazi propaganda leaflets; apparently they had been intended for dropping among British and American troops, but the German withdrawal had made the planned distribution impossible. However, distribution within the Third Battalion now was very rapid.

The leaflets were well-illustrated with skillful drawings and photographs. One pictured a British soldier leaving his wife:

When you left your wife—you tried to console her in the belief, that by "this very last, great effort of all Allies together"
the war will definitely be over within a few months
Well—in between perhaps you already changed your mind a bit, getting the first, slight impression of what means

Invasion

In order to preserve you from any further disappointments you ought to know:
You are facing German soldiers now, defending the forefield of their home.
They are equipped not only with new weapons (and you will have the honor, to make their acquaintance) but also with the experience of three years war against the Bolshies.
Besides the Jerries have been rather busy in this country and by no means only in the coastal area—you certainly heard about "German accuracy."

And don't forget:

The men, you're facing now, don't defend territorial or economical or any other sort of material interests, but a very simple and elementary thing:
The life of their women and children and their national existence!

Do you think there is only the slightest hope on a German capitulation? Happy end in a few months?

Then beside a photograph of a German soldier in the lower corner: "I tell you, these Germans are damned good soldiers."

—Statement of General Montgomery quoted by Wendell Wilkie in his book, "One World."

Did you write home already? Do it at once! A few hours from now, it may be too late![30]

Another was supposed to represent an American sergeant with an English girl who was saying:

"You Americans are sooo different!"

And on the other side it pictured a British soldier's grave and said:

British Soldiers!

You are fighting and dying far away from your country while the Yanks are putting up their tents in Merry Old England. They've got lots of money and loads of time to chase after your women.[31]

A third leaflet pictured a lonely girl saying, "Go away, Moon—you're making things *worse!*" Below the photograph, it went on to say:

...you're reminding me, over and over, that my boy is so far far away.—Darling moon, you've seen the whole story of our young love, the perfection of our happiness—our "little heaven on earth"— ...and then came war—. What a long time I've been waiting now...it's been so dreary—and the thought that my sweetheart may never come back— haunts me night and day ever since he went away.

GOOD OLD MOON—TELL ME THE TRUTH:

Shall I be one of those unfortunate ones who will be waiting in vain?[32]

While the Third Battalion waited on its objective, another dramatic episode was reaching its climax to the northwest.

Two days earlier the 1st Battalion of the 320th Infantry had been assigned the mission of making contact with a battalion of the 120th Infantry (30th Division) which was surrounded on a hill at the edge of Mortain. At 3 P.M. on the 10th, men of the 320's 1st Battalion, under command of Major William G. Gillis, Cameron, Texas (former West Point football star) mounted tanks of the 737th Tank Battalion to drive up a steep, narrow road in a move to rescue the "lost battalion". The attack was almost due north—right angles to the direction of attack of the remainder of the regiment.

With the advantage of observation, the Germans began hitting the tank column with artillery even before it started. American planes came in to bomb.

The tanks were in column and the road was deeply hedged. The Germans hit the column with everything they had. "By nightfall the identification panels on the tanks were shredded until they looked like lace." About half of the tanks were knocked out, but the column reached the hill and got part way up. When darkness stopped the heavy fighting they were on the outskirts of Mortain. There was wild confusion all during the night and hard fighting all the next day. Finally on the 12th they made contact with the beleaguered troops. Two men loaded a Quartermaster company truck with supplies and water and headed for the position convoyed by three tanks. They dodged enemy fire, raced down rutted roads to reach the battalion with supplies intact. On the return trip, 20 seriously wounded men were evacuated.[33]

Another order, with new objective for the Third Battalion, came down

30. From a copy of one of the leaflets.
31 From a copy.
32. From a copy. Interestingly enough, this same photograph—of the lonely girl saying, "Go away, Moon, you're making things worse!"—was used to illustrate Cannon Percale sheets! e.g., see **Life**, XVIII (Aug. 21, 1944), p. 12.
33. Lawrence Youngman in the **Omaha World Herald**, reprinted in **Santa Fe Express**, May, 1945, p. 9. Also Associated Press in **The New York Times**, Aug. 13, 1944, pp. 1, 4.

later in the afternoon. Colonel Moore assembled his command group and went down the sunken trail to the road. The companies would attack generally northward along the road.

The luck of the Battalion in encountering relatively light resistance thus far had run out. There was opposition almost from the first, and it was vigorous —small arms and shell fire. The aid station was busy. At the CP Captain Heffelfinger was busy with details. Presently the field telephone rang. He took the call. "My God," he exclaimed. He turned to S-2 and said, "The command group has been hit; we've got to take over."

A mortar shell had come in on the command group. Colonel Moore,[34] Captain Corroll, and Lieutenant Freitas, at least, were hit. None of the wounds was fatal, but apparently they would be out indefinitely.

The battalion commander and the artillery liaison officer already had been evacuated. Captain Heffelfinger and the S-2 arrived on the scene, but Carroll still was there. His wounds were not serious but the scores of lacerations all over his body doubtless would be painful once the excitement of battle had subsided. The S-3 would not leave until he was sure that everything was under control.

The new commander established the locations of the companies, and as darkness approached, began to "tie in" for the night. The command group established itself in a room which Company K was occupying. They took a few minutes to open a "K" ration supper when a call came from upstairs observers that some Germans were approaching. It was a group of about 25 coming in to give up. It looked as though the resistance might be breaking.

Soon after, a party of officers from the 4th Division arrived. They were to relieve the Battalion during the night.

At 10:30 the next morning the Battalion moved out once again in route column. It was moving back to an assembly area near Notre Dame.[35] Spirits rose as the troops marched down the road on another bright day. It had been depressing to come back to another week of Norman hedgerow fighting after they had been on their way to join the Third Army's spectacular drive. And this long week had not been without its cost. There had been another 250 casualties in the Battalion.[36]

When members of the Third Battalion moved into the assembly area they learned that once again they were to mount trucks to join in the Third Army's drive. The 35th Division was to move to the vicinity of LeMans to join the XII Corps.[37]

For the second time, the Third Battalion had completed its mission in one of the decisive battles of the war in Western Europe.[38] Later, members of the German General Staff stated that the war had been lost for them when their attack for Avranches failed.[39] His counter-offensive launched on August 7th, the enemy brought in reinforcements to continue his fierce attacks, and showed no signs of giving up his ambition of reaching the sea until August 12th[40]— the day of the Third Battalion's final attack.

But the enemy had caused delay—delay which was to become more important later. Perhaps more important than the diversion of troops—such as

34. 134th Inf., S-3 Journal.
35. ibid., 13 Aug. 1944.
36. 134th Inf., Battle Casualty Report.
37. 134th Inf., S-3 Journal.
38. General Eisenhower's Report, p. 121.
39. 35th Div., Santa Fe (MS.) p. 48.
40. General Eisenhower's Report, p. 43.

the rapid shift of the 35th Division—was the holding up for 20 days the construction of an oil pipe line which was to go through Vire to make available quantities of indispensable fuel for the armored columns now sweeping across France.[41]

Once again men of the Third Battalion could pause for a few moments to reflect on what they had been through, and to anticipate better days ahead.

There was one bit of news to dampen the high spirits: Colonel Thomsen was dead. After he had been evacuated on "Bloody Sunday", the surgeons had given him a 50-50 chance. Word had come that he was getting better. But no, he was dead. His men knew that this rugged leader—the symbol of the Third Battalion in the Battle for St. Lo—had gone down fighting. His influence would persist as long as the Third Battalion continued to fight.

Now perhaps men of the Third Battalion could leave behind the hedgerows and sunken roads. Yes, they might leave the hedgerows physically, but upon many minds memories had been impressed which doubtless would continue as long as life itself. They would remember the days of which they had been a part—

The United States Army is engaged in one of the most brutal slugging matches in its history in the hedgerows of Normandy.

Hour after hour, day after day—and now week after week—the grim, tired soldiers fight bloody close-in battles for 100 yards of shell-pocked meadow. Each hedgerow conquered is a minor campaign won, each pasture and orchard a bitter epic of valor and of death.

Someone once said that wars were won by the souls of men. Some day, when the full story of this phase of the French campaign can be written, some day when the Norman names of St. Lo and Pont Hebert and the forest of Mont Castro are inscribed in gold on the battle streamers and the plaques, due tribute can be paid to the men who struggled and died in the hedgerows and orchards and weeds of western France.

They are ordinary American men. The faces of so many of them, as one sees them along the front sheltering in foxholes or plodding down the sunken roads toward the enemy, are gray with fatigue and lined with the unutterable weariness of battle. They are men who have endured—a few short weeks ago they were careless youngsters; today they are veterans of one of the grimmest series of minor battles yet fought in this war.

. . . .

When they speak of "liberation," think too of devastation, for that is the price of freedom in Normandy today. From Cherbourg to Caen and from Isigny to St. Lo, war has left a drab tale of desolation. The other night down near Pont-Hebert, the war stopped an hour or so while weeping peasants—little children, old women and old men—trundling wheelbarrows or carts before them, fled from the zone of hostilities. They had clung pitifully to their homes; close to the guns one saw little children playing with the abandon born of the lack of comprehension. In the rubble and skeletons of towns one sees them, their scrubbed rosy faces strange anomalies amid death and destruction.

One gets used, as one goes along the front, to these cherubic apparitions. One gets used even to the destruction—the sour smell of plaster, to rubble and dust; to smashed and vacant towns where once life had been; to walls with no roofs, to gutted homes and piles of debris. It is more difficult to get used to the stench left in the wake of war.

Along the road of Le Desert yesterday, in an area won by bloody sacrifice and American valor, dozens of dead cattle lay thickly in the fields and roadside ditches—their bellies swollen and distended, their legs stiffly in the air. Back up the leafy lanes and amid the hedgerows were all the evidences of battle and flight—gas masks, rifles, ammunition, German helmets, motorcycles, trailers, a burnt-out tank, equipment of all sorts in wild disarray. Our dead had been buried, but down the lane by an abandoned farmouse a dead German lay stiffly, his face toward the sky.[42]

41. Randolph Leigh, **48 Million Tons to Eisenhower**, p. 26.
42. Hanson W. Baldwin in **The New York Times**, July 19, 1944, p. 3.

"The battle for France was decided among the bloody orchards and hedgerows of Normandy."[43]

Americans had had a rough time in the hedgerows. The Third Battalion had had special training in mountain warfare, in attack of pillboxes, in attack through towns, but until it arrived in France, it never had had any training in hedgerow fighting. S. L. A. Marshall asked Lt. Gen. Walter Bedell Smith (General Eisenhower's chief of staff) whether some of the American troubles in Normandy were not due to a lack of information about the bocage country. General Smith's answer was: "Not at all! That wasn't the source of the trouble. The information which we had from the French was more than adequate. Moreover, Field Marshall Sir Alan Brooke and General Sir Frederick Morgan had both come out that way in 1940. They told us about the country, describing it quite accurately. They were very pessimistic about our chances of coping with it. But we couldn't believe what we heard. It was beyond our imagination."[44]

43. General Eisenhower's Report, p. 121.
44. S. L. A. Marshall, Men Against Fire (New York, 1947), p. 108.

PART TWO—RACE ACROSS FRANCE
★ ★ ★
CHAPTER VII
★ ★ ★
INTO A NEW WAR

Happy to leave behind the onerous hedgerow fighting of Normandy, once more men of the Third Battalion mounted 2½-ton trucks for rapid transit to the east—and this time with good reason to believe that there would be no immediate recall. The Germans now battling to extricate themselves from the pocket they had created in their ill-fated drive for the sea, the Third Army was free to press its dash across France.

After the collapse of the enemy's western flank with the St. Lo breakthrough late in July, General Eisenhower had determined to destroy the German forces in Normandy by having the Third Army move eastward in a great encircling movement. This had meant the abandonment of a primary objective of the original Allied plan: capture of the Brittany ports. Actually, then, Hitler practically had played into the Allied commander's hands by launching the counteroffensive toward Avranches and the sea. This does not mean that the attack did not constitute a major threat, but its failure left large German forces in a difficult situation. The battle of the Falaise-Argentan pocket which followed was only partially successful in annihilating the enemy in the area,—he was able to keep open a withdrawal route through Falaise long enough to save a considerable portion of his strength—but it did destroy the German Seventh Army as an effective fighting force to be used in the defense of France.[1]

The trucks carried the 134th Infantry, and the Third Battalion, to an assembly area east of Le Mans[2]—a city which already had been cleared by another unit—on August 14th where the 35th Division joined the XII Corps on the Third Army's right (south) flank.[3] The column had started moving at 4:20 A.M. for a 15-hour journey.[4] The distance—about 120 miles—was several times greater than that covered during the whole preceding month. And few things could be better calculated to stimulate high morale in fighting men than a long movement forward which still fails to bring them into the presence of the enemy.

For men of the Third Battalion this trip was a refreshing one. Refreshing because instead of ghost towns of ruined bare walls, they passed through inhabited towns humming with activity—for the first time in France they saw a shop actually open for business! It was like a triumphal procession all the way: people lined the streets at every village, and often between; they called, waved, tossed fruit and flowers; whenever the congested military traffic on the highway would delay the column for a few minutes there would be wine and cider brought out for the liberators. Sometimes on a country road they would meet a French family—dressed in their best clothing—driving along in a two-wheeled cart. The men admired the fresh beauty of the country, and began

1. General Eisenhower's Report, p. 46.
2. 134th Inf., S-3 Journal.
3. 35th Div., **Attack!**, p. 13. It had been intended that the 35th should close up on the 80th and 7th Armored Divisions to form the XX Corps. Now that corps moved northeast of Le Mans, and the 35th joined with the 4th Armored Division to form the XII Corps.—Patton, **War As I Knew It**, pp. 104-5.
4. 134th Inf., **Daily Log**, V, 14 Aug. 1944.

to compare French women with English or American, and to compare the effects of the war on this part of France and on the part of England which they had seen. For themselves it was a momentary return to modern civilization from a world of 20th Century barbarism.[5]

Here combat teams were formed, (each infantry regiment of the division given its normal attachment of a field artillery battalion, an engineer platoon, a medical company, signal personnel, for independent operation) and while the 134th remained in reserve the 137th, in a task force commanded by Brigadier General Edmund B. Sebree, assistant division commander, teamed with Combat Command A of the 4th Armored Division and set out the next day for Orleans. The other regimental combat team—the 320th—took Chateaudun on August 17th in a "textbook battle."[6] General George S. Patton's whole Army was on its way.

> With his main forces trapped and broken in Normandy, the enemy had no means of checking the Third Army drive, the brilliant rapidity of which was perhaps the most spectacular ever seen in modern mobile warfare. The three corps, [XV, XX, XII] each spearheaded by an armored division, raced headlong toward Paris and the Seine with an impetus and spirit characteristic of their leader, at once guarding the flank of the armies to the north and seeking fresh objectives of their own.
>
> The primary objective of the Third Army advance was to deny to the enemy the use of the key lines of communication running through the Paris-Orleans gap, between the Seine and Loire Rivers.[7]

American forces were exploiting to the maximum their greatest advantage in equipment—motor transport. Mass production achievements of the American motor industry now made it possible to "out-blitz the blitzers." For the Germans, in spite of the reputation they had built up for their "panzer armies" in the early part of the war, still depended heavily on horses for their regular infantry divisions. No animal transport of any kind was found in this American army.[8] Now infantrymen in 2½-ton trucks—a multiple-drive vehicle not to be excelled in any army—were streaming across France in the wake of rapidly-moving Sherman medium tanks.

The rapid seizure of Orleans called for another 55-mile move forward by the 134th Combat Team on August 16th. The Third Battalion, moving early in the morning, arrived at its assembly area in a narrow grove near Lierville (northwest of Ouzouer) at 7:30.[9]

Two day's pause in this area even permitted inauguration of a brief training program. It was a far cry from the bitter battles just concluded in Normandy when men of the Third Battalion found themselves participating in mechanical training of weapons, in close order drill, in motor maintenance, and in "care and cleaning of equipment."[10] Whenever possible, any training program included periods for "orientation" in which the men were informed of latest news and the developments in the "big picture." The Battalion S-2, on this day (Aug. 17th) told them how the battle in the Falaise pocket was reported to be turning into a massacre—that the "Air Corps was having a field day," and that 3,000 German vehicles had been destroyed—and that friction was reported between the Wermacht and the elite S.S. troops; five German divisions were reported moving toward the battle zones from the Dieppe area. In the

5. J. Huston, to F. E. Webb, Aug. 16, 1944.
6. 35th Div., **Attack!** p. 13; Lawrence Youngman in the **Omaha World-Herald,** reprinted in The Santa Fe Express, May 1945, p. 9.
7. General Eisenhower's Report, p. 47.
8. General Marshall's Report, p. 98.
9. 134th Inf., S-3 Journal; 134th Inf., Daily Log, 17 Aug. 1944.
10. 3rd Bn. S-3 Journal, 17 Aug. 1944.

south of France (where the Seventh U. S. Army and the First French Army had landed in Operation Dragoon on August 15th) the beachhead had been extended to a depth of 25 miles, on a front of 80 miles, and units were six miles from Toulon. The Russians had entered East Prussia. Admiral Nimitz had announced that two fleets were ready to strike at the Japanese.[11]

Notwithstanding the mounting optimism, Captain Heffelfinger refused to be dazzled into thinking that hard battles did not remain ahead for the Third Battalion. One of his concerns was heavy casualties and loss of efficiency which the Battalion headquarters had suffered on previous occasions. Therefore he took advantage of this pause from combat to work with the staff in drawing up certain SOP's (standing operating procedure) for the organization and distribution of the headquarters during combat. It was laid down that the command group to accompany the battalion commander at the OP (observation post) should include the S-3, the heavy weapons company commander, the intelligence sergeant and one scout, two wiremen (telephone), a radio operator for the SCR 300, and two to four runners. Personnel at the CP (command post) would include the executive officer, the S-1 (adjutant), the S-2, S-4 or his sergeant, the communications officer, the ammunition and pioneer officer, the operations sergeant, the sergeant major, a representative of the Antitank Platoon, a medic runner, the transportation officer or his sergeant, and members of the communications platoon and of the headquarters section. The Ammunition and Pioneer Platoon would be located at the ammunition distributing point with the two 2½-ton ammunition trucks and the jeeps from the rifle companies which were used for ammunition resupply. Five jeeps—the ones assigned to the commanding officer, the S-1, the S-2, wire section (telephone) and the one carrying the battalion 284 radio—would be allowed at the command post; all other vehicles would remain at a separate motor pool.[12]

The Battalion S-2, for his part, drew up a priority for map distribution, for as the advance progressed, they would become more and more scarce, and though some 27 copies were required in the Battalion, that number frequently could not be obtained.[13]

This period also saw some changes in the leadership of the Battalion. Major Warren C. Wood of Nebraska, who had been executive officer of the 1st Battalion (and in training had served as commander of the regimental antitank company and later as S-3 of the 2nd Battalion) came to take command. Captain Carroll had been designated executive officer, and Captain Melcher of Company K had come to Battalion headquarters to take Carroll's place as S-3. Now this left the Third Battalion in the fortunate position of having two executive officers; Major Wood referred to Captain Heffelfinger, who had commanded the Battalion temporarily since the wounding of Colonel Moore near Mortain, as his "chief of staff." Lieutenant Jack Campbell of Chicago, who had served during the Normandy campaign as platoon leader in Company L, was appointed commander of Company K. All four of the letter companies now were commanded by lieutenants: Hyde, Company I; Campbell, Company K; Greenlief, Company L; Ruby, Company M.

On August 19th the Battalion resumed its advance, first by marching, and then by trucks which had returned from carrying the 2nd Battalion, to an

11. 3rd Bn. S-2 Notebook.
12. 3rd Bn. S-3 Notebook, I.
13. **Ibid.**

assembly area at Santilly, south of Janville, (and 15 miles north of Orleans).[14] (It was here that Lt. Hyde, unable to find his way back to Company I—out in an open field—through the black night after he left a meeting at the Battalion C.P., spent the night in a foxhole with Company L.)

When the regiment moved on the next day, the 3rd Battalion remained as division reserve.[15] Now XII Corps was on the southern, or right flank of the Third Army, the 35th Division was on the corps right flank, and now the 3rd Battalion, as division reserve, was assigned the mission of guarding the flank along the Loire River. At this point the protection of the Third Army's exposed flank was "in the hands of the Ninth Air Force and the 3rd Battalion."

Such a disregard for the flank was made possible by the very kinetics of the Corp's forward advance in disrupting the German forces, and by close liaison with the attached fighter-bomber group of the XIX Tactical Air Command—air observers could keep a watch on the flank, and their bombs and machine guns could discourage any attempt of the enemy to collect a serious force there.[16]

The Third Battalion's role in the flank protection consisted of maintaining a series of "road blocks" or outposts along the highway which paralleled the Loire River northwest of Gien.[17]

While men of Company L and tank destroyers went south to man the roadblocks, the remainder of the Battalion was formed into a task force (Wood) and prepared to make an assault in the vicinity of Bellegarde where it had been reported that there were some 2,000 of the enemy. Company I was to ride tanks, and Company K to follow on trucks. However, any enemy groups which had been in the vicinity were withdrawn, and the Battalion was able to move without difficulty to successive positions near Montigny, (northeast of Bellegarde) at Lorris, and near Oussoy.[18]

For the first time since the beginning of this "new war" Company L contacted some enemy groups near its outposts: the enemy had set up a roadblock outside Gien. Captain Heffelfinger went down to inspect the dispositions in the area, and he and Lieutenant Greenlief were walking down the highway beyond the last "L" Company roadblock toward the enemy. Suddenly two Germans jumped up, but mounted bicycles and started to flee. The executive officer was unable to get any results with his pistol, but Greenlief (perhaps with a rifle) dropped to one knee and hit both enemy soldiers. Soon reinforcements arrived for both sides, and after a brisk fire fight the squad which had come to the assistance of the two officers was able to drive 30 to 40 Germans from their roadblock, and men from Company L occupied the former enemy position. Within an hour after this incident Major Wood arrived on the scene with some new major's leaves for Heffelfinger, and a set of captain's bars for Greenlief. On receiving them Greenlief remarked, "If those Heinies had beat me to the draw, I would have ended my career a lieutenant."[19]

That same day (August 23rd) Lieutenant Ruby received notice that he too had been promoted to captain.[20]

There were no other friendly troops in the area—except some British paratroopers who had been working with the underground—being encountered.[21]

14. 134th Inf., S-3 Journal; 134th Inf., Daily Log, V, 19 Aug. 1944.
15. ibid., 20 Aug. 1944.
16. General Eisenhower's Report, pp. 47f; Patton, op. cit., pp. 112-3.
17. 3rd Bn. S-2 Notebook.
18. ibid.
19. ibid.
20. 134th Inf., Daily Log, V, 22 August.
21. ibid.

Now the Battalion moved north to an assembly area near Montargis to rejoin the regiment preparatory to another motorized advance to the east.

The 134th Infantry (led by the 1st Battalion) had entered that city previously after a brief fight on the outskirts. They had seen some tense moments that day when Lt. Col. John T. Hoyne, Division G-2, and a party of three had gone into the town under a white flag to deliver an ultimatum to the German commander to surrender. Unarmed, they had marched forward through the streets, disregarding gay French civilians, and encountering a few German soldiers riding on bicycles. However, they found that the headquarters had been abandoned, and as they returned the 1st Battalion already was entering.[22]

At 7:00 A. M., August 26th, the 134th Infantry set out for Joigny—35 miles away—over a route which had been reconnoitered only as far as Chateaurenard (one-third the distance). French reports indicated that there was a German battalion in Joigny.[23]

The Third Battalion was following the 2nd, and the motor columns moved smoothly along a good black-top highway. In order to prevent any congestion in case of trouble, and in order not to get too far behind, Major Wood assigned to the S-2 the duty of keeping contact between the head of his Battalion, and the rear of the unit ahead. In the course of these rapid advances and halts, the S-2 jeep had stopped temporarily in order to make radio contact with the Battalion coming to the rear, and was setting along the road quite alone when a cavalry armored car passed by and its occupants waved and pointed over to the field on the left. The morning haze had not cleared sufficiently for good visability, but the intelligence sergeant and the intelligence man with the party thought that they saw some one. "Probably some Free French," they agreed.

But not taking any chances they set out across the field—and a group of seven Germans jumped up. A shot over their heads was enough to dissuade them either from resisting or fleeing, and the Battalion S-2 section had seven prisoners on its hands to await the arrival of the trucks. Most annoying of the group was a contrary medic who was found carrying a pistol and ammunition.[24]

Soon thereafter the Battalion arrived at its destination in Joigny, but this was only the beginning of a busy day. The French had brought a report that there were a hundred or more Nazis down near a neighboring town (Villemer) who were willing to surrender to Americans. Company I organized a reinforced platoon to go with the S-2, and Major Godwin, regimental S-2, brought his sergeant interpreter and joined this special motor column. After one or two changes in direction the column approached the town where the enemy was supposed to be. The trucks stopped on the hill at a place where they would be safe from direct fire, and the major and the interpreter dismounted, took a white flag, and walked down the road toward the enemy position.

On arrival, they found a typical "Hollywood" Nazi captain in command. Asked to surrender, he replied that he would like four hours to think it over. Major Godwin told him to come out within 30 minutes, or all the artillery at his disposal would be brought down. (Which actually was very little). Officers with the small task force made every effort they could to get some artillery within that time, but had little success. However, some artillery from some-

22. Sgt. Saul Levitt, "Montargis...as They Wanted It," **Yank** (British ed.) III, Sept. 17, 1944, pp. 5ff.
23. 3rd Bn. S-2 Notebook; 134th Inf., Daily Log, V, 26 Aug. 1944.
24. J. Huston, to F. E. Webb, Aug. 30, 1944.

where did fall in the general vicinity. After some delay, then, a group of about 50 Germans came over the hill to surrender. A short time after, another group of 26 came up the road on bicycles. Soon a 2½-ton truck was at work hauling prisoners.

By this time the Battalion commander had arrived to see what was happening, and he and Major Godwin made one more trip back into the town, and came out with another truck load of prisoners. Now the commander and the regimental S-2 returned to Joigny, while the Company I platoon moved down to the southeast to a town on the main Joigny-Auxerre highway.

The Battalion intelligence officer and his party of three, plus two French guides who had joined them, remained to see if more prisoners might yet be picked up. They watched a group of Frenchmen deploy on a ridge to the southwest and move after a column of Germans, but when they disappeared, the S-2 sent the sergeant, with the jeep and driver, to see if they could find out what had happened.

This left the S-2 with one man and their 300 radio and the two French guides alone on the hill. Presently an artillery liaison plane came over and circled low to gain recognition. Then it came back and landed and the pilot beckoned to the S-2. He wanted to know whether there were supposed to be any friendly troops in the area to the west. When he heard the negative reply he said that there was a large column of men approaching the other side of the hill; he would return to the air and keep watch.

A few minutes later he came over low again and pointed. The S-2 turned to see a long column of Germans going across the front. Just then the 2½-ton truck which had been hauling prisoners, and two guards, returned. Anxious to go after more prisoners, they received permission to proceed with caution on down the hill toward the town—and the Germans. The guards mounted two of the discarded German bicycles, and with the truck following, disappeared over the forward slope. There was some reason for caution, for word had come over the radio that some American vehicles had been destroyed by enemy fire in a neighboring village.

Meanwhile the Battalion commander had ordered the Company I platoon to reassemble at Joigny, and now, en route back to the area, Lieutenant Hyde arrived with the platoon on this hill to see if he could offer any assistance. Now the long column of German foot troops was moving away, over the next hill. The artillery plane still was keeping watch overhead, and at last the 2½-ton truck which had gone forward after more prisoners returned with another full load (about 50). Holding their fire, some of the leaders, waving white flags, walked out toward the Germans. But there was no reaction. Then Hyde went to the .50-caliber machine gun mounted on his jeep, and, aiming high, fired a burst. The enemy soldiers hit the ground, and then started moving again. Now a section of Company M's 81 mm mortars which were attached to the platoon very quickly went into action, and Hyde, keeping up a steady fire on the big machine gun, swept the whole visible length of the enemy column. But insistant orders were coming over the radio for the group to rejoin the Battalion, for it was moving again. The mortars fired a few rounds over the hill and went out of action. The task force arrived back in Joigny just in time to catch the rear of the Battalion as it was moving on to St. Florentin.[25]

At St. Florentin (17 miles east of Joigny) members of the Third Battalion

25. J. Huston, to F. E. Webb, Aug. 30, 1946.

made their first close acqauintance with the F.F.I. (French Forces of the Interior). Already these underground fighters of the "Maquis" had gained the respect of American leaders by their active assistance in Brittany.—

> When our armor had swept past them they were given the task of clearing up the localities where pockets of Germans remained, and of keeping open the Allied lines of communication. They also provided our troops with invaluable assistance in supplying information of the enemy's dispositions and intentions. Not least in importance, they had, by their ceaseless harassing activities, surrounded the Germans with a terrible atmosphere of danger and hatred which ate into the confidence of the leaders and the courage of the soldiers.[26]

Their actions in rising up to seize towns as the Americans approached, the security they provided for such a rapid advance by protecting its rear and giving directions were worth divisions in contributing to the liberation of France.[27] These men who, for the most part, were engaging in hazardous enterpise and risking their lives under no other compulsion than belief in a cause, now were anxious to give all possible assistance to the American battalion which had established its headquarters in the city hall of St. Florentin.

Indeed it must almost have become an annoyance to members of the Battalion intelligence section as reports of enemy groups, columns, activities—each demanding immediate attention—crowded upon each other during the two days and nights in that location.[28]

As a protection to communications, the Battalion was ordered to send one company to Bouilly, more than 20 miles to the northeast of St. Florentin, and to operate jeep patrols all the way to Troyes to contact the 320th Infantry. Company I drew the assignment to Bouilly.[29] As a matter of fact the Battalion was operating motor patrols throughout the vicinity. They would bring in German prisoners, reports of civilians, and results of their own observations. There seemed to be no doubt that there were large, though disconnected and disorganized, numbers of German troops remaining in the area. One patrol found some indication of ambush when it came upon a knocked-out jeep and half-track which had been hit from the side.[30]

Following persistent reports that a large German column had been withdrawing to the south in the vicinity of Tonnerre, the Battalion S-2, together with some members of the regimental intelligence and reconnaisance platoon, made a reconnaissance in that area. The results primarily amounted to the tracing of the route of a German column—estimated at 1,200 to 2,000 strong, with horse-drawn cannon—which had passed through the area that morning. Civilians in the various towns along the road between St. Florentin and Tonnerre (about 15 miles) gave similar stories of the movement. En route the patrol picked up a flyer of the British Royal Air Force who had been living in hiding with the French in one of the villages for over a year since parachuting from his stricken aircraft. And then the group made a triumphal entry into Tonnerre—triumphal because the Germans had withdrawn only a short time previously, and there were no other American troops in the city.[31]

But the "drive to the east" was halted temporarily, and the 134th Infantry assembled in the vicinity of Aix-en-Othe (about 15 miles north of St. Florentin) on August 29th.[32] The Third Battalion went into bivouac in a woods to the

26. General Eisenhower's Report, p. 41.
27. Ingersoll, **Top Secret**, pp. 181-183.
28. 3rd Bn. S-2 Journal, 28 Aug. 1944.
29. 3rd Bn. S-2 Notebook; 134th Inf., Daily Log, V, 27 Aug. 1944.
30. 3rd Bn. S-2 Journal, 28 Aug. 1944.
31. 3rd Bn. S-2 Notebook.
32. 134th Inf., Daily Log, V, 29 Aug. 1944.

east of the town. The command post was set up, dispersed according to section, with truck tarpaulins stretched over poles to provide shelter against the rain. In the operations and intelligence sections a long table was set up to provide facility for mounting a map of the area. Here the "SOP" was followed of keeping information posted on the map: symbols drawn with blue grease pencil for friendly locations and with red for enemy upon a celluloid-like covering over the map. Leaning against the table was a large map of France and western Germany on which was shown the "big picture".[33] Staff officers took turns at duty during the night sitting by the telephone in the commanding officer's canvas-covered dug-out, reading or writing by the light of a flickering candle.[34]

By this time Paris had fallen, and optimism was mounting among all ranks. Rumors and good news continued through the week. On September 5th, Stockholm and Paris reports said that American troops had reached Perl, Germany, 12 miles northeast of Thionville, while other troops had crossed the frontier from Belgium toward Aachen; unconfirmed radio reports also announced the fall of Antwerp, Dunkirk, Boulogne, Calais, Metz, and Nancy.[35] Rumors of advances continued the next day and there was even one peace rumor.[36] It was confirmed on the 7th that the Third Army had had patrols in Germany; and the climax came with the Army's announcement of its demobilization plans that day.[37] Even officers at Supreme Headquarters were sharing the almost unbounded optimism; one general there predicted (September 7th) that the war would be over within three weeks, and the deputy G-2 had remarked: "Why, of course, we'll go right through it. [the Siegfried Line]."[38]

In the midst of all these reports of spectacular advances and bursts of optimism, the Third Battalion was conducting disciplinary drill, weapons training, conferences in small unit tactics, marches, close order drill, inspections, and continuous motor patrols.[39] There is little question but that a regular daily schedule, with appropriate bugle calls actually sounded, the first visit of a Red Cross "Clubmobile" with doughnuts and coffee—and American girls— an opportunity to see a movie (in Aix-en-Othe) for the first time since arriving in France,[40] all were welcome and refreshing experiences to the infantrymen of the Third Battalion. But they must have known, deeply, that however much they hoped for their vacation from war to last, they were living in a "fool's paradise," for each day of inactivity granted the enemy another precious day in which to gather up his disintegrated forces and form new lines for defense.

Thus far in this drive the enemy had suffered tremendously. The 134th Infantry alone had captured nearly a thousand prisoners in two days around Joigny and St. Florentin.[41] And captured and destroyed enemy equipment abounded everywhere. This included such diverse items as shovels (see photograph), mortar shells, gloves, acetylene torches, kitchenware, boots, and Ford, Buick, and Mercedes motor cars.[42]

Ironically now the Third Army was slowing to a halt for want of gasoline.

33.   J. Huston, to F. E. Webb, 30 Aug. 1944.
34.   J. Huston, to N. F. Huston, 3 Sept. 1944.
35.   The Stars and Stripes (London ed.) Sept. 5, 1944, p. 1.
36.   The Stars and Stripes (London ed.) Sept. 6, 1944, p. 1.
37.   ibid., Sept. 7, 1944, p. 1.
38.   Harry C. Butcher, My Three Years with Eisenhower (New York, 1946) p. 656.
39.   3rd Bn. S-3 Notebook I; 3rd Bn. S-2 Journal.
40.   3rd Bn. S-3 Notebook, I; Private to N. F. Huston, Sept. 2, 1944.
41.   134th Inf., Daily Log, V, 26 Aug. 1944 ff.
42.   Lawrence Youngman in the Omaha World-Herald (134th Inf., Daily Log, V, 132.)

That supply lines should be taxed in trying to support an advance at once so rapid and so far away from the bases was to be expected. Something of the problem was suggested when it was announced on September 4th that airplanes had dropped ten tons of maps to "General Patton's racing units." [43] But the Third Army was losing its race with the supply lines, and priority on supplies was going to Field Marshal Montgomery's 21st Army Group in the north.[44]

On August 24th General Bradley's headquarters (12th Army Group) had prepared its original draft of a "Blueprint for Victory"—a plan to end the war quickly by betting everything on the Third Army to crack the West Wall beyond Nancy and Metz. But it never had a chance.[45]

For ten days, in addition to the two at St. Florentin, the Third Battalion remained in its bivouac near Aix-en-Othe while the enemy prepared his defenses behind the Moselle River.

43. **The Stars and Stripes,** (London ed.), Sept. 4, 1944, p. 1.
44. General Eisenhower's Report, p. 62; Patton, **op. cit.,** p. 119.
45. Ingersoll, **op. cit.** pp. 211-213.
    Gen. Patton called the failure to rush the Siegfried Line "before it could be manned" the "momentous error of the war."—**War As I Knew It,** p. 120.

CHAPTER VIII

★ ★ ★

THE BRIDGE AT FLAVIGNY

By September 8th the Third Army had saved up enough gasoline to permit further movement of the 35th Division. And General Patton, in spite of loss of priority and hindrances of logistics, was determined to push his offensive with all the resourcefulness at his command; though wanting in fuel, he was not wanting in resolution.

It was a move of 125 miles, and took the 134th Infantry to an area around Thuilley-aux-Groseilles,[1] a town approximately at the apex of a triangle between Toul (about eight miles to the northwest) and Pont-St. Vincent (a slightly less distance to the east-northeast, on the Moselle River).[2] The Third Battalion went into bivouac in a woods—Bois le Jure—east of Thuilley.[3]

Immediately the Battalion had closed in its new area, motor patrols began to operate and French began to bring information of the enemy. There were a number of strongly-built forts on dominating hills in the Toul-Nancy area, and a determined enemy would be capable of making a great deal of trouble in any of them. French civilians reported that a group of 200 enemy occupied Fort de Pont St. Vincent—on a hill rising 460 feet above the junction of the Moselle and Madon Rivers. Mazieres (about five kilometers east of the Battalion area) had been receiving small arms and shell fire during the day. Viterne (in a valley about two kilometers northeast of the bivouac area) and a number of other towns in the vicinity also had been receiving artillery shelling from time to time. (This was the first report of German artillery since the Battalion had left Normandy.) Enemy artillery was reported to be located in the Foret-de-Haye—a large forest in the big bend of the Moselle River, between Toul and Nancy. But American troops (80th Division) had advanced eastward from their bridgehead at Toul to enter Gondreville, Dommartin-les-Toul, and Chaudeney, but the enemy still held the strong Fort de Villey-le-Sec.[4]

It soon was evident that German patrols were operating west of the river. That same evening one of the Battalion's motor patrols was fired upon when a flat tire on the jeep halted it at Maizieres. While the driver changed tires, the other members of the patrol returned the fire, and they were able to get away without injury.[5]

Next day Lt. William Chavet, of Nebraska, a recently arrived officer, led a patrol north from Viterne, through the woods, to Sexey-aux-Forges on the river. There they drew fire from across the river. Chavet reported the Moselle to be 40 to 70 yards wide at that point. He learned from the French that there were German ammunition dumps and artillery positions along the edge of the Foret de Haye, and on a wooded plateau north of Maron there were supposed to be three panzer regiments and four divisions.[6]

Lt. Vernon Kennedy of Company K led another patrol through the woods

1. 35th Div., **Santa Fe,** pp. 72-73.
2. Map, France, 1:100,000, Nancy-Mirecourt, Sheet 14G.
3. 3rd Bn. S-2 Journal.
4. 3rd Bn. S-2 Journal, 8 Sept. 1944.
5. **ibid.**
6. **ibid.**

to the northeast of Viterne. Then he contacted Company A at "Fort de Pont" where, after seizure by a mechanized cavalry unit in an attack the preceding evening, that company had moved up to occupy the dominating position.[7]

Anticipating an order from division for an advance to the Moselle next day, the regimental S-3 issued a warning order to the battalions at 1 o'clock (September 9th) and that evening the complete order was issued. First and 2nd Battalions would lead the advance, while the Third, in reserve, would follow the 2nd.[8] Objective was the wooded ridge (Moulin Bois) between the Madon and the Moselle.

The advance—on foot—to the Moselle began at 8 o'clock, and meeting only scattered artillery fire, the 2nd Battallion was approaching its objective shortly before noon.[9] Following closely, men of the Third Battalion waded the smaller Madon River at a ford at Pierreville. As reserve, they went into an assembly area in the woods about 1,000 yards in rear of the 2nd Battalion.[10]

It was to be expected that the next step in the advance would be an attack across the Moselle itself. It was regarded as something of a "break," then, when a reconnaissance party of the 2nd Battalion discovered that a bridge to its front—below Flavigny—remained intact.[11] The highway which crossed this bridge was the direct route to Nancy eight miles to the north. And here was a possibility for the 134th Infantry to get a ready-made crossing! The prospect was appealing. No infantryman was likely to harbor a relish for making a river crossing by assault boat. More than that, with a good bridge and a good highway available, tanks would be able to cross quickly without waiting for any construction, and not only would they be available for defense of the bridgehead, but they might be able to make a rapid thrust toward Nancy. Of course, as in any military operation, an attack to seize the bridge would involve risk; the extent of the enemy's defenses was not known accurately. But a success would mean a valuable prize.

Plans already were being made for a coordinated division attack the next morning at 5 o'clock. The 134th and the 137th Regiments were to make the crossing at six sites. Pursuant to this plan a regimental order was prepared at 5:20 that evening. Each battalion was assigned a forward assembly area where it was to assemble during the night, and then the Third Battalion was to cross the river at a point designated as "D", while the 2nd crossed at "E"; the 1st Battalion was to follow the 2nd and cross at "F".[12]

But then a decision was taken to make a try for the bridge, and at 7:00 P. M. the 2nd Battalion was ordered to make the attack.[13]

Even as that battalion moved down toward its precarious objective, a new order, calling for a crossing by the Third and 1st Battalions in the coordinated effort at 5:00 A. M., was prepared.[14] This would be put into effect should the 2nd Battalion's attempt fail; but in the meantime these two battalions were to get ready to cross the bridge immediately behind the 2nd.

At this point the Third Battalion almost found itself with two commanders. Lt. Col. Walker had arrived to take command, but inasmuch as plans and

7. ibid.
8. 134th Inf., S-3 Journal, 9 Sept. 1944.
9. 134th Inf., S-3 Journal.
10. ibid.
11. The entry in the 134th Inf. S-3 Journal (10 Sept. 1944) states: "1240—Flavigny—Bridge intact at this pt. Grab this if possible."
12. ibid.
13. 134th Inf., Unit Journal, 10 Sept. 1944.
14. ibid.

reconnaissance already had been made, he asked Major Wood to continue to take charge of the Third Battalion's activities, until the operation was completed. The Battalion lost one of its executive officers when Capt. Carroll was called to be regimental S-3. (For a brief period in the late afternoon it had appeared that there might be some changes in the command of Companies I and M when Hyde and Ruby ventured down into Flavigny to make a reconnaissance and were cut off by a group of Germans; however, after some close calls, they had been able to escape.)

The story of the bridge at Flavigny is mainly a story of the 2nd Battalion; but the Third was so closely associated with it, that its members hardly could have failed to retain a vivid impression of that night on the Moselle.

At first everything went well for the 2nd Battalion after it started moving at 10 o'clock. Within an hour Companies E and F, a part of G, and a heavy machine gun platoon had raced across the bridge. Then, as it appeared that success was imminent, the Nazi defenders discovered what was happening, and heavy artillery concentrations began to fall. Tank destroyers were ordered to the site; one platoon was to cross immediately. But they failed to arrive in time; and the Germans were counterattacking with tanks.[15]

Meanwhile the Third Battalion was marching down in order to cross as soon as the 2nd had cleared. Continuous flares, and an unending roar of mortar and artillery shells marked the bridge site in the night. The column halted along the open road while Major Wood went forward to contact the 2nd Battalion commander. Making his way to the highway, whose surface was covered with leaves and boughs freshly cut by flying shell fragments, and where dead of the preceding battalion lay along the shoulders where they had fallen, he walked through the continuing barrages toward the bridge.

He found the 2nd Battalion command group operating in a culvert beneath the approaches to the bridge. Aid men crowded in to work over wounded, communications men worked to keep the telephone line open; and there was no pause in the enemy shells which were bursting on and around the bridge.[16] The intensity of this fire was making it difficult to move any additional troops across the bridge, and the way was not yet clear for the Third Battalion to begin crossing; at the same time the violence of the counterattack on the opposite side of the river was making doubtful the fate of the men who already had crossed.

Then at 1:30 A. M. came a thunderous explosion on the bridge. An artillery shell—or perhaps a sympathetic detonation of a fixed charge—had destroyed one of the spans.[17] This left the men who had crossed in an extremely perilous position with neither means for reinforcement nor for escape.

Germans closed in shouting "Heil Hitler!"[18] and very soon after, the doom of the 2nd Battalion's bridgehead was sealed.

At 2:00 A. M. it was reported that Major Roecker, commanding the 2nd Battalion, had been wounded again, and Col. Walker was transferred from the Third to take command.

Details of what had happened on the other side of the river could not yet be known, and it was considered possible that some groups had been able to hold out. In any case the division's order for a coordinated attack at 5:00 A. M.

15. 134th Inf., S-3 Journal, 10-11 Sept. 1944.
16. Lt. Col. Warren C. Wood to the Author, June 26, 1946.
17. 134th Inf., Unit Journal, 11 Sept. 1944.
18. Wood, **loc. cit.**

remained. At 3 o'clock the Third Battalion received instructions to cross to the right of the 2nd Battalion by assault boats prior to daylight; boats and treadway bridge were dispatched to the vicinity of the bridge.[19]

Naturally this plan included the 1st Battalion. That battalion was supposed to move to the former assembly area of the 2nd where it would be available to support the Third, and then it was to cross as soon as the bridge could be built. However, it appears that the 1st Battalion not only was out of communication with regimental headquarters, but its specific location was not even known![20] Without benefit of any available support, then, the Third Battalion was being called upon to reinforce a bridgehead which no longer was able to maintain an effective existence.

There were delays in getting the boats to the site, and delays in trying to get any kind of accurate information about the 2nd Battalion. Soon, however, it was apparent that the bridgehead was being given up. Survivors returned by swimming. Other groups were captured. The rest of the bridge—including the span across an adjacent canal—was knocked out.[21]

The order to attack stood. Any chance for success on the part of the Third Battalion appeared to be very slim. First of all there could hardly be any hope for surprise in making a crossing in the same general area where already there had been such a violent battle. But what made a boat crossing particularly hazardous in this area was the presence of a canal (Canal de l'Est) which ran parallel to the river. This meant that, in the face of probable enemy fire, the first groups of men would have to drag their boats from the river, carry them across a few yards of open ground, and launch them again in the canal—or else attempt to swim the deep canal channel. And all of this with little supporting fire, and with no other unit immediately available to strengthen a bridgehead if one could be established. Moreover, daylight was approaching and the whole river line would be under observation. It appeared to be a case of "sending good money after bad"—of losing another battalion as an effective fighting force.

As these considerations weighed heavily on Major Wood, he became convinced that the whole situation was not clear to higher headquarters. Therefore, as the time for the attack approached he sent the S-2 back to the regimental CP to try to explain what had happened. The intelligence officer called his jeep driver, and they set out in a race against time to try to forestall what looked like certain disaster for the Third Battalion.[22]

It was not a simple decision for a regimental commander to make. To order postponement of the attack would be contrary to the letter of his instructions; and he would have to consider what effect it might have on the general plan—whether it might involve difficulties for the neighboring regiment which was to be crossing some distance to the south. On the other hand an attack into certain failure not only would fail to be of any assistance in the overall plan, but it might impair the effectiveness of the regiment to such an extent that it would be unable to render any kind of assistance to the common effort for some time to come. One of the reasons for the effectiveness of the American Army has been in the importance attached to the initiative of the individual

19. 134th Inf., S-3 Journal.
20. An entry in the 134th Inf., S-3 Journal at 0300 (11 Sept. 1944) states: "Capt. O'Keefe instructed to find 1st Bn. and transmit orders to CO ..."
21. **ibid**; 35th Div. **Attack!**
22. Wood, **loc. cit.**

soldier and the relative freedom of action in commanders of all echelons. The regimental commander was in possession of information which could not have been clear to higher headquarters. He alone was in a position to influence the situation.

He gave instructions for the Third Battalion to hold up and cover the reorganization of the 2nd Battalion.[23]

While the S-2 was rushing back to the Battalion with these instructions, Major Wood and the company commanders were proceeding with plans for their attack. They walked down toward the river to reconnoiter the crossing site. The engineers unloaded their boats on the highway at a point covered from enemy observation. Then as the major issued his order for the crossing, the company commanders, facing a situation which promised almost certain defeat, merely answered, "Yes, sir," and prepared to move out. Just then the S-2 arrived with the new orders, and, with obvious relief, the leaders planned to take their companies into positions on the hill overlooking the river.[24] The total strength of the 2nd Battalion now was reported to be 295.[25]

Whenever there is something of a disaster, or a heavy loss, or a failure, there frequently develops a tendency on the part of people to fix responsibility— to place blame on someone. There is little question but that this is fully warranted in many cases as a means toward preventing a repetition. In this instance, however, there would appear to be little to commend such an effort. Did the principal initiative for seizing the bridge arise in the 2nd Battalion commander? in the regimental commander? in the division commander? Did it fail from want of vigor in exploiting the opportunity? Specific answers matter little. It simply was a case of making a bid, against recognized risks, for a prize whose value would make the chances worth taking. The decision to try to seize a bridge whenever one is found intact is almost automatic; seizure of a Rhine bridge a few months later was to be regarded as one of the great windfalls of the war; it is an attempt to be made whenever the circumstance presents itself. On this occasion it was very near success, but the enemy counterattack proved to be too strong.

As a matter of fact the Moselle River was found to be a bitterly defended barrier all the way along the line. Indeed later that morning the 2nd Battalion of the 137th Infantry likewise was forced to abandon a crossing, although later that regiment was able to make a new attack and secure a permanent bridgehead.[26] Whether it was the 90th Division at Pont-a-Mousson, or the 80th below Toul on the north side of the big bend, or the 35th around Flavigny and Lorey and Coyviller, the results were similar. "Some of the bitterest fighting since St. Lo and La Haye du Puits was reported from the Third Army Front... Germans with their best remaining divisions along the Moselle were trying to hold the fortress towns of Metz, Toul, and Nancy."[27]

The change in the plans of the 134th Infantry did not mean, however, a cancellation of the project for the regiment to make a crossing. Plans were made to make another attempt at 4 o'clock that afternoon, and the Third Battalion moved back into the woods to an assembly area to make preparations. This was cancelled later on receipt of orders to hold the river line during the

23. 134th Inf., S-3 Journal, 11 Sept. 1944.
24. Wood, **loc. cit.**
25. 134th Inf., Unit Journal, 11 Sept. 1944.
26. 35th Div., **Attack!** p. 15.
27. **The Stars and Stripes** (London ed.) Sept. 11, 1944, p. 1.

night and the next day.[28]   (There still was some German shell fire in the area. One wounded Capt. Melcher, and the S-2 took over the duties of S-3.)

Meanwhile men of Company A who had been left to hold Fort "de Pont" when the remainder of the 1st Battalion assembled, received a sharp counterattack during the morning from an estimated two companies of Germans who had effected a river crossing of their own.   The attack beaten, division called for another company to be sent to reinforce the fortress garrison; this assignment went to Company K.[29]

The next day plans for a crossing were renewed, and Major Dan Craig (who had been regimental S-3 and now was acting as executive officer) led a party—including the Battalion commanders and S-3's—to make another reconnaissance.[30]   But now the proposed crossings sites were some distance to the southeast.   In addition to the advantage of a new location in affording some possibility for surprise, there was the added consideration that the canal there was on the near side of the river (its concrete bed crossed the river at Haut Flavigny) and there was a considerable distance between the two obstacles as well as the concealment of woods.

Farther to the south the attack of the 137th was going well, and the 320th was crossing nearby.   And the tanks of Combat Command B of the 4th Armored Division were crossing in the area of the 137th to "take off" toward Luneville. The 137th and 320th were to swing to the northeast.   The 80th Division was reported to have two regiments across to the north.[31]

Now it appeared that some new plans were in the making.   The 134th Combat Team, the 319th Combat Team (80th Division), a battalion of tanks, and a battalion of tank destroyers were to be formed into a task force probably under the command of Brig. Gen. Summers, assistant division commander of the 80th Division.   Meanwhile the Third Battalion was to be division reserve again during September 13th pending official orders on formation of the task force.   The mission of this task force would be to attack from the bridgehead which the 80th Division had established at Toul directly eastward toward Nancy.[32]

28.   134th Inf., S-3 Journal, 11 Sept. 1944.
29.   ibid.
30.   ibid.
31.   ibid.
32.   ibid.

CHAPTER IX

*   *   *

LIBERATION OF NANCY

*   *   *

Nancy, traditional capital of Lorraine and fifth city of France, was an objective to be coveted both as a military and as a political prize. Though the city itself had not been formally annexed by the Germans after their 1940 victory, it closely associated itself with and was regarded as the political leader of the region to the east which had been incorporated into the Reich. By its very size and location Nancy was bound to be a center of the German occupation forces.

With a population of more than 120,000—and 50,000 more in its suburbs— Nancy was an important communications center 200 miles east of Paris and 60 miles southwest of the German border. It was an important railway center; the Rhine-Marne canal and its branches provided other arteries of commerce for the city. An important position in industry was assured by its location near the rich Lorraine iron-ore deposits. Aside from the mining there were manfactures of shoes, glass, furniture, casks, tobacco. It was proud of its university, of its artisans. Now a city of fine public buildings and beautiful churches, it traced its colorful history back to the eleventh and twelfth centuries. And it was the symbol of these people—the cross of Lorraine—which had become the symbol of the Fighting French. (The origin of their double-barred cross is traced back to the Crusades and the conquest of Jerusalem by Godefrey de Bouillon, Duke of Lorraine.) [1]

Preparatory to the attack the 134th Infantry moved to an area east of Toul, September 14th. The Third Battalion relieved units of the 319th Infantry in holding the line Fort de Villey-le-Sec—Gondreville. Brig Gen. Sebree, assistant division commander of the 35th Division had been named to command the task force. [2]

Though it was a welcome change to cross the Moselle River over a bridge (at Toul) which already had been established by another unit, the formidable Foret de Haye—and the German troop concentrations which had been reported in it—made it look as though a bad obstacle might have been exchanged for a worse. True, medium bombers had been working over the forest, [3] but even intense bombing could not be expected to neutralize all the forces in such a large area. The forest extended all the way across the area within the river bend—about nine miles from Maron, Chaligny, and the vicinity of Pont St. Vincent on the south to Liverdun and Prouard on the north. There was no way around it, and the distance through was about six miles. (The total distance from Gondreville to Nancy—down the main highway—was about nine miles.) A few well-placed guns would be able to deny the highway; there always was an added danger of mines on a road through a forest; there would be possibility of ambush; well-concealed defensive positions could turn the attack into a difficult, slow infantry battle.

1. Information—Education Section, Lorraine District, Oise Intermediate Section, Theater Service Forces, U. S. Army, **Lorraine and Nancy,** (Nancy 1945).
2. 134th Inf., Daily Log, V, 14 Sept. 1944; 3rd Bn. S-3 Notebook, II.
3. 134th Inf., S-3 Journal, 10 Sept., 12 Sept. 1944.

General Sebree called the unit commanders to his headquarters in the sturdy Fort de Gondreville to receive his order. The objective of the task force was the high ground just west of Nancy. It would move out at 6:00 A. M. (September 15th) in a column of regiments. Leading the attack would be the 319th Infantry with the tank battalion, a platoon of TD's, and an antiaircraft platoon: its companies were to attack along the highway on a 400 to 600-yard front. One battalion of the 134th would follow closely, while the remainder of the regiment and the remaining TD's would assemble at Gondreville as reserve and be prepared to follow by motor. There was to be an artillery preparation from 6:00 to 6:15.[4]

During the night men from Company L's outpost along the highway brought in three Frenchmen who said that they had just come from Nancy; they brought the reassuring news that the Germans had withdrawn from the forest. Reconnaissance patrols from Company L confirmed this, and General Sebree cancelled the artillery preparation.

These three Frenchmen had been sent by the F.F.I. in Nancy; they informed the American staff of the types and locations of mines; they would be available to serve as guides to lead American columns into the city, and their information spared Nancy a bombing which had been planned for the next day. These men represented an active underground organization which had been working in Nancy almost from the beginning of the German occupation in 1940.[5]

Perhaps the story of the resistance movement in the Nancy area is more or less typical of that of France. In any case it was an example of close organization, determination, and an effective coordination with the nation-wide effort.

It had made a deep impression on the people of Lorraine who were not willing to accept defeat when General Charles de Gaulle had broadcast his appeal from London on June 18, 1940:

France has lost a battle but France has not lost the war. I urge all Frenchmen, wherever they may be, to join me in action, in sacrifice, in hope.

Our country is in mortal danger. Let us fight to save it.[6]

Hopeful people began to seek each other out and began to hold meetings to form the first links of what was to become the Resistance. There was clandestine passing of the line of demarcation between "occupied" and "unoccupied" France; there was receipt and distribution of weapons; prisoners were assisted in escaping. Local underground newspapers began to spring up: *Lorraine, La Voix de l'Est, Liberation, Chardon Lorrain.* The Resistance was organized and began to grow; some of its first efforts were toward assistance for refugees from the forced labor draft and their families. There were arrests, shootings, mass deportations; but the organization continued to grow. Each time that its leaders were apprehended and arrested, it reorganized quickly and resumed its activities.

In April 1943 the Secret Army of Lorraine was formed. New sites were designated for parachute operations, and acts of sabotage were planned in cooperation with national organizations. In August of that year came the "dislocation" of the first Maquis when the principal leaders were arrested or forced to leave the country. But in November the first departmental committee of liberation was formed. The following January (1944) the Resistance move-

---

4. 3rd Bn. S-3 Notebook, II.
5. Ville de Nancy, **En Hommage a ses Liberateurs** (Nancy 1945).
6. Ibid.

ment of eight departments was formed into Region C under the command of Colonel Grandval in Nancy. Then the departmental committee of liberation was reorganized along lines set forth by the National Committee, and the military and civilian movements—the F.F.I. and the F.T.P.F.—were placed under the control of the national headquarters in accordance with directives from the military representatives in London. Activities continued to mount in the face of serious difficulties. In February, for example, there was an attack on the electricity sub-station of the Nancy railroad terminal: 34 men were arrested in connection with the incident—11 were shot and 23 deported. Again in April the Gestapo was able to learn the identity of several of the members of the staff of the Lorraine Resistance movement. Its numerous arrests included the military chief of the Nancy Sector. In May the Gestapo apprehended the leader of the "liberation" movement. But that same month the government of the Free French in Algiers appointed as Commissaire de la Republique and the Prefects of the liberation the men whom the departmental committee had nominated.[7]

The coming of the invasion in June brought new calls for action. After a message from the B.B.C. the GREEN plan was put into effect for the spread of sabotage along railways, canals, and other communications lines, and for general guerilla warfare. There followed new mass arrests, and in July the Committee of Liberation, reduced to a fraction of its former membership set about recruiting new followers. The second in command of the Nancy region was arrested, but the Resistance continued to broaden its activities. By August the rapid drive of the American columns across France was sending Germans flowing through the city. (And then the Third Army ran out of gasoline!) Resistance organizations set up permanent headquarters and began to perfect plans for the liberation. Now special measures had to be taken to prevent a premature and disastrous outbreak. In fact, during the night of September 2nd, two small posters were put up on walls in the city warning the population and the F.F.I. against pillage or acts of violence without specific instructions from headquarters. That same day the German service forces had evacuated the city, but strategic points around the city were strongly occupied with about two divisions.[8]

But let us look at some excerpts from the log of what was happening inside Nancy while the men of the Third Battalion and their American comrades were approaching the city:

Tuesday, 5 September 1944

From the 4th to the 9th of September, the Liberation Committee and F.F.I. staff are in constant session watching the development of the situation which seems to be becoming serious for Nancy.

Sunday, 10 September 1944

During the night, the telephone line between Frouard and Champigneulles is sabotaged, at the place known as "la Rochotte."

At the request of the F.F.I. command, the German troop concentration in the Foret de Haye is bombarded for the first time.

Tuesday, 12 September 1944

From 1 o'clock to 3 o'clock in the morning, a German column of about 2,000 men passes along the rue de Metz and the rue de Strasbourg.

On the Avenue de Boufflers and in the rue de Toul, the Wehrmacht takes precautionary measures against a possible F.F.I. attack. Artillery pieces are emplaced to fire on the city.

7.   ibid.
8.   ibid.

LIBERATION OF NANCY

As a result of details supplied by the underground intelligence agencies, the Resistance secures a new and violent bombardment of the Foret de Haye.

Underground cables along national highway 57 are sabotaged near Houdemont and the telephone line between Maxeville and Saint Jacques farm is cut.

Wednesday, 13 September 1944

As a result of the bombardment of the Foret de Haye, the Germans withdraw part of their troops.

Reconnaissance of detonating devices of mines placed in position for destroying permanent structures.

Thursday, 14 September 1944

Three F.F.I.'s are sent on a reconnaissance mission toward the American lines.

Patrols by heavily-armed S.S. troops.

The Germans finish the demolitions decided on by their staff.

Burning of the Grand Moulins by a heavily-armed group. The Germans forbid access to the spot by rescue squads.

The survivors of the bombardment of the Foret de Haye fall back to Prouard and Flavigny.

Detached groups take prisoners.

18.00 hours—Meeting of the F.F.I. staff and of the president of the C.D.L.—Review of the situation—Sensitive points will be occupied during the night by night patrols. Telegram to London from Colonel Grandval asking for the support of American troops for the following morning. [Why this was necessary, and why it was sent to London is not clear.]

Major Lamolle-Lariviere gives the order for setting military action in motion on the 15th at 6 o'clock in the morning.

Acts of insurrection are authorized and posters are put up.

Friday, 15 September 1944

During the night: the Palais du Gouvernement is occupied and the Prefecture, City Hall, and telephone exchange are kept under surveillance.

6 o'clock: Action begun according to plan: Patrols cover the city. Mopping-up of premises occupied by the enemy or his collaborators. Arrest of suspects.

9 o'clock: Conflicting reports. The crowds are nervous.

9:30: Colonel Grandval and Major Pierret-Gerard visit the regional prefect, Jean-Faure.

10:15: At the CP of the F.T.P.F. on Place des Dames, M. Chailley Bert, M. Dieudonne, chef de cabinet de l'Intendant de police; M. Lamelle-Lariviera, chief of the F.F.I.; Majors Herr-Hemours and Stenger-Richard of the F.T.P.F. receive General Sebree and a colonel whom a group of F.T.P.F. have brought from Fonds-de-Toul.

10:45: M. Poeters, president of the Committee of Liberation, and Major Pierrot-Gerard, chief of the insurrectionists, notify M. Schmitt that he is no longer mayor of Nancy. Installation of M. Prouve as new mayor of Nancy.

11:10: Arrival of the first American tanks.

11:30: Installation of M. Chailley-Bert, Commissaire de la Republique, and of M. Blache, perfect of Meurthe-et-Moselle, by the Committee of Liberation....

Upon his installation, the commissaire de la Republique issued a proclamation to the Lorraine population:

NANCY IS FREE

but the battle is continuing at the gates of the city where Frenchmen and Americans are uniting their efforts.[9]

When a wandering German officer had gone into Nancy during the last days of the occupation he had found the city full of German troops, unconscious of their doom, drinking and singing, playing musical instruments, and dancing with and making love to French girls.

Not till the bullets began to whizz about their ears in the last hours in Nancy, did the Germans begin to suspect that these French girls who were ostensibly fraternizing with them, were secret agents of the Resistance, waiting to hear news of orders for them to pull out. That was the signal for street fighting to begin. You had to be on the inside of the underground to know that.[10]

9. ibid.
10. The New York Sun, April 17, 1946, p. 6.

The Americans who were continuing the scattered fighting were members of the 134th Infantry—mostly of the 1st Battalion. True to the reports, the Germans had withdrawn from their positions in the forest. By 8:20 the leading companies of the 319th Infantry were marching down the highway in route column with only patrols moving through the woods to protect the flanks; then infantrymen mounted tanks to rush forward.[11]

Its mission accomplished when the high ground to the west of Nancy was occupied, Task Force Sebree was dissolved, and while the 319th Infantry returned to join the 80th Division in its attacks on the north of the big bend, the 134th Infantry moved into the city. Wild, happy throngs lined the streets, and crowds filled the great open square—Place Stanislas—to acclaim the liberators.[12] Women rushed to the streets with babies, holding up their children's hands that they might touch an American soldier!

Excited Frenchmen ran about seeking to ferret out snipers, German stragglers, collaborators.[13]

Soon a big sign appeared along the Rue de Toul:

VIVE LA FRANCE
VIVE DE GAULLE
VIVE LA THIRD ARMEE

It was as though this should have been the ending of a dramatic novel in which hero and heroine "live happily ever after." But they must have known that it was not so. Liberation could not automatically bring prosperous towns, for many days of bitter war for France and her allies remained ahead; and even then a return to anything like pre-war conditions could be achieved only with the greatest difficulty. Their city would continue to be filled with foreign soldiers; but the people would consider themselves free, for to them, these soldiers represented the kind of liberty which they associated with the tradition of France.

The leaders of Nancy were not unaware of the practical difficulties which lay ahead in making necessities of food and clothing available to the population. That same day the Commissaire de la Republique issued a directive on revictualing the population. He explained that rationing would have to be maintained strictly, and he called upon the population for discipline in enforcing the rules. All acts of pillage would be punished immediately. In another declaration the commissaire declared all vehicles, equipment, merchandise left by the German army of occupation to be national property, and to be reported to the police. In addition he called upon merchants and manufacturers to cooperate in making goods available and in making available all possible means of transport: he warned that black market operations would be punished severely by court-martial.[14]

In the afternoon regimental headquarters opened in the Hotel Thier.[15] The Third Battalion moved into positions at the north edge of the city above Maxeville.

It was disappointing for infantrymen that they never could expect to pause long enough for prolonged visits in newly-liberated towns, and perhaps it was with a note of bitterness that they foresaw the entry of rear echelon men who

11.   134th Inf., S-3 Journal, 15 Sept. 1944.
12.   Ville de Nancy, op. cit. See photograph.
13.   35th Div., Historical Booklet, Santa Fe (typescript) pp. 66-67.
14.   Ville de Nancy, op. cit.
15.   134th Inf., S-3 Journal.

would have such opportunity. Franco-American friendship might have been cemented on a new high level had it been possible for all the troops to keep on moving. At the moment of liberation, the American soldiers were the heroes of the world, and they commanded universal respect and admiration. In the months to follow, however, careless behavior in some areas tended to cancel that warm enthusiasm and attitudes growing out of misunderstanding began to grow on both sides. But, except for a relatively few passes which became available later, the infantryman, to his chagrin, could have no part in the deterioration.

The fall of Nancy had been regarded as a highly significant event; perhaps Patton was going to be able to resume his rapid advance:

> The capture of Nancy, Charmes, and Epinal, all on the same day by the American Third Army, was an outstanding victory that changed the whole situation on the southern half of the Twelfth Army Group's front. With the reduction of these strong-points the way is now open for an advance toward the Siegfried Line in this sector....
>
> Nancy is an important keystone to German defenses in front of the Rhine, since it controls the main road running along the northern slope of the Vosges to Strassbourg.[16]

Nancy was free, but it could not be safe from observed artillery fire as long as the enemy retained possession of the heights across the Meurthe River to the east. There would be no time, then, for men of the Third Battalion to enjoy the attractive city, for that high ground had to be taken.

16. Drew Middleton in The New York Times, Sept. 16, 1944, p. 2.

CHAPTER X

★ ★ ★
PAIN DE SUCRE ("SUGARLOAF" HILL)
★ ★ ★

A prize requisite for a successful attack against a hostile position is an adequate reconnaissance.[1] In the hedgerow country this frequently was not possible, for time was short and observation poor. Now, however, Colonel Miltonberger was able to issue his regimental order for the crossing of the Meurthe River some four hours (of daylight) before the attack was to be launched. Therefore when Major Wood received the order at 10:00 A. M., September 16th, to seize an objective on the high ground east of Nancy,[2] his first action was to make a personal reconnaissance.

Under cover of the buildings of Nancy, the Battalion Commander, his S-3, and the artillery liaison officer moved by jeep to the northeastern section of the city. Crossing the Rhine-Marne Canal, they dismounted and made their way down to the street paralleling the river. Here, a few hundred yards upstream (south) from the destroyed bridge to Malzeville, they could observe the river approaches, and the ground on the opposite side. They themselves, however, were not immune to observation, and whenever a member of the party would venture into an open area, there would be an immediate reaction from enemy rifles.[3]

The Third Battalion was to make its crossing by wading, while, at the same time, the 1st Battalion would be crossing by assault boats at a point about a mile to the right.[4]

As the Battalion marched through the streets of the city toward the crossing site, Captain Greenlief, whose Company L was to make the assault, was able to make a reconnaissance of his own. Taking his platoon leaders to the top floor of an adjacent flour mill, Greenlief pointed out objectives and issued his company order.

Antitank guns were to be forded across the river immediately behind Company L, and then Companies I and K would follow in order. A machine gun platoon was attached to each of the two leading companies, and the mortars went into position to support the attack.[5]

Covered by heavy machine gun fire, men of Company L plunged into the river at 2:45 P. M.[6]

Major Wood and his command group had set up an observation post in the mill where they could look down upon the crossing site.[7] Lieutenant Clyde Payne was having trouble getting his antitank guns across, and while his platoon moved a short distance upstream, Company I started across at 3:40 and "K" followed at 3:55.[8] The second machine gun platoon had relieved the first as

1. cf. Infantry Field Manual 7-20 (1942) p. 82.
2. 134th Inf., S-3 Journal, 16 Sept. 1944.
3. Wood, loc. cit.
4. 134th Inf., S-3 Journal.
5. 3rd Bn. S-3 Notebook, II.
6. 134th Inf., S-3 Journal.
7. On a visit to the site a year after the event, the writer found bullet-holes still in the windows where Germans had fired at members of the group who exposed themselves too near the openings.
8. 134th Inf., Unit Journal, 16 Sept. 1944. 134th Inf., S-3 Journal, 16 Sept. 1944.

it displaced forward to join Company L, and a perfect continuity of covering fire was maintained while the riflemen, supporting themselves against the strong current by a rope, continued to go through the waist-deep water. The antitank men finally succeeded, then, in manhandling a 57 mm gun across the river and its 1½-ton prime mover was able to ford the stream.

In spite of scattered German small arms fire, casualties in the Battalion were very light.[9] In view of some rather heavy artillery concentrations which the Battalion had received as it descended the high ground at the north edge of Nancy, it seems that the movements through the city had been well concealed, and the attack was made at an unexpected place—it is likely that the Germans were expecting the attack to come nearer the Malzeville bridge.

At any rate Company L was on the flank of the German defenses of Malzeville. Here there was a pause in the attack while Captain Greenlief negotiated with a group of Germans for their surrender. Already he had taken 12 prisoners, and now a man from Company L went with one of the Germans to the enemy command post to try to arrange for the surrender of the entire force.[10] But there was delay and evasion. Two emissaries appeared from the German commander, but still the situation remained indefinite.

Finally the Battalion resumed its attack: Company L advanced northeast along the road to attack Malzeville, and Companies I and K moved north against the heights—the Plateau de Malzeville. Company L ran into difficult town fighting but by 7:40 both Malzeville and the objectives along the south edge of the plateau had been occupied,[11] and the command post moved to a house generally between the two areas.

The next day's efforts were directed toward perfecting control of the high ground in the zone which dominated Nancy. The Plateau de Malzeville rose 620 feet above the Meurthe River. Its slopes were wooded, but its summit was in a broad, open flat which extended more than two kilometers in length by a kilometer in width. It made an ideal location for one of Nancy's air fields.[12] Company G relieved Company L in Malzeville that afternoon so that that unit could join "K" in the attack. Both companies encountered some stiff opposition—particularly around Dommartemont, and it was 6:30 before they reached their objectives.[13] Now "K" controlled Butte St. Genevieve, a high, rounded appendage of the plateau, and a denial of observation on Nancy practically was complete. The CP displaced to St. Max on the side of the hill.

That evening it was directed that the two German emissaries who had come to the Battalion should be freed. (The men from Company L had escaped from the German CP so that now the Battalion had its own men back, and also had the Germans.) That evening the two men (blind folded) were taken back to Malzeville and released.[14]

The next morning (September 18th) the Battalion was to attack at 10 o'clock to seize the north edge of the plateau. Like most commanders, Lt. Campbell subscribed to the practice of sending out patrols, whenever practicable, to probe in the area to his front prior to making an attack. Such a patrol went out from Company K on this morning. It returned at 9:45 with two prisoners.

9. Lawrence Youngman in **The Omaha World-Herald,** reprinted in **The Santa Fe Express,** May 1945, p. 8.
10. 134th Inf., S-3 Journal, 16 Sept. 1944.
11. **ibid.**
12. Map; Easter France, 1:50,000, NANCY, Sheet XXXIV-15.
13. 134th Inf., S-3 Journal.
14. 3rd Bn. Journal, I, 1.

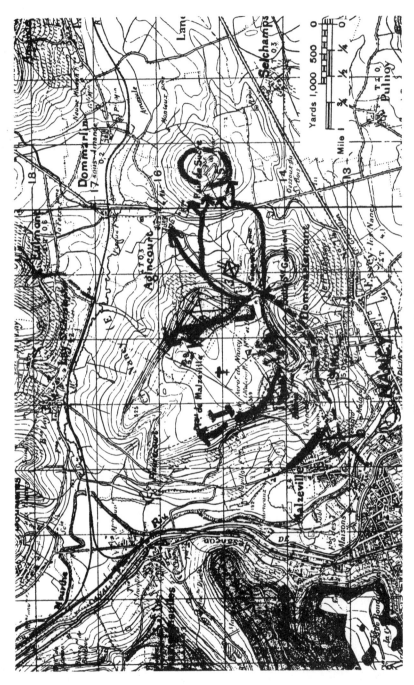

Nancy and Pain de Sucre.

Right:—**A C.P. In Minnesota:** Maneuvers, 1940 (In center is Alfred Thomsen, later C.O., 3rd Bn.). Lt. Col. Stoll and Col. McCormick are on his right and left.

Below:—**Armistice Day Parade, Memphis, 1940.** During early training, lots of time went into drill. It did a great deal for the unit, but many deplored the hours at Robinson given to "eyewash" like building little picket fences and neat walks around the tents. In those days it seemed at times more important to impress superior officers than the enemy.

Gen. Eisenhower, Gen. Baade (Division C.G.), Col. Miltonberger (Regtl. C.O.), Gen. Patton and Col. Solomon (Div. Chief of Staff). With this much brass around, the Third Battalion was convinced of its importance. And the visitors were impressed here as they watched a squad of Co. L go through a problem. (England)

Left:—**Colonel Thomsen.** The big colonel . . . had an invention for everything . . . his vigorous spirit supported a battalion.

Trucks of the 35th Div. Landing at Omaha Beach on D plus 30. One of the great American contributions to the art of war was the modern amphibious operation. Men of the Third Battalion were grateful for a secure beach when landing in Normandy.

Hedgerow Country . . . Looking south toward St. Lo. "Each hedgerow conquered is a minor campaign won."

Digging in Behind a Hedgerow in Normandy . . . Men of the Third Battalion had special training in mountain warfare, in attack through towns, in attack of a fortified position, in attack through woods, and river crossings, but nobody ever mentioned the hedgerows. And they were the toughest obstacles of all.

"The position in St. Lo was described as 'hell' by troops at the front . . . ." From high ground to the south, Germans poured artillery fire into St. Lo to make rubble of the rubble, and keep Yanks in cellars.

A Dead End Sunken Road in Normandy . . . . When they could, Americans looked around for German equipment. It is a curious thing that in the Civil War the U.S. soldier had combination knives and forks and spoons, but in World War II he had to capture such from Germans and Italians. And German leather equipment was more attractive than American web cartridge belts and harness.

Distinguished Service Cross.
Sgt. Buster Brown receives the DSC from Gen. Baade while Col. Miltonberger is looking on, for gallantry in action back in the hedgerows of Normandy.

The Burning House Became a Reference Point in the Drive Toward St. Lo.

Capt. Greenlief, Col. Wood, Capt. Campbell, Sgt. Sass have just received decorations. Whether a man happens to get the Silver Star instead of a Distinguished Service Cross or even a Medal of Honor often depended as much on what unit he was in and when it was, and who he was (a nationally known entertainer seemed more likely to get a Legion of Merit than an unknown G.I.)—and how skilfull a writer was the Hq man who wrote the citation—as upon the deed itself.

German Prisoners in Joigny. Prisoners came easier now, and that was good for American morale . . . . Many still think that, had supplies held out, the Third Army could have rolled right into Germany.

Rolling through Montargis to continue the race to the east. This was a new war—joyous crowds, champagne, flowers, fruit. If American armies could have gone right thru France, without leaving rear units for months in the cities, American soldiers would have endured as immortal heroes.

"NANCY IS FREE"

All of the German soldiers didn't get away. Here a patrol from the Third Battalion enters Habkirchen, one of the first units to enter Germany here.

Riflemen of the Third Battalion Crossing the Roer River.

They were the same two Germans which had been released the night before![15] Anxious to avoid any violation of rules of war in making prisoners of official emissaries, the regiment had given them special treatment, and had tried to rid itself of them. Now the only recourse was to commit them to the PW cage, for an attack was beginning. It seems that Company K, in capturing Dommartemont and the Butte Ste. Genevieve, had captured the German command post, and the two men had been wandering through the woods trying to find their unit.

In this attack, after a five-minute artillery preparation, Company I was to attack through the woods around the left (west) edge of the plateau while Company K attacked through the woods around the right edge. Company L would follow "K" as reserve. A platoon of tank destroyers (605th Battalion), a regimental antitank platoon, and a platoon of engineers (Company A, 60th Engineer Battalion) were attached.[16]

As a harassing measure, the antitank guns were put in position on a line along the southern edge of the plateau and fired a barrage of direct fire across the flat field just before the companies moved out.

"I" Company began meeting resistance very soon, but within half an hour some prisoners were taken and it appeared that the advance would be able to continue without too much difficulty.[17] Company K did find this to be pretty much the case, and, after some scattered rifle fire, moved through the woods toward its objective. Company I, however, found itself up against some stubborn defenders who seemed determined to hold to their well-dug-in positions in the woods. (One of the captured prisoners was found carrying a note which instructed the group to "fight to finish.") Machine gun fire was cutting through the trees, and it was exacting casualties from the attacking company. One of the platoon leaders was killed; additional men were wounded; then Captain Hyde was hit—wounded seriously. Once more Company I had lost its commander.[18]

Major Wood and his command group were following the companies on the right, and the attached tank destroyers were close behind on the road which ran along the east edge of the plateau from the St. Genevieve Farm. An enemy sniper from somewhere down the hill was annoying the group with his continuous rifle fire. The Battalion commander looked back toward a TD and said he thought something ought to be done about it. Captain Ruby thought he knew where the sniper was—in a tree down near the bottom of the hill; he ran to one of the destroyers. Its turret swung around, and a blast from its three-inch gun rent the air. The three-inch proved its superiority over .30 caliber rifle, for the latter ceased its annoyance. But other targets were appearing. The 1st Battalion, attacking through the valley toward Pain de Sucre hill and Agincourt was flushing out Germans before its advance. From their position high on the plateau, members of the Third Battalion could look down upon the fleeing enemy; some distance forward, relatively, of the other battalion, they were in an excellent position to fire down on the flank of the enemy. After checking through headquarters to make sure of the 1st Battalion's location, the Third Battalion's attached TD's and antitank guns began to fire. But they

15. Ibid.
16. Ibid.
17. Ibid. One of these prisoners, on being asked why they continued to fight against such overwhelming odds, replied that his unit commander was trying to earn the Iron Cross.
18. Ibid., pp. 1-2.

met with a quick response: tanks accompanying the 1st Battalion, apparently unaware of the location of the Third, answered with some cannon fire of their own toward the plateau. That quickly ended the attempted assistance to the 1st Battalion.[19]

Company I, meanwhile, was having difficulty in maintaining contact with the 2nd Battalion which was attacking on the left, and it stopped for the night some distance short of its goal. The Battalion had taken 26 prisoners during the day.[20]

The regimental plan for September 19th envisioned a general advance in which the 2nd Battalion was to continue its attack to the north toward the Bois de Faulx and the 1st was to attack from its positions on Pain de Sucre and in Agincourt to the northeast to seize the highground around Amance, and then continue to the north to take Bouxieres-aux-Chenes. Third Battalion, in reserve, was to follow the 1st.[21] This, apparently, was intended to be a prelude to a resumption of the rapid breakthrough warfare, for a new armored division—the 6th—had joined the corps, and 40 Quartermaster trucks had been attached to the regiment. Another "Task Force Sebree" was being formed from Combat Command B of the 6th Armored Division and the 134th Infantry.[22] (The XII Corps now was executing a brilliant maneuver: Combat Command B of the 4th Armored Division, after crossing the Moselle in the zone of the 137th, had driven in a wide arc to the northeast of Luneville; meanwhile Combat Command A had crossed the Moselle far to the north, in the zone of the 80th Division, and swung wide in a complementary arc—tanks of the two columns had passed each other in completing the big circle. Now the two infantry divisions—the 80th on the north, and the 35th on the south, were swinging toward each other inside this circle—it almost was a "wheel within a wheel." This finished, the 6th Armored Division would be in position to lead a new drive to the northeast.—The corps objectives were said to be Mannheim and Darmstadt, Germany—across the Rhine south of Frankfurt.)[22a]

The enemy, however, was not immediately cooperative. Unwilling to resign his hold on such a dominating terrain feature as Pain de Sucre, he launched a vigorous night attack in the early hours of September 19th and drove the 1st Battalion from the hill.[23]

Therefore, when the company commanders assembled in the Battalion CP at St. Max at 7:45, they could be given only a tentative plan. This was for the Third Battalion to take over the assignment of the 1st in the attack which was scheduled for 10 o'clock.[24] But obviously the first problem was Pain de Sucre—the Sugar Loaf, and its recapture was the Third Battalion's first task. Pain de Sucre was a knob independent of neighboring hills or ridges, which rose to a height about equal to that of the Plateau de Malzeville. From its summit an observer could see for miles in almost any direction; it commanded the surrounding valley,

Major Wood and his S-3, as soon as tentative instructions had been issued to the company commanders, went to the 1st Battalion CP—south of the Sugar

19. Wood, loc. cit.
20. 3rd Bn. Journal, I, 2-3.
21. 3rd Bn., S-3 Notebook, II.
22. 134th Inf., S-3 Journal, 16 Sept., 1944; Daily Log, V, 17 Sept. 1944.
22a. Gen. Patton hoped XII Corps, with three armored and two infantry divisions could reach the Rhine and beyond.—**War As I Knew It,** p. 132.
23. 134th Inf., S-3 Journal, 19 Sept. 1944.
24. 3rd Bn. Journal, I, 4.

Loaf—to learn the situation and make plans for the new attack. It appeared that the enemy was not remaining wholly passive in his defense, for one soldier came into the 1st Battalion CP and reported that the Germans were preparing to attack farther south with tanks and infantry: two heavy machine guns (.30 caliber) and a .50 caliber machine gun from the engineer company went into position to bolster the 1st Battalion's defenses. General Sebree arrived at the 1st Battalion CP and when he had familiarized himself with details of the situation, he telephoned the corps chief of staff to explain it, and to inquire whether it was necessary to retake the high ground immediately; he was told that he should retake the hill, and then prepare to hold.[25]

The Third Battalion, on the Plateau de Malzeville, was in an excellent position to make an attack against Pain de Sucre from the east; this would be across the front of the 1st Battalion, and that unit would be in a position to assist the attack by fire. It would be necessary, however, to protect the left flank by containing Agincourt—the town which lay at the foot of the hill on the northeast.

Two platoons of tanks (ten Shermans) and five M-10 tank destroyers were available to the Battalion. The plan called for an attack at 1 o'clock with men of Company K, mounted on the tanks, leading—with the remainder of Company K and Company L following on foot—in the assault on the hill, while Company I, with the tank destroyers, would attack Agincourt.[26]

The Battalion commander returned to his command post shortly after 11 o'clock and immediately issued instructions to the companies to move to assembly areas and he called to the company commanders to accompany him on a personal reconnaissance.[27] The 2nd Battalion was to extend to take over the ground on the plateau which the Third had taken.[28] To succeed Captain Hyde in the command of Company I, Major Wood called upon Lt. James Cecka of Company M.

When it was found that the hour set for the attack—1 o'clock—would not allow sufficient time for reconnaissance and for assembly of companies and tanks, it was possible to have it postponed one-half hour.

Then at the appointed time, following a ten-minute artillery preparation on the hill, Company K and the tanks "took off." From the vicinity of "Five Corners" (the junction of five roads near St. Genevieve Farm at the point where the Butte St. Genevieve joined the Plateau de Malzeville) one platoon of tanks carrying one platoon of infantry—five men on each tank[28a]—rolled down the Agincourt road to the northeast, (along the side of the Plateau) while the second platoon of tanks—and its platoon of mounted infantrymen—moved down the road running to the east (along the Butte St. Genevieve). Company K's support platoon and Company L followed on foot. As the tanks reached the bottom of the valley and crossed the highway, both columns fanned out to form a single irregular skirmish line, and, behind their own continuous machine gun fire and sporadic 75 mm cannon fire, they began their advance up Sugarloaf Hill. Until masked by the advancing troops, the 1st Battalion continued an effective diversionary fire from the south, i.e., the right flank. Meanwhile, Company I and the tank destroyers followed the left column down the slope,

25. *ibid.*, p. 5; 134th Inf., S-3 Journal, 19 Sept. 1944.
26. 3rd Bn. S-3 Notebook, II.
27. 3rd Bn. Journal, I, 5.
28. 134th Inf., S-3 Journal, 19 Sept. 1944.
28a. (Perhaps this could be called a modern version of attack by dragoons—mounted infantry!)

and when the preceding platoons swung toward the hill, this company "peeled off" and continued toward Agincourt. It was at Agincourt that the only serious opposition developed, but Company I was filling its mission of containing the town and protecting the left flank, for the attack against the main objective was moving smoothly. By 1:45 the tanks were three-fourths of the way up the hill, and by 2:10 they were on the crest. (At this point the command tank, on which Lt. Jack Campbell was riding, was knocked out, by an antitank gun or tank on a neighboring hill, but its men escaped). Forty minutes later, 22 prisoners were on their way to the Battalion cage. But still Company I battled in Agincourt for another hour or more; during this time the TD's knocked out a German tank in the streets of the town. The objectives secured, the Battalion had completed one of its most successful attacks. Adequate reconnaissance, close cooperation of tanks and infantry, clearly assigned tasks for each unit, supporting and diversionary fire, an approach from a new direction, and skilful, precise, dynamic execution had contributed to the result. The achievement had been in taking quickly and with almost negligible casualties an objective which the Germans had prized highly enough to make a counterattack to recapture from the 1st Battalion.[29]

It was not likely that the Germans would be content to give up this dominating hill so easily. Soon after arrival on the summit, Company K was receiving mortar fire.[30] With the example of the 1st Battalion before them, men of the Third prepared to defend their hill. One precautionary—though quite normal—measure was in the sending of 57 mm guns of the Battalion Antitank Platoon to the hill.

True to form, the enemy came back during the darkness of the early morning hours. At first—at 5 o'clock—it seemed to be only a minor infiltration into Agincourt, but at 5:15 Company K's 60 mm mortars opened fire, and soon it was seen that it was a full-scale attack against both Pain de Sucre and Agincourt. All the companies began reporting casualties—calling for litter bearers.[31] There was tense, close-range fighting on the hill. Technical Sergeant Charles Ostrom of Oregon, a "K" Company platoon sergeant, moved among his men, coordinating their fire to meet the attack. Then he noticed two German soldiers, armed with machine guns, crawling up the slope toward the antitank gun in the company's area. Quickly Ostrom started toward the assailants; he crawled down to close range and threw hand grenades to kill both. But as he made his way back to his platoon, he himself was killed by enemy fire.[32]

It was for good reason that the enemy had been seeking out that antitank gun, for this time the Germans too resorted to the use of tanks to assist them to capture the hill. But the result was to give the Battalion Antitank Platoon the opportunity to mark up their first enemy tank—a victim of the 57 mm gun. (And possibly it was crippled by an antitank rocket from Company K.)[33]

Company I was finding its position less tenable as the Germans moved into the town and gained control. It still was dark, and there was a heavy fog in the valley when the enemy closed in. Staff Sergeant Huston Temple of Tennessee, one of the squad leaders, found that the house which he and some of

29. 3rd Bn. Journal, I, 5-7; 3rd Bn. S-3 Notebook, II; 134th Inf., Unit Journal, 19 Sept. 1944; 134th Inf., S-3 Journal, 19 Sept. 1944; Wood, loc. cit. See Patton, op. cit., p. 134.
30. 3rd Bn. Journal, I, 6.
31. 3rd Bn. Journal, I, 7; 134th Inf., S-3 Jouranl, 21 Sept. 1944.
32. 35th Div., General Orders, No. 47, 27 Oct. 1944.
33. 3rd Bn. Journal, I, 7.

his squad occupied was surrounded—the Germans were calling upon them to surrender. He saw that he could not expect to hold out against this superior force, but, on the other hand, he was not willing to surrender. Therefore he ordered his men to withdraw and find their way out, and he opened fire to cover their withdrawal. The enemy sent up flares as they waited for the men to surrender, but Temple moved rapidly from one window to another, firing accurately in the light of the flares, and took a heavy toll among the would-be captors. Then he made his own escape without injury.[34]

Other parts of Company I were not so successful in resisting capture. Enemy groups had been able to find the company command post, and here they concentrated their efforts—the company commander, and most of his headquarters personnel were taken. Other men of the company withdrew to the edge of the town. When communications with the company had gone out at 5:45, the Battalion S-2 and four men had gone down to try to establish contact, but they found that they could not even get into the town.[35]

But the principal feature—the Sugarloaf—had held: at 6:30 it was reported "everything under control on the hill."[36] And Agincourt without Pain de Sucre was an empty holding. At noon a terrific artillery shelling was brought down on the town, and late in the afternoon it was found to be clear. Now Major Wood purposed to control Agincourt without occupying it. Company I— strengthened by the fortunate arrival of 16 replacements—undertook reorganization under Lt. William Chavet—an officer who only recently had left a platoon to join the Battalion staff as S-2. The weapons platoon and one rifle platoon, with a section of heavy machine guns from Company M, took up positions on the reverse slope of Pain de Sucre. The remainder of the company returned to the high ground near the Battalion CP at St. Genevieve Farm as Battalion reserve. Company B (Mason) had been sent to reinforce the Battalion— originally sent to help Company I at Agincourt, but unable to arrive before that issue was settled—and it took up positions on the plateau in the woods where Company K formerly had been.[37]

The next day an "M" Company patrol counted 42 German dead in Agincourt.[38]

Pain de Sucre was secure. A news dispatch had noted:

> One of the sharpest battles for strong points behind the lines is now raging at "Sugarloaf Hill", four miles from Nancy. The hill changed hands for the third time yesterday when it was retaken by American infantry, but they had to fight off a German counterassault a few hours later.[39]

The Third Battalion remained in position the next day while the 6th Armored Division moved out at 7 A. M. and then the 1st Battalion moved around to the north edge of the Plateau de Malzeville to join the 2nd Battalion at 12 o'clock in a new attack toward Bois de Faulx.[40]

That afternoon Pain de Sucre proved its value as an observation post. Already enemy had been seen withdrawing from Eulmont and generally from in front of the 1st Battalion as it attacked north of the Plateau, and General Eddy had called from Corps headquarters to say "air having a field day" on

34. 35th Div., General Orders, No. 50, 4 Nov. 1944.
35. 3rd Bn, Journal, I, 7.
36. ibid.
37. ibid., pp. 8-10.
38. ibid., p. 14.
39. Drew Middleton in **The New York Times**, Sept. 21, 1944, p. 5.
40. 3rd Bn. Journal, I, 17-18; 134th Inf., S-3 Journal, 22 Sept. 1944.

the withdrawing troops.[41]   Then at 3:20 Lt. Campbell reported that there was
a long column of enemy infantry, horse and tractor-drawn artillery, including
heavy pieces, and command cars, moving north in the vicinity of Moulins (about
three miles north of Pain de Sucre).   An air strike was requested, and in the
meantime corps artillery was to fire on the column.   Campbell reported the
progress of the column, and at 3:43 Major Wood called regimental headquarters
"begging for an air strike."   Now it appeared that fighter-bombers already
were in the air, for scarcely more than 15 minutes later planes were swooping
down on the target.[42]   Again and again planes returned to their prey in attacks
which continued for more than forty minutes.   Major Wood went across to the
hill to observe the action.   Reports were noted at regimental headquarters:

> 1600—L Co observer reports air is really working German column over.   Moving
> toward BOUXIERES.   Maj. Wood says it was a complete rout.

> 1642—Maj. Wood reports that our planes are dropping gasoline bombs on infantry.
> Horses running around and air corps just raising complete hell with the German with-
> drawal.[43]

The break had come, and the Battalion made plans for a renewal of its
attack to the north the next day.   If there was a more dominating hill in the
area than "Sugarloaf," it was that around Amance—the town nestled in a
shallow saddle on the hill about three kilometers northeast of Pain de Sucre.
A patrol of the 137th Infantry had found it undefended, and now "K" Company
was ordered to relieve a company of that regiment in occupying the high
ground.   From here men of Company K could look down upon Eulmont,
Moulins, and Bouxieres, and, together with the Battalion Antitank Platoon, they
were to fire from the heights as the remainder of the Battalion attacked to
seize these successive objectives.   But neither was this necessary, for a Company I patrol found Eulmont abandoned, and the company, after assembly and
breakfast in Agincourt, marched to that town and occupied it at 9 o'clock.   In
the afternoon Company L passed through I, and, moving to the northeast along
a secondary road—a kilometer to the left of the main highway—occupied
Moulins, and Bouxieres.   Released from its assignment at Amance, "K" Company rejoined the Battalion here.   Now the Battalion was to move, by shuttling,
to Leyr (about three miles north of Bouxieres) where it was reported that units
of the 6th Armored Division had attacked at 12:46 and had occupied the town
at 3:00 P. M.   The 1st Battalion was to follow the Third, and then occupy
Bey (three miles east of Leyr).   The truck column proceeded down the highway toward its destination, (over a road which had been reported mined at
several places, but had not been swept) but as it approached the town it appeared that a violent fire fight was going on there.   The vulnerable 2½-ton
trucks halted behind the nose of a hill to discharge their troops and return,
and the Third Battalion went into a perimeter, "wagon wheel" defense for the
night on the side of the hill.[44]   The 1st Battalion, which had been following the
Third, turned back; it went all the way back to its former location at Ley St.
Christopher, seven miles to the rear (southwest).[45]   This left the Third Battalion alone on a strange hillside in the midst of a "fluid" and not very clear
situation.

41.   134 Inf., S-3 Journal, 22 Sept. 1944.
42.   3rd Bn. Journal, I, 22-23.
43.   134th Inf., S-3 Journal, 22 Sept. 1944.
44.   ibid., pp. 25-29; 3rd Bn. S-3 Notebook II; 134th Inf., Unit Journal, 23 Sept. 1944.
45.   134th Inf., Unit Journal, 23 Sept. 1944.

Fortunately for the Battalion, however, members of the 6th Armored Division settled the issue in Leyr during the night favorably for themselves, and the next morning (September 24th) the Third Battalion moved into the town to relieve the armored units. At 2:10 P. M. a patrol from the 80th Division arrived at the Battalion CP; the "inner circle" had been cleared.

But neither had the enemy been altogether cooperative on the outer rim of General Eddy's corps "wheel." After its brilliant encircling movement which had carried it deep into enemy territory, the 4th Armored Division met fierce counterattacks in the Luneville-Dieuze areas (Dieuze was fully 22 miles to the east of Leyr). Luneville had changed hands two or three times, and some of the "largest tank battles seen in France for many weeks" had developed.[46] After a ten-day "slugging contest" it appeared by September 23rd that the 4th Armored had been able to gain the edge.[47] It was reported that the Germans had lost 257 tanks in the ten-days' fighting.[48] But reports also came in that the 4th Armored Division had suffered serious losses.[49] If the enemy had been beaten the Americans were in no position to undertake a pursuit. Hopes for another breakthrough faded. That afternoon (September 24th) Major Wood returned from a meeting at regimental headquarters, and announced that the whole Third Army was going over to the defensive.[50]

46. Drew Middleton in **The New York Times**, Sept. 21, 1944, p. 3.
47. E. C. Daniel in **The New York Times**, Sept. 24, 1944, p. 3.
48. **The World Almanac** (1935) p. 91.
49. The German communique for Sept. 24 reported that 106 American Sherman tanks had been knocked out in the Luneville area.
50. 3rd Bn. Journal, I, 31. See Allen, **Lucky Forward,** pp. 135-144.
Gen. Patton regarded Sept. 23, the day he received the call from Gen. Bradley announcing the decision of higher headquarters that the Third Army was to go on the defensive, as a bad day in his career.—Patton, **op. cit.,** pp. 135-6.

CHAPTER XI

* * *

DEFENSIVE IN THE FORET DE GREMECEY

* * *

General Patton at last had been stopped. He had been stopped primarily not by the enemy, but by a lack of supplies. Already the Third Army's rapid advance had "involved herculean tasks in the matter of supply," and when the enemy's resistance had stiffened at the Moselle, the problem of supply became increasingly acute, "to the extent that General Patton's forces were partially immobilized and physically incapable of mounting assaults on a large scale or of continuing a pursuit had the opportunity offered."[1] However, it is not unlikely that the costly encounters in which the 4th Armored Division had engaged in the Dieuze-Luneville areas during the ten days immediately preceding had had some bearing upon the decision to assume the defensive at this particular time. Indeed, the extent to which that action represented an American "victory" might be questioned in view of the fact that the Third Battalion's front-line defensive area was organized in the Foret de Gremecey which was some eleven miles to the west—i.e., to the rear—of Dieuze.

The stiffening of enemy resistance at the Moselle and beyond was rather the result of—or at least rendered possible by—the diminution in supplies which had forced the slow-down during the last week in August—the eleven days which the Third Battalion had spent in bivouac near Aix-en-Othe. At that time patrols from General Patton's racing columns had probed in the vicinity of Nancy almost unopposed.[2]

The real reasons for the halt have been attributed to two factors: (1) General Eisenhower's decision to divert priorities to Field Marshal Montgomery for a major try in the north; (2) Failure of Communications Zone—the Services of Supply—to rise to a new miracle.[3]

For weeks Montgomery had been applying more and more pressure to obtain priorities on supplies for his Northern Army group.[4] Early in August the First Allied Airborne Army had been organized with the intention of employing it in front of the Third Army to close the Paris-Orleans gap; however, the rapid advance of the ground forces had made this unnecessary. Later, then, following Eisenhower's plan to put the big effort on Montgomery, the entire airborne forces were made available to him, and three American divisions were completely immobilized in order to supply additional logistical support for the effort in the north. What supplies remained to the American armies had to be concentrated with the First Army in its attack abreast of Montgomery's forces to protect his flank.[5] The result had been a bold committment of the airborne forces on September 17th in an effort to secure crossings of the lower Rhine in Holland. It had ended in the ill-fated battle at Arnhem, though the

---

1. General Eisenhower's Report, pp. 65-66.
2. Statement of Lt. of Cavalry to the author, vic. of Fort de Pont St. Vincent, 8 Sept. 1944; Patton, op. cit., p. 121. See Allen, op. cit., p. 136.
3. Ingersoll, Top Secret, pp. 202-221.
4. ibid.; Butcher, My Three Years with Eisenhower, pp. 672-676.
5. General Eisenhower's Report, p. 62.

important bridge over the Maas at Grave, and the one over the Waal at Nijmegen had been secured.[6]

General Eisenhower gave a number of reasons for his decision to make the effort in the north: The great bulk of the Germany army was located there; the desirability of capturing the flying bomb sites; the imperative need for the port of Antwerp; the desire for the airfields of Belgium; the attractive possibility of turning both the Rhine and the Siegfried Line, and the exploitation of the shortest route to the heart of Germany.[7]

Over against these considerations of General Eisenhower, it might be observed that, while the primary aim of an army may be to destroy the enemy (rather than to capture territory), that usually is to be accomplished best by hitting the enemy where he is weakest. The very statement that the bulk of the German Army was in the north lends the more credence to the possibility that the Third Army could have achieved a decisive breakthrough in the south—through the Frankfurt gap to the heart of Germany, and thus contributed to the destruction of the enemy by maneuver and by control of his communications and resources; beyond the strategic and economic factors involved, such a breakthrough might have gained importance as a blow at enemy morale; perhaps General Eisenhower was subscribing to what Liddell Hart calls the "Napoleonic fallacy"—the doctrine that a decisive victory can be obtained only by destroying the bulk of the enemy's forces in the field.[7a] True, there was a need for the port of Antwerp, but this consideration hardly could have been a major one in the decision to attempt the crossing of the lower Rhine; as a matter of fact, the Canadian First Army did not open its attack to clear the approaches to Antwerp until October 24, and the task was not completed until November 9th—the first ship unloading there on November 26th.[8]

Any desirability for capturing air fields or the flying bomb sites must have been secondary in any plan seeking an early conclusion of the war. And of course, in this connection the possibility of turning both the Rhine and the Siegfried Line was an attractive one; perhaps it was so attractive as to be too obvious—after all, the "great bulk of the German army was located there." This seems to have been something of a change in the attitude which had led to the less-geographically desirable Normandy beaches for the invasion rather than the Pas-de-Calais—"the shortest route to the heart of Germany," but where the enemy had concentrated his strongest forces.

But it has been contended that had the communications zone been able to rise to the occasion and perform new miracles of supply—as it had been able to do in the invasion of Normandy, and in the early days of the break out, that General Patton's forces still might have been able to force a decision with a rapid drive into the Saar and the Frankfurt gap. That it did not has been attributed to its ponderous organization—the division of responsibility among base sections, intermediate sections, and Advance Section—and perhaps to some logistical difficulties of its own as its headqaurters was moving from London to Paris during the critical period.[9] There is no question but that the supply services faced serious problems:

6. **Ibid.,** pp. 67-68.
7. **Ibid.,** p. 62. It is interesting to compare Gen. Eisenhower's later discussion of these same general factors as influencing his decision to make the main effort to the north of the Ruhr during the planning **before** the Normandy invasion.—**Crusade in Europe,** pp. 225-229.
7a. See Liddell Hart, **The Remaking of Modern Armies,** pp. 38-112.
8. General Eisenhower's Report, pp. 66-69.
9. Ingersoll, **op. cit.,** pp. 202-221; Patton, **op. cit.,** pp. 114-121.

The lack of adequate port facilities to support the rapidly moving armies became a major difficulty in the European operations. Although captured on 27 June 1944, Cherbourg required extensive reconstruction and did not reach peak discharge until November. Antwerp was captured intact in September and the first ships began to unload there in November. This port filled a real need, but its full use did not become possible until 6 months after the invasion. In the meantime, almost two-thirds of the supplies for the armies in France were unloaded over "Omaha" and "Utah" beaches, the original assault areas.

The unloading conditions had two results. Since the Normandy Peninsula continued to be the supply inlet, long transportation lines were required to move supplies to the troops as they marched to the German border. The well-known "Red Ball" truck service was the answer until rail operations could be increased. But highway trucking meant greater demands upon the United States for heavy trucks, spare parts, and road maintenance supplies. The job of railway restoration was a major undertaking. About 60 per cent of French rolling stock had been destroyed. In a single marshalling yard there were 1,300 charred locomotives and freight cars. All important railway bridges in northern France had to be rebuilt. Yet French railways operated by the Army were hauling 11,200 short tons a day by October, and had moved over 6.6 million tons out of ports by V-E day. But while internal transportation was being arranged, ships awaiting unloading jammed up. There were inadequate storage facilities near ports or between the ports and the front lines until January 1945. Many improvisations were necessary to continue support of the combat armies.[10]

Frequently man seems to be embarrassed as much by his successes as by his failures; suddenly finding himself at the threshold of an achievement for which he had dared not hope, he is unequal to the occasion, and he permits the opportunity of the moment to slip from his grasp, and falls back to his more familiar mediocrity. In military operations this becomes a defficiency almost as grave as positive failure. Failure to follow up a preliminary victory— to be prepared to "strike while the iron is hot"—has been a weakness of military commanders through the ages—as McClellan at Antietam or Hooker at Chancellorsville in the Civil War, or the Germans with the introduction of poison gas at Ypres, or the British with the surprising use of tanks at Cambrai in the First World War, or the German failure to invade England following the fall of France in this war. Now, in spite of every effort to avoid it, it appeared that the Americans were somewhat embarrassed by their own success; they were unable to rise to the occasion of the moment, and the opportunity slipped from their grasp.[11] Actually, General Eisenhower felt that a rapid thrust into Germany by a single column on a narrow front was likely to be cut off.[11a]

The order of priority for the essential trilogy of supply traditionally had been "food for guns, food for motors, food for men." Obviously an army without ammunition could not operate, and while men could miss a meal and still fight, mechanical vehicles would not operate under such a flexibility. Immediately, the race across France had tended to alter the order of priority; during breakthrough operations a relatively light expenditure of ammunition was to be expected, but the tanks and tracks demanded huge quantities of fuel. The struggle for supplies was reduced largely to a race for petrol.

But to the combat infantryman—used to fighting on foot—the demand for gasoline was likely to seem more remote. Personally, he was very much

10. **Annual Report of the Army Service Forces for the Fiscal Year 1945,** p. 23.
11. The orginal plan, prior to the invasion, had envisaged a line on D-plus-90 which would extend along the Seine from Le Havre to Paris on the north, and along the Loire from Nantes to Orleans, Fontainebleau, and Paris on the south and east, with the Allied Armies standing ready to take Paris.—General Eisenhower's Report, p. 7. Actually by D-plus-90 the Third Army was 200 miles to the east of this line!
11a. Eisenhower, **Crusade in Europe,** pp. 292-3; see also Robert E. Merriam, **Dark December** (Chicago and New York, 1947), pp. 60-65. A much fuller, and more objective account doubtless is to be found in Hugh M. Cole, **The Third Army in Lorraine** (Washington, scheduled for 1950).

interested in "food for men" even though that did stand third in importance. For his benefit the Army had developed a series of field rations which were unparalleled in the history of warfare. When the Third Battalion was in a position where it could have "hot chow," the food was of the "B" ration. This was prepared in the kitchens, and included a regular garrison menu, insofar as practicable, with all perishables eliminated; the "B" ration, then was composed of such items as canned vegetables, meats, and fruits, and dehydrated potatoes and eggs. In the Foret de Gremecey the ration which most companies used was the "ten-in-one." This was designed as a "support area ration" for use in areas where it was impracticable to bring food prepared in the kitchens, but was sufficiently protected to permit small-group feeding. It provided food for ten men for one day—though it was packaged so that it could be used to feed five men at a time. Packed in a compact case, with a total weight for case and contents of 49 pounds were the components of one of five different menus. These included various combinations of 16 canned meat items—as roast pork, roast beef, bacon, or hamburgers—three types of biscuits, five types of puddings, five kinds of cereal, jam, vegetables, butter, spread, sugar, milk, beverages, confections, and accessory items consisting of cigarettes, matches, can openers, toilet tissue, soap, water purification tablets, and paper towels. Each ration (a ration being food for one man for one day) contained 4,100 calories. Of the combat rations—individual rations designed for men in combat who had no messing facilities—type C was the more palatable, though the more bulky and difficult to carry. The "C" ration was packed in six small cans, 48 cans (eight rations) to a case, with a total weight of 42 pounds. Three of the cans, one for each meal, contained one of ten different meat components— meat and beans; meat and noodles; meat and rice; frankfurters and beans; pork and beans; ham and lima beans, or chicken and vegetables—and the other three cans, again one for each meal, contained the bread component, which included biscuits, beverage, sugar, confection items, pre-mixed cereal, and jam in any one of six combinations. Again there were accessories of cigarettes, matches, chewing gum, salt tablets, toilet tissue. A "C" ration provided 3,800 calories. A "survival ration," D, was available as supplement and for emergency conditions. It consisted of four-ounce bars of chocolate made with chocolate, sugar, milk powder, cocoa fat, oat flour, and vanillin, and enriched with vitamin B-1. This ration (three bars) contained 1,800 calories.[12]

But the hard ration with which men of the Third Battalion had become most familiar was the type K. Originally developed for paratroopers, the "K" ration, largely because of its compactness and light weight, came into general use in the infantry. A meal, packed in its brick-size cardboard box, weighed only a pound. Twelve full rations, i. e., 36 meal units, were packed in a wooden box, and the total weight was only 50 pounds. Each meal included approximately four ounces of either meat, meat and egg products, or cheese, together with biscuits, confections, chewing gum, beverage, sugar, and cigarettes. Total calories for a ration (i. e., three meals) was 2,830.[13]

Delivery of a "K" ration to a man occupying a foxhole in the Gremecey Forest was the culmination of a long and complex process. The food might

12. U. S. Army Support, Survival, Assault, Combat Rations and Supplements (Quartermaster Corps Manual 17-3); General Marshall's Report, p. 97; "Chow Talk," **The Infantry Journal,** LVI (April 1945) pp. 49-54.
13. Quartermaster Corps Manual 17-3.

have been packed by any one of a number of companies in the United States,[14] but again the component parts which went into the package represented the work of food processors and farmers and importers in all parts of the country. Take, for example, the dinner unit (which really was less complex than the breakfast and supper units) packed by the Patton Company. Its principal component was a four-ounce can—painted olive drab—containing "processed American cheese" which had been prepared by one of the plants of the Kraft Cheese Company (general offices in Chicago)—probably from milk from a middlewestern farm. On the can was a small key for opening it, and packed with the can in its light cardboard wrapping was a khaki-colored book of matches which had been made by the Diamond Match Company of New York. A waxed waterproof bag contained the bread component—two small packages of cellophane-wrapped biscuits, each containing four hard biscuits about an inch wide and three inches long, one "K-3," Sunshine, and the other "K-14," Nabisco, of the National Biscuit Company—and confection, beverage, and accessories. There was a two-ounce box of vanilla caramels—made with corn syrup, sugar, sweetened condensed skimmed milk, hardened vegetable oils, wheat flour, salt, artificial flavor—manufactured by E. J. Brach & Sons, Chicago. There was a packet of lemon juice powder prepared by Henry Heide, incorporated, New York. It contained seven grams of dried lemon juice with corn syrup, citric acid, dextrose, ascorbic acid, lemon oil, tricalcium phosphate. (Vitamin C potency was listed as 60 milligrams). Then there was a cardboard box containing 23 grams of granulated sugar which had been packaged by the Patton Company; there was a package of four Chesterfield cigarettes, and one stick of Beech-Nut, peppermint flavored, chewing gum. All of this was fit snugly into a heavy, wax-covered cardboard package, and this into an outer cardboard box, and then placed with 35 similar packages into its wooden case—with water proof lining—it was ready to leave Chattanooga for the long trip which would take it to the Gremecey forest in Lorraine.[15]

Perhaps months before its ultimate destination could have been guessed, this "K" ration had moved by rail to New York or one of the other eastern ports. There, in response to a requisition from the European Theater of Operations, it had been loaded into the hold of a ship—possibly one of the newly-built "Liberty" or "Victory" ships—for its movement overseas. Perhaps it had gone to England for storage to await trans-shipment; possibly it had gone to Cherbourg. The chances are that it finally reached Normandy via the Omaha Beach.

There it would come under control of Normandy Base Section of the Communications Zone. There would be port battalions—men unloading ships—others driving DUKW's (the amphibious 2½-ton truck), lighters, barges. Then the ration would be taken to some huge depot near the beach, or possibly moved farther inland to some dump in a forest, or in a field deep with mud, or in some warehouse. Its move forward might have been over a part of the patched-up railway system, or it might have been on a "semi-trail" truck of the Red Ball

14. On a visit to the battlefield a year later (Sept. 1945) the writer found beside one foxhole in the forest, for example, a discarded container for a dinner unit which had been packaged by Patton Food Products of Chattanooga, Tennessee, and a supper unit which had been packed by the Beech-Nut Packing Company, Canajoharie, New York. (The Beech-Nut Company had begun work toward the production of "K" rations early in 1942, but it was late in September of that year before actual production began.—D. R. Grant, assistant vice president, Beech-Nut Packing Company, to the author, June 19, 1946.)

15. From a sample dinner unit packaged by Patton Food Products, Chattanooga, Tennessee.

Express. (The Red Ball had been inaugurated as a one-way, through traffic highway system for speeding trucks from St. Lo to Chartres; later it was extended to Sommesous—15 miles south of Chalons-sur-Marne.) But it would have to wait its turn, for supplies were piling up, and transportation was not available to move them forward. (Even as late as the end of October, over 75 per cent of all tonnage on the Continent was in Normandy Base.) Presently, however, it would arrive at a forward depot under control of Advance Section, Communications Zone.[16] Then 2½-ton trucks from the 35th Division Quartermaster Company—or from the regimental service company—would deliver the ration from the "railhead" to the regimental train bivouac. Here, after being broken down according to companies, the ration would go forward, under supervision of the Battalion S-4, by jeep and trailer to the company on the position. Men would carry the boxed food up to the platoon leaders, and the squads would infiltrate back to pick up each individual share, or men would pass them among the fox holes. If the final recipient paused to look at his small packaged dinner before opening it, he might have read on the outside:

RATION, TYPE K

DINNER UNIT

Open inner bag carefully. It may be used as a water-proof container for matches, cigarettes, etc.

For security, do not discard the empty can, paper, or refuse where it can be seen from the air. If possible, cover with dirt, foliage, sand, etc.

Turning the box over the soldier would have read the contents:

2—Packages Biscuits (Energy Crackers).

1—Can cheese. Should be eaten cold.

1—Envelope—Lemonade or Orange Powder:
Add contents to 2/3 canteen cup of cold
or hot water with sugar to taste, and stir well.

1—Package of granulated Sugar.

1—Package of 4 Cigarettes.

1—Book of 10 Matches.

1—Package of Candy.

1—Piece of Chewing Gum.[17]

From Leyr the Third Battalion, mainly by shuttling on its own jeeps, had moved to an assembly area near Bey on September 24th, and the next day had moved across the Seille creek to Alincourt. Then on the 26th it had gone into its defensive position in the Foret Gremecey—in an area previously secured by the 6th Armored Division.[18]

The outstanding features of a Lorraine landscape is its forest. The height and depth of the woods, the strength of the lofty oaks, beeches, elms, firs, and birches, are typical aspects of the Lorraine forest. They cannot be compared with Fontainebleau or Compiegne. They have a character of their own.[19]

Located about 15 miles northeast of Nancy, the Foret de Gremecey extended almost six kilometers in length, east-west, and its greatest north-south depth was nearly four kilometers. There was a local bend in the line in this area so that the Third Battalion's front was toward the north, while that of the 137th Infantry, on the right, was mostly toward the east. The forest was on a ridge line, and its forward (north edges) sloped down toward the small Oesen creek. Approximately a kilometer to the north of the regimental defen-

16. Randolph Leigh, **48 Million Tons to Eisenhower**, (Washington, 1945), pp. 2, 25-31.
17. Sample, K ration box.
18. 3rd Bn. Journal, I, 32-37.
19. U. S. Army, **Lorraine and Nancy**, p. 9.

sive area there was a line of towns—west to east: Malaucourt, Jallaucourt, Fresnes—two to four kilometers apart. Another three kilometers to the north there was a second tier of towns: Lemoncourt, Oriocourt, Laneuveville.[20]

Although the usual frontage for a battalion in defense was given as being from 1,000 to 2,000 yards,[21] the main line of resistance for the Third Battalion in this area extended for nearly 6,000 yards along the irregular trace of the edge of the forest and along the ridge to the west of the woods. Company K occupied, in general, the right half of the area with its right limiting point on a hill south of Fresnes, and Company L occupied the left half, with the left limiting point on the Jallaucourt-Manhoue highway. About the only way by which a concentrated attack could be repelled on such a thinly-held front would be in the employment of an effective reserve. Therefore, Company I was held in reserve, in a separate woods, about 1,000 yards in rear of the front line. The reserve would be called upon to prepare positions to give the battalion defense depth and to provide protection in case of attack from the flanks or rear; it would prepare plans and reconnoiter routes for counterattacks in case of a penetration in the forward areas; it would be called upon for reconnaissance patrols, and security patrols, and it would provide local security for the position by maintaining an outpost well to the front of the main line of resistance. Company M's heavy machine guns were disposed to put one platoon in the Company L area, one section in the Company K area, and one section in depth in the Company I area. Battalion antitank guns went into position on the left, and regimental guns on the right. Engineers worked to put in concertinas of barbed wire, and mines and booby-traps to strengthen the position. The Battalion Command post was estabilshed in the buildings of the Farme Rhin de Bois near the Company I area. The 2nd Battalion was on the left of the Third.[22]

If there was some bitterness among officers at Third Army headquarters because of the shifting of the airborne forces to Field Marshal Montgomery and because the Army had been stopped for want of gasoline rather than by the enemy,[23] that feeling probably was not reflected among the officers and men of the infantry battalions. They doubtless were quite willing for someone else to make the main effort toward terminating the war while they awaited the outcome in the relative quiet of their foxholes. (There was apprehension among some men when they first heard of the order to go over to the defensive; such a thing was so unusual after a war of continuous attack and pursuit that they feared that a major enemy counter offensive must be on the way to cause such a drastic change.)

However, the enemy was not content to leave the Third Battalion in complete quietude. Once he found himself no longer under attack, he became more and more bold, and began to hope for a recession of some of his lost ground. That the Germans had designs on this area already had been suggested on the night of September 24-25 when intelligence officers warned that two divisions were assembling to the northwest of Dieuze and were marching to the vicinity of Delme (about four miles north of the Foret de Gremecey), and another division was reported to be moving southeast from the vicinity of Metz toward

20. Map: France, 1:25,000, NOMENY (S.E.) Sheet XXXIV-14 7 & 8.
21. Infantry Field Manual 7-20, p. 155.
22. 3rd Bn. S-3 Notebook, II; 3rd Bn. Journal, I, 37.
23. Butcher, **op. cit.**, pp. 693-694.

the same destination. Their mission was said to be "to encircle and clear out woods of Foret de Gremecey and Foret de Chateau Salins."[24]

Hardly had the troops of the 35th Division taken up their new positions than the enemy began to test them. On the morning of the 27th groups attacked the 2nd Battalion, on the left, and stronger forces hit at the 137th, on the right, when six tanks and infantry succeeded in breaking through a road block at Chambrey. Then, after this news had come, the Battalion received word that the main effort was to be made through the Third Battalion's area. And it appeared that this might be the case at noon when the outpost (a reinforced platoon from Company I some 1,500 yards to the front) reported that an enemy company was between it and the main line of resistance. Major Wood authorized the outpost to withdraw; but this took some planning, for now the platoon found enemy on both its flanks. However, the men made their way back through Company L and rejoined Company I in the reserve area. The Battalion commander and the S-3 went forward to an observation post at the edge of the woods—on high ground near a north-south road running to Jallaucourt—where they could watch the enemy activity. German troops continued to move into Jallaucourt during much of the afternoon. Two supporting tank destroyers were knocked out over to the left of the Battalion's area, and they, in turn destroyed one enemy tank.[25]

Although no major attack developed that afternoon, it seemed to be evident that one was forming, and Colonel Miltonberger took steps to strengthen the regimental position. Already Company B had moved up to fill a gap between Company L and the 2nd Battalion, and now the remainder of the 1st Battalion, less one company as regimental reserve, moved up. Corps artillery was to continue heavy fire on Jallaucourt, and Division Artillery would deliver harassing fire on La Juree Woods (midway between Jallaucourt and Fresnes). In an order reminiscent of California days, the regimental commander directed that there would be a "stand-to"—during which every officer and enlisted man was to be alert—until one hour after darkness in the evening, and from 5:30 to 7:30 in the morning. Companies were to establish listening posts to the front with wire (usually sound power telephones) communication. Companies were to report hourly during the night. After a request of Company L, Lieutenant Hall and his pioneers undertook to make some "Molotov cocktails"— bottles filled with gasoline and oil and provided with a rag wick—as an added facility for stopping a tank attack.[26]

German patrols were active during the night. Shortly after midnight one the size of a squad walked by an "L" Company local outpost. Shortly after, a listening post reported that there was an enemy patrol down near the blown-out bridge on the creek. But the climax in German audacity came when a five-man patrol made its way into the "L" Company area and pulled a man out of his hole and made him prisoner. Capt. Greenlief sent a combat patrol after the intruders as soon as he learned of the episode, but it was unable to effect a rescue, and some time later the hostile patrol was seen returning to its own territory.[27]

Other enemy activity continued. Listening posts could hear tanks and motorcycles moving about in the vicinity of Malaucourt. Between 4 and 6

24. 3rd Bn. Journal, I, 32.
25. ibid., pp. 39-43.
26. ibid., pp. 39-47.
27. ibid., p. 48.

o'clock in the morning "L" Company received some shell fire which seemed to be coming from direct-fire weapons to the west of Jallaucourt. Two men of this company were killed by the shelling. Before 6 o'clock such concentrations of German troops had appeared that both Companies K and I were calling for pre-arranged artillery fires. Major Wood and the S-3 went to the Battalion OP—which had just been dug in the previous evening—where they could see what was happening, and could direct the defense of the area.[28]

Daylight revealed long columns of enemy forces. Tanks, half-tracks, horse-drawn wagons, and artillery were moving along the Jallaucourt-Manhoue highway toward the Battalion left flank, and other vehicles appeared on the ridge to the east of Jallaucourt. Obviously here was an air target, but a hurried request for an air strike brought the response that aircraft would not be available before 9 o'clock at the earliest. And the forces approaching the Third Battalion were not the only ones in the area. Others were attacking toward Manhoue (deep to the left rear of the Battalion left flank) from the north— through the 1st and 2nd Battalion areas. Nor was it reassuring to learn that tanks and infantry also were attacking the 137th Infantry, for then it did appear that the enemy was making a coordinated effort to "encircle and clear out the Foret de Gremecey."[29]

But if no air power was available, the artillery could be depended upon to bring the columns under fire. Nevertheless, tanks continued down the highway between Jallaucourt and Manhoue, and at 7:12 five of them were approaching Company L's left platoon. Two of the Battalion's 57 mm antitank guns were in positions to cover those approaches (the third was in the vicinity of the Battalion OP) and they opened fire. The north gun was able to get off only four rounds—two at a tank, and two at another vehicle—when enemy tanks returned a heavy fire; one man was decapitated, and six others were wounded. Continuing artillery and small arms fire then denied survivors access to the guns.[30]

Readily available aircraft might have prevented such advances; indeed it might well have resulted in another rout such as that in the vicinity of Pain de Sucre. For their immediate local defense, doubtless the company commanders would have welcomed the support envisaged in the table of organization in 1939 which provided that the heavy weapons company should have sixteen guns for the defensive. A doubling of the machine gun strength would have gone far toward easing the situation in which they found themselves. Now they were forced to the expedient of pressing into service on the main line of resistance their 50 caliber machine guns (one had been allowed each company for antiaircraft protection) and Greenlief even set up several German machine guns on his line in an effort to make it a real barrier. This, however, he found to be impracticable, for when they opened fire, the men of the company, though they had been informed, could only think that it might be Germans who had worked into the rear; that rapid-firing German gun had a sound too familiar and too dreaded to be disregarded.

Soon the German tanks halted, and started moving back toward Jallaucourt. One had been knocked out, and two others were dragging it back. As enemy troops moved back to the town, artillery continued firing, and at

28. **ibid.**, pp. 48-49.
29. **ibid.**, p. 49; 134th Inf., S-3 Journal, 28 Sept. 1944.
30. 3rd Bn. Journal, I, 49, 51-52.

8:40 Jallaucourt was on fire after an ammunition dump apparently had been hit. At 9 o'clock an air strike was reported to be on the way; but it did not arrive until after 2:20 P. M., and then was on Malaucourt instead of Jallaucourt.[31]

Meanwhile, however, it developed that not all of the German forces were going to be dissuaded so easily. At 8:35 machine gun and rifle fire in the sector of Company L's right platoon announced that an attack was coming directly from the front. Some enemy infantrymen got into the woods, and Capt. Greenlief committed his support platoon to counterattack. But immediately it appeared that this would not be sufficient to stand off the attack, and Major Wood ordered one platoon from Company I to go to the assistance of "L." Half an hour later a small column of enemy infantry began to ascend the road toward the Battalion OP, and then to turn into the woods toward Company L's position; but a quick warning brought a Browning Automatic Rifle and some M-1 rifles into action, and the whole group was destroyed. At 10:20 the company had nine prisoners and at 2:30 P. M. there were six more; the attack had been contained.[32]

That evening Major Wood returned from a regimental meeting to announce that the Third Army expected to remain on the defensive at least until October 15th, and probably later. Positions were to be improved and well dug-in with good fields of fire; all possible ammunition was to be dumped on the position; overcoats were to be issued to all men.[33]

The Major also had a division order which had some unique features: it opened with the categorical statement, "Enemy will attack from Fresnes at 0500 into woods..." The General proposed to meet it with an attack of his own. There was to be a 100 per cent alert in the division at 4:30 A. M. The 137th Infantry was to attack at 5:00 to regain the edge of the woods which it had lost during the day's fighting, and a battalion of the 320th Infantry was to attack on a narrow front to meet the enemy, and then was to hold Hill 282 south of Fresnes.[34]

The attack came all right, though it was a little late; but so too was the 320th Infantry late with its attack. The Germans arrived first on Hill 282, and, on directions from Company K, Lt. Hunt called for artillery on them. But the enemy succeeded in making a penetration through the left company of the 137th, and Lt. Campbell sent his support platoon of Company K to protect the right flank and to attempt to re-establish contact. One patrol which was trying to re-establish this contact ran into a group of about 20 Germans who were questioning 5 American prisoners. Fighter-bombers arrived for an effective bombing and strafing of Malaucourt and vicinity—there was a direct hit on an 88 mm gun there—and on Fresnes. Activity continued both to the left and to the right, but the Third Battalion escaped any direct attack that afternoon.[35]

But this fortune was not of long duration, for a heavy shelling of Company L at 4:40 A. M., September 30th, heralded another attack. At 5 o'clock enemy infantry hit the center of Company L. Machine guns and rifles opened fire along a 400-yard front; men of Lt. Payne's antitank platoon joined the line and

31. ibid., pp. 50, 53.
32. ibid., pp. 50-51.
33. ibid., p. 55.
34. ibid., p. 58.
35. ibid., pp. 61-66.

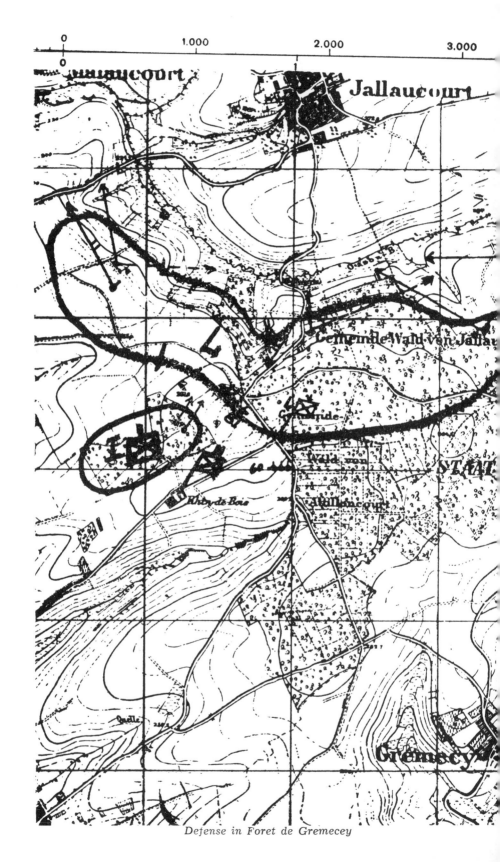

Defense in Foret de Gremecey

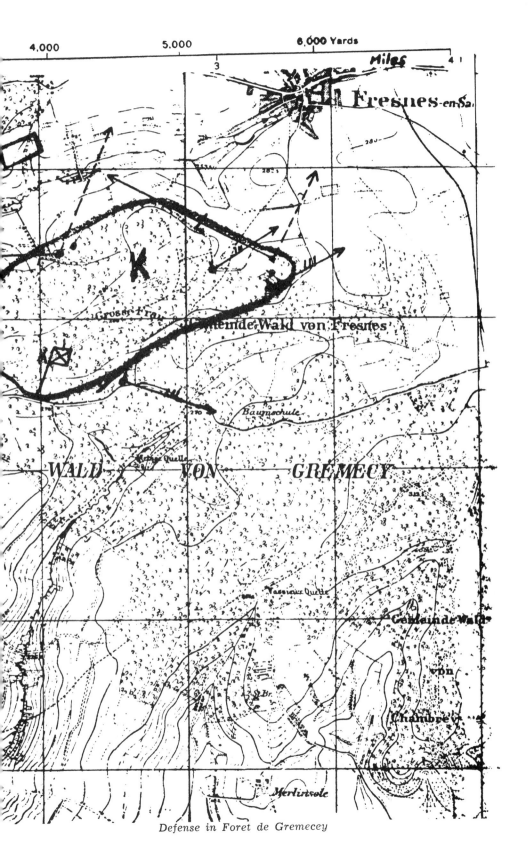

Defense in Foret de Gremecey

began firing antitank rockets; artillery and mortar concentrations fell into the ravine in front of the woods with deadly effect. But the enemy got into the woods and overran some of the "L" Company forward positions. At 6:15 Captain Greenlief reported that anti-personnel mines in the woods had killed and wounded a great number of Germans, but large numbers of others were still coming. A sergeant from the company hailed a Company I motor patrol— a patrol which had been established to maintain contact between the Battalion CP and the CP of the neighboring battalion on the right—and said that they were going to need reinforcements. By 6:45 Major Wood had decided to commit his reserve Company. Fifteen minutes later Company A—the regimental reserve—arrived to assist the Third Battalion.[36]

Lt. William Chavet led the men of Company I up a deep draw which ran along the east side of the Farme Rhin de Bois toward "L" Company's area. At 8:10 he arrived at the "L" Company command post, and at 8:36 the reserve company was in contact with the enemy. Almost at once Company I knocked out a machine gun. At 9:50 sixteen prisoners had been taken, and at 11 o'clock there were 14 more. When men of Company I reached the Battalion OP they found enemy groups withdrawing toward Jallaucourt; they watched an enemy ambulance come down the road and pick up wounded. It looked as though the attack had been stopped.[37]

It was a misleading appearance, for other groups of enemy came in to attack Company L's command post. They had penetrated all the way to "Three Corners," a road junction at the rear edge of the woods in the "L" company area—and here was located a section of Company M's 81 mm mortars. With the sudden approach of the enemy the mortar crews had abandoned their guns and joined Company L in its defense. Corporal Homer Gettler of Indiana and Corporal Paul E. Faulconer of Texas, mortar gunners for the section, were feeling rather helpless in this situation inasmuch as they were armed only with pistols. Then they remembered that they had left a considerable amount of ammunition with their mortars, and those weapons still were in firing condition. Should the enemy seize them he might turn them against the Battalion to further his attack. As soon as they had determined the main direction of attack of the enemy forces, they hurried back to the mortars—they must fire that ammunition before the enemy seized it. Just as they arrived at the position enemy fire killed Corporal Gettler. But Faulconer determined to carry out their pre-arranged plan alone—even in the face of that fire. Quickly he aimed the mortar, and then in rapid succession fired all the remaining shells. Not only did he keep the ammunition from falling into German hands, but he broke up other groups which were trying to reach the Battalion position.[38]

Meanwhile men of Company L were having a desperate fight to save their command post. Major Wood had gone to Company L after noon, and now he found himself with the small group almost surrounded. The company's 60 mm mortars kept up a steady fire, shooting at very close range from positions in the field just outside the woods from the CP (Greenlief credited the mortars with saving this particular situation). Farther out, artillery kept up its fire to prevent the arrival of reinforcements.[39] One of the defenders of the Company CP was Staff Sergeant Albert Grobe. He saw four enemy riflemen ap-

36. **ibid.**, pp. 67-68.
37. **ibid.**, pp. 68-69.
38. 35th Div., General Orders, No. 43, 1 Nov. 1944.
39. 3rd Bn. Journal, I, 70-71.

proaching. In the first exchange of fire his trigger-finger was cut off. Nevertheless he stood his ground and kept up his rifle fire until all four of the assailants were killed. Then he would not permit medical attention until after he had picked up the weapons of the dead Germans to prevent their possible use by any other infiltrating troops.[40]

This time Company K, as well, was feeling some of the effects of the attack. Again it was a "battle of the CP," for German soldiers who had penetrated Company L's position had continued laterally through the woods, and they reached the Company K command post without even attracting the attention of the front-line platoons. Lt. Campbell thought that he might have to have some help in this fight, and Major Carroll, regimental S-3, tried to get a company from the 320th Inf. (from the battalion in division reserve) to assist; however, assistance appears not to have been immediately available. In any case, the attackers were pressing for a decision.[41] Lt. Edward Kennedy of Philadelphia, executive officer of the company, quickly organized his few headquarters men for the defense; he manned a machine gun mounted on a jeep. The fire power was enough to force a withdrawal, and then Kennedy had the jeep driver advance down the forest road while he continued firing. A sudden burst from an enemy antitank rocket (or possibly a machine gun) fired the gasoline tank and demolished the jeep and seriously wounded Kennedy; but the command post had been saved.[42]

There was one element to assist Company K during this critical time: the supporting regimental antitank platoon on the right flank. The enemy was making another attack against the 320th Infantry, and was threatening the right flank of Company K even while its command post was being attacked from the left. When a machine gun opened fire on the antitank guns, Lt. Lyle Reishus, platoon leader, made his way forward and destroyed its crew with two hand grenades. Then he discovered a group of about 30 enemy infantrymen approaching Company K's exposed right flank. He hurried back to his platoon to organize a defensive line to protect the right-rear of Company K and his own guns and equipment.[43]

The situation was under control at Company K at 2:30 P. M., and then Company A moved forward to join Company I in the counterattack which sought to restore Company L's line. This turned out to be a bitter, difficult fight through woods. Prisoners continued to come in, but the attacking companies were taking casualties too. Lt. Humm, commanding Company A, was wounded, and soon that company had 16 wounded men at the aid station, while "I" had 11. Thirteen wounded Germans were receiving medical treatment. Heavy artillery fire suggested that another "battle of the CP"—the Battalion command post—was imminent; but soon the counterattacks had been able to ease conditions at Company L and the situation was stabilized.[44]

Repeated attacks already had weakened the position of the 137th Infantry on the right, and now the 134th had been seriously threatened. The corps commander ordered a withdrawal to a new position behind the Seille river. A covering force of one platoon in each battalion was to remain to cover critical roads and routes of withdrawal, and to carry on a maximum of di-

40. 35th Div., General Orders, No. 50, 4 Nov. 1944.
41. 3rd Bn., Journal, I, 70-71.
42. 35th Div., General Orders, No. 47, 25 Oct. 1944.
43. ibid.
44. 3rd Bn. Journal, I, 71-72.

versionary activity to deceive the enemy. The Third Battalion was to begin movement to the rear at 11:00 P. M., and the covering force was to come out at 3:00 A. M. In the new position, Third Battalion was to be in regimental reserve. However, just as the S-3 and his party were leaving to reconnoiter the new area, he received word at regimental headquarters that the withdrawal order had been cancelled—by order of General Patton. (The Third Army commander, on hearing of the situation, was reported to have said, "Withdraw hell, we'll attack!") At 11:20 the commander of CCA, 6th Armored Division, reported to regimental headquarters with his plan of attack.[45]

Already the keeper of the Battalion Journal had noted:

"2230—Tanks start moving into assembly area near CP. Thank God!" [46]

With enthusiasm and belligerancy, leaders of the three task forces assembled their unit commanders in the Third Battalion CP and issued orders and coordinated plans.

Guides had to be called in who would show the attacking tankmen the location of mine fields; dispositions of the Battalion were plotted on their maps; artillery was coordinated.[47]

The armor "took off" at 6:15 A. M. in its local attack to break up the enemy concentrations.[48] Sweeping around the west end of the forest, they attacked across the front through Jallaucourt, La Juree Woods, and Fresnes.

The persistent Germans too had been planning another attack—about 150 infantry came toward Company K's right flank, but some well-adjusted artillery fire quickly broke it up. The attack of the 6th Armored was as effective as that of the Germans was futile. By 8:45 there were 20 prisoners in the Battalion cage, and by evening the number rose to 100—the result of clearing out the woods in the Company L and K areas, and of groups sent back by the armored forces. This permitted a reorganization in the defensive position. Company A returned to regimental reserve, and Company I returned to its former reserve position, but left one platoon for the close support of Company L. Company L's position was further strengthened when its frontage was shortened as a platoon of Company B took over the sector of its left platoon. Another outpost—a squad of Company I and an artillery observer—was established on the ridge in front of Jallaucourt.[49]

Hon, the Chinese orderly-cook to the Battalion staff, celebrated the victory by serving up a dinner of lamb chops—the artillery barrages of the previous day had included a direct hit on a sheep pen in the vicinity of the command post! (Hon is alleged to have added vegetables to his larder under the cover of enemy artillery; it is said that when a barrage would drive the civilians to the cellars, Hon would run out to the garden with a market basket.)[50]

The vigorous, positive action of the counterattack by the 6th Armored succeeded in discouraging further plans toward reconquest on the part of the Germans in the area. From that time the Foret de Gremecey never was in real danger.

Not that German activity ceased, but it seemed to assume a design for the defensive rather than for any determined attacks. During the next two weeks there was almost continuous artillery firing, work toward improvement

45. 134th Inf., S-3 Journal, 30 Sept. 1944; 3rd Bn. S-3 Notebook, II. See Patton, op. cit. p. 145.
46. 3rd Bn. Journal, I, 73.
47. ibid., pp. 73-74.
48. ibid.,p. 74.
49. ibid., pp. 75-78; 134th Inf., S-3 Journal, 1 Oct. 1944.
50. J. Huston, to N. F. Huston, 7 Oct. 1944.

of positions, and patrols. In addition to fire on observed targets—or on specific areas where activity was heard—there were nightly, and sometimes daily TOT's on such favorite targets as Jallaucourt, Fresnes, and La Juree woods by corps and division artillery, and Captain Jack Hunt, artillery liaison officer, had a busy time trying to fill all requests for fire. Nor was the artillery alone in this pattern of destruction, for there were frequent air strikes—usually by P-47 "Thunderbolt" fighter-bombers—and Company M's 81 mm mortars, as well as some 4.2 inch chemical mortars, joined in to the extent that their ammunition ration would permit. In improving the defenses, men of the 60th Engineer Battalion worked during the night not only to restore the mines in the area of the penetration, but, at the direction of the company commanders, to extend concertinas of barbed wire along most of the front, and to fill gaps between strongpoints with antipersonnel mines and trip flares. Lt. Charles Hall and his Ammunition and Pioneer Platoon contributed to this effort by such activities as clearing an area in the woods and helping dig emplacements for a section of 81 mm mortars in rear of Company K, and in planting a series of electricially-wired charges and clusters of mortar shells in the draw in front of Company L which could be discharged on the approach of the enemy by contacting the wires. In addition, Hall went to the companies to conduct instruction in the use of the flame-thrower. Toward stability of communications, the communication platoon laid heavy German cable to the companies for telephone lines. Nearly every night two patrols—usually led by officers—went out to make reconnaissance near the enemy positions. Sometimes these patrols would be coordinated with the artillery—first to determine the target, and then to determine the results.[51] An entry in the Battalion Journal for October 7th at 0005 (12:05 A. M.) may have been a more or less typical patrol report:

Lt. James patrol — passed Co. L outpost at 2140 going along road toward JALLAUCOURT. Moved up hill to sharp bend in road, remained about 10 minutes— heard motor vehicles, sounded as though they were entering JALLAUCOURT from the east (rd north of town)—heard 2 horses and wagons in vicinity JALLAUCOURT. Moved on up over crest of hill—from here could hear enemy digging and talking loudly to front. Waited for WP shells at 2330 [which had been pre-arranged with Company M in order to give some illumination] which landed long—in the town and in the woods. (Started fire in house.) Talking stopped. Patrol waited till 2315, heard more digging; fired 9 rds 60 mm mortar—could hear no further activity. Moved about 150 yards to right along fence.—Observed gun flashes in rear of town between church steeple and water tower—could hear gun report very distinctly and then shell burst in vicinity of B Co. woods. Returned past L Co. outpost at 2345.[52]

On October 8th the other battalions of the regiment, while the Third remained in its position, together with an attached battalion of the 137th Infantry, and again with elements of the 6th Armored Division, launched an attack to gain more favorable defensive ground around Fossieux and Malaucourt. This attack resulted in another bag of several hundred prisoners, and doubtless contributed to the continuing stability of the situation.[53] That the Germans were contemplating a stable situation was indicated when a captured prisoner (in "K" Company's area) said that a group of his comrades of the 1125th Infantry Regiment were building cabins in La Juree woods with the intention of remaining there all winter.[54]

During those days of defensive warfare in France, it was World's Series

51. 3rd Bn. Journal, I, 79-145.
52. ibid., p. 117.
53. ibid., pp. 119-125.
54. ibid., p. 145.

time in the United States, and the more attractive thrills of sport gained sway as broadcasts of the Cardinals-Browns baseball games—it was night in France—were received over a German radio at the communications platoon and "piped" down to the companies over the field telephone system. Companies relayed the broadcasts down to platoons and outposts over their extensive network of sound power telephones.[54a]

In times of relative quiet, rumors had an opportunity to fly at an even greater pace than ever. Rumors sometimes can be a serious threat to morale, but in the Third Battalion they usually were recognized for what they were and contributed rather to a humorous atmosphere. In the operations section there was put up in a prominent place on the wall a "Rumor Map." Here were recorded, with appropriate symbols and arrows, the choicest bits of gossip—with names of "contributors." Latest was one which had come from the battalion clerk on "good authority." He had heard it from a friend in the personnel section at division rear echelon who had heard it from a clerk who heard it from General Eisenhower's or General Patton's chauffeur during a visit of those officers. The 35th Division was to be shifted to the north where the big attack was building—leave the Third Army and probably join the Ninth.

Other activities during the period included the adjustment of 81 mm mortar fire by an artillery observer in a liaison plane with a 300 radio, shower details to Nancy, the marking of soldier ballots for the presidential election, pay day. The enemy continued to move vehicles—tanks, trucks, wagons—about during the night, and reports of long columns moving toward the general vicinity suggested the reinforcement of the enemy troops. Sporadic artillery came into the Battalion area, and from time to time the bursting shells would take a toll of dead and wounded among the men of the Third Battalion.[55]

The 2nd Battalion, 137th Infantry relieved the Third Battalion on October 16th as the division carried out a program of rotating the units. In the exchange the Third Battalion moved to the town of Gremecey—about three kilometers to the southeast of the Farme Rhin de Bois—where it became the division's active reserve in the 320th area. (The remainder of the regiment moved back across the Seille River.) One company—rotated among the companies, beginning with "I"—occupied positions on the ridge to the east of Gremecey to fill a gap and provide depth for the 320th Infantry's defense. Counterattack plans were prepared—some for use with tanks of the 737th Tank Battalion—and the battalion and company commanders reconnoitered all the routes involved. At Gremecey there was a greater opportunity for recreation—motion pictures and Red Cross clubmobile—as well as for training. There were orientation classes, an ordinance inspection, target practice with the bazookas. Capt. Hunt conducted some classes for company officers in artillery fire adjustment technique so that they would be prepared better to adjust fire on important targets when no artillery forward observer was available. The Battalion prepared for a possible four-day period of virtual isolation as aircraft set out to bomb the dam on the Seille river near Dieuze on October 20th, and supplies of ammunition and rations were brought in to last that long. It had been estimated that the stream would rise seven feet in the Pettoncourt area, but though it did not reach that height, it did become a formidable obstacle.[56]

54a. An entry in the Bn. Journal for October 5th:
"2235—The St. Louis Cards win 3-2 in 11th inning, 2 game world Series,"—I, 112.
55. ibid., pp. 79-145.
56. ibid., pp. 146-169.

Another exchange brought the 1st Battalion, 320th Infantry, to Gremecey on October 24th and the Third Battalion took up new positions on the line with Company I in the Bois de Chambrey—a southerly extension of the eastern part of the Foret de Gremecey—Company K in the town of Chambrey—in the broad, open, valley—and Company L on the right on the high ground near Moncel. A section of heavy machine guns went with Companies I and K, and a platoon with Company L. A section of 81 mm mortars was in direct support of each company, and the antitank guns went to Chambrey in the center.[57]

Some additions to the Battalion staff had been made during this period. Lt. Shields had joined the staff as S-2 until Lt. Michael Hanna arrived from the 1st Battalion to take over that assignment. Shields remained temporarily to assist the S-3. Then Capt. Ernest Mangnuson came to the Battalion, and he was retained at headquarters to assist the S-1 with Headquarters Company. Major Wood was promoted to lieutenant colonel.

In the new position activities followed much the same pattern as in the other areas. Patrolling was refined to an extent, however. Under supervision of the intelligence section, a select group of men was organized and equipped to make the night forays into enemy territory. These men were withdrawn from the line to quarters in a house in Pettoncourt. Here their days would be spent in resting and in receiving instruction for their night's mission. This mission might be to capture an enemy soldier and bring him in for interrogation, or it might be to test the enemy strength to the front in anticipation of future attacks which undoubtedly would come before very long. The S-2 and the artillery liaison officer would coordinate their plans to provide for an artillery barrage—or a succession of them—at a given time. The patrol would go out toward its destination, and then await the artillery. It would move quickly after the barrage to accomplish its mission and return.[58]

Close liaison was maintained with the 104th Infantry of the 26th ("Yankee") Division on the right in this sector. There were local adjustments in the company areas, and then Company L was brought back to Pettoncourt and motorized to form a mobile reserve. Passes continued for officers and men to Nancy, and then passes for a fortunate few became available for Paris. Training and planning continued for a resumption of the offensive at which General Patton hinted in his speech to the officers of the regiment on November 3rd. On the night of 7-8 November the Third Battalion re-assembled at Pettoncourt in preparation for that attack.[59]

Even during two months which had been relatively quiet, the Battalion's casualties amounted to over 325, for the fighting at Agincourt and Pain de Sucre, the enemy attacks in Foret de Gremecey, and the attrition of artillery fire had contributed to a considerable total.[60] Now the casualty rate could be expected to rise, for again the Battalion would be in the attack.

57.　Ibid., pp. 171, 177.
58.　Michael Hanna to the author, June 24, 1946.
59.　3rd Bn. Journal, II, 19-57.
60.　134th Inf., Battle Casualty Report.

PART THREE—LORRAINE TO THE SAARLAND
★ ★ ★
CHAPTER XII
★ ★ ★
"BLUE MONDAY" ON RED HILL

After lying dormant for some six weeks on the defensive, the whole Third Army front broke out into an offensive on November 8th aimed at the Saar.[1] That this happened to be the day after the presidential election in the United States may or may not have been coincidental, but there had been a feeling among some in the Battalion for weeks that the approaching election was holding up the progress of the war.[2] However that may have been, the Third Army's attack presaged a general mid-November offensive involving all the Allied Armies in the West. General Eisenhower's objectives were the Ruhr and the Saar, for he felt confident that the enemy would be compelled to concentrate most of his available resources in defense of those essential areas.[3]

The Regiment remained in division reserve as the 137th and 320th Regiments led off the attack at dawn behind a 70-minute artillery preparation,[4] but as the Third Battalion assembled to be in position to move on short notice,[5] its men knew that their turn would not be long in coming. Even as the other regiments were fighting through their initial objectives—Jallacourt, Malaucourt, Fresnes—orders came on the following day for the Third Battalion to move out at 1 o'clock. In a few hours the Battalion would be on its march through Lorraine toward the Saar.[6]

Most of the members of the Battalion had been in elementary or high school back in 1935 when the people of the Saar had voted to rejoin Germany after a fifteen-year separation under League of Nations supervision as the result of a compromise provision in the Treaty of Versailles. Lying where the low hills of the German Rhineland on the north and east merge into the plateau of Lorraine on the south and west, the Saar Basin was regarded of immense strategic value both for France and for Germany, for offense or defense. A main natural pathway between the two countries, the region was important not only for its economic value in rich veins of coal and iron, steel, glass, paper, and pottery manufacture, but also for its network of roads and railways.[7] But Lorraine, of course was important too, and for largely the same reasons. Now men of the Third Battalion were setting out to tramp across ground which had borne the steps of soldiers' feet of armies practically all through European history. Now names which had the familiar, but far off ring of the class room or text book in historical settings had acquired a realness in hills and ground and trees.

1. **The Stars and Stripes** (London), Nov. 9, 1945, p. 1.
2. J. A. Huston, to N. F. Huston, Oct. 7, 1944. Chances for President Roosevelt's re-election did seem to be diminishing as the war continued a highly favorable turn. A poll by the American Institute of Public Opinion on April 23 had shown that of those questioned, 55% said that they would vote for Roosevelt were the war still going on, but 58% indicated that they would vote for Dewey if the war had ended by election day.—**The Public Opinion Quarterly**, VIII, (Summer, 1944) p. 278.
3. General Marshall's Report, p. 42.
4. 35th Division, **Attack!** p. 17.
5. 3rd Battalion Journal, II, 57.
6. 3rd Battalion Journal, II, 61.
7. Sidney B. Fay, "The Fate of the Saar," **Current History**, XLI (Jan. 1935) p. 399.

With the 2nd Battalion on its left,[8] the Third was to seize a wooded hill called Bois de Marchande northeast of Chambrey and push on to the north.[9] The plan called for Company L to lead the attack out of Chambrey. From its positions in the Bois de Chambrey Company I was able to give supporting fire; then as "L" neared its objective, "I" advanced east across the narrow valley to join "L" and "K" in the next woods. The Battalion met no opposition as it advanced under its own fire to the edge of the woods; anti personnel mines were there, however, to present some passive resistance, and one of those vicious mechanisms caused the only casualties when a Company I man stepped upon one.[10]

After a night in the woods above Coutures (one mile west of Chateau Salins), during which it was impossible to bring up jeeps with supplies, the Battalion moved into the village. The advance of other units on the left then permitted the opening of a road, and the men were able to pick up ammunition and K rations as they moved through the town toward the Foret de Chateau Salins. Shortly after noon, the Battalion, moving into a reserve position, climbed the high ridge and entered the Foret de Chateau Salins where it made contact with rear elements of the 2nd Battalion. Thus it had the protection of a friendly battalion to its front as it started through the seven-kilometer long woods; but this if anything only made worse the effect of the dreaded artillery bursts among the trees—even in reserve the Battalion was taking its casualties. As evening approached the Battalion shifted slightly to the left and made an attack of its own to come up abreast of the 2nd.[11]

Armistice Day found the 35th Division in almost the very same place where it had been on the first Armistice Day 26 years earlier.[12] (The 134th however, was not a part of the 35th in World War I). But on this Armistice Day it was just another day for attack. With the weather continuing cloudy, and becoming increasingly colder, the attack, coordinated with the 2nd Battalion on the right, moved off again at 8 o'clock with Companies I and K in assault (I on the right) and L in reserve.[13]

Again there was no opposition as the men began to move, but as they approached a small collection of buildings called Farm Mon Lorois hostile fire served notice that the enemy intended to make a stand. Soon it was found that at least four armored vehicles were supporting the defense.[14] Nevertheless the American infantrymen continued to press the attack. They were up against elements of the 11th Panzer Division.[15]

When machine gun fire and a Mark IV tank threatened to hold up his platoon indefinitely, 2nd Lt. Bartholomew J. Hanusovsky of Connecticut, determined to do something about it. Steadily men of the platoon stole nearer the tank; then, with three of his sergeants, he crept up to within ten feet of the armored vehicle and tossed a grenade into its open turret. Immediately there was a tremendous explosion. The tank was destroyed, but it was at a high price:

8.   134th Inf., After Action Report, Dec. 3, 1944.
9.   3rd Bn. S-3 Notebook I.
10.   3rd Battalion Journal, II, 61; Interview by Capt. Jacob Goldman with S-3, 3rd Battalion, Vellem, Germany, May 27, 1945: 3rd Information and Historical Section, **35th Infantry Division,** Typescript: (Combat Interviews—No. 108—35th Div.—1 Nov. 1944—23 Jan. 45; Historical Records Branch, The Adjutant General's Office, The Pentagon, Washington, D. C.) p. 1.
11.   3rd Bn. Journal, II, 62; 3rd Bn. Interview, p. 1; Cf. Drew Middleton in **The New York Times,** November 11, 1944, p. 4.
12.   **The Hutchison** (Kans.) **Herald,** (AP), Nov. 11, 1944, p. 2.
13.   3rd Bn. Journal, II, 62.
14.   **Ibid.**
15.   Drew Middleton in **The New York Times,** Nov. 12, 1944, p. 1.

the lieutenant and Sgt. Laurie Griffin of North Carolina were killed; Sgt. Albert Antone of Michigan, and William Zais of West Virginia were wounded,[16] not to mention others whose names were not learned at the time. With such a loss it was evident that Company I practically would be without the services of one of its platoons.[17]

However, the assault companies were able to drive the enemy from his positions to their immediate front by about 4 P. M. Darkness comes early in November in that northern latitude (somewhat farther north than St. John's, Newfoundland) and so as soon as the Companies were able to secure their objectives and consolidate their positions, plans were being made for their re-supply. Difficult enough in any case when undertaken in darkness in close proximity to the enemy, the problem of re-supplying became acute with the added factors of wooded, rolling terrain and absence of usable roads.[18]

However, those plans had to be abandoned when an unequivocal order came to renew the attack to capture another hill to the front. In the dark twilight at 6 o'clock, the Battalion jumped off again. It hardly more than got underway before it had run into strong resistance again; but it was not stopped.[19]

That is not to say that there were not some delays. Company K was held up by some effective machine gun fire coming from among the buildings of the Farm Bellevue. Pvt. Walter Werner was up near the front with his bazooka. He discovered that the enemy was lodged in the second story of a house; but he could not get nearer than 150 yards. Nevertheless he got his rocket launcher ready, and moved up as close as he dared; he knew that the tremendous back-flash would give him away as soon as he fired. He took careful aim, and a press of the trigger sent the rocket on its way; it flew true to its mark, right into the window and exploded. Company K resumed its advance—and found two machine guns and three dead Germans beside that second-story window.[20]

Lt. William J. Chavet of Nebraska, who had been commanding Company I, received a painful foot wound, and though he refused to be evacuated until he had his company re-organized,[21] it was without his services during the last phase of its attack. But the company executive officer, Elwood James, stepped in to face the "I Company Commander Jinx," and led the company to its objective.

This did not mean, however, that the day's work was finished. Company K, coming up on the left, had difficulty in making contact with Company I as the inevitable darkness overtook them. This was accomplished only after some firing of signal shots, and directions by radio.

Meanwhile Company L, in reserve, had moved forward some 500 yards to the vicinity of the Farm Bellevue. Col. Wood determined to use it to carry supplies up to the forward companies. During the afternoon a supply point had been established near the position occupied by the Battalion OP. To this area jeeps had come up over unimproved roads and muddy trails to bring ammunition, rations, water, radio batteries, communication wire, dry socks, and bed rolls. From this point it was necessary for men to hand-carry the supplies nearly 1,500 yards over unknown, muddy trails, through the inky

---

16. 35th Div., General Orders, No. 56, Dec. 12, 1944.
17. Michael Hanna to the Author, June 24, 1944.
18. 3rd Bn. Interview, p. 2.
19. 3rd Bn. Journal, II, 62.
20. 35th Div., General Orders, No. 57, Dec. 18, 1944.
21. **ibid.** Chavet arrived at the aid station on a self-styled travois—borne by two German prisoners—Col. Warren C. Wood to the Author, June 26, 1946.

blackness of the night. Again there was difficulty in contact; leaders of the carrying parties could not find the forward companies until there had been another exchange of signal shots (fired at the risk of enemy notice) and radio directions. A machine gun platoon of Company M was pressed into service to assist in the supply distribution. Then it was nearly 4 A. M. before the task of supply and evacuation of all wounded had been completed.[22]

How much damage had been done to the enemy's forces was evident as the Battalion resumed its advance the next morning. Always very particular in removing his dead from the battlefield, the enemy had abandoned numbers of dead and their equipment in order to withdraw before a new attack.[23] Through the cold rain of a bleak November day,[24] the Battalion's column tramped on along the wooded ridge above Gerbecourt and Vaxy, and then, leaving the Foret de Chateau Salins at a point northwest of Vannecourt, continued on over the high, now open, ridge line to a position a kilometer northwest of Dalhain.[25] Up to this point there had been no enemy opposition. Only abandoned defensive works, gun positions, and recent tracks from armored vehicles.[26] In fact there was a complete battery of 150 mm artillery near Dalhain.[27] Now men of the 3rd Battalion knew that they had penetrated deep into the enemy's rear areas; but so were they aware that soon he would be fighting again from another position.

They had warning of this when, as they prepared their defensive positions for the night on the objective, they came under mortar and artillery fire. Other rounds were going into the town of Dalhain where the command post had moved from Gerbecourt.[28]

Beyond those positions of the Battalion, high, dominating, Rougemont—Red Hill—rose. As Col. Wood looked it over he sensed that it was going to be a real obstacle: "a regimental objective," he thought.[29] The breath of winter was in the air as the night closed in.

When the regimental order was issued that night, Red Hill was an objective for the Third Battalion. The weather contributed a new factor when snow fell during the night.[30] It was in complete openness, then, that the dark figures began to move out over the gleaming whiteness of the new snow at 8 o'clock, after an effective ten-minute artillery preparation.[31]

Rougemont, the key terrain feature of the area, stood at a point where the ridgeline, and the highway, turned to a more easterly direction; that is, the Battalion would have to make a slight change in direction to the right at the hill. In setting up the previous evening's defense, Company L had sent one platoon to form an outpost on a knoll to the left of the highway, which was on the ridge southwest of Rougemont. The main positions had been about 800 yards south of the dominating hill. Now as Company L led off the attack, with Company K coming up on its right, the outpost platoon opened fire from its forward position on the left. Inasmuch as that platoon could follow the

22. 3rd Bn. Interview, pp. 2-4.
23. 3rd Bn. Interview, p. 4.
24. 3rd Bn. Journal, II, 62.
25. ibid., cf. Philip Greene in the **Philadelphia Evening Standard** reprinted, **Santa Fe Express,** May 1945, p. 9.
26. 3rd Bn. Interview, p. 4.
27. In addition to the four 150 mm pieces, four 75 mm Antitank guns and an infantry field piece were overrun in the regimental zone during the day.—135th Inf., S-2 Periodic Report, Nov. 13. 1944.
28. 3rd Bn. Journal, II, 62; 3rd Bn. Interview, p. 4.
29. Col. Warren C. Wood to the Author, June 26, 1946.
30. 3rd Bn. Journal, II, 62.

ridge, while the other troops would have to descend to the valley, and then fight up the hill, it must have seemed to the enemy that that would have been the most likely avenue for the main attack. With the assistance of that diversion, then, the remainder of Company L soon made its way across the open valley, and started up Red Hill. At first the resistance was not very great, but soon a few bursts of machine gun fire turned to the direction of the main attack, and then began a heavy and continuous mortar barrage, leaving a close pattern of black pock marks all over the white snow.[32]

Company L's 3rd Platoon was leading the attack on the left. The men were making their way through low brush, over snow covered trails, and on up the face of the hill. Again there were machine gun bursts from concealed positions in that low brush. Now four of them concentrated their fire on the platoon; one of the automatic riflemen, caught in the withering fire, dropped to the snow, dead. Staff Sgt. Eddy Teply of Nebraska, the platoon guide, picked up the automatic rifle and rushed forward to destroy two of the enemy machine guns before he himself fell, seriously wounded.[33]

Company K was having trouble advancing against the small arms and mortar fire on the right. The advance continued, however, in spite of casualties, and Company I gained the crest of the hill. The attack order had called for a continuation of the attack to the northeast once Red Hill had been secured. But the question came up concerning the plans of elements of the 4th Armored Division who were operating to the left of the Battalion zone, and whose vehicles now were coming down the ridgeline highway just to the northeast of the heights of Rougemont. There had been a suggestion that they might leave the ridge road, and take a secondary road to the right to go down into the valley to Achain, objective of the 2nd Battalion. This would mean that the Third Battalion would have to hold up its advance while the armored vehicles moved across the front.

Meanwhile Capt. Greenlief called his platoon leaders forward to a position where they could observe the next objective and began to give his order for continuation of the attack. But this pause in movement did not mean a pause in German artillery. Now it began to rake the hill—the positions just given up by its own forces. A shell burst only feet from the five Company L officers—all were wounded. Capt. Greenlief, though wounded, refused evacuation, and determined to carry on with the assistance of the one officer who had not been in the group—the executive officer.[34]

Technical Sergeant Jacob Sass of Nebraska, platoon sergeant, immediately took over command of his platoon, and Staff Sgt. Frank Nebenfuhr of Washington, finding himself the only noncommissioned officer left in his platoon, reorganized it, and made ready to continue the advance. Men of the Company's weapons platoon were determined to keep sending back fire from their 60 mm mortars. Private First Class Wayne Fleener of Indiana had been wounded, but not seriously enough to force him out of action: he carried his mortar and base plate forward and resumed firing; when his ammunition was exhausted, he returned to carry up more.[35] Meanwhile Pfc. William Hafner of New York was carrying on for his mortar squad—his squad was depleted, and

31. ibid., 134 Inf., Daily Log, IV, Nov. 13.
32. 3rd Bn. Interview, p. 4.
33. 35th Inf. Div., General Orders, No. 56, Dec. 12, 1944.
34. 3rd Bn. Interview, p. 5; 3rd Bn. Journal, II, 62.
35. 35th Inf. Div., General Orders, No. 56, Dec. 12, 1944.

he was wounded in the left hand, but he carried the mortar and base plate forward, and put it back into action.[36]

Casualties were mounting: Company L's total was rising sharply—20, 30, 40; Company K's was above 20, and its men still were facing small arms opposition as they tried to advance along the slope—along the contour—on the right side of the hill. Company I, in reserve behind Company L, had had six or seven men hit by mortar or artillery fire, and so had Company M.[37]

Col. Wood and his command group moved up forward to try to get the advance resumed. Troops from the 137th Infantry made contact on the hill, and it seemed that the enemy's resistance might soon be broken. Col. Wood hurried on, but as his party approached the forward positions of Company L, it came under the direct fire of a German tank: once again—the third time— the battalion command group was the target for a shell burst—the battalion commander, Capt. Earl J. Ruby (heavy weapons company commander), Capt. Jack Hunt (artillery liaison officer), and Sergeant Ambrose, the artillery liaison sergeant, all were wounded; the heavy weapons radio operator was killed.[38]

Within a few minutes Major Heffelfinger had come up the hill from the CP at Bellange to take command of the Battalion.[39] The principal test for a good executive officer probably was not in his ability to perform the duties normally pertaining to that position, but in his ability to step in at a moment's notice and assume command of the battalion. Now, with Col. Wood being evacuated through the aid station, the major was meeting that test.

As he made his way forward, he could have followed the route of the Battalion by the dead—both its own and the enemy's—left in its wake.[40] He could have seen the crimson blood of the lately wounded mingling with the whiteness of the snow, and snow blackened and ugly from the bursts of shells and the tramping of feet. Rougemont had indeed become Red Hill—speckled with blood drops on the snow.

When Major Heffelfinger arrived on the hill it appeared that the resistance had about been broken. Twenty-five prisoners were taken, and the Battalion was ready to move again. (The 4th Armored Division tanks had not, after all, gone across the front to Achain, but remained waiting up on the main highway). An order came from regiment to advance to the east, and capture the village of Rode. Doubtless the possibility of finding shelter for the night would have appealed to members of the Third Battalion, but occupation of Rode would have meant virtual isolation of the Battalion with no way of getting in supplies. For Rode lay nearly two kilometers directly east of Achain where the 2nd Battalion was having a very difficult time of its own, and not even a jeep could get to Rode without using the road through Achain, and the hour already was growing late. The order was modified, therefore, and the Battalion moved without opposition another thousand yards to occupy the high ground north of Achain. Control of this commanding ground would discourage any re-inforcement of enemy forces in Achain, and would permit closer coordination for a renewal of the attack.[41]

As darkness fell, the men of the Third Battalion prepared their positions,

36. 35th Inf. Div., General Orders, No. 57, Dec. 18, 1944.
37. 134th Inf., Battle Casualty Report.
38. 3rd Bn. Journal, II, 62; Col. Wood to the Author, June 26, 1944; Hanna to the Author, June 24, 1944; 3rd Bn. Interview, p. 5.
39. 3rd Bn. Journal II, 62.
40. Hanna, loc. cit.
41. 3rd Bn. Journal, II, 62; 3rd Bn. Interview, p. 6.

and as they tried to relax in their water-soaked foxholes, they could look with some longing on the warm fires of burning buildings in Achain just below them. Though widely hailed as the achievement of a "one-man Army,"[42] the capture of Achain was a bitter struggle for the 2nd Battalion; at 10 P. M. that battalion occupied one-third of town, and it continued its fight through the night, finally completing the capture at a cost of 106 casualties.[43]

Again a long hand-carry was necessary to get supplies from the road at a point west of Achain up to the positions on the high ground. A hot meal was out of the question, but it was possible to plan on hot coffee for breakfast.[44]

Once more nightfall gave a brief respite from a daily ordeal which seemed to have no end for a man except that he could expect to become a casualty sooner or later. Already weakened by days of living in bad weather, and some sharp fighting, the Battalion had launched an attack, without benefit of strong diversionary action by other units, against an objective which should have been too much for it. The men, aware of the strong position which Rougemont presented, had entered into the attack with a determination which had given results.[45]

Not since "Bloody Sunday" had the Battalion lost so heavily. The weather claimed a toll of 23—even the one officer of Company L who had not been hit finally had to give up when his swollen feet would no longer function. But bullets and shell fragments claimed the important numbers: Company L's total battle casualties rose to 59, K's to 29; I, 9; M 7, and Headquarters 1. This meant that the Battalion had lost a total of six officers and 114 men, not including the number who were slightly wounded but not evacuated.[46]

It was with some reason, then, that members of the Third Battalion remembered November 13th as "Blue Monday."[47]

42. Staff Sergeant Junior Spurrier of Bluefield, West Virginia, a Company C squad leader, won the Congressional Medal of Honor for his exploits involving successive use of Garand rifle, Browning automatic rifle, bazookas, and grenades to kill 25 Germans, and capture 20 others—35th Inf. Div., **Attack!** pp. 18-20; Joseph Driscoll in the **New York Herald Tribune**, Nov. 26, 1944; War Dept., General Orders, No. 18, 15 March 1945.
43. Interview by Capt. Jacob Goldman with Lt. Col. Frederick C. Roecker (2nd Bn. commander), Vellern, Germany, May 27, 1945 (3d Information and Historical Service. Combat Interviews, No. 103—35th Div.—1 Nov. 44—23 Jan. 45) p. 4.
44. 3rd Bn. Interview, p. 6.
45. Col. Wood, **loc. cit.**
46. 134th Inf., Battle Casualty Report.
47. 3rd Bn. Interview, p. 6; 3rd Bn. Journal, II, 62.

CHAPTER XIII

★ ★ ★

CAPTURE OF MORHANGE

★ ★ ★

The Battalion's fighting strength down to a fraction of normal, the companies and Battalion headquarters made quick adjustments at reorganization. When Major Heffelfinger took command of the Battalion, Capt. Bruce took his place as executive, and Capt. Magnunson of Minnesota, who recently had joined the Battalion from the 90th Division, assumed the duties of S-1 (adjutant). Lt. Erickson took command of Company M.[1]

The Battalion's mission now was to seize Lapotence, a key hill just northwest of Morhange, preparatory to a regimental assault against the town[2]—the site of the first important battle between the French and Germans in World War I.[3] However, there was some delay in the general advance while the other battalions worked to clear their own local objectives. From their positions on the high ground above Achain, members of the Third Battalion could see plainly a German tank setting at a tilt beside a small monument on the hill which was to be their ultimate objective. The enemy monster was nearly two thousand yards away, and it was not clear whether or not it was active. The shell burst and quick report of a direct-fire gun drew attention to another tank some distance—perhaps a thousand yards—to the right. A tank destroyer rumbled out to the edge of Achain to fire a couple of rounds in return—but those were his last: the tank up by the monument suddenly came to life and sent the very first round through the destroyer—the "destroyer" was destroyed.[4]

But the artillery liaison officer with the Third Battalion (Lt. Jefferan) was able to bring some fire from a supporting eight-inch gun into the picture. So accurate that it would respond to a correction of ten yards, the gun sent round after round onto the hill, each time enveloping the hostile tank in a huge sheet of flame and pillars of smoke, and although no direct hit on the tank itself was observed, neither were any more flashes from its hated direct fire gun.[5]

It was not until 3 o'clock that the Battalion moved out for Lapotence hill behind a thorough artillery and mortar preparation which concluded with smoke shells to blind the enemy's observation from the hill. Company L, bayonets fixed, advanced across the narrow, shallow valley with a singular demonstration of marching fire: with every weapon firing at places likely to conceal enemy, the soldiers advanced, not by rushes in small groups, but walking upright steadily to their goal.[6] Now the men of the Third Battalion began again the tedious process of digging in the cold, wet ground. Though they had cleared the crest of the hill, actually they were some 400 yards short of a

1. Hanna to the Author, June 24, 1946.
2. 3rd Bn. Journal, II, 63; 3rd Bn. Interview, p. 6.
3. Joseph Driscoll in the **New York Herald Tribune**, Nov. 14, 1944, p. 2. Morhange had been the objective of a French Corps in its ill fated offensive in Aug. 1914—John Buchan, **A History of the Great War** (N. Y. et. 1922) I, 141-2.
4. Hanna, loc. cit.
5. ibid.
6. 3rd Bn. Interview, p. 6. Many units, fearful lest the sight of bayonets would arouse a more desperate reaction on the part of the enemy, would not carry fixed bayonets; not so Company L under Capt. Greenlief—they felt rather it would instill fear into the enemy soldier to the point of making him break, and so give up.

position where they could control the approaches to Morhange.[7]

Battle casualties during the day had been light, but the second enemy—the weather—had not relented. And "the terrain was nowhere kind to a campaign out of season."[8] Six days of continous attack, through woods, over hills covered with mud and snow, with the temperature near the freezing point, and precipitation varying successively from "showers" to "snow, sleet, rain"[9] could hardly fail to have a result in the physical condition of the men who were so exposed. And so, though, "casualties were light," there were "many SIA's (seriously injured in action) due to immersion foot."[10]

By whatever name it was called, foot trouble was weakening the Battalion as definitely as the enemy's mortars. In the usual cases of trench foot which were developing, there would, first of all, be a numbness, so that the man would feel as though he were "walking on blocks of wood." Then there would be a burning, or stinging pain in the feet or toes, and then an aching of the ankles or the bottoms of the feet. Further use of the foot would lead to increased swelling—frequently when a soldier would remove his shoes to change socks he would find it impossible to get the shoes back on again. The skin would be pale and cold; blisters and blobs would develop. And then, too frequently, the skin would turn dark and the dreaded rot of gangrene set in to require an amputation.[11]

It was easy to prescribe corrective measures: keep the feet dry; put on dry socks daily; stay out of water as much as possible; exercise the feet—even by wriggling the toes when halted; wear the right footgear.[12] But it was difficult to expect men in foxholes to take the normal precautions to prevent trench foot and frost bite.[13]

Of the suggestions offered, probably the last—to wear the right footgear—was the key to the whole situation, and it was the one least under the soldier's personal control. For some ungiven reason, an order had come down to the Battalion prior to the initial attack that no overshoes were to be worn in this operation. Many men, feeling the overshoes too cumbersome, did not like to wear them anyway, but some did wear them and found protection. Later the order was eased, and a few weeks later there were complaints that replacements were arriving not equipped with overshoes.[14] But the irony of the situation was that shoepacs, which had been available for maneuvers in West Virginia, and had proved their value in protecting the feet from cold and dampness, were not now available in combat.

By this time the attrition of the enemy and the weather had reduced the fighting strength of the Battalion to something like 120 men[15]—considerably less than the "normal" strength of a company. (Fortunately, about 50 replacements arrived that evening.)[16] This did not mean, however, that the objective or zone of action was reduced to company size. On the contrary, it now de-

    7.   ibid., p. 7.
    8.   R.C.K. Ensor, **A Miniature History of the War** (3rd Ed., London, 1945) p. 88.
    9.   3rd Bn. Journal, II, 62.
   10.   ibid.
   11.   "How to Avoid Trench Foot," **The Infantry Journal** LVI (Jan. 1945) 32.
   12.   ibid.
   13.   Theoretically, trench foot could be avoided, but not frost bite; hence the Purple Heart was awarded for the latter, but not the former.—Transcript of Interview, Lt. Col. Donald M. Ashlock, G-1, 35th Division, to 1st Lt. William J. Dunkerley and T/Sgt. C. J. Angulo, Hq. III U. S. Corps, Jan. 12, 1945) 3d Information and Historical Service, Combat Interviews, No. 108—35th Div.—1 Nov. 44—23 Jan. 45) p. 6.
   14.   ibid.
   15.   3rd Bn. Journal, II, 63.
   16.   ibid.

veloped that the Third was to coordinate with the 2nd Battalion to capture the key garrison and supply depot of Morhange.[17]

The original regimental plan had called for the 2nd Battalion to cross behind the 1st, then operating on its right, and occupy the heights commanding the approaches to Morhange on the south; then, with the Third commanding the high ground on the north, the 1st would, with the assistance of supporting fire from the other battalions, move in to clean out the city. However, when the 1st became involved in preliminary encounters, the plan was changed: the Third would move on up to the commanding ground just beyond its position, and pause while the 2nd advanced east beyond the village of Rode—in the valley leading into Morhange; then both battalions would enter the city, the 2nd on the right of the main street, and the Third on the left.[18]

The Battalion began moving at 8 A. M. to cover the 400 yards to get into position at the approaches to Morhange. It was another attack over snow, and though there were more men hurt and some delay when vicious, rapid-firing 20 mm shells began bursting about the advancing troops, they soon had consolidated on their initial objective, and paused to wait for the main attack. They could see men of the 2nd Battalion advancing up the valley below them, and then commanders of both battalions notified the regimental operations officer that they were prepared to attack on schedule.[19]

This schedule called for a thirty-minute artillery preparation to begin at 9 o'clock—15 minutes of smoke, and 15 minutes of high explosive, and then the infantry attack. This was modified to eliminate the smoke, but there would be a TOT at 9:15, and then anti-personnel fire would continue until the 9:30 attack time.

Members of the Third Battalion were in an excellent position to watch the results of the artillery exhibition. Precisely at 9:15 a roar of guns announced that the TOT was on the way; as the whine of shells approached, the men waited expectantly. But then, suddenly, the whines ended in a deafening blast and smoke and flying fragments in their very midst. They buried their heads in what snow-filled foxholes the Germans had left on the hill, or whatever furrow or fold was at hand. The battalion commander grabbed the SCR 300 to notify the CP what was happening, that they might get word to regiment and to the artillery; the S-3 was calling regiment by field telephone, and the artillery liaison officer was on his radio to contact the artillery fire direction center. Fortunately, it was stopped very soon.[20] Apparently an officer of one of the battalions reinforcing the 161st had made an error of one grid square in his map references.[21]

In spite of the snow on the ground, and the hostile 20 mm fire, and the friendly artillery fire, the Battalion was ready to move on. At this point Lt. Hanna was making his way to the top of the hill with a new officer; he directed him to Major Heffelfinger. Knowing the critical officer situation in Company L, Capt. Bruce had decided to send him on up, even though a battle was in the making.

"Lt. Davis, sir."

"All right, Davis, here is Capt. Greenlief, your company commander."

17. 35th Div., **Attack!** p. 20.
18. 3rd Bn. Interview, p. 6.
19. **ibid.**
20. **ibid.**, p. 7.
21. Hanna to the Author, June 24, 1944.

Greenlief had dropped to an adjoining hole during the shelling.

"Come on, I'll take you to your platoon," he said.

There was a sniper or two at the edge of the city, but by 1045 the Battalion had entered the town,[22] and, coordinating with the 2nd Battalion, began to move through without opposition. Company K, on the right, moved through the block of buildings bordering on the main street, while Company L moved along the slope on the left. Now tanks of the 4th Armored Division were coming up along the highway on the ridge just north of the town—that is to the left, and rear of Company L.

The regimental staff was following the movement closely by radio: at 12:41 the 3rd Battalion reached the church...it was passing the "Adolph Hitler" Cafe...it was passing the "Heinrich Himmler" Cafe.[23] It was found that the German 1127th Regiment had been charged with the defense of Morhange[24] and civilians stated that German troops had withdrawn from the city at 9:30; thus they were in the streets at the very time that the artillery was supposed to have been falling![25]

Before 2 o'clock the Battalion had reached the western edge, and it appeared that its task was finished, when suddenly the air became filled with the crackling of machine gun fire. At first a feeling of almost panic gripped some of the men as they faced the unprecedented volume of fire; actually they could not tell from what direction it came. After a few minutes, some, in spite of the heavy volume and continuous loud successions of reports, could discern the familiar rhythm of American machine guns. Immediately thoughts turned to those tanks which had been coming up. There was no direct communication between the Battalion and the armor, and though regiment was notified, it would take time for a message to get down to halt the withering fire.

Lt. Shields, then with the command group, had been helping to locate a tentative Battalion CP. Sure that it was the tanks causing the trouble, he called for a messenger to accompany him, and ran out amidst the flying bullets. He dashed into a nearby house and came out with a large bed sheet, and waving this prominently, he ran to the tanks. The success of his mission permitted a lessening in high tension throughout the Battalion.[26]

Now the Battalion was to push on out to a railroad about half a mile to the east of Morhange. Major Heffelfinger directed Company L to occupy a settlement called Bellevue on the main highway running to the northeast of the city, while Company K would occupy a group of buildings along the railroad more directly east of the city; Company I would remain in reserve at the eastern edge of Morhange, near the Battalion command post.[27]

Before undertaking his attack, Capt. Greenlief contacted the commander of the tanks, and found that they were to assemble at Bellevue. "Well, I'll just let you capture the place for me," Greenlief said. Doubtless anxious to atone for the unfortunate machine-gunning incident, the tank unit commander told him to stand by. When the withering fire of those machine guns was turned on Bellevue, results were not long in obtaining—surely with a great deal of

22. 134th Inf., Unit Journal, Nov. 15, 1944.
23. ibid.
24. ibid.
25. 3rd Bn. Interview, p. 7; Hanna to the Author, June 24, 1944.
26. 134th Inf., Unit Journal, Nov. 15, 1944; 3rd Bn. Interview, p. 8; Hanna to the Author June 24, 1946.
27. 3rd Bn. Interview, p. 8.

satisfaction, men of Company L watched the enemy troops coming out waving white flags.[28]

That night, for the first time since the beginning of the operation, soldiers of the Third Battalion, with friendly tanks around giving the assurances of further security, could get a night's rest in dry shelter. As a matter of fact, it was the first time since August 27th at St. Florentine that all companies of the Battalion had been in shelter at the same time.[29]

28. 134th Inf., Unit Journal, Nov. 15, 1944; 3rd Bn. Interview, p. 8.
29. There is an interesting confusion in the date and circumstances given for the capture of Morhange. When the men received **The Stars and Stripes** for November 15th, they read that the 4th Armored division had taken Morhange and "continued the attack to the east" (Continental Edition, p. 1), and when Lt. C. D. Hall questioned this statement in a letter to the correspondent who wrote the story, the latter attributed his information to a Third Army press release. The Associated Press implied that it was on Nov. 16th that "23 miles southeast of Metz, the Americans seized the World War battlefield of Morhange." (**New York Herald Tribune** Nov. 17, 1944, p. 3), and even the 35th Division's historical pamphlet, **Attack!** states that Morhange was taken on Nov. 16th (p. 20). Drew Middleton, writing from SHAEF, had the unit and date correct, but there were other errors: "Meanwhile the Thirty-fifth cleared a woods southwest of Landreff and entered Morhange. There was a brisk street-fight in the town, but by dusk two-thirds of the town had been won by the doughboys." Officially, it was announced that "our troops are in Morhange" in SHAEF Communique 222, Paris, Nov. 16 (printed in **The New York Times**, Nov. 17, 1944, p. 2) which would mean of course, that the town was taken by the 15th.

CHAPTER XIV

★ ★ ★
"TASK FORCE LAGREW"
★ ★ ★

Reversion of the regiment to division reserve allowed a breathing spell. November 16th was a bright day for morale—first of all, the weather was fair...there was time for the regimental Personnel Officer to visit the Battalon...and for the Red Cross man...weapons could be cleaned...replacements arrived to build up the depleted strength...later five new officers arrived (Lts. Parris and Oelbeck for Company L, Neuhoff and Shapiro for Company I, and Mossel for Company K)...in the afternoon the men could watch the armor swing out toward Harprich...word came down that the First and Ninth Armies had jumped off in a coordinated attack at 9 A. M.[1]

During the September conference of President Roosevelt and Prime Minister Churchill, General Eisenhower had reported to the Combined Chiefs of Staff that it was his intention to prepare to destroy the German armies in the West with all possible speed, and to occpy the German homeland. The critical supply situation had been a strong deterrent; the supreme commander had called upon the British forces on the north flank for the difficult task of clearing the approaches to Antwerp, for he felt that the service of that port would "have the effect of a blood transfusion." The last of those positions then was cleared on November 9th. Thus, with the promise of a great increase of supplies through the port of Antwerp, and with more than 3,000,000 troops on the continent, General Eisenhower launched his general offensive aimed at penetrating the Siegfried Line and gaining a position to cross the Rhine. Preferring the northern approach into Germany through the Cologne plain, this is where he concentrated his main effort.[2]

Now with the Ninth Army, under Lt. Gen. William H. Simpson (a former commander of the 35th Division), going into action on the north of the First, six allied armies had joined in a general offensive along a 300-mile front from Holland to the Alps: the British Second, Canadian First, American Ninth, First, Third, and Seventh, and the French First. It was reported that in their initial attack, troops of the Ninth had gained 2,000 yards between Geilenkirchen and Eschweiler, and were four miles from the Roer River.[3]

Bad weather continued to hamper operations along the entire front—not in years had it been so unfavorable for a large scale military campaign; and the Nazi defenders were resisting frantically. In spite of those difficulties, the Second British Army had cleared the west bank of the Meuse River and the Ninth Army had reached the Roer, while the First battled through the bloody Hurtgen Forest. But now General Eisenhower saw that his offensive must be slowed; a principal obstacle was the flooded condition of the Roer River, and the capability of the enemy to produce a sudden rush of water by blowing the dams near Schmidt. He considered that the attacks should be continued as

1. 3rd Bn. Journal, II, 63.
2. General Marshall's Report, pp. 38-42.
3. **The Stars and Stripes** (London ed.), Nov. 17, 1944, p. 1; **New York Herald Tribune**, Nov. 17, 1944, p. 1 (Associated Press).

long as their results were so favorable, but at the same time preparations should be made for an all-out offensive when the weather should become more favorable. He felt that the Germans, "assisted by weather, floods, and muddy ground" should be able to maintain a strong defense line for some time.[4]

Men of the Third Battalion knew that those gains of armies were the gains of infantry battalions—of men suffering from trench feet, of men accomplishing deeds of valor, of men miserable in the cold rain and mud and snow. And they knew that their turn would come again soon.

The 35th Division renewed its part in the offensive toward the Saar on November 18th when the 137th and 320th regiments attacked to the northeast. Now the 6th Armored Division was assembling. Apparently the Corps commander still was hoping for a break-through in which he could send the 6th Armored dashing through to the Saar and beyond, with the 134th Infantry following on trucks.[5] But the break-through warfare of the race across France could not be re-captured during the kind of weather which was prevailing— and the kind of defenses which the enemy was offering. Therefore the infantry battalions of the sister regiments had to keep pushing—through Harprich and Bistroff and Bermering and Vallerange, against light resistance, then small arms fire, tanks and artillery, with mine fields and antitank ditches in the path. Elements of the 6th Armored Division entered into the fight, and the advance continued: Berig Vintrange, Virming, Gros-Tenquin, Erstoff, Freybouse, Francaltroff.[6]

Replacements were arriving steadily until the companies were nearing full strength. Five days in Morhange permitted a program of further training for the new arrivals to be set up in the regimental Service Company area (train bivouac), and then they still had some time to be oriented into their units. Some men even had a chance for a shower.[7]

After several "false alarms" and changes in plans, the division reserve (i.e., the 134th Infantry) moved forward, by marching, on November 21st to a new assembly position at Linstroff. (About a three hours march northeast of Morhange). The small town was much too crowded with all kinds of units to permit any kind of shelter for the Battalion. However, the distance from the enemy was sufficient that the men could get some protection from the damp and cold by pitching their shelter tents at ten-yard intervals, and bringing up straw. It was still possible, too, to bring up hot meals.[8]

Shortly after noon the next day the battalion commander went to a meeting at regimental headquarters to learn that a new plan for armor-infantry integration had been devised in an effort to speed up the advance. The 134th Infantry and the 737th Tank Battalion (the tank battalion habitually attached to the 35th Division) were to be attached to the 6th Armored Division. Combat Command B, with these attachments, would be formed into three task forces. The 737th Tank Battalion, with the 1st Battalion, 134th Infantry, would form the nucleus for TF 1 (Kroechell); the 15th Tank Battalion, with the Third Battalion, 134th Infantry, would form the basis for TF 2 (Lagrew) while TF 3 (Wall) would, initially, be formed around the 50th Armored Infantry Bat-

4. General Marshall's Report, pp. 43-44.
5. 3rd Bn. Journal, II, 66. Stronger than the average (most frequently, one armored division and two infantry divisions), the XII Corps during this campaign included the 4th and 6th Armored Divisions, and the 26th, 35th, and 80th Infantry Divisions.
6. 3rd Bn. Journal, II, 65-72; 35th Div., **Attack!** p. 20.
7. 3rd Bn. Journal, pp. 68-72.
8. **ibid.**
9. **ibid.**, p. 72; 3rd Bn. S-3 Notebook, I.

talion. The 2nd Battalion, 134th Infantry, would remain in reserve for the time being.[9]

Almost immediately the Third Battalion assembled and set out in route column to join Lt. Col. H. T. Lagrew and his 15th Tank Battalion at Hellimer. It was a march of a kilometer north from Linstroff to Gros-Tenquin, and then seven kilometers northeast, up a main road, to Hellimer. The kitchens were released to battalion control, and Lt. Stoneburner moved them up to occupy a large building in the same town.

Thanksgiving turkeys had arrived at the kitchen, and although a called meeting for 9 o'clock the next morning warned that the Battalion would be moving again, Maj. Heffelfinger decided to gamble, and he directed the kitchens to proceed with their preparations for a Thanksgiving dinner.

There was a hard rain falling at noon,[10] and although the kitchen crews erected their flies to protect the serving of the food, there was no satisfactory place where a man could seek refuge to enjoy his meal. It was "turkey with all the trimmings," but it was turkey in the rain. Nevertheless, even under these circumstances, the mashed potatoes, peas and carrots, fruit cocktail, cookies, and hard candy, with the "white or dark meat," and a few minutes relaxation was an attractive contrast to what had been a few days before, and what might come within a few hours again.[11] Yet a pause like that, however helpful to individual morale, might, at the same time, have had something of an effect to make it more difficult for him to enter vigorously in the battle of death, for he longed to share Thanksgiving again with loved ones at home.

Scarcely had the jeeps returned the food containers to the kitchens when orders came to move on to St. Jean Rohrbach. It was another two-hour march up the main road to the northeast.[12]

The Germans had been using every means at their disposal to slow the advance against them. They blew bridges, they had dug antitank ditches a mile or more long and ten feet wide, they would use deep-biting plows to tear up sections of road in order to turn it into a quagmire for vehicles.[13]

The Third Battalion's first job was to clean out a section of woods about 1,500 yards beyond St. Jean Rohrbach (about half way to the important town of Puttelange). At the woods, the high ground sloped down toward the swollen Maderbach River, on whose opposite bank Puttelange stood. At the military crest of that slope, the enemy had left a long, deep, and wide antitank ditch; there was no available detour around it; and there were mine fields in the small clearings on either side of the road where it went through the woods. Before any tank attack could be attempted toward Puttelange, it would be necessary to establish a bridgehead across the antitank ditch, and then the engineers would have to put in a bridge. To gain that bridgehead was the mission of the Third Battalion.[14]

10. 134th Inf., **Daily Log**, V, 23 Nov.

11. Robert Richards (United Press, Nov. 23, 1944), reprinted in **The Santa Fe Express**, May, 1945, p. 8.

12. 3rd Bn. Journal, II, 72. The 15th Tank Battalion had captured St. Jean in brilliant maneuver the preceding day: Col. Lagrew, anticipating obstacles on the main road, divided his task force, and sending the secondary group on down the main road, he took the major force by a circuitous route over secondary roads to the left—through Leyviller, and all the way around the woods (Bois Habst) where he suspected enemy forces to be. Then while his secondary force, held up at that woods by a blown bridge, engaged the enemy by fire, Col. Lagrew swept into St. Jean from the north, in rear of the enemy's defenses before the town.

13. Donald MacKenzie in the **Atchison** (Kans.) **Globe**, Nov. 23, 1944.

14. 3rd Bn. Journal, II, 72-73, 3rd Bn. Interview, p. 9.

Company L was to take the initial action. At 1 o'clock, one platoon, under Lt. Brigandi, moved out as a combat patrol to determine what enemy strength remained in the woods. It awaited some concentrations of machine gun fire from the light tanks, and then moved into the woods. After once gaining entry, it met very little opposition, and within an hour, Lt. Brigandi was reporting that he was digging in on the high ground just short of the far edge of the woods. Curiously, Company L's 3rd platoon was pinned down by machine gun fire as it entered the woods to go in between Brigandi's position, on the left, and the highway on the right. Company I was alerted to be prepared to move up and establish a bridgehead on the right of the highway, and when Col. Lagrew and Capt. Greenlief reported that the crossroads[15] had been secured, Maj. Heffelfinger ordered the company to move out. It was able to make contact with Company L and estabilsh a defensive line in an arc to the right without difficulty. Lt. Erickson sent both heavy machine gun platoons, and two sections of 81 mm mortars to support the forward companies.[16] Prisoners of War taken from the 8th Company, 37th Panzer-Grenadier Regiment reported that their company of 60 men, with one tank in support, had been in the woods, but that the tank and most of the infantrymen had withdrawn in face of the attack, to Bermering.[17]

There had been heavy concentrations of artillery falling in St. Jean Rohrbach at different periods throughout the day. No less than seven of the Battalion's vehicles were hit.[18] One of these was a Company M mortar jeep, but worse, a burst struck a quarter-ton trailer loaded with 81 mm ammunition. Pfc. Joseph Klinsky of Nebraska braved the treacherous fire to drive two nearby vehicles to safety, and extinguish a fire in one of them.[19]

Neither had the successful clearing out of the woods assured safety for Companies I and L, for new artillery and mortar fire was directed to their positions, and bursting shells became the more treacherous when they landed among trees. Thus, even though opposition was light, and there was no general attack, 23 casualties from the Battalion were evacuated through the Aid Station.[20]

Among those casualties there would be some who could walk back to the aid station, and after a few days, could return to their companies. There would be others which would be more serious, and those whose wounds would require several weeks to mend would find themselves going all the way through the channels of evacuation to a hospital in the United States. When one of these, possibly with a shattered arm or leg, would come in, Captain Royce would supervise immediate treatment: the race would be to ease shock and to prevent infection. Blood plasma would assist in the former object, while sulfa powder in the wounds, a sulfa bandage, and sulfa tablets washed down with water from a canteen, together with a tetanus toxoid "booster" shot would go a long way toward combating infection.[21]

As soon as practicable, an ambulance from the supporting medical collecting company (Company A, 410th Medical Battalion) would take the patient for a 10 or 15 minute drive to the collecting station where all evacuees of the

15. A short distance beyond the antitank ditch there was a secondary road running to the right to Remering, and one to the left to Diffembach.
16. 3rd Bn. Journal, II, 73-4.
17. ibid.
18. ibid., p. 73.
19. 35th Inf. Div., General Orders, No. 9, Jan. 29, 1945.
20. 3rd Bn. Journal, II, 73.
21. Ralph Morse, "George Lott, Casualty," Life, XVIII (Jan. 29, 1945) pp. 15-17.

regiment were assembled for further transportation to the rear. Here, during a ten-minute wait, another medical officer would check for shock and hemorrhage, and see that he was in a satisfactory condition for a longer trip.

Now an ambulance from Company D (clearing) of the medical battalion would pick him up, and after a 40 or 50-minute drive, would deliver him to the Division Clearing Station, some 15 miles to the rear. Staffed with 20 surgeons, the Clearing Station was equipped for major first aid treatment and emergency surgery. (Up to this time the Clearing Station of the 410th Medical Battalion had had only 20 deaths out of more than 12,700 patients.) Here dressings and splints would be changed, there would be injections of penicillin, and probably a face wash and some hot coffee. Then, warmly wrapped in a cocoon of six blankets, with four more folded double underneath, the wounded soldier would be carried out to a Third Army Ambulance.

This trip would be one of over 50 miles to the evacuation hospital at Nancy. Beautifully set-up in a former French hospital, but with army field equipment the "evac" was prepared to give complete hospital service. But the patient's stay would be only about three days. During this time he would receive transfusions of whole blood, as needed, which came from a pool donated by Army Service Forces troops in Paris. X-rays would make a complete diagnosis possible, major surgery would be performed, and casts applied. And the Red Cross girls would be making their rounds with cigarettes and good cheer.

The next move probably would take the patient to a field hospital, which would be set up in tents out by an air field. Here he would await evacuation by air to England in a plane of the IX Troop Carrier Command.

After a 24-hour wait at the air base in England, a hospital train would carry him probably to the 7th General Hospital near London where his ward would be in a concrete-floored, clean Nisson hut. First priority here would be in checking any infection or beginning of gangrene. Perhaps a new plaster cast would be applied.

A few days later he would be back out at the air base—this time possibly for a plane to Paris where he would await for a flight to the United States. Soon he would have a place aboard a C-54, and after less than 30 hours in the air, would land at Mitchell Field, Long Island, hardly a month after the artillery shell caught him back in a town of Lorraine called St. Jean Rohrbach.

For final recuperation he would be on his way to a general hospital not far from his own home.[22]

Col. Lagrew called a meeting of all company commanders for 7:30 P. M. at his headquarters. The officers of the Third Battalion had a great deal of respect for the 6th Armored Division; they recalled how it had gone into action on short notice to make a decisive counterattack in front of the Foret de Gremecey; they were attracted by the enthusiasm and the "fight talk" which the armored command leaders exhibited. And, on the other hand, the armored command officers had respect for the infantrymen who had been pressing the campaign through the soggy terrain of Lorraine. The task force commander announced that Puttelange was the objective for an attack the next morning.[23]

Task Force Lagrew included the following units:

        15th Tank Battalion
        3rd Battalion, 134th Infantry

22. **ibid.**, pp. 17-26.
23. 3rd Bn. Interview, p. 9.

Company C, 603rd Tank Destroyer Battalion (less one platoon)
Company A, 25th Engineer Battalion (armd.) (less one platoon)
2 sections of Battery B, 777 Antiaircraft Artillery Battalion
(Automatic Weapons)
128th Field Artillery Battalion (armd.)—direct support.[24]

As rifle and tank company commanders paired off to study their maps, Lagrew explained his plan. One thing about an armored unit, the leaders made their plans fluid; they were not too much concerned with unit boundaries except as general guides, and they intended to exploit weaknesses; if the enemy be found too strong at one point, attack at another. Then he announced the order of march: Company C of the tank battalion, with Company L, would lead off and after crossing the bridge over the antitank ditch, would deploy on the left of the road for the assault; the 105 mm assault guns would follow next in column, and would have priority in getting into position to lay down fire on the objective; then Company B of the tanks, teamed with Company I, would go straight in, deploying on the right of the highway. Tank Company A and Company K would follow Company I, prepared to maneuver, but initially the tanks would protect the right flank by taking Remering (a town about 1,800 yards to the right, i. e., southeast of the highway on the near bank of Maderbach River) under fire; Company D (light tanks) would swing to the left (north) of the highway and pour volumes of machine gun fire into Diffembach to protect the left flank; then following in succession, ready to speed forward on call, would be the headquarters group,[25] the tank destroyers, engineers, antiaircraft, the mortars (81 mm mortars mounted on tanks), and the "thin-skins," or "junk" (the unarmored administrative vehicles which ordinarily did not move until an objective was taken.)[26] Medical service was coordinated so that there would be one joint aid station. Infantry litter squads would remove all casualties out to the highway, and jeeps from the armored unit would be available to take them to the rear. Initially a litter squad was to follow Company L and one would follow Company I.[27]

Not content to wait for enemy action, the Company I "Commander's jinx" operated the next morning two hours before the attack was scheduled to begin. Lt. James was wounded in the leg when a "grease gun"—an M-3 submachine gun—was accidentally discharged. Maj. Heffelfinger called for Lt. Miltonberger of Company L to take temporary command of "I."[28]

As H-hour approached, the battalion commander assembled his command group—the S-3, SCR 300 radio operator, intelligence sergeant, heavy weapons company commander, and a messenger—and boarded the half-track which had been assigned to him. This was the focal point for coordination, for the major could communicate with Col. Lagrew, and listen in to instructions to tank company commanders via the radio mounted in the half track; at the same time he could keep in contact with his own rifle company commanders, and with the CP, via his SCR 300.[29]

When Company L reported German soldiers and vehicles moving about in Puttelange, it appeared that there might be some opposition. But the companies jumped off at 10 A. M.[30]

24. 3rd Bn. S-3 Notebook, I; Combat Record of the Sixth Armored Division (Aschaffenburg, Germany, 1945), p. 114.
25. This would include a tank for the commander, and one for his S-3, and a half-track for Maj. Heffelfinger and his party.
26. 3rd Bn. S-3 Notebook, I.
27. ibid., 3rd Bn. Journal, II, 75.
28. 3rd Bn. Journal, II, 76.
29. 3rd Bn. S-3 Notebook, I.
30. 3rd Bn. Journal, II, 76.

Initially the tanks were to lead off, with the infantry to follow behind to mop up, or to assist the tanks should they be held up. Almost at once there was strong enemy reaction. Artillery of heavy caliber began to fall along the highway and in the woods; enemy mortars could be heard firing from Diffembach, and as the tanks passed over the bridge at the antitank ditch they drew direct fire which was as accurate as intense. The antitank ditch was just so located that in order to cross it, a tank was forced to come under direct observation—and direct fire—from the enemy in Puttelange.[31]

Perhaps even a more adverse factor was the condition of the ground. The snows of a few days earlier had disappeared, but had left the ground completely water soaked. As the tanks tried to deploy off the road, then, they bogged down almost immediately, and tracks churning helplessly, tearing great ditches into the earth, they became easy prey for the hostile antitank guns. Losses both in tanks and men mounting, further frontal attack was impossible. Col. Lagrew called for the infantry to change direction to the right, and pass through the armor and take Remering. The change in direction, executed in the simplest manner, put Companies I and K in assault, K on the right.

Demonstrating the prowess of the "doughfoot" in that kind of terrain, the infantrymen deployed on a wide front on either side of the secondary road leading to Remering, and moved out of the woods and down the open slope to enter the town with only the slightest resistance. There they made contact with elements of the 1st Battalion which, as a part of TF 1, had attacked northeast from Hilsprich.[32]

Company L remained in its position while the tanks pulled back to St. Jean for repairs. Troops of the armored infantry battalion (Wall) moved in to make contact between Company L and Company I in Remering.[33]

The companies remained in those positions for two days. They watched the flooded Maderbach River for any signs of rising or falling; they had occasional concentrations of artillery fire. On the other hand, this afforded an opportunity to issue dry blankets to all companies. First Lieutenant George Kryder of Michigan, formerly of the 1st Battalion, came to take command of Company I.[34]

What the next phase in the operations would be remained uncertain, but on November 27th the Battalion received word that the regiment had been released from attachment to the 6th Armored Division. The next evening an order came directing the Battalion to move to Lelling: the division was going back into Corps reserve.[35]

During a lull in the day's activities it was possible to relay to the companies a transcript of the British Broadcasting Company's newscast as picked up by the Battalion Radio Section at 9 A. M.—

> American First Army troops have captured Weisweiler and advanced last night about a mile beyond it on the great motor road to Cologne. American Third Army troops, supported by 2,000 fighter-bombers, made substantial advances yesterday. Further south the enemy were in full retreat toward the Rhine. Allied planes had a big day shooting up traffic behind the German lines and bombing pontoon bridges across the river. RAF Lancasters attacked targets in Western Germany yesterday and all returned. Over 1,100 American heavies from Britain, escorted by 700 fighters, attacked targets in northwestern Germany including Germany's largest remaining oil

31. 3rd Bn. Interview, p. 9.
32. 3rd Bn. Interview, p. 9.
33. 3rd Bn. Journal, II, 77; 3rd Bn. Interview, p. 9.
34. ibid., pp. 77-80.
35. 3rd Bn. Journal, II, 82-2.

plant at Hanover, and the rail yards at Hamm. The raiders knocked out a total of 129 enemy fighters. American losses were 37 bombers and 13 fighters.

The Victoria Cross has been awarded Major David Vivien Howell of the 29th Canadian Armored Reconnaissance Regiment for his leadership in cutting one of the main escape routes from the Falaise pocket in Normandy last August....

The Russians have taken a rail junction less than 30 miles from Budapest and have gained ground in Czechoslovakia.

American Superfortresses have made another attack on Tokyo. They flew from Saipan....[36]

At 10:05 P. M., the 50th Armored Infantry Battalion completed relief of the Third Battalion.[37]

36. 3rd Bn. S-3 Notebook, II.
37. 3rd Bn. Journal, II, 82.

CHAPTER XV

* * *

CROSSING THE SAAR RIVER

* * *

Three days' respite which the Third Battalion enjoyed at Lelling while the division was in corps reserve came none too soon. The fighting through Lorraine had hurt the Battalion: its casualties for November totaled 616.[1] This amounted to a total as great as the entire "normal" fighting strength of the Battalion! Of these, 48 had been killed and two others died of wounds; thirteen men were listed as "missing," and inasmuch as there had been no important counterattacks nor reports of any captures by the enemy, it could be assumed that most of these probably were dead.[2]

The Third Battalion, representing hardly more than one-fourth of the regiment's total strength had suffered 55 per cent of its casualties during the month.[3]

But again and again replacements came up to fill the depleted ranks. Now a few days out of the line gave an opportunity for reorganization, training, and the absorption of the new men into their units.

Among those who joined the Battalion were some who were returning to combat after recuperation from wounds. One of those who had come up during the last two weeks was a sergeant of Company K named Lawrence Langdon. Now he was offered a battlefield commission, and was appointed a second lieutenant. Langdon had been wounded by German machine gun fire on July 17th as his company tried to advance against Hill 122 before St. Lo. After evacuation and hospitalization in England, he had returned to Company K on November 17th. There he had found a new company commander. Assigned to the 1st Platoon, he found it only a fraction of "normal" size, and discovered only two men who had been with the platoon when he left. All of the noncommissioned officers were new men with about two week's experience, and one of them had been a cook up until that very day.[4]

Without any relaxation of measures for security, the Battalion was able to inaugurate a full program of recreation and training. Barbers were kept busy, equipment was cleaned, there were showers and shaves. There were Catholic services, Protestant services, pay day, a regimental school for training new aid men, and a communications school. On December 1, the following activities were coordinated to insure participation of all companies: (1) Showers for 25 men and one officer from each rifle company; (2) Red Cross Clubmobile, with Red Cross girls, doughnuts, coffee, and music; (3) training in the attack of a fortified position (against a pillbox of the Maginot system); (4) two groups of 60 men to go to Lixing for a U.S.O. show; (5) a medical inspection of all troops; (6) an orientation class for each company. At 7 P. M. the Battalion was alerted for a possible move on the next day; this was made

---

1. Distributed as follows: Hq. Co., 11; Co. I, 150; Co. K, 153; Co. L, 225; Co. M, 77—134th Inf., Battle Casualty Report.
2. A soldier could not be officially reported "killed in action" until his body had been positively identified.
3. 134th Inf., Battle Casualty Report.
4. Lawrence P. Langdon to the Author, July 5, 1946.

definite at 1:30 A. M., and the order was issued at 8:30. The Battalion was returning to St. Jean Rohrbach; for the first time in its combat career it was returning to a place where it had been located previously.[5]

A new attack on Puttelange was in the making. This time it was to be a regimental proposition for the 134th Infantry. The Third Battalion was to relieve the armored battalion holding the line between St. Jean Rohrbach and Puttelange, and the 1st and 2nd Battalions were to pass through to make the assault.

By 10 P. M. (December 2) the Third had accomplished its relief. Company I occupied the wooded forward slope on the right of the St. Jean-Puttelange highway, and Company K occupied the corresponding position on the left of the road. The other battalions spent the following day in careful reconnaissance for crossing sites over the swollen Maderbach River and made plans to launch a night attack at 5 A. M., December 4.[6]

Quietly, and without benefit of artillery preparation, the attacking battalions moved out in the 5 o'clock darkness. Attacking on the left, the 2nd Battalion waded across the abnormally deep river, and moved rapidly to capture the high ground to the northeast of the town. Achieving complete surprise, its men captured several Germans asleep in their foxholes, and suffered only one casualty; they were on their objective by 6 o'clock.[7]

Meanwhile on the right, the 1st Battalon improvised a foot-bridge over a blown-out flood control gate. Company A crossed and assaulted Puttelange from the south while Company C moved into the town from due west. The result was complete surprise: German officers were captured in bed, while others were shot as they fled from their sleeping quarters barefooted. The battalion had one officer and two men wounded, and one man killed. It speedily occupied Puttelange.[8]

At 9:30 the Third Battalion, in regimental reserve, assembled in Diffembach, and after a hot dinner moved on into Puttelange.[9]

Shortly before 9 P. M. the regimental S-3 telephoned to say that the regiment would move the next morning at "banker's hour" (8 o'clock). Following the 1st Battalion by bounds, the Third marched out of Puttelange at 8:15 and arrived at Ernestviller at 9:00. As the leading battalion continued to move forward without resistance, the Third left Ernestviller at 10:55 and arrived at Woustviller at 12:00. Here it was possible to serve hot "chow" before the Battalion moved on again at 1:10. It arrived at Roth at 2:45.[10]

Here the Battalion was given a mission of its own: while the other two battalions continued on toward Sarreguemines—about three and a half kilometers to the northeast—the Third was to move directly east to occupy the town of Neufgrange.

About three kilometers directly south of Sarreguemines, and about two kilometers southwest of the Saar River town of Remelfing, Neufgrange was nestled in an open valley among patches of woods called collectively the Foret

5. 3rd Bn. Journal, II, 82-86.
6. ibid., pp. 87-88.
7. Lt. Col. Roecker, 2nd Bn. Interview, P. 6.
8. Transcript of Interview, Lt. Col. Dan E. Craig, CO, of the 1st Battalion, to Capt. Jacob Goldman, Wadersloh, Germany, May 25, 1945 (3d Information and Historical Service, Combat Interviews, No. 108—35th Div.,—1 Nov. 44—23 Jan. 45) p. 6; Apparently there is some exaggeration in the statement, "The 134th swept into Puttelange without a casualty"—35th div., **Attack!** p. 21. The AP story also said "without a single American casualty." Edward Bell, The Associated Press, Dec. 4, reprinted in **The Santa Fe Express,** May 1945, p. 12.
9. 3rd Bn. Journal, II, 88-89.
10. 3rd Bn. Journal, II, 90.

de Sarreguemines.[11] The Battalion occupied the town without resistance at 4 P. M. Its only deterrent had been a 700-pound bomb in a culvert at the entrance to the town which the engineers later removed. A supply route was opened up when the engineers put in a treadway bridge over a partially-destroyed culvert at Roth.[12]

Almost immediately patrols started toward the Saar River. Men of Company K who had just found a place to sleep, and were anticipating a good rest, reported to the Battalion CP for instructions. Sgt. Harless led his patrol down to within 400 yards of Remelfing, and while he saw civilian activity, saw nothing of the enemy, and learned from civilians that the Germans had withdrawn across the river. Lt. Langdon took two men to reconnoiter to the left, and though he ran into some artillery fire and heard some small arms fire, he was able to get to the outskirts of Remelfing.[13]

On the basis of these reports, Major Heffelfinger decided to have a platoon of Company K outpost Remelfing. Shortly after 7:30 P. M. Lt. Langdon took his 1st Platoon down to occupy the town; it was so dark then that men had to keep contact by holding on to each other, as they had learned in Louisiana maneuvers. Sgt. Brown and some men of the Battalion intelligence section accompanied the platoon in order to set up a forward observation post on the river bank. By questioning civilians and by additional patrols, they learned that there was a deep canal on the west side of the river, and that all bridges, both over the canal and over the river had been blown; however, it was possible to cross the canal on the locks. The canal was reported to be about 30 feet wide, separated from the river by about 25 to 30 yards; the river was reported as being 75 to 100 yards wide, and according to a French guide was too deep to wade.[14]

In order to reinforce his one platoon in Remelfing against a possible counterattack, and in order to avoid a possible later fight for his company, Captain Campbell asked for permission to take the remainder of Company K into that town while it was yet dark. The company closed in just prior to daylight.[15]

In the meantime Lt. Neuhoff was leading a patrol from Company I down toward the river in the sector to the left (northwest) of Company K's. He returned before 9 o'clock without having reached the river, and without sufficient information for the planning of a river crossing. However, he was anxious to make another attempt. Four hours later he returned with a report on the bridges at the south edge of Sarreguemines: the railroad bridge, though badly buckled and difficult to cross could be crossed by foot soldiers.[16]

Obviously Company K had slipped into Remelfing without the enemy's being aware of it. Next morning as the men watched from attic windows along the canal, they could see very plainly numbers of German soldiers walking about their river-bank entrenchments hardly more than 75 yards away. At one point they could see an officer with a map, whistling; sometimes a series of helmeted heads could be seen moving along the trenches; sometimes they would bail water out of their trenches, and then come out to sun themselves. Capt. Campbell began calling for artillery almost as soon as he was in position.

11. Map, Central Europe, 1:100,000—Saarbrucken—Sheet V. 1.
12. 3rd Bn. Journal, II, 90.
13. 3rd Bn. Journal, II, 91; Lawrence P. Langdon, loc. cit.
14. 3rd Bn. Journal, pp. 92-93; Langdon, loc. cit.
15. ibid., p. 93.
16. ibid., pp. 92-94.

With such promising targets presenting themselves, Captain Hart, commander of Battery C, 161st Field Artillery (the battery teamed to support the Third Battalion) went up to direct fire personally. His effectiveness was plain to see. He kept working this deadly fire as long as the Battalion remained.[17]

The opposition which the 1st and 2nd Battalions had met in Saarguemines suggested that the Germans intended to make a strong defense of the Saar River. The 38th SS Panzer Regiment and engineers from the 17th SS Division had been identified in the area.[18] Additional patrols, accompanied by engineers, continued to reconnoiter for crossing sites. The canal offered a serious obstacle to any crossing by assault boat; Major Heffelfinger considered that it might be necessary to build a bridge across the canal, and then carry the boats over for launching in the river. The closest concealed approach to the river was through the Honigwald, a woods about 500 yards to the southeast of Remelfing which extended down toward the river; a Company L patrol made its way to the forward edge of this woods, and there could see groups of enemy moving about in the town of Sarreinsming on the opposite bank. An engineer officer estimated the river to be 40 yards wide at this point.[19]

An initial tentative regimental plan had suggested that the Third Battalion, followed by the 1st, would make the crossing at Remelfing. Then this was abandoned in favor of a crossing in Sarreguemines with the 2nd and Third Battalions abreast. However, the Battalion S-2 and the company commanders found a number of objections to this plan when they made a reconnaissance of the proposed site: the route to be taken would mean a march of more than six miles for the companies; no motor route was found to take boats down to the river because of rubble in the streets; there was a good launching site, but it could take only six boats at a time, and it would be possible to carry only one boat at a time—and it with difficulty—over the narrow path through the debris; the river was about 125 feet wide, but the swift current would cause a drift of nearly 200 yards; the opposite bank was to be approached over 25 feet of slate at a 70 to 80 degree angle, which would make it virtually impossible to debark without additional equipment; and this opened into a good field of fire for the enemy. There was a suggestion that alligators—amphibious, tracked personnel carriers—would be the answer for the double crossing, but the concrete banks of the canal made them impractical.[20]

Originally scheduled for predawn of December 7th, the attack was postponed for 24 hours. Reconnaissance patrols continued. Company L reported a good launching site opposite Sarreinsming. At 6 P. M. on the 7th, Lt. Neuhoff reported that he had crossed the fallen railway bridge, and had encountered no enemy fire.[21] Then Colonel Mitlonberger decided to take a gamble: he would send the entire regiment across that bridge in column.

Company commanders and staff members gathered at the Battalion command post at 10:30 P. M. to hear the battalion order:

(1). The 134th Inf. attacks at 0500 to seize a bridgehead across the Saar, and the high ground to the northeast of Sarreguemines. The 320th Infantry seizes a bridgehead on the right; the 6th Armored Division holds its present position on the left of the 35th.

17. 3rd Bn. Journal, II, 95-96; 3rd Bn. Interview, p. 11; Langdon, loc. cit. Campbell reported on one occasion, "Rounds falling into river. Caused Krauts to put their helmets on—dived into their water-soaked trenches."—3rd Bn. Journal, II, 96.
18. 35th Div., Attack!, p. 22; 134th Inf., After Action Report, Jan. 4, 1945.
19. 3rd Bn. Journal, II, 96, 97.
20. 3rd Bn. Journal, II, 97-98; 3rd Bn. Interview, p. 11.
21. 3rd Bn. Journal, II, 98, 100.

The 1st and 2nd Battalions will cross the railroad bridge ahead of the Third, and attack to the northeast.

The 161st FA Bn. (reinf.) fires preparation on Sarreinsming, 0500 to 0700; smoke and additional fire on call. Forward Observers with Companies I and K, and at the OP in Remelfing.

Company C, 737th Tank Battalion, and Company A, 654th TD Battalion, from positions on hill 262, will support by direct fire.

2nd Platoon, Regimental Antitank Company, will be prepared to support from positions in Le Honigwald.

Antitank Mine Platoon will be attached.

Company A, 60th Engineers, will have assault boats available and will construct a foot bridge; Company C, 133rd Engineers will build an infantry support raft, and will put in the Bailey bridge at Sarreinsming.

(2). This Battalion will seize a bridgehead at Sarreinsming, protect construction of the bridge, and be prepared to continue the advance.

Formation: Column of companies in the order I, K, L,—Company K echeloned to the left.

Direction of attack: Southeast from the far end of the railroad bridge crossing site.

Time of attack: 0500 plus clearance of 1st and 2nd Battalions.

Base Company: Company I

The Battalion will move to assembly position in Le Freywald [a wooded hill just east of the railroad whose bridge was to be the crossing site.]

IP: Street at Company I area, 0430 Order of March: I, K, L, M.

(3). Company I will cross the railroad bridge on clearance of the 2nd Battalion, change direction to the right, advance along the river line, seize and mop up Sarreinsming.

Company K, less one platoon, with one platoon of heavy machine guns attached, will follow Company I, echeloned to the left. Advance to the north of Sarreinsming, seize and hold the reverse slope of Hill 271. One platoon be prepared to support by fire from positions in Remelfing.

Company L, with one antitank mine squad attached, will follow Company K, seize and hold ground to north and northwest of Sarreinsming. The antitank mine squad will sweep the road through the town to the bridge site. Company L to provide security to left flank during advance.

Company M—one machine gun platoon attached to Company K, one machine gun platoon to support by fire from positions in Remelfing to displace to positions in Le Honigwald on order. Mortar Platoon to support from position vicinity Hill 262, one observer with Company I, one observer on Hill 262.

The Battalion Antitank Platoon will be prepared to furnish AT protection and direct support fire from positions in Remelfing.

Ammunition and Pioneer Platoon—initiate reconnaissance—prepare to establish an advance ammunition distributing point in the vicinity of the crossng site, then at Remelfing.

(4). Individuals will carry one complete K ration and one D ration. Bedrolls to be stacked at present company CP's—platoons in Remelfing stack rolls at K company forward CP.

Weapons carriers—move forward with battalion motors, available for ammunition supply.

Battalion Aid Station at Neufgrange, advance collecting point vicinity the crossing site—then vicinity the foot bridge. Aid men to carry extra litters.

Extra ammunition—two bandoliers per man—will be carried.

(5). Communication wire: double to OP—to Sarreinsming on completion of bridge.

Radio: Additional call numbers—AT platoon, 6; attached AT, 7; tank company, 8. Call sign: Able (1st Battalion X-ray; 2nd Battalion, Tare). Channel: 36, Alternate, 27 (1st Battalion 39, alternate 24; 2nd Battalion 21, alternate 33.)

Signal for lifting artillery fire: green star cluster.

Battalion OP—Remelfing.

Battalion CP—Neufgrange.

Initially the Battalion Commander will be at the crossing site.

"Annex"—Plan 2:
The Battalion will cross in 24 Engineer Assault Boats.
Crossing site: Sarreinsming.
Order: Company K, I (One machine gun platoon attached), L.
8 men per assault boat; appoint a leader for each boat. First wave; Company K, 14 boats.
Boat pickup—Le Honigwald.
Company K, less one platoon, will seize Sarreinsming and mop up.
Company I, with one platoon heavy machine guns attached, will move northeast and occupy the reverse slope of Hill 271.
Company L will seize high ground to north and northwest.
Guides to boat pick-up: S-2 section.
Route from assembly position: trail to right of Honigwald.
Order of March: K, I, L.[22]

There were two important elements of risk implicit in the regimental plan. The first was in "putting all the eggs in one basket"—to cross all three battalions in a column of files over the railroad bridge. The other was in crossing at a site some three kilometers away from where the Bailey bridge was to be constructed. The success of the Third Battalion was essential. Should it fail to capture the intended bridge site at Sarreinsming, it would mean that practically the entire fighting force of the regiment would be in danger of being cut off. With the coming of daylight the enemy probably could complete the destruction of the railroad bridge, or at least make it untenable, when he found what had happened. And in any case there would be no way for vehicles to bring up ammunition and supplies, and more important, no way of getting tanks, tank destroyers, and antitank guns across to resist enemy counterattacks with armor.

To accomplish its task, the Third Battalion would have to hope that the 1st and 2nd could get across without blocking the railroad bridge; then it would have to execute a difficult change of direction to the right in the black darkness, and move three kilometers through the entrenched positions along the river bank to Sarreinsming.

There were some advantages, however, to the direction of attack. It made possible a great volume of supporting fire. Firing at very close range, the machine guns, antitank guns, and the riflemen of Company K's 1st platoon, would be able to pin down the enemy as Company I advanced along his flank. At the same time, the tanks and tank destroyers in position on Hill 262 (to the southwest of Remelfing) were in a position to protect the attacking companies' flank by firing on the high ground beyond them.

The alternate plan provided a means for action in case the advance of the leading battalions over the railroad bridge should be stopped. And very likely the movement of trucks and boats down in the Honigwald served as a demonstration to make the enemy think that that was to be the crossing. Moreover, this was a rare opportunity for gaining the effect of an artillery preparation without sacrificing surprise. While Sarreinsming was the real objective of the Third Battalion, the artillery preparation would tend to substantiate any German belief that an assault was about to be launched from directly across the river, while the Battalion actually would be crossing on the flank three kilometers away.

The Battalion assembled in the woods above the railroad tracks and awaited word that the other battalions were crossing. The artillery preparation began

22. 3rd Bn. Journal, II, 100-102.

on time but, unfortunately, there were a few short rounds again—some fell into the woods where the Battalion was assembling; others injured some engineers in Remelfing.[23]

Word came over the SCR 300 that the 1st Battalion was crossing without opposition. The Third formed into column, and marched down the railroad to the vicinity of the bridge and then after the 2nd Battalion had crossed, quickly followed. It was nearly 7 o'clock by the time the Battalion had crossed and daylight would be coming soon. Lt. George M. Kryder led his Company I down the railroad and in a rapid advance along the river bank. The company began to take prisoners almost immediately, and as soldiers took their captives back along the route of advance, they would add to their number from additional Germans who had been passed over.

A heavy volume of machine gun, antitank gun, and rifle fire from Remelfing helped to clear the way for Company I, but it was halted soon in order not to interfere with the company's rapid advance. As morning twilight approached, the tanks and TD's opened fire from their positions up on the hill. Machine gun and cannon fire from a dozen tanks and eight TD's created a terrible display. Kryder called over the 300 radio,

"Say, what's all that machine gun fire cracking over my head?"

Major Heffelfinger called back, "That's Conde and his tanks; he's protecting your left flank." There was a slight pause, then

"Oh, that's just right; tell him to keep it up!"

Captain Conde, commander of the tank company, and Major Heffelfinger had worked out a system of check points on the map. By reference to these, the Battalion commander could call for direct fire (the tank commander had one of the Battalion's extra 300 radios) on the place desired.[24]

The two TD platoons alone fired 138 rounds of 3-inch ammunition, and 1,300 rounds of caliber .50 machine gun ammunition in supporting the Battalion.[25]

The enemy finally became aware of what was happening, and as daylight approached, the rear elements of Company K and Company L were pinned down by machine gun fire about 250 yards from the railroad bridge. In spite of this, Kryder saw that the only way to complete his mission, and at the same time to gain the greatest protection for his men, was to get into the town. Therefore he kept moving.[26] The company soon moved into Sarreinsming. But there had been some men wounded; artillery fire was falling on the town; prisoners were being taken; civilians were making confusion. Seeing that it was going to be impossible to evacuate wounded or prisoners for some time, Kryder called his company aid men and some other soldiers who had had some medical training, and set up an aid station to care for the wounded. Then he set up a prisoner of war cage for his fifty prisoners, and assembled all civilians in one section of town and screened them for persons thought to be assisting the enemy.[27] The task of mopping up Sarreinsming was completed by noon.[28]

Meanwhile Company L and a part of "K" remained pinned down by enemy troops lodged in a group of buildings northeast of the railroad bridge. Proximity of the 1st Battalion, also encountering stubborn resistance in the same

23. 3rd Bn. Journal, II, 102.
24. 3rd Bn. Interview, pp. 12-13.
25. 654th Tank Destroyer Battalion, After Action Report, Dec. 31, 1944.
26. 3rd Bn. Journal, II, 103.
27. 35th Div., General Orders, No. 9, Jan. 29, 1945.
28. 3rd Bn. Journal, II, 103.

area, ruled out the use of artillery. Captain Campbell returned with a platoon of Company K to assist his own rear platoon and Company L in breaking the resistance. They got into the buildings and found the Nazis making a floor-to-floor defense. When the first floor would be cleared, the Germans would fight from the second floor; when the Americans would reach that floor, then enemy would enter the first again. It was difficult for other squads to reach the buildings because they were pinned down by German machine guns. Captain Campbell made his way to a second floor hoping to get a better view of the situation. Looking across at the next building, he found two Germans who were firing a machine gun from the window; some quick shots from his .45 pistol eliminated that particular obstacle.[29]

By 1:30 P. M. the situation with Company L was beginning to ease, but it was 4 o'clock before the buildings all were cleared out. Then Company L sent back 22 prisoners to join the 20 which "K" and "I" had sent across before 8 o'clock. Now able to advance, "K" and "L" moved into Sarreinsming to consolidate with Company I. The Battalion CP moved to Remelfing.[30] Through the night work continued. Lieutenant Hanna went across by raft to deliver supplies and make reconnaissance.

At 8:30 the next morning Companies K and L moved out to occupy Hill 271 while "I" remained in town to defend approaches to the bridge site.[31] The enemy had by no means abandoned his defense. The 1st and 2nd Battalions had received some sharp counterattacks by infantry and tanks during the preceding afternoon; these were broken up with the assistance of air strikes.[32] Accurate concentrations of artillery delayed work on the Bailey bridge. An "L" Company patrol, entering the woods beyond the crest of Hill 271, ran into a group of enemy and the man carrying the 536 radio was captured. In the afternoon "L" Company reported an 88 mm gun, a captured American jeep, and two other vehicles along the edge of the woods; artillery destroyed the gun, but the vehicles continued on into the woods. The 161st Field Artillery took a tank under fire a short distance beyond; three rounds of high explosive, and two rounds of white phosphorous disabled the threatening armor. The antitank mine squad ran into small arms fire as it swept the road for mines at the northeast edge of Sarreinsming.[33]

The site chosen for the Bailey bridge was over the ruins of a destroyed masonry bridge, a part of whose abutments still were usable. Enemy artillery fell in the Battalion area throughout the day.[34] The 81st Chemical Smoke Generator Company moved in to cover the valley with thick white smoke,[35] and "construction of the bridge across the Saar continued under heavy artillery and mortar fire."[36]

Meanwhile the engineers were able to put in a treadway across the canal at Remelfing and put a support raft into operation.[37] Company K's 1st Platoon, which had remained in Remelfing to give supporting fire, crossed the river in assault boats to rejoin the company.[38] During the afternoon the Battalion's

29. 3rd Bn. Interview, p. 13; 3rd Bn. Journal, II, 103.
30. 3rd Bn. Journal, II, 102-104.
31. ibid.
32. Donald Mackenzie in The News, Dec. 9, 1944, reprinted in The Santa Fe Express, May 1945, p. 6.
33. 3rd Bn. Journal, II, 102-4.
34. ibid., p. 104.
35. 35th Div., Attack! p. 23.
36. 134th Inf., Daily Log, V, 3 Dec. 44.
37. 35th Div., Attack! p. 23.
38. Langdon, loc. cit.

antitank guns and their 1½-ton prime movers were ferried across the river under the cover of the smoke screens, but through some enemy artillery fire. The tank destroyers, however, proved to be too heavy for the raft, and they would have to await completion of the bridge. The Communications Platoon established telephone communications by laying wire through the water from an assault boat. Rations and ammunition went across by ferry at 5 P. M.[39] A request came for cigarettes.

In order to facilitate supplying, and to consolidate defenses for the night, Companies K and L were recalled to the shelter of Remelfing in the evening, but were instructed to leave strong outposts in position on the hill.[40]

The nature of the terrain around Sarreinsming and Sarreguemines made it very difficult for any unit—battalion, regiment, or division,—to seize all of the high ground from which the enemy might be observing his artillery fire. The Battalion's occupation of Hill 271 denied any observation from that area; the 1st and 2nd Battalions occupied the high ground to the northwest; the 320th Infantry had made a crossing up stream at Letting and was coming up to seize the wooded heights to the east; the 137th Infantry crossed the same railroad bridge where the 134th had crossed and turned northwest to clean out that part of Sarreguemines lying across the river. But one suspected trouble spot remained immune: a small tip of Germany proper extended down to the very edge of Sarreguemines from the north; it was an area between the Saar and Blies rivers. There, above a bend in the Saar, an observer could look directly up the river to Sarreinsming—and a gun could shoot directly up the same course.[41] On the other hand, Lt. Col. Alford Boatsman, regimental executive officer who was in Remelfing to coordinate activities, felt that enemy gunners might be getting information from sympathetic civilians; consequently he ordered extensive counter measures: concentration of civilians in one section of town, and the searching of all houses.[42]

In spite of difficulties, the engineers continued their work while all concerned waited news of their progress. At 10:30 P. M. (December 9) it was announced that the bridge was nearing completion. Half an hour later came the word: "Bailey bridge at Sarreinsming open for business."[43] Among the first vehicles to cross were jeeps carrying cigarettes and mail.

The tank destroyers started across before 1 A. M.; however, after about two platoons had crossed further traffic had to be held up for repairs to the approaches. Traffic was resumed at 4 o'clock, and by 4:45 all the TD's and all the regiment's antitank guns were across. The battle for the bridgehead had been won.[44]

39. 3rd Bn. Journal, II, 104-5.
40. ibid.
41. ibid., 35th Div., **Attack!** pp. 22-24; map.
42. 3rd Bn. Journal, II, 104.
43. ibid., II, 106.
44. ibid.

CHAPTER XVI

★ ★ ★

HABKIRCHEN

★ ★ ★

Dec. 12...."Third Army troops crossed the Blies River into Germany and took Habkirchen, four miles northeast of Sarreguemines"—*The World Almanac*, 1945, p. 104.

Behind that statement lay one of the bitterest local battles of the war.

The bridge over the Saar completed, the Third Battalion prepared to resume its advance. At 7:30 Companies K and L moved up Hill 271 to the woods, and, encountering slight resistance, moved along the edge of the woods to an old rifle range in Le Grand Bois two kilometers northeast of Sarreinsming. Company I mounted tanks and TD's and moved up to the range over the highway. One tank destroyer was disabled when it hit a nonmetallic mine on the road near the edge of the woods. The CP moved across to Sarreinsming.[1]

Companies K and L then moved on to the northeast to occupy La Bauerwald, a low-dome-like, wooded knob between Folpersviller and Blies Ebersing, while Company I retained a position short of the ridge line highway which ran across the front just beyond the edge of Le Grand Bois. The next morning Company I moved up to join the leading companies, and shortly before noon passed through to seize Blies Ebersing. They knew that they would have to fight for the town, because not only could they see dug-in emplacements around it, but they would have to emerge from the concealment of the woods and advance down the forward slope of the knob fully exposed to the observation and the fire of any enemy on the dominating heights across the river. Surely enough there were calls for "baby buggies" (litter teams) almost at once. Nevertheless, men of Company I raced down the hill and into the Blies River town. The other companies went in by rushes of small groups.[2]

At 4:45 P. M. regiment called for patrols to reconnoiter along the river for possible crossing sites. The 1st Battalion had captured Folpersviller, on the left, and were moving on to Frauenberg, which the 137th had cleared, on the river opposite Habkirchen, about two kilometers down stream from Blies Ebersing. The 2nd Battalion, in reserve, was to move into Blies Ebersing with the Third. At 8 P. M. the regimental commander telephoned the commander of the 1st Battalion to tell him that his battalion was to cross the Blies River "by morning" and seize the town of Habkirchen. Forty-five minutes later Major Heffelfinger received a call—the Third Battalion was to cross at the same time as the 1st at a different site while the 2nd covered by fire; both the 1st and Third would go into Habkirchen.[3]

Among the traditionally most difficult of military operations are the attack of a hostile beach, and the attack of a defended river line. Now the 134th Infantry was facing its third river crossing in eight days. Army doctrine had taught: "Preparations for the crossing include the search for all obtainable

1. 3rd Bn. Journal, II, 106; 3rd Bn. Interview, p. 13.
2. 3rd Bn. Journal, II, 108; 3rd Bn. Interview, p. 13.
3. 134th Inf., Unit Journal, 11 Dec. 44.

information, both of the enemy and the terrain, in the area where the battalion is to operate. Whenever practicable, ample time is allowed for daylight reconnaissance by all subordinate leaders."[4]

The emphasis on reconnaissance and planning for any night attack has been noted previously—

"A night attack requires careful planning and preparation, special measures to preserve secrecy and secure surprise, and precision and cohesion in execution. A battalion should have a minimum of 3 hours for daylight preparation.... Night attacks are seldom justfied without ample time for daylight preparation."[5]

In face of the dominating terrain and the known enemy defenses, a night attack was the only feasible way to cross the Blies. But the need for reconnaissance and detailed planning was paramount. The 1st and 2nd Battalions had executed an attack across the swollen Maderbach River to capture Puttelange in an operation which was a model; a full day and two nights had given battalion and company commanders and platoon leaders opportunity for complete reconnaissance and detailed planning. A 24-hour delay at the Saar River had permitted the formation of a complete plan and reconnaissance to exploit a bridge which that reconnaissance revealed to be usable; the regiment had been able to cross, still with complete surprise. Now, however, detailed reconnaissance and full planning were to be sacrificed to haste. Perhaps the pressure of time was more acute because a foothold in pre-war Germany itself was the goal; possibly Army or Corps commanders were anxious to announce a new penetration of German soil. In any case, the Third Battalion was to make a crossing of the Blies River, with whatever equipment happened to be available, and with or without the benefit of what night reconnaissance it could achieve, and under what plans it could perfect and disseminate before 5:30 the next morning.

Early in the afternoon G-2 had reported that the Blies was a swift stream, that its depth in this zone was over a man's head, and that the enemy occupied well-manned fortifications on the opposite bank. But the regimental intelligence officer received information from civilian sources that the river was fordable just off the point of a small island down stream from Blies Ebersing. He reported to the Battalion S-2 at 10:10 that, according to this information, the river was 15 to 20 meters wide and at this point (map coordinates 562 590) was about two feet deep in normal times and rose to a depth of four feet during the rainy season.[6] Company L was to send a patrol to reconnoiter this point.

Meanwhile, the Battalion S-3 was called to the regimental command post (new also in Remelfing) to receive the order for the operation. He arrived there at 9:45 P. M. All available assault boats had been allotted to the 1st Battalion, and now, on the basis of the civilian report, it was assumed that the Third Battalion could wade the stream. However, the Company L patrol had not reported yet, and when the Battalion S-3 raised the question as to an alternate plan in case the patrol found the river unfordable, it was agreed to get some rubber reconnaissance boats from the engineers. The regimental S-3 telephoned the 60th Engineers and ordered all rubber boats that could be had— seven—, 1200 feet of rope, and four boat inflaters. The Battalion S-3 returned to the CP with the regimental order at 11 o'clock.[7]

4. War Department, Infantry Field Manual 7-20, **Rifle Battalion** (Sept. 28, 1942) p. 134.
5. ibid., 112.
6. 134th Inf., Unit Journal, 11 Dec. 44; 3rd Bn. Journal, II, 109.
7. 134th Inf., Unit Journal, 11 Dec. 44; 3rd Bn. Journal, II, 109; 3rd Bn. Interview, p. 15.

Apprehensive at trying to shuttle a battalion across the river in seven light rubber boats which could each carry only two men and their equipment, Major Heffelfinger called the regimental S-3 to suggest that the engineers put in a foot bridge for the crossing. But all bridging equipment, as well as assault boats, were in the 1st Battalion area; the Third would have to get along with rubber boats. The seven rubber boats arrived at the CP at 12:30, and at 1:45 Major Carroll reported that four more boats would be delivered before 5 o'clock.[8]

At 2:20, Lieutenant Brigandi, commanding Company L for the time being, called Major Heffelfinger to report the results of his patrol. Lt. Tom Parris of Georgia had led the patrol to the designated point along the river. They found a narrow island, about three feet wide, but when a man stepped into the stream he disappeared in water over his head. The men of that patrol who swam across the river probably were the first men of the XII Corps to touch German soil. They heard digging on the far bank. The near bank was reported to be marshy, while the opposite bank was steep.[9] Obviously the stream was not fordable at that point.[10] The two-man rubber boats remained as the only recourse.

The regimental plan called for the 1st Battalion to cross the river at Frauenberg and capture the northwest half of Habkirchen, moving through the town to the southeast to meet the Third. At the same time, the Third Battalion was to cross the river at a point between Blies Ebersing and Folpersviller, move into Habkirchen from the southeast and meet the 1st Battalion. For the crossing the 1st Battalion had 20 engineer assault boats (each capable of carrying eight men plus its two-man engineer crew) and a foot bridge; the Third Battalion was to have seven rubber reconnaissance boats (each capable of carrying two men alone) and 1200 feet of rope.

The battalion commander and his staff worked to form a feasible plan under the circumstances and prepared an order to relay to the company commanders:

(1) (a) The enemy is strongly defending from the woods and high ground north of the Blies River. He has prepared strong positions, and his artillery is intense. There is no information on his local reserves. Weather forecast: showers in the early morning.

(b) The 134th Infantry attacks at 0530 to capture Habkirchen, 3rd Battalion on the right, 1st Battalion on left, the 2nd will remain in present position [Blies Ebersing] prepared to support by fire. The 320th Infantry will make a crossing in their zone on the right.

Tanks will support by fire from Hill 269 [overlooking Frauenberg.]

TD's will support by fire from Hill 274 [also overlooking Frauenberg.]

Artillery support by the 161st Field Artillery (reinforced).

(2) This Battalion will move from present positions at 0500 in column of companies: L, K, I to make crossing of the Blies River and seize the right half of Habkirchen. Base company after crossing: K.

(3) Company L will furnish guides to the crossing site, make the initial crossing, post security, and assist the crossing of the other companies; post three men for each

8. 3rd Bn. Journal, II, 109.
9. 3rd Bn. Journal, II, 109.
10. A curious confusion in map coordinates may have been the cause of the misinformation on the fordability of the stream. The entry in the 3rd Bn. Journal, II, 109, at 2210 hours on Dec. 11 states that the regimental S-2 gave the coordinates for the site where the river was fordable as 562 590; an entry in the 134th Inf. Unit Journal at 0230 on Dec. 12 gives these same coordinates for the point where the Third Battalion patrol crossed the river by swimming—this would be a point on the river approximately midway between Blies Ebersing and Habkirchen. However, the entry in the 134th Inf. Unit Journal for 2120, Dec. 11 states: "Civilian information on Blies River discloses two good building sites....Fordable at 557 602. Bottom is sandy and rocky. River is from 15 to 20 meters wide." These coordinates would refer to a point on the river northwest of Habkirchen, even to the left of the 1st Battalion area.

boat on the far bank, and one on the near bank to handle the boats. On completion of the Battalion crossing, Company L will follow Company K and furnish security to the right flank and rear.

Company K, with one heavy machine gun platoon attached, will follow Company L to the crossing site, pass through on the far shore and seize the southeast section of the town; mop up the area on the right side of the street, advance through the town to the battalion boundary and hold.

Company I, with one heavy machine gun platoon attached, will follow Company K across the river, seize, mop up and hold the section of town on the left side of the main street as far as the battalion boundary.

Company M—One machine gun platoon attached to each of Company K and Company I. Mortars in position to cover approaches to the town; observer with Company K.

Ammunition and Pioneer Platoon—Furnish guides to mark routes down to the launching site; assist in making the boats ready and in handling them.

Antitank Platoon: make reconnaissance for sites for earliest possible crossing into the town.

(4) Individuals each carry two full rations and extra ammunition. Additional supplies to be hand carried to the foot bridge in 1st Battalion area.

Aid Station: Folpersviller.

(5) Radio call sign: Baker (1st Battalion, Jig; 2nd Battalion, Fox); Channel: 36. CP: Folpersviller.[11]

The only possible chance for the Third Battalion's success lay in the possibility of stealthily moving across the river in the quiet rubber boats under the cover of darkness. The plan was for the pioneers, with the assistance of two engineers who accompanied the boats, to inflate the small craft, secure a length of rope to each end, and then, with the assistance of men from Company L, to pull the boats back and forth across the river to ferry the companies to the other side by shuttling.

It was nearly 4 o'clock by the time the boats and equipment had been loaded into the Ammunition and Pioneer Platoon's 1½-ton truck and the Battalion S-2 and S-3 set out by jeep to lead the party over the dark roads from Sarreinsming to the vicinity of the crossing site northwest of Blies Ebersing. Reconnaissance had shown that bridges over creeks on either side of Blies Ebersing had been blown. Therefore it was impossible to get vehicles closer than about 600 yards from the crossing site from either direction.[12]

It was decided that the best route to follow through the black darkness with the vehicles would be via the paved highway from Sarreinsming north and northwest to Neunkirch (four kilometers) thence generally east to Folpersviller (two kilometers) and on east toward Blies Ebersing as far as the destroyed creek bridge (one kilometer). However, the boat party met its first serious obstacle when it found that the tank destroyer which had been disabled by a mine near the edge of Le Grand Bois still set in the center of the highway; steep shoulders and mud on either side made it impossible for wheeled vehicles to travel off the highway, and when the 1½-ton truck was unable to get by the TD, it was necessary to return to Sarreinsming to try for another route. The staff officers returned to the CP for another map study—it would not be possible to refer to the map again once they resumed the move through the night under black-out discipline.[13]

The party then took the road running out of Sarreinsming to the northeast. This became a difficult mud road as it went through Le Grand Bois, and the officers and men with the boats made their way through the blind darkness

11. 3rd Bn. Journal, II, 110.
12. **ibid.**, p. 109; 3rd Bn. Interview, p. 15.
13. 3rd Bn. Interview, p. 15.

of the woods to the main Neunkirch ridge line highway at the Grand Viesing Farms. Here a sharp turn to the left (northwest) on the highway brought them soon to the railroad and an adjacent secondary road which led to Folpersviller. In Folpersviller it was necessary to find the road running to the east, but the darkness was so complete that it was almost impossible even to see the road over which they were moving. With the assistance of a luminous-dialed lensatic compass they found an easterly road, and when they arrived at a creek and a destroyed bridge, they knew that they had reached the spot which they had designated on the map.[14]

Meanwhile the companies had been forming and had anxiously watched precious minutes escape. While the Battalion S-2 supervised the preparation of the boats,—unloading, inflating, securing ropes—the S-3 went down to contact the companies, nearly half a mile away, and to bring back men to carry the boats to the river. He found the companies in column ready to make the crossing, and their commanders growing impatient as they realized the short time before dawn in which to get the Battalion across with the equipment available. When he returned to the place along the road where the boats were being fitted, he found only three ready to go: the process of inflation was taking some time, and moreover, it was found that the rope was badly tangled. Already it was 6 o'clock, so that he decided to send the three boats on down in order that a beginning could be made. The southeastern sky was growing light when leading men of Company L went down to the water's edge with the boats. Company commanders and staff officers alike appealed for a postponement of the attempt as being impossible. But by this time the 1st Battalion had troops in Habkirchen and it was necessary to make every effort to support them.[15]

When the men put the first boat into the water, the swift current almost immediately swept it out of control. Enemy armor could be heard on the other side of the river. It was approaching 8 o'clock and daylight was upon them. A call for smoke to screen the observation on the opposing hills was answered by two or three rounds of white phosphorous whose billowing white pillars mushroomed against the dull green hill sides in an incongruous, lonely beauty. The regimental commander called on Division Artillery in vain for additional smoke. Men of the 3rd Battalion stood in open nakedness in the river bottom land before that dominating high ground; the buildings of Blies Ebersing, about 400 yards away, offered the only cover in the area. Capt. Campbell moved his Company K back to the protection of the first of those buildings to await the clearance of "L" Company. But the observation of the enemy was not just imagined. He opened fire almost simultaneously with machine guns, mortars, and artillery. He took a toll of casualties from the Third Battalion; but more than that, he put an end to the abortive attempt of the Third Battalion to cross the Blies River at that particular place, at that particular time.[16]

If the efforts of the Third Battalion had any effect, it might have been in making enough of a demonstration to threaten the Germans and thus facilitate the crossing of the 1st Battalion two kilometers down stream (northwest). But fanatical Nazis of the 17th SS Division were charged with the defense of the

14. ibid.
15. ibid., p. 17.
16. ibid., Langdon, loc. cit., 134th Inf., Unit Journal, 12 Dec. 1944.

Habkirchen area,[17] and the 1st Battalion had a fight on its hands from the very beginning.

Company C led the 1st Battalion, and Company B followed. The swift current presented a major problem even for the assault boats, and the company lost one boat and some men drowned.[18] The last boats drew fire, and the bitter struggle was on. "C" Comapny captured 65 prisoners during the day and herded them into the basement of the large house which became its principal strongpoint.[19]

There was a tentative plan afoot to have the Third Battalion cross on the footbridge the next day, advance to the north of Habkirchen, then swing east across the Mandelbach Creek (which flowed through Habkirchen from the northeast to the Blies River) and seize the high ground overlooking the town from the northeast. With this in view, the Battalion marched, after nightfall, down the railroad from Blies Ebersing to Folpersviller. Sergeant Joe Morahan and his intelligence scouts guided the companies through the dark streets to billets.[20]

Hardly had the men bedded down for the night when at 12:30 A.M. word came: "Red Battalion is being counterattacked by infantry and armor; 3rd Battalion alerted to move to Habkirchen."[21] The counterattack had hit the 1st Battalion a few minutes after midnight. Groups of Germans would approach a house, and after firing bazooka rounds through the windows, would toss in concussion grenades, and then rush in to capture the occupants. Much of "B" Company was "sacked up." The principal American stronghold in Habkirchen consisted of 21 "C" Company men under Capt. William M. Denney of Missouri, with their 65 prisoners in that one large house. Captain Denney called upon 1st Battalion headquarters to send more men; but when the enemy continued retaking the few buildings left to the Americans, he suggested that it might be better to delay sending any more men. However, "A" Company already was on the way, though only a part of it was able to get across before a section of the foot bridge capsized at 12:30.[22]

Regimental headquarters learned of the counterattack at 12:15, and at 12:17 the 161st Field Artillery was notified to lay down its protective fires.[23] Warned by G-2 to expect a counterattack during the night, or the next day, the supporting artillery prepared to play a major role in defense of the bridge-head. The terrain surrounding Habkirchen included flanking hills to the north and northeast with a main road in the valley between leading to the town of Bebelsheim which was reported to be the center of German supply services for this sector. A major counterattack was possible from three different directions. The 161st Field Artillery prepared a "curtain of fire" in pre-arranged missions; it relayed its data to all the other artillery capable of firing into the sector— four light (105 mm) battalions, two medium (155 mm howitzers) battalions, and some larger caliber units from corps artillery. When the call came for artillery against the counterattack, normal barrages as well as a number of pre-arranged concentrations were fired. Later in the morning, a "road runner,"

17.   134th Inf., After Action Report, 4 Jan. 45.
18.   An Associated Press story of Dec. 12, 1944 stated that the 134th Infantry had crossed the Blies River into Germany "without the loss of a man."
19.   Robert Crome, Chicago Tribune Press Service, Dec. 14, 1944 (reprinted in The Santa Fe Express, May 1945, p.11.)
20.   3rd Bn. Interview, p. 19; 3rd Bn. Journal II, 111.
21.   3rd Bn. Journal, II, 111.
22.   Robert Cromie, loc. cit.; 134th Inf., Unit Journal, 12 Dec. 44.
23.   134th Inf., Unit Journal, 13 Dec. 44.

using battery volleys, searched the road to Bebelsheim, a distance of 2,500 meters. The 9th Company, 38th Regiment of the 17th SS Division had moved to the high ground to the east of Habkirchen on December 10th; now this unit suffered 50 per cent casualties from the artillery fire, and had to withdraw to reorganize. The 3rd Company of the 37th SS Regiment was badly confused by artillery as it moved up. Other units, from the 36th Division, were coming up to join in the attack against the bridgehead. As the 5th Company, 165th Infantry Regiment attacked from the east, it was caught in the artillery fire; in one group of 30, ten were killed or wounded by a concentration at 5 A.M. A Fusilier Company of the 36th Division, moving in from Bliesmengen was stopped by the artillery; later it suffered heavy casualties as it approached Habkirchen from the north.[24]

While the artillery broke up numbers of counterattacking troops, the Third Battalion was on its way. An hour after they were alerted, the companies were beginning their three-kilometer march through the black night to Frauenberg. At 2:15 A.M. the column cleared Folpersviller and at 3:15 was assembled in Frauenberg ready to cross the river. But the enemy directed almost continuous artillery fire on the bridge site for about three hours. Not only did this prevent the engineers from repairing the capsized section of the bridge, but at 2 o'clock it hit the bridge and damaged it to such an extent that it would require at least two and a half hours to repair. The Third Battalion would have to go across by boat. At 4 o'clock Company L, using ten assault boats, started across.[25]

Company L and two platoons of Company I were able to get to the opposite bank without enemy interference.[26] Then wild screams, the flash and boom of bazookas, and finally a display of green tracer bullets along the crossing

24. 35th Div. (161st FA), "Lessons Learned," pp. 4-5.
25. 134th Inf., Unit Journal, 13 Dec. 44; 3rd Bn. Interview, p. 19; 3rd Bn. Journal, II, 111.
26. The reinforcement of the hard-pressed troops in Habkirchen presents an interesting commentary on the necessity for a critical comparison of sources. Unit citations for Company C and the 2nd Platoon of Company D imply that those units held the bridgehead without further reinforcements for about 40 hours;—War Dept. General Orders, No. 68, 14 Aug. 1945, pp. 8-9 and No. 66, 10 Aug. 1944, p. 12; that those units alone held the bridgehead for 48 hours appears in the Division History, Santa Fe (typescript) p. 107; Again, the 134th Inf. After Action Report, 4 Jan. 1945, states: "B and C Companies held this bridgehead alone for 48 hours against the repeated counterattacks of over 300 SS troops and tanks." On the other hand, the 3rd Battalion Interview, p. 19; the 3rd Bn. Journal, II, 111; the 134th Inf., Unit Journal, 18 Dec. 1944; and the 134th Inf., Daily Log, V, 13 Dec. 1944, all indicate that elements of the Third Battalion crossed the river between 4:00 and 6:00 A.M. on December 13—24 hours after "C" Company's initial crossing. The Daily Log sums it up: "0015—Companies B and C heavily counterattacked by tanks and infantry, but repulsed. Elements of 3rd Battalion began crossing Blies at 0400 in assault boats. Company L and Part of I succeeded and assisted 1st Battalion in repulsing counterattacks at 0830." In making a comparison, the nature of the sources themselves must be considered. The unit citations were written from recommendations which had been prepared, at best, several days after the action took place; Santa Fe, the division history, was written from other sources, and so it becomes a secondary source; the After Action Report was a summary prepared for The Adjutant General's Office on January 4—three weeks after this particular action. The Combat Inteview covering these events was given five months later, so that its reliability is not to be unquestioned when it is found to conflict with other sources; but the 3rd Bn. Journal, kept mainly for reference of the battalion staff, consists of entries made at the time; the 134th Inf. Journal, likewise consists of entries made at the time, and the Daily Log was a summary made at the close of each day. In most cases, it would seem logical to assume that documents prepared at the time, or nearly so, mainly for local reference purposes, would be more reliable than documents prepared some time after the action described. However, even those documents cannot be used uncritically: what is apparently a typographical error in the Daily Log for 12 Dec. 1944, states that the 1st and 3rd Battalions began crossing the Blies River at 1500 hours—the typist probably intended 0500; again, in the 3rd Bn. Journal, II, 111, is an entry at 0630 saying "L Co. is across into Germany— K is crossing—I to follow"; this was corrected by a later entry, at 0835, which indicated that K was not across. As far as the reinforcement of B and C Companies was concerned, the Daily Log, V, 12 Dec., 44, and Robert Cromie, loc. cit., show that elements of Company A crossed over the footbridge around midnight—18 hours after the initial crossing of "C"; the evidence discussed above is conclusive that Company L and half of Company I crossed the river in assault boats within 24 hours after "C" Company's crossing, and Langdon, loc. cit. and the 3rd Bn. Interview, p. 19 (as well as the context of the 3rd Bn. Journal) show that Company K crossed on the footbridge, after it had been repaired, on the evening of December 13—about 36 hours after the initial crossing. The growth of this incidental myth—that elements of the 1st Battalion defended the bridgehead alone for 48 hours—may suggest some of the difficulties which the future historian will encounter in dealing with larger issues of military history.

site announced that another counterattack was underway. Troops of the Third Battalion were unable to swing above Habkirchen toward the high ground, then, but were drawn immediately into the fight. Bitter house-to-house fighting developed and it continued all day, but there was little gain on either side. Casualties mounted on both sides, but it was impossible to evacuate the wounded from the streets under the heavy fire, much less bring them back across the river. Lt. George Kryder fell under the "Company I Commanders jinx" when machine gun bullets streaked through a window to wound him painfully in the back. Finally an informal truce developed, and there was a cessation of hostilities while German and American medical men worked side by side to pick up their wounded. Aid men would carry wounded of the 1st and Third Battalions to the river where others would put them into an engineer boat flying the Red Cross flag; litter teams would pick them up and carry them to the aid station—jeeps would pick up those from the Third Battalion and carry them to the rear aid station in Frauenberg.[27]

With the coming of darkness the engineers were able to get to work at putting a Bailey bridge across the river over a former bridge site, while the footbridge could be made usable. Supplies were shuttled across the stream by boat. Then Company K was ordered to go across to reinforce the garrison in Habkirchen.

Lieutenant Langdon, now serving as executive officer of Company K, took an advance party across the river to locate places in which to move the company. He found men of the 1st Battalion "dead on their feet." A guide pointed out two buildings which he thought were vacant; one was burning, and the other was a shambles. Langdon sent a runner back for the company, and the men moved into the two buildings. They soon realized that they were in a precarious position—the Germans held the other side of the street. There was little sleep for the men in Hakbirchen that night—they were wondering what dawn would bring—wondering how long that house would burn. At dawn there were more counterattacks. A group of Germans rushed one of "K" Company's buildings, but were repulsed. Then another group moved behind the houses to an orchard and started to climb the trees in order to carry on some sniping; but riflemen knocked them out of the trees before they could get into action.[28]

Then the enemy resorted to artillery, and direct fire guns. A solid antitank projectile came crashing through the wall of a house to miss Capt. Campbell and members of his party by inches. But the American answer was in kind. During the night, corps and army artillery had fired some ten-minute concentrations of 150 guns on the approaches to Habkirchen, and had followed up with white phosphorous "road runners." Now all day the tanks and TD's from their dominating positions above Frauenberg, as well as antitank guns and heavy machine guns, poured an effective fire into the portions of Habkirchen held by the enemy.[29]

The Germans did not intend to give in easily to any attempted penetration of the valuable Saar territory. Though it was a bit premature as far as Habkirchen was concerned, *New York Times* of December 13, 1944 said of the campaign in the Saar:

27.   3rd Bn. Interview, pp. 19-20; Robert Cromie, **loc. cit.**, Cromie, Chicago Tribune Press Service, Dec. 13, 1944 (reprinted in **The Santa Fe Express**, May 1945, p. 2.)
28.   Langdon, **loc. cit.**
29.   3rd Bn. Interview, p. 20; 3rd Bn. Journal, II, 112.

The Third Army, battling its way through the thick German defenses of the Saar Basin today (Dec. 12), hammered out a new crossing of the German frontier, this time over the Blies River, and captured the German town of Habkirchen, four miles northeast of Sarraguemines. This was the only important progress on Lieut. Gen. George S. Patton's front. The Ninetieth and Ninety-fifth Infantry Divisions in the Dillingen and Saarlautern bridgeheads, on the left flank of the attack are holding their own in the face of furious enemy counter-attacks and a deluge of artillery fire.[30]

Again the next day:

The Third Army was still locked in violent battle with the Germans from Dillingen to Habkirchen in the arc of the defense protecting the Saar in the center of the Western Front.[31]

Thus far the reinforcement of the troops in Habkirchen had accomplished little. Rather it served to overcrowd dangerously the few buildings in American hands, and with the bridgehead too small to permit maneuver, it made no contribution toward expansion of the area. The situation in the large house which had been Company C's strongpoint worsened when command groups of both the 1st and Third Battalions moved into the building already crowded with men of Companies C and D, stragglers from other companies, and the 65 German prisoners—and then in the afternoon a battalion of the 137th Infantry crossed over on the foot bridge, and when German fire caught them many of its men sought temporary refuge in the house before moving on toward their objective on the high ground to the northwest of the town.[32]

Consequently it was decided to withdraw Company K from the town to make a maneuver from another direction. During the night of 12-13 December, the 2nd Battalion moved upstream from Blies Ebersing to cross the river in the zone of the 320th—who had established a bridgehead below Bliesbruck—and occupied the high ground northwest of Hill 312 (about two kilometers east of Habkirchen). Now Company K would cross the 2nd Battalion's bridge and, moving up on the left of that battalion, would seize the heights dominating Habkirchen from the northeast.[33]

On the night of 14-15 December, Company K marched out of Habkirchen over the footbridge. Capt. Campbell led the men up to the other crossing site, and the column began moving up the hill toward its objective. As the Company, marching in close column in order to keep contact in the darkness, moved quietly up the slope, another platoon fell in on the rear of the column and continued on up the hill. It was not until the newcomers were within a few yards that the men of Company K's last platoon noticed that they were speaking German. Both groups were so surprised that each fired one shot and then the Germans ran back toward the town while the American platoon ran for the woods on the hill. However, "K" Company did take three prisoners. Capt. Campbell estimated that there were 50 Germans in the group leaving Habkirchen. The prisoners stated that the Germans had withdrawn from Habkirchen by truck early in the morning.[34]

At any rate, Company K was on its objective by 8 A.M., and the Bailey bridge between Frauenberg and Habkirchen was nearing completion. When the tanks and TD's began to roll across the bridge, the crisis was over.

The two platoons of Company I which had remained as security in Frauenberg moved across to join the other "I" Company men in Habkirchen, and

30. Drew Middleton, pp. 1, 3.
31. Drew Middleton in **The New York Times**, Dec. 14, 1944, p. 1.
32. 3rd Bn. Interview, p. 20; 3rd Bn. Journal, II, 112.
33. **ibid.**
34. Langdon, **loc. cit.**; 3rd Bn. Journal, II, 112.

under the command of Lt. Hunt, moved through the right half of the town while Lt. Brigandi took Company L, with Company A attached (both far understrength) to mop up on the left. The town was all clear by noon and the Battalion CP moved to the southeast edge of Habkirchen.[35]

But there was to be no rest. The Third Battalion renewed the attack at 1:30 to gain the high ground northeast of Habkirchen on the left of the 2nd Battalion. Company I contacted Company K, and the two attacked abreast through the strip of woods on the hill while Company L remained in reserve. There was a sharp fire fight in the far edge of the woods, but the companies were able to gain their objective and consolidate for the night.[36]

The advance continued at 8 o'clock the next morning after a Company K patrol had found the next small patch of woods to be free of enemy. The companies were changing direction to the right in order to advance on through the grove to the larger Bannholz woods where they were to contact the 2nd Battalion. But bursts of machine gun fire pinned down the whole battalion; vicious direct fire began to raise havoc with the troops caught under the tree bursts; a stream of machine gun bullets over the Battalion command group caught Lt. Jefferan, artillery liaison officer, in the leg. Presently Major Heffelfinger and his party recognized that the machine gun fire was the slow cyclic rate of American Brownings. Once again the Third Battalion was caught in friendly tank fire. The 137th Infantry was making an attack for the high ground to the left (west) of the deep Mandelbach Creek valley, and supporting tanks of the 737th Tank Battalion (the battalion habitually attached to the 35th Division) were firing out of their zone. Notified of what was happening, the Battalion CP was out of communication with the regiment at the moment. Lt. Mike Hanna called for his jeep and raced through Habkirchen to contact the tanks and have them cease fire.[37]

The Third Battalion had hardly more than 100 riflemen for its attack. The bitter fighting, and now additional casualties from the tank fire, left Company K with approximately 60 men and 3 officers; Company I, 30 men and 2 officers; Company L, 11 men and 2 officers.[38]

Nevertheless, the Battalion moved on its battalion-size task. Entering the Bannholz woods, it made contact with the 2nd Battalion, and then the two battalions advanced to the north to enter the Rheinheimwald. During this advance, German artillery began to fall in greater and greater quantities. There was almost a continuous firing of battery and battalion volleys. For the first time men of the Third Battalion heard enemy volleys fired with the precision and coordination of American artillery; and it was one of the few times that they saw enemy artillery exceed the American in volume. It was one of the greatest demonstrations of German artillery which they encountered throughout the war.[39] The Associated Press reported that German artillery barrages were "reaching 250 rounds an hour on the Third Army front in the Saar Basin."[40]

Even when the companies halted to dig in for the night the artillery fire did not cease altogether. And again that evening Company I was without a commander. At 6 P.M. Second Lieuteant Hunt was reported killed in action.[41]

35. Ibid.
36. 134th Inf., Daily Log, V, 15 Dec. 44; 3rd Bn. Interview, p. 21.
37. 3rd Bn. Interview, p. 21.
38. Ibid., p. 22.
39. Ibid.
40. The New York Times, Dec. 17, 1944, p. 1.
41. 3rd Bn. Journal, II, 113.

During the afternoon the regimental Cannon Company and the 161st Field Artillery had moved across the river to Habkirchen, even though the bridge was under almost constant enemy artillery fire. At twilight machine guns were supporting the attack of the 137th Infantry to the northwest of Habkirchen from positions in *rear* of the 105 mm howitzers, and the enemy was using his mortars for counter-battery fire.[42]

During the night aircraft reported three columns of vehicles, each two to five miles long, moving toward the Habkirchen area, and another convoy of 75 to 90 vehicles to the northeast in the vicinity of Homberg. But if a major counterattack were developing, the nearly-depleted Third Battalion would not be there; on the morning of December 17th it was relieved by the 1st Battalion of the 137th Infantry, and by 5 P.M. it had closed in back at Folpersviller.[43]

42. Ibid.
43. 3rd Bn. Journal, II, 113; 134th Inf., After Action Report, 4 Jan. 45.

PART FOUR—THE ARDENNES BULGE

★ ★ ★

CHAPTER XVII

★ ★ ★

TOWARD BASTOGNE

When the Third Battalion returned across the Blies River to Folpersviller on December 17th the Third Army was facing the necessity of stabilizing its positions. Although General Eisenhower had hoped that it would be possible to achieve a complete victory in the Saar, he had ordered that the Third Army's final attack was to begin on December 19th, and then, regardless of results, divisions were to be shifted to the north for the main effort against the Rhine.[1]

The Battalion was able to undertake a program of training for newly-arrived replacements, and activities of recreation. The 1st Battalion re-entered the line in the woods southeast of Habkirchen near where the Third had been, but a sharp counterattack of tanks and infantry on the 20th forced that battalion to withdraw. Thereupon the Third Battalion was alerted to be prepared to move on a half hour's notice to protect the bridgehead at Habkirchen.[2]

That crisis passed, however, and on the 22nd the entire regiment was withdrawn to the vicinity of Puttelange; the Third Battalion went into assembly at Luberhouse.[3] Important developments were coming to pass in the Ardennes of Belgium and Luxembourg; the Seventh Army was extending its line to take over the Saar defense.[4]

Field Marshal Walter Model had launched a counteroffensive in the north which threatened to disrupt the whole Allied disposition in that area. Aimed at seizing bridgeheads over the Meuse, the almost indispensable port of Antwerp, and Brussels, the attack—24 divisions strong—rolled through the four divisions of the VIII Corps deployed along the thinly-held Eifel-Ardennes sector, with the benefit of complete surprise, on December 16th. The American commanders had taken a "calculated risk" to leave lightly defended that difficult avenue— but previously used by the Germans—in order to concentrate forces for their own offensive father north. A combat command of the 10th Armored Division moved into the important road center of Bastogne, and on the 18th was joined by the 101st Airborne Division, moving up from SHAEF reserve near Reims. Shortly after, the Bastogne garrison found itself surrounded.[5]

Stories of the confusion and action reached the Third Battalion.

At first everything was wild confusion. Germans suddenly appeared over the crest of hills and shot up towns. They overran rear-area supply points, pounced upon U. S. artillerymen before they could get to their guns. Germans surrounded a field of artillery-spotting planes, whose pilots were fast asleep. U. S. divisional generals found their command posts the centers of battles, their defenders hastily armed cooks, clerks, medics, runners. Trucks filled with German soldiers dashed through areas where rear-echelon G.I.'s went about their routine tasks.[6]

1. General Eisenhower's Report, p. 73.
2. 3rd Bn. Journal, II, 115.
3. ibid., p. 116.
4. General Marshall's Report, p. 44.
5. General Eisenhower's Report, p. 76; Crusade in Europe, p. 348-353; General Marshall's Report, p. 44; Ingersoll, Top Secret, pp. 243-247; Robert E. Merriam, Dark December (Chicago and New York, 1947) pp. 103-120. S-2 Periodic Reports of 6th Armored Division had mentioned capability of German attack and had raised question of whereabouts of Sixth Panzer Army.
6. Time, Jan. 1, 1945, p. 18.

The German radio announced that the 106th Division had been wiped out, and that its 212 survivors were wandering around lost in a snow storm.[7]

The Luftwaffe returned to the skies in the greatest strength employed since D-day. The Germans resorted to every kind of trick and device: parties of paratroopers dropped along the north flank of the battle area; agents in American uniforms were sent through the lines for sabotage and reconnaissance behind Allied lines; a panzer brigade was operating in capured American equipment.[8]

During the breathing spell permitted him by the American halt in September, Hitler had been able to begin the building of a new striking force. Young, fanatical Nazis were formed into the Sixth SS Panzer Army, with complete and new equipment. Other troops were re-formed into *Volksgrenadier* divisions to support the new army. And for home defense the *Volkssturm* was created of men who had been considered unfit for military service, but they would be able to man fortifications while other divisions were freed to make the attack.[9] Altogether Rundstedt had assembled three armies; the Fifth and Sixth Panzer Armies, and the Seventh Army, with a total of some 14 infantry divisions and 10 panzer (armored) and panzer grenadier (armored infantry) divisions.[10]

General Eisenhower and General Bradley had sensed very soon that this was the "real thing," and plans were made for swinging the Third Army to the north. Because of the difficult situation in the Bastogne region, Bradley felt that the Third Army should be attacking northward from the Arlon-Luxembourg area no later than December 22nd. Patton was authorized to attack, but was instructed to make sure that his right flank was safe, and to advance by phase lines.[11]

When General Patton heard of the German counteroffensive his reaction was: "Fine. We should open up and let 'em get all the way to Paris. Then we'll saw 'em off at the base."[12] He received orders from the Supreme Commander, through 12th Army Group, to assume command over the units of the VIII Corps south of the break-through, and to attack north to cut off and destroy the enemy. Patton quickly issued orders to his corps commanders to get movement started. The 35th Division was to be withdrawn to the vicinity of Metz.[13] Once again the superior mobility—the superior automotive power— of the American Army was to be a decisive factor.

A light snow fell around Puttelange on December 22nd. At 4 A.M. the next morning the Third Battalion, on 19 trucks and its own organic transportation, joined the motor column of the 134th Infantry in moving to Metz. Soldiers were ordered to have a blanket available during the trip, for it was bitterly cold in the open or canvas-covered trucks. Before noon the regiment arrived at its assigned area in permanent French barracks in the military city of Metz.[14]

With a hope which the men must have known was forlorn, the regiment and battalion immediately reverted to garrison life. However, the commanders felt it highly important to undertake as much training as possible before they were called upon to go into the critical battle farther north. Replacements came

7. 35th Inf. Division, Official Program: Dedication of the Santa Fe Stadium (Coblenz, Germany, July 1, 1945), p. 4.
8. General Eisenhower's Report, p. 76; Merriam, **op. cit.**, pp. 126-131.
9. **Ibid.**, pp. 6-8; Ingersoll, **op. cit.**, pp. 229-232.
10. General Eisenhower's Report, p. 76.
11. General Eisenhower's Report, pp. 76-77; Ingersoll, **op. cit.**, p. 261.
12. Butcher, **My Three Years with Eisenhower**, p. 274.
13. Third U. S. Army, After Action Report, I, 169.
14. 3rd Bn. Journal, II, 116-118.

in to fill the Battalion to full strength, and it required some time for the companies to reorganize—for squad leaders to be appointed, for men to be assigned, and then for squad members to become acquainted. Therefore a daily schedule was set up calling for six hours of training a day. Plans were made for range firing of weapons during the week.[15]

The regimental commander called a conference with each battalion the next afternoon. He emphasized the need for preparation to meet the tests which lay ahead; he warned of the tricks and the ruthlessness of the German attackers in the area to the north; he told them that the 134th Infantry would be called upon to deliver the "Sunday punch." But he did declare Christmas a holiday—provided there was no move.[16]

Word came early on the 24th that the 26th and 80th Divisions already were attacking north in Luxembourg. But it looked as though the 35th Division would be fortunate enough to have a Christmas holiday in Metz.[17]

Groups of men collected Sunday evening to celebrate Christmas Eve. Major Heffelfinger decided that the Battalion Staff should invite the company commanders over for a party. With the enthusiasm of their school days the staff officers began to make preparations. They were housed in quarters along the Moselle River across the street from the main garrison buildings. A furnished parlor made an appropriate place. The first need was for a Christmas tree. The artillery liaison officer and the S-3 found a hand axe and a flashlight and went hunting. A few minutes later they returned—they had found a pine tree already felled, and had cut the top out of it. Shiny foil from radio battery wrappers, tissue paper, and toy balloons provided decorations, and illumination came from flashlights set up at the side. On the table beneath the tree was a spread of refreshments: nuts, candies, cakes, cookies, cigars—contributions from boxes which had been received from home. Using the discarded Christmas paper from those boxes, the officers neatly wrapped a box of K ration as a "Christmas present" for each of the company commanders. When the guests arrived the party was not wanting for entertainment. For a moment they captured a fleeting bit of gaiety. There was laughter and talking and singing. Hon made up "orange blossoms" from powdered orange juice, and Vlascious served the group. "Fluff" Greenlief boomed forth with a loud, "St. Louis Woman" . . . Mike Hanna danced a slow jig while they whistled "Swanee River" . . . Jack Campbell gained the praises of everyone when he sang a group of old Irish favorites in his excellent tenor voice . . . Chaplain Walker brought roars of laughter as he sang "So Long Mule."

Then shortly after midnight, the party quieted down. The chaplain rose. He noticed that most of the members of the group, in spite of all the rapid turnover which the Battalion had experienced, had come through the war from the beginning: Captain Gibson, newly-appointed commander of Company I, had been with regimental headquarters; Captain Campbell had started with Company L, and now was commanding K; Capt. Greenlief had been with Company L, as platoon leader and commander, all the way; Lt. Erickson had started as a machine gun platoon leader; Lt. Hanna had been with Company C before coming to the battalion as S-2; Capt. Bruce had been with Battalion Headquarters since England; Capt. Magnunson had been with the 90th Division;

15. *Ibid.,* pp. 118-119; 3rd Bn. S-3 Notebook, I.
16. *Ibid.*
17. 3rd Bn. Journal, II, 119.

Major Heffelfinger had been with the 1st Battalion but joined the Third in Normandy. Several had been wounded, but returned. That others of the group would be wounded in the days to come there could be no doubt.

"Perhaps we have been spared for greater tasks which lie ahead," the Chaplain observed. "In the midst of war we are celebrating in peace and happiness the birth of a babe nearly two thousand years ago. It is a wonderful thing that one man could bring such joy into the world when others bring such misery. In our homes back in the States tonight the greatest joy obtained by men is being reached because a man named Jesus lived in a country called Palestine. Around us tonight the most terrible destruction and pessimism hovers because that man was forgotten."

Quietly the group went out to the doorstep. A nearly full moon was shining down through snow-covered evergreens. Softly the male voices of the Battalion's leaders blended in "Silent Night, Holy Night."[18]

Reconnaissance of firing ranges in the Metz area, and preparation of training schedules was of no avail. Third Army was conducting its troop movements smoothly enough and rapidly enough to permit the Arlon highway to the 35th Division on December 26th. The Third Battalion moved into the small Belgian town of Attert, six miles north of Arlon.[19]

In order to provide adequate security while in assembly, the practice had grown up in the Battalion of naming one company each night to be the alert company, or "fire company." This unit would be on call in case of any disturbance during the night, and would furnish an "officer of the day" to supervise the security and inspect sentries, and roving patrols to patrol the streets and contact the various outposts guarding entry into the town.[20] Now, as the Battalion approached enemy-held territory, Major Heffelfinger directed security patrols and guards to be especially alert. On this night, for example, Company K was designated the alert company, and was directed to have three two-man patrols touring the streets continuously from "sunset to sun up." Lt. Keary was made officer of the day, and he reported to the Battalion CP for his instructions. In addition, jeep patrols from Company M patrolled the roads in the vicinity and contacted the other battalions located in neighboring towns.[21]

The 134th Infantry remained in division reserve the next morning when their attack was launched at 8 o'clock by the 137th and 320th through knee-deep snow across the Sure River. The 35th Division was attacking between the 26th Division on the right, and the 4th Armored Division on the left as the III Corps drove to raise the siege of Bastogne and to secure the Arlon-Bastogne highway.[22] To be sure, tanks of the 4th Armored Division had made contact with elements of the 101st Airborne Division the preceding day,[23] but as long as the main north-south highway remained in enemy hands, and the enemy, still occupying ground around most of the town, continued his efforts to close in, that corridor remained extremely tenuous.

Although to some observers that initial contact—by tank—had meant that the "Battle of the Ardennes was over,"[24] the Third Battalion had "not yet

18. Chaplain A. C. Walker to the Author, July 15, 1946 and July 26, 1946; J. Huston, to N. F. Huston, Dec. 25, 1944.
19. 3rd Bn. Journal, II, 120.
20. ibid., pp. 82, 91, 120.
21. ibid., p. 20.
22. 35th Div., **Attack**, p. 26.
23. General Eisenhower's Report, p. 77.
24. Ingersoll, op. cit., p. 273, et. al.

begun to fight," and for all those battalions attacking the Bulge, it was far from over. Indeed, American losses sustained *after* December 26th exceeded those for the preceding ten days—including all the units which had been overrun in the German's initial break-through.[25]

As a matter of fact the First Army was not able to attack against the north side of the Bulge until January 3rd,[26] and therefore, Model was in a position to deploy his main defensive strength against the Third Army's attack from the south.[27] The rapid shift of the Third Army from an offensive in the Saar to an attack in the Ardennes was recognized as a brilliant military achievement, involving army and corps staff work of the highest order.[28] But this attack did contribute much to halting the German drive, for now Model had to turn his main effort away from the Meuse to try in greater force to take Bastogne and to hold against the Third Army. Moreover, the weather had cleared for the first time since the break-through and Allied planes were able to attack columns throughout the area for four days in succession. (According to stories which made the rounds, the break in the weather had followed General Patton's order to the Chaplain to pray for clear weather.)[29]

As the 137th and the 320th attacked, the Battalion moved forward—still along the Arlon-Bastogne highway—in another ten-mile motor move to an assembly position in the woods north of Warnach.[30] The 134th Infantry was preparing to join the attack.

Before noon (December 28th) Major Heffelfinger was called to the regimental CP to plan an attack in cooperation with CCA of the 4th Armored Division. While the Battalion would not be attached to the armored division, it was instructed to cooperate with it completely. Brig. General Ernest, Commanding CCA, was attempting to drive into Bastogne via the Arlon-Bastogne highway. To do that, he told Major Heffelfinger, it would be necessary for the Third Battalion to seize the town of Lutrebois—a village five kilometers south of Bastogne, and a kilometer and a half east of the highway—in order to protect the right flank. That afternoon the Battalion moved by shuttling to relieve the 3rd Battalion, 318th Infantry (90th Division) in a woods north of Sainlez. It had entered the line on the left (west) of the 137th Infantry, prepared for an attack toward Lutrebois—three kilometers to the north-northeast —on the next morning (December 29th).[31]

Later that day it developed that the whole regiment would enter the attack, but it was to be in a column of battalions, the Third leading, and instructions for close cooperation with CCA of the 4th Armored Division remained. Colonel Miltonberger was determined to make contact with units of the 101st Airborne

25. Eisenhower, **Crusade in Europe**, p. 359; Commager, **The Story of the Second World War,** p. 461. Shugg and De Weerd put it this way: "Rundstedt's offensive was over, and the Battle of the Bulge began."—**World War II,** p. 325. Also Merriam: "During this time the heaviest fighting ensued in the battle for Bastogne; the casualties were much worse."—**Dark December,** p. 196.

26. "Allies Squeeze the German Bulge," **Life,** XVIII (Jan. 15, 1945) 15-19; General Eisenhower's Report, p. 78.

27. Ingersoll states that plans had been made and orders issued for a simultaneous attack by the First Army, on the north, and the Third Army, on the south, when General Bradley's command was split to give Field Marshall Montgomery control of all the troops north of the penetration. Montgomery then abandoned the offensive, and the 82nd Airborne Division and the 7th Armored Division, prepared to make a stand at St. Vith like that of the 101st and CCB of 10th Armored at Bastogne, were withdrawn—**Top Secret,** pp. 263-271.

28. General Marshall's Report, p. 44.

29. Ingersoll, **op. cit.,** pp. 272-273; Merriam, **op. cit.,** pp. 196-198; Allen, **Lucky Forward,** p. 239 gives the text of Patton's own prayer.

30. 3rd Bn. Journal, II, 127.

31. 3rd Information and Historical Service, Combat Interviews, No. 108—35th Div.—1 Nov. 44 —23 Jan. 45, p. 24; 134th Inf., Daily Log, V, 28 Dec.

Division in his zone with the greatest possible speed. Hence the column formation: should one battalion become involved in a fight, the next would by-pass to the left, and keep going, and then, if necessary, the next.[32]

Officers from units which had been designated to support the Third Battalion's attack reported to the CP in Sainlez that evening: Lieutenant Merschany and Lt. Budeznarick of the 4.2 inch chemical mortars (code name: SATIRE CHARLIE) who were given an SCR 300 radio set on the Battalion's channel; Lt. Dunn of the 2nd Tank Destroyer Platoon, who also was given a 300 radio for close coordination; Lt. Evans of the 66th Field Artillery Battalion (Corps). Others came and joined the meeting with the Battalion staff and company commanders at 9:30 P.M. for the Third Battalion's first attack order against the bulge:

1.a.) Enemy continues to defend in Division sector with capability of counterattack. There is a warning of a counterattack from the north to northeast tonight or tomorrow.

b.) 134th Infantry attacks at 0800 in column of battalions, 1st Battalion follows 3rd, 2nd follows 1st. 1st Battalion moved initially to assemble area in rear of present position of Companies I and L. 2nd Battalion moved to assembly in woods south of SAINLEZ. 137th Infantry attacks on right, 4th Armored Division on left.

In direct support:
161st Field Artillery Battalion (Observer with Company L.)
Cannon Company
Company C, 3rd Chemical Mortar Battalion.
2nd Platoon, Company A, 654th TD Battalion
3rd Platoon, Antitank Company
3rd Platoon, Company A, 60th Engineers.

2.) This Battalion will attack to seize LUTREBOIS, prepared to continue the attack north to MARVIE.
Formation: Column of Companies, L, I, K.
LD: Present front line of Company L.
Direction of attack: north
    Time of attack: 0800.

3.a.) Company L will attack to the north, seize and mop up LUTREBOIS.

b.) Company I will follow Company L by 200 to 300 yards, prepared to attack on right. Provide security patrol to right flank (contact 137th). Be prepared to pass through Company L at LUTREBOIS and continue the attack.

c.) Company K will follow Company I by 200 to 300 yards, prepared to attack on either right or left, provide security patrol to left flank.

d.) Company M—one machine gun platoon direct support Company L, one prepared to support Company I.
    81 mm mortars in position to fire on Lutrebois and area to front. Observer with Company L.

e.) Antitank Platoon—Initiate reconnaissance to provide AT security, particular attention to front and right flank. Reconnoiter for positions to give direct fire on LUTREBOIS.

x.) Possible contact with friendly troops in vicinity of MARVIE.

4.) Rolls—stacked vicinity present CP's (men carry 1 blanket) with 2-man guard.
    Rations—one complete K on individual; hot coffee available for breakfast 0600.

5.) Radio channel 27, call sign PETER.
        Battalion CP—present position
                OP—Vicinity road north of Company L area.
    Password: REVOLUTION; reply: FRENCH[33]

32. 134th Inf., Daily Log, V, Dec. 28, 1945.
33. 3rd Bn. Journal, II, 129.

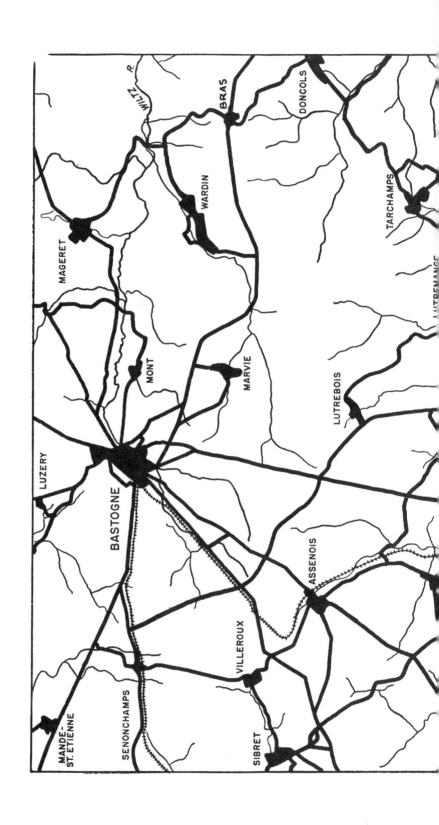

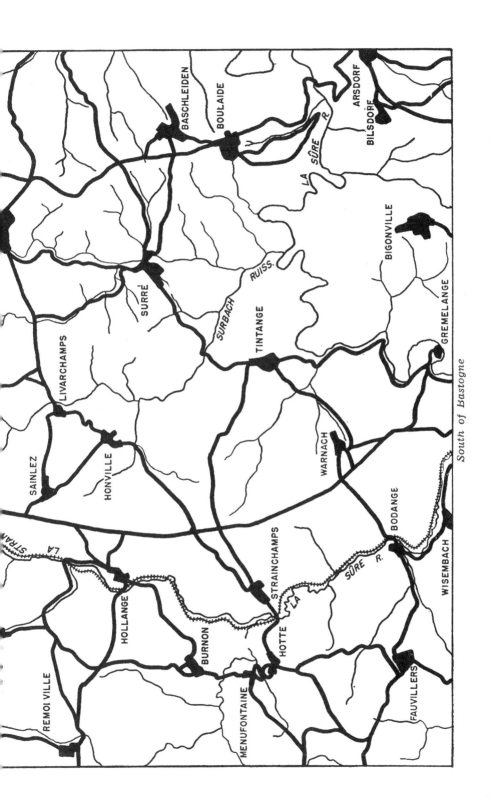

South of Bastogne

Captain Greenlief sent out a patrol two hours before H-hour and it returned with the reassuring news that it had been able to advance to the front nearly 1,000 yards before it drew fire from machine pistols.[34]

The Battalion column advanced through the woods without opposition to reach the high ground overlooking Lutrebois. The town, mainly along a single street, stretched a thousand yards across an open valley between the wooded hill which Company L occupied, and other tree-covered heights to the northeast.[35]

In order to get into the town it was necessary for the men of Company L to move out of the edge of the woods and down the open forward slope. The first men drew some small arms fire. Greenlief paused to call for smoke on the hill across the valley, then as the chemical mortars, and the 81 mm mortars built up a screen with white phosphorous, platoons, moving in small groups, rushed into the village.[36]

As it advanced along the narrow street between scattered houses, the leading platoon surprised an enemy vehicle which was driving toward it. Quick volleys of rifle fire wrecked the motor car and killed the occupants.[37] In all, the company left 17 enemy dead in the streets as it consolidated its position, and took a few prisoners.[38]

In order best to make secure the position in Lutrebois, and to provide the best flank protection for the 4th Armored Division's tanks, it was desirable to gain a hold on the wooded high ground to the northeast of Lutrebois. Greenlief sent one platoon to accomplish this. The platoon crossed the road which ran across the far end of the town and entered the woods beyond. But as it moved up the slope, it found that it had been lured into a trap. Enemy automatic weapons opened fire from all sides. It was only with the assistance of artillery and a hard fire fight that the platoon was able to extricate itself and get back into the town.[39]

Meanwhile Companies I and K changed direction to the right and moved across the valley to the southeast of Luterbois. They took up positions, Company K on the right, Company I on the left, in the woods just short of the road, overlooking the southeasterly approaches to the town.[40] Greenlief kept his Company CP on the high ground to the southwest of Lutrebois, and there the machine gun platoon took up its positions where it could cover the southwest approaches to the town and give depth to the defenses.

When the Third Battalion became involved at Lutrebois, Colonel Milton-berger sent the 1st around it to go on into Marvie where it made contact with elements of the 101st Airborne Division.[41] Now the armor was able to fight its way on up through Remoifosse along the highway. The Arlon-Bastogne highway was open. The immediate question was to keep it so.

34. **ibid.**
35. 3rd Bn. Interview, p. 24; Map: Belgium & N.E. France, 1:100,000 (ARLON) Sheet 17.
36. 3rd Bn. Interview, pp. 24-25.
37. **ibid.,** p. 25.
38. 3rd Bn. Journal, II, 134.
39. 3rd Bn. Interview, p. 25.
40. **ibid.**
41. 134th Inf., After Action Report, 4 Jan. 45; 35th Div., **Attack!,** p. 27.

CHAPTER XVIII

★ ★ ★

COUNTERATTACKS AT LUTREBOIS

★ ★ ★

While the companies were approaching Lutrebois, the Battalion command post moved up to share a shell-torn chateau already occupied by the headquarters of an armored infantry battalion of the 4th Armored Division. The chateau was in a small open-hollow about 1,500 yards southwest of Lutrebois and about 400 yards east of the Arlon-Bastogne highway. A tree-covered hill lay between it and the town. Now troops of the Armored infantry battalion occupied a position along the forward edge of the woods from a point near the highway, about 1,500 yards north of the chateau, southeast to a point about 500 yards from the approaches to Lutrebois—in other words, the men of the armored infantry battalion held a line some distance to the left (north) of the position occupied by the Company L headquarters and support group, and the heavy machine gun platoon. On the open ground to the north of the armored infantry, tanks and tank destroyers of CCA (4th Armored Division) were deployed along the highway; the TD's in direct support of the Third Battalion were on the open hill in the same vicinity, in position to cover Lutrebois and its valleys. The Battalion's 57 mm antitank guns were in position in the area of Company L's support platoon after Sergeant Frank Stephan's Antitank Platoon had man-handled them through woods and over soft ground.[1]

The 137th Infantry had been stopped by difficult fighting in the vicinity of Villers la Bonne Eau. This meant a serious gap between that area and Lutrebois. The 2nd Battalion, therefore. was moved to fill partially that gap. But this still left Company K, across the valley, with an open right flank.[2] Now Company E of the 2nd Battalion was the only reserve available in the area.

Lt. Col. Warren C. Wood returned to the Battalion during the attack on Lutrebois,[3] but he did not re-assume command until the day's mission had been completed. It had been only six weeks since Col. Wood had been wounded—on "Blue Monday," west of Morhange in Lorraine.

As the Battalion prepared its security for the night, it was evident that the enemy still was active in the area. The Air Force had reported knocking out 25 enemy tanks and 25 half-tracks during the afternoon; a civilian reported that there had been 500 Germans—half of them in American uniforms—with five tanks and a large-caliber gun in Lutrebois the preceding evening; from Marvie the 1st Battalion reported much vehicular traffic during the night in the vicinity of Wardin, a town about 3 kilometers to the east of Marvie which was thought to be a supply center; Captain Campbell reported that tanks and infantry seemed to be withdrawing from the right front of "K" Company.[4]

1. 3rd Bn. Interview, p. 26 ff., map.
2. 134th Inf., After Action Report, 4 Jan. 45.
3. 3rd Bn. Journal, II, 129.
4. Ibid.

The enemy struck back at 4:30 A.M. the next morning (December 30th) when infantrymen began moving from the woods opposite Companies I and K toward Lutrebois. Immediately the company commanders called for artillery— "concentrations 228 and 229." The quick response was effective in disorganizing the enemy, but only momentarily. He reformed, and by 5:15 had reached Company L's position in the forward (northeast) end of Lutrebois. Here again the attack was delayed as the Company L light machine gun section held up the whole German force. However, the enemy deployed, and while one column moved to by-pass the town to the northwest, and another by-passed it to the southeast, a third gained a foot-hold in the town and started to work through. Soon Lutrebois was surrounded, and the enemy infantrymen started up toward the wooded hill to the southwest.[5]

Colonel Miltonberger sensed early that the enemy was aiming for something more than just the recovery of the village of Lutrebois. Accordingly at 6:00 A.M. he ordered Company E, in reserve in the 2nd Battalion area, to counterattack to assist the Third Battalion. However, it still was dark and enemy groups already were in the woods; the Company, advancing along the paths north toward Company L's position was unable to make an effective attack before enemy groups succeeded in infiltrating through to disorganize its own ranks. Now, with no effective American reserve in the area, groups of enemy were able to advance toward the 2nd Battalion's left flank: Company F found enemy in its rear; a platoon of Company G was cut off.[6]

Enemy airplanes came in to bomb Bastogne at 7:10.[7] This looked to be a coordinated, all-out attack.

Company M's 2nd Machine Gun Platoon (Shapiro), with the Company L headquarters and mortar section, waited in the midst of this confusion for the enemy to reach their position. Lines of enemy infantrymen started over the open slope from the direction of a small cemetery just outside the town. The temperature had dropped during the night, and a fresh snow covered the ground.[8] Even in the winter twilight the dark figures of the approaching enemy stood out plainly against the white background as they came near the woods. Lieutenant Shapiro and Technical Sergeant Homer Wolfe, platoon sergeant, had prepared coordinated fire. The heavy machine guns opened fire. The enemy soldiers fell. But others kept coming. When enemy groups infiltrated around the flanks, Captain Greenlief began to organize the remnants of his company to withdraw from the woods. As he did so, the machine guns kept up their fire. For more than an hour they held their positions, inflicting heavy casualties, and repelling three successive assaults. Finally with little rifle protection and the enemy about to enter the positions from the flanks, the platoon leader ordered his men out of action and organized an orderly withdrawal in which every man and every gun was brought out without loss.[9]

In recognition for this stand every one of the 24 members of the 2nd Machine Gun Platoon later was awarded the Bronze Star Medal. They represented a cross-section of the Third Battalion—and of their nation: Sgt. Wolf of Illinois; Staff Sergeant William Brown of California, section leader; Sergeant Carl Brady of Ohio, section leader; Sgt. Carl Corley of South Caro-

5. 3rd Bn. Interview, p. 26; 3rd Bn. Journal, II, 130.
6. 3rd Bn. Journal, II, 130; 3rd Bn. Interview, p. 26.
7. 3rd Bn. Journal, II, 130.
8. 134th Inf., Daily Log, V, 30 Dec. 1944.
9. 35th Division, General Orders, No. 14, 26 Feb. 1945.

lina, squad leader; Private Joseph Conlen of Ohio, squad leader; Sgt. Refiel Duffek of Nebraska, squad leader; Private First Class Clyde McGlothlin of Virginia, squad leader; the first gunners: Corporal Kermit Meltz of New York, Cpl. John Miller of Ohio, Pfc. Dean Anderson of Indiana, and Pfc. John Scritchfield of West Virginia; the number 2 gunners: Pfc. Guierimo Cardone of New York, Pvt. Jack Covington of Kentucky, Pvt. John Gullett of Texas, and Pvt. Florian Kowalske of Wisconsin; and then the ammunition handlers: Pfc. Albert Atliff of Pennsylvania (who went back 250 yards for a re-supply of ammunition in the midst of the fight), Pfc. Lloyd Morley of Michigan, Pfc. John Myers of Michigan, Pfc. Edwin Rosenthal of New Jersey, Pfc. Carmine Trovato of New York; Pfc. Harold Wigginton of Indiana, and Pvt. Albert Narvid of Pennsylvania; and the aid man: Pfc. Bert Bogan of Virginia.[10]

The Battalion antitank guns, which had been man-handled into the difficult position, had to be abandoned.[11]

Captain Greenlief then led his men west through the woods to the main highway, and thence south to a position in rear of the Battalion CP.[12] Now there was nothing between the command post and the woods.

Meanwhile Companies I and K, in a good position to be cut off in their trans-valley woods, took measures to protect their flanks. Captain Campbell called repeatedly for artillery concentration 228 as enemy infantry seemed to be forming for a new attack against his right flank. The company captured a few prisoners in the vicinity—and found some of them wearing American overcoats.[13] But now enemy groups were approaching the CP.

Second Lieutenant William Bomberger, who recently had been commissioned and assigned to Company I as a platoon leader, happened to be at the Battalion CP awaiting a chance to return to his company. Colonel Wood charged him with setting up a perimeter defense around the CP. The lieutenant quickly organized a complete circle around the chateau and the adjacent buildings where the aid station was located. Members of the Ammunition and Pioneer Platoon, the men of Company L who had made their way back, members of the Antitank Platoon, who had come back from their guns, stragglers, members of the armored infantry battalion headquarters, all joined in the defensive circle. Other men took positions at the windows—or at shell holes in the walls—of the chateau. A medium tank, a light tank, and a half-track or two (with 50-caliber machine guns) provided close-in defensive fire power. The heavy machine guns of the Company M platoon which had withdrawn through the woods set up to cover those woods. The 81 mm mortars, located near some farm buildings about 250 yards up the road, east, from the chateau, shortened their range, and began firing into the woods which Company L and its supporting units had just abandoned.[14]

But now the enemy injected a new element into the picture: tanks. Evidently the preceding infantry were considered to have completed their mission with the capture of Lutrebois and the occupation of the woods behind (and they had succeeded in overrunning three antitank guns which had been disposed to meet just such a threat as this). The enemy was calling upon some of the best troops at his disposal in a bid to (1) capture a sup-

10. Ibid., and General Orders, No. 15.
11. 3rd Bn. Interview, p. 26.
12. Ibid.
13. Ibid.
14. Ibid.

ply dump which was thought to be in the vicinity of the chateau; (2) cut the Arlon-Bastogne highway; (3) swing north to reduce Bastogne itself.[15] About 600 troops of the 331st Regiment, 167th Volksgrenadier Division had participated in the initial attack.[16] Now the elite were prepared to enter: elements of the 14th Parachute Regiment, 5th Parachute Division, and the 2nd Regiment, 1st SS Panzer (Adolph Hitler) Division.[17]

Captain Campbell could count the tanks as they rumbled slowly past his position; a few minutes later Captain Gibson would report their rolling along the road in front of Company I's position. Men of the rifle platoons, scarcely more than fifty yards from the road which the "iron monsters" were following, watched the column halt. Officers from a command car at the head dismounted—and, almost as by reflex, riflemen of Company K opened fire. Campbell hastened to stop the outburst, for he felt sure that their position had not been discovered; nevertheless the order was too late to save the Germen officers, and doubtless those riflemen had gone a long way toward disrupting the enemy's organization and leadership for the attack. Then the men waited apprehensively to see what the tanks were going to do—they knew how deadly would be the tree bursts if the tank guns started firing high explosive shells in their direction; but they could take some hope in their knowledge of the difficulty of locating rifles merely by the sound of the bullets. They watched the turrets of the Mark IV tanks swing around, and the long, ugly barrels of the guns point toward them; and then, strangely, the tanks only fired a few bursts from their machine guns, then the turrets turned back to the original direction, and the tanks rolled on toward Lutrebois—200 yards beyond. Companies K and I now were "out like a sore thumb," but the Company commanders were in excellent positions to bring down artillery fire on the armored column and its supporting infantry.[18]

Meanwhile the German's leading infantry groups were closing in on the Battalion CP. Fifteen rounds of 120 mm mortar shells burst in patterns about the chateau; a German rocket flew wide of the Sherman tank in the yard; now enemy riflemen, coming through the woods, began to fire—a man near one of the chateau windows was wounded. But the CP defenders were quick to reply: machine guns—heavy 30 caliber of Company M, light 30 of tanks and 50 caliber of tanks and half-tracks—sent steady streams of bullets into the woods; the medium tank fired its 75 mm gun; supporting artillery laid down heavy concentrations on what had been Company L's position; 81 mm mortars shortened their range to 300 yards to send their shells bursting into the trees on the slope. Even then, some enemy groups persisted in their advance.[19] A hostile machine gun team found a position where it could neutralize the 81 mm mortars with machine gun fire!

Pfc. Edward Lentz of Indiana, a member of the Battalion Ammunition and Pioneer Platoon, heard the dangerous machine gun on the slope. He asked permission to leave his post in the perimeter defense in order to attempt its destruction. Then he stole around the nose of the hill until he

15. PW statements—134th Inf., Unit Journal, 30 Dec. 1944, and 3rd Bn. Journal, II, 131; a captured map showed that one battalion was to turn north in the vicinity of the chateau and attack on the right of the Arlon highway, while two others were to continue west across the highway and then swing north toward Bastogne.—3rd Bn. Interview, p. 27.
16. P.W. statement, 134th Inf., Unit Journal, 30 Dec. 1945.
17. 134th Inf., S-2 Periodic Report, 30-31 Dec., 1944.
18. 3rd Bn. Interview, pp. 26-27.
19. ibid.; 3rd Bn. Journal, II, 130.

located the gun; with his M-1 rifle he killed the three members of the crew.[20] This permitted the mortars to get back into action effectively.

Yet others were descending out of the woods toward the chateau itself, but quick adjustments of fire stopped most of this. Finally a German major and a small party made their way into the yard, and ran toward the CP. The soldier manning the 50-caliber machine gun on top of the medium tank cut them down. "Let him have another burst," a comrade shouted, "he's still kicking." The German major died just 400 yards short of the Arlon-Bastogne highway.[21]

While all this counterattack had been going on, Hon had been busying himself in the kitchen. He was happy when he was able to find some pancake flour, and he had wanted the Battalion staff to enjoy a change from a "K" ration breakfast. He was becoming impatient as the morning wore on and some of the staff members still had not come in to eat. Never one to hurry away to safety, he was distressed to find himself left all alone in the kitchen with dirty pans to clean; but he was still saving his pancake batter in the hope that some of the officers would come to eat soon. Naturally he had heard the shooting going on about the CP, but he felt that he had other worries. But then Hon happened to look out; there he saw Germans coming across the yard. Quickly he ran for his pancake batter and threw it out the window "so damn Germans won't get it."[22]

The attacking tanks at this point were faring little better. The Battalion requested an air strike, and in the meantime kept up the artillery fire. Gibson watched 15 tanks go by his position, and at 10:35 A.M. they were "fanning out" to the north of Lutrebois, preparing to attack across the open ground to the southwest. Five minutes later the number had grown to 20. Now Gibson was giving a running account of the knock-outs. Artillery shells from 155 mm howitzers knocked out two of them; one hit a mine, and then a shell from a 4.2 inch mortar finished it—just as the mortar lieutenant came into the CP to announce that he could fire no more missions. Campbell reported that 29 tanks had gone by his position, and he in turn brought the 155 mm fire on other vehicles farther down the road. As artillery became effective some of the crews and accompanying infantry abandoned the tanks and went back into the woods. But most of them kept coming. And now the tank destroyers opened fire with deadly accuracy. Lieutenant Dunn had been able to follow developments on his radio, and he was watching for them. Two of the M-10 TD's were hit by direct tank fire from the enemy, but they continued operational. Very quickly the 3-inch guns of the TD's were able to destroy four of the tanks. As others came on toward the hill where the machine gun platoon had made its stand they exposed their sides to the tanks of the 4th Armored Division along the highway, and even the 75 mm tank guns of a Sherman could very easily penetrate the sides of a Mark IV. Tanks and TD's together accounted for 11 more enemy tanks. And in addition to 44 rounds of 3-inch ammunition, the TD's fired 1,000 rounds from their 50-caliber machine guns at enemy infantry. At 1220 P-47 Thunderbolts flew in for a strafing run near the front lines of Companies I and K, and then returned to fire rockets at other tanks in the woods or on the road to the southeast of Lutrebois. Of an estimated 40 tanks in the at-

20. 35th Div., General Orders, No. 13, 20 Feb. 1945.
21. W. C. Wood to the Author, June 26, 1946.
22. **ibid.**

tack—including those which never reached Lutrebois—at least 25 were destroyed by the combined efforts of artillery, TD's, tanks, and aircraft. Barely short of one of its major goals, the attack had spent itself.[23]

With Lutrebois now in enemy hands, with enemy troops in the woods to the southwest of that town, and with a gap of nearly a thousand yards separating Companies I and K from the 2nd Battalion, Colonel Wood decided to bring those companies back across the valley to take up a more tenable position in the woods on the left flank of the 2nd Battalion. The commander, and the companies, were reluctant to leave the favorable ground, but a consolidated defense and a feasible supply line demanded it. Just after dark, then, at about 5 o'clock, the companies marched back across the valley to form a new line on the left (north) of Company E. Major Heffelfinger made arrangements to send a 12-man patrol with the supply party. Lieutenant Bomberger, as he was going up to rejoin Company I, would lead the group up as soon as the companies were in position. Company K was able to make contact with the 2nd Battalion, but as Company I tried to extend its line to the left it ran into machine gun fire. And the armored infantry battalion, trying to push down from the north, also was held up by machine gun fire. Company I finally was able to consolidate its position, but a dangerous gap remained between it and the armored infantry on the left. Nevertheless the supply party started out over the snow-covered paths at 7 o'clock, and returned at 10, its mission accomplished.[24]

That the whole situation remained unstable was illustrated by a report from the 2nd Battalion at 8 P.M. That battalion had been able to make contact on the right with the 137th Infantry at a point between Lutrebois and Villers la Bonne Eau, but that regiment had been having a counterattack too; two of its companies had not been heard from since 10:30 that morning.[25]

The next day found a condition in which both antagonists were seeking to attack. However, the first task of the Third Battalion was to consolidate its own position in the woods southwest of Lutrebois, and the immediate problem was the enemy pocket which remained between its left flank and the armored infantry battalion to the north. In order to extend the line in that direction, Col. Wood sent Lt. Joseph L. Brigandi with the survivors of Company L—amounting to about 25 men—to take up a position on the left of Company I. (Capt. Greenlief, after five and a half months' continuous service as platoon leader and company commander, had drawn a "leave to the States," and Brigandi took command of the company.) Even as Brigandi moved up, a sharp counterattack came against the 2nd Battalion's right flank which cost it 90 casualties during the afternoon. It was not until 7:30 P.M. that the men of Company L and those of the armored infantry were able to make contact; they had had to drop back into the woods to get around the German pocket which still remained.[26]

The only other course open for action against the enemy that day was continuous firing of artillery and mortars, and this was undertaken

23. 3rd Bn. Journal, II, 131; 3rd Bn. Interview, p. 27; 654th Tank Destroyer Battalion, After Action Report, 31 Dec. 1944; 134th Inf., Unit Journal, 30 Dec. 1944; 134th Inf., After Action Report, 4 Jan. 1945; Third U. S. Army, After Action Report, I, 186; Robert Cromie, Chicago Tribune Press Service, Jan. 3, 1945—reprinted in The Santa Fe Express May 1945, p. 6. Gen. Patton described this as "probably the biggest coordinated counterattack that troops under my command have ever experienced"—War As I Knew It, p. 207. See Allen, op. cit., pp. 259-260.
24. 3rd Bn. Journal, II, 131; 3rd Bn. Interview, p. 27.
25. 3rd Bn. Journal, II, 132.
26. 3rd Bn. Journal, II, 133, 3rd Bn. Interview, p. 27.

in the greatest concentration of fire since St. Lo. Ammunition for the 81 mm mortars had been rationed sharply almost from the beginning of combat, but Company M had been able to save enough so that at 2:30 P.M. Lt. Erickson could announce that the company's mortars already had fired 1,000 rounds that afternoon.[27] The supporting 161st Field Artillery Battalion, though receiving a ration of only 393 rounds on the 27th, 221 rounds on the 28th, and then 1,084 rounds on the 29th, had fired 2,226 rounds on the 30th, and now 2,895 rounds on the 31st.[28] Altogether 35 battalions of field artillery had participated in the operation to relieve and establish solid contact with Bastogne during the period December 22-31st. They had expended 94,230 rounds.[29]

This artillery had been made all the more effective by the introduction of "pozit" or proximity-fused ammunition.[30] A closely guarded secret, this new shell was equipped with a miniature five-tube radio receiving and sending set. As the shell went on its way, the sending set would radiate waves, then, when it came within 70 feet of its target—woods, hill, tank, airplane— the reflected electromagnetic waves, passing through the receiving set, would touch off the explosion. This amounted to a devastating perfection of time fire, and the flying shell fragments would scatter through forest and into foxholes.[31]

The battles were reaching a climax. The indication was that the enemy was trying to reinforce Lutrebois.[32] In fact a German prisoner reported that the 339th Volkgrenadier Regiment had been scheduled to make another attack that day (December 31st), but it had been broken up by the artillery fire.[33] But now the enemy was reaching the culmination of his efforts to seal-off Bastogne. Now he had all of his armor in action. All of the German's original panzer reserve in the west either had been committed or was disposed close to the battle area.[34] If the Third Battalion, and the other battalions in the vicinity, could regain the initiative, it was likely to be decisive.

Members of the Third Battalion found a new reason for hope with the arrival in the area of another group of former team-mates—the 6th Armored Division. The Battalion S-2 guided the group through the area, and "Task Force Lagrew" and the others prepared to attack to the east and northeast from Bastogne.[35]

At midnight all the artillery and mortars in the area joined in a "New Year's serenade."[36] And "South of Bastogne, as the New Year comes in, there are still the Old Year's dead, with ice matting their eyelashes, and the burnt tanks softened by the drifting snow."[37]

The Third Battalion, with 2nd Battalion on the right, renewed its attack at 1:30 P.M. January 1st. The 1st Battalion, still in Marvie, three kilometers north of Lutrebois, was making an attack to the south at the same time.[38] Attacking with Company K on the right and Company I on the left, the Battalion ran into the enemy pocket on its left almost at once. Com-

27. 3rd Bn. Journal, II, 132.
28. 161 FA Bn. Daily Ammunition Report: After Action Report, 10 Dec. 1944-1 Jan. 1945.
29. Third U. S. Army, After Action Report, I, 188.
30. 35th Div. History, Santa Fe, MS, p. 115.
31. Newsweek, Oct. 1, 1945, p. 26.
32. Third U. S. Army, After Action Report, I, 187.
33. 3rd Bn. Journal, II, 134.
34. Third U. S. Army, After Action Report, I, 187.
35. 3rd Bn. Journal, II, 132.
36. 3rd Bn. Journal, II, 133.
37. Sgt. Saul Levitt, "They Held Bastogne," Yank (British Edition), III, (Jan. 28, 1945) p. 6.
38. 3rd Bn. Journal, II, 134.

pany I took a prisoner who said that there were 250 Germans dug-in there. The attacking companies were only able to reach the edge of Lutrebois before nightfall.[39]

As long as that pocket remained, the Battalion's flank and rear would be insecure. Therefore when companies I and K made their "jump off" for the town the next morning, "K" would attack to get into the edge of the town immediately, while "I" would attack against the pocket, and then, swinging wide, would work through the town on the left side of the street. Company L was to support by fire from the high ground in the woods. Almost immediately on moving out at 6:30 A.M., Company I was in a brisk fire fight, but within an hour the Company took 20 prisoners, and leading men were able to get into the town.[40]

Company K, on the right, was held up by a well-placed machine gun in a house at the edge of town, and an ominous-looking antitank gun set in front of the house. Second Lieutenant David Cunningham of Virginia looked across the short snow field between the woods and the house. He took one of the company's rocket launchers, put some white phosphorous grenades in his coat, and made his way along the slope to the rear of the house. There, to his dismay, he found the walls too thick for penetration by the rocket—quick action was imperative, for now he was out in the open, near the enemy's position, and liable to discovery before he could move very far. Soldiers had learned in training, "whenever practicable, attack a building from above."[41] And though this had been done in the practice "attack of a Nazi village," one perplexing question had been, where would they find a ladder when in actual combat? Now Cunningham looked about—and near the house he saw a ladder! Quickly the platoon leader made his way to the roof and started dropping his white phosphorous grenades down the chimney. His platoon gained a foothold in Lutrebois.[42]

By shortly after noon the prisoner total had grown to 30. The Battalion's casualties were eight. But one of those wounded was Captain Jack Campbell of Company K.[43] He had defied the law of averages longer than any other rifle company officer in the regiment—he was the only one who had served since the beginning—but now his turn had come.

But the capture of prisoners had not meant a collapse of the enemy's resistance. Rather, it was requiring stubborn efforts to make any advance at all. However, Company I had succeeded in neutralizing the enemy pocket in the woods, and a few men had gained entrances to outlying buildings. Now the company prepared to enter in force. Leading the assault platoons were two young second lieutenants who only recently had been commissioned: Walter Bomberger, who had been busy with the CP defense two days earlier, and Lester Clark, who had been called back that same day to receive his commission, and only had rejoined his company as an officer two hours before this attack. These men were "freshmen" in the officer corps, and as all "freshmen," could expect little sympathy and much work. In garrison they would receive the extra assignments as officer of the day, and as duty officer on week-ends. As junior officers they would be in a position to receive full blame for any failures and little credit for successes. But

39. ibid., pp. 134f.
40. ibid., p. 136.
41. "Combat in Towns," War Department Training Circular, No. 41, April 3, 1943.
42. 35th Div., General Orders, No. 13, 20 Feb. 1945.
43. 3rd Bn. Journal, II, 136.

they would be expected to set an example as "officers and gentlemen." On the battlefield their responsibility was heavy and the danger great. Before any thought of rest for themselves they always would have to check their security, see that their men had food and ammunition, make sure that weapons were functioning, and often be called to the company command post late in the night to receive the order for the next day's attack. And when the attack came, its success would rest in their hands. For once the companies were committed to action toward their assigned objectives, there actually was little that the battalion commander, or the regimental commander, or General Patton could do to influence the immediate situation. The task of leading the men forward went to the platoon leader. Men would "freeze" in their foxholes; it was up to the junior officers to lead them forward. Men impelled by fear might tend to fall back, or become stragglers; the lieutenants must have the courage to face danger in spite of fear; their failure might mean failure and even disaster for the platoon, and for the battalion.

Now an intense mortar barrage and machine gun fire caught Company I's platoons as they prepared to cross the open ground to the front. Instinctively the men began to hold back. But their newly-commissioned platoon leaders knew that if the attack were to succeed, they must move forward out of the fire. No, they had no desire to face enemy guns, but now they had gold bars on their shoulders; they had a high sense of duty and an obligation to their men, to their superiors, to themselves.

Bomberger moved along the line shouting words of encouragement to his men, and calling on them to follow him. They moved across the open ground, under the enemy fire. Then as they were approaching the immediate objective the fire became more intense. Walter A. Bomberger, second lieutenant, junior officer, rifle platoon leader, was killed in action.[44]

In the same action Lieutenant Clark was wounded, but when he was taken back to the aid station he went to the Battalion CP to point out on the map the location of what he had estimated to be some 200 enemy.[45]

The 2nd Battalion too was having a difficult time in its attack across the valley toward the positions formerly occupied by "I" and "K". A patrol from that battalion had crossed the small stream at the bottom of the valley, only to be captured. Later in the day, however, the battalion was able to get across the valley and take up positions just short of those where "I" and "K" had been—but then enemy fire cut off those companies to the extent that they could be resupplied only with the aid of strong combat patrols.[46]

The Third Battalion hardly was able to fight its way half-way through Lutrebois, and the leading platoons consolidated for the night in an area short of the creek. A few men of Company L who had been in the town when it was recaptured had managed to conceal themselves from the Germans and to survive the heavy shelling, and now were able to rejoin their company.[47]

Enemy forces in the area included troops from the 2nd Regiment, 1st SS Panzer (Adolph Hitler) Division, and the 901st Regiment of the 130th (Panzer Lehr) Division.[48]

Little progress was made on January 3rd, but in the evening patrols crossed the creek and located enemy positions in the far end of the town.

44. 35th Div., General Orders, No. 18, March 16, 1945.
45. 3rd Bn. Journal, II, 137.
46. 134th Inf., After Action Report, 1 Feb. 1945.
47. 3rd Bn. Interview, p. 28.
48. 134th Inf., After Action Report.

Captain John Strader came to the battalion to take command of Company K, and plans were made for a continuation of the attack on the next morning. This time the companies were able to complete the occupation of Lutrebois with little opposition as they approached the woods beyond. Recovered from captivity, the Battalion Antitank guns assisted the companies with direct fire on point targets.[49]   At the same time the 1st Battalion, attacking from the north, was able to surprise the German 331st Volksgrenadier Regiment in the woods northeast of Lutrebois in a pre-dawn attack, and to overrun its positions. Unfortunately, however, Company C drove deep into the enemy area, and then lost contact in the woods and had a number of men captured; later Company A was surrounded, but finally most of the men were able to fight their way out and build up a defense with Company B.[50]

Now in order to protect the rear, and to afford a stable position from which to attack, special units had been sent up to build up a line along with Company L in the woods west and southwest of Lutrebois. Counterattacks still were being reported at various points in the area and Third Army warned all its units to be alert for any desperate attempt of the enemy to break through.[51]

On this particular day (January 4th) a Major General Brown, a War Department observer, visited the Battalion. He looked around briefly in the battered village of Lutrebois—warned the men to take care of the sanitation in the buildings. As he started back through Company L's area he heard sniper fire down in the valley. Approaching Brigandi he said, "Hasn't anyone been through there?"

"Yes, sir, two battalions," the company commander answered.

"Well weren't two battalions enough to clear that out?"

"No, sir, not the size that our battalions are now."

"How many men do you have in your company, lieutenant?"

"Twenty-eight, sir, counting myself."

"Who is on your left flank here?"

"A and P [Ammunition and Pioneer] Platoon, sir."

"Who is on your right?"

"I and R [regimental Intelligence and Reconnaissance] Platoon, sir."

"And who is on their right?"

"Regimental MP's" [a provisional military police platoon].[52]

Hot coffee each morning was the only approximation of a hot meal which could be delivered to the companies during those cold days at Lutrebois. Captured German heat tablets were issued, and with the fire from these, or, when necessary, with fire made from the waxed pasteboard containers, the men were able to heat the ground meat units of their "K" rations, and to make additional coffee from the powdered Nescafe. On the 2nd the temperature dropped to six degrees above zero, and outside the buildings, water in canteens soon would freeze.[53]

It was, perhaps, as much due to a desire to find protection from the cold as to promote deception that German soldiers were wearing American overcoats when they counterattacked against Companies I and K after those units had gained entry into the woods beyond Lutrebois on January 5th. But

49. 3rd Bn. Journal, II, 138, 147.
50. **ibid.**, pp. 138-140; 134th Inf., After Action Report, 1 Feb. 1945. 3rd Bn. Journal, II, 138.
51. 3rd Bn. Journal, II, 138.
52. Lawrence Langdon to the Author, July 5, 1946.
53. Robert Cromie, Chicago Tribune Press service, Jan. 3, 1945—reprinted in **The Santa Fe Express**, May 1945, p. 6; 3rd Bn. Journal, II, 134-143.

whatever the motive, the results were confusion among the Third Battalion troops, and they had to be satisfied with holding the town itself again that day.[54]

Another step for security was taken in the evacuation of the civilians who had remained in Lutrebois. Men of Company K had pulled a civilian "sniper" out of a haystack in the village, and his wife had protested with wild screams; another woman shouted crazily as headquarters men moved in to set up a company CP. And there was some suspicion that some of the inhabitants had been giving assistance to the Germans.[55] Consequently officers from the CIC (counter-intelligence corps) came to supervise the evacuation of the civilians—about 60 were taken out one day, and 20 on another.[56]

The importance which was being attached to the current operations was suggested by the repeated visits of interested officers to the Battalion CP during this period: Colonel Miltonberger and Major Carroll (S-3) and Lt. Col. Boatsman (executive officer) from regimental headquarters; Major General Brown, the War Department observer; Major General Baade, division commander; Colonel Solomon, 35th Division chief of staff; Colonel Renfroe from the 101st Airborne Division; Brigadier General Ernest of CCA, 4th Armored Division; Brigadier General Sebree, assistant division commander (35th Division), Lt. Col. Ashlock, Division G-1; as well as battalion commanders from the 2nd Battalion and from the 320th Infantry, and from the supporting 161st and 66th Field Artillery Battalions.[57]

One change had come in the Battalion staff: Captain Bruce, who had been acting as executive officer during the period when Major Heffelfinger had commanded the battalion in the absence of Colonel Wood, now was transferred to the 2nd Battalion as executive officer. Lt. Col. Frederick Roecker, commander of the 2nd Battalion, had been evacuated again, and when Major McDannel succeeded to the command, that battalion was without an executive.[58] Captain Mangnusson remained as S-1.

In a new effort to break the stubborn German defenses around Lutrebois, the 1st Battalion, 320th Infantry, was brought into the area and attached to the 134th Infantry. Now that battalion, with the 1st Battalion, 134th, on its left, launched an attack southeast along the edge of the woods north of Lutrebois to try to eliminate the resistance to the front of the Third Battalion. But this attack (January 6th) was stopped in the same section of the woods where Companies I and K had received their counterattack the preceding day. Now four battalions were in the area, and none was able to make any substantial progress. Two of them were facing generally to the northeast, and the other two were trying to attack to the southeast. All of them either were partially cut off by enemy small arms fire, or had dangerously exposed flanks and rear: indeed there was no real contact between any of them.[59] "The Bulge

54. **ibid.**, p. 144. At this point it is difficult to arrive at an accurate estimate as to the extent the Germans actually did resort to the device of wearing American uniforms, and the extent to which it became an exaggerated rumor. In this particular case, the Germans were reported to be wearing American overcoats, but were wearing the distinctive German helmets.—**ibid.**; Third Army reported on Dec. 29 that the handling of American dead at cemeteries was being hampered by the receipt of German bodies in American uniforms and with American identification tags; and photographs were being taken to establish identity in uncertain cases.—Third U. S. Army, After Action Report, I, 187; the Third Battalion Graves Registration officer found among the hundreds of German bodies which were removed from the vicinity of Lutrebois only one which was clothed in an American exterior garment, and that was a raincoat; many were found to have on parts of American uniforms, but not in such a manner that they would be conspicuous.—E. C. Reischel to the Author, July 14, 1946.
55. Langdon, **loc. cit.**
56. 3rd Bn. Journal, II, 145, 149.
57. 3rd Bn. Journal, II, 138-166, **passim.**
58. 134th Inf., Daily Log, V, 31 Dec. 1944.
59. 3rd Bn. Journal, II, 146-148; 3rd Bn. Interview, p. 30.

was now a confusing maze of attack and counterattack, and counter-counter-attack."[60]

Two more days of fighting similarly were indecisive. The 2nd Battalion tried to assist by making an attack from its position toward the northeast, but was stopped in its tracks by machine gun cross-fire. The only favorable development was the possibility of getting hot food up to the Third Battalion's companies in Lutrebois during darkness; but even this was a risk, for the town was being shelled at intervals, and there still were threats of further German counterattacks—one morning the whole regiment was put on a 100 per cent alert at 3 A.M. on the basis of a PW report that a new attack was preparing.[61]

The attacks frustrated, and the confusion in the situation clearing very little, Colonel Miltonberger determined to regroup his forces and launch a new, coordinated attack. He conferred with leaders of the 6th Armored Division to arrange cooperation with another battalion of the 320th which had been attached to that organization, and called the interested commanders to his CP to discuss the plan. This was to extricate the Third Battalion, and the 1st Battalion, 320th, and then, with the 2nd Battalion, 320th, to make a vigorous attack from the north deep into the woods. A concentration of fire power, and a concerted attack from a new direction would, he felt, force a break in the situation.

Wood and his Battalion staff made plans for executing the Third Battalion's role. The battalion commander and S-3, and the company commanders went up to make a reconnaissance late in the afternoon of January 8th. They chose final assembly positions in a woods north of the one into which they were to attack, and noted how the companies would have to be guided in during the hours of darkness. From a corner of this woods, company boundaries and directions of attack were pointed out on the ground as they looked over the stretch of snow-covered open ground across which the troops would have to advance to get into the bigger forest. In order to avoid further confusion, this attack was to be made in daylight, and therefore, other measures would have to be taken for protection in crossing the open ground. Two measures were planned: smoke, and direct fire of accompanying tank destroyers.[62]

There was a suggestion, during this time, for a tactical device which might have had some merit had there been aircraft immediately available to the division. That was that one or two flights of fighters might support the infantry attacks of the battalions on the ground. Perhaps there would be a preparatory bombing and strafing run, but then, after H-hour for the attack, the airplanes, while refraining from further actual firing, would remain to zoom down upon the positions while infantrymen advanced. From their own reactions to the relatively limited operations of "Bed-Check Charlie," members of the Third Battalion could guess that a long session of zooming and diving probably would keep German defenders huddled deep in their foxholes as effectively as additional battalions of fire power. In such state, the enemy would be ill-prepared to offer very effective resistance as infantrymen overran his positions. And here might well have been an effective expedient for night attack. If the flares of "Bed-Check Charlie" tended to move members of the Third Battalion to hide in their foxholes, why would not it have worked as well to keep Germans down while attackers approached? Here the at-

60. Miller, **op. cit.**, p. 795.
61. 3rd Bn. Journal, II, 146-152.
62. 3rd Bn. Journal, II, 152-153.

tacker would have had the advantage of observation by the light, while, at the same time, his adversary would have been driven to hiding by that same light. But such speculation was idle, for aircraft simply was not available for such close infantry support.

The leaders returned to the CP where they could study their maps further, and could make notes. The staff and commanders gathered at 7:30 P.M. for the battalion order:

1.a.) Elements of 1st Battalion, 331st Volksgrenadier regiment (167th Division)

Elements of 339th Volksgrenadier Regiment (167th Division). Their only reinforcements have been 200 field artillery men who form the 137th Fusilier Battalion. Their mission is to continue to defend in the woods in our zone. They are capable of counterattacking. (One division remains in reserve.)

b.) 134th Infantry, with 1st Battalion, 320th Infantry attached, and a task force from the 6th Armored Division attacks from left flank vs. enemy right to clean out woods to our front. 1st Bn., 320th, will attack on our right, 2nd Bn., 320th (part of armored TF) will attack on left. 1st Battalion, 134h, holds present position, relieves present position of 1st Battalion 320th. 2nd Battalion remains present position, one company to secure Lutrebois.

Support: 161st Field Artillery Battalion reinf.—Fires smoke from H minus five minutes to H plus 15. Fires from H-hour to H plus 20 minutes on objective, then shifts to rear areas, and will be on call. Forward observer with Company I, and at O.P.

2nd Platoon, Company A, 654th TD Battalion—fires direct fire preparation, H minus 30 to H-hour from woods in the vicinity of the LD.

3rd Platoon, Antitank Company

3rd Platoon 60th Engineers

81 mm mortars of 1st and 2nd Battalions available for reinforcing fires.

2.) This Battalion will attack, companies abreast: Company I on left, K on right, L in reserve. Base company, Company I; contact right to left. Assembly area: woods in vicinity 565545.

LD [line of departure]: Trail south of assembly area.

Direction of attack: Azimuth of approximately 110 degrees.

Battalion left boundary: trail through woods; right boundary: second trail.

Time of attack: 1000

Objective in Zone: Portion of Lutrebois trail [a trail running northeast from Lutrebois through the woods.]

Battalion will move from Lutrebois to assembly area under cover of darkness. Guides: S-1.

IP [initial point] road junction northeast of town.

Time and order of march: Company I, 0500; Company K, 0530; Company L, 0600.

Route: Trail to northwest along edge of woods directly to assembly area.

3.a) Company I will attack on left, maintaining contact with 2nd Battalion, 320th; seize and hold left half of Battalion objective. Prepare for defense.

b.) Company K will attack on right, seize and hold right half of Battalion objective. Prepare for defense.

c.) Company L, Battalion reserve. Remain in assembly area prepared to repel counterattack to right or left. Move on order to follow Company I.

d.) Company M: one section heavy machine guns attached to Company I, one section attached Company K; one platoon support from positions forward of assembly area, displace forward with Company L.

Mortars: One section displace to position behind assembly area; prepare to reinforce smoke on edge of woods at H-hour. Other mortars in present position. Observer with Company I.

e.) Antitank Platoon—move to position in vicinity of assembly area, prepared to displace forward when objective is seized.

f.) Ammunition and Pioneer Platoon—Reassemble at 2000; maintain advance ammunition DP. Keep bazookas with HE and WP ammunition well forward for assault fire.

    4.) Hot coffee in assembly area at 0730. Complete K ration on the individual. Bed rolls left under guard at present CP's.

    Ammunition DP, present location; forward DP in vicinity of assembly area (trail crossing).

    Aid Station—present location; advance collecting point in vicinity assembly area.

    5.) Radio channel: 30 alternate 21 call sign, NAN
        2nd Battalion: 18 alternate 39 call sign DOG
        1st Battalion: 24 alternate 15 call sign VICTOR
        CP—present location.
        OP—to be selected by S-2—vicinity high ground northwest of woods.[63]

Preparation for the attack meant work for staff members and headquarters men that night. The 1st Battalion had to be notified of the route which the Third planned to follow to the assembly area so that there would be no mistaken shooting. A wire team from the Communications Platoon left Lutrebois at 10:25 P. M. to lay a telephone line to the assembly area—company runners from Battalion headquarters accompanied them so that they would be able to guide the companies later—at midnight the party became momentarily lost until they called back over their telephone line and Major Heffelfinger gave them directions. The executive officer checked to see that the medics had a radio, and found out the radio channels of the battalions of the 320th to be able to coordinate with them. At 1:40 A. M. Captain Magnunson, S-1, and his party left for the assembly area; at 4:55 Company I was formed to march the mile across the snow—along the edge of a woods occupied partly by the 1st Battalion, and partly by the enemy. At 6:30 telephone communication was established with Company I in the assembly area. At 6:40 Lt. Hanna, S-2, left to set up the O. P. At 6:55 Lt. Stoneburner, S-4, arrived at the C. P. with hot coffee. At 7:00 Lt. Hall, ammunition officer, left to set up the advance ammunition distributing point. The companies arrived in the assembly area on schedule—some men from Company K were lost in the darkness, but they came in with Company L, the TD's prepared to move into position, and at 8:10 the battalion commander, the artillery liaison officer, and the S-3 left for the OP.[64]

This command group established itself in the attic of a farm house on the right flank of the area. Here too was the battalion commander and party of the 1st Battalion, 320th. Here the battalion commander had telephone communication with the command post back at the chateau, and with the regimental CP at Sainlez. He had radio communication with each of the companies and with the special units and the CP. The artillery liaison officer could reach his fire direction center by radio or telephone. And the group could watch the coordination of fires and they could see the men "jump off" in their attack.

As H-hour approached they watched a perfect smoke screen being built up along the edge of the woods toward which the battalions were to attack. Explosions from the tank destroyers' three-inch guns reverberated throughout the area. Then promptly at 10 o'clock a whole line of men began to move out of the near woods across the open ground. The TD's moved forward with them, pausing at intervals to fire their deadly high explosive shells into the forest. The effectiveness of the supporting fires became apparent almost at once as the Third Battalion moved through the woods. There was some small arms and mortar fire, but the resistance quickly was overcome and the com-

63. 3rd Bn. Journal, II, 153-155.
64. ibid., pp. 155-156.

panies went on to overrun four enemy mortars and capture about 50 prisoners—some stunned Germans had to be routed out of their foxholes at the point of a bayonet. They were from a newly committed element: the 387th Volksgrenadier Regiment. Company L moved up skillfully to protect flanks and rear as the Battalion forged ahead of its neighbors on the right and left, and well before noon it reached the Lutrebois trail which was its objective. Soon thereafter the 2nd Battalion of the 320th was abreast on the left, and the left company of the 1st Battalion came up on the right, though a group of enemy held out longer on the right flank. But the width of the attack had completely overrun the enemy's immediate rear, and that portion of the woods was clear.[65]

However the enemy pocket still remained in front of the 2nd Battalion (134th) east of Lutrebois, and the trail to the town could not be used for supplies. Rather it was necessary to follow the long way around and reach the companies by the route over which they had attacked. Engineers opened a roadway for jeeps to a point in the woods about 600 yards in rear (northwest) of the companies' position, and from here it was necessary for carrying parties to take the ammunition, rations, water, radio batteries, and bed rolls over the rough, wooded terrain to the front.[66]

A pause in the attack the next day afforded an opportunity for further consolidation, for getting up hot food and certain needed supplies—like overshoes for the men who did not have them—and for reorganization—absorption of replacements, or now as they were ordered to be called, "reinforcements." It was opposed to policy to send up new replacements—or "reinforcements"—while the companies were on the line, but the attrition of two weeks' hard fighting in cold weather had seriously weakened the strength of all the battalions, and Colonel Miltonberger personally spoke with the battalion commanders on the importance of absorbing these men into the platoons and squads.[67]

These were the first reinforcements to arrive to the division since the beginning of its operations in the Ardennes. Many had been switched from other duties; former rear area clerks and cooks had been transferred to combat duty. Although all of them had had basic training, the units preferred to get men who had been trained as riflemen in the infantry replacement training centers. Whenever raw reinforcements joined the companies, casualties tended to become heavier among officers and noncommissioned officers, for the leaders were forced to expose themselves to make clear their orders and directions. New men frequently either were afraid or foolhardy, and in either case greater leadership was required for them. On arrival at the division rear echelon headquarters, reinforcements were subdivided and assigned directly to the companies. After a brief talk and orientation they were sent to their units via the regimental trains (the kitchen and supply areas). At the trains they were checked for equipment, and, if they were not required immediately in combat there would be some additional training, indoctrination talks, and an attempt to build up an *esprit de corps*. They were sent to the front on kitchen trucks. Often they would go up at night, and see their new buddies and leaders for the first time the next morning—and sometimes be called upon to participate in an attack before they had had a chance to become acquainted with anyone in the unit. Sometimes during this great demand for replacements, ports of

65. 3rd Bn. Interview, p. 30; W. C. Wood to the Author, June 26, 1946, 3rd Bn. Journal, II, 156f.; 134th Inf., After Action Report, 1 Feb. 1945; 134th Inf., Daily Log, VI, 9 Jan. 1945.
66. 3rd Bn. Journal, p. 158.
67. Ibid., p. 159.

embarkation had been changing the military occupation specialty numbers of soldiers without requiring the 30-day training period prescribed for a change in classification. On December 16th, 437 "retrained riflemen" came to the division who had had two days' infantry training. Some units had men in the line on December 29th who had had their Christmas dinners in America and then had been flown to Europe.[68]

Now with five battalions under his control, Colonel Miltonberger planned to change the direction of the attack to the northeast—to sweep along the longer axis of the forest toward the division objective at the northeast corner five kilometers away. A prime consideration was protection of the right flank and rear as the units moved deep into the forest away from their supplies. The formation, therefore, provided for a long tail which would extend all the way back to Lutrebois. The Third Battalion on the right; the 2nd Battalion, 320th Infantry, on the left; the 1st Battalion, 320th echeloned to the right, following the Third Battalion; 1st Battalion, 134th, following 1st Battalion, 320th, and 2nd Battalion, 134th, to occupy and defend the wooded area just beyond Lutrebois, and to protect the town.[69]

Resuming the attack at 8 A. M. January 11th, men of the Third Battalion soon saw testimony to the effectiveness of the artillery and mortar fire which had been pouring into the woods, for they found scores of German dead in their path. They soon had picked up 34 more prisoners, and did not run into serious opposition until noon when they approached a relatively open plateau and came under enemy small arms and mortar fire. Here light tanks which had been accompanying the 2nd Battalion, 320th, came forward to lend real assistance; rapidly shifting up and down the front, the armored vehicles sprayed enemy positions with machine gun and 37 mm gun fire, and the companies were able to continue their advance to reach "phase line B" at the far side of the clearing before nightfall.[70]

Now it was necessary for the engineers to bring up a bulldozer to lengthen their roadway down to the Lutrebois trail to take jeep traffic up to the company areas. Later the 2nd Battalion was able to clear the enemy from the area northeast of Lutrebois, and then, after engineers had cleared fallen trees from the path, that route was opened for supplies.[71]

The forest was thickest, and the trails fewest, in the area which remained between Companies I and K and the final objective. It is difficult to locate oneself accurately with respect to a map in a thick, strange woods under any circumstances, and with snow covering what few trails might have appeared on the map, accurate location would be virtually impossible. This would render the supporting artillery practically useless. As a means of determining the location of the base company on the map at a given time, an arrangement was made whereby the artillery forward observer would communicate with an air observer in a liaison plane flying over the woods; on a signal the company would fire a flare above the trees, and then the air observer would read back the coordinates of the location.[72]

In addition, Colonel Wood ordered a wire crew to accompany the reserve company and lay a heavy (No. 110) telephone line. This was as necessary for

68. Lt. Col. Donald M. Ashlock, G-1, 35th Division, in interview with 1st Lt. W. J. Dunkerly and T/Sgt. C. J. Angelo, 12 Jan. 1945 (3rd Information and Historical Section), Combat Interviews— No. 108 35th Division—1 Nov. 44—23 Jan. 45.
69. 3rd Bn. S-3 Notebook, I, 10 Jan. 1946.
70. 3rd Bn. Journal, II, 162f.; 3rd Bn. Interview, p. 30; Wood, loc. cit.
71. 3rd Bn. Journal, II, 164.
72. 3rd Bn. Interview, p.51.

marking a trail through the woods to the companies as for telephone communication.[73]

The next day's attack (January 13th) was delayed while the light tanks refueled, but then it moved forward without opposition. Shortly the other battalions were ordered to halt, and the Third Battalion was on its own to reach the final division objective. The enemy remained cooperative, however, and, taking a few prisoners from companies of the 331st Volksgrenadier Regiment which had been virtually destroyed, the Battalion occupied its assigned area early in the afternoon. This was a position in the woods to the west of the town of Bras, and immediately south of the Bras-Bastogne highway. Dead German soldiers and dead horses abounded in the area.[74]

But now the question was contact with the 90th Division, coming across the front from the south, and with the 6th Armored Division, attacking from the west. When that was accomplished the Third Battalion would be "pinched out" and would be withdrawn. At 3:15 o'clock that afternoon a report came that Task Force Lagrew of the 6th Armored Division had occupied Wardin (1,000 yards north of the Battalion's area) and that the 90th Division had cleared Bras and advanced several hundred yards to the north. However, when members of a patrol from Company L went over to make contact with the "friends on the right" they found the town (Bras) unoccupied, and then the next morning an "M" Company jeep got lost and went into Bras and drew fire. But then Company K made contact with a unit of the 90th Division, and as the 6th Armored came up the Third Battalion was withdrawn.[75] At last there could be a few days rest.

The "attacks, counterattacks, and counter-counterattacks" around Lutrebois had cost the Third Battalion approximately 400 casualties, of whom 32 were killed.[76] But the enemy had suffered terribly. Now instead of the five Germans to one American dead as he had found in Normandy, the Graves Registration Officer found the ratio nearer eight to one. Indeed, here was the greatest number of German dead which men of the Third Battalion ever encountered. Salvage crews—four to five men with each vehicle—worked for four days with two jeeps and trailers hauling dead, and three other jeeps and trailers hauling equipment—and there still was a full day's work for them to do when the Battalion was ordered to another area.[77] Much of this was the result of 100,000 rounds of artillery shells which had been fired into the woods east of Lutrebois.[78]

Among the American dead there was a group of six which obviously had been murdered in cold blood. Four of the group had been wounded, and the wounds dressed with American bandages, but a small bullet hole through each of their heads showed that they later had met instant death from a small arms weapon fired at close range. The other two had no other wounds, but only these same kind of bullet-holes in their heads. Overcoats, field jackets, and shoes had been removed from most of them.[79]

The Battalion had made a heavy contribution to the protection of the road center of Bastogne, and to the seizure of the initiative from the Germans. Some time later General Eisenhower sent a memorandum to Generals Bradley

73. Ibid.
74. 3rd Bn. Journal, II, 166, Wood, loc. cit.
75. 3rd Bn. Journal, II, 167f.
76. 134th Inf. Battle Casualty Report.
77. E. C. Reischel to the Author, July 14, 1946.
78. 3rd Bn. Journal, II, 168.
79. Reischel, loc. cit.

and Devers suggesting that the divisions were not being published sufficiently. In this dispatch he stated:

"An exception to this rule was the account of the action of the 101st Airborne Division at Bastogne. Yet, in many instances other units have performed in equally gallant fashion—and under almost equally spectacular conditions."

"To return to the example of the 101st Airborne Division: little has been said of the exploits of the 4th Armored, or of the 35th and other units in battling their way forward under appalling conditions to join up with the Bastogne position."[80]

On January 14th the Third Battalion moved back several miles to the southwest to a town called Remoiville, and neighboring villages, for three days of rest, training, and reorganisation (in the course of which Sgt. Buster Brown of Company L was presented with the Distinguished Service Cross for his heroism in the vicinity of St. Lo.)[81] On January 16th, the First and Third Armies made contact at Houffalize and turned their strength eastward.[82] By the 17th the Bastogne campaign could be regarded as closed, and a new phase was entered upon as the enemy continued to retire under pressure.[83]

Difficult times lay ahead for those men who had been taken prisoner in Lutrebois. While the Battalion continued its attacks, they were on the way to prison camps. After their only ride in German motor trucks, they spent New Year's Day in Clewaux. Rations initially consisted of a can of cheese, equivalent to a No. 2½ can, for each ten men. From Clewaux, they walked and walked—through Prum, where they saw 13 Americans killed by the strafing of an RAF Mosquito bomber—Gerelstein, where they had to carry heavy logs down from the mountains to railway tracks, and where a German guard, a Sergeant Eisenhower, entered their crowded room one evening in search of more "volunteers," and fired a shot from his pistol into the room, and killed one American—Kelberg—Mayen—Koblenz—Bad Ems—and, finally, Limburg. Here was located Stalag XIIA, and it was the first time that any of the group was registered as a prisoner of war. There was no such thing as consideration. A Canadian paratrooper had been told at Prum that he had a piece of shrapnel near his heart, but he had to march the distance, and he dropped dead as he entered the prison camp. There was no heat at the Limburg enclosure;\ men of Company L slept on small piles of straw over a frozen floor inside frame buildings. Now rations consisted of one-tenth of a loaf of bread a day, ersatz tea in the morning, hot soup at noon (a cupful), and either three potatoes boiled with jackets on or a potato soup at night. After an interrogation in an old castle at Diaz, the group with Sergeant Ralph E. VanLandingham returned to Limburg where they were given small portions of bread and placed aboard a locked box car for three days of travel. The weather was so cold that frost formed inside the car every afternoon at about 1600, and remained until about 1000 the next morning. There was no water to be had during the trip, and the guards tried to sell the rations to the hungry prisoners for fountain pens, pencils, watches. Some men's feet were frozen during the trip. When they arrived at their destination, Hammelburg, on 31 January, each was handed

80. Butcher, op. cit., p. 770.
81. 3rd Bn. Journal, II, 170-176.
82. General Eisenhower's Report, p. 79.
83. Third U. S. Army, After Action Report, I, 221.

about a pound of cheese and told that it must be eaten by the time they reached the camp—it was rations which the guards had been holding back in the hope of making sales. But at the camp at least there was one thing which was a real boost to their morale—the arrival of Red Cross Parcels.[84]

On the 18th the Third Battalion went back into the line.[85]

84. Ralph E. VanLandingham to the author, 15 August, 1947.
85. 3rd Bn. Journal, II, 178.

CHAPTER XIX

★ ★ ★

STEEL ON ICE

★ ★ ★

Once again the 134th Infantry was attached to the 6th Armored Division. While this combat team—the infantry regiment plus attached artillery, engineers, and medical units—was left behind to assist in reducing the dwindling Bulge, the remainder of the 35th Division was shifted to the south—there was a five-day stop-over in Metz, and then the division moved on down to Alsace to bolster the overstretched defense lines of the Seventh Army in a region where the Nazis had created a threatening "Little Bulge."[1]

Initially the 134th Infantry was ordered to take up a defensive position in the sector of the 6th Armored Division—an area generally between Bourcy and Longvilly—about nine kilometers northeast of Bastogne, and a slightly greater distance southeast of Houffalize. To be sure, this defensive situation would not be long duration, but inasmuch as this was only the third time in which the Battalion ever was ordered into a deliberate defense, and since this is one of the few complete Battalion defense orders which has been preserved, it may be well to note its provisions:

    1.a) Front lines are receiving artillery, nebelwerfer ("screaming meamies") and SP [self-propelled guns] fire.

    b.) (1) CT 134, attached to 6th Armored Division, relieve 320th Infantry and elements of 6th Armored Division to defend generally the line BOURCY—No. 3 Highway, southeast.

        (2) The 2nd Battalion on our left, 1st Battalion in reserve, 9th Armored Infantry on our right.

        (3) In support: 161st FA Battalion—FO with Company L.

        3rd Platoon, Company A, 60th Engineers.

        Elements 6th Armored Division.

    2.a.) This battalion will organize a holding garrison to occupy and defend the sector between RJ [road junction] at 635 626 and a point along the highway at 641 619 [map coordinates], Company L on the right, Company K on the left, Company I in reserve. MLR [main line of resistance]—suitable ground along No. 3 Highway, limiting points generally as above.

    b.) The Battalion will move by motor from present position.

    c.) Order of march: Company L, Company K, Company M (—), Headquarters, Company I.

    d.) IP [initial point]—Company M, Headquarters Company—Company L, CP at 0700.

        Company L, Company K—Company L CP at 0715.

        Company I, CR [crossroads] at CLOCHIMONT at 0800.

    e.) Trucks: Company I—5 report to Company I at 0730.

        Company K—6 report to RJ north side REMICHAMPAGNE at 0645.

        Company L—6 report RJ north side of REMICHAMPAGNE at 0645.

    f.) Route: REMOIVILLE — REMICHAMPAGNE — CLOCHIMONT — ASSENOIS — BASTOGNE — MARGARET — ARLONCOURT.

    g.) Guides—S-2 and MP guides.

    h.) Detrucking Points: Company L and I at AL HEZ; Company K, vicinity MICHAMPS; Headquarters and M, ARLONCOURT.

    Return trucks to MTO [motor transportation officer] at ARLONCOURT.

---

1. 35th Div., **Attack!** p. 29; Allen, **Lucky Forward**, pp. 274-275.

3.a.)   Company L will organize, occupy, and defend right of Battalion sector.

b.)   Company K will organize, occupy, and defend left of Battalion sector.

c.)   Company I—Battalion reserve. Organize reserve line vicinity AL HEZ, reconnaissance for routes to repel attacks and areas to defend Battalion flanks. Establish OPLR [outpost line of resistance] when practicable.

d.)   Machine Guns—Company L area: light machine guns on right flank, section of heavy machine guns on left flank; Company K area: light machine guns on left flank, section of heavy machine guns on right flank. One platoon heavy machine guns in area of Company I for long range support. Company I light machine guns: left flank.

e.)   81 mm mortars—positions in rear of reserve area to fire on woods to front. Observers, Company K and Company L. Register primary targets.

f.)   Heavy weapons Company Commander, coordinate final defensive fires.

g.)   Antitank guns: Initially Reserve area, sited to front and flanks (present position of 1st Battalion guns).

x.)   Priority of work:
Clearing fields of fire.
Individual entrenchments.
Obstacles—Antitank mines, booby traps, wire.
Camouflage, continuous.

4.   Forward Ammunition DP [distributing point] vicinity AL HEZ.
Motor Pool—ARLONCOURT.
Aid Station—ARLONCOURT.
Hot breakfast tomorrow 0530.
Hot coffee to all companies on position when practical—K rations initially—hot chow to reserve company when practical.

5.   Communications: wire command in right to left; wire to all companies
Password: BAZOOKA; Reply: ROCKET
Radio: GEORGE; channel, 39—alternate, 27.
CP: ARLONCOURT
Kitchens: BASTOGNE[2]

Actually the defensive situation lasted for just three days. During this time there was some shifting of units on right and left, light tanks and TD's were added to the defensive system, communications were improved, and there was almost continuous patrolling.

Lieutenant Hall and his pioneers worked hard to open a satisfactory supply route through the snow and forest—and over a creek—to the forward companies. But even then it was only by the use of "M" Company's "weasel"—the light track-laying "country cousin to the jeep"—that carrying parties were spared making the haul to Company K.[3]

Patrols reported enemy activity in the town of Moinet—a place about a kilometer to the front (northeast) of Company L's position—on the 19th, but the next day it appeared that the enemy had left.[4] Now with the enemy apparently withdrawing, the 6th Armored Division prepared to resume the offensive. Combat Command A would go through Moinet while the 2nd and Third Battalions of "Combat Team Miltonberger" would clear the woods—called Bois du Maister and Gros Bois—on the left. Preparatory to this the Third Battalion was to send out a strong patrol "to go till the enemy is contacted." As most of the patrols, it was sent out from the reserve company (I)—but an intelligence scout from Battalion Headquarters, and two men from Company K—so that the base company would have guides for the next day's attack—went along. Equipped with a 300 radio for communication, and with a strength of 12 men,

2. 3rd Bn. Journal, II, 176-178. The Battalion relieved the 1st Battalion and elements of the 44th Armored Inf. Battalion—134th Inf., After Action Report, 1 Feb. 1945.
3. **ibid.,** p. 182.
4. **ibid.,** pp.180-183.

the patrol was prepared to fight. However, this did not prove to be necessary, and, after reporting Moinet "all clear," the men pushed on through deep snow, reporting in their position from time to time, and made their way finally all the way to the vicinity of the Battalion's assigned objective. That night a platoon from the 44th Armored Infantry Battalion moved into Moinet. The stage was set for the advance.[5]

It was with a considerable assurance of success, then, that men of the Third Battalion started moving across the highway and through the woods on the morning of January 21st. Five medium tanks, four light tanks, and 12 tank destroyers took up positions to the left of the woods—east of Bourcy— where they could support by flanking fire. A man from the 2nd Battalion (the 2nd was advancing on the left of the Third) carried a cerise air-identification panel on his back and walked at the edge of the forest abreast of the leading squads; this served as a marker so that tank gunners could direct their cannon fire well forward of the friendly troops should any hostile resistance develop. The Battalion commander and his command group watched the advance from a high building at the edge of Bourcy where they could see all the way to the far edge of the woods which was the objective. It turned out that the snow was the greatest deterrent to a rapid advance: men were walking through waistdeep drifts as they wondered whether the enemy might open fire at any moment from the next group of trees; the exhausting task of trail-breaker had to be rotated among the men of the leading squads. It took until noon to cover the 4,000 yards to the objective, but a whole day of fighting the snow would be better than ten minutes of fighting machine guns and artillery. The Battalion's area was squarely astride the Belgian-Luxembourg frontier. The command post opened at Bourcy in mid-afternoon.[6]

Now there was no supply route open to the companies which approached nearer than two or three miles. Carrying parties for that distance over the snow would be almost out of the question. But the means for resupply was at hand: the light tanks. The tanks picked up the supplies which jeep trains brought to Bourcy, and, following a route in the clearing to the north of the woods, and generally along the right of a railroad, the tracked vehicles easily made their way through the snowfields. And again the weasel proved its indispensability. It was the only means available for getting into the area where men of Company L had stacked their bedrolls. Lt. Reischel, the Battalion motor officer, as well as the engineers, improvised snow plows and tried to clear a route for jeeps, but they were only partially successful, and tracked vehicles had to be called upon either to pull out jeeps which had become stuck, or to transfer the loads and carry them to the companies.[7]

Meanwhile the armored column on the right had made good progress, and the next day the 2nd and Third Battalions could be moved to a new area to the northeast. This move was made on the tanks of the 68th Tank Battalion. Men of the Third Battalion had ridden the "iron horses" into the battle, but it was something of an innovation for them to ride tanks in an "administrative" move. But that was one advantage of being attached to an armored division; a doughboy usually would welcome *any* substitute for walking. The tanks carried the 2nd Battalion to Hoffelt, and then returned to pick

5.   Ibid., pp. 183-185.
6.   Ibid., pp. 185f.; 3rd Bn. Interview, p. 33.
7.   Ibid.; 3rd Bn. Journal, II, 186.

Chateau C.P. Near Lutrebois (South of Bastogne):—The C.O. and Exec look over the situation on their map. To men of the rifle companies, battalion headquarters was "rear echelon." And there was reason for their view. On the other hand, the Battalion had one commander killed, two seriously wounded, and a fourth who had been wounded three times while commanding another battalion.

S-2 and S-3 After the Battle of the C.P.

Heavy Machine Gun (Cal. .30) Covers the Roer Crossing.

Medics Bringing a Wounded Man Back Across the Roer.

Medics Bringing Wounded Out of Lutrebois:—A brave band of Co. L men under Lt. Davis, held out as Germans encircled them. For a while they had artillery support from an unknown "Bill" whom they chanced to contact on the radio; for a while friendly airplanes came over. Then all support disappeared. They were overwhelmed and lined up for march to imprisonment.

Steel on Ice:—Infantrymen of the Third Battalion mounted tanks and TD's for move to Heinerscheid.

Another Roer Bridge.

Heavy Weapons Moving Through Hilfarth: Numerous mines forced infantrymen to step gingerly.

Machine Gun in the Ardennes:— The .30 caliber Browning heavy machine gun was the "Old Reliable" of Infantry weapons. It was too heavy, and that is a serious objection to any infantry weapon, but its stable mount made it accurate, it was water-cooled and so could not stand long firing, and it did not jam often. It should have been used more than it was for long-range fire in supporting attacks. But it was a master of defense, and it proved itself in the Ardennes. Except for the guns of Co. M, it is likely the Germans would have surrounded Bastogne again. On the other hand, the German air-cooled machine gun was much lighter, fired twice as fast, and had smokeless powder.

Jeep on the Supply Route to Bastogne:—The sturdy quarter-ton truck became indispensable.

Poised for Attack Toward the Rhine.

Infantry Attack Toward the Wesel Pocket in the Rhineland.

Here They Crossed the Rhine.

A Factory in the Zone of the Third Battalion Near Buer.

Mertens and Belbke, of S-2 Section, Look Over Nazi Records and Money in Police Headquarters at Recklinghausen. "Pop" Mertens was a character always on the lookout for Nazi secrets. In Buer he went out on his own, late at night, while skirmishes still were going on, to investigate the house of a Nazi official; he returned with valuable rosters and documents and a load of firearms. After the capture of Recklinghausen, he undertook another lone night mission; he went to a bunker a thousand yards beyond the Battalion's position, and there he found 15 soldiers and 50 civilians hiding. In Buer Erle, Mertens discovered a secret underground passage in a mine which led to a large cache of weapons and ammunition; his inquiries led to the discovery of food stocks, the capture of a concentration camp official, and more documents.

Flak Gun, 128mm. The Germans had set up heavy flak guns to protect the industrial Ruhr against air attack. The Battalion found them also disturbing against ground attack. Co. L overran this near Buer.

Occupation for awhile . . . Competitions . . . Parades . . . Then Home.

Top:—City Hall at Hannover . . . Headquarters for 134th for occupation duty.

Center:—A platoon from Co. M wins a regimental platoon drill at Kottenheim.

Right:—Advance detachment of the 35th Division prepares the way home.

up the Third. The column moved cross-country about a mile and a half to a road northeast of Troine, and then travelled northeast for another five miles to a town just a kilometer beyond the 2nd Battalion's area called Hachiville.[8]

That same night the Battalion was alerted to be prepared to attack the next day. But then came a succession of changes and delays.[9] Now changes in orders may be irritating to the soldier in garrison, or when pertaining to administrative matters, but the infantryman is not likely to be disappointed when an attack order is changed or delayed. At this particular time the rest of the 35th Division was known to be in Metz, and with the memory of an enjoyable Christmas in their minds, members of the Third Battalion could hope that they might rejoin their own division soon. Not that they disliked working with the 6th Armored; in fact they probably welcomed the change. But infantrymen were prone to lend their hope to anything which might promise to put them out of reach of the enemy even for a little while.

Finally, the result for January 23rd was an attack on Basbellain (referred to by members of the Third Battalion as "Baseball.") Again tanks carried the men to the final assembly position, and then at 1:00 P. M. Company I led the attack into the town, and Company K went in to share the occupation. Company L remained in reserve on the high ground overlooking the objective.[10]

During the night there was some shelling in Basbellain, and some men from Company I were wounded. As Captain Gibson stepped outside his CP at 2:00 A. M. a shell fragment hit him in the leg, and he had to be evacuated, another victim of the Company I "commander's jinx." The weasel went up to evacuate the wounded. Colonel Wood sent Lieutenant Frank Fulgham of Company K to take command of "I." This made the turnover of rifle company commanders during the campaign in the Ardennes complete. Captain John Strader had taken command of "K" back at Lutrebois after Captain Campbell was hit, and Lt. Tom Parris of Georgia had taken Lt. Brigandi's place with Company L. Brigandi, whose feet—once frozen during ski-troop training— had gone bad during the cold exposure of those days, had been evacuated just prior to the opening of this latest phase.

Again during that night and the following morning there were plans made for a renewal of the attack, but these were delayed, and then cancelled. There seemed to be some confusion in the assignment of objectives with the 17th Airborne Division which now was operating on the left. Then came word that the Battalion would be "relieved in zone" by elements of that unit. Tanks and half-tracks brought troops of the Third Battalion back to the shelter of Hachiville.[11]

There were more orders and changes the next day. The Battalion commander, S-3, and Company commanders made a reconnaissance with a view to relieving elements of the 44th Armored Infantry Battalion in a defensive position along the "skyline drive" some eight miles to the east of Hachiville. The Battalion was to "move by tanks, TD's, half-tracks, and assault guns" to an assembly area at Breidfeld. These plans were changed, however, and late that evening the Battalion received orders to move to Heinerscheid, another town along the "skyline highway" which ran along the ridgeline above the narrow valley of the Our River. This time Colonel Wood and the S-3 had to

8. **Ibid.**, p. 187; 134th Inf., After Action Report, 1 Feb. 1845.
9. 3rd Bn. Journal, II, 187f.
10. 3rd Bn. Journal, II, 189-191.
11. 3rd Bn. Journal, II, 194f.; 3rd Bn. Interview, p. 31.

make their reconnaissance by the light of a bright moon. They were to relieve the 3rd Battalion, 357th Infantry, (90th Division).[12]

In order to make the relief it was necessary for troops to go into the town on foot during darkness, for the skyline exposed them to enemy observation and artillery. Therefore the Battalion would move initially to a protected assembly area in a canyon behind the main ridge—about two miles from the destination. It was an assorted column that left Hachiville at 11:15 A.M. that day, (January 26th). Men were mounted on 32 armored vehicles—mostly tanks of one kind or another—and five 2½ trucks; and then followed the Battalion's own 1½-ton trucks and jeeps.[13]

The column churned through the snow of a little-used road between Weiler and Asselborn[14] and then, over a road where the snow had been packed by heavy traffic started through the town. Then one of the tanks hit a mine. Fortunately, the force of the explosion was weak, and the damage was slight, but here was an instance in which traffic of all kinds had been moving over the road, and it just happened that this particular tank hit the mine. As the column went through the canyon toward the assembly area, traction became difficult for the vehicles. There was one stretch where the road ran along a ledge with a drop-off of about ten feet to the bottom land of the Clerf creek. And it was at this point that one of the tanks chose to leave the road—the iron monster rolled all the way over and came to a rest upright on the bottom land. Again the crew and passengers escaped serious injury.

At first each of the three rifle companies of the Third Battalion occupied the position of the corresponding company of the 3rd Battalion, 357th Infantry in Heinerscheid, and the Battalion CP was set up in Hupperdingen, a town, on the high plateau, about two kilometers west of Heinerscheid. Later, in order to lend better depth to the position, Company L was withdrawn to a reserve area at a farm settlement called Kaesfurt which was about midway between Hupperdingen and Heinerscheid.[15]

As in most defensive situations where attacks are not being launched against the position, patrol activity was of paramount interest. Officer-led foot patrols from the companies, from friendly units on right and left, and from the cooperating 86th Cavalry Squadron, probed down through the woods to the river, and around the town of Kalborn which lay down the slope about a kilometer—or half way to the river—to the front (east) of Heinerscheid. One afternoon Lt. Mike Hanna, the Battalion intelligence officer, made plans for a new kind of air-ground reconnaissance: a patrol from Company L would be equipped with a 536 radio as it went out on its assigned mission; then an artillery liaison plane, equipped with a 300 radio tuned to the same channel as the Battalion's net, would fly over the designated area; then the air observer would be able to relay directions to the ground patrol to investigate suspicious localities, and, on the other hand, would be able to warn the patrol should he see any enemy groups; at the same time, the air observer would be in a position to help the patrol out of trouble, or to assist it to approach close to enemy positions, by calling for artillery fire on the exact spot where it would do the most good. Much to the disappointment of the S-2, all the airplanes were assigned to other missions just before the time set for the patrol to start, and

12. 3rd Bn. Journal, II, 196-198.
13. 3rd Bn. Journal, III, 3-6.
14. ibid.
15. ibid., pp. 5, 6, 15.

the experiment had to be cancelled—he had bet 200 Belgian francs with the 2nd Battalion S-2 that it would work.[16]

Isolated prisoners began to be taken almost at once. They represented such diverse elements as the 78th Regiment of the 26th Division, the 340th Volksgrenadier Regiment, a heavy mortar battalion of the 5th Paratroop Division, and members of the Nazi labor "Todt" organization.[17]

Patrols reported several times finding enemy activity around Kalborn. Division and regimental commanders were anxious to eliminate all enemy west of the Our River; as long as the enemy held Kalborn he would have a convenient base from which to send patrols to gather information on American dispositions. The assignment to seize the town fell to Company I.

It was a pre-dawn attack on January 29th. While a tank rolled down to the forward slope and engaged the enemy's attention with diversionary cannon fire, men of Company I swept down through the snow drifts and into the town. Resistance was only momentary; they picked up half a dozen prisoners from the 39th Regiment (26th German Division)—others withdrew across the river— and one platoon set up a defense so that the rest of the company could return to its former positions in Heinerscheid.[18]

Part of the surprise which Company I had been able to achieve probably was due to the use of white snow suits by the men of the leading platoon.[19] Similar white camouflage suits had been found to be highly effective when the Germans used them in their early attacks in the Bulge. Now men of Company I were using snow suits—and patrols made continuous use of them too—whose manufacture had been begun by a Third Army salvage repair company on December 29th—the day the Third Battalion first went into Lutrebois—from 5,000 mattress covers which had been delivered on that date.[20]

Now, in this area, the American line of December 15th had been restored. Elimination of the Bulge had been completed. "When Eisenhower was ready, he had a place to leap from."[21]

Commanding that leading platoon which went into Kalborn, and charged with the holding of that town after its capture, was a husky young first lieutenant from Kansas named Warren Hodges. He had joined the company only a couple of days before, and already found himself leading an assault platoon in an attack, and then commanding an outpost; in fact he had celebrated New Year's in the States—and was still there while the Third Battalion was making its recovery of Lutrebois and a battalion of the 320th was attacking in the woods to the front. Hodges was the latest officer to arrive to the Battalion via the replacement system. Actually, of course, replacement officers had long since come to include most of the officers of the Battalion.

Satisfactory replacement of officers presented a difficult problem for the G-1. During this period many captains and lieutenants who had been commanding service units, or had been in some other branch, like the antiaircraft (coast artillery), were sent forward to infantry units. Many lacked the experience required of an infantry commander, and reconversion was difficult for them.[22] Hodges happened to be one of those officers with a training background and a personal character which permitted rapid adjustment.

16. **ibid.,** pp. 10-11.
17. 134th Inf., After Action Report, 1 Feb. 1945.
18. 3rd Bn. Journal, III, 22, 27f.
19. **ibid.**
20. Third U. S. Army, After Action Report, I, 187.
21. **Time,** Feb. 5, 1945, p. 23.
22. Lt. Col. Donald M. Ashlock, G-1, Interview.

The new "I" Company platoon leader had been sent into the replacement "pipe line" on December 23rd—at a time when losses in the Bulge were known to be serious and could be estimated to continue so for a while. On that date he reported to Fort Meade, Maryland, and, with three other officers, was processed and assigned a packet of 200 men for which he would be responsible on the movement overseas. A week later—January 1st—Hodges and his group reported to Camp Shanks at the New York Port of Embarkation. There they spent six days checking equipment, correcting service records, making out new allotments of pay, and attending to all the other administrative details and instruction incumbent upon all troops moving overseas. Hodges' provisional company boarded the *Queen Elizabeth* on January 6th as an advance party; it drew an assignment to kitchen, fatigue, and guard details for the voyage. Two days later the giant ship sailed, and, making the mid-winter crossing of the North Atlantic in six days, dropped anchor in a harbor of Scotland on the 14th. Since it had served as advance party, this group was the last to debark, so that Hodges did not reach land until the 16th. A train carried the new men to Southampton, and immediately on arriving (on the 17th) they boarded LST's (landing ship, tank). However, a storm in the English Channel delayed their departure one day, and, sailing the evening of the 18th, they arrived at Le Havre the next afternoon. After a walk of some seven or eight miles they arrived at a camp at 6:00 P.M., and by 8:00 the troops had been fed and issued two additional blankets per man, and had marched a mile back to railroad depot. Around midnight they boarded a train of the small "40 and 8" French box cars; they were very crowded—39 men to a car—but in the cold weather the men rather welcomed the crowding as a means for keeping warm. During the long, tiring, rail movement, the train stopped three times a day and the troops had hot meals from the kitchens on the train. They arrived in Neufchateau in the afternoon of January 22nd where they were given billets, and their American money was exchanged for French. At noon the next day they boarded a "40 and 8" train again for an all-night trip to Metz. There the packet of replacements was dissolved and divided into groups for assignment to various divisions—another one of those occasions when a chance assignment to one group or another might mean life or death for a man. At this point the responsibility of Hodges and his three fellow-officers with the packet was completed; but they too waited eagerly for their unit assignments. Two of them went to the 5th Division; Hodges and the other went to the 35th. At noon on January 25th these two officers joined a large number of replacements in a convoy of 2½-ton trucks, and after a bitterly cold journey arrived at Service Company, 134th Infantry, in Bastogne at 2:00 A.M. Assigned to Company I, Hodges, on the 26th, went through regimental headquarters and Battalion headquarters, and that evening joined his platoon in Heinerscheid, Luxembourg.[23]

January's battle casualties for the Battalion were 406, and the total for the month was 450, making it second only to November in losses for a month—and the 1st Battalion had suffered even worse. Total for the five weeks in the Bulge would be about 550.[24]

Temperatures approaching zero, infrequent opportunities for hot meals, lack of shelter during much of the time all had added to the hazards as well as to the discomforts of combat. Ironically, when men of the Third Battalion

23. Capt. W. D. Hodges to the Author, July 5, 1946.
24. 134th Inf., Battle Casualty Report.

had participated in winter mountain maneuvers in West Virginia, they had been equipped with shoepacs, down sleeping bags, mountain tents, heavy mittens, small gasoline stoves, and "wind breaker" outer garments; now in mid-winter combat they only had the addition of heavy overshoes, a heavy, cumbersome, wool overcoat, wool gloves, and a wool skull cap, to fit under the helmet, to their regular wool uniform. There were a few gasoline stoves in the Battalion, but a man relied mainly on an issue of captured German heat tablets for heating his unsavory "K" rations.

Finally shoepacs—the boot with a rubber foot and leather upper worn with two pairs of heavy wool socks and fitted with a thick felt insole—were delivered to the Battalion during the last week of the campaign.[25]

When troops of the 86th Cavalry relieved the Third Battalion on January 31st,[26] the Battalion had completed its role in the biggest "battle" of the war.

A total of 35 American divisions had participated in the six-week's operations.[27] German losses amounted to an estimated 220,000 men, including 110,000 prisoners, and more than 1,400 tanks and assault guns. During the month ending January 16th the enemy had lost an estimated 1,620 aircraft, and in addition, the Allied air forces claimed 6,000 motor vehicles and 550 locomotives destroyed during the period. Possibly "more serious in the final analysis was the widespread disillusionment within the German Army and Germany itself which must have accompanied the realization that the breakthrough had failed to seize any really important objective and had achieved nothing decisive."[28]

But if the counteroffensive "was not without its effects on the enemy"[29] neither was it without its effects on the Americans. Total American casualties in the Ardennes were reported to have amounted to 55,421, including 18,418 prisoners, by January 21st.[30] Losses in material, among other items included 4,000 caliber .30 machine guns, 70,000 bayonets, 24,000 rocket launchers, 10,000 rifles, 2,600 two-and-a-half-ton trucks, 684 medium tanks, six complete hospitals, 21,000 radio sets, 11,000 telephones, 280 heavy guns.[31]

Men of the Third Battalion could think back over a grim struggle and recall the words of General Eisenhower's order of the day which had come to them as they had prepared to join the attack:

> The enemy is making his supreme effort to break out of the desperate plight into which you forced him by your brilliant victories of the summer and fall.
>
> He is fighting savagely to take back all that you have won and is using every treacherous trick to deceive and kill you. He is gambling everything, but already in

25. 3rd Bn. Journal, II, 198.
26. 3rd Bn. Journal, III, 41-42.
27. Major James M. Whitmire, Jr., exec., Historical Division, War Dept. special staff, to the Author, Sept. 5, 1946.
28. General Eisenhower's Report, p. 79; General Marshall's Report, p. 45.
29. Gen. Eisenhower's Report, p. 79.
30. **The Encyclopedia Americana** (1946 ed.), XXVIII, 855. General Eisenhower's Report. General Marshall's Report, Miller, Shugg and DeWeerd, and Commager, all avoid or omit mention of American losses either in men or material. Gen. Eisenhower estimates total Allied casualties in the Ardennes as 77,000.—**Crusade in Europe**, p. 365.
31. War Department, Annual Report of the Army Service Forces for the Fiscal Year 1945 (Washington, U. S. Govt. Print. Off., 1945), p. 23. Randolph Leigh, **48 Million Tons to Eisenhower** (Washington, 1945), p. 77 lists the American ordnance losses for the month of December as follows: 22,259 rifles and similar arms, 7,012 mortars and machine guns, 782 artillery pieces, 13,820 binoculars, compasses and watches, 10,478 trucks and trailers, and 1,349 tanks, half-tracks, and armored cars. Gen. Eisenhower gives total tank and tank destroyer losses as 733.—**Crusade in Europe**, p. 365.
In the Battle of the Meuse-Argonne in World War I, 24 American and 7 French divisions had engaged in the American First Army's offensive, and a total of 1,200,000 American soldiers had participated in the 47 days of fighting. German losses amounted to about 100,000 casualties (Americans took 26,000 prisoners) and 874 cannon, 3,000 machine guns, and large quantities of material. American casualties totaled approximately 117,000 killed and wounded.—John J. Pershing, **My Experiences in the World War**, 2 Vols., (New York: Frederick A. Stokes Company, 1931), II, 388-389.

this battle your gallantry has done much to foil his plans. In the face of your proven bravery and fortitude, he will completely fail.

But we cannot be content with his mere repulse.

By rushing out from his fixed defenses the enemy may give us the chance to turn his great gamble into his worst defeat. So I call upon every man of the Allies to rise now to new heights of courage, of resolution, and of effort.

Let everyone hold before him a single thought—to destroy the enemy . . .

United in this determination and with unshakeable faith in the cause for which we fight, we will, with God's help, go forward to our greatest victory.[32]

32. **Time,** Jan. 1, 1945, p. 23.

PART FIVE—ROER TO THE RHINE

★ ★ ★

CHAPTER XX

★ ★ ★

THE NINTH ARMY

Another move to the north impending, company commanders assembled at 4 P.M. on January 31st in the Battalion command post to hear the movement order:

1.) Combat Team Miltonberger moves to the vicinity of Maastricht, The Netherlands, on 1 February 45, reverting to the 35th Infantry Division on departure from the zone of the 6th Armored Division. Battalions move in the order, 2, 1, 3. Artillery with respective attachments.

2.) This Battalion will move with 27 Quartermaster trucks in three march units; and, with Service Company in two march units will form March Group No. 3, March Units 9, 10, 11, 12, 13.

      Composition of March Units:

      March Unit No. 9 (24 vehicles)

      1—¼ ton, message center jeep with 2 messengers

      22—2½ ton QM personnel carriers, Company I, K, L, (I—7 trucks, K—7, L—8)

      1—¼ ton trail jeep (Co. K)

      Ambulance.

      March Unit No. 10 (23 vehicles)

      3—2½ Ton QM trucks: Co. M (one for weasel)

      18—¼ ton, Co. M

      1—¾ ton, Co. M

      March Unit No. 11 (23 vehicles)

      2—2½ ton QM personnel carriers (Hq. Co.)

      4—2½ ton cargo trucks (ammunition and blanket carriers)

      4—1½ ton trucks (Hq. Co.)

      5—¼ ton (I, K, L.)

      4—¼ ton (Hq.)

      1—¾ ton (Hq.)

      2--¼ ton (Medical Det.)

      1—¼ ton (Chaplain)

      Recapitulation of Quartermaster personnel carriers: Hq—2; I—7; K—7; L—8; M—3.

   3.a.)   March Unit No. 9:

      Major Heffelfinger commanding, Capt. Strader, second in command. Personnel of I, K, L, in that order.

      March Unit No. 10:

      Lt. Erickson command, Lt. Brush, second in command.

      Personnel carriers and organic vehicles of Company M.

      March Unit No. 11:

      Lt. Reischel commanding, Lt. Hall, second in command

      Headquarters Company personnel battalion organic vehicles (less Co. M), medics, chaplain.

      March Unit No. 12:

      Capt. Brown, commanding

      Service Company and Kitchen and Baggage trucks of 1st Battalion

      March Unit No. 13:

      Lt. Stoneburner commanding, Lt. Reed, trail officer.

      Kitchen and Baggage trucks of 2nd and 3rd Battalions and maintenance trucks.

b.) Entrucking area: vicinity of road fork at southwest edge of town. S-2 will post guides to meet companies as they enter Hupperdange by respective roads at 0745. (Order of march from Heinerscheid: I-K) IP—Farm buildings southwest of Hupperdange

Time to cross IP: March Unit 9—0830
March Unit 10—0835
March Unit 11—0840
March Unit 12—Join column at road junction south of
Boxhorn—0900
March Unit 13—0845
Head of March Unit 9 to cross regimental IP, road
junction at Lullierkamp, 0910

e.) Route: Urspelt—Clerf Station—Highway
N12 to N28
N 28 to Bastogne
N 4 to Marche
N 35 to Liege
N 43 to vic. of Maastricht

x.) Five minute interval between march groups. Three minutes between march units.

Ten-minute rest stops: 10 minutes before the even hour; first halt: 0950.

Thirty-minute halt for dinner at 1130. All men to detruck and exercise during scheduled stops—well to right of the road.

Speed: 25 miles per hour for lead vehicle

S-2 will reconnoiter route ahead, maintain contact with March Group 2.

Quartering Party left with S-1, 30 Jan. to prepare billets.

6th Armored Division furnish MP guides to Bastogne, 134th Inf. MP's Bastogne to destination.

4.) Hot breakfast tomorrow 0530. Individuals carry full K ration. Individuals carry bedrolls. Organic transportation will report to companies to pick up basic loads after breakfast. Rifle company organic report to Lt. Reischel at Battalion CP at 0800.

5.) Bn. C.O. will move throughout column.
Direct messages to Exec. Off. at head of column.
Air panels will be displayed.
Radio silence until further orders, or contact with enemy.
S.O.I. 1-40, 35th Div., in effect.
Password, 011200 to 021200: Rough; Reply: Gentle.[1]

The motor column wound down from the snow-covered plateau around Hupperdange on schedule, and, as a cold rain fell from time to time, moved northward to its destination. After almost nine hours on the road, the Third Battalion closed in at Berneau, Belgium, in the area south of Maastricht.[2]

Berneau was an oasis in the destruction of war. It set amidst flat meadows —patched here and there with small woods—and its trim brick houses, with gleaming glass windows, offered a welcome contrast to the rubble of the towns which the Battalion had visited ever since leaving Nancy. The men could find comfortable billets in warm houses with electric lights and running water.[3]

Four days in Berneau gave an opportunity for rest, recreation, further training. The companies carried on training programs which emphasized fighting in towns, map reading, patroling, use of compass, use of weapons, marching fire, enemy tricks, history of the regiment and the Battalion's record in the war. Lt. Hanna gave some orientation lectures on the progress of the war as a whole. There were showings of a motion picture on non-fraternization which all per-

1. 3rd Bn. Journal, III, 42-45. Gen Patton expressed regret at losing the 35th. He wrote: "This division was one of the oldest in the Third Army and had always done well.—War As I Knew It, p. 231. Also, Allen, Lucky Forward, p. 275: "One of Third Army's oldest and best divisions, it had been in combat practically continuously since July.
2. 3rd Bn. Journal, III, 45.
3. J. A. Huston to N. F. Huston, Feb. 4, 1945.

sonnel were required to see. And then there were entertainment films, and opportunities for shower baths, and USO shows, and visits of a Red Cross Clubmobile, and church services.[4]

But the men were aware that soon they would be moving against the enemy once more—this time on German soil. There was emphasis on what to expect in Germany—of the attitudes of the German people, of German propaganda and the Nazi Party, and warnings against fraternizing with any of the enemy people.[5] General Eisenhower's earlier proclamation was recalled:

> We come as conquerors but not as oppressors . . . . We shall overthrow the Nazi rule, dissolve the Nazi party and abolish the cruel, oppressive and discriminatory laws and institutions which the party has created. We shall eradicate that German militarism which has so often disrupted the peace of the world.[6]

Men of the Third Battalion knew that in the operations ahead they would not be able to depend upon members of an FFI to guide them to favorable routes, nor would there be friendly French civilians to rout out hiding Germans. The Third Battalion would be fighting in the enemy's homeland—driving for the heart of the Fatherland.

The move to German soil came on February 6th. Division shoulder insignia removed, bumper identification markings on all vehicles painted over, the 35th Division—after a 300 mile shift by rail and motor from Alsace for all its units except CT134—moved under secrecy orders to relieve the 52nd British Division in the Roer River sector. It was joining the army of its former commander: Lt. Gen. William H. Simpson's Ninth Army—XVI Corps[7] (Maj. Gen. J. B. Anderson).

Since its vicious mid-November battles in moving up to the Roer River, the Ninth Army had occupied a quiet sector, and its troops had ample time for preparation and training for the crossing of the river.[8] After its capture of Brest in September, the Ninth Army had moved under official secrecy until its commitment on the left (north) of the First Army in the November attack. Then it was hailed as a "long-hidden" and "ghost" army[9]—(though German propaganda had announced correctly that it had moved north and established its headquarters in Maastricht.)

The 134th relieved the 155th British Brigade, and the Third Battalion took over the reserve positions from the 55th Battalion (7/9 Royal Scots) in the area southwest of Heinsberg. Headquarters and Company I went into a small town called Nachbarheide, while Companies K, L, and M went into nearby Breberen. A thaw had turned the roads in the vicinity into a quagmire, but at 3 P.M., four hours after leaving Berneau, Belgium, the Battalion CP opened at Nachbarheide, Germany.[10]

The stay in Breberen and Nachbarheide was of brief duration, for the next day the Battalion moved on short notice to another reserve position farther east. Company commanders were given warning at 1:00 o'clock. At 1:30 they assembled at the Battalion CP to receive the order; at 1:50 the motor column was moving out of Breberen. The Battalion relieved elements of the 406th Infantry (102nd Division) in Randerath, and then the 1st Battalion passed

4. 3rd Bn. Journal, III, 46-55.
5. U. S. Army, Pocket Guide to Germany.
6. Quoted in Henry Steele Commager, The Story of the Second World War (Boston, 1945) p. 453.
7. 3rd Bn. Journal, III, 55-56; 35th Div., Attack!, p. 31.
8. Sidney Grusan in The New York Times, Feb. 24, 1945, p. 3.
9. (AP). The New York Herald Tribune, Nov. 17, 1944, p. 1; The Stars and Stripes (London ed.), Nov. 17, 1944, p. 1.
10. 3rd Bn. Journal, III, 56-58; 134th Inf., After Action Report, 1 March 1945.

through to occupy forward defensive positions in Horst and Himmerich, a kilometer to the north and northeast. A couple of creeks and two thousand yards of open, water-soaked bottom land separated the 1st Battalion's positions from the Roer River. Hilfarth, a town on the near (southwest) bank of the Roer, two kilometers northeast of Himmerich, remained in enemy hands. The regimental train (kitchens) set up in Geilenkirchen, six kilometers to the southwest.[11]

The special measures taken to preserve secrecy before the departure from Belgium were being maintained and implemented in this lesser shift. News release blackout continued. Steps toward signal deception were taken in the 134th's maintenance of radio nets of the 406th Infantry with transmission continued by operators of that regiment. The British 692nd Field Artillery Battalion (25-pounders) continued firing on its previous missions.[12] The regiment now was on the right flank of the XVI Corps. The 84th Division, operating under a secrecy code designation as "Control Peter" was on the right, and the 320th Infantry occupied positions on the left.

If the crossing of the Blies River had seemed somewhat hasty, the crossing of the Roer would not be. There was immediate emphasis on planning and reconnaissance—with time to carry it out. Colonel Miltonberger, in a meeting of battalion commanders on February 8th, outlined the plans for "Operation Grenade"—the operation which would bridge the Roer and drive to the Rhine— and the part which the regiment would play.[13] Already the British and Canadians of the Canadian First Army were attacking in the north from the Nijmegan bridgehead.[14] Two days later, tentatively, the right wing of Field Marshal Montgomery's 21st (Northern) Army Group—the Ninth U.S. Army— was scheduled to launch its offensive to coordinate with the drive coming down from the north. And orders had been issued and reconnaissance initiated for the crossing of the 12th (central) Army Group to the south.[15]

According to the regimental plan the 1st Battalion would clear the near bank of the river—which would mean the seizure of Hilfarth—while the 3rd would be prepared to assist, and cross the river on order; reconnaissance parties would accompany the attacking echelons to prepare for the crossing. The 2nd Battalion would be prepared to cross in the left of the regimental zone, or to follow the Third Battalion.[16]

A personal message from the Commander-in-Chief of the 21st Army Group was read to all troops. "Monty" predicted that soon they would "crack about on the plains of northern Germany," and "chase the enemy from pillar to post." "We stand ready for the last round . . . ." his order said, "We will go for the knockout blow . . . . and "good hunting!"[17]

Immediately the battalion commander and his S-3 began ground reconnaissance, and made plans for further reconnaissance from the air. Col. Wood called a meeting of the company commanders for 6:30 P.M. to give a warning order for the coming operation. Companies K and L, each with a section of heavy machine guns, would be in assault, with Company I in reserve.[18]

---

11. 3rd Bn. Journal, III, 61-62; 134th Inf., After Action Report, 1 March 45.
12. 134th Infantry, After Action Report, 1 March 45. For a commentary on the efficacy of these efforts see **infra.**, p. 401f.
13. 134th Inf., After Action Report, 1 March 45.
14. General Marshall's Report, p. 46.
15. 134th Inf., After Action Report, 1 March 45.
16. 3rd Bn. S-3 Notebook, I, 8 Feb. 45.
17. 3rd Bn. Journal, III, 63; Time (Feb. 26, 1945) p. 32.
18. 3rd Bn. Journal, III, 63-64.

Intensive preparations continued that night and the next day. Patrols probed into the enemy's defenses; commanders studied a series of excellent aerial photographs and reconnoitered for routes. The companies spent the next morning in training with engineers in using assault boats; they left Randerath at 8:30 by truck to go down near Geilenkirchen to participate in practice crossings of the Wurm Creek.[19]

However, the Germans had blown a sluice gate in the Schwammenauel Dam, on the upper Roer, and, with the water making an average rise of five feet, the operation scheduled for February 10th was postponed 24 hours. The flood still threatening, another 24-hour delay was announced the next day. By February 11th water from the Wurm, swollen by thaw and the opening of the Roer dam, was only 200 yards from the 1st Battalion's positions. General Simpson, at a meeting at the 35th Division command post, announced an indefinite postponement of the operation.[20]

Seizure of those Roer River dams in the vicinity of Schmidt was a necessary prelude for the drive to clear the enemy from the Rhineland. Troops of the First Army were undertaking this mission. By February 10th they had succeeded in gaining control of the Erft and Schwammenauel Dams, and on the following day, infantry battalions cleared the entire west bank of the Roer in that area. While this action did not prevent the flooding of the Roer valley, it forced the Germans to release the water at a time when the operation would not be endangered. With that threat removed, the Ninth Army could await the recession of the water, and choose the most desirable time for its attack.[21]

That wait gave an opportunity for further preparation—reconnaissance, planning, training. Each of the company commanders, as well as the battalion commander and the S-3 were able to make reconnaissance flights in artillery liaison planes. They could see the barbed wire and trenches and minefields protecting Hilfarth; they could see the ground on the other side of the river over which they would operate; they could see a stone bridge and a footbridge intact over the Roer River.[22]

In addition, the leaders of the Battalion, together with an officer of the engineer battalion, made plans and reconnaissances for several kilometers to the rear for a main line of resistance, a secondary defense line, and "switch lines" to be occupied should the enemy make a serious counter-attack.[23]

Night reconnaissance patrols, coming first from one battalion and then from another, operated across the regimental sector throughout the waiting period. Two patrols from the Third Battalion were scheduled to go out on the night of 9-10 February. Major Godwin, the regimental S-2 came to the Battalion CP early in the afternoon to orient the members of the patrols. Their mission was to find possible crossing sites over the Roer, and to get an estimate of the enemy strength on either side of the river. One patrol was to reconnoiter to the right of Hilfarth, the other to the left. Two engineer soldiers were to accompany each patrol. The intelligence officer gave the results of previous patrols, and pointed out that Hilfarth had been converted into an enemy strong point. He warned the members not to carry any kind

19. *Ibid.*, Boat groups were formed which included these variations: 12 riflemen, or 10 riflemen with a light machine gun and ammunition, or 10 men with a 60 mm mortar, or 7 men with a heavy machine gun.
20. 35th Div., After Action Report, 4 March 45; 134th Inf., After Action Report, 1 March 45.
21. General Marshal's Report, p. 46.
22. 3rd Bn. Journal, III, 67.
23. *Ibid.*, p. 81-82.

of identification or valuables. They were to leave at 7 P.M. and be back by
2 A.M. They studied aerial photographs of the areas, and then patrol leaders
went forward to make a daylight reconnaissance of the routes they would
follow.[24]

Both patrols left a Company C outpost at 9 o'clock and proceeded a
thousand yards on the road northeast out of Himmerich to the Teich creek
where they crossed on planks. From this point one patrol went to the left,
following another road for about 500 yards, and then proceeded north and
east along a trail toward a bend in the Roer River west of Hilfarth. They
found a German sentry before they had crossed half the remaining distance
to the river, but they went around him to the north. Very shortly they found
the whole landscape lit up by flares, and a machine gun opened fire from a
cluster of buildings on the westward outskirts of Hilfarth. About 200 yards
short of the river they ran into criss-crossing barbed wire which was strung
about 18 inches off the ground, and extended to a depth of 15 to 20 feet;
the whole area appeared to be mined. Accompanying engineers saw no
feasibility in trying to open a gap through that minefield and that thickness
of barbed wire. The patrol worked its way to the northwest in an effort to
find an opening through the wire, but it appeared to cover the entire area.
A machine pistol gave a short burst on their left. With little to be gained by
remaining longer on the enemy's doorstep, the patrol retraced its steps (a
questionable procedure), and, after pausing briefly to examine an enemy
observation post—a tree platform with a ladder—made its way back to
Himmerich shortly after midnight.[25]

The second patrol turned to the right off the road 300 yards beyond
the creek and passed through a water-logged area to a position just south of
Hilfarth. After drawing steady fire from three machine guns, located in a
line running to the west from a roadfork at the south edge of the town,
the patrol returned to Himmerich at about 1:45 A.M.[26]

Company training schedules called for four hours a day to be devoted to
assault team training with engineers in practice attacks against Siegfried Line
pillboxes in the area, instruction in mines and booby traps, test firing of
weapons, village fighting, and special techniques.[27]

In addition there were periods of special training. On Sunday, February
18th, the Battalion went by motor back to the Maas River in the vicinity of
Sittard, Holland, for further training in the attack of a river line. Monday
morning each rifle company took its turn in going to Geilenkirchen for training with the 784th Tank Battalion in tank-infantry coordination. Its personnel made up of Negroes, the 784th was attached to the 35th Division to replace the 737th Tank Battalion which had been left in the south, and though
new to battle, its men were full of enthusiasm and immediately gained the confidence of the infantrymen in this preliminary training.[28] Although the Third
Battalion relieved the 1st in the forward defensive positions (K and L on the
line) on Monday evening, training continued in the area of the reserve company in Randerath. In anticipation of pill box defenses on the other side of
the Roer, eight more hours of training in assault of a fortified position were

24. Ibid., pp. 66-67.
25. ibid., pp. 67-68.
26. Ibid., p. 69.
27. 3rd Bn., S-3 Notebook, I.
28. 3rd Bn. Journal, III, 87; 3rd Bn., S-3 Notebook, I.

scheduled for the remainder of the week. The 1st Battalion returned to its former forward positions on the 22nd, and the Third re-assembled in Ran-derath.[29]

Another training development was an emphasis on the use of the anti-tank rocket launcher, or "bazooka," and the formation of bazooka teams in the Antitank Platoon.

Under the tables of organization, the rocket launcher was an extra weapon; they were assigned to the companies but there was no designation of par-ticular individuals or sub-units to carry them within the companies. There were a total of 29 in the battalion: five for each rifle company, six for the heavy weapons company, and eight for headquarters company.[30]

The weapon itself was a simple smooth-bore tube, open at both ends, fitted with batteries and wiring to transmit an electrical impulse on depres-sion of the trigger to ignite the propelling charge in the rocket. Of two types in general use (one folded for more convenient carrying), one was 54 inches long and weighed something over 13 pounds, while the other was 61 inches long and weighed 15 pounds. Its internal diameter, or caliber, was 2.36 inches. The effective range against a point target was about 300 yards, though it could be fired on areas as far away as 600 yards.[31]

The projectile was a two and one-half pound rocket which looked like "a sharp-nosed egg attached to a finned stick a few inches long."[32] Unlike the conventional antitank guns, the rocket's penetrating power did not de-pend upon its own velocity, but upon the force of its explosion. This in-volved a wholly different principle from that used in other ammunition. The tremendous penetrating force of the explosion was due not only to the strength of the explosive, but also the design of the ammunition—it was the hollow charge, or the Munroe ring, principle. Charles E. Munroe, a Columbia University chemistry professor, had discovered the principle in 1900 while experimenting on safes. He found that while a given charge in solid form did not damage a heavy steel plate at all, it blew a hole all the way through it when the charge was arranged in the form of a deep cylinder and one end placed against the steel plate. Such a tubular charge proved to be of the order of ten times as destructive as a similar solid charge. The professor pub-lished his findings in 1901, but it aroused little attention, except for some unsuccessful German attempts to pirate the discovery in the same year, and again in 1911. Thereafter, it was ignored until 1939 when both Germans and Americans took it up. The bazooka made its first appearance with the American troops in Africa, but it was not long before the Germans were mak-ing them by the thousands in two models: one considerably larger than the American, and the other, a small "fist bazooka" or faustpatrone.[33]

Previously members of the Third Battalion had seen the bazooka's effec-tiveness demonstrated, but there was a feeling that it could play a greater role, particularly in attacks against pillboxes and in fighting in town, in the pending operations. At the same time, the 57 mm antitank gun, primarily a defensive weapon, had not proved to be of a very great value in offensive operations. Antitank officers and other leaders felt that the antitank platoons

29. 3rd Bn. Journal, III, 87, 106.
30. Table of Organization 7-15, Feb. 1944.
31. Leonard Engel, "Rockets," **The Infantry Journal**, CIV, 61-62.
32. Ibid.
33. Ibid., pp. 61-62.

ought to be able to make a more effective contribution to a battalion's attack than the tying up of whole platoons in displacing seldom-fired antitank guns. These considerations, then, led to the formation of bazooka teams and an intensive program of training under the supervision of the regimental antitank company.

With six of Headquarters Company's eight rocket launchers, the Antitank Platoon formed three teams, each armed with two bazookas. Of the ten men in a full strength antitank squad, seven were organized into a bazooka team as follows: two launchers, two loaders, two ammunition bearers, one squad leader. The other three men remained with the 57 mm gun and its 1½ ton prime mover to keep the gun up where it would be available on short notice. Six rocket launchers ready for action would be a powerful addition to whatever rifle company they might be supporting.[34]

During this period, in addition to training and preparation for the river crossing, there was time for recreation and other activities. A large room of one of the houses was cleared for almost continuous showing of motion pictures; there was a "jeep show" appearance by radio entertainer Bobby Breen. Some of the men had passes to Brussels or to nearby Dutch towns;(a few went to Britain. The chaplain had a full schedule of church services and visits; Mr. Tom Kairns, formerly a Boy Scout Executive from Philadelphia, the Red Cross representative with the division, was able to make several visits to the companies to bring up useful hard-to-get articles and to assist the men in pressing personal problems.[35]

The medical detachments, with inspections of kitchens, quarters, and personnel gave special attention to the health of the command as a few cases of jaundice, mumps, and measles developed.[36] There was additional training in control of trench foot and of venereal disease.[37] And now a new foot ailment—"shoepac foot" was reported to be appearing in the other battalions, though none had been found yet in the Third. This condition was attributed to the failure of the men to make daily changes in their felt inner soles. In any case, the members of the Third Battalion changed their footgear from shoepacs to combat boots on February 24th (to the extent that the latter were available).[38]

All this activity did not mean that members of the Battalion were beyond the danger of enemy artillery fire. At 10:30 A.M., February 12th, men in Randerath were startled by a sudden, jarring explosion. It left a crater eight feet in diameter and four feet deep just 40 yards from the Battalion CP. Inasmuch as there had been no warning of any kind, first guesses were that it must be a time bomb or a mine of some kind.[39] But, at intervals of five to 15 minutes, there were three more similar explosions in the same area. Lt. Erickson brought in a shell fragment that measured one and a quarter inches thick, five inches long, and one inch wide. Other fragments, as they were found, were sent over to the 161st Field Artillery.[40] Artillery officers estimated that the enemy weapon sending over those shells was about a 280 mm piece. And they noticed a dual action shell: there would be fragmen-

34. 134th Inf., After Action Report, 1 March 45; 3rd Bn. Journal, III, 92, 100, 103.
35. 3rd Bn. Journal, III, pp. 57-104, **passim.**
36. ibid., 3rd Bn. S-3 Notebook, I.
37. 3rd Bn. Journal, III, 90.
38. ibid., p. 103. During this period a Mr. Shepard of the War Production Board in Washington, and two officers, visited the Battalion to discuss the problem of footwear.
39. ibid., p. 72.
40. ibid., pp. 72-73.

tation from an air burst or a super sensitive point detonation, and then a secondary delayed action explosion.[41] A shell struck an artillery command car (the 161st was located in Randerath) as it proceeded down the narrow main street one morning and completely demolished it and killed its occupants.[42]

Robot planes or "buzz bombs" passed overhead carrying potential death, but most of them continued on a course toward Antwerp or Liege.[43] One night one of the "things" fell in the area to the rear of Randerath. Some who heard it recognized the quaint-sounding "put-put" of its motor, then the cut-off, and, seconds later, the explosion. Others who heard it thought at first that it was an airplane crash.[44]

A concentration described as the "most severe artillery barrage since the days of St. Lo" fell on Randerath[45] between 1:00 and 1:30 A.M., February 18th.[46] Men hurried to basements and cellars—they found that buildings usually afforded adequate protection against artillery. Hon's first thoughts were on the safety of the battalion commander and his staff, and he rushed upstairs to arouse those who were sleeping to get them to go to the basement.[47] Telephone lines were knocked out and an "M" Company jeep was destroyed, but, at least at the time no casualties were reported.[48] An estimated 300 rounds had fallen on Randerath within the space of half an hour.[49]

Now division insignia and unit markings on vehicles were to be restored. And regimental insistance was as strong for putting them on now as it had been for removing them prior to the move from Berneau. With a deadline set for noon, February 24th, the priority for sewing shoulder patches on garments was: (1) field jackets, (2) shirts, (3) overcoats.[50]

A change in the command of the regiment came when Colonel Miltonberger went to division headquarters to become assistant division commander, and Lt. Col. Alford Boatsman assumed command.[51]

Meanwhile, on February 23rd, other infantry battalions of the Ninth U. S. Army attacked across the Roer River for the beginning of their action in "Operation Grenade."[52]

---

41. 134th Inf., After Action Report, 1 March 45.
42. 3rd Bn. Journal, III, 75, 76.
43. Late in November the V-weapons had been falling on Antwerp at a rate of one every 12½ minutes. There were doubts for a time as to the advisability of continuing to operate the port.—General Marshall's Report, p. 38; of Edmund Antrobus, "V-Bombs on Antwerp," **Yank, The Army Weekly**, (British ed.), III, April 13, 1945, pp. 4-5.
44. 3rd Bn. Journal, III, 75.
45. 134th Inf., After Action Report, 1 March 45.
46. 3rd Bn. Journal, III, 90.
47. Col. Warren C. Wood to the Author, June 26, 1946.
48. 3rd Bn. Journal, III, 90.
49. 134th Inf., After Action Report, 1 March 45.
50. 3rd Bn. Journal, III, 100, 103.
51. 134th Inf., After Action Report, 1 March 45.
52. General Marshall's Report, p. 46.

CHAPTER XXI

* * *

ACROSS THE ROER AT HILFARTH

* * *

General Eisenhower's plan envisaged the destruction of the German armies west of the Rhine; he sought to gain the decision before the Rhine had to be crossed. While the Ninth Army prepared for its drive, Germany's divisions were being pinned down all along the front: the Seventh Army had cleared the Colmar pocket in the south, and now held a loosely-defended line along the Rhine from Strasbourg to the Swiss border; the Third Army was advancing steadily through and beyond the Siegfried Line in the Prum-Trier area; the British and Canadians continued their bitter attack across flooded terrain in the north.[1]

In preparation for the Ninth Army's offensive, the air forces, flying from bases in Britain, France, and Italy, flew nearly 10,000 sorties on February 22nd to cover rail and transportation targets throughout Germany in a pattern designed to isolate the western battlefields.[2] The next day troops of the Ninth Army, behind a tremendous artillery preparation, "jumped off" in a pre-dawn attack.[3]

But while infantry battalions of the 29th Division fought through the rubble of Julich—and battalions with the First Army took Duren—the Ninth Army's left remained passive for two more days. The order came for the 134th Infantry to attack on February 26.[4]

Elements of the German 343rd Infantry Regiment (183rd Division), with headquarters across the river in Huckelhoven, were defending the sector in front of 134th Infantry. They had been maintaining a garrison of approximately 125 men in Hilfarth. But covered by a thick mesh of barbed wire, and hazardous mine fields in great depth, Hilfarth did not depend upon manpower alone for its defense. A bend in the Roer river protected the flanks of the town, and the vicious mine fields—there were S-mines ("Bouncing Bettys"), Shu mines, "rail mines," all contrived to destroy men, as well as the big Teller Antitank mines—and barbed wire and machine guns covered the approaches. The thaws had uncovered minefields which frozen ground and snow had rendered ineffective during the November attacks. The whole area around Randerath was sown with treacherous mines.[6] And weeks of relative inactivity had permitted the Germans to turn Hilfarth into "the worst nest of mines which the Americans have had to cross for two months."[7]

The clearing of Hilfarth was assigned to the 1st Battalion; it was to make a night attack against the town at 8 P.M. (February 25th). An hour later the Third was to leave Randerath to assemble in Himmerich, there to await the cap-

1. General Marshall's Report, pp. 45-46.
2. Ibid., p. 46.
3. The New York Times, Feb. 24, 1945, p. 1.
4. The New York Times, Feb. 25, 1945, p. 1, Feb. 26, 1945, p. 1; 3rd Bn. Journal, III, 111.
5. Ibid., pp. 109, 111.
6. Ibid., p. 62.
7. The Associated Press, Feb. 26, 1946, reprinted in The Santa Fe Express, May, 1945, p. 9.

ture of Hilfarth before moving up to cross the river and seize Huckelhoven. Companies K and L would make the assault with "I" in reserve. The 137th Infantry was to cross upstream in the zone of the 84th Division.[8]

It was after 9 o'clock before the 1st Battalion moved out to cross the creek to the front, over a treadway which engineers had put in two nights earlier. An hour and a half later leading squads were moving into Hilfarth. Moving on in spite of some machine gun fire and, worse than that, the mine fields, Companies A and B occupied the town by 1:45 A.M., but the process of mopping up took until almost daylight.[9] The antipersonnel mines had exacted a toll:

> A doughboy whose right foot had just been blown off by a mine lay on a stretcher in the aid station and said,—"and I used to be a jitterbug."
> . . . the bottom lands west of here were littered with wrecked American equipment, and tired medics were bringing in a seemingly endless stream of wounded. Several medics were wounded and one was blown to bits, but when the sun came up this morning only six mine casualties remained to be brought in, and these were removed when engineers cleared the path.[10]

They found the stone arch bridge intact, though seriously damaged by American artillery fire, and soldiers stripped from it demolition charges which the Germans had left. Vehicles could not use this bridge immediately, but it was passable for foot troops.[11]

However, in order not to play into the German defensive organization, and to gain protection for the flanks, Col. Wood chose to make the crossing at a military bend in the river (a bend curving in toward friendly territory) just to the west of Hilfarth.

A heavy machine gun platoon of Company M went into position on the southwest bank of the river to support the attack, (of the other platoon, one section was attached to Company K and one to Company L), and the 81 mm mortars went into position to fire on Huckelhoven. The bazooka teams of a regimental antitank platoon had joined Company K, and the Battalion Antitank Platoon's rocket launchers were with Company L. The Aid Station moved up to Hilfarth.[12]

Inasmuch as the Third Battalion was not crossing at a bridge site, it would be necessary either to cross in assault boats, or for engineers to construct a foot bridge. Col. Wood preferred the latter course, and at 6:45 A.M., soldiers of the 60th Engineer battalion, covered by a platoon from Company L began construction of a footbridge. The channel actually amounted to hardly more than a creek, (see photograph) though its current was swift, and the engineers rapidly completed their bridge.[13]

Company K started across the bridge at 8 o'clock, and minutes later its men were cleaning out some scattered buildings on the opposite side.[14] Enemy opposition was not determined, but it was daylight now, and the Third Battalion was drawing enemy fire and losing a few men. Just as Company L was starting across, the First Sergeant of Company K, ahead, was hit; immediately one of the medics with "L"—Corporal Almon N. Conger—rushed forward to help him. Too busy and excited to be mindful of the continuing fire, he

8. 3rd Bn. Journal, III, 106f.
9. Ibid., p. 108; 134th Inf., After Action Report, 1 March 45.
10. The Associated Press, Feb. 26, 1945, reprinted in **The Santa Fe Express,** May 1945, p. 9.
11. 134th Inf., After Action Report, 1 March 45.
12. 3rd Bn. Journal, III, 107.
13. 134th Inf., After Action Report, 1 March 45; 3rd Bn. Journal, III, 109.
14. 3rd Bn. Journal, III, 110.

continued to work with his patient—and presently a sniper's bullet wounded him; afterwards "at least nine doughs" told him that "they got him" (the sniper). Conger, who entered the military service from Tacoma, Washington, received a Distinguished Service Cross for his heroism.[15]

Co. M's 1st Machine Gun Platoon fired a thousand rounds of caliber .30 ammunition as men of "K" and "L" scurried across the foot bridge. Within half an hour "K" Company had secured the approaches to the stone arch bridge from the other side, and had taken 15 prisoners. Company L crossed, and, deploying on the left, advanced across open ground and roads toward Huckelhoven a thousand yards to the north. Small arms fire from the southern edge of Huckelhoven temporarily pinned down the attacking troops. The enemy even undertook a local counterattack, but mortar and artillery broke that up, and then an artillery TOT on Huckelhoven eased the situation there. The Battalion took 45 prisoners—second rate soldiers from two companies and a battalion headquarters of the 340th Volksgrenadier Regiment in Huckelhoven, and some from the 216th and the 343rd VG regiments who did not seem to be too sure what they were doing there. By noon the assault companies were in the objective town, but it took the remainder of the afternoon to search out the buildings for hiding enemy.[16]

The reserve company (I) and the Battalion Command Post moved to Hilfarth during the afternoon. Tanks of the 784th Tank Battalion and TD's of the 654th Tank Destroyer Battalion moved up to support the rifle companies in holding the ground. The right flank was secured as battalions of the 137th Infantry, moving rapidly in a wide swing from their crossing approached Huckelhoven from the north and east. The 2nd Battalion, crossing behind the Third, now held positions on the left.[17]

Meanwhile troops of the 60th and 202nd Engineer Battalions worked to insure communications to the rear to support the bridgehead: in addition to completing two infantry foot bridges and repairing the stone arch bridge so that tanks could cross it that evening, they began construction on two class 40 floating treadways and one class 6 infantry support bridge.[18]

While opposition had not been absent, casualties in the Battalion had been light, and men of the Third Battalion, doubtless apprehensive in making their first attack after several week's delay, looked to the continuation of the attack with confidence.

The delay in the Ninth Army's offensive had given it time to build up a supply reserve to be prepared for fast action. Moreover, during this time the Germans had committed three divisions against the Canadian First Army which might have been used on this front.[19]

After a hot breakfast the next morning at 4:30, the Third Battalion "jumped off" again at 6:30. The direction of attack now was *northwest* and the Battalion moved along the flanks and rear of the enemy's Roer River defense positions. It was taking time to flush out the enemy from houses and mine shafts and factory buildings, but the Battalion was advancing steadily against light resistance. Companies K and L cleared Siedling quickly and took 13 prisoners from the 2nd Company, 343rd V. G. Regiment. Prisoners

15. 35th Div. Press Release, (The Information Section, Analysis Branch, Headquarters Army Ground Forces.)
16. 3rd Bn. Journal, III, 110-113.
17. **ibid.**
18. 134th Inf., After Action Report, 1 March 45.
19. Sidney Grusan in **The New York Times,** Feb. 24, 1945, p. 3.

reported that the defenders of Hilfarth had been ordered to assemble in Schauffenberg . . . an hour later the attacking companies were in Schauffenberg;(at noon prisoners reported that the command post of the German 343rd Regiment was in Gendorf . . . at 4 P.M. the CP of the Third Battalion opened in Gendorf. Nineteen PW's had been taken by 9 A.M.; 15 minutes later 51 were on the way to the rear—the latter were from the 4th company (heavy weapons) of the 330th Regiment (183rd Division), and their morale appeared to be broken. By 2:30 the Battalion was prepared to "jump" for its day's objective: Wassenberg.[20]

Company I mounted tanks at Schauffenberg, and, while K and L cut across along a railroad, the tank-infantry team found its way through minor obstacles and then moved up over a parallel paved highway. There was a pause at Gendorf, a mile short of the objective, while foot troops cleared road blocks of movable rails from the path of the tanks, and coordination was completed for the final attack. Then as Company L, followed by K,[21] moved along the railroad, 600 yards to the right of the highway which was to be the tank's route, the column of Shermans began to roll over the road and soon was approaching Wassenberg. However, German defenders halted the approaching column as infantrymen sought cover from a burst of fire.[22] The leading tank opened fire in reply. As though this were a signal, the turrets of the other tanks—now strung out a thousand yards over the slightly curving highway—turned to the right and opened fire all along the line. Firing across the railroad, they raked the woods beyond with machine gun fire—and pinned down the leading elements of Company K; their tracer bullets set fire to a hay stack just in front of the Battalion observation post; the leading tanks engaged in a sharp exchange of cannon fire. When the voluminous shooting finally subsided—much to the relief of "K" Company—a small group of Germans came out of the woods to surrender. But an antitank gun had sent a round directly through the side of one of the leading tanks, killing one of the crew; a comrade walked away from the tank, and said sadly, "Po' Leroy, he won' never see Georgia no mo'."

After that brief counter, the Third Battalion occupied Wassenberg in short order, and took out 47 more German prisoners.[23] (Wassenberg was an important road center across the six kilometers of Roer River lowland—and the parallel creeks and canals—from Heinsberg, and connected with that destroyed city by a main highway.)

The next day's operation (February 28th) was almost a repetition of the previous ones: Company L, followed by Company K, moved out at 7 A.M. and seized Birgelen, a kilometer to the north, hardly more than half an hour later. Then "I" Company mounted tanks again in Wassenberg, and passing through L, raced on up the highway to the northeast to occupy Objective No. 2 five kilometers beyond Birgelen. Companies K and L moved on up on foot to join "I" in an area around an important road junction near the northeast corner of a woods called Birgeler Wald. As they passed through Elsum, Rosenthal, and the Ophoven and Effelder Woods, the only enemy encountered were small groups of stragglers. Armored Cars of the 35th Reconnaissance

20. 3rd Bn. Journal, III, 116-118; 134th Inf., After Action Report, 1 March 45.
21. Capt. Strader had become ill and Lt. Langdon had taken over command of "K"—Lawrence Langdon to the Author, July 5, 1946.
22. 134th Inf., After Action Report, 1 March 45; 3rd Bn. Journal, III, 118.
23. 3rd Bn. Journal, III, 119.

Troop passed through in pursuit to attempt to locate what positions the enemy might be defending.[24]

When men of the Third Battalion arrived in Birgelen, they were surprised to find printed greetings awaiting them in some of the houses. Nazis had printed leaflets, with the division insignia in blue in the upper left corner, flanked by words in bold red letters:

WELCOME MEN OF THE 35TH DIVISION:

They read on:

> Considering the fact that you are newcomers, we would like to do everything to make you feel at home. We extend to you a cordial greeting and a hearty welcome to the Rur [Roer] Valley!

They were puzzled to read at the bottom of the page:

> You have tried to veil your arrival here by doing such things as removing your divisional insignias. Nevertheless, a little bird told us all about it.

And on the back:

> Before you arrived, there were other divisions here who didn't fare so well; namely: the 84th, the 102nd, the 29th, and, not to be forgotten, the British. They all got knocked about a bit. You can see that you won't have an easy time of it against the Rur [Roer] defense lines.
>
> As we said before, we shall try to make you feel at home. We hope to make every day here seem like "the glorious Fourth"—there'll be plenty of fireworks.

Apparently the "welcoming committee" had not had an opportunity to send over its greetings before its "Rur defense lines" were overrun.

There was another leaflet of a different nature. It carried a picture of the score board at the Berlin Olympic Games showing the American flag waving in triumph for the first three places. Perhaps the words on the back, printed in red and black, carried some prophecy:

> Many Americans have been in Germany to see the Olympic Games. You yourself have listened to the radio reports and vividly followed up the competitions.
>
> You recall that all nations had been present—all but the Russians; they were too busy arming, of course!
>
> Have you ever heard or seen in these reports that the German people then was "unhappy, oppressed and enslaved by the Nazibosses?"—NO. You have seen a peaceful, sporting, gay people, at work and at festivals and contests. But today you are told to liberate the German people.
>
> Now listen!
>
> Since 1933 we have built up a new nation. We know no unemployment, no hunger. And then WAR came, and later YOU came, you Americans. And together with you came the terror of unscrupulous bombing, death and destruction for our families and homes and the prospect of forced labor in Siberia. Your liberation brings us nothing but destruction and the threat of deportation. We know that. And we act accordingly.
>
> Every house, every farm, every settlement will bring you high losses, and losses only. And when you hope to have achieved your aim—then our time will come. And all your sacrifices will have been in vain.

There were some other leaflets intended for the British.

As the Company I tank column had rolled on through Birgelen, an artillery liaison plane, in communication with a forward observer in one of the leading tanks, scouted ahead for possible enemy activity. But the biggest obstacle which the force ran up against was an antitank ditch. Some drivers found that it was possible, at one point, to get across by easing into the ditch

---

24. 3rd Bn. Journal, III, 120-123; 134th Inf., After Action Report, 1 March 45.

and then pulling out on the not too steep opposite bank.[25] However, there were to be no detours for one enthusiast; as he approached the ditch, he "gave her the gun" to hurtle the obstacle; and although the precarious jump of the "iron horse" sent one of its infantry riders to the hospital, he did make the other side and keep going.

The companies organizing on their objective, Col. Wood and the S-3 went forward to visit him. As they stood at the road junction, Lt. Fulgham, the Company I commander, pointed out how an "M" Company machine gun covered the roads from a house a hundred yards away, and then the three gathered about the lieutenant's map so that he could point out his company's dispositions. Then, without any warning there was a burst of machine gun fire. Lt. Fulgham dropped to the ground in pain; a series of bullets had gone through his forearm as he held the map with the other officers. This time the Company I "commanders jinx" had worked again through a friendly weapon—the bullets had come from an accidental discharge of that "M" Company machine gun which was covering the road junction.[26] That evening First Lieutenant Warren D. Hodges became the combat commander of Company I. He must have crossed his fingers as he thought of the fate of his 13 predecessors: two killed, ten wounded—five very seriously—and one captured.

Examination of the villages which the Battalion occupied revealed that numbers of innocent-appearing houses were in reality camouflaged pillboxes of the very strongest type. The companies were directed to search them out. Engineers blew some of the outlying concrete positions.[27]

In view of the rapid advances and low casualties, morale of the men was bound to be high. Indeed, casualties for February were the lightest for any month thus far; it was the first time that the total for a month had been less than 100.[28]

Meanwhile the 320th Infantry, which had been in division reserve, was motorized, and the tank battalion was attached to form Task Force Byrne. This force was to pass through and drive rapidly to the northwest toward Venlo.[29]

25. 3rd Bn. Journal, III, 120.
26. Col. Warren C. Wood to the Author, June 26, 1946.
27. 3rd Bn. Journal, III, 123.
28. 134th Inf., Battle Casualty Report. Company I had 20; K, 35; L, 22; M, 14.—and seven men from "K" had been evacuated with "shoepac foot" on Feb. 28—3rd Bn. Journal, III, 123.
29. 134th Inf., After Action Report, 1 April 45.

CHAPTER XXII

✶ ✶ ✶

THE WESEL POCKET

✶ ✶ ✶

"Operation Grenade," both in planning and execution, was one of the more skillful maneuvers of the war. Its objective was the destruction of the German armies in the Rhineland. While the First Canadian Army, its flanks secured by the Rhine on the left and the Maas on the right, drove to the southwest, (Operation VERITABLE) the Ninth Army caught the enemy off balance; instead of driving directly eastward toward the Rhine, it swung the main force of its attack to the north—in the direction of the oncoming British Empire troops. But the objectives assigned the divisions in the Ninth Army were echeloned in such a way that each had protection on its flank from the pressure of a neighbor. Actually, by the time the big "wheel" completed its turn toward the north, its right elements were at the Rhine opposite Dusseldorf. At the same time, the First Army's attack for Cologne secured the right flank (and rear) of the Ninth.*

On the Ninth Army's left flank, along the Roer and Maas Rivers, (the Roer flows into the Maas at Roermond) Task Force Byrne "took the ball" for an "end run" to Venlo (again inside the Netherlands border). The mechanized-motorized force covered the 24 miles from Wassenberg to Venlo and swept in to capture the Dutch city so rapidly on March 1st that British, who had seen the capture from the opposite side of the Maas, could hardly believe it until their reconnaissance boats came across the river to investigate.[1] Venlo's 15,000 people—of a normal population of 60,000—put on one of the wildest demonstrations which soldiers of the 35th Division had seen.[2] It was reminiscent of the race across France.

Men of the Third Battalion who had survived the Saar and the Ardennes could permit themselves a bit of exhilarant anticipation as they envisaged, for the first time since France in September, rapid advances and light casualties.

The Third Battalion, with a platoon of engineers and a platoon of tank destroyers attached, set out for Venlo early on March 2nd. Relieved by the 2nd Battalion, the companies had assembled in Wassenberg and Birgelen. With certain exceptions, the Battalion's motor vehicles—including the TD's with a squad of men riding on each destroyer—left from Birgelen at 3:15 A.M. Forty-five minutes later the foot troops—130 from I, 86 from K, 128 from L—moved out along the road in a column of files on each side. The radio jeep (SCR 284), the artillery liaison jeep, a medical jeep, and Company M's 1st Machine Gun Platoon and one mortar section accompanied the foot column. Their machine guns mounted on jeeps, one section patrolled the roads to the

---

* General Simpson's instructions were based upon alternative plans: one, in case resistance should be strong, called for an attack of the three corps abreast to the Rhine—after the initial bridgehead had been broadened. The other contemplated swift break-through operations. On the basis of early reports, then, Simpson put the second plan into effect.—Lt. Gen. W. H. Simpson, "Rehearsal for the Rhine: an account of the Ninth United States Army Operation 'Grenade.'" **Military Review**, XXV (Oct. 1945), 22.
 1. 35th Div., **Attack!**, p. 31; 134th Inf., After Action Report, 1 April 45.
 2. Wes Gallagher, (AP), **The Omaha World-Herald**, March 5, 1945.

left to protect the flank, and the other remained with the foot troops for immediate protection.[3] The regiment was using its 2½ ton trucks for shuttling the troops, and after carrying the 1st Battalion to Venlo, they returned to pick up the marching column of the Third. At 7 A.M. the Battalion closed into its assigned area in settlements immediately to the southeast of the city.[4]

From Venlo, Task Force Byrne turned northeast to head for the Rhine. After some sharp local encounters, the tanks and infantry pushed through Straelen, Sevelen, Nieukirk, Kamp. Combat Team Murray (137th Inf.) and a combat command of the 8th Armored Division moved up on the right and drove for Lintfort and Rheinberg.[5]

Given the mission of protecting the Ninth Army's flank as its attack moved to the northeast, Col. Boatsman sent the 1st Battalion northward from Straelen to seize a part of Geldern and attempt to make contact with the First Canadian Army.[6] With tanks accompanying, the 1st Battalion moved out on its assigned task, but near the objective ran into groups of bitterly resisting Germans. The tanks opened fire. A round almost hit British troops attacking from the north. A British officer organized a small patrol, and, accompanied by an American war correspondent, hurried along what cover was at hand to find the Americans and stop the tank fire. German bullets still cracking overhead, the British met Major John E. Davis of the 1st Battalion, and the long awaited juncture between the First Canadian Army and the Ninth U. S. Army was achieved on March 3rd.[7]

The Third Battalion, in reserve—with side missions of setting up road blocks and guarding bridges—moved successively from Venlo to Straelen, to Sevelen. As Task Force Byrne encountered increasingly stubborn resistance in the area north of Lintfort—about five miles from the Rhine—members of the Third Battalion began to speculate on whether the 134th would not have to be called upon for the final push to the river.[8]

Up to this point the gains all along the front had been spectacular: Rheydt, Munchen Gladbach, Krefield had fallen in rapid succession (and the highly-rated Panzer Lehr Division had been back in action to defend Munchen Gladbach). Cologne fell on March 7th after strong resistance, and on the same day occurred one of the greatest windfalls of the war when elements of the Ninth Armored Division seized the Ludendorff Bridge at Remagen intact.[9]

But, reduced to an area eight miles long by five to seven miles wide, the enemy's bridgehead across the river from Wesel remained, on March 7th, his most important holding on the west bank of the Rhine north of the Moselle;[10] and here the German defenders were fighting a bitter delaying battle. Five German divisions had been thrown in to try to stop the advance of the Canadian Army from the north.[11]

3. 3rd Bn. Journal, III, 126-131.
4. 134th Inf., After Action Report, 1 April 45; 3rd Bn. Journal, III, 131.
5. 35th Div., **Attack!**, p. 31; 3rd Bn. Journal, III, 133-147. Task Force Byrne escaped a possible disaster in taking Sevelen. Moving at night, the tanks rolled into the town, drawing only a few rounds of fire. Allowing the tanks to get into the town, the Germans then blew out a bridge (over a creek) behind them and opened fire on the following trucks and on the tanks from all sides. In a wild melee of bazooka, machine gun and mortar firing, the Negro tankers succeeded in holding their own and when daylight came most of the Germans were gone.—Wes Gallagher, The Associated Press, **The Santa Fe Express**, May 1945, p. 8.
6. 134th Inf., After Action Report, 1 April 45.
7. Ned Nordness (AP), **The New York Times**, March 4, 1945, p. 4.
8. 3rd Bn. Journal, III, 133-147.
9. **ibid.**; General Marshall's Report, p. 46; Shugg and De Weerd, **World War II**, pp. 326-327.
10. "World War II Chronology," **The World Almanac**, 1946, p. 65; General Marshall's Report, p. 46.
11. 3rd Bn. S-3 Notebook, I.

The advance of Task Force Byrne slowed to a halt, orders came down on the afternoon of March 8th for the Battalion to relieve the 1st Battalion, 320th Infantry. Col. Wood, after alerting the companies for a possible move, took his S-3 and went forward by jeep to the area southwest of Alpen to contact the commander of the battalion to be relieved and to make a reconnaissance. However, the order was cancelled at 8 P.M.; the 320th was to continue the attack for one more day.[12]

At 8:30 the next night, eighteen 2½ ton trucks—6 each for Companies I, K, L—began to roll through the dark streets of Sevelen. Following the lead of Major Heffelfinger in a jeep ahead, they turned onto the highway and headed northeast. Two machine-gun jeeps followed the first six personnel carriers, and another section followed the rear. Antitank trucks—loaded with extra men —pulled their guns into the column. Jeeps, tanks, TD's joined it. By the time its leading trucks reached Horstgen, where the highway made a turn to the east, the column had extended out to its distance and was moving along smoothly. The familiar purr of running 2½-ton trucks drifted through the night to be lost in the clash of armored tracks a kilometer to the rear. The highway was paved, but its surface was muddy from the droppings of earlier vehicles, and the thick rubber tires—and the 2½-ton trucks were "6x6" (six wheeled, six wheel drive) with ten tires on the road—set up a steady hum until delayed by some brief obstacle or congestion.[13] The trucks formed dim silhouettes against the pale glow of man-made moonlight in the northern sky where British searchlights reflected against low clouds to furnish some illumination over the battle area.[14]

A kilometer short of Kamp the column turned north to find its way over muddy gravel roads along the edges of dark woods, around numerous deceptive turns, to the village of Bauern. There Captain Magnunson and his quartering party met the companies to lead them through the darkness to their billets for the night.

After an hour and fifteen minutes on the road, the Battalion moved into its assembly area for a brief rest for its early morning attack.[15]

But company commanders would find little time for rest that night. They would have to make sure that adequate guards were on duty for local security; that the men had a place to sleep; they would have to see that men had ammunition and rations and water; they would have to study their maps and discuss plans with platoon leaders in anticipation of the battalion order; then, between 2 and 3 A.M. they would be called to the battalion C.P. for the battalion order; there would be more study and planning, and they would have to issue their company orders to the platoon leaders, and give them time to orient the squad leaders and pass the information down to all the men; then they would very soon have to see that the men were ready to go, and then would lead their companies through the night toward another German town—and danger: the battle against the Wesel pocket had become bitter all the way across its front.[15a]

12. 3rd Bn. Journal, III, 147-148; 134th Inf., After Action Report, 1 April 45.
13. 3rd Bn. Journal, III, 150.
14. cf. "Attack in Holland," **Life**, XVII, Dec. 18, 1944, p. 69. The use of "artificial moonlight" came into prominence during the Canadian Army's operations through Holland. It was first used by the British at Caen; Americans used it to some extent in the Ardennes,—supra.; **The New York Times** (U.P.), Jan. 10, 1945, p. 4.
15. 3rd Bn. Journal, III, 150.
15a. "The hardest fighting of the operation was produced by the frontal attacks on the Wesel pocket."—Simpson, loc. cit., p. 27.

German infantrymen of the Luftwaffe were resisting troops of two Allied Armies "with all the valor customary of elite corps." The Canadian 2nd Infantry Division, joining with the Canadian 4th Armored Division, pushed in from the north. Scottish troops in the center were attacking from the west and southwest, while the American 35th Division bit into the German bridge-head from the southwest and south.[16] After some intense house-to-house fighting, the British 52nd Division had taken Alpen, on the left flank of the 320th Infantry, during the morning.[17] On the other flank, the 137th Infantry had taken Ossenberg, three kilometers northeast of Rheinberg and within a kilometer northeast of the Rhine. However, as battalions of the 137th attempted to push on into the open ground north of Ossenberg, Germans strongly entrenched in near-by woods and across the river, had stopped them—they were calling it another "88 Alley." One of the sergeants of the 137th had described it, "They are throwing everything in the book at us; there have been more mortar shells plopped in on us today than we ever encountered anywhere—St. Lo, Bastogne, or Gremecey Forest. I guess they don't want to ferry any stuff across the river with them."[18]

This attack was going to be made without any opportunity for the commanders to make any kind of reconnaissance of the ground: the 1st Battalion, 320th Infantry was still fighting for the town from which the Third Battalion, 134th, was to "jump." Before being relieved, the 1st Battalion, 320th was to clear Drupt. The companies had entered the town shortly before midnight but fighting still was going on.[19]

In the zone of the 1st Battalion, 320th Infantry, and now in that of the Third Battalion, 134th, there was a series of towns of varying sizes. Something over a kilometer northwest of Bauern, the Third Battalion's assembly position, was a village called Huck (just southeast of British-held Alpen). It was from Huck that the 1st Battalion, 320th Infantry had launched its attack over the open ground toward Drupt, nearly two kilometers to the north. Two kilometers northeast of Drupt was Borth, and finally, on the banks of the Rhine was the larger town of Buderich—about four kilometers farther to the northeast, on the main highway to Wesel (via a bridge over the Rhine two kilometers beyond).

With the issue of Drupt still not completely settled, Col. Wood, on the assumption that it would be cleared before morning, called in the company commanders at 2 A.M. They made their way through the dark streets of the strange German village to the Battalion CP. There, in the room of a house with windows and doors covered with blankets to hide their bright light from the Battalion's portable German generator, Hodges, Langdon, Parris, Erickson, and members of the Battalion Staff, looked at their maps, and opened notebooks to take down details of the order:

> 1.a.) The enemy continues to defend his bridgehead west of Wesel. Intense mortar fire and some armor is reported in our zone.
> b.) 1st Battalion, 320th, has two companies in Drupt. 1st Battalion 134th will attack on our right. First Canadian Army (52nd British Division) attacks on our left.
> Supporting troops: 3rd Platoon, Company A, 60th Engineers (To Co. L)
> 161st Field Artillery Battalion, reinforced.—Artillery on call, FO's with Companies

16. **The New York Times,** March 11, 1945, pp. 1, 3.
17. 3rd Bn. Journal, III, 149.
18. Everett Walker, **New York Herald-Tribune,** March 10, 1945 (reprinted in **The Santa Fe Express,** May 1945, pp. 1, 8.
19. 3rd Bn. Journal, III, 150.

K and L; planned fires on Borth will lift at 0500. 89th Chemical Battalion (4.2 in. mortars). Observer to Company L.

2.) This Battalion, with Company C, 18th Tank Battalion (8th Armored Division) ; 3rd Platoon, Company A, 654 TD Battalion, and 3rd Platoon Antitank Company attached, attacks to seize BUDERICH and continue attack to northeast.

        L.D.—Creek through DRUPT
        Time of Attack: 0545
        Direction of Attack: Azimuth of 65° initially.
        Formation: Column of Companies: L—K—I.

3.a.) Company L will leave present assembly area at 0400—meet 320th guides at edge of HUCK and move to final assembly position in vicinity of DRUPT. Company L will attack at 0545, seize and mop up BORTH, be prepared to continue attack to northeast.

b.) Company K will move from present position to HUCK at 0500. Move to DRUPT at H hour, be prepared to support Company L. Send contact patrol to friends on our left: vicinity cross roads northeast of ALPEN.

c.) Company I—move from present position to HUCK at H prepared to follow Company K—attention to Battalion flanks and rear.

d.) Company M—one machine gun section in direct support of Company L, one section in direct support of Company K. One MG platoon move with Company I prepared to support the attack.

81 mm mortars: from positions in vicinity of HUCK be prepared to fire on BORTH and vicinity. Observers with K and L.

e.) Tanks: direct support of Company L. Move to DRUPT from present position at 0530.

f.) Battalion Antitank Platoon: Reconnoiter for positions in vicinity of DRUPT, provide AT protection to Battalion right flank and rear.

g.) Regimental antitank platoon: Bazooka teams in direct support of Company L; report to Company L CP at 0415. [?]

h.) TD's—go into positions in vicinity of DRUPT to provide AT protection to left flank and front—fire on targets of opportunity; be prepared to displace forward.

4.) Weapons off carriers at HUCK—vehicles return to battalion control.
        Aid Station initially, BAUERN—collecting point at HUCK.
        Drop rolls at present CP's and leave under guard.

5.) SCR 300 Radio calls and channels:
        3rd Battalion — William — Channel 39 — Alt. 21.
        1st Battalion — Oboe — Channel 27 — Alt. 18.
        Tanks call number William 8; TD's, 9; AT Co. Platoon, 10.
        Battalion CP: BAUERN
        OP: HUCK[20]

One element of hope, so far as the infantry attacker was immediately concerned, might be found in the report of a prisoner from the 1226th German Regiment which the 320th had taken the preceding night: that he had been told that his unit was scheduled to withdraw across the river on this date (March 10th).[21]

As the commanders were leaving, they could hear the violent explosions of barrages of the German rocket "artillery"—the nebelwerfers, or "screaming meamies," up in the area through which they were to attack within three hours. Tom Parris looked back toward the S-3 and grinned; this might very well indicate that the German field artillery was out of action in the area—that the enemy was finally withdrawing from his bridgehead.

Just half an hour before "L" Company was to start moving, regimental headquarters announced that the 320th Infantry had completed the capture of Drupt. Col. Wood called for communications platoon to lay a telephone wire to Drupt while it was still dark.[22]

20. 3rd Bn. Journal, III, 152f.
21. ibid., p. 148.
22. ibid., p. 153.

Moving out on schedule, Company L's men marched up the dark road to reach Huck; at 4:30 they were leaving the place, and at 5:10 they must have felt some uneasiness as they approached Drupt now still in the night after its capture had been completed only two and a half hours earlier. Inside the town Lt. Parris walked through the streets looking for someone from the 320th who could point out his route out of the town, but all remained quiet. He called in on the radio to explain his difficulties and estimated that he would be 15 minutes late in "jumping off." After half an hour of searching, the Company L commander still had not found the positions of the other battalions, and he was anxious to move across the open ground ahead before daylight. As his doubts were mounting higher and higher, he finally found some of the friendly troops, and at 6:15 Company L was on the way. Quietly, their thoughts to themselves, the infantrymen moved toward Borth. Did death await them there? or would it be abandoned? Soon they found that it had not been abandoned altogether, but neither was it being defended frantically. German defenders must have wondered what manner of soldiers were these men—an attack nearly all night, till 3:30; and now, before the night had passed to dawn, another full-scale attack! (Without knowing that it was a fresh battalion coming at them.) After a short exchange of rifle fire along a creek in front of Borth, 20 prisoners were on their way back before 7:30.[23]

An early bag of prisoners often meant that the enemy's defense had disintegrated. Company L swept into Borth against slight resistance, but spent the next hour and a half mopping up: at 8:45 they had rounded up 36 more PW's, and five minutes later that number jumped to 50.[24]

Even as the mopping up went on, engineers were putting in a treadway bridge over the creek between Drupt and Borth, and, at the same time, Lt. Munroe had others sweeping the roads for mines.[25]

Company K closed into Borth at 8:38 to help with the mopping up job, and "I" displaced to Drupt. The OP displaced to Borth.[26]

The attack against the Wesel Pocket was moving all along the line. Companies of the 137th were on their first objective at 8 o'clock and ready to continue their attack to the north. The 1st Battalion, 134th, was advancing on the right of the Third. At 9:10, behind a terrific 20-minute artillery preparation—intense from beginning to end, and to the disturbance of near-by Americans on the right who were not prepared for such a violent action, the British "jumped off" on the Battalion's left. Before noon they had patrols entering Menzelen, approximately abreast of Borth (four kilometers to the northeast).

Under the circumstances of the rapid seizure of Borth and the apparent breaking of enemy resistance, Colonel Wood felt that he could bring this operation to a swift conclusion: "L" Company would attack for a second objective—a factory located along the Geldern-Wesel highway about two kilometers north of Borth—and, that successful, Company I would mount the tanks again to go for the Battalion objective, Buderich.

"L" was on its way again shortly after 10 o'clock. Reporting a roadblock of fallen trees on the highway, the company moved on and was mopping up in the factory buildings by 12:40; here the infantrymen captured a

23. ibid., pp. 153f.
24. ibid., pp. 154f.
25. ibid.
26. ibid.

German half-track, an 88 mm gun, and some more prisoners—bringing their total PW count for the day up to 100. The stage was set for Company I's dash to the Rhine.[27]

The tank company and the mounted doughboys came rolling into Borth and prepared for its new thrust. The end of a campaign now in sight, the men became enthusiastic to get it finished. Lt. Warren Hodges gave final instructions to his platoon leaders, and climbed up on the command tank. Someone from the Battalion command group called up, "They say Courtney Hodges led the First Army to the Rhine; now 'Courtney' Hodges is going to lead the Ninth Army to the Rhine. Let's go, 'Courtney'!"

The tank column roared out of Borth on the road to the north, cut around the roadblock, and angled up on the highway toward Buderich. Artillery and chemical mortar smoke shells burst across the Rhine to screen the movement, for, as the highway approached Buderich it ran almost parallel with the river, and the flanks of the column would be exposed to observation and fire from the opposite bank.[28]

Halted by an antitank ditch at the edge of Buderich, the tanks came under enemy artillery fire. But here was a *raison d'etre* for mounted infantrymen: they scrambled off the tanks and swept into the city. They took some more prisoners, but found no organized resistance. The objective was captured at 2:30. Both the highway bridge south of Wesel, and the railroad bridge on the north, had been blown.[29]

Only one possible source of trouble remained: a minor fortification called Fort Blucher at the approaches to the Wesel bridge about two kilometers down the river (northeast) from Buderich. Waiting for the cover of darkness, a patrol from "I" Company moved out toward the fort; but when they heard digging in the vicinity, there was some question as to whether this might be British troops outside their zone, and the attack was delayed till morning. But that fort had to be taken before the division could report its mission completed. Next morning a platoon seized the fort and took 25 more prisoners.[30]

The mission was completed, but the area was not without some danger for the individuals in it. Intermittent German artillery continued on Buderich that morning, and one of Company I's jeeps was blown up by a mine in the streets.[31] On the other hand, some Germans were killed by their own mines as they retreated near Fort Blucher.

"With the collapse of the Wesel Pocket . . . when [the] 134th Infantry of [the] 35th Division reached [the] Rhine opposite the city, [the] Germans lost their last foothold west of the river between Nijmegen and Remagen."[32]

The Allied Armies stood before a Rhine barrier which was left practically undefended, for the enemy had played into their hands by insisting on fighting where he stood. Armies intended for the defense of the homeland had been shattered in the campaigns between the Roer and Maas and the Rhine, in the Eifel, and in the Saar. "The war was won before the Rhine was crossed."[33]

27. Ibid., pp. 155-157. The men with the 88 gun had marched to Wesel from Osnubruck four days earlier.—ibid., p. 158.
28. ibid.
29. ibid., pp. 157-158.
30. ibid., p. 160.
31. ibid., pp. 160, 162.
32. The Stars and Stripes (Liege ed.), March 11, 1945, p. 4.
33. General Eisenhower's Report, p. 121.

Relieved on March 12th by the 1st Battalion, Glasgow Highlanders, 157th British Brigade (52nd Division),[34] men of the Third Battalion looked forward to sharing in a rest period before the final big drive.   For the first time since landing in France, the entire 35th Division was to have a period of rest.[35]

34.   Though reporters had speculated on possible use of the "big" British Second Army in this operation, (**Time**, Feb. 26, 1945, p. 32) that army had become a shell, most of its units transferred to the Canadian First Army for the period. The British War Minister revealed in the House of Commons that two-thirds of the forces which Gen H. D. G. Crerar had received for his February offensive were British.—Clifton Daniel in **The New York Times**, March 14, 1945, p. 4.

35.   3rd Bn. Journal, III, 161f; 134th Inf., After Action Report, 1 April 45.

PART SIX—THE FIFTH STAR: EAST OF THE RHINE

★ ★ ★

CHAPTER XXIII

★ ★ ★

URBAN OFFENSIVE

Soon after getting settled in the area assigned for a rest period in Alst, Germany (near Bracht, about 12 kilometers south of Venlo, Holland) the Battalion commander was called to a meeting at regimental headquarters in the next village east. He returned with voluminous notes to pass on to the company commanders in an afternoon meeting (March 14th):[1] a commendation from the division commander for the work done in the operation just finished—mission during this period: maximum rest, rehabilitation, cleaning up —cleanup to include billets, clothing, equipment, motors; civilians could be used for area clean-up—daily inspections of quarters, kitchens, latrines, and an "old fashioned garrison Saturday morning inspection"—check that all men have on shoulder insignia—keep all uniforms pressed; civilians authorized for laundry and pressing; take steps to improve each company mess; improvise seats for greater comfort while eating—do not relax on discipline and saluting—review instructions on calling attention and reporting to an inspecting officer—helmets and arms to be worn when out of doors—take strict measures to prevent looting—any report of rape to be investigated at once; official investigation to be completed within six hours, charge sheets filed within 24, and trial by court-martial held within 48 hours—non-fraternization regulations to be strictly enforced; no civilians to be quartered in same house with soldiers; $65 fine for fraternizing—blackout to be complete in buildings, but vehicles permitted to use headlights—check on AWOL's—take steps to prevent spread of VD—no captured enemy vehicles to be retained unless registered with "W" number after approval of letter of request—any soldiers found riding bicycles, motorcycles, or driving unauthorized vehicles will be tried by summary court—duffle bags being brought up to this area—all shoepacs still with units to be turned in—have all vehicles properly marked; keep 60-yard interval on the road—all men going on pass to wear complete uniform and insignia—watch police and control of German civilians—each company commander to make a visit to the personnel section at division rear echelon to look over his company's personnel records—keep men busy; the war is not yet over, and much work remains to be done; future operations remain top secret; there will be only little training; 25% of unit strength authorized to be on pass (to Dutch towns; German towns off limits)—schedule full program of athletics and recreation—men going on pass to rest centers will not carry arms—schedule lectures to complete requirements for instruction of all personnel on the Articles of War and sex morality. There was even an official daily schedule of calls and a bugler on duty.[2]

1. 3rd Bn. Journal, III, 167.
2. 3rd Bn. S-3 Notebook, I, 14 March 45.

Later a scale of fines for petty offenses in the regiment was published: failure to salute, $2.00; wearing of knit cap without helmet, $2.00; other uniform violations, $2.00; failure to obey military police, $25.00; speeding, $15.00.[3]

And as always, it was necessary to maintain local guards, and certain jeep motor patrols. During the ensuing week there was a schedule of activities similar, but on a larger scale, to that which the Battalion had followed during previous halts: motion pictures, USO shows—one day a group of men went to Krefeld for a performance by Lily Pons and Andre Kostelanetz—religious services (Catholic, Protestant, Jewish), softball games.

The most important training was the firing of weapons—rifles, machine guns, mortars, rifle grenades, bazookas. A large open area in the midst of thick woods to the west of the Battalion's billet area made an almost ideal range for the purpose—except that mortar shells started a brush fire one afternoon. Here too the companies tried out for the first time the new "knee mortars"—a 60 mm mortar, without a base plate, fired with a trigger. All the Battalion's weapons were inspected by an ordnance team.

The Third Battalion was chosen to organize a drill team—two platoons of 24 men each—to participate in a ceremony where French officers presented a number of decorations to the members of the division. Company M's commander, Chauncey Erickson (now promoted to Captain) commanded the picked unit in its perfect performance.

But probably the outstanding spectacle of the Battalion's sojourn in this area was its retreat parade. A large green field just outside of Alst served admirably as a parade ground. Men erected a flag pole at one end of the field, and there, standing out in sharp contrast to its green background, the Stars and Stripes waved over the German field like a long-absent friend met in some strange, far-off place. The flag had to be borrowed from regiment, but it was the first time that the men had seen an American flag since arriving on the Continent. The regiment's extra baggage had arrived in the area, and now the Battalion's national colors, and company guidons were brought out. Some companies had to improvise staffs, and others to borrow guidons, but when time came for the formation, all carried the blue burgee-like flag of the infantry company. Dressed in immaculate, pressed uniforms, netting removed from newly-painted steel helmets, chin straps buckled beneath the chin, rifles with tight gun slings, carried at the right shoulder, the men marched onto the field in a demonstration of precision and broke into company mass formations, just as the Battalion had done it back at Ojai, California. The Battalion antitank platoon had prepared some blank ammunition and now one of its freshly-painted 57 mm guns set near the flag pole pointing down the field. As trumpeters in the regimental band sounded the final note of "retreat," the gun fired its salute. An old German farmer, following a one-horse plow in a neighboring field paused to watch; he doffed his hat as the band played the National Anthem and the flag came down. Precise company phalanxes marched in review behind the band in what was probably the most inspiring parade of its career. The Battalion seemed to be prepared for whatever might lie ahead. How many of these fine-looking soldiers would fall in the battles to come?

3. 3rd Bn. Journal, III, 169.

One other important development during the rest period involved some key personnel changes. Joseph L. Brigandi, who had been evacuated after the Battle of the Bulge, rejoined the Battalion as a captain and was re-assigned to the command of Company L. Lt. Langdon, who had taken over Company K temporarily during the campaign to the Rhine, left for a furlough to the United States, and Lt. Tom Parris, who had been commanding "L" was shifted to the command of Company K. Lt. Norman Wardwell who had been wounded while with Company I in Normandy returned to the Battalion, and was assigned to Company K as executive officer. In Battalion Headquarters, Major Heffelfinger was transferred to division headquarters as assistant G-3, and Capt. Donald C. Rubottom of Nebraska, formerly heavy weapons company commander and S-3 in the 1st Battalion, came to the Third as executive officer.

The men of the Third Battalion watched hundreds of heavy bombers going over each day now in the clear spring weather. The impression which the intrinsic beauty of the sight made was exceeded only by the personal appreciation that those bombers probably were hitting cities through which they would be marching within a few days.[4]

Infantry battalions of the XII Corps, Third Army, achieved a brilliant surprise crossing of the Rhine south of Mainz on the night of March 22nd. Battalions in the Remagen area had extended their bridgehead to a length of about 30 miles and a depth of ten miles. But the "main show" of the general trans-Rhine offensive was scheduled to take place north of the Ruhr: this would permit a quick sealing off of the Ruhr industrial area, the north German plains would be suitable for tank operations, and the Rhine between Wesel and Emmerich was most suitable for an assault crossing. The stage was set for the final campaign into the heart of Germany.[5] Men of the Third Battalion knew that their rest period was drawing to a close.

Word was flashed to the companies at 7:45, March 24th that a crossing of the Rhine had been effected.[6] British Commandos had spearheaded the attack in crossings north of Wesel during the evening of March 23rd. Troops of the 30th and 79th Divisions had made the crossing south of Wesel in the Ninth Army's zone in a pre-dawn assault. Later in the morning the First Allied Airborne Army began the greatest single airborne operation in history when parachute troops of the U. S. 17th and the 6th British Airborne Divisions began descending.[7]

Company commanders assembled at regimental headquarters at 9 o'clock for further orientation.[8] They learned that the 30th Division had "jumped off" at 2 A.M., using assault boats at three crossing sites, and by 4 o'clock had six battalions across, and had advanced inland 2,000 yards. The 79th Division had begun crossing an hour later, and by 4 o'clock had three battalions across and had captured Walsum. Opposition had been light. Troops from two British Corps had attacked at midnight, and Commandos were taking Wesel. It was expected that the 35th Division would cross the river on about D plus 4 to exploit a breakthrough.[9]

4. 3rd Bn. Journal, III, 165-179, et. al.
5. General Marshall's Report, pp. 46-47.
6. 3rd Bn. Journal, III, 180.
7. ibid., pp. 181-182; General Marshall's Report, p. 47; Drew Middleton, Frederick Graham, in The New York Times, March 25, 1945, p. 1; SHAEF Communique, March 24, 1945 (in The New York Times, March 25, 1945, p. 2.) The German communique stated: "penetrations of our positions have been sealed off."—ibid., p. 19.
8. 3rd Bn. Journal, III, 180.
9. 3rd Bn. S-3 Notebook, I, 24 March 45.

However, that same afternoon the 134th Infantry, and so the Third Battalion, was alerted to prepare to move. While the men were kept informed of progress at the front by reports from liaison officers, from information passed down from higher headquarters through command channels, and from radio newscasts, they prepared for a "one way trip" across the Rhine. Once across, vehicles would not be permitted to go back across the river. There was to be radio silence until further notice. Gas masks, carried since the Ardennes campaign, would not be carried during this operation, though they would be kept available on 24-hour notice.[10]

While considerably below authorized strength, Lt. Col. Warren C. Wood's Third Battalion was decidedly above the strength at which it had fought many of its battles, and it enjoyed one other advantage of effectiveness—nearly all of its men were veterans of previous engagements; never before had the Third Battalion, a "veteran battalion" from St. Lo, been able to enter into an operation with its ranks nearly filled with veteran soldiers. And the return of wounded officers actually put it in the almost unique position of having an overstrength of officers. Company I (Hodges) had 152 men and seven officers; Company K (Parris) had 137 men and seven officers; Company L (Brigandi) had 136 men and eight officers; Company M (Erickson) had 110 men and seven officers. In Battalion Headquarters and Headquarters Company there were 112 men and ten officers.[11]

The next afternoon the 134th Infantry, with its normal combat team attachments plus a company of tanks, a company of tank destroyers and a battalion of medium artillery was formed into "Task Force Miltonberger," under the former regimental commander who now was a brigadier general and assistant division commander. Ordered to precede the 35th Division across the river, this task force, under operational control of the 79th Division, moved by motor to the vicinity of Rhineberg. At 6:30 P.M. the Battalion Commander, S-3, and company commanders went forward by jeep to make what reconnaissance they could and to contact the friendly unit commanders in the assigned area to orient themselves into the situation. At 8 o'clock, the Third Battalion, leading the regiment, marched down to cross the Rhine River on Love Bridge at Blue Beach.[12]

The river banks had taken on an appearance reminiscent of Omaha beach —barrage balloons, busy tractors and trucks, columns of troops. Riflemen, posted at intervals all along the long ponton (floating treadway) bridge, were firing at any bits of floating debris which came down the river—they were taking precautions against the possibility of any floating mines which might find their way through the barriers to the bridge.

But darkness had come when the Third Battalion started across. Though kept high by the barrage balloons and heavy concentrations of anti-aircraft fire, enemy airplanes were zooming overhead and coming in for strafing runs. Searchlights and long dotted arcs of tracers lit up the sky in a colorful display.

One man of the Third Battalion was wounded during the air activity.[13]

10. **ibid.**; 3rd Bn. Journal, III, 180-182.
11. **ibid.**, 3rd Bn. S-3 Notebook, 24 March 45.
12. 3rd Bn. Journal, III, 182; 134 Inf., After Action Report, 1 April 45.
13. Michael Hanna, **Trans-Rhine Operation**, (typescript. Summary of the Battalion's operations from 25 March to 1 April, 1945. Also included in 9th Historical Section, Combat Interviews —The Adjutant General's Office, Historical Records Section, Washington, D. C.) p. 2.

While the troops marched the leaders were planning. Conferring with the commander and staff of the 2nd Battalion, 315th Infantry (79th Division) at the Battalion CP near Hiesfeld (east of Dinslaken) they found that resistance had not been heavy thus far. Principal obstacles to the advance had been ground-firing flak guns and small groups of infantry.[14] But those leaders well knew that a major river-crossing operation could not be regarded as decisive until the enemy's counter-attack had been beaten back. Up to this time there had been no counter-attack, and if the enemy was going to make one effective, the time for it had arrived. As they huddled around maps in the dimly-lighted house serving as a command post at midnight that night, awaiting the arrival of the foot troops, the company commanders could wonder whether they were not entering the line just in time to catch the brunt of any counter-attack which might be in the making. But then came a flash that General Patton's Third Army was 32 miles east of the Rhine; the 4th Armored Division, team-mate of the 35th across France and at Bastogne, had raced 40 miles in 18 hours to seize a bridge over the Main below Frankfurt.[15] Relieved, the company commanders could sense that there would be no major counter-attack.

Marching along dark roads whose only light was from the irregular reflections of burning buildings, the troops covered the twelve miles to their assembly area in five hours. Captain Mangnunson, S-1, and his quartering party directed the companies into quarters and set up the Battalion CP in Lohberg. The companies settled, the commanders and staff assembled at the Battalion CP at 1:30 A.M. for their first attack order in the new campaign:

1.a.) The enemy is resisting in delaying action with infantry, artillery, and aircraft.

b.) The 30th Division, to our north, has advanced eastward 10,000 yards. The 79th Division (315th Infantry) holds present position in the vicinity of 3431.

The 2nd Battalion attacks on our left, 1st Battalion in reserve.

161st and 127th Field Artillery Battalions in support. Artillery forward observers with Company K and L.

2.) This Battalion with the 3rd Platoon, Company A, 784th Tank Battalion, 3rd Platoon, Company A, 654th Tank Destroyer Battalion (SP), 3rd Platoon, Company A, 60th Engineers, 3rd Platoon, Regimental Antitank Company attached, will attack at 0800 and seize the high ground at coordinates of 2732.

Line of Departure—present front line of 2nd Battalion, 315th Infantry.

Direction of attack: northeast.

Formation: Column of Companies—L, K, I.

3.) Company L, with platoon of tanks and one platoon of heavy machine guns attached, will seize battalion objective, hold, and prepare to continue attack on order.

Company K, with one section of heavy machine guns attached follow Company L, prepare to assist, and maintain contact with the 2nd Battalion on the left.

Company I, with one section HMG's attached, follow Company K, prepare to assist in attack, move by bounds, and maintain contact on the right with the 79th Division—314th Infantry.

81 mm mortars prepare positions to support the attack.

Engineers move with Company K.

Tank Destroyers reconnoiter for positions at front.

Battalion Antitank Platoon—positions to left flank and rear.

Antitank Company Platoon—positions to right flank and rear.

4.) Bedrolls released to companies. K ration for breakfast unless otherwise notified. Full ration to be issued tonight.

5.) Battalion CP at Lohberg.

Radio silence lifted at 0730.

14. 3rd Bn. Journal, III, 180-183.
15. The New York Times, March 26, 1945, p. 1.

Call signs:
1st Bn. YOKE   Channel 24, Alt. 30
2nd Bn. JIG   36,   18
3rd Bn. DOG   21,   39
Password: ONE; reply: WORLD[16]

Strangely enough, the Battalion's first attack in the Ruhr area—in this "urban offensive"—was through the heart of a woods called Forst Wesel. At 6:35 A.M. the Battalion commander, the S-3, and the company commanders went forward to make a daylight reconnaissance before H-hour.[17] They found the front line of the battalion through whose area they were to attack along the forward edge of a narrow woods just beyond the graded roadbed of an uncompleted section of the Reichsautobahn—the German super highway. To reach the assigned objective it would be necessary to advance over some open ground, over gently rolling terrain, and through some small villages before gaining the high ground in the edge of the larger forest. It would require an advance of some 3,000 yards.[18]

At 8 o'clock Capt. Brigandi began deploying his men of Company L. Artillery fire began to fall in the area soon after the advance began and then demoralizing fire from dual purpose 88 mm guns and 20 mm guns began to plague the advancing troops. The attached tanks were having a bad time in the muddy ground around the autobahn bed, but some got into position and opened fire on the enemy positions. This proved to be effective and Company L began to move forward again. By 10 o'clock 20 prisoners were on the way to the rear. However, the enemy had not yet given up; his rapid-firing cannon were still in the picture. A Sherman tank moved up with Company L, but a round from an 88 mm gun to the left flank knocked it out; the other tanks were bogged down in the mud. General Miltonberger, then at the Battalion CP, ordered the tanks attached to the 1st Battalion (in reserve) to join the Third; then as the 1st displaced forward, the tanks left by the Third in the mud could join the former. Under the pressure of heavy artillery concentrations directed on the woods ahead, a Mark IV tank withdrew to the east.[19]

After the Battalion S-2 had guided the newly arrived tanks from 1st Battalion to the position of Company L, that Company, with Company K now moving up on the left, "jumped off" again at 2 o'clock. Within an hour they were on the battalion objective. They had found a bridge across the Schwarger Creek intact and engineers began to sweep the gravel road so that jeeps could get up with hot "chow" and supplies.[20]

The 41 prisoners taken during the day represented a mixture of organizations: some from the 2nd Company, 881st Flak Battalion, others, mostly replacements, from the 116th, 146th, 180th Divisions. Some were aircraft pilots, some tank men, even some navy men.[21] This did not appear as though there was a very well organized defense.

For its part, the Battalion had sustained 16 battle casualties; one man died at the aid station. Of these, 13 had been from Company L, the assault company, two from K, and one from M.[22]

16. 3rd Bn. Journal, III, 184.
17. ibid.
18. Map: Central Europe 1:100,000—Essen—Sheet Q1.
19. 3rd Bn. Journal, III, 185f.
20. ibid., pp. 186-188.
21. ibid., pp. 185-187.
22. ibid., p. 188.

Task Force Miltonberger was dissolved and the 134th Infantry returned to control of the 35th Division. During the night the 137th Infantry moved up to relieve the 314th Infantry on the Battalion's right.[23]

Night reconnaissance patrols, whether the Battalion was on offense or defense, were almost a standard procedure. On this night, patrols from Companies I and L moved a thousand yards to the front without encountering any enemy positions. Company commanders could hope that their opposition would be light when they resumed the advance through the woods at 6 o'clock the next morning (March 27th).[24]

For their hot breakfast at 4:30 A.M. the men may have had "scrambled" (powdered) eggs, or dried beef gravy on toast ("slop on a shingle"), or French toast, or wheat cakes—and the inevitable "G.I." coffee. In any case, breakfast finished in good time, the companies prepared to move out.

Again the attack was to begin with a formation of a column of companies, but with Company I leading. A series of company objectives had been assigned and plotted on operation maps. Company I was to seize No. 1, about 400 yards southeast of the present position, then turn northeast to seize No. 2, a trail junction 2,000 yards deeper into the woods, then swing southeast again and move nearly 3,000 yards to seize a small town at the far edge of the woods (No. 3); from here the company would move on order almost another 3,000 yards—over varied terrain, including another 1,000-yard neck of woods, to seize another village (No. 5). "K" Company was ordered to follow Company I as far as the edge of the woods, but from here that company would advance 1,500 yards to the east to seize a village designated as No. 4. From this point Company K would guide along a road some 500 yards to the left (north) of Company I's route, and advance to the east to take No. 6—a village abreast of Company I's final objective, No. 5. Company L was to remain in reserve and furnish protection to the flanks, following Company K to the far edge of the woods, and then following Company I on the right of the Battalion zone. The Battalion CP displaced to a group of buildings near the edge of the woods where Company K had set up its CP the preceding evening.[25]

When the Third Battalion moved out at 6 o'clock, the 2nd Battalion on the left, and the 137th Infantry on the right were attacking abreast in a coordinated division attack. True to the reports of the patrols, no opposition was encountered during the first hour and a half. Company I cleared objective No. 2 and the leading scouts, wary for enemy fire—which they were out to draw—came under enemy small arms fire at 8:30 when they were yet about 800 yards from reaching the edge of the woods. Hodges deployed his men to bring all possible rifle and machine gun fire to bear on the enemy standing between him and Objective No. 3. In a sharp fire fight which lasted less than 20 minutes, Company I gained fire superiority, and, leaving 45 enemy dead, and taking 30 prisoners, swept into the village at the edge of the woods. Simultaneously Company K moved up to debauch from the woods and clean out the houses in Objective No. 4.[26]

The climax of this encounter had come when Staff Sergeant Gene Fletcher of Missouri, an "I" Company squad leader, and two riflemen, Private

23. 134th Inf., After Action Report, 1 April 45.
24. Hanna, "Trans-Rhine Operation," pp. 3; 3rd Bn. Journal, III, 189.
25. Hanna, "Trans-Rhine Operation," p. 3.
26. ibid.; 134th Inf., After Action Report, 1 April 45.

First Class Joe Kelley of Arizona, and Pfc. Virgil Lockwood of Oklahoma made their way forward. As his two comrades covered his approach with rifle fire, Kelley worked in close enough to throw his hand grenades; then all three rushed the enemy position. With their wounding of two Germans and capture of three others, a break in the enemy resistance had been set.[27]

The voluminous rifle fire which Company I had poured out had made a re-supply of ammunition necessary before the attack could be resumed. The trail through the woods, deep with mud, was impassable even for a jeep. Once again the M-29—the track-laying "weasel"—provided the solution.[28]

Captured prisoners reported that there were 150 men and two Mark VI tanks to the Battalion's immediate front, and 1,000 additional men in the sector. (The total of prisoners taken was 46 at 11:15 A.M.).[29]

The companies were ready to move on to the final objectives. By 2:30 they were in those towns (No. 5 and No. 6) and after 20 minutes of mopping up, 66 more prisoners were taken. The attached tanks had had difficulty in moving up because of a crater in the road. However, they found an alternate route and joined in the mopping up operations. At 4:15 an additional 30 PW's were added to the bag and it appeared that the day's assignment had been completed.[30]

But this was not enough. The division commander wanted the advance to continue to Phase line "Uncle"—a railroad running across the front about 1500 yards beyond the forward companies' positions. Already the Third Battalion was sticking out like the proverbial sore thumb. The 2nd Battalion was at least two kilometers to rear on the left, and the 137th Infantry had been able to keep up no better on the right. That there was some danger in this situation was made clear when the 137th warned that about 75 enemy soldiers which they had flushed out would be coming toward the right flank and rear of the Third Battalion. In order to give some protection in this gap in depth, the regimental commander committed the 1st Battalion on the right of the Third. Now the Third was to attack northeast, in the zone of the 2nd in an effort to assist the advance of that battalion. This new attack would take the companies through another woods (of a maximum depth of 1,000 yards) to another small town along the railroad.[31]

The regimental commander obtained permission to continue the attack after dark in an effort to reach the objective. At 8 P.M. all three battalions resumed the attack. Company I received some rocket fire from the right flank, but this did not stop them. At 11:45 a platoon from "K" Company occupied the objective, and then the remainder of "K" and "I" moved in by infiltration. At 2:20 A.M. Company L moved in to the village vacated by "K" to set up a reserve position. Friendly artillery fire kept Company I's patrol from actually reaching the railroad until 6 A.M.[32]

This latest advance had netted 16 more prisoners—including three wounded. This brought the total of prisoners taken during the day to 152. The Battalion had suffered eight battle casualties.[33]

Outstripping its neighbors did have one advantage for the Third Battalion; its men could salvage a little rest during daylight of March 28th while

27. 35th Division, General Orders, No. 28, 29 April 45.
28. 134th Inf., After Action Report, 1 April 45.
29. Hanna, "Trans-Rhine Operation," p. 4.
30. ibid.; 3rd Bn. Journal, III, 192.
31. ibid.; 134th Inf., After Action Report, 1 April 45.
32. 134th Inf., After Action Report, 1 April 45; 3rd Bn. Journal, III, 193f.
33. Hanna, "Trans-Rhine Operation," p. 4; 3rd Bn. Journal, III, 193f.

the other battalions attacked to come up abreast. However, there was additional patrolling to assist the other battalions, seven more PW's were picked up, artillery observers had a full day. At one point five enemy tanks appeared out in front of Company I's position. Tank destroyers took them under fire and knocked out two; artillery disabled a third, and the other two withdrew. A platoon of Company I attacked at 2:20 to the southeast to assist the 1st Battalion and establish contact; even as it moved out an enemy mortar shell fell in its midst and wounded six men; but the platoon reorganized and moved on.[34]

Another night attack was scheduled. As the 1st and 2nd Battalions fought their way up abreast of the Third, plans were made for a resumption of the attack at 9 P.M., 2nd and Third Battalions attacking for the west edge of the city of Gladbeck: urban operations were about to begin.[35]

In a column of companies, K, L, I, the Battalion moved down north of its position to Highway 2, a good paved road, and, with the 2nd Battalion in a similar close column on its left, went through an underpass at 9 P.M., and set out over the dark road toward the Moeller mine at the edge of Gladbeck, about four kilometers away. A platoon of heavy machine guns was with Company K; 81 mm mortars were being hand carried. (This meant a load of about 45 pounds for each of the three men who carried a mortar: tube, bipod, base plate; the machine gun broke down into two-man loads—40 pounds for the gun and 51 pounds for the tripod.) There was little reassurance in a report that the 1st Battalion had received a counter-attack at 8 o'clock, but the front had quieted by 9, and the attack went off on time. Apparently "K" Company slipped through enemy outposts without being noticed, for first opposition encountered was machine gun fire against "L" Company. The source of trouble was in the town of Hagenhaff. This delayed the advance for an hour, but finally the resistance broke when 13 of the enemy surrendered. But the black darkness gave Parris and Brigandi a very difficult reorganization problem. To get their men out of the houses and back into formation when they had scattered in the darkness in seeking out the enemy was no simple matter. This finally accomplished, the companies moved into the objective at 2:10. Mopping up and organization required another two hours. The prisoners total for the night had reached 52 by 4:30. At 8:15 the Battalion CP opened in the west end of Gladbeck.[36] Company I occupied the vicinity of the mine on the right flank.

The Third Battalion now ran into new problems—the forced laborers of the Ruhr area. More than 6,000 of these "DP's"—displaced persons—were found hiding in the Moeller coal mine. Soon they would get out to clog the roads as they started walking toward their homeland—France or Belgium or Holland or Italy.[37] But the Third Battalion's primary concern was combat, and there remained much to be done.

The Battalion took 24 more prisoners in mopping up operations during the morning of March 29th, and at noon patrols probed across the railroad in the main part of the city preparatory to a new attack at 3:30 P.M. Again coordinating with the 2nd Battalion the Third "jumped off." Against light opposition featured by some fanatical resistance on the part of some old men and

34. 3rd Bn. Journal, III, 195f.; Hanna, "Trans Rhine Operation," p. 4.
35. 3rd Bn. Journal, III, 196.
36. 3rd Bn. Journal, III, 197-199.
37. Wes Gallagher, The Associated Press, March 29, 1945.

boys of the city, the companies advanced through the blocks of buildings, here destroyed by bombs, there still intact, until "K" reached its objective at 5:40, and "L" at 6:10. In cleaning out Gladbeck the three companies had taken another 70 PW's.[38]

The city secured, tank destroyers moved up to reinforce the defense for the night, and jeep trains brought up hot supper and supplies.[39]

Although the 190th VG Division was known to be in enemy reserve,[40] no contact had been made with that unit thus far. However, when an "L" Company patrol returned from a reconnaissance of the road to the vicinity of Buer it brought along two prisoners who had been manning an outpost for the 7th Company, 1225th regiment of the 190th VG Division. The patrol also found that the road, unpaved, but hard-packed, was suitable for tanks.[41]

After a night of harassing artillery fire on the objective, the Third Battalion, again with the 2nd on the left, crossed the line of departure—a creek at the east edge of Gladbeck—at 7 A.M. and advanced toward Buer four kilometers to the east.[42]

Companies I and K were in assault and Company K in reserve. Company I was to swing wide to the right, and then, guiding along a road to the east, was to move through a series of settlements and seize the southern portion of Buer. Company L would attack through successive objectives along a parallel road about 600 yards to the left (north) of "I" and seize the heart of the city in the vicinity of the city hall. Company K would move by bounds behind Company L and mop up and occupy the southwestern section of the city. (The successive objectives were indicated on large-scale operation maps issued to the company commanders).[43]

If the men of the Third Battalion thought that they were going to see the Ruhr area completely in ruins from the repeated allied air attacks, it must have been with some surprise that they not only saw great industrial plants standing intact; they could see smoke rising from their chimneys! From a distant, casual observation, they could see a striking resemblance between this area—particularly as they looked southward toward Essen—and, for example, the Great Lakes industrial region of Chicago and northwestern Indiana, or the Cleveland area. But certain differences would at once make themselves apparent on the ground:

> This dissimilarity is accentuated in Spring by the sea of green which laps round the towns, making them appear as dark islands in a well-cultivated countryside. Its green arms even stretch into the ruins, so that much of their base ugliness is concealed.
>
> Instead of running mile after mile through smoke blackened streets with one town merging imperceptibly into the next, and with only a few fields and trees to bear witness to the existence of nature, the towns of the Ruhr have preserved an easy contact with the country-side; it separates most of them by belts of woods, fields and allotments in which every yard of ground is cultivated with intense care. The ratio of country to town in the Ruhr is insufficient to provide any substantial contribution to the feeding of the large urban populations within it, but it does provide the possibility of black market operations close at hand for those who can afford them, and an easy escape from the every day sights of destruction.[44]

38. 3rd Bn. Journal, III, 198-200.
39. **ibid.**—Gladbeck had a peace-time population of something over 61,000—Encyclopedia Britannica World Atlas, (1942) p. 56.
40. 3rd Bn. Journal, III, 200.
41. Hanna, "Trans-Rhine Operation," p. 5.
42. 3rd Bn. Journal, III, 203.
43. **ibid.,** p. 201.
44. "The Ruhr in Spring," **The Economist,** CL (June 8, 1946), 929.

A city of 100,000, Buer is one of those cities whose importance and reputation have been eclipsed by a location in the midst of many cities. Its growth and development present a parallel to that of Gary, Indiana in the "American Ruhr."[45] "Greater Buer" might be said to include Buer-Schelven on the northwest, Buer-Hassel to the north, Buer-Resse to the southeast, and Buer-Erle to the south.

"Courtney" Hodges led his men of Company I in a rapid advance through their successive objectives, and skirting along a large factory, collected some 30 prisoners, and at 9:36 occupied the assigned area in the Battalion objective.[46]

Meanwhile Company L was having a little more difficulty. Capt. Brigandi's men picked up five prisoners straightway, but then came under the fire of two tanks. And not the least obstacle to a continuation of the advance was a series of emplaced 128 mm antiaircraft guns and some machine guns. Located for aerial defense of the Ruhr, these big flak guns (see photograph) were capable of depression to a point where, the muzzle just clearing the surrounding embankment, highly effective ground fire could be directed at attacking troops. Brigandi committed his support platoon and assaulted the enemy position. Four of the 128 mm flak guns with 200 rounds of ammunition, and three machine guns were overrun. Immediately south of the gun positions other men took a large, completely equipped radar station. They took 40 prisoners out of the area. (Company I practically had passed "under the noses" of the guns!)[47]

Once again the Third Battalion was outstripping its neighbors on right and left, and a group of enemy in the 2nd Battalion's zone was holding up "L" Company. During the delay Company I sent a combat patrol into the area to be occupied by "L" in order to assist in the advance. As the 2nd Battalion came up on the left, "L" was ready to move again. Evidently growing impatient at waiting, Private First Class Henry Alonzo, a member of the company's light machine gun section, approached his captain and said that he wanted out of that "rear echelon outfit." Brigandi was reluctant to consider any requests for reassignments under the circumstances, but finally he said, "all right, you are a member of the 1st Platoon; report to the sergeant right over there."

As the company advanced into the outskirts of Buer, Alonzo fixed his bayonet, paused for a sip from his canteen (witnesses would not swear that the canteen contained pure water), and "took off" up the street. Hearing enemy rifles overhead, he ran into a building and quickly stole up the stairway. He burst in upon a group of Germans and accounted for three with bayonet and rifle shots. He came back down the street marching seven prisoners.[48]

While Alonzo was off on his private war, the remainder of the company encountered a strong point lodged in the City Hall. Tanks and TD's rolled up to fire at point-blank range and soon this obstacle was reduced. Company L was on its objective at the east edge of the city shortly after 3 o'clock.[49]

45. Buer is noted as a "village" of Prussia with a population of 9,589 in 1900 in Lippincott's Gazateer (1922) p. 292; it is not even listed in the **Encyclopedia Britannica World Atlas** (1942); in **The New World Loose Leaf Atlas** (New York: C. S. Hammond and Company, 1946—) it is not included in the General Index of Cities and Towns of the World, but is listed in the Index of Germany with a population of 99,058. **The Times Atlas and Gazateer of the World** (London, 1922) includes it in the map index, but does not give the population.
46. Hanna, "Trans-Rhine Operation," p. 5.
47. Ibid.; Capt. Elbert B. O'Keefe, "Artillery was the Answer," **The Infantry Journal**, CVI, (June 1945) p. 25.
48. Hanna, "Trans-Rhine Operation," p. 6; "Splinters," **The Gering** (Nebr.) **Courner**.
49. Hanna, loc. cit.

This did not mean, however, that the day's task was finished. Company K found that it had a considerable amount of mopping up to do in order to secure the southwest section of Buer. As the company approached its assigned area, the men of one of the leading platoons noticed that everything seemed to be too quiet. Sergeant Walter Janken of Illinois, platoon sergeant, halted his men. It was just in time to avoid walking into an enemy trap. Their plan frustrated, the enemy group opened fire on the platoon where they stood. Moving about under this intense demonstration of small arms fire, Sergeant Rankin organized his men, then upon a pre-arranged signal, he led the platoon forward to rush the enemy position. With eight prisoners and a number of enemy killed, the platoon had eliminated another strong point.[50]

A group of die-hard Nazis took refuge in solidly-constructed building near a coal mine to attempt to hold out as a thorn in the side of Company K. Two platoons pressed in toward the building from two sides, but while the German occupants could rake the approaches with machine gun fire, the small arms fire available to rifle platoons was ineffective against the thick walls. Lt. Tom Parris commandeered a German motorcylce and sped through the streets—he paused briefly to explain the situation to the Battalion commander and received permission to use the tanks which had been supporting Company L—and led the tank platoon down to the relief of his company. With this addition of heavy striking power, the stalemate was broken at dusk.[51]

Even though the city now was secure, activity continued during the night. Companies had to consolidate their positions; jeeps had to come up with supplies; Lt. Charles Hall, the Ammunition and Pioneer officer took some men from Company L and went back to destroy the guns which had been overrun; the inevitable patrols had to probe out to the front. Amidst this activity, Company L reported at 10:45 P.M. that newly-commissioned Second Lieutenant Thomas Patrick Ryan and his platoon were out of radio contact and could not be found. Patrols sent out during the night to locate this platoon—abroad on enemy streets after midnight—returned with no information. Inquiries at 2:30 A.M., at 4:00, and at 5:10 received no encouragement. As fears that the platoon had met with foul play neared a climax, Ryan, a bullet hole through his helmet (but only a minor scalp wound), his platoon intact marching 15 German prisoners ahead of it, reported to his company commander at 7:45. In the course of their adventures members of the platoon had encountered a German staff car carrying a Wehrmacht major and his staff; their rifle and automatic rifle fire had riddled the car and killed all the occupants. Their 15 prisoners sent the Battalion's total for the day (24 hours) to 182.[52]

At 1:45 A.M. a skirmish broke out near a hospital in the Company I area. A platoon picked up 15 prisoners in the action.[53] The intelligence section of Battalion headquarters was called upon to relieve guards posted by a company of the 2nd Battalion on another hospital at 1:45 A.M.[54]

Ideally a commander likes to keep his best unit in reserve during an attack so that it will be available for commitment at the critical moment to make a success decisive. But during tiring days of successive combat, the reserve position tends to become a devise for recuperation—an assignment to be

50. 35th Division, General Orders, No. 31, 8 May 45.
51. Hanna, loc. cit., p. 6.
52. ibid.; 3rd Bn. Journal, III, 205-207.
53. ibid.
54. ibid., p. 206f. One of the hospitals had 250 patients from the German Army, three Canadian and one American prisoners, and 80 civilians—134th Inf., After Action Report, 1 April 45.

hoped for by attacking infantrymen. In any case the Third Battalion, for the first time since the crossing of the Rhine, reverted to regimental reserve on the morning of March 31st when the 1st Battalion passed through, and, with the 2nd Battalion on its left, continued the regiment's attack to the east.[55]

This reserve position, however, was not to be of long duration. The Battalion marched to a new assembly position at Westerholt in the afternoon. About four kilometers northeast of the Battalion's position in Buer, Westerholt was in the zone of the 2nd Battalion; the Third was to pass through the 2nd and continue the attack the next morning (April 1st). It appeared that Recklinghausen would be the objective.[56]

The rapid turnover of company commanders and other leaders, as well as the prime importance of complete understanding, had led to the policy in the Battalion of issuing a complete field order, with leaders taking full notes, before each new attack. At 10:30 P.M. the company commanders met together for this new attack order:

1.a.) 2nd Battalion has been receiving small arms and direct fire from the vicinity of HOCHLAR. PW reports enemy withdrawing from RECKLINGHAUSEN.

b.) For 2nd and 1st Battalion positions—see operation map. The 1st Battalion coninues its attack on the right; the 75th Division, relieving the 8th Armored, will be on the left.

Artillery forward observers with I and K.

2.) The Battalion attacks at 0615 to seize HOCHLAR, prepare to continue the attack to capture RECKLINGHAUSEN. No change in attachments.

LD—Railroad crossing at STUCKENBUSCH.

Formation—Two companies abreast, I on the right, K on left, L in reserve. Move to vicinity of STUCKENBUSCH: K, I, L, IP—"Five Corners" in WESTERHOLT; IP time—0445 (H-1½ hours). Guides by S-2.

3.) Company I will attack on the right, seize right portion of HOCHLAR, prepare to continue the attack.

Company K attack on the left, seize left portion of HOCHLAR.

Company L in reserve. Take up position in vicinity of SCHLAGEL mine, attention to flanks, patrols to settlement northwest of mine. Prepared to assist attack.

Company M—One section heavy machine guns to Company I, one section HMG's to Company K, one platoon in support in area of Company L.

81 mm mortars—support the attack from positions in vicinity of SCHLAGEL mine.

Battalion Antitank Platoon—bazooka teams to Company K, reconnaissance for guns on left.

Regimental antitank platoon—bazooka teams to Company I, reconnaissance for guns on right.

Tanks and TD's—from positions in vicinity of DISTELN be prepared to fire on HOCHLAR. Tanks prepared to move forward on call from Company K, TD's prepared to move forward on call from Company I.

4.) Hot breakfast at 0345
Weapons on carriers to BACKUM
Ammunition DP—vicinity of BACKUM
Aid collecting point—North of BACKUM

5.) Radio—3rd Battalion   TARE   27—18
1st Battalion   NAN   21—30
2nd Battalion   OBOE   36—24
Map Code Word—REGULATION
OP—BACKUM
CP—WESTERHOLT to HOCHLAR.[57]

55. ibid.
56. 3rd Bn. Journal, III, 209.
57 3rd Bn. Journal, III, 208f. The Division attack had been set for 0700 but Col. Wood received permission to attack earlier in order to take advantage of the early morning haze.—134th Inf., After Action Report, 1 May 45.

Recklinghausen was a city whose peace-time population was 87,429[58]—larger than Terre Haute, Indiana, or Lincoln, Nebraska—and it had been noted for its manufactures of damask, cabinet ware, tobacco, as well as its coal.[59] It looked to be at least a regimental objective should it have a well-organized defense. The field artillery's plan called for more than 4,000 rounds on the city during the night.

The companies arrived at the line of departure as dawn was breaking on a gray morning; it was Easter sunrise. Heavy machine gun and mortar fire opened up as the companies began their advance, but they fought their way through to occupy Hochlar at 8:30 and reorganized to attack toward the objective. "L" Company moved in to mop up and took 27 prisoners. To get into Recklinghausen the companies had to advance up a broad, gentle slope for about 1,200 yards northeast of Hochlar; it was nearly a perfect field of fire for the enemy. At 11:43, with the armor in close support, they "jumped off" again. "K" moved directly northeast to go into the city from the southwest, while "I" followed a route wide to the right to enter from the south. Effective enemy mortar and machine gun fire all along the front indicated that, for the first time in this operation, the Battalion had met a coordinated defensive line. But in "an excellently executed attack; artillery followed closely by tanks and infantry"[60] the Battalion broke through what proved to be the enemy's main line of resistance. With the enemy "on the run" the artillery poured in successive battalion volleys—some 500 rounds—of time, percussion, and white phosphorous shells. The howitzers pursued by fire when about 80 German infantrymen, three tanks, and two horse-drawn guns were seen fleeing to the north and east; meanwhile time on target barrages of three to four battalion strength continued to fall on Recklinghausen every 15 minutes in continuation of a program begun with the initial attack for Hochlar. By 12:35 the assault companies were in the outskirts of the town, and at 12:55 reached the "Wall Street" which, on the site of the wall which had surrounded the town, encircled the heart of the city. A Mark IV tank still was burning in the city square. As the companies mopped up, the Battalion CP opened at Recklinghausen at 4:45 P.M.[61]

Patrols moved out to uncover hiding Nazis and investigate important buildings during that evening and the next morning. An "M" Company patrol found 35 Russians and 23 Holland Dutch in one of the Blumenthal mines, looked into an air raid shelter to find 600 civilians living, 16 seriously wounded German soldiers, and 64 civilian patients, including four maternity cases; then brought in six 20 mm antiaircraft guns. There were 200 German soldiers in a modern hospital at the south edge of the city, and 53 in another. An "I" Company patrol uncovered an ordnance warehouse, Battalion Intelligence Section men examined secret documents in the police headquarters (see photograph). Stores of military supplies and equipment made Recklinghausen a gold mine of authorized loot, and the infantrymen exploited it feverishly, for they knew that the city would not remain long in their hands; Corps Headquarters was preparing to move in.[62]

58. **Encyclopaedia Britannica World Atlas,** p. 99.
59. Lippencott's Gazeteer, p. 794.
60. Statement of captured German officer—Hanna, "Trans-Rhine Operation," p. 7.
61. **ibid.,** pp. 6-7; 3rd Bn. Journal, III, 209-212; 134th Inf., After Action Report, 1 May 45; 161st F.A., After Action Report, 1 May 45.
62. 3rd Bn. Journal, III, 213f.; 134th Inf., After Action Report, 1 May 45.

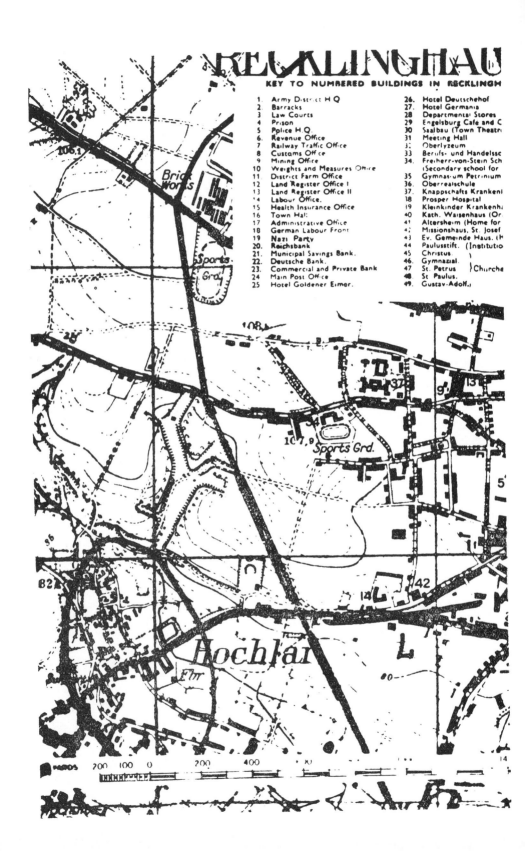

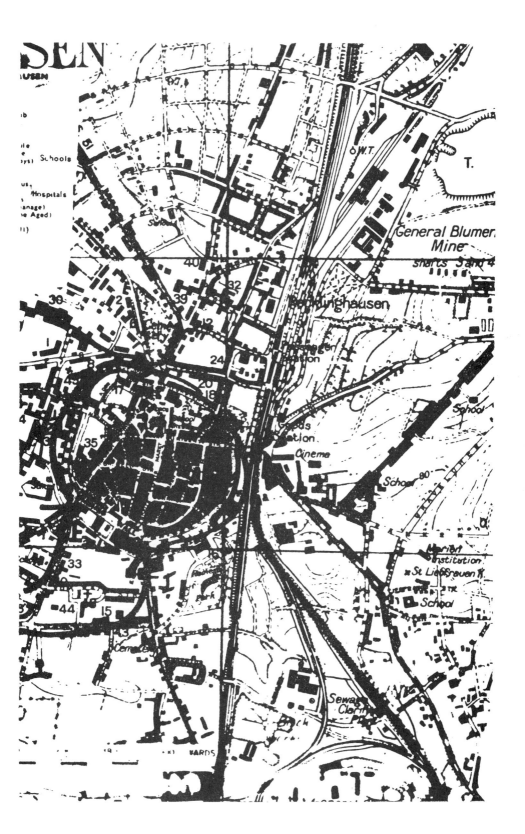

At 1:40 P.M. (April 2nd) the Battalion received word that armored columns of the Ninth Army, breaking through in a zone to the north, had effected a link-up with elements of the First Army to seal off the Ruhr. This left a tremendous pocket to be cleared out.[63]

Excluding about 500 German wounded in Recklinghausen and Buer hospitals, the Battalion had taken 479 prisoners of war in its battles east of the Rhine. Its total casualties had been 96, and 20 of these had been returned to duty after treatment at the aid station. And the Battalion listed the following captured or destroyed enemy equipment:

> 2—150 mm howitzers
> 4—128 mm antiaircraft guns and 200 rounds of ammunition
> 1—88 mm gun with prime mover
> 1—88 mm tank gun (unmounted)
> 4—tanks, Mark IV
> 2—radar stations, complete
> 20—carrier pigeons
> 300 to 500—dual, 30 cal. antiaircraft machine guns (in ordnance warehouse at Reckinghausen)
> Cache of rifles estimated at 1,000 (in Gladbeck mine)
> 500—additional rifles
> 500—gas masks
> gasoline storage dump: 500—50 gal. bbls.[64]

63. 3rd Bn. Journal, III, 214.
64. Hanna, "Trans-Rhine Operation," pp. 7-8.

CHAPTER XXIV

★ ★ ★

THE RUHR POCKET

★ ★ ★

From the beginning of operations in western Germany, an encirclement of the Ruhr was an attractive goal.[1] After the First Army had built up its bridgehead in the Remagen area, and the 21st Army Group had concentrated strong forces north of the Ruhr area, this became the quite obvious move. Ordinarily American doctrine holds that if a military commander is to achieve decisive success he must look primarily not to the capture of ground, but to the destruction of the enemy troops. However, the Ruhr, the greatest industrial area of Europe, was of such intrinsic value that it presented a worthwhile prize in itself; the German war machine could hardly remain effective without its industrial heart. Moreover, the Nazis could hardly allow this heart to be severed without a strong fight, and so there was known to be a large number of troops of Army Group "B" in the area. Thus the Ruhr presented an opportunity to eliminate an industrial area indispensable to the German war effort, and, at the same time, to destroy a sizeable portion of the enemy's remaining troops. And there was little that the enemy could do to prevent the encirclement which he saw closing in on him. Obviously he could not defend the whole Rhine River line with the forces remaining at his disposal; to withdraw his Ruhr garrisons to the east would have been to give up a part of his war potential as essential as were the troops; and he did not have sufficient forces to launch a counter attack—the only way in which he could have saved himself. Perhaps, with greater mobility and sufficient armor he could have mounted a counter-attack with the troops manning the Ruhr defenses, but in the circumstances this did not prove to be practical.

When elements of the First and Ninth Armies made contact on April 1st west of Paderborn to form the "largest pocket of envelopment in the history of warfare,"[2] this did not mean necessarily that the defenses in the whole area would collapse automatically. In an area so immense, it would make little difference immediately on a battalion front that encircling troops had made contact some fifty miles to the east. And encirclement on such a large scale should have little effect on the supply situation; it was not unlikely that there were great stores of food in the area, and as for military equipment, it would have been more appropriate to say that the rest of Germany was cut off from the Ruhr—that the encirclement's more immediate effect would be to ease the opposition to the east, outside the pocket. But cities have been famous for their ability to withstand siege, and house-to-house fighting through built-up areas never was an attractive assignment for soldiers. Were the Germans to make of each city an Aachen and of each town a Habkirchen, they might delay for months any complete Allied victory.

---

1. As early as May 1944 the SHAEF Planning Staff had envisaged an encirclement of the Ruhr in the Kassel area.—General Eisenhower's Report, p. 7.
2. General Marshall's Report, p. 60. Major General Karl Haushoffer, leader of German geopolitics, regarded urban concentrations as particularly vulnerable, because they lack the self-sufficiency pre-requisite to a successful defense. He said that cities should not be attacked frontally, but should be surrounded, and they would fall automatically.—Andreas Dorpalen, **The World of General Haushoffer** (New York and Toronto: Farrar and Rinehart, 1942) pp. 292-293.

Reporting on the operations in the Ruhr area General Eisenhower wrote to the Chief of Staff on April 6:

"You must expect, now, a period in which the lines on your map will not advance as rapidly as they did during the past several weeks because we must pause to digest the big mouthful that we have swallowed in the Ruhr area. It should not take too long and, of course, in the meantime, maintenance will be pushed to the limit to support our next main thrust. My G-2 ([Major General Strong of the British Army]) figures that there may be 150,000 German soldiers left in the Ruhr, but a number of these will change into civilian clothes before we liquidate the whole thing. He is confident, however, that we will capture at least 100,000.. ([Actually 300,000 were captured.]) The enemy has been making efforts to break out of the area but our persistent policy of knocking out his communications to the eastward, and his lack of mobility within the pocket, both make it very difficult for him to launch a really concerted attack. I am confident that he can do nothing about it."[3]

While other units pressed on in the breakthrough to the east, it fell to the 35th and other divisions of the XVI Corps to participate in the "digestion" of the Ruhr by attacks from the north; troops of the Ninth Army would be attacking into the pocket from the north; troops of the First Army would be attacking into the pocket from the south, while the relatively small, newly-committed Fifteenth Army would contain the pocket in the west along the Rhine.[4]

Wary of "pockets of resistance" from experiences of Mortain and around Lutrebois, men of the Third Battalion moved on April 4th by truck from Recklinghausen to an assembly area in Buer Resse,[5] prepared to face fanatical city fighting of trapped Nazis within the next few days.

But the Battalion's first assignment was to occupy a defensive sector—a front of some 4,000 yards along the Rhine-Herne Canal in the vicinity of Buer Erle. With a heavy machine gun platoon in each sector, one section in each platoon sited in depth, Company K relieved Company C of the 320th Infantry's 1st Battalion, to "organize, occupy and defend the right of the battalion sector," and Company L relieved Company E of the 320th Infantry's 2nd Battalion on the left. Company K's men occupied buildings along the southern edge of Buer Erle from a Blumenthal mine on the right to a railroad and highway crossing on the left—there never was any compunction against doubling up the enemy civilians in the area to make room for the conquering soldiers. Company L, though sharing a defensive sector in the industrial and urban Ruhr area, found itself out in the woods again, and considered itself fortunate to find a house in the area for a CP. Company I went into position as reserve in buildings of a government housing project in an opening in the woods—on relatively higher ground—about 1,000 yards in rear of the center of the front lines. Regimental anti-tank guns took up positions in Company L's area, while the Battalion guns went into position on the right. A platoon of TD's (90 mm) of the 654th Tank Destroyer Battalion took up positions in front of Company I.[6]

Occupation of this relatively quiet sector was to continue for five days. To say that the sector was quiet, does not mean that there was any lack of daily activity in this populous community located some seven miles northeast of Essen and two miles north of Gelsenkirchen. This activity, in the main, took the form of nightly patrols, measures to reduce the enemy positions on the south side of the canal, and dealing with the problems of the civilian population and displaced persons.

3. General Marshall's Report, pp. 50-51.
4. Ibid.; et. al.
5. 3rd Bn. Journal, III, 216.
6. 3rd Bn. Journal, III, 217f.

Patrols came from the reserve company (I). The first (of four men) was given a mission of crossing the canal by rubber boat in the "L" Company sector, and then of following a railroad on the opposite side into a small woods to investigate the enemy positions. Two nights later another patrol attempted a crossing in the same general area; but as their boat reached the middle of the waterway two German automatic weapons, as well as several rifles, opened fire. Two of the men got back safely by swimming, but the other two were listed as missing. Nevertheless another group of four men from Company I was ready to venture into enemy territory the following night. But this patrol did not get as far as its predecessor. As the men carried their boat down to the water, three flares went up on the opposite bank; then bursts of fire from machine pistols, and a mortar barrage prevented them from even getting the boat afloat.[7]

In addition to the reconnaissance patrols Company I, with jeeps and drivers from Company M, operated two motor security patrols to the rear— one covered the area to Westerholt, and the other covered Buer.[8]

When Company L called for a cessation of all fire (artillery and mortar) to their front at 10:25 one morning, investigation revealed that Capt. Brigandi was down at his Company OP negotiating for the surrender of a group of enemy facing his company. Two civilians had come across the canal under a white flag to tell about a group of 29 soldiers on the other side who were ready to surrender. The civilians pointed out the location of the enemy positions, and then the artillery and mortar observers prepared to fire concentrations on the indicated points. Brigandi sent an ultimatum by one of the civilian "middle men" that he would give them until 12 o'clock to surrender, or would bring down all the fire at his disposal on their positions. The civilians moved from foxhole to foxhole trying to get the soldiers to come out; it seemed that all were willing except an SS man who would not permit them to give up. For a while it seemed that they were getting ready to surrender when observers saw them changing clothes, but at 11:45 it was clear that they did not intend to surrender, and Brigandi called for the barrage. Then it was agreed that a civilian would go across at 8 o'clock that night and attempt to infiltrate the enemy soldiers back to surrender. But when the civilian went to his boat the oars were missing —he claimed that some women took them. After an hour's search the oars were recovered, and the negotiator rowed across the dark, concrete-bedded canal. Company L observers could make out a group of about 15 men on the other side, but they were not sure whether this was an enemy patrol, or part of the group getting ready to surrender. The net result was that the civilian returned four hours after his departure—with *two* prisoners.[9]

The most active measures taken for "softening" the enemy's positions were the almost continuous firing of artillery—accurately adjusted from the companies and from the excellent Battalion observation post high up in a building at the Bismark mine (shafts 2 and 6), direct fire from the tank destroyers' 90 mm guns, and concentrations from the 81 mm mortars—though the ammunition for the latter was under a strict ration. An 8-inch gun sent "half a dozen direct hits" into a power plant some distance south of the canal. One day the TD's sent 97 rounds into factory buildings; another day they fired for half an

7. ibid., pp. 231, 229, 230, 236.
8. ibid., p. 226.
9. ibid., pp. 224-228.

hour on enemy pill boxes or emplacements.[10] And then between 2:45 and 3:00 A.M. on April 6th, the Battalion made an "attack by fire" to support an attack toward Essen launched down on the right by the 79th Division. The heavy machine gun section which was sited in depth in each company area, and the light machine guns of Company K set up a steady chatter; 81 mm mortars fired both light and heavy ammunition—and included a 54-round concentration fired with extreme rapidity; the 60 mm mortars of all companies went into action; the TD's opened fire both with their 90 mm guns and with their 50-caliber machine guns.[11]

In order to carry out military operations it was necessary to give some attention to the problems of the civilians living in the area which the Battalion occupied. Capt. Jack Campbell, who had been wounded at Lutrebois, rejoined the Battalion,[12] and Col. Wood kept him at Battalion headquarters as special "civil affairs officer" to cooperate with Lt. Hanna and his intelligence section, and with the regimental military government officer. Combat units had to improvise some means of dealing with these problems pending the assumption of control by regular military government teams from higher headquarters. The Battalion had taken a step in this direction during the campaign west of the Rhine when Hanna called in three German-speaking soldiers to form a civil affairs team within his intelligence section.[13] Most ambitious of the group was Private First Class George T. Mertens of New York, who joined the section from Company M. Now, with a few days' pause in Buer Erle, "Pop" Mertens was in his element. He undertook organization of the distribution of certain food supplies, he got the power plant to working—so that the Battalion could have electric lights without operating its mobile generator—he investigated reports of Nazi activity. One of his most promising—but apparently futile— projects was down at the mine near the canal. He found that not only was there a deep tunnel running under the canal from here, but there was a functioning telephone cable connecting the other side. He tried to put through a call to the enemy authorities to negotiate for their surrender.[14]

Guards were placed on food stores and warehouses to prevent looting. Stray prisoners continued to be picked up from time to time; one fellow, dressed in civilian clothes, had come home on furlough from another part of Germany— only to be captured and see his home overrun by the American invaders; Company K brought in a vicious uniformed young woman—an example of the German "WAC." All civilian passes which the burgomaster had issued previously were recalled, and new ones issued with the approval of Battalion headquarters; priority for passes would go to employees of the coal mine which would be listed by the operator and the burgomaster: men from the division Counterintelligence Corps team coordinated with the Battalion S-2 in approving the passes—Mertens brought in a complaint from some woman that a man had used a 134th Infantry pass to enter her house and take her belongings. Regimental military government officers announced that civilians would be permitted to circulate in the streets only between the hours of 7 and 8 A.M., 10 A.M. and 1 P.M., and 5 to 6 P.M. No one was permitted to ride a bicycle; no one was to go across the autobahn which ran between Buer Erle and Buer. And

10. ibid., pp. 219-232, **passim.**
11. ibid., pp. 227f.
12. ibid., p. 229. After this operation Capt. Campbell left the Battalion to take command of antitank company.
13. ibid., pp. 143f.
14. ibid., pp. 226f.

there were charges of looting and of rape to be investigated, appeals for permission to ride bicycles to work, requests for medical assistance. Capt. Royce, Battalion surgeon, went down to inspect a group of Italians and Russians who had been held prisoners in one of the coal mines; he found them to be suffering from tuberculosis and malnutrition—several already had died—and so medical men evacuated them back to the rear area.[15]

There was one local facility which had a great appeal for the American soldiers: a clean, modern bath at the mine. Of course it was in a building adjacent to the Battalion OP, and was right on Company K's front line, but there were long rows of private, white-tiled rooms with huge tubs and showers, and with plenty of hot water—and German employees kept the power and boilers going. It was a rare opportunity for front-line luxury—even if it was necessary to go *forward* for a shower.[16]

Attacking toward Essen, the 79th Division was reported to be making progress on April 8th—150 prisoners had been taken, and a bridge across the canal has been put in—but apparently its left battalions were having some trouble with their exposed flank.[17] The time had come for the 35th to attack.

The battalion commanders and S-3's, the artillery commander, the TD commander, and the engineer commander met with the regimental commander and his S-3 in the Battalion CP that afternoon to discuss plans for attacking across the canal.[18] Originally the plan called for an assault by the Third and 1st Battalions together. (The 1st had relieved the 1st Battalion, 320th Infantry, and now occupied the sector on the right (west) of the Third.) There was some objection to this, however, on the grounds that the objective could be attained more economically by obtaining permission from the 79th Division to cross on their bridge, and then swinging northeast along the canal to hit the flank of the enemy's defenses while machine guns and cannon held him by fire from north of the canal. Later a compromise was arrived at; the Third would make the direct assault across the canal, while the 1st would swing wide through the 79th zone and attack the flank. It still was necessary for the Third to make a frontal attack across a difficult obstacle known to be defended, but now it would have the advantage of an envelopment coming against the enemy's left flank.

In spite of the fact that it had been attacking cities, it is probable that the Third Battalion had been able to operate more according to the pattern of its training during its operations east of the Rhine than at any other similar period during the war. Now it was spring and extreme weather no longer loomed as such an important condition. There had been no really coordinated systems of defenses in depth with mutually supporting flanks; now the companies had found it possible to maneuver, to turn flanks, and to make full use of their fire power and supporting arms. Again, casualties had been relatively light and officers and men had been able to work together in successful combat long enough to develop team work and confidence; now the vicious circle was tending to operate the other way—the lesser turnover in personnel permitted the greater development of efficiency and skill, which tended further to reduce casualties. During these days leaders had been able to experience that deep satisfaction—rare enough in any warfare—of seeing their units move into

15. 3rd Bn. Journal, III, 219-232, **passim**.
16. J. Huston to N. F. Huston, 6 April 45.
17. ibid., pp. 231, 233.
18. ibid., p. 231.

successive "goose eggs" as assigned—of seeing operations go "according to plan." For the regiment to have failed to use a maneuvering force in this instance could have been unfortunate.

An artillery air observer was called upon to get the latest information on the state of the three bridges—a railroad bridge on the right of Company K's sector, a highway bridge in the middle of Company K's sector, and a highway bridge near the boundary between "K" and "L"—in the Battalion sector. He reported that the railroad bridge was broken and its roadway in the water, but that it might be possible for foot troops to cross on the superstructure. There was about a 10-foot gap of water between the exposed parts of the center highway bridge, and was an unlikely crossing site. The third was broken and twisted at the near end with a six to eight foot gap between the bank and the exposed parts, but it offered the possibility of making a crossing by throwing some planks across the gap.[19] The canal presented serious difficulties to any attempt to cross by assault boats. To be sure the channel was not wide nor the current swift, but the water was deep and the bed was concrete; the steeply-sloping concrete banks would be an obstacle both to launching the boats and to disembarking on the other side· in addition to that the canal was double in front of K Company, and though the bridge spanned both channels, it would be necessary for boatmen to put craft on both—an almost impossible task in the face of enemy fire. (The channels separated to the east and Company L's left platoon occupied a woods between the two; but there was only a weak bridge over the first canal, and boats could be taken down to the second only with great difficulty.

His reconnaissance and plans completed, Col. Wood called in the company commanders—who too had been making reconnaissance for the inevitable attack —to the CP for another attack order:

1.a.) Map: The Ruhr, 1:12,500, sheets 4,5,8,9
Light artillery has been falling in sector. Enemy defends south of RHEIN-HERNE Canal with automatic weapons from positions which seem to be occupied at night. Company L received some SP fire last night on its right flank.
b.) 134th Infantry attacks south across RHEIN-HERNE Canal to seize bridge-head to relieve pressure against left flank of the 79th Division.
2nd Battalion will continue to hold present position, [on left] to assist 3rd Battalion by fire with preparation of machine gun and mortar fire, 0615—0630.
1st Battalion, with platoon of tanks and AT platoon attached, will cross bridge in 79th Division area, attack northeast, seize and hold objective to our right, prepare to continue attack to the east to assist this battalion.
In support:
161st Field Artillery Battalion, reinforced by 216th F.A.
Co A (less one platoon), 654th TD Battalion
3rd Platoon, Company A, 60th Engineers
Artillery F.O.'s with I-K-L.
Artillery and TD's fire harassing fires during night. Close-in preparation 0620-0630—TD's from area of the hut camp; [front of Company K] one platoon crosses with 1st Battalion, joins 3rd on contact. After preparation, artillery shifts to targets south of objective.
Engineer detail with companies K and L to prepare foot crossings; prepare to assist Company I with boats.
2.) This Battalion, with Company A (less one platoon), 784th Tank Battalion, and 2nd Platoon Antitank Company attached, attacks to seize and hold area south of GELSENKIRCHEN-BISMARK passenger and goods station.
Time: 0630
LD: present front line

19. ibid., pp. 231f.

Direction of attack: south southeast

Formation: Two companies abreast, K and L in assault, I in reserve—K on the right.

3.a.) Company K will cross at railroad bridge (No. 41) and highway bridge to west (546275) seize power station and coke oven area of GRAF BISMARK mine (1 and 4). Continue attack to seize and hold objective A (see operation map).

b.) Company L will cross canal at highway bridge (No. 42), attack through objective C and seize and hold objective B. (see operation map).

c.) Company I in reserve. Remain present position initially, prepared to assist attack by crossing an assault platoon in rubber boats; prepare to follow either K or L on order, occupy area C, provide security to left flank. One platoon, Company I, with light machine gun section and bazookas, support by fire from the present area of Company L. 60 mm mortars fire 0620 to 0630.

d.) Company M: One section heavy machine guns direct support of Company K, one section direct support of Company L. One platoon HMG's in general support—fire from vicinity of Company L 0620 to 0630.

81 mm mortars prepared to support from present positions, prepared to displace forward to canal. Smoke on call. Observers—I, K, L.

e.) Tank platoon: From positions forward of BISMARK mine and northeast of No. 42 [highway bridge]—fire machine gun and HE 0620 to 0630, additional fire on call. Prepare to cross canal to Battalion objective on completion of bridge.

f.) Regimental antitank platoon: Two guns fire harassing fire from present area of Company L tonight—fire preparation from those positions 0620-0630; one squad of bazookas with Company L. On completion of bridge cross guns to protect Battalion left flank.

g.) Battalion Antitank Platoon—bazookas teams direct support of Company K—prepare to cross guns on completion of bridge to protect right flank.

h.) Ammunition and Pioneer Platoon—Establish ammunition DP; be prepared to lay smoke pots to cover crossing sites on order.

4.) Battalion Aid Station—present location; collecting point—vicinity of BISMARK mine entrance.

Ammunition DP—BISMARK Mine (2 and 6)

Breakfast—0500

Carry full K ration

Bed rolls—present CP's

Gas masks will be carried.

5.) Battalion CP—present location

OP—present location

(Bismark mine)

Radio: call sign, GEORGE; Channel 33, Alt. 27.[20]

Col. Wood deliberately had made his plan elastic. If crossings could be made at all three sites, that would be all to the good, but should only one of the attempts be successful, then the entire Battalion would be prepared to cross at that point. And should all attempts to cross at the destroyed bridges be thwarted, then Company I would have a platoon ready to make a crossing in boats. Or this platoon would be available to cross in case a counter-attack should come against "L" before its bridgehead was secure. At the same time, there was to be an impressive display of firepower—a rifle platoon, light machine guns, a heavy machine gun platoon, rockets, 57 mm antitank guns, and mortars along the left of the sector to pin down the troops which had been occupying the positions opposite Company L. This would be in addition to the disturbance which tanks and TD's—not to mention artillery and mortars—were calculated to create farther to the right just before the "jump off."

20. *ibid.*, pp. 232-235. Commanders were given operation maps with objectives marked, and with a system of numbered check points to be used as reference in radio communication. To facilitate coordination marked maps were exchanged with the 1st Battalion. Whether gas masks were being carried because of a threat of military use of poison gas, because of fear of escape of gas from some damaged industrial plants, or because of lack of space for transporting them is not wholly clear; the second suggestion appears to be the most likely explanation.

Opposite the Third Battalion the Germans had deployed the four companies (each with a strength of about 90 men) flanked by a group of Luftwaffe personnel under a Lt. Col. Bierle on the west, and a group of "Volkssturm Saarland" on the east.[21] Actually the Third Battalion did not enjoy a real numerical advantage for attacking across an obstacle as formidable as the canal presented. But much of the Germn force consisted of stragglers; a number were sick, mortar ammunition was very low, and there was no immediately available artillery support; morale could not have been very high.

In these circumstances the designated weapons opened fire at 6:20 A.M. and ten minutes later the companies moved down to their crossing sites. "K" Company drew machine gun fire almost at once—one of the leading men fell wounded. Doubts began to arise as to whether this attempt would be successful.[22]

Meanwhile Company L had not yet attracted so much attention. Its leading squad was able to make its way over the first canal on the broken bridge, but it soon was obvious that the bridge could not be used as it was for crossing the second. Sergeant Keith Dowell of California was leading this squad, and he knew that he must act quickly; his men would be exposed to close-range enemy fire without any protection; but he did not intend to turn back. The squad leader slipped down into the water and swam for the opposite bank. On gaining it he found two German guards on duty; immediately he attacked them and killed one and wounded the other. Then he seized a boat which he brought back for his squad to cross the canal and secure the bridgehead. The squad over, the platoon leader put the boat to use as support for an improvised foot bridge, and the remainder of the platoon made its way across.[23]

All of "L" Company was across by 8:40, and Brigandi called for some boats to be used in crossing heavy weapons and succeeding units.[24] If the company had found the use of rubber boats impractical in the attempted crossing of the Blies, now it put them to good use: a ferry service was established with German prisoners pulling the boats back and forth by attached ropes to shuttle across men and supplies.

The assault platoons eliminated six pill boxes, but still received troublesome fire from the left flank; Brigandi requested that the Company I platoon keep up its effective fire from across the canal.[25]

Hostile resistance and inability of expedients to span the gap in the bridge rendered Company K's attempt unsuccessful. However, the 1st Battalion was moving up rapidly from its crossing down on the right in the 79th Division zone. At 9:20 the 1st Battalion called for a cessation of friendly fire in front of "K" Company, and Company A entered the rear of long buildings whence enemy troops were firing at K. By 10 o'clock Company A had taken 20 prisoners out of the area and that obstacle had been removed.[26]

Col. Wood quickly shifted his plan to take advantage of the situation. Both Company I and Company K would cross at the Company L site; "K" would advance to the objectives originally assigned, and Company I would pass through "L" to capture that company's former objective. Company L would

21.   Ibid., pp. 238f.
22.   Ibid., p. 237f.
23.   35th Div., General Orders, No. 33, 16 May 45.
24.   3rd Bn. Journal, III, 237; 134th Inf., After Action Report, 1 May 45.
25.   3rd Bn. Journal, III, 237f.
26.   Ibid., pp. 237f., 134th Inf., After Action Report, 1 May 45.

continue to work along the left flank. The platoon of TD's which had come with the 1st Battalion joined Company L.[27]

The attack now progressing well—Company L had 18 prisoners at 10 o'clock, and at 11:15 the total was 70—at 11 o'clock Col. Wood received notice from regiment that a new order would be down for continuation of the attack. This arrived on a map overlay at 1:00 o'clock, and the Battalion commander went forward to confer with the company commanders. Moving out again the companies met only scattered resistance and at 5:30 occupied objectives about four kilometers southeast of the crossing site. At 6 o'clock the Battalion CP opened at Havercamp. There had been delay in building a bridge at Buer Erle and the Battalion's vehicles rejoined the Battalion via the circuitous route over the 79th Division bridge. (The tanks and TD's [less one platoon] remained with the 2nd Battalion north of the canal.) During the night Company K made contact with a unit of the 137th Infantry on the left.[28]

Lack of a bridge made it impracticable to bring up a hot breakfast the next morning (April 11th), and a K ration unit had to suffice before the resumption of the attack at 7 A.M. This proved to be a "short working day," for the companies advanced through successive towns to their objectives by noon. They met little more than sniper fire—the PW total went up to 142. Now they were facing east in positions around Riemke and adjacent communities (north of Bochum); the Battalion CP moved to Eickel.[29]

During the afternoon there was recorded one of those minor details which served to irritate battalion and company commanders during combat operations. The regimental S-3 relayed an order to the battalion to send a detail of ten men to relieve a 2nd Battalion warehouse guard. Ten men from Company L and an antitank truck were made ready, but there were no definite instructions as to where they were to go. The Battalion S-3 called the 2nd Battalion to inquire about the location, only to be told, "No one knows their location: MG [military government] grabbed 10 men off the tail of G Company as they marched by."[30]

When the order came that night the company commanders could sense that the climax of the Ruhr operations—as far as they were concerned—was at hand: "This Battalion attacks to secure ground commanding Ruhr River west of STIEPEL. Time: 0700."[31]

This meant a march to the south of over 11 kilometers; but the city of Bochum (pop. 303,000) was reported to have been cleared by the 315th Infantry (79th Division). If the enemy were going to make a stand north of the Ruhr it would have to be met on this day; and it seemed that there would be little point in his retreating across the river, for battalions of the First Army would be approaching it from the south within a few days. Yet the company commanders could hope that withdrawal or surrender woud be the enemy's reaction. Once the enemy were cleared in this area, they knew that the Battalion would be out of contact for a few days—the nearest enemy would be across the river in the zone of the First Army, and beyond a boundary which only an order from General Bradley could change; and the active front of the Ninth Army had moved on 200 miles to the east.

27. 3rd Bn. Journal, III, 237f.
28. ibid., pp. 238-240.
29. ibid., pp. 239-241; 134th Inf. After Action Report, 1 May 45.
30. 3rd Bn. Journal, III, 241.
31. ibid., p. 242.

It was with some anxiety mixed with hope then that the battalion column started moving through Bochum the next morning. Weapons were taken off jeeps at the south edge of the city, and the column divided in two—Company L with a platoon of tank destroyers on the right, and Company I with a platoon of tanks on the left—to move along parallel roads. The advance continued steadily toward the river. Although the 1st Battalion ran into a pocket of fanatical paratroopers on the north bank (to the right of the Third), the enemy in front of the Third was cooperative, and the heights overlooking the Ruhr River were occupied in the early afternoon. The enemy marked his withdrawal with the destruction of a bridge to the left of the Battalion sector. Then artillery observers with both companies—as well as the liaison officer, Capt. Jack Hunt— went to work on columns of enemy troops and vehicles which could be seen withdrawing up a series of three valleys which joined the valley of the Ruhr opposite the Battalion position.[32]

On this sunny afternoon in April the landscape could make its most effective appeal to the eye; here indeed "the towns of the Ruhr have preserved an easy contact with the countryside . . . . accentuated in Spring by the sea of green which laps around the towns, making them appear as dark islands in a well-cultivated countryside."[33] Here in the midst of an industrial area were beautifully-kept green meadows, trim lawns, and thriving gardens.[34]

During the late evening the frontage of the Battalion was extended when Company K took over the sectors of both "A" and "B" to permit those companies to join in the 1st Battalion's final assault the next day to eliminate the pocket still remaining to its right front.[35]

The Battalion's total of prisoners for operations in Ruhr pocket now amounted to 173. There was a camp of Russian laborers in the area most of whose 130 inmates were suffering from malnutrition; 22 had died when the camp was caught between German and American artillery.

Once the Germans had had time to reorganize on the other side of the river, heavy artillery began to harrass the Battalion area. One tremendous explosion dug a big crater right next to the house being used for a CP, and others interdicted a crossroads to the front.[36]

Combat Team 134 was left behind and attached to the 79th Division on April 13th when the remainder of the 35th Division moved from the Ruhr area to join the XIX Corps nearly 200 miles to the east. However, this regiment's turn came a day later. That afternoon the 3rd Battalion, 315th Infantry (79th Division) relieved the Third Battalion, 134th Infantry, and the Battalion marched back to an assembly area in the south section of Bochum.[37]

At midnight on April 12th the Battalion had learned of the death of President Roosevelt.[38] Used as they were to death and the loss of close friends, men of the Third Battalion felt deep personal loss. They knew that this would not alter the inevitable outcome of the war, but they wished that he could have seen the victory completed.[39]

32. Ibid., pp. 242-244.
33. The Economist, loc. cit.
34. J. Huston to F. E. Webb, April 12, 1945.
35. Ibid., p. 244, 134th Inf., After Action Report, 1 May 45.
36. Ibid., p. 245; Warren C. Wood to the Author, June 26, 1946.
37. 134th Infantry, After Action Report, 1 May 45; 3rd Bn. Journal, III, 247f.
38. 3rd Bn. Journal, III, 248.
39. J. Huston to N. F. Huston, 25 April 45.

CHAPTER XXV

* * *

THE DASH TO THE ELBE

* * *

In almost any military attack, generally it is assumed that the attacker must possess a considerable superiority in numbers—from 2 to 1 to 5 to 1, depending upon the type of defense—if he is to be successful. Yet the American Army repeatedly demonstrated its ability to carry through a major offensive against a numerically superior foe. To do that it was necessary to maintain a local superiority. Several things contributed to make this possible. One was the efficiency of the Air Forces in being able to "isolate the battlefield" and immobilize the enemy—at the same time neutralizing the hostile air power. Another was the tremendous fire power of American divisions—from semi-automatic rifles, to rapid-firing, highly effective artillery. But not the least of these factors was the American Army's superior mobility—based largely on the fast, sturdy 2½-ton truck. This capability for rapid shifting of troops is hardly more strikingly demonstrated than by the actions of the 35th Division in mid-April. While Combat Team 134 was participating in operations against Army Group "H" to reduce the Ruhr pocket, the remainder of the division was pursuing the enemy east of the Weser River. The next day the 134th was back with the division, over 200 miles from the scene of its latest operation.

The Third Battalion, with the Antitank Company, formed the first serial in the combat team's "SOP administrative move" to rejoin the division on April 14th. The column moved out of Bochum at 6 A.M. Its destination was Peine.[1] Steadily the trucks moved along the highways to the east—through Bielefeld, across the Weser River on a pontoon bridge at Hameln, through once picturesque, but now bombed-out Hildesheim. By mid-afternoon the column was opposite Peine, but instead of angling north toward that city it followed directions of posted guides and continued to the east. Soon the leaders found that they were off their maps, and they could only estimate their location and guess at their ultimate destination. Division military police gave way to men of the reconnaissance troop as guides, and when these ran out, men of the TD battalion were posted. The column continued on through Braunschweig (Brunswick), and finally, about 30 miles to the northeast, came to its assigned area near Oebisfelde-Kultendorf—about mid-way between Brunswick and Gardelegen.

The Third Battalion went into the town of Niendorf and neighboring villages between 7 and 8 P.M. Distance covered during the day was more than 230 miles. The Elbe River was only about 40 miles away.[2]

Lt. Stoneburner, Battalion S-4, was leading the kitchen train in the last serial of the column. He telephoned the Battalion CP at 3:15 A.M. to report that, of the Battalion's five kitchen trucks, two had turned over in a ditch, two were delayed en route, one had arrived.[3]

1. 3rd Bn. Journal, III, 249; 134th Inf., After Action Report, 1 May 45.
2. Ibid., 3rd Bn. Journal, III, 250.
3. Ibid., p. 251.

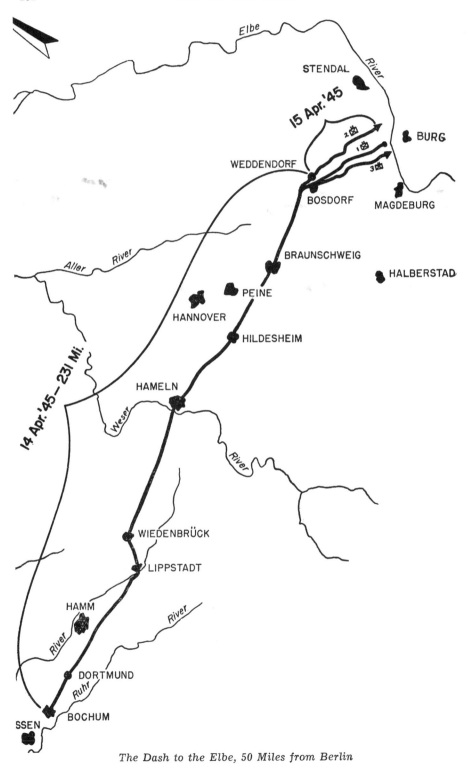

The Dash to the Elbe, 50 Miles from Berlin

Though the hour was growing late and the travel had been long, neither men nor vehicles were to have very many hours for rest. Col. Wood and the S-3 were called to regimental headquarters at 1:30 A.M., and they returned at 3:45 with plans for a continuation of the advance to the Elbe.[4] Up to this point the advance had been covered, i.e., it was through territory through which friendly troops already had passed. But now the regiment was to make a *tactical* move by motor—without any support from armor (it would be some time before the tanks and TD's could complete the 230 miles covered the previous day)—through enemy territory. Here was the boldest kind of use of the superior American automotive power, though it was not a type of operation which had been completely neglected in training.

Even the renowned German motorized divisions of the "blitzkrieg" had anticipated no such use of motors as this. In fact the German doctrine had been opposed to it. This a member of the German general staff had expressed to General Wedemeyer during a visit of the latter to Germany in the late 1930's when he said: "The truck has no place on the battlefield." He meant that an unarmored vehicle was too vulnerable to be brought within immediate fire areas.[5] Even the American teaching had said: "It is contemplated that marches to gain contact with the enemy will be made on foot."[6]

Company Commanders were not called in to receive the Battalion order until 6 A.M.—

1.a.) There appears to be no organized resistance this side of the ELBE RIVER, though isolated groups have been contacted. The 137th moved through the FOREST [on a route to the north of the 134th zone] without opposition. Elements of the 30th Division on our right have received scattered artillery fire from across the ELBE—first encountered since crossing the WESER.

b.) CT 134 moves by motor into defensive positions on the ELBE RIVER between CT 137 and the 30th Division, clearing area between present location and objective. 1st Battalion will move on our left, then become regimental reserve. 2nd Battalion moves on route to the left of the 1st, then occupies defensive position on our left. 30th Division occupies area on right of our sector (ROGATZ)

2.) This Battalion, with 3rd Platoon and Mine Platoon of Antitank Company; Battery C, 161st Field Artillery, and one squad regimental MP's attached, moves by motor to occupy defensive positions east of UTZ on the ELBE RIVER and to clear the area intervening.

Order of March: L, Battalion AT Platoon, K, Hq, AT Mine Platoon, M (—), I (—), FA Battery.

RP—RJ, NIENDORF [0745?]

IP —RATZLINGEN, 0800

LD—WIEGLITZ, 0900

ROUTE — BOSDORF—RATZLINGEN—GRAVINGEN—BUDDENSELL—WIEGLITZ—BULSTRINGEN—SATUELLE—FOREST—COLBYTZ—ANGERN—UTZ.

Detrucking Area: UTZ

3.a.) Company L with one platoon HMG's and one section 81 mm mortars attached, will furnish advance guard; will seize, organize, defend area vicinity SAND-FURTH—contact 2nd Battalion on left.

b.) Company K, follow Company L by 300 yards, prepared to assist Company L by attacking either to right or left. Seize, organize, defend area vicinity KEHNERT.

c.) Company I, follow Company M (—) prepared to defend either flank or rear, or to attack to assist leading companies. One 2½-ton truck, with MG and mortar sections, and regimental AT platoon, follow artillery battery, furnish rear guard. Occupy area vicinity BERTINGEN; make contact with 30th Division on right.

4. *ibid.*, p. 251.
5. General Marshall's Report, p. 98.
6. **Training Notes, The Infantry School, 1939–40,** IV: "Security and Marches," (Fort Benning, Georgia, 1942), p. 6.

d.) Company M—One platoon HMG's attached to Company L, one platoon, security to flanks, patrol down intersecting roads. On objective—one platoon heavy machine guns with Company L, one section with Company K, one section with Company I. One section 81 mm mortars attached to Company L, two sections move with Company M prepared to support advance.

e.) Battalion Antitank Platoon: direct support Company L—occupy postions on left of Battalion objective, prepared to fire across ELBE.

f.) Regimental Antitank Platoon: Direct support Company I—occupy positions on right of Battalion objective, prepared to fire across river.

g.) Mine platoon—Move with Battalion headquarters prepared to assist advance by removal of obstacles.

h.) Ammunition and Pioneer Platoon—coordinate with mine platoon in removal of obstacles.

i.) MP's—move with Battalion headquarters, control of S-2, prepared to assist in handling PW's and civilians.

j.) Light Tank Platoon—if and when it arrives—attached to Company L.

k.) Field Artillery battery—follow Company I, prepared to go into position to assist advance of the Battalion.

x.) All machine guns mounted and manned, including .50 calibers on personnel carriers and other vehicles.

Have bazookas available.
Personnel carriers will join companies at 0720.
Interval between vehicles: 60 yards.
Guide speed: 20 MPH—hold on phase lines until further orders.
S-2 men guide through RATZLINGEN

4.) Gasoline is available at Service Company.
At 0600, 1⅓ K rations to be issued.
Kitchens revert to Service Company
Bed rolls carried by individuals on trucks.
Organic vehicles—company control
Aid station—move with Battalion headquarters

6.) Battalion CP will move to UTZ
March CP—follow Company K
Radios open at 0700—call sign, GEORGE, channel 36, alternate, 27.
First Battalion, WILLIAM, 24—29;
2nd Battalion, NAN   30—18.
Password: NILE, reply: GREEN.[7]

The enemy offered a prelude to the day's move when aircraft appeared overhead at 7:20 and came in to bomb and strafe. Supporting antiaircraft guns shot down one of the planes,[8] and men from the Battalion brought in the frightened young pilot.

Most dangerous obstacles to the advance by motors were large areas of forest—the route of the Battalion went through about 18 miles of woods. Here the enemy would be able to ambush a column not completely alert; and should enemy groups be encountered, it would be difficult to deploy the companies; the enemy's artillery would be rendered more dangerous by the trees, while it might be difficult or impossible for the artillery attached to the Third Battalion to go into action against a particular position located deep in the woods. Though there would be an important saving in physical effort, there would be some sacrifice to nervous strain. However, the regimental commander had appraised the state of disintegration of German troops in the area, and had taken account of the successful advances of friendly units to the north and south; the risk really was not too great. The main weight of the nervous apprehension had to be borne by the men from Company L who were riding in jeeps out in front as the point, and to the men of Lt. Archer's "M" Company machine

7. 3rd Bn. Journal, III, 251-253.
8. Ibid., p. 254.

gun platoon who were patrolling on the flanks. To them fell the task of preventing an ambush or disastrous encounter with a defensive position. That
there were some enemy in the area became apparent very early when the point
captured a group of Germans in the village of Satuelle at the near edge of the
forest. When the column seemed to be delayed, Lt. Mike Hanna and men of his
intelligence section went forward in their jeep to reconnoiter. The forest trails
were difficult enough to follow under any circumstances, but the whole question
of direction was confounded when the column came to a modern concrete highway and a broad cleared area which were not indicated on the map. Hanna
questioned a civilian who happened along, and on the basis of his information
and compass readings, the column continued.

The great open area was found to be an artillery range and ordnance
proving grounds.[9] The men could feel a strange nakedness as they emerged
from the woods and their trucks rolled by the concrete emplacements—were
enemy eyes watching their every move while they were falling into some trap?

Actually the selection of trails and roads proved to be the biggest obstacle
as the column moved on toward the Elbe. It encountered one other notable
enemy installation shortly before reaching its objective. A German motor park.
There were staff cars—Cadillac, Mercedes, Ford—there were new Ford and
Chevrolet trucks, and trailers, and motorcycles, and special equipment. Fleeing
Germans had tampered with most of the new vehicles—some had been set on
fire. A few tardy German soldiers were taken prisoners.[10]

When the Battalion arrived at a crossroads in the woods near Utz and
Bertingen, it found one of the reasons for the few delays in its advance: Lt.
Archer and his machine gun patrols met the column; their jeeps were crowded
high with prisoners—the platoon had taken about 30 during the day. Not only
had they patrolled deep to the flanks—and broken up one group of enemy by
their machine gun fire—they already had patrolled into Bertingen, Kehnert,
and Utz, and found them to be clear. It was with a welcome feeling of reassurance that the men of the companies started for their respective objectives. It
was found possible to take trucks up to Bertingen for Companies I and K,
whence the latter would have a short march to Kehnert. Company L detrucked
in Utz, and the men had a march of about three kilometers to Sandfurth.

As some of the Company L soldiers took over one of the houses to set up
defensive positions and billets, a woman came wailing to Captain Brigandi. She
pointed to a crucifix in the hope of winning sympathy. The captain paused and
showed his own rosary. "If you had believed more in God, and less in Hitler,"
he told her, "all this might not have happened!" Sobered, the woman turned
away.[11]

The Battalion CP opened at Utz at 4 P.M. Utz was a village about 2,500
yards from the Elbe, at the apex of an almost equilateral triangle formed with
Sandfurth (Company L) and Kehnert (Company K)—on the banks of the river
—and Bertingen (Company I) was outside the triangle on the right flank about
equidistant between Kehnert and Utz. The command post moved into the com-
modious quarters of the local "Simon Legree"—the overseer of groups of
imported foreign workers in the vicinity. There was steam heat, bath with hot
and cold running water and luxurious furnishings which filled admirably

    9.   134th Inf., After Action Report, 1 May 45.
    10.   Eldephonse C. Reischel to the Author, July 14, 1946, 134th Inf., After Action Report,
1 May 45.
    11.   J. Huston to I. W. Langston, 25 April 45.

optimum requirements for the headquarters installations and afforded ample comfort for its personnel.[12]

Now the Battalion had reached the banks of the Elbe River. Berlin was scarcely more than 50 miles away—a distance not much greater than that which they had travelled that day! The men might have felt a surge of excitement and anticipation as they thought of being in on the capture of Berlin. Berlin—that was the big objective toward which they had been working since early training days. Everything had been pointed toward the moment when the capital of the foremost enemy would fall; now it appeared to be at hand, and perhaps they of the Third Battalion, 134th Infantry, would be among the first to enter that city. But infantrymen found little joy in contemplating the liberation or capture of any city. To them it would mean just another attack. Any joy would have to be reserved to the completion of the task. Any tendency toward exaltation would be cancelled by the dread of facing hostile guns again. And it appeared that the enemy was going to make a fight for his capital.

Two bridgeheads had been established across the Elbe in the Magdeburg area to the south of the positions which the Third Battalion occupied—one by the 2nd Armored Division, the other by the 83rd Infantry Division. However, the enemy, in a resurgence of power, sent a savage counterattack against the 2nd Armored, and that bridgehead was wiped out.[13] One regiment of the 35th Division—the 320th—went down to reinforce the 83rd Division in maintaining its bridgehead.

The role of the Elbe River bridgeheads in the strategy of the Western Allies is not altogether clear. Perhaps they were meant to facilitate a further advance to the east to meet the Russians. To the small unit observer in the Magdeburg area it looked as though the Ninth Army were making a bid for a rapid drive to Berlin, until the German counterattacks put an end to that notion. If the decision to hold the line of the Elbe River already had been made, there certainly was little point in undertaking the risks of river crossings and setting up a defense in a vulnerable bridgehead with such a formidable defensive barrier as the Elbe River at its back.[14]

In any case it was with some relief that the company commanders, in a meeting at regimental headquarters, learned that the Ninth Army was to await the Russians on its present line.

Nevertheless reconnaissance for crossing sites continued in preparation for a possible change in orders as the 35th Division passed to the control of Maj. Gen. A. C. Gillem's XIII Corps.[15]

Responsible for a frontage of nearly 10,000 yards, the Third Battalion organized its defense on the basis of company strong points. Company I was

---

12. J. Huston to N. F. Huston, 25 April 45.
13. Drew Middleton in **The New York Times**, April 16, 1945, p. 1; John MacCormac, **ibid.**, p. 12; Eisenhower, **Crusade in Europe**, p. 410.
14. General Eisenhower states that he regarded Berlin as no longer having major military importance, and was more interested in reducing the "National Redoubt"—**Report by the Supreme Commander**, p. 107; Butcher reports that as early as March 11, Eisenhower had parried a question on whether he intended to drive for Berlin by discounting its military importance and speaking of the Ruhr as a more important objective—General Bedell Smith explained that the halt at the Elbe was not due to any arrangements with the Russians, and he re-emphasized the greater importance of cutting Germany in two, and of concentrating resources to the south—But Prime Minister Churchill pressed for an Allied entry into Berlin.—**My Three Years with Eisenhower**, pp. 768, 804, 809-810. Ralph Ingersoll maintains that General Bradley made the decision early in April to meet the Russians on the Elbe rather than drive for Berlin, and that this received the approval of General Eisenhower and the American Chiefs of Staff, but was opposed by the British, and led to important differences between President Roosevelt and Prime Minister Churchill—**Top Secret**, pp. 320-325. All this, however, does not explain the bridgeheads across the Elbe river near Magdeburg. cf. Eisenhower, **Crusade in Europe**, pp. 398-403.
15. 3rd Bn. Journal, III, 255.

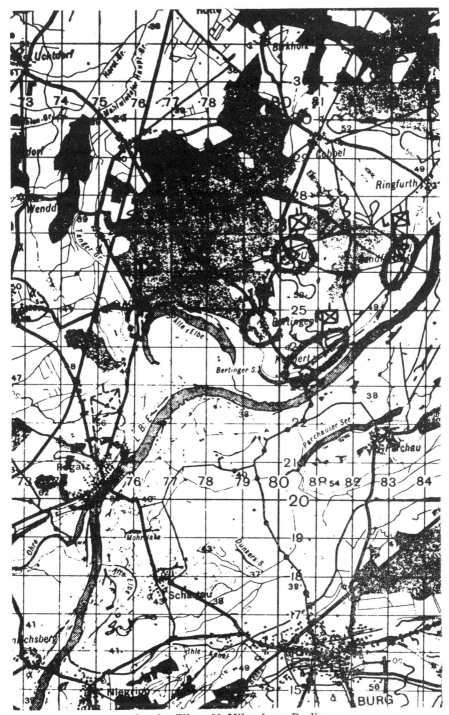

On the Elbe—53 Miles from Berlin

in a position to give protection to the right flank where the large woods called Bertinger Wald was a possible avenue of enemy approach, and at the same time, this company, with a platoon of tank destroyers which reported to it, would be an effective striking force to make a counterattack in case of an enemy penetration. Even this wide frontage was extended by another 4,000 yards when the Battalion received orders to relieve elements of the 30th Division in Rogatz.[16] Actually Rogatz was too large a city to be defended very effectively by one company, (the 30th Division was holding it with a battalion) and even to send one company would deprive the Third Battalion of its reserve. However, Company I, with a section of heavy machine guns and an antitank platoon, made the relief on April 16th.[17]

A reserve is an essential to any defense. There must be depth to the defense, and there must be a force available to make a counterattack. Otherwise if the enemy is able to find an opening or force a penetration through the front line, then the day is his, and he is in a position to overrun the communications and supplies to the rear. And the wider the front, the more essential is a counterattacking force, for it becomes easier for the enemy to find undefended gaps. Therefore, when Company I moved to Rogatz on the right flank of the Battalion sector, Col. Wood brought Company L's 1st Platoon (Ryan) back to Bertingen as reserve.[18]

The other normal defensive measures were taken—mines, trip flares, prepared artillery and mortar concentrations and normal barrages, plans for counterattack. But only the most likely approaches could be covered with available flares and mines, and these were difficult to choose on such a front as this. Contact patrols operated between the companies each night, and motor security patrols operated through the woods to the flanks and rear each day—and usually brought in a few prisoners.[19]

It seemed that there was about as much danger from the rear as from across the river. The 35th Reconnaissance Troop took 480 prisoners out of the forest areas to the rear (through which the Battalion had passed in its final advance) in a week's patrolling.[20] There was the constant threat of "werewolves"—it was not yet known whether the German threats of ruthless guerilla warfare were to be taken seriously. One night a man from the 161st Field Artillery was captured by Germans who took his name, rank, and serial number, and then shot him in the leg and turned him loose.[21] Another night an artillery liaison pilot and his driver were shot to death by machine gun and rocket fire as they drove a jeep along a road in the rear area.[22]

But a testimonial to the disintegration of the enemy's forces was to be seen in the prisoners which were being picked up in small groups. During one week prisoners were found in the regimental area from a pilot training unit, from "Parachute Regiment Von Emmon," war academy personnel, "Task Force Zugek," and an infantry replacement unit.[23]

Yet there was one threat from farther to the rear which might have brought some danger. A force referred to as "Combat Team Clausewitz." It appears that a force of some 1,000 men, with about 40 tanks and self-propelled guns,

16.   134th Inf., After Action Report, 1 May 45.
17.   3rd Bn. Journal, III, 256f.
18.   Ibid.
19.   Ibid., pp. 257-265, passim.
20.   The Santa Fe Express, May 1945, p. 10.
21.   3rd Bn. Journal, III, 259.
22.   Ibid., p. 274.
23.   134th Inf., S-2 Periodic Report, 17-24 April 45.

30 half-tracks, and a considerable number of American trucks and jeeps, had collected, and was bent upon moving south to the Harz Mountains.[24] As far as the Third Battalion was concerned, the principal implication of "Combat Team Clausewitz" was the uneasiness of having an enemy force moving across the lines of communication.

Nor was the enemy entirely passive to the front during this period. On the night of April 16th, two patrols from Company I went down to explore crossing sites on the river. As they went toward the river, the men of one of the patrols noticed a boat carrying about 10 persons across the river at a point in Company K's sector some distance away. Later it turned out that these were civilian women and children, but the warning to Company K had served to put that company on the alert. The patrol continued on its mission: it was to cross the Elbe to reconnoiter the approaches, investigate the current, see if there was a good landing site on the opposite bank. (The second patrol was to undertake a similar mission in the sector of Company L.) As the men floated across the dark river toward the hostile shore, they could hear some activity over there. When they reached the other side a flare went up and they were challenged— but were not fired upon, and were able to return safely.[25] The strange benevolence of the enemy in failing to shoot undoubtedly was due to certain confusion on his part, and to his reluctance to draw attention to himself at this particular time. He was planning a little party of his own.

At 2:30 A.M. Lt. Tom Parris reported that "Krauts" were in his (Company K) sector. Enemy troops made their way through the streets and isolated the 1st Platoon. One group attacked the platoon command post with hand grenades and "bazookas" and knocked out the communications.[26] Private Richard Stoll of New York had seen the enemy coming from his outpost down near the river bank, and, opening fire with his M-1 rifle, he was able to divert and delay the leading groups. Soon it was clear, however, that his position would be overrun; nevertheless he stood his ground and kept firing until he had expended his last round of ammunition. Then Stoll started toward his platoon command post, and though he was wounded badly by enemy fire, he was able to get back in time to give information on the enemy movements.[27] Enemy attackers began to infiltrate through the 1st Platoon's position. One of its squads, in turn, was surrounded. It was imperative that the platoon maintain its integrity if it were to withstand the enemy assault. Staff Sergeant Bertice Womack hurried out into the dark street—a darkness emphasized by contrasting streaks of tracer bullets and an occasional brilliant double flash from the discharge and detonation of a rocket. He ran through the intermittent bursts of fire to reach a building near the surrounded squad; as he entered, the concussion of a rocket knocked him down; but he recovered and went over to a window where he hurled hand grenades out toward the assailants. At once this had effect, and the squad was able to reorganize and repel the enemy from its position.[28]

Meanwhile the platoon and the section of heavy machine guns (Company M) in its area stood fast and poured out fire. The artillery forward observer,

24. 3rd Bn. Journal, III, 264, 266. When a delegation of officers and men from the regiment went back to the vicinity of Corps headquarters on April 19th for a demonstration of recoilless weapons, they found troops disposed in anticipation of possible attack by this force.
25. ibid., pp. 257, 258.
26. ibid., p. 257f.
27. 35th Div., General Orders, No. 34, 22 May 1945.
28. ibid.

isolated at his observation post, remained at his station to keep the artillery fire going. For 40 minutes the artillery continued firing "concentration 221 and 223"—pre-arranged fires covering enemy avenues of approach. The 81 mm mortars added their pre-arranged fires. Some of the enemy seemed to be getting behind "K" Company's right flank, between Kehnert and Bertingen; but Lt. Ryan moved his reserve platoon (Company L) out to set up a defense in front of Bertingen. Lt. Parris sent "K" Company's support to the streets to try to reestablish contact with the 1st. At 4 A.M. the platoon reached the artillery observer. Finally the heavy machine guns brought their fire down on a group of 10 or 12 of the enemy and they broke and fled toward the river. The crisis had passed, though tension remained until daylight. Three dead German paratroopers were found in the street; "K" Company lost one man.[29] Later, civilians reported that the attack had been a planned raid by about 70 men who had been told the location of the Battalion's positions by some of the civilians.[30]

Amidst the heroes that night it seems that there were some who let their comrades down. The company commander sent two men back to Battalion Headquarters; one was charged with fraternizing, the other with drunkenness and being asleep on outpost.[31]

Two companies of the 2nd Battalion relieved Company I in Rogatz on April 16th, and the Third Battalion restored, with one exception, its original disposition of troops. This exception had Company I's 3rd Platoon (Neuhoff) garrison an outpost on an ox-bow lake or bayou (Alte Elbe) in a group of buildings along the Battalion's right flank—3,500 yards of woods separated this platoon from the remainder of "I" Company in Bertingen.[32]

Trip flares around the Company I outpost platoon had to be replaced almost every day, as there were encounters with enemy patrols about every night. Enemy artillery was coming into various parts of the Battalion area from time to time now too. On the other hand, the liaison officer and the forward observers with the Third Battalion directed fire on observed targets throughout the days: small groups of enemy soldiers, river barges, activity in Burg, or around the Blumenthal mine, all came in for their share of fire.[33]

One evening Lt. Hodges thought that he might lure some of the enemy into a trap. He had learned that the enemy was sending parties across the river to pick up civilians on a signal of making a circular motion with a lighted cigarette. The enemy password that night was supposed to be ELBE-ERTEI-DIGUNG. A patrol went down to the river—tramped up and down the river bank a thousand yards, then waited at the designated spot, lit cigarettes and waved them—but nothing happened.[34]

Moved by repeated reports that the enemy across the river was receiving information from civilians, military government officers made plans to evacuate all civilians who were within five kilometers of the river. A warning that such a move was anticipated was given to the Battalion April 18th. Next evening rules were published to govern the evacuation which would take place between 7 A.M. and 5 P.M. the 20th. U. S. transportation would be furnished for the aged and lame; only necessary clothing and bedding were to be taken along;

29.   3rd Bn. Journal III, 257-259.
30.   ibid., p. 263.
31.   ibid., p. 259.
32.   134th Inf., After Action Report, 1 May 45; 3rd Bn. Journal, III, 260-262.
33.   ibid., pp. 262-280, passim.
34.   ibid., pp. 265, 266.

extra food was to be packed, one box per family, and left in front of the door to be picked up later; no livestock would be permitted on the highway except that drawing wagons; all traffic was to keep to the right side of the road; civilians could return to their homes only when authorized by the military government.[35]

The departure of the civilians was a boon to the frustrated farmers of the Battalion. Now they found an opportunity to practice such domestic arts—so long unused—as tending gardens and looking after and milking cattle. In fact a number of measures were taken to relieve the food shortage when extended lines of communication could furnish little more than K rations for some time. The S-4 took over the town bakery, and one man from each company kitchen worked there to turn out rolls and pastries; in addition to that he supervised the pasteurization of milk for local consumption. Meat supplies were replenished occasionally with rabbits or a deer from the Kaiser's former hunting grounds—the victims of a carbine, or rifle, or possibly even automatic rifle or machine gun.[36]

Much as he had been opposed to the acquisition of any enemy motor vehicles—he felt that the extra work which they always required meant neglect of the regular organizational vehicles, and the extreme difficulty of replacing parts and keeping them in repair made them more a liability than an asset—even Lt. Reischel, the Battalion motor officer, was proud of the three trucks—Chevrolets and Ford—which had been picked up at the enemy motor park. In fact, one of them was a well-equipped ordnance truck which he turned into a very efficient maintenance vehicle—"We Fix 'Em." Crews painted the trucks olive drab, and got them in running order against the day when the Battalion would be making another move.[37]

Another change in the leadership of the Third Battalion came on April 19th when Lt. Col. Frederick C. Roecker, Jr., youthful West Pointer from Walla Walla, Washington, took command of the Battalion. Lt. Col. Warren C. Wood, who had taken command of the Battalion during the race across France, had been wounded on "Blue Monday," and then had rejoined the Battalion during the "Battle of the Bulge," was returning to the United States on leave. Col. Roecker had been commander of the 2nd Battalion, but he had been evacuated with wounds repeatedly. He had come back to the regiment lately—during the final operations in the Ruhr pocket—and now was taking over a new command.

Immediately the new commander set upon reconnaissance of the river, and began to make tentative plans for an attack across that barrier. He and the company commanders, the executive officer (Captain Rubottom), the S-2, and S-3, all made flights in artillery liaison planes for an aerial reconnaissance of the river.[38]

It turned out, however, that the enemy was more bent on making attacks across the river in that particular sector than were the Americans. An observer out on the night of 22-23 April would have noticed about the usual activity of the area—flares going up occasionally—the usual flares and firing down in the direction of the Company I outpost platoon—friendly artillery firing an occasional round of interdiction and harassing fire—an occasional burst of machine gun fire in the distance. But around 5:15 A.M. his attention would have been

35. **ibid.**, pp. 261, 265, 267.
36. J. Huston to N. F. Huston, 25 April 45.
37. Reischel, **loc. cit.**
38. 3rd Bn. Journal, III, 267.

drawn toward Kehnert by sharp bursts of a "burp gun," and soon after an opening up of all kinds of fire. Company K was being attacked again.[39]

The first action was against Company K's outpost down near the river in front of the town, when machine pistols opened fire. Men on the outpost moved back to a building, and the Germans closed in for a frontal attack against the 3rd Platoon. A rocket fired a barn next to where the outpost had withdrawn. The enemy gained entrance to the buildings along the southeast side of the main street, but the platoon held firm and fired back from across the street. Now three or four buildings were ablaze to lend a reddish light to the eerie scene. But the enemy was making his main effort against the left flank. Here the approach to the town was across a flat meadow, and the light machine gun section had been set up at the edge of the field—beside one of the last buildings in town—to cover this flank. As the German squads deployed to come across the meadow the machine gun section opened fire. One gun failed to fire after the initial burst, but the other increased its rate; firing from free traverse it covered the whole area with grazing fire. The house next to the machine gun position was set on fire by grenades and panzerfaust; but the gunner kept up his rapid firing—some enemy were killed within five yards of his position. Combining with the machine gun to halt the attack was the other section of the company weapons platoon: the 60 mm mortars. The "60" was only a simple, 28 inch-long, 12-pound tube with a 16-pound bipod, and a 12-pound baseplate; its maximum range was listed as 1,935 yards, and its minimum range was 100 yards. It was the latter—minimum range—that the mortar men were interested in on this particular morning. As the machine gun pinned down enemy troops, the "60's" sent out round after round in a pattern of bursts that covered the whole field. The observer had gone up to a post near the machine gun. Closer and closer he called for the fire, until mortar tubes seemed to be pointing almost straight up; the fire was brought in as close as ten yards to the friendly positions. Artillery forward observers from Company K and Company L brought down fire on the far side of the river to break up additional enemy groups. Again the attack was beaten off. Company K had three men wounded—one of these an aid man—and one man killed.[40]

With the coming of daylight it was possible to see what had happened. The battalion commander and the S-3 went forward to visit the scene. They were impressed by the row of dead Germans on the flat meadow who had been caught by the light machine gun and by the 60 mm mortars. They paused beside the dead American in the street—his head had been riddled by machine pistol bullets. "That is probably the last man of the Third Battalion to be killed in this war," the S-3 said. The battalion commander nodded.

"I suspect that is right," he said, "let's hope so."

The enemy's toll had been 17 killed, seven wounded and captured, and 12 others taken prisoner. They said that 50 had been in the attacking force, and 50 others had been waiting on the other side of the river to come over afterward.[41] Meanwhile Company I's 3rd Platoon sent in eight prisoners who had come from Rogatz and run into the trip flares.[42] With the American position improving daily, with the Russians approaching from the east, what the enemy

39. **Ibid.**, 275f.
40. **Ibid.**, pp. 276-279.
41. **Ibid.**, p. 279; 134th Inf., After Action Report, 1 May 45.
42. 3rd Bn. Journal, III, 277f.

hoped to achieve by dissipating the meager forces remaining to him in these futile local attacks is difficult to see. Even had he been successful in capturing Kehnert, he did not have sufficient strength to build up an effective bridgehead. That it was a nuisance value against the Third Battalion there is no doubt, but it is no less certain that it had no permanent effect on contributing to the German defense in those final days.

In order to discourage any further attempts of that kind, Col. Roecker obtained permission to launch another of the Third Battalion's "attacks by fire." An impressive ruse might persuade the enemy to become more defense-minded. Units on right and left were notified so that they would not think that a counterattack was coming, and a program of fires arranged. Artillery fired a 10-minute preparation beginning at 4 A.M. At 4:10 the 81 mm mortars and heavy machine guns began firing; at 4:15 the light machine guns and 60 mm mortars joined the firing. All ceased at 4:30. There was no reaction from the enemy—but neither were there any such attacks.[43]

The 1st Machine Gun Platoon was planning to fire long range harassing fire on Blumenthal No. 2—reported to be headquarters for enemy activity—after dusk the next evening. But a new development prevented carrying out the plan. For all except observed enemy targets, the Elbe River had been established as a no-fire line! This meant the Russians must be coming.[44]

Not until very lately had General Eisenhower been able to make any arrangements with the Russians for mutual identification. (It is not unlikely that the danger of a collision had led to the arbitrary selection of the Elbe River as the limit of American advance in this sector.) There had not even been any coordination or exchange of information at the strategic level until the Supreme Commander had sent a military mission to Moscow in January 1945. Already in early April there had been unfortunate exchanges of shots between the air forces, and as ground forces approached each other a system of identification became more imperative. "Solutions were not forthcoming until the last minute." After recommendations by the army group commanders, "a system of recognition signs and signals was eventually arranged by 20 April."[45]

This information got down to the Third Battalion on the evening of April 22nd. The Russian identification signal was two red flares, and the American answer was to be three green flares—but the companies were warned to beware of enemy ruses.[46]

Lt. Frank Snyder, Communications Officer, sent up a supply of the green pyrotechnics to each of the companies. Either the power of suggestion had an immediate effect or company observers at once became more watchful, for although no *red* flares had been reported previously, there were no less than five reports—from all companies—within three hours after the information had been given out. When both "K" and "L" reported red flares at 10:05 P.M., the latter answered with three green.[47] Whether the red signals were from distant Russian troops, or whether they represented enemy activity never was determined. In view of the enemy's attack the next morning, however, the latter suggestion probably is the least unlikely. Newspaper corres-

43. *ibid.*, pp. 281, 284.
44. *ibid.*, p. 285.
45. General Eisenhower's Report, p. 110.
46. 3rd Bn. Journal, III, 274. As a matter of fact the Germans who attacked Company K on the following morning were carrying a Vary pistol with green flares.—*ibid.*, p. 278.
47. *ibid.*, p. 275.

pondents were moving along the front trying to guess the place where contact would be made. High-ranking officers shared the excitement with the front-line soldiers in anticipating the long-awaited meeting.

There had been a rumor on April 22nd that troops in the 83rd Division's bridgehead had observed Russian tanks and aircraft.[48] Then at 4:44 P.M. on April 24th the Battalion received word that, according to a German report, Yanks and Russians had made contact at Torgau.[49]

That same evening Lt. Tracy, regimental liaison officer, brought a message to Battalion headquarters which was calculated to be more cause for exaltation among infantrymen of the Third Battalion than any possible order for an attack on Berlin: the 35th Division was to move back very soon to clear out any remaining groups of enemy and "occupy and govern" an area in the vicinity of Hannover—duration: indefinite.[50] Apparently the European war was just about over for the Third Battalion. Men could permit themselves to hope to reach home; a thing which had seemed so far away as to be almost beyond hope sometimes now was at hand.

The men felt very deeply the need for preventing the repetition of such a conflict as they had seen. Efforts aiming in that direction were forming back in the United States: the United Nations Conference on International Organization was opening that April 25th in San Francisco. Churches throughout America would be joining in a day of prayer for the success of the conference.[51]

Hours before dawn's light came to San Francisco, men of the Third Battalion met in a sunrise service of their own. They met in a small white church, a church which had stood unused for 15 years, in a small village called Utz, near the Elbe River, in Germany. The attendance was not large—church percentage of attendance among military men seldom was very much greater than it was among the general civilian population, and in view of the recent early-morning attacks, the companies' defensive strength could not be impaired. Nevertheless the battalion commander and members of his staff were there, and officers and men from each of the companies were there. As the steel-helmeted soldiers, all carrying loaded weapons, filed into the little church, now brilliant as the white morning sunlight poured through its windows, Sergeant Paul Lundmark sat down to the chaplain's field organ to play a prelude. After the Chaplain's call to Worship, the group joined in singing "Saviour like Shepard." One of the staff officers read from the Bible:

48. **ibid.**, p. 272.
49. **ibid.**, p. 285. Ensor, **A Miniature History of the War**, p. 98, and Shugg and DeWeerd, **World War II**, pp. 351, give April 26th as the date for the link-up. General Marshall's Report, p. 51, General Eisenhower's Report, p. 107, and Miller, **History of World War II**, p. 846, give April 25th as the date. Drew Middleton in **The New York Times**, April 28, 1945, states that the first official contact was at 4:40 P.M. on "Wednesday"—which would be April 25th; but on p. 3 of the same paper is a dispatch from London dated April 27 which refers to the link-up "yesterday." Marshal Stalin's Order of the Day (**The New York Times**, April 28, 1945, p. 3) states that contact was made "at 1330 on April 25th in the area of the town of Torgau; General Bradley's Order of the Day (**ibid.**) gives the time as 1640 hours. The British report from London (U.P. **ibid.**) stated that General Eisenhower had reported that American and Russian division commanders had met at 4 P.M. on April 26th at Torgau, but that first contact was made at 4:40 P.M. on the 25th. In a report written on April 27th, Richard C. Hottelet (in **From D-Day Through Victory in Europe**, reprinted in Commager, **The Story of World War II**, pp. 549f.) describes a contact by one patrol at 1:32 on Wednesday afternoon (25th), and states that a few hours later another patrol made contact at Torgau, and some Russian officers returned to the American headquarters, which "made it official." The link-up first was announced by SHAEF in its communique 385, April 28th (**The New York Times**, April 29, 1945, p. 2.) but no date for it is given. Some of the confusion probably was due to the fact that news dispatches were datelined the 27th, which might suggest that it occurred on the 26th, and some of the references may be to the meeting between division commanders on the 26th. Possibly the entry in the 3rd Battalion Journal for 1644 hours, 24 April, is due to another example of "uncanny" German prophecy.
50. **ibid.**
51. **The New York Times**, April 26, 1945, p. 6.

The people that walked in darkness have seen a great light: they that dwell in the land of the shadow of death, upon them hath the light shined.

Thou hast multiplied the nation, and increased the joy: they joy before thee according to the joy in harvest, and as men rejoice when they divide the spoil.

For thou hast broken the yoke of his burden, and the staff of his shoulder, the rod of his oppressor, as in the day of Midian. For every battle of the warrior is with confused noise and garments rolled in blood; but this shall be with burning and fuel of fire.

For unto us a child is born, unto us a son is given: and the government shall be upon his shoulder: and his name shall be called Wonderful, Counsellor, The Mighty God, The everlasting Father, The Prince of Peace.

Of the increase of his government and peace there shall be no end, upon the throne of David, and upon his kingdom, to order it, and to establish it with judgment and with justice from henceforth even forever. The zeal of the Lord of hosts will perform this. (Isaiah 9:2-7)

Corporal Gordan Cross, medical technician, sang a solo, "Be Still My Soul" *(Finlandia)*. Then the Chaplain rose to the pulpit for a brief talk. He spoke of the conference which would be opening that day, of how difficult the task would be which the delegates would face, but of how important their success would be. Against a background of organ music, the chaplain prayed for the early return of peace to the world, and for the success of the United Nations Conference in its efforts to make peace lasting. Another member of the staff read a selection of poetry, and then another passage from Isaiah 55:8-13 :

For my thoughts are not your thoughts, neither are your ways my ways, saith the Lord.

For as the heavens are higher than the earth, so are my ways higher than your ways, and my thoughts than your thoughts.

For as the rain cometh down, and the snow from heaven, and returneth not thither, but watereth the earth, and maketh it bring forth the bud, that it may give seed to the sower, and bread to the eater:

So shall my word be that goeth forth out of my mouth: it shall not return unto me void, but it shall accomplish that which I please, and it shall prosper in the thing whereto I sent it.

For ye shall go out with joy, and be led forth with peace: The mountains and hills shall break forth before you into singing, and all the trees of the field shall clap their hands.

Instead of the thorn shall come up the fir tree, and instead of the brier shall come up the myrtle tree: and it shall be to the Lord for a name, for an everlasting sign that shall not be cut off.

And they sang a hymn—"I Would Be True"—and, with the Chaplain's benediction, went out.[52]

---

52. Chaplain Alexander C. Walker to the Author, July 26, 1946; J. Huston to N. F. Huston, April 25, 1945, and to I. W. Langston, April 25, 1945.

CHAPTER XXVI

★ ★ ★

WAR'S END

★ ★ ★

Continuing patrol activity, the discharge of flares, scattered firing, additional enemy stragglers all required that the Third Battalion maintain its vigilance during the remainder of its stay on the Elbe.[1] But elements of the 407th Infantry (102nd Division) relieved the Third Battalion on April 26th, and the companies assembled in Utz and Bertingen to prepare for their first major move to the west.

When it came off the line that day the Battalion possibly was at the peak of its combat efficiency. At any rate its personnel was made up, for the most part, of veterans of at least two campaigns. In earlier operations, in Normandy, or Saarland, or the Ardennes, few veterans had survived. Still men had been hurt, and crippled, and killed, but not in the numbers of other days. During the operations in the Ruhr pocket (after April 1st) and to the Elbe, the Battalion had had 81 casualties: Company I, 29; K, 24; L, 13; M, 15.[2] A greater number had *died* in *two weeks* in the Normandy campaign. The Battalion had lost more men both on "Bloody Sunday" and on "Blue Monday" than it lost during any of the three months February, March or April. Moreover, Lt. "Courtney" Hodges, had broken the jinx with Company I!

Enemy material destroyed or captured by the Battalion during its "dash to the Elbe" included 30 staff cars and motor trucks, 25 motorcycles, 30 electric generators, four searchlight batteries, three multiple antiaircraft machine guns, 50 machine pistols, 500 faustpatrones ("fist bazookas"), a signal equipment depot including scores of batteries, radios, and parts.[3]

But now combat had ended. Men of the Third Battalion looked forward to their new assignment, and anticipated the announcement of the end of the war in Europe.

The Third Battalion's motor caravan—a column of 65 vehicles—crossed the IP at Bertingen at 7:35 A.M. on April 27th and moved to the west over a route well-marked as the "Santa Fe Trail." After a journey of seven and one half hours, the Battalion arrived in its assigned area—an area south of Hameln, 30 to 40 miles southwest of Hannover. "Heinie trucks" and four-wheel trailers, carrying supplies, travelled in a separate regimental march unit.[4]

Though some local adjustments were made later, Company I was assigned a sector around Kirchback, Company K an area around Ottenstein, Company L Baarsen, Company M, Berry. Headquarters Company was not assigned a separate area—except for Hehlen, the town it occupied—but the Antitank Platoon and Ammunition and Pioneer Platoon were to be for motorized "riot squads" to be available for despatch to any part of the area.[5]

1. 3rd Bn. Journal, III, 286-293.
2. 134th Inf., Battle Casualty Report. Company I had had four men wounded when a grenade dropped off a pack and exploded.—3rd Bn. Journal, III, 256.
3. 3rd Bn. Journal, III, 290f.
4. ibid., pp. 292-296.
5. ibid., pp. 293-295.

Companies were widely separated, and each was given the responsibility for a number of towns. The company itself maintained its integrity as a unit in some central location, but guards would be posted on important installations wherever they might be found, and jeep patrols toured the areas to maintain order. Company officers visited the burgomasters in the respective towns to coordinate the dissemination and enforcement of rules of the military government. In their own garrison towns, the companies established interior guards and had formal guard mounts and relief of guard each day. New emphasis was put upon discipline in order to command the respect of the enemy civilian population.[6]

Distance between companies was great. It required an hour and a half for a messenger to make a round trip to Companies I and M, and the route to Companies K and L, in the other direction was just as long.[7]

The regimental CP was 30 miles from the Battalion CP; telephone messages were inaudible much of the time.[8] All of this meant greater independence for the local commanders.

Most men of the Battalion had been able to find quarters the like of which they had not dared dream a few months earlier. Away from the centers of population, the beauty of the rolling—frequently wooded—countryside and the neat towns had escaped the ravages of the war. Battalion headquarters located in a picturesque, finely-furnished castle, at the edge of Hehlen, on the Weser.

But it was for Company L to acquire the greatest luxury—and the greatest headache—when a boundary change extended the area to the west, and the company moved in to take over the resort town of Bad Pyrmont. There were in the city approximately 80 hospitals and convalescent homes with a total of 3,000 patients from the German army. With the facilities at their disposal, medical staffs, under the command of a German Colonel, were functioning with the usual German efficiency.[9] Here men of Company L had an opportunity to see some of the results of American artillery fire; here black, decaying feet showed them how the German too had suffered from the cold during his Ardennes offensive; and they saw lingering wounds, full of infection, failing to heal for want of a "wonder drug" like penicillin. Regimental medical officers and CIC teams undertook the big task of inspecting and screening the patients with a view to evacuating them.

Captain Brigandi divided most of his time between his company and the city hall. There was a constant stream of visitors seeking an audience with the American commander—food rationing had to be adjusted, order maintained, banks opened, bakeries and other shops kept functioning. Brigandi assigned a lieutenant to full time duty with the burgomaster at the Rathaus. "Being mayor of Syracuse [New York] ought to be a cinch for me," he said.

The administrative tasks of organizing and governing an area were not small, but there appeared to be little diffiuclty from the German civilians, and activities seemed to function smoothly. Straggling German soldiers continued to be picked up from time to time, but they caused little trouble. What local disturbances did occur occasionally to irritate the occupying troops stemmed mostly from sources other than the indigenous population. There

6. Ibid., p. 296ff.
7. Ibid., p. 297.
8. The regimental area covered 1,000 square miles and included 166 towns. 134th Inf.,. After Action Report, 1 June 1945.
9. 3rd Bn. Journal, III, 299; 134th Inf., After Action Report, 1 May 45.

was a report that some American colored engineer troops had been teaming up with Poles to make trouble in the vicinity of Lauenstein in Company M's area; some previous authority had posted a few French guards in Bad Pyrmont, and they were reported to be creating disturbances among the civilians; there were a few Belgian soldiers in the area, and though they made every effort at cooperation with the Americans, sometimes their unannounced rifle practice was not calculated to allay battle-worn nerves.[10]

An important boost to morale developed during this period: furloughs to the French Riviera for a small number of lucky men.[11] And now other activities could be conducted. One day the companies were able to show a motion picture, "A Tree Grows in Brooklyn;" the next day a quota from the Battalion went to Hannover for a concert by violinist Jascha Heifetz; the next day there was a USO show made up of Russian entertainers, a "PX" ration was distributed, the regimental band played for Retreat.[12]

Meanwhile the Battalion watched developments on the fighting fronts. A war map in the operations room showed graphically the complete disintegration of the German resistance. At 6:45 P.M. on May 2nd the Battalion learned that the German armies in Northern Italy had surrendered; at 10:30 that evening came the news of the fall of Berlin to the Russians; at 8 A.M. May 5th, a news flash announced the capitulation of all German troops in Northwestern Germany, the Netherlands, and Denmark to Field Marshal Montgomery.[13]

A shift in assignments was effective May 6th. Elements of the 137th Infantry relieved Company L in Bad Pyrmont, and the 654th Tank Destroyer Battalion moved in to assume responsibility for the remainder of the area. The Third Battalion moved to the city of Hannover.

A city of 472,000,[14] Hannover had enjoyed a long history as a royal, and later a provincial, capital. Its prominent buildings, its opera house, theater, polytechnic institute, its noted library, had established it as a cultural center; manufacturers of machinery, chemicals, precious metals, pianos, had given it prominence as an industrial city.[15] But for this importance it was doomed to destruction by Allied air forces.

British officers already had set up military government on three levels: province, region, and city, and the German administration was functioning. The American units would not have the same responsibility here which they had had in the other area. But the Third Battalion was assigned a major section of the city to occupy and supervise. Principal duties now involved the maintenance of guards at certain points, controlling the population and the displaced persons and investigating and guarding SHAEF " 'T' Targets" in the area.

As might be expected under the circumstances, the restless displaced persons presented the biggest problem, and constant patrolling was necessary to enforce curfew regulations.[16]

10. 3rd Bn. Journal, III, 303, 304, 306.
11. ibid., p. 300.
12. 134th Inf., Daily Log, V, 3-5 May 1945.
13. ibid., pp. 304, 305, 307.
14. The World Almanac, 1946, p. 381.
15. Lippincott's Gazetteer, p. 794.
16. But it seemed that the Russians were so happy to see the Americans that the latter could do nothing to offend them. When patrols picked up groups of the roaming DP's who were on the streets after curfew and committed them to a large, above-surface, concrete air raid shelter for the night, the gay Russians only appeared on the streets again the next night carrying musical instruments and blankets—they were waiting for the Americans to pick them up and take them to their "Night Club"

During its first 12 days on occupation duty the regiment evacuated approximately 30,000 French, Belgian, and Dutch displaced persons from the Hannover area. People were being returned to their homelands by train at approximately 1,400 a day. Approximately the same number of Poles and Russians remained in the area. Two Russian officers were assigned to the Division military government team to locate camps where the Russians could be assembled. There were seven Polish officers in the area to assist in handling the Polish DP's.[17]

Although there was sure to be some errors, the descriptions of the key "SHAEF Targets" which Army intelligence had prepared were found to be highly accurate—and in most cases this accuracy had been matched by Allied bombardiers. The task of checking these locations fell to Lt. Charles Hall who had come to Battalion Headquarters (from the Ammunition and Pioneer Platoon) as S-2 when Lt. Hanna left that post to fill the vacancy as adjutant and S-1 created by Capt. Mangnuson's leave to the United States. The companies inspected those in their areas and posted guards. Outstanding among these targets was the giant Hanomag Works—where armored vehicles and very large caliber artillery had been produced; it had been only partially destroyed. Another was the destroyed Continental Gumms Works rubber factory: there was a smaller hardly damaged plant which had manufactured parts for airplanes and naval machinery; another, half destroyed, had made ammunition boxes; there was another rubber factory which was not damaged; other "targets" which had escaped destruction included a pair of large stone buildings—one a finance building, the other a police station.[18]

In the absence of Col. Roecker who was on a three-day leave, Captain Rubottom was called to regimental headquarters on the morning of May 7th for a meeting of battalion commanders. When he returned to the Battalion CP at 10:15 he handed a typewritten note to the S-3. Traditionally the dispenser of bad news to company commanders, the operations officer welcomed the opportunity for a new role. He stepped to the telephone and put in a conference call to all the companies; then he read slowly from the slip of paper the anticlimactical news:

General Miltonberger called the following message:

A representative of the German High Command signed the unconditional surrender of all German land, sea, and air forces in Europe to the AEF and simultaneously to the USSR at 0141 B.C.E. time, 7 May 45, under which all forces under the German command cease operations at 0001, 9 May 45. Effective immediately all offensive operations by AEF cease and all troops will remain in present locations. Troops on occupation duty continue mission. Due to communication difficulties, there may be some delay in similar announcement reaching enemy troops so full offensive resource will be taken. No release will be made to press, pending an announcement by England, the United States and USSR.

C. G., XIII Corps.[19]

17.   134th Inf., **Daily Log**, V, 9 May 45.
18.   3rd Bn. Journal, III, 308-310.
19.   **Ibid.,** pp. 310-11.

EPILOGUE

I

Though the news that at last hostilities had ended in Europe doubtless brought joy to the hearts of the men of the Third Battalion, there was no reason for enthusiastic demonstrations, and there were none. After all, the Third Battalion already was performing occupation duties, and the fact that the German forces had surrendered formally would have, little immediate effect upon the situation in Hannover. Yet, now a soldier could permit himself to dwell upon thoughts of returning home with an added assurance that such thoughts would be realized. Now it appeared unlikely that any critical situation would develop to require a recall to fighting fronts.

However, there still was war in the Pacific, and men began to speculate on their chances for avoiding or participating in that Japanese phase. Although the War Department had announced plans for beginning demobilization after VE (Victory in Europe) Day—with priority for discharges to be arranged according to a point system based on credit for length of service, overseas service, campaign stars, awards, and dependent children[1]—it likewise took steps to emphasize that the task of eliminating Japan remained to be done. Weeks before the termination of hostilities against Germany, a motion picture had been prepared for showing to all troops as soon as practicable after the German surrender. Titled "Two Down and One to Go," the film presented statements from Army chiefs in Washington which pointed out that two of the three Axis partners—Italy and Germany—had been eliminated, but now effort must be concentrated toward elimination of the third— Japan. Five days after VE day, members of the Third Battalion saw the film in Hannover.[2] The success of such appeals as this film in generating enthusiasm among these infantrymen in Europe for a continuation of the war in the Pacific remains problematical. This was the same disheartening reward for success on the strategic level with which the infantryman had become familiar on a tactical level—on the successful completion of a mission or capture of an objective, there always was a new assignment to be expected. "Two Down and One to Go" probably even had somewhat of a depressing effect— here was a threat to that newly-found security which V-E day had promised. One consolation was that the unit probably would go via the States if it drew an assignment to the Pacific. (Actually it developed later that a rather large proportion of the men elected to remain even though they had sufficient points for discharge; but other considerations doubtless entered into this decision— one principal one was that sooner or later they probably would have to go to the Pacific anyway, and, that being the case, they would rather go with their own regiment.)

When movement orders came two weeks later, they prescribed further occupation duties, but there was the advantage that the movement was to be to the southwest—a direction more likely to mean an earlier return home. However, whether or not this would be an advantage would depend upon the

---

1. General Marshall's Report, p. 116.
2. 134th Inf., **Daily Log**, VI, May 12, 1945.

point of view. An early return to the United States doubtless would mean that this was only the first step toward redeployment to the Pacific Ocean Area. All American troops in northern Germany were moving south and west to new areas, for the regions around Hannover and Hamburg and the Ruhr were in the British zone of occupation, while those around the Elbe River had been assigned to the Russians. There was an indication, however, that the 35th Division's occupation mission was not to be of long duration, for its new area under the Fifteenth Army, was to be in the vicinity of Coblenz— an area destined to come under French control.

There was an interim stop of five days for the Third Battalion, however, in the vicinity of Beckum (approximately 30 miles southeast of Munster). Moving by motor, the Battalion had travelled much of the way over the smooth super highway known as the "Autobahn," (Reichsautobahnen) and it established its command post just off the highway in Vellern.[3]

Orders for the longer trip came on May 26th. This time only the organic transportation went by highway—a distance of 185 miles. For the men not assigned to motor vehicles, it was a movement by rail—a military movement in the European tradition. It required two days for the trains—made up of box cars of the "40 and 8" size, each crowded with men—to reach their destination over a circuitous route which took them across the Rhine at Wesel, then all the way to Roermond (in the Netherlands), and on through Maastricht, Aachen, Duren, and back to the Rhine at Bonn. At last, on the 29th, the troops arrived at Neidermendig where they detrained to proceed to assigned areas in neighboring towns.[4]

Adopting a pattern of organization similar to that under which it had administered its area south of Hannover, the Battalion quickly adjusted itself to the new assignment. Headquarters set up the command post at Kottenheim (about five miles northeast of Mayen and 18 miles west of Coblenz), and the companies moved to convenient locations in other towns through the Landkreis. Again Company L went to the largest city—Andernach, on the banks of the Rhine about 12 miles northwest of Coblenz.[5]

Men of the Third Battalion were on occupation duty in an area not far distant from that which some of their fathers had occupied with the Third Army in 1919, and their activities seemed to be not very different from those of 26 years earlier. Men of 1919 had found themselves participating in training programs calling for drills, exercises and studies in the morning, and athletics and recreation in the afternoon; there had been a system of granting leaves and furloughs to France, Belgium, England, and three-day passes to nearer points; there had been shows and exhibitions, and football games, and baseball games, and there had been general and vocational education schools, and special schools for officer training.[6] And so men of the Third Battalion now, aside from motor patrols and other duties of local supervision, participated in training programs—drill and instruction and inspections in the morning, and athletics in the afternoon; there were leaves and furloughs to France and

3. 3rd Bn. S-2 Notebook.
4. 134th Inf., **Daily Log**, V, 26-29 May, 1945; **Santa Fe Express**, June 1, 1945, p. 6.
5. **Ibid.** The American 3rd Division had occupied Andernach after World War I.—Col. Elbridge Colby, "A Soldier Looks at Military Government," **The Infantry Journal**, LII (March 1943, 52.
6. Society of the First Division, **History of the First Division** (Philadelphia: 1922), pp. 248-250.

England; there were U.S.O. shows and motion pictures, and baseball games, and a school for officer training.[7]

In fact one of the big sporting events of the occupation—a baseball game between the 35th Division's "Santa Fe Indians" and the 106th Division's "Lion Cubs"—was a part of a program dedicating the re-opening of a stadium at Coblenz which first had been used by American occupation troops in 1920. American engineers had built the arena at that time. With the withdrawal of American forces, the French had taken over the area and soccer replaced baseball. It reverted to German control in 1929 and became the scene of track meets, football games, and horse races. In 1932 an afternoon crowd of 15,000 people had gathered to hear Adolf Hitler plead for election to the German presidency. Two years later, swastikas and bright lights greeted Propaganda Minister Joseph Goebbels when he came to the stadium to speak. The concrete structure had been completed in 1937 when it was renamed "Hermann Goering Stadium." Bombing raids in July and August 1944 had damaged the stadium badly, but engineers of the 35th Division had worked with several hundred German prisoners—and used 150 truckloads of rubble to fill craters in the field—to repair the stadium for its dedication July 1st.[8]

Shortly after the dedication of the Santa Fe Stadium, the Third Battalion participated in the dedication of a regimental baseball park. Here bleachers had been erected to seat 500, and companies had contributed big signboards to make a colorful board fence. The dedication program had included a flag-raising ceremony, an appearance by the regimental band, some brief speeches, an exhibition by Company I's Battalion championship drill platoon, and a victorious baseball game with the Division Special Troops.[9]

The Company I drill platoon, mentioned above, had won its distinction as Battalion champion as the result of a drill contest conducted on the Battalion field at Kottenheim. Subsequently, however, a platoon from Company M edged out the Company I unit in a regimental contest.[10]

Men found additional worthwhile activity in the schools and study courses offered by the Information and Education program.[11] Designed to keep the soldier informed about the events of which he was a part as well as of news from home, the I & E Division's program throughout the war had included radio service, publication of newspapers and magazines, orientation lectures, educational projects, information films, distribution of books and popular magazines.[12]

Soon it became known that the 35th was among the divisions scheduled for "redeployment" to the Pacific. But if men were concerned about the ultimate destination of their division, they soon found that its fate did not necessarily include their own. Already the "readjustment" program was beginning to operate: "high point men who would not be eligible for service with the 35th Division in the Pacific were transferred to units destined for eventual return to the United States for discharge and inactivation. Low point men were assigned to the 35th to replace those with longer service."[13] However, the

7. 134th Inf., **Daily Log**, V, 29 May-10 July, 1945.
8. 35th Inf. Div., **Dedication of the Santa Fe Stadium; Official Program**, July 1, 1945, pp. 12-13.
9. E. C. Reischel to the author, July 14, 1946. Both the division baseball manager and the regimental manager had come from the Third Battalion: Lt. W. D. Hodges, and Lt. E. C. Reischel respectively.
10. 134th Inf., **Daily Log**, V, 30 June, 1945.
11. **Santa Fe**, p. 196.
12. General Marshall's Report, pp. 111-112; **Santa Fe Express**, June 4, 1945, p. 1.
13. **Santa Fe**, p. 196.

process was a gradual one, and numbers of officers and men elected to remain with their unit—to serve with it until the war should be finished in all theaters. This made possible, then, a preservation of some of the unit's continuity and integrity.

The first step in a division's "redeployment" was to move to one of the camps—tent cities—which had been set up in the vicinity of Reims under a newly-organized Assembly Area Command. For the 35th Division, this movement began on July 11th.[14] Relieved of occupation duties by elements of the 5th French Regiment (10th Division) on July 10th, the Third Battalion assembled in Andernach on the 12th and entrained for Camp "Norfolk." This was to be the last move in those small European boxcars. The Battalion arrived at the Sommesous station in the heat of mid-day on the 13th, and motor trucks carried the men to their area in the camp hardly more than a mile away.[15] (Camp Norfolk—named, as were the other camps of the Assembly Area, for an American city—was about 15 miles southwest of Chalons - sur - Marne.) Next day, men were taking passes to Troyes to join in the celebration of Bastille Day.

The work for units in the Assembly Area was cut out for them: personnel rosters would have to be prepared, a physical profile completed, showdown inspection, some equipment turned in, other property crated for shipment, certificates prepared for baggage and freight, identification tags checked, service records checked and brought up to date, steps taken to discontinue mail service, certain training requirements to be met. All this must be done as prescribed in the theater directive, "POM-Red" (Preparation for Overseas Movement—Redeployment) before the division could leave for the United States.[16]

Soon after arrival at the camp, Col. Roecker outlined to the company commanders this work that had to be done. And there were other points of detail for the commanders to note—all weapons to be collected, American or enemy, and including all straight razors and knives having a three-inch blade—commanders to submit a certificate that this had been accomplished . . . kitchen grease traps to be cleaned daily—on penalty of a fine for failure . . . a latrine orderly to be on duty 24 hours a day . . . all soldiers to shave daily, "whether they need it or not" . . . daily inspection of quarters . . . police call each morning after reveille . . . battalion vehicles to be turned in . . . men not to leave camp area without pass . . .formal guard mounts to be held daily . . . emphasis on prevention of venereal disease . . . men having 85 points (toward discharge) would be transferred from the unit prior to departure . . . barbers to be kept busy . . . Allied marks to be exchanged for francs . . . cooking would be done on stoves provided by the camp; company stoves to be prepared for packing . . . athletic officers and noncommissioned officers to be appointed . . . and there was to be new emphasis on security discipline—on maintaining secrecy of troop movements (in spite of the fact that *Stars and Stripes* was carrying complete announcements of movements of divisions in the redeployment program).[17]

It was contemplated that the division would have a thorough retraining program under more favorable conditions in the United States; nevertheless certain minimum requirements—whose reasons were not always clear—had to

14. Ibid.
15. 134th Inf., **Daily Log**, V, 12-13 July 1945.
16. 3rd Bn. S-3 Notebook, III.
17. Ibid.

be met before the division could leave its assembly area camp. A list of deficiencies which came down from Headquarters, Assembly Area Command, at one point, for example, noted the following:

(1) Personnel have not been adequately trained in malaria discipline.
(2) Anti-malaria details have not been appointed and trained.
(3) Chemical decontamination squads have not been appointed and trained.
(4) Personnel have not been trained in scrub typhus fever.
(5) Status of military courtesy and discipline not satisfactory.[18]

In addition, there was a requirement for all men to participate in range firing of their weapons (in spite of the fact that all weapons had been turned in!); finally this was interpreted to apply only to men who had not fired their individual weapon during the preceding 12 months.[19]

After several delays it became apparent that the 35th Division would be leaving Camp Norfolk in mid-August. But as that time approached, rapid developments began to occur in the Pacific to attract the attention of members of the Third Battalion. Perhaps, after all, they would not be called upon to engage in further military operations:

On 6 August the bomb was dropped. The results are well known. Two days later the Soviet Union declared war on Japan . . . . The first Red offensives were across the Manchuria border and southward on the island of Sakhalin . . . . Then, on 9 August, the Strategic Air Forces loosed a second atomic bomb on Nagasaki, which displayed greater destructive blast and fire than the Hiroshima bomb . . . . On 10 August the Japanese Government sued for peace on the general terms enunciated by the Allied powers at the Potsdam conference.[20]

At 7:00 P.M., August 14th (1:00 A.M., August 15th in Europe) President Truman announced that the Japanese had accepted the surrender terms.[21]

Had the Japanese surrender come a few days earlier it is not unlikely that the 35th Division, now made up largely of low point men, would have been delayed to make way for units filled with men of longer service. But processing had been completed, and any delay hardly could have contributed to any earlier return of men to be discharged. It was to the good fortune of the men of the Third Battalion, then, that they were scheduled to leave Camp Norfolk the very morning after news of the surrender came.[22]

Sixteen trains—this time made up of passenger coaches—were required to transport the personnel of the division to the Port of Le Havre. Of these, the sixth was for the Third Battalion. A light rain was falling when the Battalion's train departed at 9:05 P.M., August 15, 1945.[23] After transportation across the English Channel, the division—less the 137th Infantry which had gone to Brussels to serve as honor guard for Presidnet Truman—sailed from Southampton on September 5th aboard the great Cunard-White Star liner, *Queen Mary*.[24]

18. Camp Norfolk, S-3 Notebook.
19. Ibid.
20. General Marshall's Report, p. 86. However, it is likely that Japan would have surrendered soon had there been no atomic bomb, no Russian attack, no invasion. See U. S. **Strategic Bombing Survey, Japanese War.**
21. **The World Almanac,** 1946, p. 95.
22. A commentary on the inability of some types of army organizations to adapt themselves quickly to new situations is to be found in the maintenance of training requirements in the Assembly Area Command, for several days after VJ Day, calling for training in malaria control and chemical decontamination (a gas chamber was required to be set up after VJ Day) and familiarization firing of weapons before any unit could leave for the United States—where it would be inactivated!—Camp Norfolk, S-3 Notebook.
23. Ibid.
24. Santa Fe, p. 196-197.

Five days later the Queen, covered with so many unit signs and banners that she was described as looking "like a huge floating billboard," slipped into New York Harbor. One of the first divisions to return to New York since VJ Day, the 35th enjoyed a tremendous welcome.[25] There even was a personal message from President Truman to greet the comrades of his "old outfit"—the division with which he had served in World War I.[26]

II

Trains returned the Battalion to the place where it had come just 16 months before—Camp Kilmer.[27] It had taken the long road home; the circle was completed. As the men scattered for 30 or 45-day recuperative furloughs,[28] their thoughts must have been dwelling at once on anticipation of reaching their homes and on the photographs of memories which had impressed themselves upon them in the course of the preceding 16 months. The extent of the experiences and memories would vary radically with each individual—after all, most of the present members of the Battalion had joined it only recently. But there would be amongst them those who would recall the departure from Camp Kilmer a year and third before—how they had boarded those same trains, carrying full packs and heavy duffle bags, marching up in their chalk-marked helmets to the recorded music of "The Stars and Stripes Forever." They would recall the voyage in convoy to England . . . the training in Cornwall . . . how they had listened for news of the invasion and read the English newspapers: "General Eisenhower visits Beachhead—Panzer Drive Beaten: All Beaches Free of Enemy—Bridgehead 25 Miles Wide, say Nazis"[29] . . . their anticipation of their own call to join in the fighting in Normandy . . . then the busy beachhead, the shattered stone and plaster of destroyed towns standing ghost-like in the white moonlight . . . nor could they forget the awful battling in the hedgerows—against those rapid-firing machine guns and fearsome "88's"—toward St. Lo and beyond . . . dead horses[30] . . . "Bed-Check Charlie" . . . vin rouge . . . motor convoys . . . the liberation of Nancy . . . warm summer days . . . great air fleets overhead . . . rain and mud and cold and snow . . . the French towns of Lorraine[31] . . . the dangers of Habkirchen . . . the uncertainties and distress in the snow around Lutrebois—and Hon's throwing out the pancake batter to save it from capture . . . the fun of escape on furloughs to Paris and London . . . the great ponton bridge across the Rhine . . . the DP's—"les miserables"—of the Ruhr . . . the gardens on the Elbe . . . the music from German phonographs coming out of Bat-

25. Associated Press dispatch on file in the Information Section, Headquarters Army Ground Forces (Analysis Branch), the Pentagon, Washington, D. C.
26. **The New York Times**, Sept. 11, 1945.
27. **Santa Fe**, p. 197.
28. **Ibid.**
29. **The Daily Telegraph and Morning Post** (London) June 8, 1944, p. 1.
30. cf. Henry David Thoreau, "There was a dead horse in the path to my house, which compelled me sometimes to go out of my way, but the assurance it gave me of the strong appetite and inviolable health of Nature was my compensation for this."—**Walden** (Everyman's Library ed.) p. 280.
31. The memories of Lorraine might be very similar to those of Americans who had been in the same area during World War I:
"When you know Lorraine it seems fitting that it should have given Joan of Arc to France. Today you may still see such peasant girls as she was, straight as young birch trees. . . . The villages have changed little since she tended her flocks and the character of the people is much the same as when she went forth from shepherding her flocks to lead an army. From high ground clusters of red roofs break into view on the rich river bottoms and in valleys mottled with woodlands and pastures, but proximity removes some of the charm and picturesqueness as you enter narrow streets where manure is piled in front of the house door."—Frederick Palmer, **America in France** (New York, 1918) p. 36.

talion Headquarters—"When Yuba Played the Tuba down in Cuba" the piano melodies of Charlie Kuntz, "Pagan Love Song," "Tea for Two," "Tiptoe through the Tulips" . . . the crowded "40 and 8" cars of the troop train moving back to France—and men singing to accompaniment of guitars, and, during a halt, German children gathering about them to join in singing "Lili Marlene" . . . the hot summer days in the tent camp of the Assembly Area—strains of "The Sunny Side of the Street" filling the air from loud radios tuned to the Armed Forces Network.[32]

Such memories doubtless would accompany the infantryman of the Third Battalion during the remainder of his days. For some time to come he would be overly conscious of an airplane flying overhead; at the sound of a riveter he could find himself searching automatically for cover from machine gun fire; a loud noise likely would recall to him narrow escapes from artillery shells; the thought of a "K" ration would bring a tightening of his stomach and a tenseness in his throat; in a beautiful valley he would see an "avenue of approach;" a river, a "defense line;" a graceful hill, an "observation post;" a clump of bushes, a "machine gun position;" a broad meadow, a "field of fire." At last he, a fortunate one, had achieved the objective which had dominated most of his thoughts—return to the States—to get back home—away from it all—peace! And yet, as time went on, he would find himself annoyed sometimes by a tugging nostalgia for the dangers and comradeship of those European fields—or at least to see those places, under more peaceful conditions, once again. Certainly those days of combat held little happiness for him; but sometimes he would feel an attraction to those sites of danger and triumph almost as irresistible as that of a flame of destruction for a May beetle. This longing most likely would find expression in the form of discussion and recounting those experiences whenever he found himself in the company of other veterans of similar experiences.

That his responses to such things as noises and terrain features would indicate some conditioning by war experiences seemed to be evident. Perhaps more questionable would be the extent to which such war conditioning would extend to other types of responses as the soldier set about to adjust himself to civilian life.

Not of a little interest to his family and friends—and of no inconsiderable significance when multiplied by the several millions representing American overseas veterans—would be his impressions of Europe and its inhabitants. What did he think of the French and the English? Did he like Germany? There would be a tendency on the part of his listeners—particularly friends who had remained at home—to grant his answers and observations the weight of authority. "Joe served in France, and he says the French are neurotic and irresponsible." Actually, the answers will reflect "Joe's" background, and more than likely his observations will have served to confirm the convictions which he already held. But this tendency will serve only to increase the weight of his authority, for now his friends and relatives—with similar backgrounds—will discover, much to their satisfaction, that "Joe's" observations tend to confirm their own previously-held opinions; then "Joe" must be right— he was there, and he saw it. Far from serving to foster a great dissemination of internationalism in thought, this generalizing from the particular may

32. 3rd Bn. S-3 Notebook, IV.

serve more to aggravate international feelings and strengthen a nationalistic superiority outlook. To the chagrin of hopeful internationalists and religious brotherhoods, they may discover that America's "ambassadors of good will in uniform" have served a contrary purpose.

The American soldier in Europe was likely to emphasize in his thought cultural differences and small differences in folkways. Many white soldiers would be offended at the absence of a color line and the free association of British girls with colored troops. They would become impatient with the English custom of pausing for tea. But it seemed that the American soldier's ultimate test of any culture was the nature and extent of its plumbing. To discover a general lack of central heating and a relatively primitive plumbing would be sufficient to describe a country as being "fifty years behind the times."[33] At the same time European cultures were likely to suffer further in the American soldier's comparison as he tended to attach an exaggerated attractiveness to things associated with home—its very remoteness gave an added appeal to home.[34]

Beyond that, the returned American soldier likely was to appear less favorably inclined toward the Allies in the war, and more favorably inclined toward Germany, the enemy, than might have been expected by those at home. As between soldiers of different Allied armies, there was bound to be intergroup rivalry. But it was easy to fall into the "habit of categorizing all one's real or potential competitors by the convenient label of nationality." Rivalry extended from the winning of the favor of the women and drinking up the limited stocks of beer to resentment over exaggerated notions of Lend Lease[35] and lack of recognition that America had won the war. Americans seemed to reason that if the United States contributed most to victory, then America won the war. They permitted themselves severe criticism of the British and French press for glorification of their own forces.[36] "To read those Limey papers you would think they were winning the war all by themselves." A member of the Third Battalion might read with satisfaction headlines in an Omaha newspaper recounting the action of "Nebraska's Own" 134th Infantry in France, and then resent a similar play-up of a proud English regiment in a Manchester newspaper.

Differences in soldiers' attitudes, then, would result from their previous education and prejudices and opinions on the one hand, and from differences in their actual experiences on the other. That is to say, a soldier who fought with the Third Battalion only through the Normandy campaign, for example, would carry away a far different impression of France than a soldier who might have joined the Battalion after the Mortain battle and left shortly after the liberation of Nancy. Again the differences in the situation in France and Germany would influence comparisons to be drawn later. When one regards the difference in casualty rates in Lorraine or Belgium and those in Ger-

33. Daniel Glaser, "The Sentiments of American Soldiers Abroad toward Europeans," **The American Journal of Sociology**, LI (March 1946) 434.

This disappointment in European plumbing facilities likewise was to be found among the predecessors of these men in France—the A.E.F. in 1918. What they missed more than home food, it was reported, was bathtubs . . . "a habit which some of our men thought had become a necessity until they were billeted in a French village. They felt sticky at first, but after a while it seemed quite natural."—Frederick Palmer, **America in France**, p. 132.

34. Glaser, **Loc. cit.**; see W. Edgar Gregory, "The Idealization of the Absent," **"The American Journal of Sociology**, L (July 1944) 53-54.

35. This superiority in material was a marked contrast to the situation in 1918 when the British and French might have had reason for such feelings. "Except for four 14-inch naval guns on railway mounts, the American First Army never fired an American-made cannon or shell, and no American-made tank was ever available for battle in Europe."—American Battle Monuments Commission, **American Armies and Battlefields in Europe** (Washington, 1938), p. 19.

36. Glaser, **loc. cit.**, p. 436.

many, a difference in conditions will be apparent at once.   Then when one adds to that such considerations as the dispersal of companies away from higher control in attractive German towns untouched by war destruction in the Hannover area or the Coblenz area—and the relatively greater civilian populations —and the warm weather and good shelter in contrast with mud and cold rain and snow and foxholes in Lorraine, and further, the absence of gun fire, the lack of great danger, and an opportunity for sports as well as training, hardly could it be expected that a combat soldier would find France more enjoyable than Germany.

As far as personal adjustment was concerned, it appeared to be unlikely that most men would have serious difficulty in adapting themselves to civilian life. Doubtless there would be large numbers, however, who would find themselves dissatisfied with old jobs; there would be those seized by a surprising restlessness after a few weeks; there might be some who would feel an annoyance at the lack of order and organization in civil doings; others would find difficulty in readjusting to family life; some might find it difficult to reassume lost responsibility. Soldiers in the main came to be dependent upon authority. They would be guided and led through every kind of activity. Men who had been heads of families and in responsible positions would become so dependent that they would not turn in worn-out shoes for a new pair at the supply room—where they could be had for the asking—until ordered to do so after some superior had discovered the worn-out pair in the course of an inspection.

Yet, at the same time, there would be resentment against authority and privilege sometimes, and some, noticing officers' clubs, and liquor rations for officers, would find satisfaction in hoping, after the war, to see the officer in an usher's uniform. The extent to which such resentment existed in any particular unit is very difficult of measurement, but certainly there was a great deal of variation as among different units. It is most likely that there would be less resentment of officers—at least insofar as they proved themselves capable—in an infantry battalion than in some non-combatant unit. Members of an infantry battalion came to recognize the terrible responsibility borne by the officers—some men, offered commissions, refused to accept them during combat. Rather, there was too much at stake in the life and death combat of the infantry. The men knew that their fate rested in the hands of their officers, and the officers knew that theirs lay with their men. It was as parts of a whole, then, that they combined their efforts to the advantage of all concerned. There was little room for such expressions of pettiness in a combat infantry battalion. "Enlisted men do not often indict the officers' military competence in battle, but they spare no words in criticizing the officer's abuse of his special privilege."[37] This is not to suggest a light dismissal of "GI Gripes" which found expression after hostilities had ended. They were widespread and often bitter. Too frequently, no doubt, there was justification for complaint. But that complaint centered, for the most part, around grievances which would have sounded ridiculous to an infantry battalion in combat—inequitable distribution of Coca Cola between officers and enlisted men (during combat no bottle of Coca Cola ever was seen in the Third Battalion except an occasional bottle sent to some individual from home), unfair distribution of liquor,

37. See Ralph Lewis, "Officer-Enlisted Men's Relationships," **The American Journal of Sociology**, LII (March 1947), 410.

poor food in the enlisted man's mess (the K ration is a great leveler!), attractive officers clubs, (fox holes are even more of a leveler!)[37a]

More justifiable, perhaps, was the allegation that sentences of military courts showed much greater leniency toward officers for similar offenses. Even here comparisons are not as easy as might be supposed, for circumstances surrounding cases include such great differences. But as far as criticism of military justice in general is concerned, it does not always rest on firm grounds. Most anxious to make themselves heard, no doubt, have been those men who are acquainted with court-martial procedure through the experience of having earned one of its sentences. Such experience and interest will not hold, of course, for the greater number of soldiers. Some would seek to discredit the military courts by pointing to the relatively high number of convictions which it finds in the cases tried; but the reason for this result should be known—that a thorough pre-trial investigation determines whether there is evidence to warrant a trial, and failing such complete evidence, the case is dropped. Sentences which appear long by civilian standards did not seem such to the combat infantryman. It seemed to him that a man sentenced to prison was getting something of a break; at least the prisoner was in relative safety. For his shirking of duty he now at least had greater assurance of survival at a time when his comrade's life might be snuffed out at any moment. No, a few weeks under fire robbed from the combat infantryman feelings of sympathy for an AWOL sentenced to long years of hard labor. With restoration of peace, doubtless reviews would be in order, but the circumstances of those sentences in time of war would remain a force in the background.

Recommendations of the special board headed by James H. Doolittle[37b] followed in general those non-combatant complaints. Some of them, like equality of treatment in courts-martial, and an overhauling of the system of decorations, were valid enough. Others, however, seemed to go too far (a view adhered to by the Secretary of War).[37c] The dangers of favoritism and loss of discipline and respect might well accompany the acceptance of those recommendations seeking to eliminate all distinctions and all barriers between officers and enlisted men. The undesirable features of such differences tend to disappear in combat units anyway. For a peace time morale, on the other hand, such considerations may come in for greater importance.

Perhaps the attitudes of returned soldiers would be most significant, as far as the local community was concerned, among the men of returning National Guard units. Here attitudes would gain weight through similarity—a relative similarity of background and of experiences. Indeed one objection to the National Guard organization—that is the assignment of units to communities —has been the effect upon the home town of a disaster to its National Guard company in combat. Before departure overseas, therefore, most National Guard units had a considerable exchange of personnel, and so, the Third

37a. see Hanson W. Baldwin, "GI Gripes—Causes and Cures," The New York Times Magazine, May 31, 1946, pp. 12-13.
A letter to The New York Times put it this way:
"Judging from the testimony presented before Secretary of War Patterson's special committee investigating the officer-enlisted men relationships—or lack of it is perhaps the better way to put it—what the GI apparently resents most is that he can't buy liquor in his NCO club the way the officers can, can't sleep between sheets the way officers can, can't look pretty in pinks the way officers can."—April 23, 1946, p. 24.
37b. Appointed by Secretary of War Robert Patterson, the Doolittle Board heard 40 witnesses, including 21 former or actual enlisted men, 14 officers, two war correspondents, one Red Cross woman worker, a Federal Bureau of Investigation agent, and a Congresswoman.—The New York Times, April 5, 1946, p. 17.
37c. The New York Times, May 26, 1946, p. 5.

Battalion, made up originally from Omaha, Lincoln, and Seward, Nebraska, included members from all parts of the United States before it completed its
training program. Nevertheless the Nebraska nucleus remained, and when, in
late July 1944, casualty lists began to mount high for Omaha and Lincoln and
the other Nebraska cities, citizens could deduce that the 134th Infantry was in
action at St. Lo.[38]

III

Now that the fighting was over the infantryman of the Third Battalion
would begin to feel more and more a sense of pride in having served with
the Battalion. During his combat days he might have considered himself an
insignificant member of the great common body of men who were unable to
get into safer, more attractive branches of the service. It appeared to him that
most of the army was made up of infantry. It was the infantry which marked
the front line of battle; it was for the support of the infantry that the other
branches existed. Perhaps it was somewhat to his surprise when he returned
to find that he was a member of a highly respected branch whose members
were relatively not so very numerous after all.[39] His pride would grow in his
Combat Infantryman's Badge as he found that its award was not as general
as he had imagined. Having survived, his experience was one which, as
one officer put it, he "would not take a million dollars for, nor a million to
go through again."

Really, this pride in belonging to the infantry began to develop early
in the training of a soldier, and although most agreed that the Infantry was
the most undesirable of the service, and its members would give anything to
be elsewhere, once it was over they were proud that they were infantrymen—
proud that they had demonstrated that they could "take it."[40] For many, the
most highly valued decoration was the Combat Infantryman's Badge.

In common with members of other arms and services, the infantryman looked with disdain upon those troops farther removed from the front
than himself. Men wanted to be as near the front as they could be—safely.
To the battalion, the regiment was "rear echelon"—and the division "way
back" and army headquarters was "practically out of this world." The "front"
tended to be a relative term. For the combat infantryman there was only
one definition for the front—the line beyond which there is nothing but
enemy. From his point of view, General Eisenhower on a "rapid tour of the
front" probably would not come near the front—he would be visiting army
and corps headquarters—possibly a division here and there—most of the time.
But this was not to suggest that it should have been otherwise. The infantryman was as likely to be no less scornful of visits all the way up to his foxhole by the "brass." They appeared to him as useless efforts to demonstrate
personal bravery, with the result that an uninitiated general was likely to expose himself unnecessarily and so draw enemy fire to the position.

It seems doubtful, however, that the infantrymen's pride extended to
the enthusiasm for action at the front which one finds ascribed to units clamoring for action—for an opportunity to attack—in World War I,[41]

38. **The Omaha World-Herald**, July-August 1944.
39. "In the Army at large, the infantry comprises only 20.5 per cent of the total strength
overseas, yet it has taken 70 per cent of the total casualties"—General Marshall's Report, p. 108.
40. (Anonymous), "The Making of the Infantryman," **The American Journal of Sociology**,
LI (March 1946), 376.
41. Palmer, **America in France**; Society of the First Division, **History of the First Division**,
et al.

but the old tradition prevailed in the minds of soldiers as well as the public: being in France meant being at the front. Sitting at a desk at headquarters in France and reviewing troops back of the battle lines—that was action; whereas sitting at a desk in Washington and reviewing troops in training camps had the look of inaction.[42]

Even replacements learned the pride of the infantry in their training under the Infantry Replacement Training Command. After six weeks of difficult training and orientation doubtless they were convinced that they were among the toughest of the army. "You're an infantryman," they were told, "act like one. Don't be sloppy like them Air-Corps guys."[43] Master of a dozen weapons, the infantryman was a trained specialist. And after a few weeks of the rigors of basic training he decided that if could go through that he could endure worse things.[44] Indeed the Third Battalion met nothing in combat which called for greater physical endurance than the winter maneuvers in Tennessee and West Virginia.

Comradeship—a sense of belonging together—grew up among members of an infantry unit. There grew out of combat that "comradeship of catastrophe" or "fellowship of the dangerous or spectacular" which springs up in all kinds of such situations. Passengers on a wrecked bus, spectators at a great fire, victims of a flood, however inhospitable or strange to each other they may have been previously, suddenly become communicative and feel a deep comradeship growing out of sharing common experiences. The sharing of hardships and "gripes" and achievements and danger promoted a high *esprit de corps* among infantrymen. And participation in combat encouraged that pride originating in training:

It is out of the agonies of training that they develop pride in having done what they believe many of their former friends could not have done and which they themselves never thought they could do.[45]

IV

Now that his war was over, the infantryman might wonder whether, after all, his contribution and his role had been appreciated. Perhaps most other "G.I.'s" would appreciate his lot, and there would be some satisfaction in that, but would the appreciation of the public go beyond romanticizing him as the "foot-slogging dogface tramping through weary miles of mud"? However certain he might feel in his own mind of the decisive role of the "Queen of Battles" in gaining victory in Europe, there would be those who would permit their enthusiasm for air power to carry them to the position that, after all, it was the terrific aerial assaults which had brought Germany to her knees. Indeed there would be even those who would look upon the invasion of Europe as a deplorable waste of lives whose only justification was to beat the Russians to the control of Germany.[46] (If that were the object, the American retreat from the Elbe at the termination of hostilities certainly was not a very convincing expression of it.)

Now to question the decisiveness of air power in the European war was not to deny its tremendous importance. No one appreciated the value of air superiority more than did the infantryman who was fighting on the ground

42. Frederick Palmer, **Newton D. Baker;** America at War, II, 156.
43. "The Making of the Infantryman," p. 377.
44. Ibid., p. 378.
45. Ibid., p. 379.
46. e.g. Radio broadcast, American Forum Guest Panel (Mutual Broadcasting System) March 11, 1947, 7:30-8:15 P.M., Eastern Standard Time.

below. But far from being brought to her knees by a deluge of more than two million tons of bombs, Germany was able to produce in 1944 more aircraft, more tanks, more weapons and ammunition, and even more submarines (measured either by number or tonnage) than ever before! A production of aircraft totalling almost 40,000 in 1944 is to be contrasted with a production of less than 9,000 in 1939, about 12,000 in 1942, and 25,000 in 1943.[47] German panzer production reached its peak in the *last quarter of 1944.* Total production for those three months amounted to 5,236 tanks, assault guns, and self-propelled guns, and even during the first quarter of 1945—the period which saw the Allied occupation of the Rhineland and the crossing of the Rhine—the Germans were able to turn out 3,932 panzers; the best production figures for preceding years were 1,880 in the fourth quarter of 1942 and 3,781 in the fourth quarter of 1943.[48] Assigning the weapons and ammunition production of January-February 1942 a production index number of 100, we find an almost continuous increase in output of weapons from that time until December 1944 when weapons production reached a maximum index of 408. And so 1944 was the big year for ammunition production; its index was above 300 for every month except January and December.[49] Likewise, December 1944 was the peak for submarine production, but it should be noted that although 288 submarines, plus another 99 midget U-boats, were produced in 1944 as against 270 in 1943 and 196 in 1941, the number actually put into operation in 1944 was less than in 1941.[50]

Even the air attacks upon the railroad system—though they had, by the end of 1944, imposed serious delays on military operations—"had not seriously reduced the ability of the Army to originate tactical moves in volume."[51] Furthermore, "when the war ended, German rubber plants had not been damaged sufficiently to be a major factor in the defeat,"[52] and, in spite of the heavy attacks against the very concentrated anti-friction bearing industry, the Germans could boast: "No equipment was ever delayed because bearings were lacking."[53]

Most effective of the air attacks were those directed against oil,[54] and the shortage of aviation gasoline resulting in the curtailment of flying training and thus a deterioration in quality of pilots was "the principal cause of the defeat of the German Air Force."[55] Here was the great contribution of the Allied Air Forces—control of the air which permitted a freedom of operation to the ground forces. It is possible that a continuation of the air attacks could have brought victory alone, but the lack of a major effort on the ground certainly would have extended the time of Germany's survival:

> There is no evidence that shortage of civilian goods reached a point where the German authorities were forced to transfer resources from war production in order to prevent disintegration on the home front . . .
> The indications are convincing that the German armies, completely bereft of ammunition and motive power, would have had to cease fighting—any effective fighting—within a few months.

47. The United States Strategic Bombing Survey, Over-all Report (European War), Sept. 30, 1945, p. 12.
48. Ibid., p. 66.
49. Ibid., pp. 81f.
50. Ibid., pp. 68f.
51. Ibid., p. 66.
52. Ibid., p. 49.
53. Ibid., p. 29.
54. Ibid., pp. 39-45.
55. Ibid., p. 25.

In the actual case—as in most other cases in the histories of wars - - the collapse occurred before the time when the lack of means had rendered further resistance physically impossible.[56]

But "Within a few months" the Germans might have been able to accomplish their project of completing an effective force of "high-performance jet-type aircraft manned by qualified personnel and operating on low-grade fuels."[57]

Constant and unending effort was required . . . to overcome the initial advantages of the enemy and later to keep pace with his research and technology. It was fortunate that the leaders of the German Air Force relied too heavily on their initial advantage. For this reason they failed to develop, in time, weapons, such as the jet-propelled planes, that might have substantially improved their position. There was the hazard, on the other hand, in the fact that Allies were behind the Germans in the development of jet-propelled aircraft. The German development of the V-weapons, especially the V-2, is also noteworthy.[58]

In June 1944, the Germans are reported to have had 8,500 of the V-1's on hand, and a production of 1,200 a month. These "buzz bombs" killed 5,476 persons, and destroyed 23,000 buildings and damaged a million more. Within three months' time they killed a tenth as many people as the grand total of the previous aerial assaults on Britain.[59] More vicious were the supersonic V-2 rockets. Production of these weapons totalled 7,500 in 1944, and 2,500 were produced even during the first three months of 1945.[60] On the drafting boards were designs for other weapons which, "within a few months," might have brought casualties to far higher totals, and might even have prevented Germany's defeat. Plans for such advanced weapons as winged rockets—discharging secondary rockets—to have a range to span the Atlantic, or for a huge long-range, pilot-controlled bomber to fly 154 miles high to reach the American coast might have changed the whole picture.[61] In view of these developments it would appear to have been quite fortunate that infantry battalions had been able to force their way into Germany without waiting for a complete reduction by air.

With the hindsight we now have as a result of our discoveries, several things become clear. One is that the Nazis' off-repeated threats concerning the "secret weapon" they would shortly direct against the Allies were far from being purely "propaganda." Hitler had boasted that England and the whole world would soon feel their effect. Examination of Germany's missiles at war's end left very little doubt that Der Fuehrer had come uncomfortably close to making good his boast.[62]

And paralleling the Nazis' research on atomic explosives was their accelerated development of the V-2 program. Linking these two programs together makes credible another theory which is current among Allied guided missiles groups: namely, that it was the intention of Nazi technicians to put some sort of atomic device in the warhead of the V-2.[63]

Even now, . . . it is still frightening to imagine what might have happened had we not halted Germany when we did. We now know that it *was* later than we thought.[64]

And not to be disregarded is the effect of the 13-month aerial campaign against the launching sites of those V-weapons in the course of which some 100-000 tons of bombs were dropped. While these attacks probably delayed the beginning of launchings, "there is no evidence that bombing reduced

56. Ibid., p. 38.
57. Ibid., pp. 25f.
58. Ibid., p. 108.
59. Charlotte Knight, "German Rocketeers," **AAF Review**, XXIX (July 1946), 24.
60. Ibid., p. 48.
61. Ibid., p. 26.
62. Ibid., p. 24.
63. Ibid., p. 26.
64. Ibid., p. 48.

the volume of the fire of V-1's after launching had started except during a 2-week period following the attack on the supply depot at Nucovert . . . . In the case of the V-2, bombing of launching sites did not delay firing, since technical difficulties with the weapon were not overcome until September, at which time launchings began."[65] No, the "buzz bombs" and rockets did not cease until infantry battalions on the ground had overrun the launching sites.

The infantryman had no reason, then, to doubt the need and effectiveness of his part in accomplishing the Victory in Europe. If he noted signs of discrimination against him or a lack of appreciation, they must have stemmed from sources other than a valid assumption that his was a subordinate role. Yet those signs were present, and he could hardly fail to contrast his own position with what he found accorded members of the Air Corps. Was there a valid basis for a preferential treatment of members of flying crews—specifically in the matter of higher ratings and increased pay?

The most obvious advantage to the airman was in the matter of pay— all officers and enlisted men who were on flying duty received an increase of 50 per centum in their pay.[66] When it is recalled that most members of flying crews either were commissioned officers or non-commissioned officers of the higher grades, this will be seen to have been relatively not an inconsiderable amount. (An amendment in July 1944 provided that his "flying pay" should not exceed $100 a month for officers or $50 a month for enlisted men.[67]) The only comparable compensation for the infantryman was an additional $10 a month to holders of the Combat Infantryman's Badge (except officers).

Or there was the matter of recognition in the way of decorations. Of the decorations awarded in the European Theater of Operations, 83.32 per cent went to members of the Air Corps while 9.3 per cent went to members of the Infantry. Yet the Infantry took 75.02 per cent of the casualties in Europe, while the Air Force suffered 9.36 per cent of the total casualties in that theater.[67a]

It already has been suggested that differences in accomplishment were not such as to have justified such differences in pay and recognition. Was the justification to be found in the greater danger of flying? Casualty figures for the Third Battalion indicate well enough the hazards of action with an infantry unit: in nine months of combat the Third Battalion suffered 2,900 casualties[68]—a turnover of 347 per cent! Assuming a replacement for each casualty, this means that a total of 3,735 officers and men served with this battalion in action, and 78 per cent of them—regardless of their length of combat service—became casualties. But wait; how about the number of deaths? It is in this connection that the hazard of flying should become most apparent. Deaths in the Third Battalion amounted to 346—a figure representing 41 per cent of the original strength, or 9 per cent of the total number of men who served with the Battalion. As a basis for small unit comparison, probably there would be no example more appropriate among the Air Forces than that of the First Fighter Group. This group—equipped with P-38 fighters—flew a total of 20,955 sorties in the Mediterranean and European Theaters in the course of which 204 pilots were killed, captured, or missing in action.[69] In the

65. ibid., pp. 88f.
66. U. S. Code, Title 37, S.118 (1940 ed.) suppl. V 1941-1946, p. 789.
67. 58 U. S. Statutes at Large 682.
67a. Leigh, **48 Million Tons,** p. 113.
68. 134th Inf., Battle Casualty Report.
69. Maj. Charles P. Beazley, "Air Force's Oldest," **AAF Review,** XXIX (July 1946), 42.

Air Forces as a whole, some 40 per cent of those listed as "killed, captured or missing in action" returned to duty or were repatriated, and 60 per cent were killed in action, died, or were declared dead;[70] therefore we may assume that about 40 per cent of those 204 pilots ultimately returned safely. This would mean 122 deaths in 20,995 sorties, or a rate of 5.8 deaths per thousand sorties.

It is very difficult to arrive at a fair standard for comparison with a ground unit, but perhaps the nearest approach would be in an attempt to arrive at an approximate number of deaths in relation to actual "man-days of combat" (though this has the objections that an infantryman may be called upon to participate in several local attacks in one day, just as the airman may fly several sorties in one day). Including quiet days as well as active ones—all days on which the Battalion either was in contact with the enemy or had a specific mission (though it might have been nothing more than patrol activity or a quiet defense), it may be estimated that the Battalion was engaged on 200 days from July 1944 to April 1945. A liberal enough estimate of the average fighting-strength of the Battalion would be 500 officers and men. Further assuming that one-third of the Battalion's 196 men "missing in action"[71] actually died (a fraction half as great as that for the "missing in action" among the air crews) it will be seen that the Battalion suffered about 400 deaths in approximately 100,000 "man-days of combat" or a rate of 4 deaths per thousand man-days.

It would seem to be questionable enough to justify such a difference in ratings and pay as existed between the Infantry and the Air Corps on the basis of a difference in action death rates of something like 1.8, but even this difference disappears when we consider other advantages to the airmen. That is, nearly the whole of the turn-over of the infantry battalion was attributable to casualties; in other words, the few men who were fortunate enough to escape wounds or death had to continue through that whole period of combat. Air crews, on the other hand, had the advantage of being returned to the United States on the completion of a prescribed number of missions—amounting to 50 missions in the Mediterranean, and 25 later in the European.[72] Even in 1943, pilots of the First Fighter Group could expect to complete their 50 missions—if they escaped the casualty lists—within about four months' time.[73] The hazard of death, as far as the individual was concerned, probably was greater for the rifleman than for the pilot.

If we look at the broader picture in comparing casualty figures, the lack of a real basis, on account of danger, for the discrimination in favor of airmen becomes more striking. "In the Army at large, the infantry comprise[d] only 20.5 per cent of total strength overseas, yet it [took] 70 per cent of the total casualties."[74] Of the total of 589,269 casualties in the European Theater,[75] 75.02 per cent went to the Infantry.[76] Taking as a guide the distribution in the 134th Infantry Regiment, we find that 94 per cent of those cas-

70. Casualties among flying officers included 12,954 killed in action, 367 died of wounds 34 who were taken prisoner or interned and died of wounds, and 6,610 of those "missing" were declared dead; on the other hand 3,016 "missing" returned to duty and 10,431 prisoners and internees were repatriated.—Lt. Col. Charles A. Brown, executive, Office of Public Relations, Director of Information, AAF, to the author, Aug. 27, 1946. (Figures are based on reports of June 30, 1946).
71. 134th Inf., Battle Casualty Report.
72. General Marshall's Report, p. 104.
73. Beazley, loc. cit., p. 19.
74. General Marshall's Report, p. 108.
75. Ibid.
76. Leigh, op. cit., p. 113.

ualties were among members of the battalions. At the end of hostilities in Europe (May 7, 1945) there were 42 Infantry divisions in that theater, or a total of 378 battalions which, at full strength would comprise 324,080 men, and adding approximately 24,000 infantrymen from the four air borne divisions, we arrive at a total of 348,080 men. Now 75 per cent of the casualties in Europe would mean 441,951 for the infantry regiments, and 94 per cent of this figure would give us a total of 403,434. In other words the total strength of infantry battalions—including even those which had arrived only a few days or weeks before V-E day—amounted to approximately 348,000 while casualties among the same groups amounted to about 403,400. That is to say, infantry battalions as a whole—with no corrections made for the several which saw little action—had a turnover due to casualties of 116 per cent. Or to put it another way, if we again assume a replacement for each casualty, a total of 751,000 men served in infantry battalions, and of these, regardless of whether they served one day or three hundred days, 52 per cent became casualties.

Let us attempt to find a comparison with air crews. Total casualties in the Air Forces in the European Theater are given as 45,545[77]—a figure which might be equaled by any two of several infantry divisions. But we are interested in casualty rates for the *air crews*. Perhaps a fair estimate could be found in the figures for total aircraft in operation and total losses. The maximum number of bomber planes assigned to American combat units in Europe was 7,177, and the greatest strength in fighters was 6,203.[78] Aircraft losses totalled 9,949 to 8,320 respectively. Now if we assume that each aircraft loss meant 100 per cent casualties for the crew, we see that the turnover resulting from casualties amounted to 138 per cent for bombers and 137 per cent for fighters, or about 57 per cent of all airplanes assigned to combat units (making no allowance for replacements of worn-out machines) were lost. But this figure does not reflect a true picture as far as personnel losses —the hazard to the individual—is concerned, for we must take into account the fact that it came to be the practice in the Eighth Air Force to provide *three combat crews per operating plane* and to return the men to the United States after 25 missions.[79] On the grounds of hazardous duty, then, it would be very difficult to justify such special consideration for members of the Air Corps.

Then what was the reason? Was additional pay and rank a lure necessary to attract sufficient numbers of men to the Air Corps? It would seem hardly necessary to provide additional attractions for air-minded American youth. Indeed, the Air Corps was so attractive that sometimes infantry commanders were forced to resort to strict measures to prevent the complete disintegration of their well-trained units by a flood of applications for transfer to air training.

Nothing could have been calculated to stimulate morale among infantrymen in combat more than friendly aircraft zooming overhead. The "doughboy" respected those pilots deeply and felt a real comradeship with them. He envied them their hot chow waiting in warm quarters, and fancied their comfort with clean sheets on their beds, but he did not begrudge them—any combat man was welcome to whatever measure of comfort he could salvage

77.   General Marshall's Report, p. 108.
78.   U. S. Strategic Bombing Service, p. X.
79.   General Marshall's Report, p. 104.

in this war—but when he thought of differences in treatment, then morale
was likely to suffer.

This situation—special privileges for flyers was not new; the problem
had grown up with flying itself, as the American Chief of Staff during World
War I later pointed out:

> The early trouble with planes was accompanied by continuous trouble with per-
> sonnel. At an early stage of the development of army flying, Congress authorized
> additional rank and pay for them, the dangers of flying having been made much of by
> skilful propaganda.
>
> In the face of the enemy, however, the danger to the other arms of the service was
> certainly as great, if not greater, and the effect of the special favors granted the
> Air Service was to make that arm feel that they were entitled to special consider-
> aion in other things; particularly that they should be freed from the discipline and
> control which applied to all the rest of the army[80]

V

And so, now that he had time for reflection, the returning infantryman
might begin to wonder whether his lot had been appreciated. He would
wonder why 82.32 per cent of the decorations in the European Theater went
to the Air Corps while the "Queen of Battles" received only 9.3 per cent.
Other, small, items would come to his attention. He might wonder whether
considerations other than the merits of the case did not play a part in such
awards as that of the Legion of Merit—fourth highest of decorations, rank-
ing immediately below the Distinguished Service Medal and above the Silver
Star[81]—to Heavyweight Boxing Champion Joe Louis (Sgt. Joe Barrow) " 'for
exceptionally meritorious conduct in the performance of outstanding services
as a member of a group that toured Army camps in the United States, Europe,
the Mediterranean area and Italy in the course of which he put on 96 exhibitions which entailed considerable risk in his boxing future as the champion
heavyweight of the world . . . .' "[82] Well might the infantryman wonder about
the risk to promising futures which pertained to lawyers, teachers, farmers,
business men and laborers who were his comrades in the Battalion.

Some of the returning infantrymen—in common with other veterans—
would be seeking compensation in the form of bonuses. They would consider it as no more than fair to receive a substantial sum of money as a partial
retribution for their lower income and sharing hardships of military campaigns while their friends at home received handsome wages in some relatively
safe industrial plant. A rapid rise in the cost of living would give further
impetus to such demands.

There would be others, however, who would feel that the American soldier
had been paid adequately,[83] and in view of the large percentage of the

80. Payton C. March, **The Nation at War** (Garden City, N. Y., 1932) p. 209. Of more than
5,000 pilots and observers sent overseas during World War I, 583 were casualties.—**The Encyclopedia Americana,** (1946 ed.), XXVIII, 457.
81. **The Infantry Journal,** LIV (June 1944), 43.
82. The New York Times, Sept. 24, 1945, p. 32.
83. Scale for base pay was as follows:

Officers: (per annum)		Enlisted Men ((Per month)	
Colonel	$4,000	Master sergeant	$138
lt. colonel	3,500	technical sergeant	114
major	3,000	staff sergeant	96
captain	2,400	sergeant	78
1st lieutenant	2,000	corporal	66
2nd lieutenant	1,800	private first class	54
		private	50

In addition both officers and men received an increase of 5 per cent for each three years
of service.—United States Code (1940 ed.) Title 57, Sec. 118 (Supl. V, 1941-1946, p. 782). And
overseas pay amounted to another 20 per cent for enlisted men and 10 per cent for officers.—ibid.,
sec. 102 (p. 778). One also should take into account dependent's allowances and all personal
living expenses which were provided.

economically productive population which would be veterans of this war, they would frown on attempts of pressure groups to get bonus bills through Congress and the state legislatures. Rather than an enterprise designed to contribute to the national welfare they would see such campaigns as attempts on the part of sponsoring veterans organizations to attract favor and membership to themselves and as lure for votes on the part of the political representatives.

VI

If history is to have a utilitarian value beyond an academic interest or a literary fascination, its study should reveal important lessons from past experience to guide future activities. But always there is a double danger: either a tendency to fail to recognize similarities in trends or activities on the grounds that no two situations can be alike, or such a complete reliance on the past experience as to permit striking similarities to blind one to a recognition of fundamental differences and to rob the imagination of its vigor. Both tendencies become apparent in military activity. During peace time, interest in military subjects—outside the professional services—is likely to lag; people, hoping that such study will be futile, come to believe it to be so. Perhaps one result is the truth in the old saying that "an army begins one war with the weapons of the last."

When the "First Expeditionary Division" arrived in France late in 1917 it had to depend upon foreign weapons to bring it up to date: the Hotchkiss machine gun, the Chauchet automatic rifle, a new 37 mm gun, the Stokes trench mortar.[84] The Third Battalion began its training in World War II with the Springfield rifle (model 1903), the Enfield rifle (1917), the Browning heavy machine gun (1917), the Browning automatic rifle (1918), an improved 81 mm mortar, and a new 37 mm antitank gun. By war's end the Battalion was using the Garand semi-automatic rifle, antitank grenades, the "bazooka," and a 57 mm antitank gun as well as the old heavy machine gun and automatic rifle. And already a new table of organization had appeared which provided for new 57 mm and 75 mm recoilless rifles.[85]

Among some there was the feeling that "old timers" would be unimaginative and see everything in terms of World War I. On the other hand, it is likely that greater use could have been made of the earlier experiences in small unit preparation. The members of the Third Battalion could find a mixture of the familiar with the quaint in examining the story of the earlier American operations in Europe.

The surroundings of Lorraine, of course, would be familiar, for that landscape changes little with the years. The billets in the villages with quarters in barns and stables and lofts[86] would seem common enough, and so would the rain and mud and sleet and snow, but wood-burning kitchen stoves would be outmoded.[87] Menus of American food would still look good to the infantryman of 1944: bacon, canned corned beef hash, fresh beef and canned "willy", fresh white bread, Boston baked beans—or a breakfast of corn cakes and syrup and fried ham and coffee.[88]

84. **History of the First Division**, pp. 20-21.
85. Table of Organization and Equipmetnt 7-16, 7-17, 7-18, 1 June 1945.
86. **History of the First Division**, p. 14.
87. **ibid.**, p. 17.
88. Palmer, **America in France**, p. 132.

As far as military action is concerned, the conditions of trench warfare—with positions remaining stabilized for weeks at a time, was something which would furnish little precedent for this war, but in the numerous American attacks there would be many lessons. Greatest similarity, perhaps, would be found in the attacks against position defenses in 1918, and those against Normandy hedgerows and works of the Siegfried Line in 1944.

It seems that perhaps the action, during some major attacks, was somewhat more vigorous in 1918, but the length of time for the continuation of this action was rather less as far as a particular unit was concerned. For example the 1st Division fought five days continuously at Soissons in July 1918 and suffered 7,317 casualties.[89] This would imply an approximate 545 casualties for each of that square division's 12 infantry battalions—a number only slightly less than the 574 which the Third Battalion suffered in the last two weeks of July 1944 in Normandy (but, on the other hand, casualties in the Third Battalion on such a day as "Bloody Sunday" would be greater.) One other feature of these casualty figures should be noted: about 23 per cent of those casualties at Soissons were "killed in action," while the Third Battalion's casualties in Normandy included just about 10 per cent "killed in action." Yet, taking the casualty figures for the two wars as a whole, we find the opposite to be true. That is, 20 per cent of the American battle casualties in World War I were killed or died,[90] while in World War II the battle deaths equaled 26 per cent of the total killed and wounded.[91] Members of the Third Battalion might have known that, based on World War I experience, they could have expected to have something like 480 casualties, including 50 killed, in five days of attack against a position.[92] But cold figures could not impress their full meaning; it was only after the days in combat that members of the Third Battalion came to realize the implications for themselves as individuals of such rapid turnover in the Battalion personnel.

But American operations in World War I were not limited to local attacks and trench warfare. Doubtless much similarity in infantry attacks of a generation later could have been found in the story of the attack against the St. Mihiel Salient. There the Americans were able to break into the open warfare which Pershing had maintained would win the war.[93] After four hours of artillery preparation early on September 12, 1918, infantry battalions of the American First Army, supported by light tanks and an American air force of 12 pursuit squadrons, 12 observation and three bomber squadrons, plus twice that number of Allied aircraft, began to move forward through the salient which had been in German hands for four years. So rapidly did the troops advance that shortly after daylight the next morning elements of the 1st Division, driving from the south, and the 26th Division, attacking from the northwest, made contact 18 kilometers northeast of St. Mihiel. By the afternoon of September 13, all assigned objectives had been taken, and during the next two days the divisions on the American right advanced to new objectives beyond.[94]

89. **History of the First Division,** pp. 140f.
90. In World War I, American casualties included 36,926 killed in action, 13,628 died of wounds, and 198,059 wounded.—**The Encyclopedia Americana** (1946 ed.) XXVIII, 650.
91. Army casualties in all theaters from December 7, 1941 included 201,367 killed and 570,783 wounded.—General Marshall's report, p. 107. (Further correction of the figures for prisoners and missing might make even greater the ratio of battle deaths to wounded.)
92. The Infantry School, **Reference Data,** (September 15, 1942) Table 25: Casualties in Combat. (p. 71).
93. **History of the First Division,** p. 19.
94. General John J. Pershing, "Final Report," printed in **Encyclopedia Americana** (1946 ed.) XXVII, 499f.

By the 14th members of the 1st Division were resting in a captured German recreation camp and going on tours to Mont Sec, the key terrain feature of the area from whose heights the Germans had dominated the American lines.[95] The result had been the capture of nearly 16,000 German prisoners and large stores of weapons and supplies, at a loss of only 7,000 casualties to the 19 divisions (four French and 15 American) and 500,000 men participating.[96] Perhaps the Third Battalion's attack toward Morhange in November 1944 would not have seemed too strange to veterans of St. Mihiel.

An examination of the record of the Meuse-Argonne offensive—"America's greatest battle"—would have revealed confusion and difficulty along with success. Only the fighting in hedgerows of Normandy could have been compared with the early phase of that fighting. But as far as the old 35th Division was concerned, its difficulties in the Meuse-Argonne were far greater; it had the heaviest casualty list of any division in the first phase, September 26th to October 1st.[97]

Attacking in column on that first day, the 35th Division ran into trouble almost at once. When one regiment was stopped by casualties, a second went through it, but soon there was confusion among the units as they became disorganized in fog and struggled forward without adequate direction. There was congestion in the rear areas as two divisions attempted to bring up supporting artillery and supplies over one bridge. In spite of delays it was expected that the artillery would be in position by 8:00 A.M., but higher authority could not wait—corps orders called for the attack to begin at 5:00 A.M., and they had to be obeyed. The division advanced, then, with the support of one battalion of light artillery! And it did not contribute to the morale of the troops when the daily ration arrived in the form of raw meat and potatoes with no way to cook them. It was rather to the credit of those infantry battalions that they were able to make an advance of about four miles during the first hectic day.[98]

But succeeding days became more, rather than less, difficult. The infantrymen met a virtual torrent of fire as they attempted to renew the advance on the second day. Their only recourse was to seek what protection they could by digging where they were or finding shell holes or depressions in the earth. The third day was little different—the congestion continued, there was slow evacuation of wounded, and there was another issue of raw meat and potatoes with no way to cook them. The division transport was short 1,400 horses. Losses among officers were becoming high as they made efforts to maintain liaison: "The division, in short, was "unprepared for a much less onerous task."[99]

On the fourth day the advance literally was blasted to a standstill:

Some men actually reached the village, but they could not remain there alive. Groups charging for what seemed cover only ran into more shell-bursts. The dead and wounded lay in "bunches" under the continuing blasts which disrupted organization, while officers in trying to restore it sacrificed themselves . . . . Every spurt of initiative was as futile as thrusting a finger into a stove door. Confused orders were further confused in transmission.

When night of the 29th came, there was nothing to do but for the 35th to withdraw

95. **History of the First Division,** p. 170.
96. Pershing, **loc. cit.,** p. 500.
97. Frederick Palmer, **Our Greatest Battle** (New York 1919) p. 184.
98. **ibid.,** pp. 186f; Historical section, Army War College, **Analytical Study,** 35th Division, 1917-1918 (1921-1922), pp. 29-33.
99. Palmer, **op. cit.,** pp. 188-190; Army War College Analytical Study, p. 33.

(. . . . A willing horse had been driven to death. The 35th's units had been crowded into the front line until the only reserves it had were men too exhausted from fighting to move.[100]

The 35th organized a defensive position on September 30th, and a fresh battalion came up from the 82nd Division to renew the attack. But straightway it ran into a killing barrage to impress a lesson: sending in one fresh battalion was only "throwing more cannon fodder into the ravine."[101] That night the 35th Division was relieved by the 1st. In advancing about six miles during those four days (and remaining on the defensive on the fifth) it had suffered 6,312 casualties. Half of its infantry was dead or in hospitals, and the other half was in a coma from fatigue.[102]

In reserve during the first phase of the offensive, the 1st Division had been able to continue its program of training and inspections. A twelve-hour march on the night of the 27th preserved its availability as the attack moved forward, and on the 29th it had moved up in French trucks, so that it was in position to relieve the 35th on the night of September 30th.[103]

When the battalions of the 1st Division jumped off in a renewal of the offensive on October 4th, they had the support of 108 guns of all calibers. There was no long artillery preparation—only a five minute preliminary barrage 200 meters in front of the line of departure. Then a rolling barrage, advancing 100 meters in four minutes, preceded the riflemen. There were 47 serviceable tanks with the division—of which five reached the first objective and three remained at the end of the day.

Let us follow the 3rd Battalion, 18th Infantry as it advanced with the attacking echelon. Soon it was engaged in trying hand-to-hand fighting; it was passing the bodies of men of the 35th Division who had been left there to die. On the second day it continued the attack, but on the third it held its position, and the next day (October 7th) the division was transferred to the V Corps. After a day of waiting and reorganization—during which casualties continued from enemy artillery and gas, this battalion was attacking again—in a general attack of the First Army—on October 9th. Once again the attack continued on the following day, but the battalion held its positions on the next, and on the night of October 11-12 the division was relieved by the 42nd Division.[104]

In the absence of trucks, then, the men had to march 75 kilometers south to the Vavincourt area. There 8,000 replacements (most of whom had been inducted in July) arrived—the division had suffered 7,520 casualties in those few days of attack—and there was delousing and re-equipping and training. The move back up to the front—again by French motor trucks—came on the nights of October 25th to 29th so that the division would be available as corps reserve when the V Corps renewed the attack to open the third phase of the Meuse-Argonne offensive on November 1st. This time the attacking divisions—the 2nd and 89th—were supported by 234 and 252 guns respectively. All the machine guns in the three divisions participated in the two-hour preparation which began at 3:30 A.M. A rolling barrage 150 meters deep prepared the way as infantrymen began the advance again. With attack-

100. Palmer, p. 191.
101. ibid. See also, Maj. Paul C. Greene, "The Corporal," **The Infantry Journal**, LII (Feb. 1943), 25-30.
102. Palmer, **op. cit.,** p. 192.
103. **History of the First Division**, p. 174.
104. ibid., pp. 186-212, 222.

ing battalions advancing nine kilometers on the first day, even the marches to keep up became rather exhausting for the 1st Division. On the night of 5-6 November the division was called upon to make a hard march over muddy roads and execute a relief—without benefit of reconnaissance—of the 80th Division (I Corps), and then to launch an assault prior to daybreak. Our 3rd Battalion, 18th Infantry, remained in "support" for this attack. But it resumed the advance toward Sedan between 7 and 8 P.M. that night. Between 4:30 P.M., November 5th, and midnight, November 7th, it covered 53 kilometers. Then the division reverted to corps reserve.[105]

Probably the days in World War II which would have seemed most familiar to a veteran of the 35th Division's attacks in the Meuse-Argonne would have been those in Normandy—the attack in the early morning fog toward St. Lo—the terrible enemy fire on "Bloody Sunday"—the confused situation around Mortain. But strange to him would have been the direction to small units provided by hand radios, the complete lack of horses among American units, the ever present volume of American artillery. He would have seen little in the way of meat and potatoes in any form during those days, but always there would have been "K" rations available which at least were edible. He might have been surprised to see the battalions' staying in for continuous assaults on as many as ten successive days, and remaining in active contact with the enemy for as many as 20 and more days without any relief—no unit in the Meuse-Argonne offensive (at least none in the 35th or 1st Divisions) remained in the attacking echelons for more than eight days, and even then the days of successive attacks were not more than four, and usually not more than two. But press reports to the contrary notwithstanding, he would have seen very little in the way of hand-to-hand fighting or bayonet assaults. Nor would he have been troubled by gas attacks. But he could have given some good advice on the dangers of "bunching." This veteran's counterpart in 1944, on the other hand, would have wondered how in the world a battalion was able to operate in 1918 without 300 and 536 radios and jeeps.

The 1st Division veteran would not have been surprised at the number of tanks which he saw supporting the Third Battalion's attacks, but he would have been intrigued by their power, speed, armor, and firepower; and he would have been not a little surprised to see how many remained operational at the end of the day. He would have found the 2½-ton trucks somewhat more efficient than the French models of 1918 in which he rode, and he would not have been called upon to make any marches as long as 75 kilometers to a reserve area. But there would have been times—like the night after the Rhine crossing when the Third Battalion marched up to relieve elements of the 30th Division and then continued the attack the next morning—to remind him of that relief of the 80th Division at night, without reconnaissance, and the continuation of the assault next morning. On the other hand, about the only time he ever could have seen a rolling barrage would have been on the occasion of the opening attack of the 1st and 2nd Battalions toward St. Lo on July 15th. Again, he probably would have found the greatest similarity to the operations in the last phase of the Meuse-Argonne in the Third Battalion's November-December advance through Lorraine—when casualties were high, but

---

105. **ibid.**, pp. 213-235.

the advance was relatively rapid, and it was on foot all the way from the Foret de Gremecey to Habkirchen. But the vigorous continuation of operations during the winter months in Belgium and Luxembourg doubtless would have seemed a little unusual.

Alike and unlike, infantry in battle in World War I and World War II was strikingly similar and strikingly dissimilar.

VII

Of lessons to be learned from military experience, probably none is of more immediate concern than whatever implications can be drawn for military training. First of all, the importance of military training should receive the emphasis of a realization that in vigorous combat there is no such thing, as far as individuals are concerned, as a "veteran" battalion. The men of the Third Battalion which went into action in the drive for St. Lo on July 15, 1944 had been through long and repeated programs of training. Many had been in training since December 1940—and most of those had had prior training as members of the National Guard. But many transfers had taken place, and many trained men had been sent out to other units. Even the relative newcomers to the Battalion had had over a year's training—including the exacting maneuvers of Tennessee and West Virginia. The noncommissioned officers were the kind whose officers would say, "I would like to have that man with me in combat."

But within two weeks that well-trained battalion—to the extent of two-thirds of its strength—was gone. Now it was a "battle-wise, veteran outfit," but two-thirds of its men were replacements: Within another month the turnover equaled 100 per cent. Of what value now all that year of training and rigorous maneuvers? Well, the most obvious advantage was in the creation of efficient battalion and higher staffs and competent commanders, and in providing an effective framework for the rapid assimilation of the replacements into the organization.

It would be difficult to show, however, that a unit whose men had had such long training was more effective than one whose ranks were filled with men of 13 weeks' training or less. Any comparison must be artificial because of the lack of similarity in any two situations. But in the Third Battalions' experience perhaps no better examples for comparison could be chosen than the operations in Normandy, on the one hand, and those against the Ardennes Bulge on the other. Already it has been pointed out that the men entering into combat in Normandy had had the advantage of long training.

Badly depleted as a result of its battles around Habkirchen, the Third Battalion had received enough replacements before leaving Metz to bring it up to full strength. Now these were men whose training had run from 6 to 17 weeks, and many were men who had been "retrained" from other branches with an infantry training amounting to two days. Yet in the Ardennes operations the Third Battalion was able to advance against a foe as determined, with the added hardship of winter campaign, and succeed in completing its mission with no greater casualties in four weeks than it had suffered in two in Normandy. The only advantage in the Ardennes was that of experienced commanders and staffs.

The experience of World War I had been rather similar. Then General Pershing had set up a program calling for an additional three months of training for each division after its arrival in France. The first month was to be for acclimatization and training in small unit tactics from the battalion down; during the second month battalions would go into the trenches alongside French battalions in a quiet sector, and the third would see combined training for the division in open warfare.[106] General Peyton C. March, Chief of Staff, considered that this program took too much time. Considering the draftees to be above the average as soldiers, and driven by a tremendous enthusiasm, he felt that while it "may have taken two years to make a soldier in the old army," it required "nothing like that in the new."[107]

Secretary of War Newton D. Baker wrote to Pershing in July 1918:

> We have just discovered two things about training in this country which apparently nobody knew or thought of before we went into the war. First, that while it may take nine months or a year to train raw recruits into soldiers in peace time, when there is no inspiration from an existing struggle, it takes no such length of time now, when the great dramatic battles are being fought, and men are eager to qualify themselves to participate in them. We are certainly able to get more training into a man now in three months than would be possible in twelve months of peace time training. And second, we have learned that to keep men too long in training camps in this country makes them grow stale and probably does as much harm by the spirit of impatience and restlessness aroused as it does good by the longer drills.[108]

An example was to be found in the action of the 42nd Division at St. Mihiel. Just prior to the opening of that offensive, the division had received about 9,000 replacements. Anxious to test their combat efficiency, General Douglas MacArthur, then a brigade commander, persuaded the commanding general of the division to use the men in the battle even though they had been in France only a week or so. "The men did splendidly . . . . If there was any difference, it was in favor of the new men." On inquiry as to the length of their training in the United States, MacArthur found one for whom this period had been only two months.[109]

Even General Marshall concedes that while

> It required more than a year to train the many elements of a new division because of the difficulties of teaching men and units the team-work so essential under the trying conditions of battle, . . . it was possible and practicable in a much shorter time to train an individual soldier so that he was competent to join a veteran team as a replacement . . . . At the replacement training centers men were made ready to join the divisions and replace casualties in a concentrated training period of 17 weeks.[110]

Whatever carry-over value any system of universal military training might have, it would hold for individuals rather than for units. On the basis of war experience it would seem to be questionable whether a year of peacetime infantry training either would cut down appreciably the time which would be required for training after the mobilization of units for an emergency on the one hand, or whether it would add to the combat efficiency of those units for their men to have had such training, on the other. At the same time, however, the importance of trained cadres and pools of officers trained to fill important assignments in command and staff was demonstrated thoroughly. This would indicate that American military policy, as far as organization into components of Regular Army, National Guard, and Organized Reserves is concerned, is sound. A greater emphasis toward more thorough military

106. **History of the First Division**, p. 19.
107. March, **op. cit.**, pp. 256f.
108. **ibid.**, pp. 258f.
109. **ibid.**, pp. 259f.
110. General Marshall's Report, pp. 104f.

education for key personnel, and increasing efforts toward improvement of the educational system of the country as a whole may go further toward providing real military security than any attempt to include the whole male population in a program of military training. Ever increasing importance of technology in warfare would seem to point to this field for the main effort of national preparedness—constant planning for industrial mobilization on a "total" scale—unending improvement of weapons and organization and methods —progress to the point where the army can escape its habit of "entering one war with the weapons of the last."

One other point in this connection should not be forgotten. Military men point to the truth that had it not been for the time which the resistance of the British Empire and the Soviet Union bought, the United States, might have met disaster before it could have mobilized its strength.[111] But, mobilized in December 1940, the Third Battalion should have been ready for combat at least by the time of the attack on Pearl Harbor. Yet it did not enter the battle lines until July 1944. But the deterrent to earlier entry into combat was not due to a lack of training, but rather to the slowness of the *industrial mobilization.*

In fact much delay in training arose out of a lack of equipment. At the beginning of the war in Europe

There were the bare skeletons of three and one-half divisions scattered in small pieces over the entire United States. It was impossible to train even these few combat troops as divisions because motor transportation and other facilities were lacking and funds for adequate maneuvers were not appropriated . . . . We lacked modern arms and equipment.[112]

It is doubtful that the war could have ended any sooner even had there been a pool of ten million men trained under a universal training program. The invasion of Western Europe was delayed, not for lack of trained men, but for want of equipment. At a conference in London in April 1942,

a tentative target date for the cross-channel operations, designated by the code name ROUNDUP, was set for the summer of 1943. However, the immediate necessity for an emergency plan was recognized. It was given the code name SLEDGEHAMMER and was to provide for a diversionary assault on the French coast at a much earlier date if such a desperate measure became necessary to lend a hand toward saving the situation on the Soviet front.

Here the Western Allies faced a shortage of assault craft, LST's, LCI's, and smaller vessels . . . . An extensive building program for landing craft was agreed upon, which necessitated a heavy cut-back or delay in the construction then underway of certain major combat ships for the Pacific Fleet. Also there were added to the production program in the United States a great many items which would be required for build-up—engineering and railroad equipment and rolling stock, pipelines, hospital set-ups, communication material, and a multitude of items to be required for airfields, camps, docks, and depots in the British Isles for the actual Channel crossing and for the support of our troops once they were in France.

In July, [General Marshall] went to London for further meetings with the British Chiefs of Staff, to determine if there were not something that could be done immediately to lessen the pressure on the Soviet, whose armies were facing a crisis. Poverty of equipment, especially in landing craft, and the short period remaining when the weather would permit cross-Channel movement of small craft, ruled out the diversionary operation SLEDGEHAMMER for 1942.

After prolonged discussions, it became evident that the only operation that could be undertaken with a fair prospect of success that year was TORCH, the assault on North Africa. . . . It was therefore decided, with the approval of the President and the Prime Minister, to mount the North African assault at the earliest

111. *ibid.*, p. 120.
112. *ibid.*, p. 117.

possible moment, accepting the fact that this would mean not only the abandonment of the possibility for any operation in Western Europe that year, but that the necessary build-up for the cross-Channel assault could not be completed in 1943. TORCH would bleed most of our resources in the Atlantic, and would confine us in the Pacific to the holding of the Hawaii-Midway line and the preservation of communications to Australia.[113]

The chief military lesson of this war was that "wars are not won by 'big battalions,' but by big industries."[114]

VIII

In the matter of organization the Army has demonstrated quite a progressive attitude in recent years. Even while the Third Battalion awaited redeployment to the United States—for eventual service in the Pacific—new tables were published which sought to correct the deficiencies in organization and equipment which had become evident from combat experience, and to provide for use of proved technological advances in the addition of new weapons. Boards and commissions had been at work during the course of combat to try to evaluate the organization and equipment in its actual applications. There were questionaires to be filled out by battalion commanders, and a conference at regimental headquarters in which a representative of one of these boards sought the views of the leaders of the regiment and battalions.

Some experimentation and improvisation during combat itself was to be expected on the part of the battalion. Thus there had been the organization of bazooka teams out of the antitank squads. The 1st Battalion had experimented with taking the 60 mm mortars out of the rifle companies, and concentrating them in a special platoon under the heavy weapons company—on the grounds that the companies were not making full use of their "60's," and ammunition was strictly rationed for the 81 mm mortar, while it was plentiful for the smaller model. The Third Battalion's company commanders, however, were reluctant to give up this "personal artillery." However, there was general agreement that the 57 mm gun had not proved to be very useful, but that battalions needed the close support of self-propelled guns or tanks.

Later, a demonstration of recoilless weapons—75 mm and 57 mm cannon that a man could carry on his shoulders!—convinced observers that here was a type of weapon to fit the needs of an infantry battalion.

In the way of other items of equipment, there was reference to the irony of the lack of shoepacs for the winter campaigns; there was some suggestion that the cumbersome enlisted men's overcoats ought to be replaced by field coats of the type which many officers wore. There was further irony to be noted in the fact that American soldiers had had to depend upon captured German heat tablets to heat their rations (a situation remedied by inclusion of such tablets in the Army's new "E" ration); again, most battalions—and companies, when the situation permitted—had acquired German portable electric generators to light their command posts.

It is best not to undertake too general a reorganization in combat if that can be avoided, but now, prior to the beginning of a new training period preparatory for further operations in the Pacific, the carrying out of desirable changes was practicable.

---

113. **ibid.,** pp. 8f.
114. Hanson W. Baldwin, "America at War: The Triumph of the Machine," **Foreign Affairs, XXIV** (Jan. 1946), 241.

According to the authorizations of the new tables of organization the battalion antitank platoon was eliminated, but a new "gun platoon"—armed with six 75 mm recoilless rifles—was added to the heavy weapons company.[115] The addition of two new sections in the weapons platoon and a small increase in the size of company headquarters extended the strength of the rifle company to a total of seven officers and 235 enlisted men. The first was an "assault section" which would carry six rocket launchers (thus filling a need for which the Third Battalion had reorganized its antitank platoon for the advance through Germany), and the other was a "special weapons section," armed with three 57 mm recoilless guns.[116] There were other lesser changes: the battalion supply officer was made a member of the battalion rather than of the regimental service company, the grade of the battalion S-2 was raised to captain, mortar section leaders were to be staff sergeants again rather than officers.

Most notable change in the regimental special troops was the provision that the antitank company should be equipped with nine heavy tanks, mounting 90 mm guns, and the cannon company likewise was to have nine heavy tanks, but they would carry 105 mm howitzers.[117]

Not content to rest on these accomplishments the army announced further changes in infantry organizations in December 1946. The most important "local change" for the infantry battalion was in the reduction in the size of the rifle squad from 12 men to 9—squad leader, assistant squad leader, automatic rifleman and his assistant, and five riflemen. (This on the theory that one man could not control a larger group effectively in combat; actually there were few times when a squad leader in the Third Battalion ever was called upon to lead a 12-man squad into battle.) The advantage which officers of the Third Battalion had found in making reconnaissance in artillery liaison planes was reflected in the assignment of a "Grasshopper" to each regiment. There was further emphasis on recoilless weapons, and an improved 3.5 inch bazooka was to replace the 2.54 inch rocket launcher. Other changes affected the regimental special troops. The antitank and cannon companies now were completely eliminated in favor of a full tank company—equipped with heavy M-36 "General Pershing" tanks—and a 4.2 mortar company. A medical company replaced the medical detachment. Additions to the division included an organic tank battalion (in addition to the three regimental companies), an organic antiaircraft battalion, and the addition of two howitzers to each of the firing batteries of field artillery.[118]

Looking toward the future, General Jacob L. Devers, commanding general of the Army Ground Forces, pointing out that the strength of the infantry division had been increased one-fifth, but the number of its artillery weapons had been tripled, and its fire power more than tripled, went on to say:

The Infantry division of the future will not be merely amphibious, striking at the enemy by land or sea. It will be "triphibious," capable of swift mechanized movement by land, sea and air. . .

In World War II V-2 rocket attacks upon our troops and upon the civilian population in Belgium and England did not stop until our ground forces had penetrated to the launching sites, destroyed the Nazi covering forces, and demolished the sites and stockpiles.

In any future war the mission of our ground forces would be the same. Attacks upon the civilian population of the United States itself would not cease until

115. Table of Organization and Equipment, 7-16 and 7-18, 1 June 1945.
116. T/O & E 7-17, 1 June 1945.
117. T/O & E 7-11, 1 June 1945.
118. **Army and Navy Journal**, LXXXIV (Dec. 21, 1946), 395f.

our Army's ground forces—infantry, armored cavalry and artillery—descended upon the enemy's airfields, launching sites, depots, and factories to seize or destroy them.

Atomic and other weapons will not alter the nature of warfare to such an extent that the ground combat need for a versatile, mobile and hard-hitting division will be diminished or altered.

The infantry division will remain the versatile combat unit of a field Army, organized basically for hard-hitting shock action. It will have a degree of training in special operations that will permit its rapid conversion for jungle, arctic, desert or mountain fighting, and for movement by motor, ships or plane.[119]

After contemplating on the decline which had come to successive military organizations during the course of history, one almost is moved to recommend change for the sake of change. In society, as a whole, there is a demand that the individual conform, and insofar as this is successful, looking beyond certain desirable features of conformity, it leads to stagnation. In the Army, where the need for discipline and standardization, and uniformity is necessary for military success, the impulse to conform is considerably more pressing, and so the danger of stagnation proportionately greater. An assurance of continued success must depend upon a fine balance between uniformity and variation, conformity and non-conformity.

Looking at the course of military history, it would seem to be the case very frequently that success begets defeat. That is, a new weapon or a new tactical organization becomes the means for decisive victory; its success proved, it then is retained until forced into defeat by another new development. Thus the phalanx, invincible under Alexander the Great, is retained until it must defer to the Roman legion. The English long bow, successful at Crecy, becomes the standard dependence of English armies who, resisting the changes demanded by the introduction of gun powder, fall to defeat before the primitive French cannon. Or the French, convinced of the superiority of the noted '75 during World War I, find it wholly inadequate in 1940. It is almost an expression in military affairs of that observation of politics, "Today's radicals are tomorrow's conservatives."

The theory of army organization seems to be fully in accord with present-day thought on organization in general. Barnard, for example, offers a number of controlling factors in any system of objective authority which have immediate implications in military organizations:

(a) . . . *Channels of communication should be definitely known.* [This becomes a definite function of military training in acquainting all members of a command with the organizational pattern and with the persons exercising the function of command.]

(b) . . . *Objective authority requires a definite formal channel of communication to every member of an organization.* In ordinary language this means "everyone must report to someone," . . . and everyone must be subordinate to some one. [This factor is exploited with a vengeance in military responsibility.]

(c) . . . *The line of communication must be as direct or short as possible.* . . . In great complex organizations the number of levels of communication is not much larger than in smaller organizations. In the Army the levels are . . . nine or ten [in Europe, from squad to the President (War Department) included eleven levels.] In the Bell Telephone System . . . the number is eight to ten.

(d) . . . *The complete line of communication should usually be used.* [In Army administration one always is cautioned to "go through channels."]

(e) . . . *The competence of the persons serving as communications centers, that is, officers, supervisory heads, must be adequate.*

(f) . . . *The line of communication should not be interrupted during the time when the organization is to function.* [There must always be a "duty officer" at each level of command, and vacancies in command are filled immediately.]

119. *Ibid.,* pp. 370. 395.

(g) . . . *Every communication should be authenticated.* [Again, this becomes a function of training.][120]

Looking to formal organization, Barnard observes that the size of a unit usually is determined by the limitations of effective leadership, and that these limitations depend upon:

(a) The complexity of purpose and technological conditions; (b) the difficulty of the communication process; (c) the extent to which communication is necessary; (d) the complexity of personal relationships involved, that is, of the social conditions.[121]

The pattern of tactical organization responds to technological developments both directly and indirectly. That is, new weapons affect tactics immediately by exposing old formations to new vulnerability. Then, at the same time, technological developments may operate to influence the size of the units and to influence those other factors affecting its size. Thus a new weapon will make possible the delivery of as great a volume of fire with less men; motor trucks may demand smaller divisions for greater ease of rapid transport; radio communication makes possible the control of larger companies and battalions, but the need for dispersal imposed by modern weapons renders personal communication within the squad more difficult, and so suggests a reduction in the size of the squad. Here again is another implication for military training:

Moreover, if men know what to do from previous experience and can work on the basis of habit and acquired skill, a minimum of communication is required; or if they are accustomed to working together; a special language which they evolve cuts down the time of communication.[122]

There remains yet another consideration of paramount importance for military organization and training: the function of informal organization.[123] Only through a period of military training with a *particular unit* can a person become familiar with its essential informal organization—with the way that particular organization does things, its standing operating procedure (SOP), its peculiar division of detail, its methods of meeting certain situations.

Though the battalion itself was primarily a tactical unit, it did come to be recognized that it did have some administrative functions. This was recognized in the new table when the supply officer was made a member of the regular battalion staff. But as far as administrative records were concerned, this was a matter for company and regiment.

"Old Timers" would be disappointed that the regimental band, lost in 1943, was not restored in the new organization. The 134th had resorted to the device—as had numbers of regiments—of instituting an unofficial regimental band. For members of the Third Battalion, the days in Europe doubtless would have been considerably more dreary had the music of that band—in concerts, programs of popular music, parades, and ceremonies—been absent.

But as far as adaptability for tactical employment, the changes in organization would seem to deserve praise. The test will be, however, to keep the organization and weapons continually improving. More may be done, for example, in the way of integration.

Since the time of Gustavus Adolphus, at least, military victories have been the result, largely, of close coordination of the various arms. Traditionally this coordination has concerned the infantry, artillery, and cavalry. The infantry-artillery team has reached a state of near perfection in the at-

120. Chester I. Barnard, **The Functions of the Executive** (Cambridge, Mass., 1938), pp. 175-181.
121. **ibid.**, p. 107.
122. **ibid.**, p. 108.
123. see **ibid.**, pp. 120-123.

tachment of artillery liaison sections to infantry battalion headquarters and the sending of forward observers to the rifle companies. Other weapons— machine guns, mortars, and now recoilless guns—have become, at one time or another organic to the battalion. Much progress was made during combat in Europe toward effective infantry—tank coordination. This promises to become closer with the inclusion of tanks as organic equipment in the regiment and division; coordination with the cavalry's successor appears to be assured.

There remains, however, that relatively new arm which threatens a domination as complete as that of the cavalry in another age—air forces. Here there is much to be desired in the matter of air-ground coordination. How effective air support can be when cooperating with infantry was demonstrated at Pain de Sucre, east of Nancy, when aircraft happened to be available on call of the Third Battalion. How disappointing it can be was demonstrated at the Foret de Gremecey when the Third Battalion watched approaching columns of German vehicles but could get no response from the air for a matter of three or four hours.

Perhaps a solution would lie in adding flights of fighter-bombers to *the infantry division.* This would not mean to take away aircraft from an independent air force; this would not mean to deny the principle of concentration; this would be *in addition* to whatever might be the requirements of the Air Force. If the Marine Corps is to retain its aircraft, why should not the Army as well retain tactical aircraft? The German and French divisions included observation squadrons in their divisions back in the 1920's. Now it would appear expedient for the infantry division to have its air arm not only for reconnaissance, but as well to support the attack and to provide protection against local attacks of enemy aircraft. Strafing runs, specific bombing missions, feints of zooming and diving, and reconnaissance over enemy territory (for which a liaison plane is not practical) could make a tremendous contribution to a division's attack, particularly if air liaison officers—with direct communication with the planes—should be assigned to the battalions making the main effort. The difference would be as noon is to twilight if such direct access to air power could replace the necessity for going all the way to corps for such assistance. Theoretically the division is supposed to include all combat arms. Now it does include all with that major exception—it has no combat aircraft.

IX

After completion of recuperation leaves and furloughs, members of the Third Battalion assembled, with the other units of the division, at Camp Breckinridge, Kentucky. Very soon, however, it melted away. High-point-men were discharged to return to civilian life; low-point-men were transferred to other units. On December 7, 1945—just four years after the attack on Pearl Harbor—the 35th Division ceased to exist as an active unit of the Army of the United States.[124]

The Third Battalion returned to the state whence it had come; it would live on—prepared for new emergencies which might appear in the future— as the 3rd Battalion, 134th Infantry, Nebraska National Guard.

Of the three episodes which General Eisenhower listed as being the most decisive in insuring victory in the West—Normandy, the Falaise Pocket, the

124. **Santa Fe,** p. 197.

Rhineland[125]—the Third Battalion had played an important part in every one. In the battle to gain and then to hold the footing in Normandy during June and July, the Third Battalion had played a major role in the capture of the key communications center—St. Lo. In setting the stage for the Falaise pocket, the Third Battalion had been in the midst of the action south of Mortain. In the third decisive phase—the battles west of the Rhine during February and March, the Third Battalion had led the final attack to eliminate the Wesel pocket.

Beyond this the Battalion had had a major part in the campaign through Lorraine, in the battles around Bastogne, in the Ruhr, and finally had gone all the way to the Elbe River. No major campaign in the European Theater escaped it.

What a long way we have come since the early days in Normandy around St. Lo.

Looking back, there are three or four actions which stand out as being the really rough ones—almost beyond imagination in severity. These would be (1) St. Lo, (2) Mortain (this did not last so many days), (3) the push through the Saar: Chambrey to Morhange to Sarreguemines to Habkirchen, Germany, (4) the "Bulge" around Lutrebois and Bastogne. By comparison, the rest has seemed easy. Yes, there were always boys getting hurt—worse; there were some sharp battles east of Nancy, and some nerve-racking close shaves in the Rhineland and in the Ruhr, but it was a different war from those four mentioned.

The greatest thrill: liberation of NANCY.

The worst night: the incessant mortar and artillery fire as we waited our turn to follow the 2nd Bn. across the Moselle River—they never made it.

The worst artillery: one day in the woods above Habkirchen (included some of *our own* tank fire, and that was terrific).

The toughest nuts to crack: (1) Habkirchen, (2) Lutrebois.[126]

The worst days for the battalion: "Bloody Sunday," July 30, 1944 and "Blue Monday" on "Blood and Guts Hill," November 13th.

Best performances of the battalion:
(1) Chasing the Krauts into St. Lo on July 17th. [sic]
(2) Crossing the Moselle at NANCY.
(3) Capture of Pan de Sucre Hill (Sugar Loaf).[127]

Others would have added the Battalion's stand against counterattacks in the Foret de Gremecey, and the difficult but decisive action at Lutrebois.

Perhaps such a characterization as that given the 1st Division in World War I would not have been completely appropriate for the Third Battalion:

It never complained; it never criticized others; it never asked to be relieved; it was never shot to pieces; it was never held up by machine gun fire; it was never tired.[123]

The Third Battalion did complain sometimes; it did hope to be relieved; it was shot up; it was held up by machine gun fire; it was tired—very tired.

And yet it could remain secure in the knowledge that it never gave up a piece of ground without itself recovering it (albeit not without some assistance sometimes), that it had played an important part in the greatest military struggle of all time, that among infantry battalions there was no finer.

125. General Eisenhower's Report, p. 121.
126. The orientation program and the emphasis on disseminating information to all ranks was successful, for the most part, in overcoming the traditional lack of comprehension of the military situation in the lower units. Something of an exception to this might have been found at Mortain, or possibly at Lutrebois. There members of the Third Battalion might have shared in such a conversation as that assigned to an earlier age:
"Oh, if a man should come up an' ask me, I'd say we got a dum good licken'."
"Lickin'—in yer eye! We ain't licked sonny. We're going down here aways, swing aroun', an' come in behint 'em."
"Oh, hush, with your comin' in behint 'em. I've seen all a that I wanta. Don't tell me about comin' in behint—"—Cain, **The Red Badge of Courage**, p. 264.
127. J. A. Huston to N. F. Huston, May 3, 1945.
128. **History of the First Division**, p. xvii.

APPENDIX

T/O & E 7-15

TABLE OF ORGANIZATION)
AND EQUIPMENT)
No. 7 - 15)
with)   26 February 1944
Changes)
No. 1)
30 June 1944

INFANTRY BATTALION

	Hq	Hq Co	3 rifle companies (each)	Hvy Wpns Co.	Total Battalion
Lieutenant colonel	1				1
Major	1				1
Captain	1	1	1	1	6
First lieutenant	1	2	3	3	15
Second lieutenant		2	2	4	12
Total commissioned	4	5	6	8	35
First Sergeant		1	1	1	5
Technical Sergeant		3	4	3	18
Staff Sergeant		9	16	15	72
Sergeant		6	15	11	62
Corporal		5	1	15	21
Technician, grade 4		6	2	3	15
Technician, grade 5		11	4	2	25
Private, first class		52	104	76	440
Private, including		19	40	28	167
Basic		(6)	(17)	(8)	(65)
Total enlisted		112	187	152	825
Aggregate	4	117	193	160	860
Carbine, cal. . 30	2	51	28	82	119
Gun, machine, cal. . 30, heavy, flexible				8	8
Gun, machine, HB, cal. . 50, flexible		2	1	1	6
Gun, submachine, cal. . 45		2	6		20
Gun, 57mm, towed		3			3
Launcher, rocket, 2.36-inch		8	5	6	29
Mortar, 60mm			3		9
Mortar, 81mm				6	6
Pistol, automatic, cal. . 45	2	15	10	34	81
Rifle, automatic, cal. . 30			15		45
Rifle, cal. . 30, M-1.		51	143	44	524
Rifle, cal. . 30, M1903A4			3		3
Trailer, ¼-ton		2	2	14	22
Trailer, 1-ton		1			1
Truck, ¼-ton		9	2	19	34
Truck ¾-ton, weapons carrier		1		1	2
Truck, 1½-ton, cargo		4			4

BIBLIOGRAPHY

I. Documents and Records:
  A. Journals.
    3rd Battalion, 134th Infantry, **Journal** (MS, 3 vols)
    134th Infantry Unit Journal.
    134th Infantry, **S-3 Journal** (MS).
    134th Infantry, S-3 Situation Reports; S-2 Periodic Reports.
  B. Papers of Major General Butler B. Miltonberger, Chief, National Guard Bureau (commander of 134th Infantry during most of its combat)—then in National Guard Bureau, The Pentagon, Washington, D. C.:
    134th Infantry, **Daily Log and Diary** (typescript, bound in 6 vols) Includes copies of operation reports, clippings, some letters, as well as "Daily Log."
  C. Combat Analysis Section, Operations Branch, The Adjutant General's Office, The Pentagon, Washington, D. C.:
    134th Infantry, After Action Reports (Typewritten)
    161st Field Artillery Battalion, After Action Reports (35th Div.)—"**Lessons** Learned" (12 pp., typewr.)
    35th Infantry Division, The Story of the 35th Inf Division
                    —(Pamphlet, **attack!**—printed in Germany)
                    History (mimeographed sketch)
                    Historical Booklet (Typewritten ms of the division history, **Santa Fe**, published in 1946 by Albert Love Enterprises, Atlanta, Ga.)
    Third United States Army, After Action Report, I: Operations (Reproduced 1945, by 652nd Engr (topo) Bn and Co. B, 942nd Engr Avn (topo) Bn)
  D. Historical Records Section, War Department Records Branch, The Adjutant General's Office, The Pentagon, Washington, D. C.:
    134th Infantry, After Action Reports (copies)
              Unit Journal (MS)
              S-2 Periodic Reports
              S-3 Situation Reports
    3rd Information and Historical Service, 35th Infantry Division: Combat Interviews No. 108—35th Div—1 Nov 44—23 Jan 45.
  E. Decorations and Awards Branch, The Adjutant General's Office, The Pentagon, Washington, D. C.:
    35th Infantry Division, General Orders, 1944, 1945
  F. Demobilized Personnel Records Branch, The Adjutant General's Office, 4300 Goodfellow Blvd, St. Louis, Mo.:
    134th Infantry, Battle Casualty Reports
              Service Records
              Qualification Cards
  G. Historical Division, War Department Special Staff, The Pentagon, Washington, D. C.:
    St. Lo (mimeographed copy of ms published in 1947 as one of the War Department's **American Forces in Action** series)
  H. The Information Section, Analysis Branch, Headquarters Army Ground Forces, The Pentagon, Washington, D. C.:
    Information File: 35th Inf. Division
    (a collection of historical sketches, press releases, clippings, etc.)
  I. Still Pictures Branch, Army Pictorial Service, The Signal Corps, The Pentagon, Washington, D. C.
    Nearly a million photographs, filed according to divisions, branch of service, location, and under every conceivable subject practically opens up a whole new avenue for research.
  J. Miscellaneous:
    Personal Notebooks:
              3rd Battalion S-2 Notebook
              3rd Battalion S-3 Notebooks
              Camp Norfolk S-3 Notebooks
    Personal Correspondence:
              (see acknowledgements)
    Battalion Training Schedules
II. Official Published Reports
    Annual Report of the Army Service Forces for the Fiscal Year 1945. Washington: U.S. Government Printing Office, 1945.
    Arnold, H. B., **Second Report of the Commanding General of the Army Air Forces to the Secretary of War.** Washington: U.S. Government Printing Office, 1945.
    ————, **Third Report of the Commanding General of the Army Air Forces to the Secretary of War.** Washington: U.S. Government Printing Office, 1945.
    First U.S. Army, Report of Operations, 20 Oct 43-1 Aug 44; 1 Aug 44-22 Feb 45.
    Eisenhower, Dwight D., **Report by the Supreme Commander to the Combined Chiefs of Staff on the Operations in Europe of the Allied Expeditionary Force, 6 June 1944 to 8 May 1945.** Washington: U.S. Government Printing Office, 1946.
    Marshall, George C., **Biennial Report of the Chief of Staff of the United States Army, 1943 to 1945, to the Secretary of War.** Washington: U.S. Government Printing Office, 1945.
    Third U. S. Army, After Action Report.
    The United States Strategic Bombing Survey. Over-all Report. (European War). September 30, 1945.
III. War Department Publications.
  A. Field Manuals
    100-5 Field Service Regulations: Operations.
    100-10 Field Service Regulations: Administration.
    100-20 Field Service Regulations: Command and Employment of Air Power.
    7-10 Rifle Company, Rifle Regiment (1942).
    7-20 Rifle Battalion (1943).
    22-5 Infantry Drill Regulations (1941).
    23-5 U.S. Rifle, Caliber .30, M1 (1940).

23-7 U.S. Carbine, Caliber .30, M-1 (1942).
23-10 U.S. Rifle Caliber .30, M1903 (1940).
23-15 Browning Automatic Rifle, Caliber .30, M1918A2 with Bipod (1940).
21-15 Equipment, Clothing, and Tent Pitching.
23-25 Bayonet (1940).
23-30 Hand Grenades (1940).
23-35 Automatic Pistol, Caliber .45 M1911 and M-1911A1 (1940).
23-45 Browning Machine Gun, Caliber .30, Heavy Barrel, M1919A4, Ground (1940).
23-55 Browning Machine Gun, Caliber .30 M1917 (1940).
23-60 Browning Machine Gun, Caliber .50, Heavy Barrel, M-2, Ground (1940).
23-65 60mm Mortar, M-2 (1940).
23-90 81mm Mortar, M-1 (1940).
  B. Tables of Organization and Equipment:
7-15 Infantry Battalion.
7-16 Headquarters and Headquarters Company, Infantry Battalion.
7-17 Rifle Company.
7-18 Heavy Weapons Company.
  C. Training Circulars.
  D. War Department Circulars.
  E. General Orders.
  F. Miscellaneous.
The Infantry School. Conference Course, Training Bulletins (1943).
The Infantry School. **Reference Data.**

IV. Newspapers and Periodicals.
  A. Official and semi-official military publications.
AAF Review; Official Journal of the U.S. Army Air Forces.
Army and Navy Journal
The Infantry Journal
Military Review
The Santa Fe Express (35th Division newspaper)
The Stars and Stripes (London and Paris Editions)
Army Information Digest
Yank, The Army Weekly
    (British and Continental editions)
  B. Civilian Newspapers:
The New York Times
The New York Herald-Tribune
The Omaha World Herald
Kansas City Star
Gering (Nebr.) Courier

V. World War II: General Works and personal accounts.
Allen, Robert S., **Lucky Forward,** New York: The Vanguard Press, 1947.
Baldwin, Hanson W., "America at War: The Crisis," **Foreign Affairs,** XXII (July 1944), 521-531.
————————, "America At War: The End Begins," **Foreign Affairs,** XXIII (Oct. 1944), 1-16.
————————, "America At War: The End in Sight," **Foreign Affairs,** XXIII (Jan. 1945), 167-181.
————————, "America At War: Victory in Europe," **Foreign Affairs,** III (July 1945), 527-542.
————————, "America At War: The Triumph of the Machine," **Foreign Affairs,** XXIV (Jan. 1946), 241-261.
Butcher, Harry C., **My Three Years With Eisenhower.** New York: Simon and Schuster, 1946.
Commager, Harry Steele, **The Story of the Second World War.** Boston: Little, Brown, and Company, 1945.
Eisenhower, Dwight D., **Crusade in Europe.** Garden City, N. Y.: Doubleday, 1948.
Ensor, R. C. K., **A Miniature History of the War; down to the End of the War in Europe,** 3rd edition. London: Oxford University Press, 1945.
Ingersoll, Ralph, **Top Secret,** New York: Harcourt, Brace, and Company, 1946.
Kehn, E. J., Jr. and McLemore, Henry, **Fighting Divisions.** Washington: The Infantry Journal, 1945.
McInnis, Edgar, **The War: Fifth Year.** London, Toronto, New York: Oxford University Press, 1945.
————————, **The War: Sixth Year,** London, Toronto, New York: Oxford University Press, 1946.
Montgomery, Bernard L., **Normandy to the Baltic.** Boston: Houghton Mifflin Co., 1948.
Miller, Francis Trevelyn, **History of World War II.** Philadelphia: The John C. Winston Company, 1945.
Patton, George S., **War As I Knew It.** Boston: Houghton Mifflin Co., 1947.
Shugg, Roger W., and DeWeerd, H. A., **World War II: A Concise History.** Washington: The Infantry Journal, 1946.
United States at War, December 7, 1943-December 7, 1944. Washington: Army and Navy Journal, 1945.
United States at War, December 7, 1944-December 7, 1945. Washington: Army and Navy Journal, 1945.

VI. Books and Articles on Special Topics.
"Allies Squeeze the German Bulge," **Life,** XVIII (Jan. 16, 1945) 15-19.
Antrobus, Edmund, "V-Bombs on Antwerp," **Yank** (British ed.) III, (April 13, 1945), 4-5.
"Attack in Holland," **Life,** XVII (Dec. 18, 1944) 69.
"Battle of France—Ruins of St. Lo," **Life,** XVII (Aug. 21, 1944), pp. 36-37.
"Battle of the Hedgerows," **Life,** XVII (Aug. 7, 1944), pp. 17-23.
Beazley, Charles P., "Air Forces' Oldest," **AAF Review;** Official Journal of the U. S. Army Air Forces, XXIX (July 1946), 17-21, 42-43.
Boring, Edwin C. (ed.), **Psychology for the Armed Forces.** Prepared under supervision of the National Research Council. Washington: The Infantry Journal, 1945.

Dager, H. E., "Modern Infantry," **The Command and General Staff School Military Review, XX** (March 1940), 5-18.
Davidson, Bill, "Barrage by Bombers," Yank (British edition), III (Aug. 13, 1946), 5-6.
Dollard, John, **Fear in Battle.** New Haven: Institute of Human Relations, Yale University, 1943.
Dorpalen, Andreas, **The World of General Haushoffer.** New York and Toronto: Farrar and Rinehart, 1942.
Engel, Leonard, "Rockets," **The Infantry Journal,** CIV (Jan. 1944), 58-63.
Fay, Sidney B., "The Fate of the Saar," **Current History,** XLI (Jan. 1935) pp. 399-403.
Glaser, Daniel, "The Sentiments of American Soldiers Abroad toward Europeans," **The American Journal of Sociology,** LX (March 1946, 433-438).
Gregory, W. Edgar, "The Idealization of the Absent," **The American Journal of Sociology,** L (July 1944), 53-54.
"Hedgerow Figthing," **The Infantry Journal,** LV (Oct. 1944), pp. 9-13.
"How to Avoid Trench Foot," **The Infantry Journal,** LVI (Jan. 1945) 32.
Ingersoll, Ralph, **The Battle Is the Pay-Off.** New York: Harcourt, Brace and Company, 1945.
"It's a Tough Racket," **The Infantry Journal,** LVI (March 1945), pp. 27-28.
Knight, Charlotte, "German Rocketeers," AAF Review, XXIX, (July 1946), 24-26, 48.
Leavitt, Saul, "They Held Bastogne," Yank (British ed.) III, (Jan. 28, 1945), 6-7.
————, "Montargis . . . as They Wanted It," **"Yank,** (British ed.) III, (Sept. 17, 1944), pp. 5-8.
————, "St. Lo Was no Cinch," Yank: The Army Weekly, (British Edition), III (Aug. 13, 1944), pp. 2ff.
Leigh, Randolph, **48 Million Tons to Eisenhower; the Role of the SOS in the Defeat of Germany.** Washington: The Infantry Journal, 1945.
Lewis, Ralph, "Officer-Enlisted Men's Relationships," **The American Journal of Sociology,** LII (March 1947), 410-419.
"The Making of the Infantryman," **The American Journal of Sociology,** LI (March 1946), 376-379.
Marshall, S. L. A., **Men Against Fire.** New York: William Morrow & Co., 1947.
Meier, Herman C., **Military Psychology.** New York: Harper and Brothers, 1943.
"The Mind in Combat," **The Infantry Journal,** LII (Feb. 1944), 53-55.
Merriam, Robert E., **Dark December.** Chicago: Ziff-Davis, 1947.
Mira, Emilio, **Psychiatry in War.** New York: W. W. Norton and Company, 1943.
Morse, Ralph, "George Lott, Casualty," Life, XVIII (Jan. 29, 1945) 15-17.
"New Division Organization," Army and Navy Journal, LXXXIV (Dec. 21, 1946), 370, 395-396.
O'Keefe, Elbert B., "Artillery was the Answer," **The Infantry Journal,** CVI, (June 1945), 25.
Pyle, Ernest, **Brave Men.** New York: H. Holt and Company, 1944.
"Psychology for the Fighting Man," **The Infantry Journal,** LII (Jan. 1943), 54-61.
Rose, Arnold, "The Social Structure of the Army," **"The American Journal of Sociology,** LI (March 1946), 361-364.
"The Ruhr in Spring," **The Economist,** CL (June 8, 1946), 929.
Scofield, John, "German Infantry Weapons," **The Infantry Journal,** LIV (Jan. 1947), 37-40.
Simpson, William H., "Rehearsal for the Rhine: an Account of the Ninth United States Army Operation 'Grenade'," **Military Review,** XXV (Oct. 1945), 20-28.
Stone, Robert C., "Status and Leadership in a Combat Fighter Squadron," **The American Journal of Sociology,** LI (March 1946), 388-394.
Thompson, Paul W., "Why Normandy?" **The Infantry Journal,** LVIII (Feb. 1946), 8-14.
United States Military Academy. Department of Military Art and Engineering. **The Invasion of Western Europe.** 2 parts. West Point: U.S.M.A. Printing Office, 1946.* **(Restricted)**
War Department. Historical Division. **St. Lo** (American Forces in Action Series). Washington: U. S. Govt. Printing Office, 1947.
Warndof, C. R., "German and Japanese Infantry Division," **The Infantry Journal,** LIV (April 1944), 33-35.

VII.   Miscellaneous

Barnard, Chester I., **The Functions of the Executive.** Cambridge, Mass.: Harvard University Press, 1938.
Information-Education Section, Lorraine District. Oise Intermediate Section, Theater Service Forces. United States Army, **Lorraine and Nancy.** Nancy, 1945.
Ville de Nancy, **En Hommage a ses Liberateurs.** Nancy, 1945.
Quartermaster Corps Manual 17-3: **U. S. Army Support—survival—Assault—Combat Rations and Supplements. Army Service Forces. Office of the Quartermaster General.**
Santa Fe: 35th Infantry Division. Atlanta: Albert Love Enterprises, 1946.
Twelfth Army Group, **Battle Experiences.**

VIII.   Military History, Tactics, Background

Albion, Robert Greenbalgh, **Introduction to Military History.** New York & London: The Century Co., 1929.
American Battle Monuments Commission. **American Armies and Battlefields in Europe.** Washington, U. S. Govt. Printing Office, 1938.
Army War College. Historical Section, **The Genesis of the American First Army.** Washington: U. S. Govt. Printing Office, 1938.
————. **Order of Battle of the United States Land Forces in the World War; American Expeditionary Forces; Divisions.** Washington: U. S. Govt. Printing Office, 1931.
Bond, P. S., and McDonough, M. J., **Technique of Modern Tactics.** 3rd ed. Menasha, Wisc.: George Bants Publishing Company, 1916.
Buchan, John, **A History of the Great War,** 4 vols. New York, 1922.
Carter, William Harding, **The American Army.** Indianapolis: The Bobbs-Merrill Company, 1915.
Colby, Elbridge, "A Soldier Looks at Military Government," **The Infantry Journal,** LII (March 1943), 50-57.
Ellis, O. O., and Garey, E. B., **The Plattsburg Manual: a Handbook for Federal Training Camps.** New York: The Century Company, 1917.

Fuller, J. F. C., **Armament and History.** New York: Charles Scribner's Sons, 1945.
——————, **Tanks in the Great War.** London: J. Murray, 1920.
Ganoe, W. A., **The History of the U. S. Army.** rev. ed. New York: D. Appleton-Century Company, 1942.
Greene, Paul C., "The Corporal," **The Infantry Journal,** LII (Feb. 1943), 25-30.
Horne, Charles F. (editor-in-chief), and Austin, Walter F. (directing editor), **The Great Events of the Great War.** 7 vols. National Alumni, 1923.
Hoyt, Epaphras, **Practical Instructions for Military Offirers: comprehending a Concise System of Military Geometry. Field Fortifications, and Tactics of Riflemen and Light Infantry.** Greenfield (Mass.): John Denio, 1811.
Huidekoper, Frederic Louis, **The Military Unpreparedness of the United States.** New York: The Macmillan Company, 1915.
Liddell Hart, B. H., **A History of the World War.** Boston: Little, Brown, and Company, 1935.
Liddell Hart, B. H., **The Real War, 1914-1918.** Boston: Little, Brown, and Company, 1931.
Liddell Hart, B. H., **The Remaking of Modern Armies.** London: J. Murray, 1927.
Liddell Hart, B. H., **Thoughts on War.** London: Faber and Faber, 1944.
March, Peyton C., **The Nation at War.** Garden City, N. Y.: Doubleday, Doran and Company, 1932.
Montrose, Lynn, **War Through the Ages.** New York, London: Harper and Brothers, 1944.
Morrison, John F., **Seventy Problems: Infantry Tactics, Battalion, Brigade, and Division,** Ft. Leavenworth: U. S. Cavalry Association, 1914.
Moss, J. A., **Manual of Military Training.** 2nd ed. Menasha, Wisc.: Geo. Banta Publishing Co., 1917.
Palmer, Frederick, **America in France.** New York: Dodd, Mead, and Company, 1918.
Palmer, Frederick, **Newton D. Baker: America at War.** 2 vols. New York: Dodd, Mead and Company, 1931.
Palmer, Frederick, **Our Greatest Battle.** New York: Dodd, Mead and Company, 1919.
Pershing, John J., **My Experiences in the World War.** 2 vols. New York: Frederick A. Stokes Company, 1931.
Society of the First Division, **History of the First Division.** Philadelphia: The John C. Winston Company, 1922.
Spaulding, O. L., **The United States Army in War and Peace.** New York: G. P. Putnam's Sons, 1937.
Upton, Emory, **The Military Policy of the United States.** Washington: Govt. Printing Office, 1912.
War Department. Document No. 453, **Infantry Drill Regulations, United States Army, 1911, With Corrections to November, 1913.** Washington: Government Printing Office, 1914.
War Department. **Manual for Noncommissioned Officers and Privates of Infantry of the Army of the United States,** 1917. Washington: U. S. Govt. Printing Office, 1917.
Wintringham, Thomas Henry, **The Story of Weapons and Tactics from Troy to Stalingrad.** Boston: Houghton Mifflin Company, 1943.

IX. Reference Works.

Encyclopedia Britannica World Atlas. Chicago, London, Toronto: Encyclopedia Britannica, 1942.
Heilprin, Angelo and Louis (editors), **A Complete Pronouncing Gazetteer or Geographical Dictionary of the World.** Philadelphia and London: J. P. Lippincott Company, 1922.
Irvine, E. Eastman, (editor), **The World Almanac and Book of Facts for 1946.** New York: The New York World-Telegram, 1946.
McDonnald, A. H., editor-in-chief., **The Encyclopedia Americana,** 1946 ed., 30 vols., New York and Chicago: Americana Corporation, 1946.
The New World Loose Leaf Atlas, New York: C. S. Hammond and Company, 1946.